FINANCING GOVERNMENT

FINANCING GOVERNMENT

SIXTH EDITION

HAROLD M. GROVES
UNIVERSITY OF WISCONSIN

HOLT, RINEHART AND WINSTON
NEW YORK · CHICAGO · SAN FRANCISCO
TORONTO · LONDON

PREFACE

In this revision the author has substantially rewritten some four chapters of this book, notably Chapters 27 and 28 dealing with the public debt and Chapters 11 and 24 on consumption taxes and budgeting. All chapters have been modernized and revitalized. Since the fifth edition a crop of excellent books and research papers has been harvested, including such well-known contributions as Musgrave's *Theory of Public Finance* and Galbraith's *Affluent Society*. Comments on these and other important additions to the literature have been woven into the text. The book has evolved directly out of experience—in teaching, writing, research, and government work.

In the author's opinion, a book ensured against obsolescence would not meet the needs of the audience this book should serve. No book on public finance that uses current practices to exemplify principles can avoid being dated. As this is written there are proposals before Congress that would change a considerable number of federal income tax provisions including the rates. Commitment to revise having been made, it seemed wisest to proceed as scheduled, relying on teachers to supply latest information from tax services, newspapers, and other sources.

The new edition, like its predecessors, provides a balanced treatment of the subject to meet the needs of most undergraduate students. It strives toward a judicious presentation of descriptive, analytical, and philosophical aspects of the subject; of international, national, and local problems; and of economic, political, and legal content. It has been designed to serve both the apprentice economist and the general student in quest of citizenship qualification. It emphasizes rather than ignores problems that can be resolved only by value judgments; but it aims to present these matters judiciously without undue emphasis upon the author's point of view. Much could be said for a treatise that presents and defends the author's opinions, but it would fail badly to meet the needs of those students for whom a single textbook must constitute the principal source of their reading.

Continued and increasing attention has been given to such teaching aids as problems, summaries, and footnotes. Thus the problems at the end of each chapter have been revised along with the text and their num-

22736

ber considerably augmented. Where possible, they have been designed to make the student apply what he has learned in a context different from that in which he learned it. The problems also provide a built-in syllabus that can be used both to stimulate discussion and to formulate provocative examinations. Summaries at the ends of chapters or parts have been retained or added. They afford a running survey of the content covered and are especially helpful in facilitating a review of the material. Since a course in public finance is ideally adapted to teaching by the tutorial method, considerable documentation has been included in the text partly to facilitate topical work.

As in previous editions, the order of the chapters is neither orthodox nor logical, but it does, we believe, meet the pedagogical test of teachability. For instance, among the taxes considered, the general property tax provides an ideal beginning because it focuses upon local problems and can be associated with the student's home and college surroundings. The chapters are, of course, sufficiently independent so that they may be assigned to suit the instructor's taste with little or no loss of continuity.

Although this book was originally designed for a two-semester course, it can readily be adapted for one-semester instruction. For this purpose, the following may be omitted or studied extensively rather than intensively: Chapters 4 and 5, most of 9, 13 through 24 (except Chapter 21). Chapter 6 can be shortened and simplified by confining the treatment of incidence to the industry (omitting the firm, except in the case of monopoly) and ignoring "Shifting in Imperfect Markets." In the case of the single-term student, the book offers the important advantage of reading material beyond formal assignments.

Acknowledgment is made of assistance in this revision from Robert Berney who contributed very substantially in reviewing and rewriting Chapters 27 and 28.

It has been said that only professors with limited capacity for scholarship bother to write textbooks, and that textbook writing is the lowest form of scholarship, if indeed it can be dignified at all by that description. Be that as it may, there can be no doubt that an effort at scholarly attainment never did a textbook any harm, and a scholar who enjoys and takes some pride in his teaching may feel the urge occasionally to perfect the most important of his teaching tools. It is considerations of this sort that have sustained the author in the laborious task of writing and rewriting this book.

H.M.G.

Madison, Wisconsin
January, 1964

CONTENTS

LIST OF FIGURES

LIST OF TABLES

1

NATURE AND SETTING
OF PUBLIC FINANCE

IMPORTANCE OF THE SUBJECT

It has been said that taxes are the price we pay for civilization; anyway, an understanding of the ways and means by which governments do and might order their financial affairs is surely a major obligation of citizenship. Most citizens have considerable tax obligations which they are expected to assume on their own initiative; tax compliance and self-defense in such cases depend in high degree on tax-literacy. The topics with which public finance deals are prime favorites for the editorials of newspapers and magazines; they occupy a large share of the attention of legislators and judges; and they constitute the raw material with which many specialists (lawyers, accountants, estate planners, and so forth) make their livings. The potentialities of the subject for improving many aspects of life and culture are great and increasing; education, for instance, is largely dependent upon it for nourishment. While it was once largely confined to the meal ticket of government, public finance now carries high responsibilities for stabilizing and fostering the growth of the economy. Thus the study of public finance is readily motivated. Moreover, whether one's interest is "practical," philosophical, or analytical, he should find a great deal in this field to suit his taste.

1

SCOPE OF THE SUBJECT AND APPROACH HERE TAKEN

Public finance is a field of inquiry that treats of the income and outgo of governments (federal, state, and local). In modern times this includes four major divisions: public revenue, public expenditure, public debt, and certain problems of the fiscal system as a whole, such as fiscal administration and fiscal policy.

Several approaches to public finance are possible. One is that of the lawyer and accountant, both of whom treat the subject from the standpoint of the individual taxpayer, coaching him in tax compliance and tax minimization to his personal advantage. Another is that of the economist who concentrates on the economic effects of financial measures. In this book our principal concern is the citizen and the questions constantly before him: "How do I vote? What policies are in the public interest?" To be sure, these approaches overlap. The student should acquire, incidentally, some sophistication in the ritual and art of "making out an income tax return." But the aim here is to develop social intelligence concerning the nature and place of the income tax. The student should cultivate an eye for the economic effects of financial policies, and this should facilitate his understanding of economics in general. But there is much to the voter's problem outside economics. Many of his problems are political in character, and in addition there are involved aspects of ethics, law, psychology, and accounting. In other words: "Public finance is a part of finance in general, and finance is a part of economics. But in a more important sense it is an independent or separate discipline." [1]

RELATION OF PUBLIC FINANCE TO OTHER FIELDS

PUBLIC FINANCE AND POLITICAL SCIENCE

A few examples will help to make clear the wide spread of the roots of financial policy. First, as an example of the political science aspect, it has long been recognized that there is a reciprocal relationship between taxation and voting. The battle cry of the American Revolution was, "Taxation without representation is tyranny." (Perhaps equally plausible is the reverse of this proposition, namely, that representation without taxation is tyranny—or at least is conducive to the irresponsible spend-

---

[1] E. R. A. Seligman, "Public Finance," *Encyclopedia of the Social Sciences* (New York: The Macmillan Company, 1930).

ing of "other people's money.") The close association between taxpaying and the franchise is eloquently testified by British constitutional history, much of which consists of a long struggle between king and parliament for the control of the national purse. The victory of the Commons survives curiously in our own constitutional provision that so-called money bills must originate in the House of Representatives.

Taxation is thought by some to be akin to robbery. The element in the former that makes it respectable and otherwise defensible is *consent*. The voters' participation in making tax decisions is the "due process" of taxation. To be sure, the connection between voting and taxation is not adhered to without exception—aliens sometimes pay taxes even though they cannot vote; the reciprocity in this latter case is the beneficial share of governmental services rather than consent. But, in the main, the association beween the voting privilege and the tax obligation in modern times is a close one.

Perhaps the irate taxpayer will hasten to complain that he never did, or will, consent to any such taxes as he recently paid. Of course, his vote is only one among many, and his individual wish may have been smothered by an avalanche of opposition at the polls. But anyway he had his chance to participate and, what is more, he was free to influence public opinion in the public discussion that preceded the vote. Thus, for example, the opportunity for swaying sentiment afforded the large taxpayer who frequently controls the instruments of communication, such as radio and press, may compensate for the relatively small number of voters who are in his group.

Not unknown, by any means, is the system of plural voting under which one with high financial stakes in the result can cast more than one vote. A stockholder of a private corporation at a stockholders' meeting can usually cast as many votes as the number of shares that he owns. The tradition of the town meeting, like that of the cooperative association, is usually "one man—one vote." But in the British dominions numerous cases can be found where local jurisdictions allow "property to vote"— that is, the owner can participate in the local election in any unit of government (including wards of cities) in which he owns property. This privilege is extended to corporations and absentees as well as residents. Of course, in both this country and abroad there is some survival of a property qualification for voting.[2]

---

[2] Constitutional limitations sometimes also protect minorities from majorities. The amendment guaranteeing free speech is of this character. By way of protecting the large taxpayer, the latest thus far unsuccessful attempt in this direction has been to write into the Constitution an income and death tax ceiling. For discussion of this movement in its early phase see *Proceedings of the National Tax Association Conference,* 1945, pp. 307–320.

PUBLIC FINANCE AND PSYCHOLOGY

Public finance, like economics in general, deals with people, and this means that many of its problems depend on human behavior which, in turn, is the subject matter of psychology. The concern that taxation may undermine incentive, for example, requires a study of human motivation. Or take the old riddle: Is risk irksome? The solution may influence considerably a decision on the taxation of profits ("rewards for risk taking"). At first thought an affirmative answer seems inevitable, but one confronts, among other things, the formidable propensity to gamble that is all too apparent everywhere. Of course, even gamblers do not play games that offer no prizes, but they do occasionally seem indifferent to the probabilities of their success. Public finance systems have sometimes capitalized directly on this propensity to gamble. Australia and other countries do this with public lotteries, and the Soviet Union, on occasion, has used prizes rather than interest as an incentive in the sale of securities. Giving away a set of dishes, so to speak, with each hundredth bond may seem beneath the dignity of a sovereign government, but it "works."

PUBLIC FINANCE AND ETHICS

Is it true that the strong have an obligation to support the weak? If so, how does one establish the validity of this proposition? May it not be that this is only a rationalization of the weak (or lazy), excusing their own lethargy while coveting the fruits that others have produced? What are the meanings of the terms "justice" and "equity" so frequently found in tax literature? Answers to such questions constitute the basic assumptions which underlie a consistent public policy. They probably involve value judgments and are deeply rooted in the fields of philosophy and ethics.

PUBLIC FINANCE AND ACCOUNTING

In arriving at the net income of a firm for tax purposes, it is customary and logical to allow a deduction for depreciation on the capital used by the firm. Should the capital be "written off" over the years according to the relative annual output of each year, evenly over the life of the asset, or in some other way? Should a government's budget present a balance sheet of assets and liabilities as well as an operating statement of current income and outgo? These are two of the countless cases where public finance and accounting overlap. The concept of income, playing a major role in public finance literature, is an accounting concept.

PUBLIC FINANCE AND LAW

Public finance also involves many legal problems. By legal problems in this connection we mean questions of law involved in issues of public policy. For example, the World War II Excess Profits Tax, and particularly its Section 722, was criticized on the score that it involved voluminous and endless litigation; and Section 534 of the present federal Income Tax Law, which imposes a special tax when corporations reinvest income with intent to avoid the personal surtax that might otherwise strike their stockholders, is criticized on the ground that in litigation a motive is extremely difficult to establish.

PUBLIC FINANCE AND ECONOMICS

Economics deals with the administration of scarce resources to satisfy human wants. Since it is the function of the state to satisfy the wants of its citizens, the issues involved in taxation are essentially a part of economics. Public finance considers not only how individuals satisfy some of their collective wants collectively through government but also how this affects problems of satisfying private wants privately. For example, special excises are frequently thought to shift resources from what the consumer regards as more important to what he regards as less important goods.

The public finance problem of the incidence of taxes lies almost exclusively in the field of economics. Legislative bodies may impose a tax on merchants, specifying that the latter shall absorb the levy—that is, not pass it on to their customers. In so doing they forget perhaps another relationship, that between supply and demand, which may operate in effect to repeal the legislative intent. This may occur independently of how the merchants feel about the matter. The issue is not one of politics or psychology but of economics.

Fiscal policy, a recently acquired and highly important domain in the public finance kingdom, is largely in the field of so-called *aggregative economics*. For instance, it is said that more aggregate taxation may relieve the pressure on prices (deflationary), while less aggregate taxation would increase such pressure (inflationary). Here we confront also the great paradoxes of public finance: under certain conditions allegedly the way to balance the budget is to unbalance it further and the way to reduce the public debt is to incur more of it. The way to save more is not to try to save so much. And so on. Like the new physics, this doctrine is beyond the reach of common sense. This control aspect of the tax level now commands a great deal of attention. The role of taxation here is strictly economic.

CONTROVERSIAL QUESTIONS AND VALUE JUDGMENTS

Many questions in public finance cannot be given an answer with which all reasonable and well-informed critics will agree. Moreover, as previously suggested, there are some problems in the field the answers to which depend upon the values (preferences, ends, desires) of the critic. It is difficult and a bit egotistical perhaps to claim that one's values are superior to those of some other observer. Philosophers and students of methodology differ as to whether values (as distinct from facts) and ends (as distinct from means) can serve as material for scientific inquiry.[3] Common sense suggests that all desires are not entitled to an equal rating and that the matter is not one in which the verdict of an opinion poll would be conclusive. It is meaningful to speak of right and wrong as dependent upon consequences and independent of the feelings of the actor. For instance, human sacrifice as a religious rite can be condemned on the evidence even though those engaged in it have no sense of wrongdoing. Anyway, it can be said with confidence that inquiry and study are of importance even in areas where they have led or can lead only to controvertible answers. If one's judgment on certain issues is based on one's values, it can at least be an informed judgment. The questions of public finance are mostly of the type that are answered ultimately at the voting booth; but this does not mean that inquiry both concerning their analysis and the related evidence is unimportant. On the other hand, controversial material does call for tolerance. A student is entitled to resentment if he is graded down because he concludes on an examination that the tax law passed by the 80th Congress was not inflationary, provided that he defends his position with competent evidence or analysis. The situation is different where he is asked the question: "Which contributes more to the revenue, the income tax or the estates tax?" Perhaps there is only one correct answer in both cases, but in the first no one can know it so certainly that he is entitled to rule out a difference of opinion.

THE NATURE OF THE STATE

The *state* has been defined in many ways, but for our purposes we may use the term as synonymous with what is popularly called *the government*. The origin and nature of the state are matters of considerable dispute. Some of our ancestors, at least, believed that the state arose

---

[3] See John Dewey, *Theory of Valuation* (Chicago: University of Chicago Press, 1939).

from an actual or implied contract (or compact) among the individuals of a community. Others held that sovereigns got their power by divine appointment and that the subject owed certain duties to his king by the same authortiy.

This is not far removed from the so-called organic view of the state in which the state takes on a personality of its own and instead of existing for the good of the individual has an independent purpose and authority.[4] Anthropologists have presented the plausible hypothesis that historically the state evolved from the family in an extension of family discipline. There is also the view that the state is an instrument of class warfare, to be captured and used by one socioeconomic group until, ultimately, a classless society has evolved. Probably most people in the Western world would now agree that the state exists because public opinion holds it to be the best vehicle for accomplishing certain social objectives. To give the state a "monopoly of violence" may be dangerous, but it is safer than other alternatives.

Our own tradition regards the state as resting fundamentally on the consent of the governed—that is, the people have the ultimate sovereignty and the state is theirs to use as they see fit for their welfare. The individual not only has a voice in determining the role of the state; the state exists only to serve him. Moreover, the individual who may dissent from majority views is provided with some protection from the encroachment of majorities (the right of free speech, for instance). As we shall see, this protection extends to the prohibition of arbitrary taxation, and some have argued that it should also ban "excessive taxation." The totalitarian view of the state is radically different; it holds that entity to be self-perpetuating, apart from and above the individual, and a sacred trust of those in control.

Attitudes toward the state can differ substantially even in a democratic society. At the time our federal Constitution was established, there was widespread fear and distrust of government which had grown out of abuses and indiscretions of British kings. This attitude has persisted in some degree, though now it is more often attributed to American skepticism of concentrated power, be it ecclesiastical, economic, or political. Contrast this view with that in New Zealand, for instance, where it is said: [5]

> The people, or at any rate most of them, look upon the state . . .
> as being themselves under another form. When it acts, they feel that

---

[4] See for instance Hans Ritschl, "Commercial Economy and Market Economy," in Richard A. Musgrave and Alan T. Peacock, eds., *Classics in the Theory of Public Finance* (New York: The Macmillan Company, 1958), pp. 233–241.

[5] Leslie Lipson, *The Politics of Equality* (Chicago: University of Chicago Press, 1948), p. 482.

they are acting. What it owns, they own. They do not endow it with
metaphysical properties or ascribe to it any transcendental personality. To them it is simply a utilitarian instrument for effecting their
will.

It seems that the New Zealanders view the state much as members view
a cooperative. However, the view that the essence of the state is coercion
finds equally wide support.

FINANCING THE STATE—CHARACTERISTICS OF THE
PUBLIC ECONOMY

We have stated that government activity is for the purpose of satisfying
human wants. Some wants are satisfied by individual action, but most
of them require cooperation for the best results. Very often cooperation
takes the form of an organization dedicated to the satisfaction of individual or collective wants. To mention only a few, recreational wants
are satisfied through country clubs, social wants through fraternal organizations, political wants through political parties and clubs, professional and vocational wants through professional associations and trade
unions, religious wants through churches, economic wants through private corporations and cooperatives. Most of these organizations have a
constitution and by-laws as well as a budget of some sort, a treasury,
and a financial problem. The government is one of these organizations,
but it differs from the others substantially.

To begin with, membership in the government is compulsory and
so also (with qualifications) are the financial obligations that go with it.
The usual privilege of resigning is not recognized. To a higher degree
than elsewhere, we enjoy the services of the government collectively;
usually any division of the benefits among individuals seems artificial
and forced. In the private sphere, at least in our trade relations, we pay
for what we buy, but in the public economy we rarely conceive "buying"
a bit of government. Then too, the public economy is motivated less by
self-interest; social utility rather than profit is more often its goal. (This
is not to say that government provision of goods and services always
yields the better results.) The measuring rod of efficiency in government
(usually without a competitive profit test) is difficult to find and apply.

Attempts have been made to apply exchange-economics to define
the optimum scope of government, but they are not very persuasive.[6]
In the last analysis the decisions in this area must rest on fortified value
judgments and in setting the pattern of both expenditures and taxes they

---

[6] Richard R. Musgrave, *The Theory of Public Finance* (New York: McGraw-
Hill Book Company, 1959), chaps. 1–6.

extend not only to public goods but private goods as well. Preferences of individuals are important in achieving consensus but they cannot serve as the basis of distributing burdens. No one seriously contemplates the (financial) exemption of pacifists from support of the army. As a matter of fact many collective decisions in the private sphere are also based on the convention that the minority must take its chances with whatever strategy for the achievement of common goals the consensus may select.

In the United States the public sector of the economy is large and growing but it is small compared with the private sphere. In 1961 including military personnel, about one out of every eight persons in the labor force was employed by governments. This was more than half as many as were employed in manufacturing.[7] Even though private business activity is greater in the aggregate, it is important to note that no other single economic unit can add to or withdraw billions of dollars from the volume of transactions as can the federal government. Its transactions, therefore, are of strategic importance to the economy in an incremental rather than a numerical sense; its withdrawals and additions contribute heavily to the difference between inflation and deflation.

INTRODUCTION TO THE FOLLOWING CHAPTERS

In the following seventeen chapters (Part I), we shall pass in review the considerable variety of taxes and other sources of income that have evolved to meet the needs of government. An attempt will be made, among other things, to explain their nature, the arguments with which they are attacked and defended, the economic effects and special problems involved, and, finally, their role in the revenue system. No analysis of taxation can proceed far without encountering the important allegation that those who pay taxes pass on the burden to others; this problem will receive special attention in Chapter 6. Moreover, the sources of revenue are alternative sources. In order to judge the place, if any, that should be given to each tax, it will be helpful to consider in general some of the qualifications of a good revenue source, certain general standards or principles of distributing governmental burdens, and certain alternative ways of setting up tax rates. These general aspects of apportionment will be considered in the next chapter.

Later parts of the book will consider problems of the revenue system as a whole, public expenditures, public debt, financial administration, and fiscal policy.

---

[7] Tax Foundation, *Facts and Figures on Government Finance* (New York, 1963), pp. 36, 42, 43.

PART 1 PUBLIC REVENUE

2

DISTRIBUTION OF GOVERNMENTAL BURDENS

What principles should guide the government in distributing the burden of its financial needs among its citizens? One time-honored approach to determining such principles is to consider the criteria of a good revenue source. These criteria generally constitute a list of so-called canons of taxation. Adam Smith in his *Wealth of Nations* (1776) set the fashion in this respect and provided a list of canons that have stood the test of time. In the frequency of their repetition and perhaps the degree to which they are sinned against, these canons resemble the Ten Commandments. They have attained such currency and venerability that it seems useful to repeat them again, if only to enrich the student's vocabulary. Moreover, with some pardonable degree of modernization, they constitute even today a not too inadequate list.

It is true that tax recommendations must be tailored to suit the conditions of time and place. The present tax system of the United States would not have suited eighteenth-century England or France. And many a so-called tax-mission from the United States to some other country with a different tradition and economy has been embarrassed to find how little that it has learned to regard as "tax wisdom" can be transferred. Nevertheless, there are some generalizations about taxes that have some validity anywhere, any time.

13

CRITERIA TO BE CONSIDERED IN CHOOSING REVENUE SOURCES

SMITH'S CANONS

First, said Smith, taxes should be equal or *equitable,* falling upon individuals "like the expense of management to the joint tenants of a great estate, who are obliged to contribute in proportion to their respective interests in the estate." Secondly, taxes should be *certain* and not arbitrary, "clear and plain to the contributor and every other person." Otherwise, the taxpayer may be subject to extortionate administration. Then, too, taxes should be *convenient* as to the time and manner of their levy. And finally, they should be *economical*—that is, not too expensive to collect and not unduly obstructive and discouraging to the taxpayer.

EQUITY—REASONABLE CLASSIFICATION

Relevance. Discussing these canons as they suit a modern setting, one may observe that *equity* and *certainty* require a high degree of rationality in methods of taxation. Mr. Brown and Mr. White are not to be treated differently because one of them is tall or the name of one appears in the beginning of an alphabetical list or their ancestors were of different origins. Tax differentiation must be based upon a *relevant* difference between the two men. A relevant difference is one which pertains to the relation of each of these men to the government and to the payment of taxes. A difference in their annual incomes is an example. If one buys a mechanical refrigerator during the year whereas the other saves (banks) his money or spends it on books and magazines, a relevant difference may conceivably exist, but the case is much more doubtful.

Neutrality. Lawyers consider the presence of relevant differences the basis for reasonable classification. Justice in taxation can be achieved only if taxpayers are assured of impartiality of treatment. This impartiality is here referred to as *neutrality* in taxation. At first thought impartiality might seem to require identical treatment for everyone, but this would ignore many relevant differences in circumstances. Revenue requirements would be met by a single, universal poll tax with no exemption for babies, old men, lunatics, and others. This would be a very simple tax system, but few people would proclaim it just.

Suppose the issue to be: "Who shall bear arms during a war?" Identity of treatment would require that the selection be made on the sole basis of drawing names out of a hat, so to speak. Actually, conscription during both World War I and II followed a very different procedure. People were divided into several classifications according to certain relevant circumstances, such as sex, age, dependents, physical condition, ability to produce in the civilian sphere, and so on. This classification met with wide approval, and few, if any, thought it unjust. Selection on the basis of the candidate's wealth or influence would have been a different matter. Why? Because these circumstances would not commend themselves to the public as relevant to the individual's ability to perform the needed service.

Hence, it is unjust to treat *A* and *B* alike when their relevant circumstances are different, and it is likewise unjust to treat them differently when their circumstances are the same. There is something wrong with a tax system that imposes a 50-percent tax upon one person with a million dollars of wealth or income and only half as much on another with equal economic status. This principle of *reasonable classification* may seem obvious. Yet people have not always enjoyed this blessing, and even today they do not enjoy it in full by any means. Before the French Revolution, French taxpayers in like economic circumstances were treated unequally if they belonged to different orders or carried different titles. And the American income tax is now criticized because it exempts certain people who derive their income from "tax-exempt securities," and allegedly favors interests which derive profit from the exploitation of natural resources.

Along with the idea of reasonable classification goes that of rough approximation. Students of taxation in the fields of law and economics recognize that it is no simple technical task to raise the revenue of a modern government. Thus we frequently hear it said that "rough justice" is the best that can be expected.

These ideas of equality, impartiality, or neutrality have a very wide application in the tax field. Veritable political revolutions have been staged over the issue of whether railroads or mining properties were paying their full share of taxes—that is, the same in proportion to income or wealth as other taxpayers. Expensive research projects have been launched to ascertain whether competing forms of transportation (railroads and trucking, for instance) were receiving neutral treatment from the tax system. The corporate income tax, as presently applied, has been criticized because it is said to be unneutral toward corporations as against partnerships, profit against interest, and distributed as against undistributed income. Evasion and avoidance are important problems for those who are concerned about neutrality. What appears to be the best tax in the world will and should lose favor rapidly if it cannot be enforced beyond, say, an 80-percent level. And a levy that is unimpeachable in its objective is none the less vulnerable if it cannot be defined so that those in essentially similar circumstances contribute alike. Discrimination is the essence of tax wisdom, but it sheds its curse only when it is proved to rest on genuine differences, the recognition of which is required by the public interest.

Progressive Taxation and Equality. What shall we say of taxation that discriminates between *A* and *B* according to the quantity of their income or wealth, taking more (both absolutely and relatively) from the more fortunate? Or what shall we say of measures that aim not at equality of taxation but at equality of taxpayers after taxation? Certainly one should not cite Smith in support of any such modern trends. A case can be made for them in terms of rational discrimination in the public interest. However, discussion of these interesting and highly controversial subjects are best deferred to later sections of this chapter dealing with the ability-to-pay principle and with progressive taxation.

CERTAINTY

Adam Smith's second canon includes the idea that taxes should be intelligible to the taxpayer. Although everyone recognizes simplicity as an important value, in our era of complicated economic activity this principle is easier to state than to follow. Much progress has been made in simplified reporting for those with simple patterns of income (short forms and standard deductions). But each new law seems to add complications for those with retirement income and dividends. Exemption of food from general sales taxes removes some of their inequities; but this exception raises difficult questions of definition. Importers complain that uncertainties in tariff classification are even more obstructive to trade than the tariffs themselves. In some countries minimizing taxes is not a matter of *what* one knows but *whom* one knows; here there is said to be a government of men rather than of laws.[1]

CONVENIENCE

Consumption Taxes. Smith's third canon finds application in the many sales and excise taxes that still feature our tax systems. Not only are these taxes paid bit by bit with consumer purchases, but they are frequently so inconspicuously mixed with prices that the consumer fails even to recognize them. It is said that this is the easy way to pay taxes and that taxation is hard enough to take without being administered "the hard way."

[1] Harley H. Hinrichs, "Certainty as Criterion: Taxation of Foreign Investments in Afghanistan," *National Tax Journal,* XV (June 1962), pp. 139–154.

It will be observed that this application of Smith's third canon may conflict with the requirements of his first. Consumption taxes are not given a high rating on the score of rationality and neutrality.

Convenience in taxation is not confined to and need not lead to an endorsement of sales taxation. Changes in the income tax that introduced withholding were designed to make compliance easier and more convenient. Installment payment of property and death taxes have the same objective.

ECONOMY

Effect upon Production. Other things being equal, that revenue source is best which interferes least with the private production of wealth. It is commonly observed that taxation should be so devised as "not to kill the goose that lays the golden egg." To the altruistic, it can be said that perhaps the lot of the underdog can be improved much more (at least in the absolute sense) by a taxation policy that enlarges the total income to be divided than by one that improves his relative status but limits the aggregate available for distribution. There is agreement on this objective but not on how to accomplish it. A tax system designed to impede production as little as possible should conserve the resources of the country, particularly the human resources. A sensible nation does not skimp the rations of its army—and during both war and peace the country's civil personnel as well as its regiments are "in the army" in the broad sense. Thus a heavy tax on food would be open to the criticism that it threatens adequate nutrition and consequently maximum industrial productivity.

Important also is the economic effect of uneven taxes upon the allocation of resources. The uneven incidence may arise either in the selection of taxes & or the exceptions that are made to their general application. The clearest case of the former occurs in excise taxation; a tax on liquor, for instance, is supported in part on the ground that it would be desirable to discourage the consumption of liquor and reduce the size of the liquor business. But many excise taxes affect resource allocation without design and presumably with ill effects upon the economy. They alter patterns of consumption deemed to provide maximum satisfaction before alteration.

Many tax proposals are based on the assumption that certain actions may be encouraged or discouraged by offering tax *incentives* to business; that economic activity and initiative respond to differential rewards that cannot safely be wiped out by the tax system. This is another way of saying that taxation must be restrained when it is leveled at sources that have an elastic supply. Thus it has been argued that land is an especially suitable subject for taxation because its supply is relatively fixed.

A FIFTH CANON

Later writers on public finance have frequently added a fifth canon to Smith's four. They say that taxes should be *adequate*. Other things being equal, that revenue source is best which yields the most revenue. It is highly important that public revenues be sufficient to maintain essential governmental functions. Beyond that, occasion may arise where public opinion is far more interested in a generous program of public expenditures than in the means of financing it. Inadequate taxes may mean unbalanced budgets which in turn may be the cause of inflation. At least it can be said that a tax which is perfect except that it brings in no money has no financial usefulness. The first question that any practical critic will ask about a new tax is: "How much will it yield?"

So much for some of the factors that must be weighed in sizing up the social advisability of a revenue source. A second approach to the problem of apportioning governmental burdens is to examine certain standards or general principles of distribution that have been advanced. Consideration will now be given to these general principles.

PRINCIPLES OF APPORTIONING GOVERNMENTAL BURDENS

THE PRINCIPLE OF BENEFITS RECEIVED

In the commercial world it is a rule that every commodity or service carries a single price for all buyers regardless of class or circumstances. When *A* and *B* go to the grocery store to buy a sack of flour, they are not subjected to an inquiry concerning their fortunes. On the contrary, to the grocery clerk a purchaser is a purchaser; he is quite happy to sell to anyone willing to pay the market price.[1a] It has been contended by many that this simple rule of paying for what one gets should be applied to the goods and services supplied by the government as well as to those supplied by the grocer. If those who received benefits always had to pay for them, there would be less clamor for government help.

[1a] There are exceptions, of course, particularly in the professions where the charge for services is likely to be gauged somewhat by the individual's capacity to pay.

No Definite Measurement of Benefits Possible. The benefit theory appears plausible, but it is open to fundamental difficulties and criticisms. The first is that, for many governmental services, no very clear accounting of benefits can be made. One of the characteristics of government is that its services in the main are rendered for the benefit of all, and the particular interest of any one taxpayer is not determinable. Unfortunately, one is equipped with no mechanism to measure the benefits he receives from government as he is, for instance, with a meter to gauge his services from the gas company. How is the benefit of a new atomic research laboratory or a new highway to be divided among the people of the United States—people with varying wealth and income and in all parts of the country? Similarly, by what process of accounting could the benefits of the national capitol be prorated?

The problem of benefit accounting is complicated by the fact that many of the benefits of government are indirect. Public charity may on first thought seem to benefit only relief clients. But indirectly it may also benefit the well-to-do taxpayer: for example, it may make his property more secure; it may reduce expenses associated with future delinquency; it may ensure him against radical and foolish politics; and it may serve his altruistic wish to avoid starvation in a rich country. The Elizabethan Poor Law was adopted more as a defense against vagrancy than as a kindness to the unfortunate.

When A attends the public school for a year, who gets the benefit and how much? First of all, the benefit may be greater or less than the cost to the government. Waiving this complication, we may ask what about the division of benefits? Presumably A and his family have some direct interest in this education; both stand to gain, at least if the result is increased earning power for A. It would not be easy to calculate in quantitative terms the value of this direct interest. Certainly many others are interested in A's education besides himself and his family. Employers of labor are interested because some of them may wish to employ A. At least a certain amount of education will make him a more efficient employee. To make matters more complicated, A may be educated in Bangor, Maine, and end up as an employee in Sacramento, California. The publishers of a national magazine in Philadelphia are interested in A's education, for he may become a potential subscriber. The voters, both of the country at large and of A's state, are also interested. A will soon have the powers and responsibilities of a voter, and it is dangerous to leave the complicated problem of government in ignorant hands. And so on.

Who Receives Greater Benefits—the Rich or the Poor? There is no clear consensus as to whether the rich receive more benefit from the government than the poor, or vice versa. On the one hand, it is contended that the rich are clearly the greatest beneficiaries of government, that in fact government exists mainly to protect property rights and to prevent those who have not from encroaching upon those who have. Rousseau, for example, in his *Discourses on the Causes of Inequality,* held that government was a device of the rich and the strong to protect their property against the poor.[2] But it also can be argued that the poor have a greater stake in government than the rich. The poor must rely upon the police force to protect them, whereas the rich can buy protection in the form of private guards, barbed-wire fences, bulldogs, and other protective equipment. The medieval castle was an example of such privately provided protection. Further, the rich man can either send his son or daughter to a private school to be educated or employ a special tutor for this purpose, but the poor man is entirely dependent upon the public schools. It is not necessary to arbitrate between these two contending points of view. The argument illustrates well the difficulty of measuring benefits from the government.

The benefit concept is ambiguous and it encompasses several more or less distinguishable types: (1) the direct and separable benefit discussed below; (2) the subjective benefit associated with the satisfaction of an individual's preference; and (3) the objective benefit that one enjoys along with others if and when the strategy chosen by consensus is successful in achieving common goals.

Benefit Principle Incompatible with Wide Consumption. The second main difficulty with the benefit theory is that public opinion supports the wide use of many public services that would be impossible under our existing system of distribution of wealth and income were beneficiaries to pay an equivalent for the benefits. What would become of the poorhouse, for instance, were the inmates to pay for their publicly furnished board and lodging? The answer is that the poorhouse would become a hotel and would, of course, lose the function for which it was intended. We are not content to confine education to those who can afford it and who have the inclination to seek it. On the contrary, we pass compulsory education laws requiring all children below a certain age to attend school, whether or not they wish to and whether or not their parents can afford to send them. "It is felt that, when . . . government compels a man to accept . . . that service at its hands, whether he wishes to or not, it would be unfair to ask him to pay for it."[3]

Governments have expanded partly by adding to their free list— that is, to those goods and services furnished without direct compensa-

---

[2] A. T. Williams, *The Concept of Equality in the Writings of Rousseau, Bentham, and Kant* (New York: Columbia University Press, 1907), p. 14.

[3] A. C. Pigou, *A Study in Public Finance* (London: Macmillan and Co., Ltd., 1928), p. 47.

tion from the immediate beneficiaries. A strong case is now being made for the addition of housing, medical service, and even, in some cases, food to this free or partially free list. As a matter of fact, the government is urged to provide these services or aid in their provision mainly because of the view that it would be in the social interest for all to have them and that private incomes in many cases are inadequate to purchase them in suitable quantity or quality.

Payment for Special Benefits. Although the benefit theory is thus open to some valid criticism, it finds much reasonable application in the revenue system. Where governments engage in more or less commercial activities (for example, operation of public utilities), they usually collect for their services in full from the beneficiaries. Charges are made according to the cost of the service—which differs little from the benefit principle. *"Prima facie* it is fair that the users of ordinary services should pay for them in proportion to their use, and should not receive a subsidy at the expense of other people." [4] The term *public prices* rather than *taxes* is ordinarily used to designate these payments. The stamp system of paying postage is an illustration, though the cost-of-the-service principle in this case is tempered by other considerations; the Detroit publicly owned street railway charges its patrons like any other street railway. Similarly, certain special services of government are paid for by fees. Students at state and city universities and colleges usually pay fees to cover part of the cost of their instruction. Many public improvements are also paid for in full or in part by special assessment—that is, by a special levy upon the abutting or near-by property that is supposed to derive special benefits and probably an increment in value because of the improvement.[5]

The above applications of the benefit principle for the distribution of governmental burdens are mainly outside the field of taxation. They are supported, and in most cases plausibly, on the ground that the government has performed a special and clearly discernible benefit for private beneficiaries. It is proper that the government should collect from these beneficiaries accordingly.

Payment for More General and Partly Discernible Benefits. Within the broader field where the services of government are paid for by taxes and the benefits are only partly discernible, the benefit principle still has wide application—much of which is entirely defensible. The benefit principle is not nearly as antiquated and obsolete as many recent critics would have us believe. Perhaps the best-known case of its application in taxation is the gasoline tax. Gasoline consumption is regarded as a fairly

---

[4] *Ibid.,* p. 46.
[5] Some account of these sources of public revenue other than taxes is presented in Chapter 18.

good measure of the service one obtains from a publicly constructed and maintained system of highways. It is generally thought that those who enjoy this service should pay for it. Social security taxes, perhaps more properly called contributions, are assessed on the benefit and cost principles. Business and property taxes also rest to some extent upon these principles. They are defended on the ground that government is an important "factor of production" and an overhead cost of doing business and owning property. It is true that, at best, these benefits and costs are but very roughly measured. And it is at least debatable whether business and property taxes are not based more on opportunism and rationalization than on equitable principles. Nevertheless, it would be difficult to conceive a tax system with no such taxes.

Lastly, the benefit theory has wide application in determining which unit of government should pay for a given public service. It would be regarded as unjust to require that the taxpayers of Albany, New York, pay for an ornamental street-lighting system installed by local ordinance in Syracuse. The Supreme Court of the United States has stated the importance of benefits in a ruling that a governmental unit may not tax those who are beyond its jurisdiction:

> The power of taxation, indispensable to the existence of every civilized government, is exercised upon the assumption of an equivalent rendered to the taxpayer in the protection of his person and property, in adding to the value of such property, or in the creation and maintenance of public conveniences in which he shares. . . . If the taxing power be in no position to render these services, or otherwise to benefit the person or property taxed, . . . the taxation of such property within the domicil of the owner partakes rather of the nature of an extortion than a tax.[6]

THE ABILITY-TO-PAY PRINCIPLE

More often urged as proper to use in distributing taxes is the ability-to-pay principle. Within the family it is customary for each to contribute toward common ends according to his ability. The church solicits funds among the parishioners with the thought that each should give as God has prospered him. To hundreds of common enterprises (community chests, Red Cross, and the like) people are presumed to contribute according to their means. Governments are one of these common enterprises fostered to serve the citizens as a group, to protect them, enhance their prestige, and add to their general welfare. What is more natural and appropriate than to distribute governmental burdens according to ability to pay?

---
[6] *Union Refrigerator Transit Co. v. Kentucky,* 199 U.S. 194, 202 (1905).

Measurement of Ability to Pay. Ability to pay, like benefits received, does not easily lend itself to measurement. There is not even a general agreement as to what should be the measuring rod. Some advocate property or wealth as the proper criterion; others prefer net income; still others support expenditure; and some advocate a combination of two or all three of these. If net income, perhaps the most popular of the many standards, were to be selected as the proper yardstick, there would still be the problem of defining net income—by no means an easy task. In addition, many would like to qualify net income with allowance for dependents. Some would also differentiate between various sources of income and ascribe more ability to property income than to service income. Finally, and most important, is the question of how fast ability advances as income advances. Does the principle call for a 90-percent tax on a million-dollar income? We shall soon see that ability to pay gives no quantitative answers. But neither does any other principle.

Minimum Sacrifice. One pillar in the support of the ability-to-pay principle is the contention that it involves a minimum of sacrifice on the part of the taxpayer. Minimum sacrifice is but a corollary of the utilitarian principle that governments should seek the greatest good for the greatest number, or the maximum aggregate welfare. As applied to taxation, this means that the inconvenience and loss to the people as a whole should be kept at the lowest possible total. Application of minimum sacrifice and ability to pay is further based upon the marginal utility theory as applied to income, according to which the value of a dollar to the recipient decreases as income increases. If the less important dollars are taken by the taxation of persons according to their means, the total sacrifice of these individuals collectively will be minimized.

The principal argument against the minimum-sacrifice theory of taxation is that the logical outcome of its application would lead further than its proponents want to go. As long as incomes are unequal, the minimum aggregate sacrifice can be attained by taxing only the larger incomes. A tax on a smaller income would hurt its owner more than if the amount were added to the tax bill of one whose income were greater, since the value of the dollar to the latter would be still less than to the former. It is obvious that if the principle were followed in practice, with the existing wide inequalities of fortune, there might not be "taxation enough to go round, so to speak" until "complete equality of fortunes" were attained.[7] This is seen in Figure 1. In order to get dollars with the least area (importance), one would not start taxing *C* until *A* and *B* had been taxed to equality with *C*.

---

[7] F. Y. Edgeworth, "The Pure Theory of Taxation," *Economic Journal,* VII (1897), reprinted in his *Papers Relating to Political Economy* (London: Macmillan and Co., Ltd., 1925), II, p. 103.

It is also said against the minimum-sacrifice doctrine that it would indeed be a strange concept of equity which would share common burdens by placing the whole load on the wealthier taxpayers.[8]

Equal and Proportional Sacrifice. Some proponents of the sacrifice theory, unable to accept the extreme program that it seems to require, have largely accepted an alternative for practical application—the principle of equal sacrifice. Thus they would approve some levy on the smaller incomes, up to the point perhaps where the sacrifice would equal that involved in levies on the larger incomes. In other words, everyone would be required to make a contribution, but small contri-

FIGURE 1

The Minimum Sacrifice Dilemma

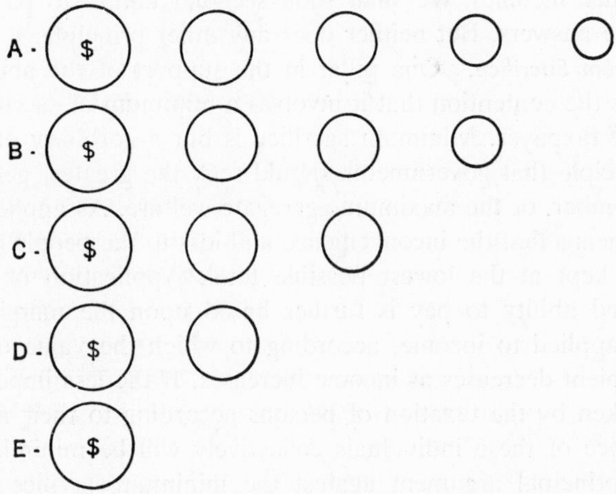

butions from the poor would be assumed to equal in sacrifice the large contributions from the rich.[9] Proportional sacrifice has also been proposed; it would adjust burdens according to the relative total utilities assumed to attend the various incomes. Others prefer to apply the concept of minimum sacrifice but to temper its logical application with consideration of the effect of extreme taxation upon production.

The principal objection to all sacrifice theories is that the utility of income is either immeasurable or, as a practical matter, not amenable to any precision in measurement. A downward direction of the marginal-

[8] Walter J. Blum and Harry Kalven, Jr., "The Uneasy Case for Progressive Taxation," *University of Chicago Law Review*, 19: 2 (Spring 1952), pp. 417–520, 470–471.

[9] See T. N. Carver, "The Ethical Basis of Distribution and Its Application to Taxation," *The Annals of the American Academy of Political and Social Science* (July 1895), pp. 79–99; Edgeworth, *op. cit.*, pp. 100–125.

utility curve is all one needs to know in order to apply rigorously the dictates of marginal sacrifice. But no one wants to carry taxation to the point of leveling incomes completely. Moreover, some critics have even challenged the thesis that utility drops with the expansion of income, at least steadily for all income ranges. The marginal-utility theory seems most realistic when applied to consumption; its validity is doubtful for the dollars that satisfy only acquisitive interests. In the latter case it may often be true that the more one gets, the more one wants (and perhaps needs).[10] Sacrifice analysis involves interpersonal comparisons ignoring the fact that A and B may have different capacities to enjoy the good things that income makes available. Recent economic literature has challenged the view, acceptable to common sense, that a more equal distribution of income, even assuming that the total to be divided remains the same, would necessarily add to human welfare.[11]

Objective Aspects of Sacrifice. It has been contended that sacrifice is a subjective matter and that it differs from individual to individual, even among those in the same economic circumstances. This is true, but only partially, as there are objective as well as subjective aspects to sacrifice. Even though A may feel the loss of dental care less than B feels the loss of his second automobile, society feels it more, in the sense that A's teeth have more social importance than B's automobile.

The social interest in minimum sacrifice is much broader than that of keeping pain and inconvenience as low as possible. There is a social interest in allowing individuals to retain enough means after taxation to maintain themselves in health, vigor, and informed citizenship. Thus it would seem unwise in these days to tax people of little means to such an extent that they could not afford to buy a newspaper—even admitting the imperfections of the newspaper as an instrument of adult education. Taxation according to ability to pay simply means that a nation, viewed as a family, satisfies its most urgent wants before it indulges in superfluities. The urgency of wants has a social as well as an individual calculus and the two may disagree substantially. More will be said about this matter of social priorities in discussing arguments concerning progressive taxation.

Other Elements in Ability to Pay. The case for the ability-to-pay theory may be approached from another angle, namely, the power of the individual rather than his sacrifice. Thus viewed, the emphasis is laid on one's capacity to bear responsibilities. Accordingly, one is expected to shoulder as much of the public burden as his capacity permits. Sir Josiah

---

[10] M. Slade Kendrick, "Ability-to-pay Theory of Taxation," *American Economic Review*, 29 (March 1930), pp. 92–101.

[11] For an excellent discussion of the difficulties in utility-sacrifice theory see Musgrave, *The Theory of Public Finance*, chap. 5.

Stamp has described this principle as it would be applied in a non-monetary economy, which, he says, would call for direct service to the common good and would expect more from the powerful man than from the decrepit; in some tasks, more from the taller or swifter members of the community than from the slower; and in teaching the young, more from the educated than from the ignorant.[12] In the terms of today's world, possession of wealth or receipt of income is itself an evidence of faculty or power not only to pay taxes out of one's income but also to earn additional income. Money earns money. The first thousand dollars "come the hardest." He who has a bank account has three hands: his right hand, his left hand, and his bank account.

It also may be argued that the receipt of income or the possession of wealth represents ability because it contains elements of privilege. Society plays a heavy part in the production of every income.

Promotion of Equality.   Some students favor higher taxes on the rich than on the poor but find the ability principle unconvincing. They would dispense with all talk about equity in the tax system and take their stand frankly upon their (nonfiscal) interest in reducing inequalities. Their interest is centered not upon equality of contribution toward the revenue but upon the equality of taxpayers after taxes.

Two kinds of equality should be distinguished: equality of opportunity and equality of reward. The first calls only for the elimination of special privilege. It proposes to allow full reward for differential economic achievement resulting from subjective variations but to render the objective environment neutral to all comers. Equality of economic opportunity is a generally accepted ideal in the United States, but it is very imperfectly realized. Equality of reward is a much more ambitious goal, and few would proclaim its desirability except in degree. Arguments for greater equality overlap those for ability taxation except that the former are not necessarily concerned with taxation principles as such. Opposition arguments are also much alike, emphasizing heavily the concern for incentives.[13]

The Possibility of Reducing Inequalities.   Questions have been raised, too, as to whether it is possible to obtain greater equality even if we want it. Some doubts were cast on the matter by certain studies of Vilfredo Pareto, an Italian economist, that showed much the same pattern of distribution in different countries at the same time and in the same countries at different times. But A. C. Pigou [14] has rebutted the conclu-

---

[12] Sir Josiah Stamp, *The Fundamental Principles of Taxation* (London: Macmillan and Co., Ltd., 1921), pp. 7–8.

[13] Important economic considerations involved in applying the ability-to-pay doctrine will be treated later in the section on progressive taxation.

[14] *Economics of Welfare* (London: Macmillan and Co., Ltd., 1920), Part IV, chap. 2.

sion from these data that the distribution of income is beyond the control of mortal man. He calls attention to the fact that, in the main, the same institutional framework prevailed in all the situations tested by Pareto. Moreover, Pigou suggested that the underlying reason for a tendency of incomes to assume a constant pattern, if it exists, must be found in a constant scale of biological differences. But biological differences should follow a bell-shaped curve characteristic of chance variations in natural phenomena. If one were to measure the length of maple leaves or the weight of walnuts or the height of students, the results would follow the well-known curve, showing a few dwarfs and a few giants but mostly middle-sized items. The curve of income distribution, on the other hand, is sharply skewed to the right.

THE SOCIAL-EXPEDIENCY PRINCIPLE

Finally, a third principle of distribution may be mentioned; one that either abandons or includes all the others. The proponents of the social-expediency theory take the pragmatic view that those revenue sources and that revenue system are best that work best. In order to determine what sources such a theory would support, the specific taxes must be examined and their operation observed. Much of this book will be occupied with such examination and observation.

Stated another way, the whole system of public finance may be viewed as a matter of value judgments concerning priorities in the distribution of resources, public and private. As to the latter, individual choice is sanctioned (with some qualifications), but with quantitative restraints imposed by taxation. It comes to this: Which is more important in terms of national goals as viewed by the voter, a potential automobile or some other private good for *A* and *B* and others, or a new school for the community? Value judgments are not susceptible to definitive answers; that is why we vote on public finance questions. But value judgments can be improved both by information and analysis of how one arrives at an intelligent decision. That is why we study public finance. This approach dispenses with the need for either benefit or ability-to-pay principles.

MAJOR PHILOSOPHIES OF TAXATION

While none of the major approaches to taxation are accepted by many critics without qualification, it can be said that public finance literature has featured four main philosophies. One along lines previously discussed has given major weight to equity and especially to ability to pay and personal taxation of income and wealth. Another, recently and ably promoted by a British author,[15] has departed from this standard to recommend the personal and progressive taxation of personal expenditure as the basis for the tax system. The thought here is that the government should not ignore expenditure from wealth as contrasted with income (living high on one's capital) and that what one does with his receipts is more important than the income he has to do with. A third approach departs from this philosophy in that it settles for heavy impersonal taxes on consumption; it gives great weight to the practical considerations of collecting revenues with minimum friction. A fourth approach is functional in character and recommends so ordering the tax system that it will least effect production and doing this by levies that strike "windfall" income, that is, income that requires no incentive and makes no return to the commonwealth. The principal source of such income, it is said, derives from private ownership of natural resources or gifts of nature.

THE RATE STRUCTURE

DEFINITION OF TERMS

Students of taxation speak of tax rates as *regressive, proportional, progressive,* and *degressive.* Before examining what kind of rate structure is in accord with the requirements of equity, it will be necessary to give some attention to the meaning of these terms. A tax base is the object upon which a tax is laid, and a tax rate is the amount of tax (usually expressed as a percentage) which is levied per unit of base. The total amount of the tax is equal to the base times the rate. This may be conviently expressed by the formulas

$$B \times R = T \text{ and } R = \frac{T}{B}$$

where R represents the rate, B the base, and T the amount of tax.

Rate structures have to do with the behavior of the rate (R), when the base (B) increases or decreases. Thus, if the rate (R) decreases as the base (B) increases, the rate structure is said to be *regressive;* if the rate (R) remains constant as the base (B) increases, the structure is said to be *proportional;* and if the rate (R) increases as the base (B) increases, the structure is called *progressive.* Progressive rates may advance regularly or irregularly, at a slow rate of increase or at a rapid

---

[15] Nicholas Kaldor, *An Expenditure Tax* (London: George Allen and Unwin, Ltd., 1955).

rate, with a constant or a changing acceleration. If the increase is at a decreasing rate—that is, if the acceleration becomes constantly less as the base increases—the rate structure is said to be *degressive*.

Actually, what is frequently done in appraising and designating rate structures is to compare the tax paid by different taxpayers with their net income. If the rate, or ratio, thus calculated is higher for large- than for small-income recipients, the tax is said to be progressive. This leads to an alternative definition of the terms used above according to their effects on inequalities. According to this definition, a tax is said to be progressive if it reduces inequalities, regressive if it aggravates them, and so forth.

Illustrations. To choose some illustrations from the tax system, the property tax usually operates with proportional rates. The base is the value of property owned by an individual. If the value is $1000 and the rate 1 percent, the tax will be $10. If the value is $10,000, the rate will still be 1 percent, although the amount of tax in this case will be $100. A frequent complaint against the property tax is that in practice it is regressive. The regressivity arises from an administrative failure which takes the form of underassessment of the more valuable properties. The rate remains constant on the nominal base, but it falls as the actual or proper base increases.

Consumption or sales taxes are usually regressive. The federal cigarette tax, for example, is based upon the number of cigarettes sold. If it is paid by the consumer in higher prices for cigarettes, it is paid by him according to the number of cigarettes he purchases and consumes. As the rate remains the same regardless of the number of cigarettes consumed, the tax is, according to our first definition of terms, proportional. But the amount of cigarettes consumed, and consequently the cigarette tax paid, may not increase with the wealth and income of the individual. The rate at which the tax is paid with respect to wealth and income decreases as wealth and income increase. Thus the tax augments inequalities of income and is said to be regressive.

Income taxes usually follow a progressive schedule of rates. If a $1000 income base is taxed at a 1 percent rate, a $10,000 income may be taxed at 3 percent, a $20,000 income at 6 percent, and so on. Rate structures in many income tax laws are complicated by the use of the bracket system, under which, rather than one rate applying to the total, different rates are applied to the different parts of the income. Under the bracket system, that portion of a net income which falls between $1000 and $1999 may be taxed at 1 percent, while the part falling between $2000 and $2999 is taxed at 2 percent. To determine what the true or effective rate is on any one income, it is necessary to compute the tax and divide it by the base. Thus, with the rate schedule given above, if the individual has an income of $2500, the first $1000 of which is exempt, he would have to calculate his taxes as follows:

Tax base		*Tax rate*	*Amount*
1st	$1000	exempt	none
2d	1000	1%	$10.00
3d	1000/2 = $500	2%	10.00
Total	$2500	0.8%	$20.00

Then, to calculate the effective rate from these total figures, he would have to divide the tax ($T = \$20$) by the base ($B = \$2500$), which in this case would make his true or effective rate equal to 20/2500 (T/B) = 0.8 percent (R). The bracket system is used in order to obtain a smooth progression. Without it, the amount of tax one would pay on an income of $2001 might be so much greater than the amount he would pay on an income of $1999 that actually he would be better off with the smaller income. The embarrassment that governments experience when they graduate a tax by totality is customarily called the "notch problem."

The calculation of an effective rate may also take account of income not taxed because of special provision of law exempting it for other reason than differences in family responsibilities. Our present federal law contains many provisions of this kind and the result is an effective rate schedule far lower and less progressive than the rate scale in the statute might lead one to expect.[16]

The lower part of the progressive scale of the federal personal income tax which prevailed at the end of World War II (and has been used more or less as a standard since then) is shown on the opposite page.

Taxable income	*Percent*
Not over $2000	20
Over $2000 but not over $4000	22
Over $4000 but not over $6000	26
Over $6000 but not over $8000	30
Over $8000 but not over $10,000	34
Over $10,000 but not over $12,000	38
Over $12,000 but not over $14,000	43
Over $14,000 but not over $16,000	47

[16] See Richard A. Musgrave, "How Progressive is the Income Tax?" *Tax Revision Compendium,* Committee on Ways and Means (Washington, D.C., 1959), vol. 3, pp. 2223–2234.

There is no apparent consideration to account for the fact that the rate of acceleration over these brackets of similar range varied from 2 to 5 percentage points.

To illustrate progression in another way, we may present the following data:

Taxpayer	Income	Tax 1	Tax 2	Tax 3
A	$4000	$30	$40	$50
B	2000	30	20	10

Tax 1, though equally distributed in absolute amounts, is regressive, tax 2 is proportional, and tax 3 is progressive.

Income tax schedules in practice are usually degressive—that is, they flatten out at the top, applying higher rates to wider and wider brackets until finally all income over a certain figure is taxed at a constant marginal rate.

Graphic Presentation. It is customary to present rate structures graphically with the rates measured on the vertical and income on the horizontal axis. The marginal and effective rates for a taxpayer with a $1000 personal exemption and the federal scale as previously indicated are thus plotted in Figure 2.

APPLICATION OF THE CONCEPT OF PROGRESSION TO RATE CHANGES

If there is some confusion in the definition of progression, there is much more uncertainty in some of its many applications. Thus, much ambiguous argument centers on the question of whether income tax rate changes as such are progressive and more or less progressive as compared with other possible changes. Suppose that effective rates on a $5000 and on a $10,000 income are respectively 5 and 10 percent. These rates might be increased by doubling each one or by adding equally to each rate (say 5 percentage points) or by applying an additional levy on "take-home pay" (after existing taxes). To illustrate the confusion, one may call attention to the fact that the second alternative (adding a flat percentage) seems to weaken progression by compounding a progressive and a proportional tax. But if the relative stake in total take-home pay after and before this change be calculated, it will be found that the change does reduce inequalities while, if the change were made in reverse (reduction of all rates by a flat percentage figure), the effect would be regressive.[17] Thus

---

[17] See R. A. Musgrave and Tun Thin, "Income Tax Progression, 1929–48," *The Journal of Political Economy*, LVI: 6 (December 1948), pp. 498–514; Harold M. Groves and C. Harry Kahn, "Stability of State and Local Tax Yields," *American Economic Review*, XLII: 1 (March 1952), pp. 87–102.

on one concept of progression, progressiveness is a function of the level of rates as well as the spread between them.

The same problem arises in a comparison of the relative progressiveness of different rate scales. To present a simple model, assume only two taxpayers: *A* with an income of $10,000 and *B* with $20,000. As-

FIGURE 2

Schedules of Marginal and Effective Income Tax Rates

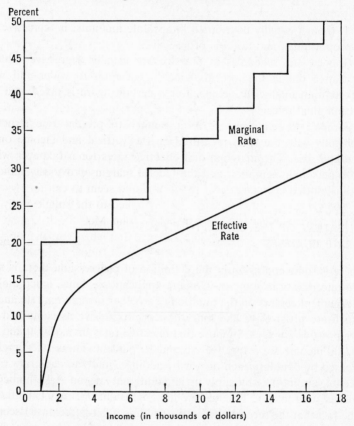

Income (in thousands of dollars)

sume one tax system in which *A* pays at an effective rate of 5 percent and *B* at 10 percent; another in which *A* pays at 10 percent and *B* at 15 percent; and a third in which *A* pays at 10 percent and *B* at 20 percent. How do the systems compare in progressiveness? The answer depends on the measure of progression chosen. *A* pays a lesser proportion of total taxes under the first system but in terms of relative income after taxes *A* does better under the second system. *A* does equally well in terms of relative taxes under the first and third systems but better in terms of take-home pay under the third system.

PROGRESSIVE TAXATION

ARGUMENTS CONCERNING THE PROPRIETY OF PROGESSIVE RATES

The proponents of progressive taxation hold that the proper application of the ability doctrine requires that a $10,000 income contribute not only ten times as much as a $1000 income but something more than ten times as much. This contention has been the subject of more debate, perhaps, than any other in tax literature.

Measurement. The proposition stated above might seem to be in accord with the theory of the diminishing marginal utility of income, but in reality it does not necessarily follow since no one knows with any precision how fast utility diminishes; some in fact deny that it diminishes at all except in the lower ranges of income. Moreover, if *A*'s income is $4000 and *B*'s $2000 and the utility at the margin of *A*'s income is half that at the margin of *B's,* equal sacrifice would seem to call for twice the tax on the larger income than would be applied to the smaller one. This is proportional, not progressive taxation. John McCulloch argued in a classic statement opposing progressive rates that when you abandon proportionality in taxation "you are at sea without rudder or compass, and there is no amount of injustice and folly you may not commit." [18] Being at sea, he went on to explain, is due to the fact that there is no scientific and objective information to indicate how fast rates should advance as the base increases. Perhaps the $10,000 person should be required to pay more than $100, if the $1000 person is charged $10. But how much more? John Stuart Mill, though favorably disposed toward an exemption of the necessities of life and progressive rates as applied to death duties, accepted this argument against the graduated principle in general as conclusive. The difference in ability to pay as income advances, he said, is not "capable of being decided with the degree of certainty on which a legislator or a financier ought to act." [19]

A rejoinder to this criticism of progressive rates has been made by Professor E. R. A. Seligman. His argument is that although the degrees of progression warranted by considerations of equity cannot be deter-

[18] J. R. McCulloch, *A Treatise on the Principles and Practical Influence of Taxation and the Funding System* (London: Longman, Brown, Green, & Longmans, 1845), p. 143.
[19] J. S. Mill, *Principles of Political Economy,* ed. Ashley (London: Longmans, Green & Co., Ltd., 1936), p. 807.

mined with mathematical exactness, it is better to approximate justice than to be clearly unjust. If it is clearly unjust to ask the $1000 income to contribute to the state at the same rate as the $10,000 income, should we not apply a higher rate to the $10,000 income even though we cannot be altogether certain just how much higher the rate should be? [20]

Social and Economic Effects.   It always makes sense to appraise any institution in terms of its effects, and in the case of progressive taxation these effects can be presumed to cover a wide range in the economic, political, and other areas. It is true that this approach does not escape the problem of measuring the immeasurable and does not give answers concerning which reasonable men may not differ. The quest for certainty in this as in many other areas is doomed to failure. It seems likely that the setting of progressive rates is a pragmatic phenomenon; legislators feel their way along, bearing in mind a host of consequences that are in the balance.[21]

Incentive.   Beginning with economic effects, one confronts first the concern for incentives. Those who innovate, who assume responsibility, who take chances and employ their capital in an active role, need somehow to be encouraged.

The effect of graduation upon the differential rewards for risk taking can be seen in the following illustration: A man leaves a million dollars to each of his three sons, *A, B,* and *C.* At considerable risk to his inheritance, *A* invests in stocks that yield him an average 10 percent return on his outlay. But the return is subject to a high effective rate of tax, let us say 75 percent. This will reduce his net yield after tax to 2.5 percent. *B* invests in high-grade bonds yielding 3 percent. At his lower income level the tax is only 33 percent, and his yield after tax is 2 percent. *C* does not invest at all but lives on his principal, thus avoiding the income tax entirely. Instead of yields of 10, 3, and 0 percent that would prevail without the tax system, returns after taxes are reduced to 2.5, 2, and 0 percent. In these circumstances, are any of these investors justified in taking a risk? It can be argued of course that we do not need millionaires to do our risk taking and to provide venture capital. But in that event we must develop channels by which middle-class savings can be shunted into the ownership of stocks.

When this is said, it should be added that incentives are probably much more resistant to tax impairment than might be supposed. One reason is that a general tax such as the net income tax is ordinarily so

---

[20] E. R. A. Seligman, *Progressive Taxation in Theory and Practice,* publication of the American Economic Association, IX: 1 and 2 (1894), pp. 193–194.

[21] See Elmer F. Fagan, "Recent and Contemporary Theories of Progressive Taxation," *Journal of Political Economy,* 46: 4 (August 1938), pp. 457–498; Harold M. Groves, "Toward a Social Theory of Progressive Taxation," *National Tax Journal,* IX: 1 (March 1956), pp. 27–34.

devised that the relative rank of the taxpayers is not disturbed. Perhaps what makes the most difference to the individual is whether his income is higher or lower than the general level. Much of the cost of the factors of production is "opportunity cost," that is, the price that must be paid to attract them from competitors. But the income tax circumvents opportunity cost by taxing all competitors. Another factor (and this distinguishes taxes from tribute) is that the taxpayer counts some return on what he contributes to government. Finally, there is the point that once a standard of living has been established, the taxpayer will fight to preserve it. He may under some circumstances even intensify his economic effort because of the tax.

Supply curves for effort may have either a positive or a negative slope. For instance, wives may be repelled from the labor force because additional family income is so largely absorbed by taxes. On the other hand, they may be enticed into the labor market because disposable income after taxes is no longer considered adequate.

In the case of risk-capital incentives, there is reason to believe that risk is not irksome to all people (witness the success of the slot machine) and in income taxation governments also reduce risk to some extent by sharing losses as well as gains.

Certain empirical evidence on the matter of incentives has been gathered by interview. It indicates that with some exceptions business executives have continued at their posts with about as much enthusiasm as before high income taxes. And investment patterns also do not appear to have radically changed. On the other hand, there can be no question about the effectiveness of the incentive to avoid taxes that high income tax rates induce. Success in creating and applying avoidance devices reduces not only the effectiveness but also the even application of high rates.[22]

Other Economic Considerations. Whatever may be the effect of progressive taxation on incentives there can be no doubt that it inhibits the ability to save. Professor Pigou distinguished here between what he called the "announcement effects" of taxation and the income effects. The former have to do with the changes in the taxpayer's outlook because of the tax; the latter with his material circumstances. Historically the fear of impairing capital was the strongest single objection to progression. However, what constitutes adequate saving under given conditions of time and place is a matter of considerable disagreement.

---

[22] See Thomas H. Sanders, *Effects of Taxation on Executives,* 1951, and J. Keith Butters, Lawrence E. Thompson, and Lynn L. Bollinger, *Effects of Taxation Investment by Individuals,* 1953, Harvard Graduate School of Business Administration, Boston. An excellent summary of empirical studies in this area will be found in Earl R. Rolph and George F. Break, *Public Finance* (New York: The Ronald Press Company, 1961), chap. 7.

There are those who hold that in the present state of our economic development, the limiting factor in output is usually the unavailability of markets. We would and could produce more if we knew how to dispose of it. On this view progressive taxation may be positively favorable to production. However, it is also said that markets can be created equally well either by wide consumption or high investment (such as new building). Taxes that promote the former may discourage the latter.

A progressive tax system contributes toward "built-in flexibility," a term which is used to describe the tendency of federal revenues to fluctuate, producing deficits when times are bad and surpluses when times are good. Rising incomes not only provide a better base, but they are also taxed at a higher effective rate. This fluctuation is regarded as having a salutary and automatic stabilizing effect upon the private economy. At the state and local level, however, governments are more concerned with stable revenue than in compensating for instability in the private sphere.

Associated with the distribution of income after taxes is the improvement of human resources. Here one recalls the argument of Pigou that the marginal net product of resources wisely invested in persons is likely to exceed that of resources wisely invested in material capital.[23]

Political and Social Effects. As to political effects, there is concern about the taxpayer retaining the means and leisure to keep himself informed on the issues of government. There is also concern lest wealth become so unequal that only part of the people can afford the important and expensive means of political communication—such as radio, television, and press. In a democracy any minority has small protection indeed if it has no effective way of making itself heard and seen by large numbers of people.

Considerations of this kind support the conclusion that one of the requisites of a democracy is a large middle class. There is also the matter of political stability; it may or may not be true that the discontent associated with wide inequality is more important on this score than the resentment of those who regard extreme progression as a flagrant case of "spending other people's money."

Clearly related to political considerations are those concerning international security. The illiteracy and physical defects of youth needed for military manpower may be associated with poverty aggravated by an oppressive tax system. A propaganda point in cold warfare concerns the degree of inequality prevailing in competing economic systems.

Considerations that may be classed as social include such matters as the relation (if any) of poverty and riches to crime and delinquency, ill health, and unstable family relationships.

------

[23] Pigou, *The Economics of Welfare,* Part V, chap. XI.

Revenue Requirements. A very high rate on the relatively few incomes in the highest brackets would not yield nearly enough to support the state. If the federal government were to confiscate all income in excess of $10,000, the result in terms of revenue would be only a small fraction of what it is now spending. The income structure is like a pyramid in shape; small increases in taxes at the base of the pyramid will produce as much revenue as very much larger increases at the peak. One recent study concludes that the basic rate of our present federal income tax structure yields 85 percent of the total revenue from the tax, and that were the present surtaxes limited to 50 percent (instead of 90 percent) the yield would be reduced by only 2 percent.[24]

Administration. As to administration, one can say that the higher the tax the more reward there is in escaping it. Whatever effect the high tax may have on the incentive to earn, there can be no question about its efficacy as an incentive to avoid paying taxes. The alternative to substantial graduation may be the collection of a light tax from very large numbers of taxpayers in the low strata of incomes. This latter policy, too, involves administrative difficulties. That the attempt to apply progression causes many administrative and avoidance problems, will become quite evident in later chapters. Indeed it is said that one reason why high-rate taxes are not so potent a blow to incentives as might be expected is that most taxpayers contrive to reduce their effective rates of tax by avoidance. It is evident that effective rates of tax rarely exceed 50 percent though nominal rates go much higher. Assuming that loopholes and avoidance are a concomitant of high rates and could be eliminated without the latter, a trade of fewer loopholes for reduced rates would constitute a clear gain for the tax system.

Offsetting Other Taxes. Concerning other taxes, it should be pointed out that a progressive tax and a progressive tax system are two quite different institutions. Alfred Marshall described the difference as follows:

> Onerous taxes, imperial and local, must be treated as a whole. Almost every onerous tax taken by itself presses with undue weight upon some class or other; but this is of no moment if the inequalities of each are compensated by those of the others, and variations in the several parts synchronise. If that difficult condition is satisfied, the system may be equitable, though any one part of it regarded alone would be inequitable.[25]

A tax system is likely to consist of many taxes, some of which are regressive, some proportional, and others progressive. The regressive taxes may

---

[24] Tax Foundation, *Are High Surtax Rates Worthwhile?* (New York, 1957).
[25] Alfred Marshall, *Memorandum on Imperial and Local Taxes* (C.9528), p. 113; quoted from Pigou, *A Study in Public Finance,* p. 75.

offset the progressive taxes, with the result that the entire tax system may be proportional. Before the progressive income and inheritance taxes were added to the tax system of the United States, the latter was regressive, and it is probably still regressive within certain ranges of income.[26] It was clearly progressive in the ranges of income above $5000 even before World War II, and the more intensive application of the net income tax to a broader base has now probably reduced the range of regressivity, particularly if noncash income be taken into account. (The latter refers mostly to the production of goods that are consumed directly as in the cases of owner-occupied homes and subsistence farming.) Statistically, the personal exemptions, which avoid application of progressive rates at the lowest levels of income, contribute to give the tax-distribution curve a negative slope or at any rate a distinct flatness in the early ranges of income. Of course, regressive consumption and property taxes, mostly state and local, are important factors.

EFFECTS OF PUBLIC FINANCE ON DISTRIBUTION

Statistical Method.   Public expenditures as well as taxes may have a progressive effect—that is, they may contribute to the reduction of inequalities. Statistical calculation of the effect of public finance on the distribution of income involves, first, a theoretical analysis of the incidence (final burden) of taxes; secondly, a distribution of total taxes among the levels of income; and finally, a calculation and comparison of effective rates of tax. Complicated as this seems, it is only half the task. Some public expenditures (particularly social security and certain social service items) can be apportioned to the income levels. Ultimately the statistician may emerge with a figure that shows the amount of real income transferred from those with incomes above $7500, for instance, to those with lesser incomes. One study of this kind purported to show that public finance in the United States in 1950 tripled the share of total income going to the lowest bracket (below $1000) and reduced the share going to the top bracket by about one quarter.[27]

---

[26] Twentieth Century Fund, Inc., *Facing the Tax Problem* (New York, 1937), p. 237; Gerhard Colm and Helen Tarasov, *Who Pays the Taxes?* Monograph No. 3, Temporary National Economic Committee, 1940. For recent study and discussion of this matter see R. A. Musgrave, J. J. Carroll, L. D. Cook, and L. Frane, "Distribution of Tax Payments by Income Groups: A Case Study for 1948," *National Tax Journal*, IV: 1 (March 1951), pp. 1–53; Rufus S. Tucker, "Distribution of Tax Burdens in 1948," *ibid.*, IV: 3 (September 1951), pp. 269–285; *Proceedings of the National Tax Association Conference*, 1952, pp. 179–221; R. A. Musgrave, "Incidence of the Tax System and its Effects on Consumption," in *Federal Tax Policy for Economic Growth and Stability*, papers submitted to the Joint Committee on the Economic Report, 84th Cong., 1st Sess. (Washington, D.C. 1955), pp. 96–113.

[27] Alfred H. Conrad, "Redistribution Through Government Budgets in the

Of course taxation involves horizontal as well as vertical redistribution of income. Such redistribution might for instance favor urban as against rural taxpayers or vice versa; it might favor those with large families against those with small ones; and it certainly does favor those who abstain from liquor and tobacco against those who are heavy consumers of these economic goods.

FIGURE 3

Effect of the Federal Income Tax on the Distribution of Income

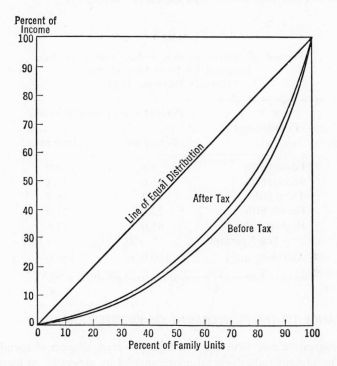

Graphic Illustration. The effect of public finance upon income distribution may be shown graphically. A favorite device for doing this is the so-called Lorenz curve. This curve shows the percentage of total income received by any given percentage of recipients. The percentage of income is measured along the vertical axis, and the corresponding percentage of recipients along the horizontal. If, in Figure 3, every family received the same income, the Lorenz curve would indicate that any given

United States," in Alan T. Peacock, *Income Redistribution and Social Policy* (London: Jonathan Cape, 1954), p. 240.

percentage of recipients received the same percentage of total income. In
this case all data would be plotted along the line of equal distribution
which is drawn diagonally from the lower left to the upper right corner of
the graph. Thus, if 50 percent of the families received 50 percent of the
income, the datum will be registered on this line. The larger the area between the line of equal distribution and the Lorenz curve, which shows
the prevailing distribution of income, the greater is the degree of inequality. In the diagram, the distribution of income in 1947 before and after
federal individual income tax is shown. The student will note how, owing
to the progressivity of the income tax, the curve "after tax" is closer to
the line of equal distribution than the curve "before tax."

TABLE 1

Percent of Money Income, before and after Tax,
Received by Each Fifth of the
Nation's Families, 1961

Family units	Percent of total money income	
	Before tax	After tax
Lowest fifth	4.6	4.9
Second fifth	11.0	11.5
Third fifth	16.3	16.8
Fourth fifth	22.6	23.0
Highest fifth	45.0	43.8
Top 5 percent	20.	18.1
All family units	100.0	100.0

SOURCE: *Survey of Current Business,* April 1962, p. 14.

RESISTANCE TO THE DEVELOPMENT OF PROGRESSION

The progressive rate structure is a high-powered weapon of social control. The present rather general acceptance of its propriety, at least as a
feature of some taxes, was not achieved without resistance. William Glad-
stone, liberal as he was, once said of progression that when a stone of that
character gets rolling no one can tell when or where it will stop. Conservative writers exhausted their invectives in abusing the principle. Some
thirty years before the adoption of the progressive principle in the British estate tax in 1894, one of them wrote: "The very name, graduation,
stinks in the nostrils of wealthy men . . . graduation is unjust . . .
graduation is a filching from rich men a payment for that which they do
not receive . . . it is a demand on rich men to pay a shilling for the loaf

which men of moderate means are to get for ninepence." [28] William New-march, the eminent economist and statistician, said that it was not the task of taxation to correct "the vicissitudes of fortune," and further that graduation is "confiscation, punishing prudence and virtue, taxing a man for being good to himself and doing good to others." [29] The combination of progression and the universal franchise was regarded as particularly dangerous.

The Supreme Court of the United States has accepted the principle of progressive taxation. Justice White, in an opinion sustaining the federal estate tax enacted during the Spanish-American War, stated that "The grave consequences which it is asserted must arise in the future if the right to levy a progressive tax be recognized involves in its ultimate aspect the mere assertion that free and representative government is a failure, and that the grossest abuses of power are foreshadowed unless the courts usurp a purely legislative function." [30] However, Justice Brewer, in an earlier opinion on the subject, expressed a vigorous dissent:

> Equality in right, in protection, and in burden is the thought which has run through the life of this Nation and its constitutional enactments from the Declaration of Independence to the present hour. . . . When a tax law directly, necessarily, and intentionally creates an inequality of burden, it then becomes imperative to inquire whether this inequality thus intentionally created can find any constitutional justification.[31]

Most recent attacks on the progressive principle have taken the form of proposed amendments to the Constitution. One such proposal contemplates a 25-percent ceiling on income taxes with the proviso that the ceiling may be broken with a favorable vote by three fourths of both houses of Congress, but not to establish a rate structure in which the top rate is more than 15 percentage points above the starting rate. The issue of a constitutional amendment to check progressive taxation goes to the fundamentals of the democratic process. It can be argued that progressive taxation is too powerful a weapon to be trusted to "the masses"—that it leaves minority interests too exposed to the vicissitudes of politics. One writer put the matter as follows: "A great and vital question today is whether a political system based on the Rights of Man, as against the Power of the State, can long survive when the *unlimited power to tax is*

---

[28] William Lucas Sargant, "An Undiscriminating Income Tax Reconsidered," *Journal of the Statistical Society of London,* XXV (1862), p. 352.

[29] Quoted by Sir Josiah Stamp, *The Fundamental Principles of Taxation,* pp. 39, 56.

[30] *Knowlton v. Moore,* 178 U.S. 49, 109 (1900).

[31] *Magoun v. Illinois Trust and Savings Bank,* 170 U.S. 283, 301 (1898).

coupled with the unlimited power to vote—that is, when the majority, through their representatives, can levy taxes on a minority at rates which the majority do not pay." [32] The extension of the ballot to the "have nots" involved a risk—perhaps a calculated risk. But it may still be doubted that property rights and income status are of such vital concern to the national interest that they should be elevated to the bill of rights.

In the last analysis, whether or not one believes that the progressive principle is desirable depends considerably upon one's general philosophy of life. In this respect people are generally divisible into two groups. One group would prefer a world in which a free hand is given to the strong and the clever. This group holds that a free struggle makes for strong, vigorous character and that large inequalities are necessary to support the economic incentives. These people accept the progressive principle, if at all, with reluctance. They feel that progressive taxation, especially if the rates are steeply graduated, violates the moral law against one's "reaping where he has not sown." They also contend that many who wish the tax system to reduce inequalities would confine its role in this respect to incomes above their own. The second group holds that the strong have a decided obligation to the weak and stresses the solidarity of human interests. It dislikes and doubts the wisdom of great inequalities. Those who belong to this latter group are very likely to approve the progressive principle with enthusiasm. [33]

TAXATION FOR NONFISCAL PURPOSES

Much is said these days about the use of taxation for social control or for nonfiscal purposes. Taxation for nonfiscal purposes is usually defined as tax legislation motivated mainly by some purpose other than raising revenue. For example, the protective tariff has as its primary aim the elimination of foreign competition; taxes on oleomargarine in some states are designed mainly to reduce competition and improve the market for the products of the dairy farmer. It should be remembered, however, that taxation itself is social control, and no tax or fiscal policy can be judged apart from all of its consequences whether they are classed as fiscal or

---

[32] Samuel B. Pettingill, "The History of a Prophecy: Class War and the Income Tax," *American Bar Association Journal,* 39 (June 1953), p. 474.

[33] For other studies of the subject of progressive taxation, in addition to those mentioned in the footnotes, see Henry C. Simons, *Personal Income Taxation* (Chicago: University of Chicago Press, 1938); William Vickrey, *Agenda for Progressive Taxation* (New York: The Ronald Press, 1947); F. Shehab, *Progressive Taxation* (New York: Oxford University Press, 1953); Musgrave, *The Theory of Public Finance,* chaps. 1–6.

nonfiscal. Professor John R. Commons states this idea in the following words:

> Taxation, then, is the most pervasive and privileged exercise of the police power. . . . Even when not consciously intended to be regulative, taxes nevertheless regulate, for they, like the protective tariff, determine the directions in which people may become wealthy by determining directions in which they may not become wealthy. They say to the business man: Here is profit, there is loss. It is impossible to avoid these effects of taxes, therefore impossible to escape the police power of taxation, therefore impossible to look upon taxes of any kind whatever as merely a means of obtaining revenue according to any principle of equality, or ability to pay, or accumulation of wealth, or any standard that looks solely to the acquisitions of the past.[34]

Taxation for nonfiscal purposes or social control is objected to by some critics because, it is said, the revenue system is complicated enough without saddling upon it a load of regulation and, further, because regulation can be accomplished more effectively and economically by direct, regulatory legislation than by tax laws.

The first answer to these arguments is that nonfiscal motivation behind legislation is a matter of degree; no clear line can be drawn between tax legislation that is nonfiscal and that which is fiscal in character. This point is very aptly expressed by Sir Josiah Stamp's excellent analogy, "that it is wrong to marry for money, but all right to marry where money is."

The second answer is that each proposal of tax legislation with nonfiscal ends must be weighed on its merits. If there are other better ways of accomplishing the ends sought, certainly the proposal should be turned down. However, this may not always be true, and no tax measure need be defeated because it seeks to accomplish some nonfiscal end. For example, it is said that Peter the Great at one time levied a tax upon beards. He held that the beard was a superfluous and useless ornament. The tax is said to have been proportional according to the length of the beard and progressive according to the social position of its possessor. Every person paying the tax received a token which he had to wear so it could be seen. Inspectors were provided with scissors and were ordered to cut off ruthlessly the beards of those who did not show badges.[35]

Peter's tax on beards seems objectionable, not on the ground that

---

[34] *Institutional Economics* (New York: The Macmillan Company, 1934), p. 820.

[35] M. D. Cobleigh, "Some Queer Provisions of Former Tax Statutes," *Bulletin of the National Tax Association,* XIV: 4 (January 1929), p. 107.

it constituted an abuse of the taxing power but that possibly the object was not a proper one or that it might have been accomplished through a better means. It is probably true that social control through taxation has often been ill advised and ineffective. But the most to be deduced is that this creates a presumption against such use and one that is not conclusive. Each proposed use of taxation for nonfiscal purposes must be judged on its own merits.

SUMMARY

The problem of finding general principles to use in properly distributing governmental burdens may be approached in a number of ways, of which one is to develop a list of canons or attributes of a desirable revenue source. Most venerable is the list of Adam Smith who said that taxes should be equitable, certain, convenient, and economical.

Another approach is to consider certain standards that have long been advocated as suitable guides in the problem of properly apportioning governmental revenues. One of these comprises the benefit principles which, however, encounters the objection that benefits from government are not measurable and that the principle limits the distribution of governmental services more than is thought to be in the social interest. Nevertheless, the benefit principle has much reasonable application in the revenue system. Of more recent development and much more popular is the ability-to-pay principle. This is championed in part on the ground that it minimizes sacrifice and takes account of the diminishing importance of income to the taxpayer; it encounters the difficulty that sacrifice is largely immeasurable. Closely related and subject to similar argument is the contention that taxes should aim at a reduction of inequalities. Finally, the student may prefer the social-expediency principle which contents itself with judging taxes according to the sum of their total effects.

The rate structures that may be used to raise governmental revenue vary, and there are several types in application in current revenue systems. The justice and wisdom of progressive rates have been for many years the subject of much argument. Against them is argued that they cannot be supported by a utility curve since no one can draw such a curve with precision. It is answered that rough justice is better than none, and that on balance the economic, political, and social effects of progressive taxation are in accord with the public interest. Some concern for incentives should temper the use of progressive rates, but both on reason and experience incentives are likely to withstand more pressure than might at first be supposed. In practice, the determination of progressive rates for a specific tax is likely to be a compromise involving considerations of revenue, incentive, saving, administration, equality, and rates of other taxes. In appraising taxation for nonfiscal purposes, probably the preponderant view is that taxes must be judged by all their effects, whether or not such measures are designed to raise revenue.

PROBLEMS

1. Why would it be inequitable to tax people according to their (physical) weight? Would it make more sense to tax them according to their economic capacity (faculty)?
2. Is it possible to follow all of Adam Smith's canons of taxation or must we choose among them? What tax in our present tax system stresses equity? What tax stresses convenience?
3. Explain what is meant when it is said that "government must be regarded as preeminently the concern of all citizens enjoyed by all in their corporate capacity."
4. Why is it not true:
   a. That progressive taxation means simply that the rich should be called upon to pay more in taxes than the poor?
   b. That equality of sacrifice necessarily involves progressive rates?
5. Comment on the proposition that where marginal utility drops as income advances, and in the same proportion, equal sacrifice will require proportional taxation.
6. With progression by totality (rather than bracket) with a 20-percent rate on incomes up to $2000 and a 22-percent rate on incomes above $2000, what tax will be paid by incomes of $1999 and $2001? What take-home pay will this leave the two taxpayers?
7. If Smith has an income of $5000 and personal exemptions of $1000 and the progressive scale on taxable income provides rates of 20, 22, and 26 percent, respectively, on successive $2000 brackets, calculate Smith's tax and effective rate of tax.
8. Using the scale in Problem 7 and assuming the personal exemption there specified, plot for graphic presentation the effective rate of tax on incomes of $2000, $4000, and $6000.
9. Assume three tax systems with the following rates at respective levels of income:
   System A—1,2,3,4,5
   System B—2,3,4,5,6
   System C—2,4,6,8,10
   Compare the relative progressivity of the three systems.
10. Comment on the proposition that income beyond subsistence has little or no absolute value; it is relative income that is important, and progressive taxation, while it may reduce the degree of rela-

tive difference, preserves incentive because it does not change relative rankings.

11. John McCulloch was of the opinion that when you abandon proportionality in taxation, "you are at sea without rudder or compass, and there is no amount of injustice and folly you may not commit." What did he mean? How was he answered by E. R. A. Seligman?

12. Submit an extensive outline of the case either for or against progressive taxation.

13. Comment on the proposition that progressive taxation is the sort of question we decide by ballot and that therefore it requires neither research nor analysis.

14. Explain the steps that need to be taken to determine the fact of progression or regression in the tax system as a whole, and the further steps that are needed to determine the effects of public finance on the distribution of income.

15. Comment on the following propositions:

    a. "Improving production matters far more than fidgeting over fractions of distribution, and too much preoccupation with distribution may easily militate against the maximum production."

    b. Progressive taxation is a pet device of the socialists to weaken the capitalist system in preparation for "the socialist kill."

    c. If a capitalist society wants a high standard of living, it must check the tendency toward excessive inequalities.

    d. Progressive taxation is unjust because it is a violation of the principle that every man is entitled to the fruits of his own labor.

    e. The function of taxation is to supply adequate funds for the public services; ulterior objectives, such as the improvement of tastes, morals, and the distribution of wealth, should be avoided.

16. A has an income of $2000 and B one of $4000: If A pays a tax of $20 and B one of $30 is the tax system regressive, proportional, or progressive? If A pays a tax of $20 and B one of $40 could their sacrifice in making these payments be equal? Why?

17. Give two reasons why it would be difficult to apply a benefit theory of taxation to poor relief.

3

THE GENERAL PROPERTY TAX— NATURE AND CRITICISM

The previous chapter was devoted to the discussion of certain theories of how governmental burdens should be distributed. The task of the coming chapters will be to examine in the light of those theories the various means now employed for that purpose. Of these, the general property tax will be considered first.

IMPORTANCE OF THE PROPERTY TAX

With three exceptions the property tax has not been used by the federal government, but it is the backbone of the local revenue system in the United States.[1] In 1960 the property tax produced about $16,405 million for state and local governments, of which all but $60 million was for the

---

[1] Once, in 1798, a direct tax was apportioned among the states to be levied on dwellings at a rate of 0.2 percent of value, on slaves at the rate of fifty cents per head, and on land for the difference between these two taxes and the amount apportioned to the states. Again during the War of 1812 a direct tax was levied as above. It yielded approximately $4 million in 1814 and 1815. The last use of this tax was during the Civil War when a $20 million levy was apportioned among the states for collection.—W. J. Shultz and M. R. Caine, *Financial Development of the United States* (Englewood Cliffs, N.J.: Prentice-Hall, Inc., 1937), pp. 110–111, 141–142.

TABLE 2

Taxes in Order of Fiscal Importance: 1932 and 1960

(exclusive of payroll taxes)

1932

Tax	Federal Amount (in millions)	Federal Percent	State Amount (in millions)	State Percent	Local Amount (in millions)	Local Percent	All Units Amount (in millions)	All Units Percent
Property	$ —	—	$ 335	18.1	$ 4,361	92.5	$ 4,696	55.5
Income	1,057	55.9	152	8.2	—	—	1,209	14.3
Gasoline	—	—	534	28.9	—	—	534	6.3
Tobacco	399	21.1	15	.8	—	—	414	4.9
Customs	328	17.3	—	—	—	—	328	3.9
Motor vehicle	—	—	310	16.8	—	—	310	3.7
Inheritance, estate, and gift	47	2.5	148	8.0	5	.1	200	2.4
Alcoholic beverages	9	.5	1	.1	—	—	10	.1
General sales, use, and gross receipts	—	—	7	.4	—	—	7	.1
Other	51	2.7	349	18.9	350	7.4	750	8.9
Total	$ 1,891	100.0	$ 1,851	100.0	$ 4,716	100.0	$ 8,458	100.0

	1960							
Income	$62,209	80.8	$ 3,389	18.8	$ 254	1.4	$ 65,852	58.3
Property			607	3.4	15,798	87.4	16,405	14.5
Motor Fuels	1,984	2.6	3,335	18.5	33	.2	5,352	4.7
General sales, use, and gross receipts			4,374	24.3	875	4.8	5,249	4.6
Alcoholic beverages	3,106	4.0	734	4.1	23	.1	3,863	3.4
Motor vehicles	2,097	2.7	1,632	9.0	127	.7	3,856	3.4
Tobacco	1,927	2.5	923	5.1	65	.4	2,915	2.6
Death and gift	1,606	2.1	420	2.3			2,026	1.8
Customs	1,105	1.4					1,105	1.0
Other	2,969	3.9	2,621	14.5	909	5.0	6,499	5.7
Total	$77,003	100.0	$18,035	100.0	$18,084	100.0	$113,122	100.0

SOURCE: Tax Institute, *Tax Policy*, XIX: 7–8 (July–August 1952); XXVII: 10 (October 1961).

local units.[2] The local units are under the control of the states and as a
rule are allowed only such discretion in taxation as the legislatures may
give them. They are generally permitted to levy such property taxes as
seem suitable, but beyond this they have little tax discretion. In general,
the smaller the unit of government, the more exclusively it relies on
the general property tax. Leaving aids from the state out of account,
the property tax in 1960 constituted 87.4 percent of the local revenue
system. Because of an impressive upsurge in federal taxes (predominantly on income), the place of the property tax in the entire revenue
system is no longer major (about 14.5 percent in 1960), and the trend
in its relative importance has been distinctly downward. However, the
trend appears to have halted and changed direction in the last few years
with their rising cost of education. Table 2 presents the tax system of
the United States in 1932 and 1960, indicating the relative importance
and the long-run trend in rank of the various taxes. The states as such
have sought and found other more lucrative sources of revenue, and they
have come to the relief of the local property taxpayer with aids and
shared taxes. Some municipalities have broadened their local tax systems
with other levies such as municipal income and sales taxes. Anyway the
absolute amounts (and usually the rates) of local property taxes are
trending upward. The typical city or rural taxpayer would be surprised
indeed were anyone to tell him that the property tax is decreasing in
importance.

NATURE OF THE GENERAL PROPERTY TAX

Definition.   What is commonly called the general property tax is
such an important part of the local revenue system in the United States
that a knowledge of its definition and nature is essential. In its broadest
meaning the general property tax is a tax upon all wealth, tangible and
intangible, that possesses exchange value. It is levied according to exchange value, at least in theory, and at a common rate for all property
in the same district. It is thus a uniform and universal tax based upon
value of goods owned. Usually it is levied upon property in the jurisdiction where it is located, and the tax is paid by the owner. In actual
practice, as we shall see, the general property tax is nowhere near so

------

[2] See Table 2. For an excellent account of the place of the property tax in
the revenue system, now and in past years, see also Mable Newcomer, "The
Decline of the General Property Tax," *National Tax Journal,* VI: 1 (March
1953), pp. 38–51; I. M. Labovitz, "The Property Tax: Quicksand or Bedrock?"
Proceedings of the National Tax Association Conference, 1960, pp. 58–70.

universal or so uniform as the above brief statements would appear to indicate.[3]

Nature of General Property. It goes without saying that the kinds of goods which are owned and which have value in a modern state are numerous and varied. If one were to list all of the property which he might observe on a mile walk through a city, he would have an impressive array of items. The two most important classes would be real estate and personal property.

Although not complete, perhaps the simple diagram on the opposite page will illustrate the more common categories of property as classified for tax purposes.

The line of demarcation between real estate and personal property is not too distinct but, in general, real estate consists of immovables and personal property of movables. Frequently this distinction is clearly a relative matter; many buildings are movable, and very little, if any, personal property is so fluid as to move without some difficulty. But these distinctions sometimes are quite important in property taxation.

Classification of Real Property. Real property or real estate consists mainly of land and buildings (or what are called *improvements* on the land). It may further be classified according to the purpose for which the real estate is used; for example, residential, mercantile, manufacturing, agricultural, forest, and so on. In Wisconsin this classification is used for statistical purposes and as an aid to the local assessor in valuing each piece of property. Other states with *classified property tax systems* group real property into numerous classes so that each may be taxed differently. Minnesota thus makes a distinction between unplatted (rural) and platted (urban) real estate.

The distinction between land and improvements is not always made in our tax laws, but the differences between the two are very important in taxation. As we shall see in Chapter 6, the ultimate burden of the taxes on these two subjects may be quite different. Moreover, some jurisdictions apply different tax policies in the treatment of these two classes of real estate. Favorable treatment for improvements (either the temporary exemption of new improvements or the outright exemption

---

[3] Originally in the United States the property tax began its career as a specific rather than a general tax. Only gradually did it acquire those features of uniformity and universality that are its present characteristics. Classification and special treatment were once the rule rather than the exception. Only selected types of property were taxed, and they were listed at prescribed arbitrary values. And the present trend, as we shall see, is toward its original status when less uniformity and universality prevailed. Today the general property tax is a greatly modified and restricted tax, the extent of coverage depending upon the constitution, laws, and administrative practices in each state. In fact there are practically as many property tax systems as there are states. See Jens P. Jensen, *Property Taxation in the United States* (Chicago: University of Chicago Press, 1931).

of all of them) may be inaugurated to encourage building or on the
ground that land, as a gift of nature, is an especially fit object for taxation. Land values and building values are subject to different conditions.
Land may increase in value while the buildings on it are decreasing in
value. Quite different methods are used in evaluating the two kinds of
property. For instance, depreciation must be considered in the case of
buildings and is not encountered in evaluating land.

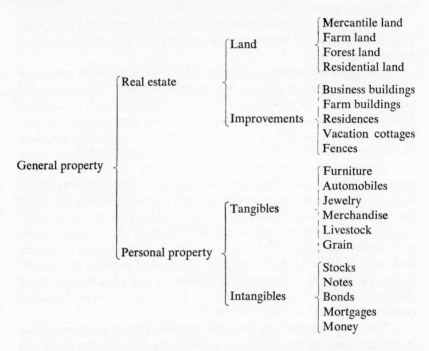

Personal Property—Tangible and Intangible. Personal property is
classified into two main categories—tangible and intangible. Tangible
personal property includes a great variety of goods: merchants' and
manufacturers' stocks (inventories); business furniture, fixtures, and
equipment; machinery, tools, and patterns; rolling stock of railways; farm
machinery; harvested crops; logs; household furniture, clothing, jewelry,
and "other personal effects." When a student "goes off to college," what
he takes with him is tangible personal property—his books, his clothes,
his traveling bags, his study lamp. He looks forward to receiving intangible property from his parents on the first of each month.

The second main category of personal property is intangible prop-
perty. This class consists mainly of contractual rights that have been
acquired by individuals or corporations in the tangible property of
others and its earnings. The more familiar items are stocks, mortgages,

deposits, money, and book credit. These are representative property; if the tangibles they represent were destroyed, the paper assets would lose all of their value. Copyrights and patents are intangibles of a somewhat different type, and good will, franchise value, and corporate excess are names given to the capitalized earning power of a business in so far as it exceeds the tangible assets of the business. Thus, in Illinois taxes are levied on the "corporate excess" of corporations in the same manner as property taxes are levied on all other property.

Often states distinguish between intangible and tangible property in arriving at a policy of tax exemption; intangibles have tended to disappear from the tax rolls as more and more states have adopted the income tax as a substitute for the general property tax on intangibles. Also, intangible property can more easily escape taxation either by migration or by hiding. It is indeed difficult to hide a barn from even the most perfunctory assessor, yet a bond can be safely hidden from the most diligent assessor. Many states classify intangibles separately and apply a low flat-rate tax to them as a substitute for the general property tax. As we shall see later, most intangible property, because it is representative of rights in the property of others, involves difficult problems of double taxation.

CHARACTERISTICS OF THE GENERAL PROPERTY TAX

The United States general property tax is characterized by (1) its gross property base, (2) its advalorem (according to value) measure, (3) uniformity, (4) universality, (5) proportionality, (6) impersonality, and (7) local collection—central sharing.

The Gross Property Base. As previously indicated, the property tax is a wealth tax. It belongs to a different family than the income tax, the latter being based upon what flows to the taxpayer between two points of time. The property tax, in contrast, is based upon what the taxpayer owns at a given point of time. The difference is familiar to the accountant—it is much the same as the one he observes between an operating statement and a balance sheet. The fixed point of time is sometimes modified in the case of certain tangible personal property—circulating capital, an element in the wealth structure that is highly dynamic. Thus, in the meat industry what was on hand on the morning of assessment day may have moved to another owner before evening. This creates certain difficulties for the general property tax that will be considered later. Moreover, it is not always easy to distinguish between property and income. Obviously, a dollar received as salary shortly before assessment day, and not spent by then, is both income during the taxpaying year and property on "A-Day." Much litigation at many points in the law attends the question of if and when a contract for personal services is property. Thus a baseball club may sell for a consideration the exclusive right to contract the services of a professional player; here exchange involved meets the qualifications of a property transaction.

The property tax is said to be based on gross wealth because the taxpayer cannot as a rule offset debts against the value of his property.

Ad Valorem Measurement.   As to the ad valorem measurement, one notes that while property differs in a multitude of respects it all has one attribute, namely, value. Of course there are many kinds of value, but the property tax sticks quite closely to the one that most concerns economists—exchange value. *A*'s farm may consist of 1000 acres and *B*'s of 10, but if the former could sell his property for only $1000 while the latter could get $10,000, *B*'s tax would be ten times as high as *A*'s. The facts that *A* may place a high subjective value on his land because his grandfather owned it or that he may have added unmarketable improvements for his own pleasure usually will not matter.

Uniformity.   The uniformity characteristic of the general property tax apparently was regarded by our forefathers as of great importance, for they often wrote it into state constitutions where, in many cases, it defied the erosions of time. Constitutional uniformity clauses vary, but generally they call for uniform treatment of taxable property within the same jurisdiction. Usually this gives the legislature power to exempt property but, curiously, not to half-exempt it—that is, to provide for lower burdens for some classes than others. In this case, oddly enough, the greater power does not include the less. Where no uniformity clause exists or where it has been amended, legislatures may have the power to classify at will, limited only by the general rule (discussed in Chapter 2) that classification must be reasonable. Apparently the fathers thought that uniformity of property taxation would ensure neutrality of treatment. If so, they have hardly been sustained by later experience. Differences in incidence alone would tend to defeat their purpose as would double counting (presently to be explained). And there are other genuine differences among properties ignored by uniformity.[4]

Universality.   The original idea of the general property tax was to include all wealth, excluding only a few items that could qualify for specific exemption. Here again the aim was neutrality and the reasoning plausible. Why should *A,* a real estate dealer, pay taxes on all of his capital, consisting of real estate, while *B,* a wholesaler, escapes on more than half of his assets, the latter largely in inventory?

Plausible as may have been the early objective, the universality

---

[4] A Wisconsin city containing within its boundaries certain agricultural property undertook to give such property a more favorable tax rate than other property in the city. This was overruled. *Knowlton v. Board of Supervisors of Rock County,* 9 Wis. 378 (1859).

program has been sadly riddled by exceptions. The slow but steady spread of personal property exemptions has tended to make the property tax more and more a real estate tax. But there is no uniformity in exemption policies among the states. New York and Delaware go farthest by exempting all personal property entirely. Wisconsin ranks among the most liberal, exempting intangibles, household goods, motor vehicles, farm machinery, and horses as well as other miscellaneous property. As to the treatment of intangibles, the states are divided among complete exemption, taxation under low valuation or tax rate, inclusion under the general property tax, and mixed treatment (including taxation under a special income tax). A long list of real estate exemptions is also customary.

In Britain and most of the British Dominions, no attempt at all is made to extend the property tax to personal property, and in Australia, New Zealand, and to a lesser extent in western Canada, the property tax is also often confined to land. As we shall see later, there is ample ground for a distinction between taxation of land and improvements. However, confining the property tax to land seriously limits the local tax base, and many feel that it also violates neutrality.

Some of the world's property tax institutions can be presented diagrammatically, according to breadth, as follows:

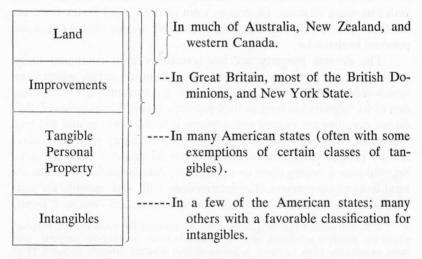

Land	In much of Australia, New Zealand, and western Canada.
Improvements	--In Great Britain, most of the British Dominions, and New York State.
Tangible Personal Property	----In many American states (often with some exemptions of certain classes of tangibles).
Intangibles	------In a few of the American states; many others with a favorable classification for intangibles.

Proportionality. X may have ten times as much wealth as Y, but the property tax will aim to apply the same rate of tax to each if they are in the same taxing district. As we shall see this feature is often more nominal than real but the rate structure itself generally follows the pattern of proportionality.

Impersonality.   Some taxes are said to be impersonal and others personal. Those levied upon things, business, and transactions are generally considered to be impersonal, whereas those levied upon individuals are regarded as personal. The property tax belongs mainly to the first of these classifications. In the last analysis all taxes are paid by persons, but there is a difference, nevertheless, in the two types of taxes. The following features of the property tax are evidence of its impersonal character: (1) for the most part it follows the location of the property as far as jurisdiction is concerned;[5] (2) security for collection is the property itself and sometimes is confined to that alone; (3) property is listed by parcels and description rather than by name (except for personal property which may be listed in alphabetical order by owners); (4) the tax is ordinarily upon the owner, but if he cannot be found, the occupier must pay or the tax can be placed on the property itself; (5) the taxpayer cannot offset his debts against the value of his property; (6) rates are proportional rather than progressive; and (7) no account is taken in one jurisdiction of what the taxpayer may own in other jurisdictions. If the tax were strictly personal, probably none of these features would prevail.

The property tax in Europe has often had a more personal character. A person's property was and is regarded as one indication of his ability to pay, and taxes were and are assessed against him personally with this index in mind. Of course, even in the United States there are members of the property tax family (notably the death tax) that are personal in character.

The general property tax has sometimes been compared to an equity in property possessed by the government, an equity which commands a regular rental. As a landlord, the government pays little attention to its "tenants" as long as they pay their taxes. When, however, they do not pay, they are evicted and someone is found who can and will pay.

Local Collection—Central Sharing.   In this country state legislatures usually provide the framework of the general property tax and sometimes impose a ceiling upon its application. Administration is left to the local units of government. The intermediate units and, usually, the state itself share in the collection. This "multigovernmental" use of a locally

---

[5] It is well settled that real estate must be assessed for property tax purposes where the property is located, and the same rule holds for tangible property, with some exceptions. (For instance, a taxing district wherein tangible personal property is customarily kept ordinarily has the right to tax rather than the one in which the property happens to be on assessment day.) The rule is not so clear with regard to intangible property. It is well established that such property may be assessed at the domicile of the owner. Intangible property may also have a "business situs" and be taxed at the place where it is used by the taxpayer's agent as a "stock in trade." And there are other possibilities of territorial multiple taxation.

determined base creates the difficult and frequently demoralizing problem of equalization (about which more later). It also means that local legislative bodies are frequently held responsible for a tax rate predominant components of which are determined by independent school districts and counties.

A different situation prevails in western Canada, for instance, where typically there is no intermediate layer of government between municipalities and provinces and where the central unit relies exclusively upon nonproperty sources. This makes the property tax a much more strictly local concern and accounts in part for the generous grant of discretion to municipalities in selecting a base (local option). Thus, in the same province improvements may be exempt, partly derated, or fully taxed.

CRITICISM OF THE GENERAL PROPERTY TAX

Criticisms of general property taxes fall mainly into two classes—those applying to its theory or conception, and those applying to its practical and administrative difficulties. It has been said that the general property tax has only two faults: first, it is wrong in theory, and second, it does not work in practice. Others have said that administrative defects of the tax somewhat compensate for its conceptual shortcomings. These people believe that if the tax worked the way it were supposed to, it would be quite unbearable. Consideration will now be given to some of these criticisms, first, from the viewpoint of equity and then, from the viewpoint of practical application.

THEORETICAL LIMITATIONS

A Poor Measure of Benefits Received. It was observed in the previous chapter that benefits received may not be a proper gauge with which to measure the amount of support that a government may require of its taxpayers. But even if benefits were a proper gauge, the possession of property would not be a very defensible measure of benefits.

For many governmental services supported wholly or partially by property taxation, no clear accounting of benefits can be made. Does a $1000 lot receive the same fire and police protection as a $1000 automobile? Does a well-constructed building worth $100,000 receive ten times as much protection from the fire department as an old "fire-trap" building worth one tenth as much? How can one determine how beneficial the city hall is to a particular taxpayer? Or the beautiful boulevard on the other side of the city where one takes out-of-town guests to "show off" the community? Or the city jail? Or the "little red schoolhouse" to the childless farmer? Almost anyone will concede that property owners are benefited in some way by these expenditures of government, but to say that the property tax payment is the index of that benefit is another matter. Perhaps it would be more realistic to conclude that local units of government require revenue for public services; that the property tax is the only important source of local revenue available; and that, therefore, we have the property tax.

It is certainly true that some services of government are more properly considered "land services" than others. Thus garbage collection and sewage disposal represent services that property owners might reestablish on some basis of payment not very different from the property tax if the government discontinued their provision. Education and health service are more personal in character, and the benefits of these functions to property owners are indirect. Garbage collection and sewage disposal might be regarded as more suitable for financing through the property tax than education and health. But in neither case is benefit accounting a very precise matter.[6]

Double Taxation.   Let us suppose that there are two identical farms on opposite sides of the road, as shown in the following diagram. Let us assume that *A* and *B* are legal owners of these farms. The *A* farm is clear of debt, but the *B* farm is encumbered with an $8000 mortgage (intangible property) which is owned by *C*. According to the theory of the general property tax, the assessments would be as follows:

---

[6] Edwin H. Spengler, "Is the Real Estate Tax a Benefit Tax?" Memorandum No. 5, *Report of the New York State Commission for the Revision of the Tax Laws* (Albany, 1932).

Years ago the Pennsylvania legislature included Collins township in the city of Pittsburgh. A taxpayer named Kelly owned a farm in Collins, and his farm was assessed for city taxes. He claimed that he received no benefit from city expenditures since his real estate was unplatted and he was not served by the city light and water systems and so forth. The court commented on this claim as follows:

"It may be true that he does not receive the same amount of benefit from some or any of these taxes as do citizens living in the heart of the city. It probably is true, from the evidence found in the record, that his tax bears a very unjust relation to the benefits received as compared with its amount. But who can adjust with precise accuracy the amount which each individual in an organized civil community shall contribute to sustain it, or can insure in this respect absolute equality of burdens, and fairness in their distribution among those who must bear them?

"We cannot say judicially that Kelly received no benefit from the city organization. These streets, if they do not penetrate his farm, lead to it. The waterworks will probably reach him some day, and may be near enough to him now to serve him on some occasion. The schools may receive his children and in this regard he can be in no worse condition than those living in the city who have no children, and yet who pay for the support of the schools."—*Kelly v. Pittsburgh,* 104 U.S. 78 (1881).

A............$10,000
B............ 10,000
C............ 8,000
  Total......$28,000

A $10,000

B $2,000	C $8,000

It should be apparent that an error has arisen in this procedure. The earning power and value of the two pieces of property are equal. Why should *A* on one side of the road be listed at $10,000 and the property on the other side at $18,000? Or to put it another way, how can there be listed $28,000 of wealth when $20,000 is all that exists? Does a state get wealthy when some of its property owners borrow from others?

Alternative Procedures with Debts and Credits. This difficulty is not easily eliminated by modifications of the general property tax. If the proposal is to exempt *C* from the tax and assess *B* for the entire $10,000, the objection will be made that this compels *B* to pay taxes upon his liabilities as well as his assets. And why should *C*, who probably has more ability to pay than *B*, be exempt from all obligations under the general property tax? Two arguments may be made in answer to these objections. First, since B owns the farm and has control over its use, he should be responsible for the tax, and the latter should really be considered a charge against the farm regardless of its ownership. In the end, however, all taxes are a burden upon people, and one can hardly ignore the personal status and interest of the debtor and creditor on the theory that the physical property pays the taxes.

The second argument is that, regardless of the division of taxes between *B* and *C*, no injustice will result because an adjustment will be made between them through the interest rate. If *B* pays taxes on the physical property, *C* will loan for less; if *C* is required to pay some of the taxes, he will require more interest. This is a problem of shifting which will be discussed in Chapter 6. Suffice it here to say that no such precision in shifting has ever been proved as to warrant entirely ignoring the creditor under the property tax; and if there is doubt about such shifting, why not give the creditor the burden and let him shift it, if he can?

The imposition of taxes upon debtor and creditor each according to his equity would seem to be the most logical procedure, but it has seldom been attempted in the United States. Administratively, it is

simpler to assess the legal owner of the tangible property. Moreover, the
theory of the property tax, that it falls on property rather than persons,
has favored the creditor under the property tax. The theory is so thoroughly established that any attempt to graft personal elements to an impersonal tax might result only in confusion.

The truth is, of course, that property has two attributes: one, a
physical existence, and the other, a bundle of ownership rights. If all the
wealth of the country were double-listed accordingly, there might be no
injustice in property taxation, but where half is double-listed and the
other half single-listed, grave injustice may result. Moreover, through
the device of the intangibles instrumentality, a value may be multiplied
to an almost infinite degree. For example, real estate may be mortgaged,
bonds based on the mortgage may be issued, a corporation may be
formed and issue capital stock with these bonds as its asset, and so on.
However, it should be added that there is a large amount of intangible
personal property that is not representative and that involves no aspect
of double taxation. The earning power of a large corporation (over and
above its tangible assets) is such an intangible.

Illustrations. In Wisconsin intangible personal property is entirely
exempt from taxation, except for the fact that the debtor and creditor
are permitted to make their own arrangement concerning taxes by contract. Actually, by means of a standard contract form, the debtor almost
invariably assumes liability for the tax. The exemption of intangible property in Wisconsin occurred for the most part when the income tax was
adopted; it was defended in large measure on the ground that the income
tax would reach the creditor. However, the state income tax is a much
lower geared tax, particularly as applied to lower incomes, than is the
property tax.

In Illinois credits are subjected to the property tax, as are other
forms of property. The only concession made to the double taxation
argument is that debts may be deducted against certain credits when
the same taxpayer has both. Stocks of domestic corporations assessed
under the Illinois property tax are exempt to the Illinois stockholder.

In Iowa, Oklahoma, Nebraska, and several other states, credits are
taxed at a low flat rate—6 mills in Iowa, 2–4 mills in Oklahoma and
2½–8 mills in Nebraska. More will be said of this attempted solution of
the problem later, but at this point it may be observed that the attempt is
more of an administrative device than an effort to eliminate theoretical
defects.

California at one time attempted to tax the mortgagor and the mortgagee, each upon his equity. This appears to be the equitable solution of
the problem, but Professor C. C. Plehn concluded from his observation

of this system that the creditor regularly shifted all of his share of taxes to the debtor through higher interest and that he added an extra charge for good measure.[7] On the other hand, the circumstances of the California experiment were rather special ones; it would be rash to conclude that it is impossible (whether or not desirable) to tax creditors under the property tax.[8]

Property Taxation of Personal Abilities. Not only has the property tax failed to solve the theoretical (and as will later be observed, the administrative) problems of taxing creditors, but, in addition, it ignores one important kind of intangible asset, personal in nature and not capable of exchange, except in person. This asset consists of skill and education. In 1960 the percentage of the personal income distributed as compensation for employee's services was estimated at about 70 percent.[9] The first American property taxes in the colonial period sought to tax personal "faculty" as part of the property tax. Thus in Massachusetts, a statute of the General Court provided that "in all rates and public charges the town shall have respect to levy every man according to his estate, and with consideration of all other his abilities whatsoever." An order explaining this added that "all men" were "to be rated in all rates according to their whole ability wheresoever it lyes." [10] Not infrequently, large salaries were listed along with the capital value of property to pay taxes at general (or special) property tax rates. In later years, this feature of the property tax was abandoned.

If education has the economic value claimed for it by its proponents or even a value equal to its cost to the state, it must be a considerable factor in the national wealth (using that term in its broadest application). In addition, of course, some persons have natural talent. Still others, perhaps, have valuable "connections." Of course, all of these forms of wealth have limitations; they cannot be exchanged except in person, a point which is sometimes in their favor. More important, no doubt, is the fact that they are highly perishable, depreciating or disappearing with age, death, sickness, and unemployment. Thus personal "faculty," if made taxable, would be very difficult to assess.

Where urban and rural property support a common budget as in the case of some joint school districts and most counties, it is often argued that urban property is more potent than rural because the former is accompanied by personal income. This creates a situation where a

---

[7] *Introduction to Public Finance* (5th ed. New York: The Macmillan Company, 1926), p. 130.

[8] See Chapter 6 for a further discussion of this issue.

[9] *Economic Report of the President,* 1961, p. 138.

[10] C. J. Bullock, *The Finances of Massachusetts,* p. 2; cited in Jensen, *Property Taxation in the United States,* p. 27.

local income tax or a state aid financed by a state income tax might produce a better balance. To this problem is often added that of equalization of assessments (later discussed).

Inconvenience of the Property Tax.   If it be conceded for the sake of argument that most property has value because it brings its owner an income and that the value has a more or less definite relationship to the amount of income, still it remains true that much property may go for long periods without bringing the owner an income. Thus, forest property may require fifty years in which to produce a crop. The property tax does not wait for the crop but hammers away year after year while the property is yielding no revenue. It is partly for this reason that over half the states have placed forest land in a separate classification and given it special treatment. But forest land is not unique with respect to delayed yield. Idle urban lots held for sale may have the same characteristics. During a depression, property that retains value and prospects of future income may go for several years without any net return, if indeed it does not produce a deficit. Thus, the property tax is not at all discriminating; it strikes the taxpayers both when their ships are in and when they are out at sea.

It should be said that this feature of the property tax can be urged in its defense as well as in its attack, for governments must continue even though some property taxpayers have no ready cash. It is precisely because the income tax waits upon the taxpayer's convenience that the income tax is likely to be a "poor producer" in times of depression. The landlord and the creditor do not wait for the property owner to realize upon his investment. Why should the government?

The property tax was designed mainly for a rural civilization and still retains its rural cast. Thus, the assessment date is likely to be at a time when the assessor formerly could "get out with his buggy," and the payment date at the time when the farmer had sold his crops. These dates may be poorly adapted to an urban civilization. For instance, installment payment by the quarter or month is now required for the taxpayer's convenience, and considerable tardy progress in this direction is being made. Assessment dates that differ from state to state afford considerable opportunity for cosmopolitan taxpayers, like chain stores, to manipulate inventories so as to have a minimum of stock on hand in a specific state on its assessment date.

Poor Correlation Between the Property Tax and Income from Property. The poor correlation between property taxes and the income from property may be partly a matter of timing, as discussed above, partly one of differences in management or fortune, and partly one of the legal interpretation of the property tax base. With three general bases for valuing property—(1) capitalization of current income, (2) appraisal of present value of anticipated future income, and (3) market prices at which similar properties are being sold or can be sold—there is plenty of room for a discrepancy to occur between the time of income receipt and the tax payment.

In a static society these values might usually be the same, but in a dynamic society they are seldom equal. Legally the property tax is generally levied on the market value of taxable property. Often there are very great differences between a value obtained by capitalizing current income and one obtained by using prospective income. To illustrate, Mr. *S* rents two city blocks of vacant land for $15 a year on which he pastures a cow. By capitalizing this current income at 5 percent, a value of $300 is obtained for this land. But the land is on the tax rolls for $20,000. Why? Simply because the present owner could obtain that sum for the property if he sold it for residential or business purposes. Yet the present property owner has to pay taxes on the $20,000 valuation irrespective of the fact that his current income from the land justifies an assessment of only $300.

The poor correlation between property taxes and the current income from property is most vividly portrayed on the fringe of cities where land is in the process of transfer from agricultural to urban uses. Before the influence of an expanding city is felt, a farmer may be operating his farm quite successfully and meeting his tax bills out of the income from the sale of his farm products. His land is valued and taxed according to its agricultural productivity. But as the near-by city expands and new subdivisions are created, the value of his farm begins to increase. It is reflecting the added income that will be present when his farm ultimately becomes urban residential or industrial property. The assessor cannot long disregard this increase in value, for the law tells him that market value shall be the basis for assessing property for property tax purposes. As time goes by, the farmer is forced to meet higher and higher taxes out of his agricultural income. For a time he may be able to intensify his farming operations, but eventually a point is reached where he must succumb to the tax burden and either subdivide his property for much more intensive urban uses or sell to someone who will. Because the farmer's present agricultural income is insufficient to bear a tax on land valued not for agricultural purposes but for urban purposes, the property tax is instrumental in forcing a change in land use. Ultimately this may be to the existing owner's benefit, but much agricultural land has been taken out of production near cities that might well have remained in agricultural use until ripe for urban occupancy. Moreover, the assessor, like buyers and sellers, is sometimes forced to speculate on future prospects. The British property tax based upon the annual or rental value of real estate traditionally ignores expectations and escapes these difficulties. A few of our states have special legislation dealing with the problem.[11]

Farmers as a class frequently find the property tax onerous not because of any feature of timing but because as a group they are "property-rich and income-poor."

A Burden on Shelter. Our property tax on housing has been variously estimated at around 25 percent of shelter rent, and this ranks it with liquor, tobacco, and motor fuel among the items of family expenditure that are singled out for special punishment by the tax system. Housing is properly regarded as one of the top amenities of life and especially important as an environment for children. The untidy appearance of many of our large cities can be traced to inadequate outlays for housing. What kind of a paradox is this, that we single out for special taxation the very function that we wish to encourage?

Elderly householders claim a special grievance; they may be recipients of small fixed incomes depleted by inflation, and their demand for shelter is inelastic because of sentimental attachment to family property. Perhaps they eat less as they grow older; perhaps they are no longer able to drive an automobile; their main compensation in life is a fairly high standard of shelter. This subjects them to a heavy property tax burden.

The problem has two main aspects. One is the unhappy distortion in the allocation of resources that the property tax may perpetrate. Here a relevant factor is the elasticity of demand for housing especially at the lower levels of income. The second aspect involves discrimination. One whose special fancy runs to housing pays the piper not only directly but in terms of the property tax as well.

Historically the idea of using expenditure for housing as an index of ability to pay was widely accepted in eighteenth-century England when and where it was thought that income as such was an unavailable measure. Local governments today find themselves in somewhat the same position as did national governments then. But no empirical study was ever made as to how well actual expenditures for housing correlate with income.

Residential property bulks very large as a proportion of a typical property tax base. In Wisconsin in 1960 the equalized value of residential property (not including farm homes) amounted to almost 50 percent of the value of all property locally assessed.[11a]

Regressivity. Regressivity of the property tax may be viewed alternatively in terms of either wealth or income. As wealth, the phenomenon

[11] Frederick D. Stocker, "How Should We Tax Farmland in the Rural-Urban Fringe?", *Proceedings of the National Tax Association Conference,* 1961, pp. 463–471.

[11a] Wisconsin Department of Taxation, Bulletin No. 460, 1961; public utility property is assessed centrally (by the state).

may occur because the assessor often assesses property of high value at a lower ratio of assessed to true value than properties of lesser value. This may be due to the fact that the assessor is more familiar with properties of low value. Frequently he lives in a moderate-cost home himself and may have had other experience with similar property. When it comes to assessing more expensive properties, he is less sure of himself and may give the taxpayer the benefit of the doubt. He is intimidated by large numbers. Or regressivity may appear because the owner of more valuable property is more influential in the community and with the assessor than his poorer neighbors. Many studies have indicated regressivity of this sort, but the phenomenon is by no means universal.

More serious is the regressivity of the property tax conceived in terms of income. Among farmers this could be due simply to the fact that poor farmers have a higher ratio of capital to income than rich farmers. More often property tax regressivity of this sort is related to housing and is based on the contention that the proportion of consumers' income devoted to shelter decreases as income advances. Thus the poor might spend 30 percent of their incomes for housing and the rich only 10 percent. In this case the ratio of property taxes to income will follow similar proportions. Many studies have purported to show that regressivity of this sort does regularly occur and in marked degree.[12] However, one recent study—by taking account of nonmoney income represented by the service value of the owner-occupied house; by including tenants in the calculation (assuming that they bear the incidence of the landlord's tax); by allowing for certain federal tax concessions that affect disposable income; and by relating taxes to the budgetary needs of families of different size—concludes that the property tax on housing is substantially proportional.[13]

The property tax and sales tax in some situations are rivals, and interest attends the controversy as to which is more regressive. Some data applying to the money income of owner occupiers has suggested that this dubious distinction goes to the property tax, but the matter has not been resolved by adequately sophisticated study.

Maladaptation to Modern Conditions. Critics of the general property tax frequently take a historical approach. They say that in an agricultural era of a former day, when wealth was the principal index of ability to pay and when the principal form of wealth was land and buildings, the property tax may have been suitable as a major source of revenue. Today these conditions no longer prevail, but the property tax

---

[12] See for instance, Walter A. Morton, *Housing Taxation* (Madison: University of Wisconsin Press, 1955); Raleigh Barlowe, *Michigan Tax Studies* (Lansing, 1958), p. 187.

[13] James N. Morgan, *et al., Income and Welfare in the United States* (New York: McGraw-Hill Book Company, Inc., 1962), chap. 19.

remains because the taxmakers have not been intelligent or courageous enough to replace it. In an urban and industrial community much property is intangible.

PRACTICAL AND ADMINISTRATIVE LIMITATIONS OF THE PROPERTY TAX

If the property tax is subject to much valid criticism on the ground that it is theoretically inequitable, it is even more open to attack on the score that it does not work out in practice as planned.

Fractionalized Assessments. One of the strongest critics of the property tax is the statistics. As previously indicated, the property tax presumably aims at taxing the privately held national wealth. Actually the property tax base represents only a minor fraction of this total. To be sure much property is legally exempt from tax. But according to the census calculations for 1956, taxable real property that had market value of $700 billion was assessed at only $208 billion. State averages of the ratios of assessed to sales values ranged from 66 percent in Rhode Island to 7 percent in South Carolina.[14]

Much of the discrepancy between national wealth calculations and the property tax base is due to the deliberate practice of underassessing all taxable property. Although this practice is usually contrary to statute, courts have usually sustained it, noting that it causes no necessary inequity providing individual properties are all assessed at the same standard. Assessors contend that this procedure reduces complaints from taxpayers. But by the same token it greatly increases the difficulty of taxpayers in protesting against unjust assessments. And critics argue further that when assessors depart from reality in making assessments they usually err more widely in maintaining equal relative levels.

Inequalities. Inequalities among counties in average ratios of assessed to exchange value need not be an indication of unfairness in the application of the property tax. Where the local tax base is used only for local support, it does not matter mathematically whether property is assessed at 100 percent or 50 percent. A lower ratio simply means a higher tax rate. And where the taxes of the overhead units of government can be distributed without reliance upon the local assessment, the same conclusion holds. But where a county, for instance, relies upon local assessments to determine the proportion of county tax to be paid by each village, town, and city within its borders, great unfairness can arise from inequalities in district assessments. Moreover, assessors may

---

[14] See 1957 Census of Governments, vol. 5; Frederic L. Bird, *The General Property Tax in the United States: Findings of the 1957 Census of Governments* (Chicago: Public Administration Service, 1960); I. M. Labovitz, *loc. cit.*

have an incentive to undervalue property in order to reduce their district's share of the county or state tax. This is known as competitive undervaluation.

Much more serious usually are the inequalities among taxpayers in the same district. *Coefficients of dispersion* is the term used to designate inequalities of this kind. The concept will be explained in more detail in the next chapter. The census study of 1956, previously referred to, revealed that in only one fifth of the districts studied was the cofficient of dispersion as low as 20 percent. Frequency distributions of assessment ratios in a Kansas study show rural properties within a county assessed at levels ranging from 5 percent to 50 percent of sales value. This could result in the burdens of a nominally proportional tax which are 10 times higher in some cases than in others.[15] Some of the reasons for this poor administrative performance will be discussed in the next chapter.

Evasion. The attempt to apply the property tax universally was and is resisted with a large amount of evasion. This is especially true of intangible property, but some kinds of tangibles, such as household furniture and automobiles, also frequently avoid listing. As to intangibles, a Texas report showed that the rendered value of money and deposits in the state on assessment day in 1946 "was only .27 percent of the actual amount of bank deposits on the previous day." [16]

Avoidance by Migration. It is sometimes argued that the property tax is especially adapted to satisfy local revenue requirements, among other reasons because property is less migratory than other tax bases and cannot and will not leave high tax districts for those with lower rates. This is not true, of course, of intangible property, much of which is highly migratory. Where even a feeble attempt is made to apply the property tax to bank deposits, they often are withdrawn from banks before assessment day. This not only defeats the tax but is also very embarrassing to the banks. It is true that real estate can be moved only with great difficulty, if at all, but taxes can be saved by judicious selection of the location where one buys.

Throughout the United States central cities have been disturbed by the drift of population to the suburbs and outskirts. This phenomenon has many causes, including the improvement of transportation and the important advantages of more space and sunshine in the outlying districts. In addition, the suburbs frequently offer substantial tax advan-

[15] William H. Heneberry and Raleigh Barlowe, *Assessment of Farm Real Estate for Property Taxes in the North Central States,* Special Bulletin 439, Agricultural Experiment Station (East Lansing: Michigan State University, 1962), p. 23.
[16] Lynn F. Anderson, *The State Property Tax in Texas,* Bureau of Municipal Research (Austin: University of Texas, 1948), p. 92.

tages. The property tax rate is largely a matter of the ratio of population to aggregate real estate values. A concentration in one municipality of well-to-do small-sized families with relatively high investment in residential property is an innocent but effective form of tax avoidance. Sometimes an advantage may be had by locating a factory adjacent to but outside a city. Here the gain lies in the separation of the factory from the workers; the former provides a rich tax base and the latter occasion most of the expenditures of government. Sociologists and city planners sometimes divide a city into "plus" and "minus" areas, the former designating zones which provide more taxes than expense, the latter, the reverse. A rich suburb is a case of separately incorporating one of the "plus" areas.

The issue is complicated by the fact that the central city frequently performs numerous services for the suburbanites for which the latter render a very inadequate return or no equivalent. The central cities usually seek to convince the suburbs of a solidarity of interest. They urge consolidation of governments to match the fact that the entire metropolitan area constitutes one community. But the suburbs stoutly and successfully resist such courtship.

Some observers have predicted that the future American city may function as a service station for the surrounding area, to provide the theaters, public buildings, and certain shopping facilities for those who sleep outside its corporate limits. They visualize a large fluid population for the city in the daytime but with few on hand during the late hours of the night.

The cities have attempted to adapt themselves to this situation in many ways. There have been attempts to rebuild the slum or blighted areas. These efforts aim at providing attractive apartment houses for those who prefer to dwell close to their work or cannot afford life in the suburbs. They also aim at support for the city's real estate tax base. Cities, if permitted to do so, also often annex outlying territory piecemeal.

Metropolitan agencies have been created to provide certain functions that cut across municipal boundaries. The city of Toronto and its suburbs have improved upon this idea, organizing their area into a "little federal system" with a strategic division of a whole array of functions.[17] Finally, where they are permitted to do so, cities are making some attempts to adapt the tax system in order to collect some revenue from those who use the city but reside elsewhere. But the property tax is not adapted to this end.

---

[17] Gordon Gathercole, "The Toronto Plan," *Canadian Tax Journal*, 1: 4 (July-August 1953), pp. 366–373.

WHY THE GENERAL PROPERTY TAX IS TOLERATED

So much for the indictment of the general property tax. It is a strong indictment. To it might be added the judgment of innumerable commissions and students of public finance, the overwhelming majority of whom feel that the property tax has been tested in the crucible of experience and found badly wanting. As an example we may take the statement of Professor Seligman: *"Practically,* the general property tax as actually administered is beyond all doubt one of the worst taxes known in the civilized world." [18]

Why then do we continue to tolerate the general property tax? Several answers may be made. Many states have sought to improve the tax by modifications; more will be said about this in a later chapter. We are creatures of habit and do not easily surrender an old instrument, even when it is proved to be a poor one. Moreover, the long tenure of the tax means that many people have bought and sold property on the expectation that the property tax would continue. They have paid a price for their property lower than they might have paid had there been no property tax. To eliminate this tax now would simply amount to handing over the government's equity to private owners who may not have paid anything for it. Moreover, there are difficulties in all alternative ways of raising the necessary revenue. The sales tax, which is a principal alternative, is thought by many critics to rest on even less rational ground than the property tax and to be even more inequitable. It may be better to "bear those ills we have than fly to others we know not of."

The property tax includes land values as one of its components; to some extent, at least, land is a gift of nature and has long been regarded as a specially suitable subject for taxation. In general, taxes on wealth are levies on the potential yield of assets and thus tend to be less inimical to incentives than taxes on yield. The case is similar to that of the poll tax which in some African countries is levied with the specific purpose of inducing people to work harder and longer.

Finally, and above all, the property tax in many ways has proved a reliable source of revenue for local governments. In addition to availability, it has the virtue of flexibility; it is the ideal source to squeeze a wee bit more to finance a new service that most local people want and are willing to help finance. Moreover it provides a tolerable measure of the contributions that diverse local units must make to an intermediary level of government, such as the county.

---

[18] E. R. A. Seligman, *Essays in Taxation* (10th ed., New York: The Macmillan Company, 1925), p. 62. (Italics are his.)

A large number of the numerous local units of government in the United States could hardly administer an income tax, even a simple one, and a sales tax is excluded on the additional score that they have no merchants. Very likely some redrawing of local governments' boundary lines is long overdue. But government in a big and populous country needs and will continue to need a very large amount of subdivision. With a few exceptions, countries that do not have something similar to our general property tax do not have much autonomous local government.

Thus the case for the general property tax is in large part the case for decentralized decision making and home rule. The local community is in some sense but the extension of the family, and a free society, it seems, should leave some considerable part of decision making to each of these institutions. But this is not to say that the general property tax cannot be imposed upon with an unnecessarily heavy load, or that improvement in its quality is beyond human capacity.

PROBLEMS

1. State some reasons why the property tax has been decreasing in relative importance.
2. Find the fallacy in the following proposition. The general property tax as used by American states differs in its coverage: some states tax only land; others, only real estate; others, real estate and tangible personal property; and still others, tangibles and intangibles, the latter sometimes at a special rate.
3. What is meant when it is said that the property tax is impersonal?
4. On what basis is it alleged that the property tax as presently applied in the American states is partial to creditors and unfair to debtors?
5. Why is the general property tax called a locally collected centrally shared tax? Indicate two problems which this characteristic creates.
6. Relative tax burdens are said to affect the allocation of resources. The American people are said to spend excessively on automobiles as compared with shelter. Can these propositions be related and if so how?
7. Write a short essay on the contention that the property tax is regressive. How would one go at a comparison of its regressivity with that of a sales tax, with or without food exempt?
8. Explain the ground on which the property tax is said to be unjust to elderly homeowners.
9. What problems of the rural-urban fringe does our property tax involve and the British one escape?
10. In what respects does a suburbanite tend to have a tax advantage

over one living in a central city? What financial and other measures can the central city use to defend itself?

11. Account for the allegation that the property tax may be well enough adapted to play an exclusive role as a local tax in rural communities but that this is not the case in urban communities.

12. What is meant by the term "fractionalized assessment"? Account for the existence of the phenomenon it describes and the difficulties the latter is said to create for equitable property tax administration.

13. Comment on the proposition that the property tax goes with local self-government and abandonment of the one would mean the surrender of the other.

14. The property tax on rural land is said to be easier on incentives than the net income tax because the former taxes the capacity of the farm and the latter taxes the capacity of the farmer. Comment.

15. Why is the joint rural-urban school district said to be unjust to farmers?

16. A central city has a population of 300,000, general property of $1,000,000,000, and expenses of $100 per capita. A suburb has a population of 30,000, general property of $300,000,000, and expenses of $200 per capita. If all expenditures are met from the general property tax, what will be the effective rate of tax in each city?

17. What studies of property tax assessment have been made in your state? What do they indicate with regard to the regressivity and inequality of assessments?

4

THE GENERAL PROPERTY TAX—
ADMINISTRATION

As previously explained, the same property tax often is divided to support several units of government. An understanding of property tax administration therefore depends upon a clear conception of governmental structure.

UNITS OF GOVERNMENT

The United States tops the list of nations both in the importance of the property tax in the revenue system and in the number of governmental units. As to the latter, the Bureau of Census in 1957 recorded 102,392.[1]

With only very minor exceptions, the entire United States, rural and urban, is covered by counties, and these are supported mainly by the property tax. Towns and townships are less general. As a rule they include rural territory only, though the New England town is often highly urbanized and some midwestern towns include villages which also have an independent existence. Urban and partly urban incorporated areas are variously known as cities, boroughs, villages, and incorporated towns.

[1] *Statistical Abstract of the United States,* 1960, p. 401.

72

Some of these have enormous budgets, surpassing in size those of many states. New York City, for instance, has a larger budget than some dozen of the Rocky Mountain and Great Plain states combined. Next to the states, these cities have made most progress in diversifying their revenue systems and supplementing the property tax. Most numerous of all units are the school districts which may or may not be coterminous with county, town, village, or city lines. In general they may be regarded as the atom in government. While as a rule they have few if any independent sources of revenue other than the property tax, they are often substantially supported by central governments through grants-in-aid. Finally there are miscellaneous and special districts, such as sewerage and irrigation districts.

THE PROPERTY TAX CALENDAR

The administration of the general property tax is a long and highly "ritualized" process. Briefly outlined, the steps in administration are as follows:

1. Levy,
2. Original assessment of property,
3. Review of the original assessment,
4. Central assessment or equalization,
5. Apportionment of taxes and setting of rates,
6. Collection,
7. Collection of delinquent taxes,
8. Appeals to some judicial or quasi-judicial body.

As an alternative to the procedure outlined above, direct state assessment is often provided for certain property such as railroads. The outline is not always followed chronologically, but it will be most easily traced and remembered if one thinks of it as a series of steps throughout the year.

Levy.   Each of the units of government discussed above has a legislative body which proceeds to make a levy on the property within its jurisdiction. The levy consists of a legislative enactment to the effect that a certain specified amount shall be raised from the property tax.[2] In some states the levy for local units may be voted by the residents of the district (at town meetings, for example); for many others, and particularly the county, state, and municipal governments, representative legislative bodies determine the amount to be raised.

___

[2] Sometimes instead of deciding to raise a certain amount, the legislative body merely authorizes a certain rate to be charged against all taxable property within its boundaries.

Original Assessment of Property. Since the general property tax is based on the value of all taxable property within the taxing district, it is necessary for someone to evaluate the property. This is done by the local assessor. On a certain day of the year the assessor is supposed to value all property lying within his district. Since in practice it would be impossible for him to complete this task in one day, he usually values property not *on* that day but *as* of that day. Assessment day varies all the way from January 1 to October 1. In the north and east, and particularly in areas with the town unit of government, it is usually April 1 or May 1.

Review of the Original Assessment. Completion of the assessment roll by the local assessor is not always the final proceeding in the determination of the assessments of individual parcels or holdings of taxable property. Due process of law requires that every taxpayer be given the right to a hearing before the tax becomes final. This hearing may be before the original assessing agency, before a separate administrative review agency, or before a court. Because original assessment agencies lack the impartiality of ideal review agencies, and because review by the courts is too slow and too expensive, all but a few states have established administrative agencies to hear protesting taxpayers and to check and double-check the work of the local assessor. The function performed by these agencies is commonly known as *review*.

Typically, review agencies are composed of ex officio members such as the town chairman, town clerk, city mayor, city attorney, and so forth. Generally the board has power to raise and lower assessments and to add and remove property from the rolls. Action adverse to a taxpayer's interest requires notice and opportunity for a hearing. In some states the board has no power to change assessments except on sworn evidence presented by the taxpayer and other witnesses. In others it may do so at its own discretion. This power has been defended as a desirable check on the assessor; in practice, it often results in an undesirable division of responsibility.

Central Assessment or Equalization. Unfortunately the local assessor's work, as previously observed, cannot be regarded as a satisfactory basis for the distribution of state tax levies among counties or (in the case of town, village, and city assessment) of county taxes among the smaller units. Adjustments made by central units to facilitate the equitable distribution of overhead taxes among districts is called *equalization*. It would be possible, of course, for central units to provide a separate assessment of all taxable properties within their borders, but this would involve heavy duplication of work. On the other hand, it would be possible to let the state do the assessing in the first place, but assessment has always been a local function, and attempts to centralize it have been vigorously resisted. Moreover, it is claimed that local assessors have the advantage of familiarity with local property. A third alternative, and the one usually accepted, is central assessment or equalization by state and county agencies, frequently called state and county boards of equalization.

These central assessments either start with the local assessments as a base and make some corrections in the totals for the counties, towns, villages, and cities, or they make a "mass assessment" of the districts as a whole. As will be more fully explained later, these assessments are based upon such knowledge concerning the towns, villages, and cities as the central agency may gather. The comparative data and analysis may be scientific or very unscientific. Under township assessment, central assessment is vital to the county in order to defeat competitive undervaluation of property by local assessors. Even in a state with county assessment and no state property tax, central assessment may fill important functions in the taxation of railroads, the distribution of state aids, and in other respects.

In practice, equalization boards often exercise functions shading into what has been described as review. They make "en masse" changes in assessments by classes of property or divisions of territory and even, in some cases, alter individual assessments.

Apportionment of Taxes and Setting of Rates; Collection. As soon as the central and local assessments have been completed, it is possible to apportion taxes and calculate rates. Taxes for the central units may be divided among the subordinate units according to the central assessment. For example, if one county has been found by central assessment to have 10 percent of the state's taxable property, it is allotted 10 percent of the state taxes. Once it is known how much a given district is required to raise for the central units, a local official (probably the town, village, or city clerk) calculates the tax rate for the district. He adds the central levies to the local levy and divides the sum by the assessment roll—that is, the total valuation of property in his district. The quotient obtained shows the necessary tax rate to be imposed upon each dollar's worth of property in order to raise the required revenue. Thus, if $10,000 is required and the local assessment roll is $1,000,000, the rate will be 10,000 divided by 1,000,000 or 1 percent. Each individual's tax is then computed by multiplying his assessment by the tax rate.

If, as in some states, equalization either corrects the local rolls or assumes that they are correct in the first place, then the central apportionment can be made exactly like the local assessment—that is, a state rate is determined by dividing the state tax by the total of all assessments in the state. All districts are then given a common state rate to add to their varying local ones.

Collection of Delinquent Taxes. If all the taxes levied were paid at the proper time, the only step remaining in the tax collection procedure would be for the treasurer to forward the county and state shares to the

proper officials. But it practically never happens that all taxes are collected on time, and this necessitates further procedure in the tax calendar.
Methods of dealing with delinquent taxes differ widely from state to
state. For instance, in Wisconsin if some of the tax "goes delinquent,"
the local treasurer, after an attempt to collect, must turn over uncollected
taxes to the county which then credits the local district with their face
value. If the real property taxes are not paid before a certain time, the
county treasurer must offer the taxes for sale.[3] The buyer of the taxes
secures a claim upon the property against which they were levied, and
after several years (now three) have elapsed, he may obtain title to it by
one of two means: he may either obtain a tax deed from the county clerk,
after properly notifying the recorded owner and other lien holders; or,
at his own option he may instead of taking a tax deed, foreclose on the
tax certificate in the same manner as a mortgage is foreclosed on real
estate. The principal distinction between the two is that in the former case
he obtains a tax deed, whereas in the latter he receives a warranty deed
—that is, the deed which the recorded owner had to the property. The
distinction is important because a tax deed, while simpler and cheaper
to obtain, is not nearly so secure as is a warranty deed. In lieu of a tax
sale the county itself may take tax certificates, and after it has obtained
the required number of successive tax claims for any parcel of property,
it may secure a tax deed.[4]

---

[3] Tax delinquency procedure in the case of personal property follows a different ritual. The county treasurer turns over the unpaid taxes to the sheriff for
collection, and if he is unsuccessful, they may be charged back to the local unit
the following year.

In Wisconsin, competition at tax sales is according to the least proportion of
property upon which the bidder is willing to accept a lien. Some states provide
for competition in terms of the lowest interest rate any bidder will offer, and still
others according to priority of bids.

[4] For a period after the sale the original owner may clear his title to the
property, in so far as taxes are concerned, by payment of back taxes and certain
penalties; the usual provision is that he must pay either a high rate of interest
and penalty or the two combined in the interest rate. Even the acquisition of tax
titles does not always mean an end to delinquency proceedings. Tax titles are
usually insecure for a definite or indefinite period, depending upon the presence
or absence of a statute of limitations designating the period beyond which such
titles cannot be upset. Upsetting such title consists of establishing some imper-
fection in the procedure followed during the delinquency period. This procedure
is quite complicated, and some error can usually be found. The courts have gone
very far in allowing the original owner to re-establish his claim.

Criticism of delinquency procedure usually asserts that the period from old
ownership to new ownership (with secure tenure) is too long and results in the
wasteful use of resources. Principal reform has consisted of cheapening the process
by which foreclosing governments can secure warranty deeds.

To the layman, tax-delinquency procedure is likely to leave the impression of
ritual "of the lawyers, by the lawyers, and for the lawyers." A simpler (and in
our opinion better) procedure would be the following: Delinquent property might
be sold after six months to the highest bidder above an upset price established by
the municipality. The old owner would then be given one year to redeem, paying

Appeals to Some Judicial or Quasi-judicial Body. Mention has been made of the board of review as a "court" of first resort for the taxpayer who is dissatisfied with his assessment. The taxpayer is frequently given an additional appeal to the state tax department and always a final appeal to the courts.[5] On its own motion or on petition from a certain percentage of property owners in a given district, the state tax department may consider and grant a reassessment for a district and may in some cases appoint the assessor and charge back the cost for the work to the district.

PROBLEMS OF THE LOCAL ASSESSMENT

The need for reorganizing the assessment process is widely recognized, but such reorganization is extremely difficult to achieve. Structures, procedures, and customs of local government are as resistant to change as a granite peak to erosion.

The Assessor. Assessment districts are frequently too small to give the assessor a full-time job. The assessor of a small village, for instance, may be expected to complete his task in a month. Where the county is the assessment unit, smaller units are sometimes permitted an additional assessment of property within their boarders for local tax distribution only; this creates what is known as overlapping assessment districts and adds to the confusion. Frequently the compensation paid is too small to attract good talent or to warrant more than a perfunctory job.

The position of assessor commonly involves no special statutory qualifications. Not a word is said concerning training, ability, intelligence, or other qualifications. Eligibility requirements for office frequently have to do only with state and federal citizenship and residence in the district. Ability to get, not to do, the job appears to be the prime requisite. Removal provisions in statutes are frequently unworkable. "It is more probable that a man would be ousted for misappropriating $10 of the taxes collected than for failure to place a million dollars' worth of property on the assessment rolls." [6]

taxes, interest, and penalty. Failing this, the purchaser would be given an indefeasible title, and any claim of the previous owner would be confined to a suit for damages. Surplus realized from sale would be returned to the original owner.

[5] The taxpayer's rights in court depend on the state's law. He may have no recourse except to prove illegality in procedure; sometimes he can make a case by proving that the assessment of his property is higher than that of considerable other similar property or (less likely) than the statutory standard.

[6] M. G. Toepel, *The Assessment of Property for Ad Valorem Tax Purposes in Texas Cities,* Bureau of Research in the Social Sciences (Austin: University of Texas, 1939), p. 66.

Except in the sizable urban centers, the local assessor in the United States is usually chosen by election. Yet it is a well-recognized rule of government that positions requiring technical skill should not be filled by popular vote. In addition, the assessor who does his work fearlessly is likely to tread on the toes of influential people, and he should be shielded against "standing for election" after each roll is completed. In some states, the strong propensity for direct popular government leads to the choice even of surveyors by popular acclaim. Of course, no one could argue that it matters at all whether a surveyor is a Socialist or a Republican—all that matters is that he be able to survey. The local assessor's office in Canada is filled by appointment rather than by election and the incumbent presumably continues during good behavior.

Generally speaking, villages and small cities are the units of government that suffer most from poor property tax administration. Large cities have professionalized the assessment office and the property of rural towns is largely homogeneous and easily assessed. Villages and small cities may offer as diversified an assessment problem as larger urban centers; yet, they turn this job over to part-time amateurs, not infrequently to provide some work for a retired person or someone out of a job. Some small cities have solved their problem by combining local offices to create one full-time position.

It can be said, however, that considerable ferment is occurring in the administrative machinery of the general property tax in many states. Thus, in Illinois a law enacted in 1949 created a full-time county supervisor of assessments, vested with the responsibility of making and equalizing assessments, in each county. Elected township assessors were continued but as deputy assessors. Supervisors were to be appointed by the County Board with the approval of the State Department of Revenue. Minnesota has given counties the option of a county assessor or a supervisor. Iowa, beginning in 1948, replaced 2500 part-time city, town, and township assessors with 120 full-time county and city assessors.[7]

The Local Assessment. Best procedure requires the assessor to assess property by actual viewing and such other information as he is able to obtain. Some states still rely mainly (and in some cases exclusively) upon sworn statements submitted by the owners of property. The latter as a sole reliance has seldom proved adequate and has served principally to make perjury respectable. In any event, it is a well-known fact that lazy and incompetent assessors are the greatest plagiarists of all time; they simply copy the work of their predecessors who, in their time, followed the same procedure.

Much personal property is difficult for the assessor to find, and

---

[7] Tax Institute, "Recent Improvements in Assessing Procedure," *Tax Policy* (May–June 1950).

some is extremely difficult to evaluate even after it is found. A variety of techniques are employed in the effort to get personal property on the tax rolls. In the case of merchants' and manufacturers' inventories, an examination of the company's books or of state and federal income tax returns is often effective. Intangibles cause special difficulties and are rarely, if ever, well assessed. Some states have used what is known as "tax ferrets" in aiding property tax administration. Special agents were induced by compensation in the form of a commission or fee to seek out and disclose information leading to the assessment of property that escaped the assessor. The consensus seems to be that this weapon, too, has not been very effective and certainly not popular. Another device is to require the payment of taxes on credit instruments as a condition of the legal enforcement of such instruments. Information on state and federal income tax returns could be used quite effectively. Administration of this remnant of the general property tax is usually demoralized by the fact that administrators have no appetite for their prescribed objective.[8]

Special Problems of the City Assessor. A description of the techniques and problems of urban assessment would require more space than can here be allotted to it. The assessor's office must be adequately equipped with maps. The most useful and important of these are the lot-and-block maps and the land-value-unit maps. The former shows the size, shape, and location of all the lots in the city. The latter gives the key value for each block, the key being the value of a lot of a certain standard size and depth in the center of the block. Over a period of years assessors, through a study of many sales of property, have built up tables for determining the influence of depth and location at or near a street corner. These are known as depth-factor and corner-influence tables. If over a period of years it is observed in a business district that lots that are 125 feet deep sell on the average for 112 percent as much as lots 100 feet deep, it may be concluded, other things being equal, that the 25 extra feet add 12 percent to the value. City assessors should have an extensive file of information concerning personal property and buildings, including for the latter, dimensions, age, nature of construction, and many other relevant facts.

Calculation of a Coefficient of Dispersion. The quality of a property

---

[8] None too good at its best, the assessment of intangible property at its worst degenerates into a first-class racket. Undervaluation of property results in high property tax rates, and assessment of credits at par then may well be confiscatory of income. In these circumstances, the assessor becomes a person of great power and can capitalize on this fact by "fixing" assessments for a secret consideration. Complaints can be penalized with high assessments, particularly on intangible property. See Herbert D. Simpson, *The Tax Situation in Illinois* (Chicago: Northwestern University, 1929).

tax assessment can be tested by computing deviations from an average. The problem is one of comparing relative, not absolute, magnitudes. Given a sample of assessments *in the same district* and acceptable sales or appraisals of these properties, four steps are involved in the process. First, one calculates the individual assessment ratio of each item. Secondly, these ratios are averaged to obtain an average assessment ratio for the sample. Thirdly, the deviations of the various assessments from the average are totaled (without regard to signs) and divided by the number in the group. The resulting average deviation cannot be compared with that of another district unless both have been converted to comparable bases—that is, to their equivalent in terms of a 100-percent assessment. Thus, a deviation of 1 with an assessment of 50 percent is equivalent to a deviation of 2 with an assessment of 100 percent. Fourthly, therefore, the average deviation is divided by the average assessment ratio from which it was measured. The resultant is the *coefficient of dispersion*. A margin of tolerance of 10 percent may be allowed for imperfections in the data; a coefficient above this figure is cause for concern. As previously noted, a census survey indicated that in only about one fifth of the districts in the United States was the coefficient of dispersion less than 20 percent.

To illustrate, assume that three parcels of property are each appraised at $10,000. They are assessed at $5000, $6000, and $7000, respectively.

1. Individual assessment ratios: 50%, 60%, 70%
2. Average assessment ratio: 60%
3. Average deviation: (10% + 0 + 10%) ÷ 3 = 6.6%
4. *Coefficient of Dispersion:*   6.6% ÷ 60% = .11   or   11%

As assessments usually go, this is a very low coefficient. To gauge the entire work of the assessor, the sample must be adequate and representative of different kinds of property.[9]

Supervision of the Local Assessment.   Formerly, local assessors were left very largely to their own resources in performing their tasks. Most states now have tax departments or similar agencies to which has been given the function, among others, of supervising local assessment work. As a rule the tax department has very limited financial resources and works at long range. In these circumstances, supervision may be confined to the preparation and distribution of an assessment manual or some other help of this nature. Some states offer their local assessors absolutely no help whatever. However, the tax department, if properly manned and financed, can render very effective assistance to them.

---

[9] There are other and more refined methods of calculating the coefficient; the above is the simplest and most readily understood.

State supervision of local assessments has received much emphasis in Wisconsin. Supervision is largely in charge of six supervisors of assessment, constituting the property tax staff of the tax department and chosen by the latter under merit appointment. Each supervisor is responsible for a specific district in which his office is located.

Among the many contributions which supervisors can make to property tax administration, only a few can be mentioned here. One is the holding of annual county meetings for the local assessors, who can then get the benefit of instruction in the fine and difficult points of property tax procedure. The local assessor can be given a field book with which to work and can be instructed as to how property should be recorded and classified. Assessors can be encouraged to compare their estimates of the same or similar properties.

Following this short course in assessment procedure, the supervisor may work in the field with the assessors. The supervisor may make himself available for consultation and advice. Supervision of this character can exercise an exceedingly favorable influence upon assessments. It follows this same general pattern in all states, but it is sometimes purely nominal and is almost universally a badly neglected aspect of property tax administration.[10]

The Standard of Value. As was stated in the preceding chapter, the law usually calls for the assessment of property at exchange value or market value. The law may state simply that property shall be assessed "at the full value which could ordinarily be obtained therefor at private sale." In this definition the word *ordinarily* is of special significance. It suggests that a market is a consensus and is not fully established by a particular sale. It also suggests that the assessor should aim at what the economists call "normal values," and this may require discounting strong upward or downward trends in real estate values. The assessor, unfortunately, may not be highly endowed with the gift of prophecy. In the real estate boom following World War II assessments lagged more than usually behind sales. A good case can be made for the abandonment of this troublesome language, leaving the assessor free to follow the current market or perhaps a two- or three-year average of market values.

Market value as a standard appears entirely reasonable, at least upon first examination. Original cost would make an untenable standard, since ability to pay must be measured by what the individual can get out of his investment, not what he put into it. Cost of reproduction, or replacement value, also falls short, in that it takes no account of the future prospects and present productivity of the property. Moreover, it could

---

[10] Harold M. Groves and A. Bristol Goodman, "A Pattern of Successful Property Tax Administration: The Wisconsin Experience," *Journal of Land and Public Utility Economics,* XIX: 2 (May 1943), pp. 142–152.

not be applied to land. The subjective value of the owner brings in psychological and personal attitudes which are impossible to ascertain. The difference between value in use and value in exchange goes back to Aristotle; both are valid concepts but the latter is more amenable to objective evidence.

Nevertheless, many cases arise where market value as a basis of assessment proves unsatisfactory. This is especially true in the case of properties that were built for a particular purpose. As such they are good investments, yet they cannot be sold on the market except for use for a less productive purpose and at a great sacrifice. A classic example is the New York Stock Exchange building. It was constructed especially for use by a very large stock exchange and would have little or at least much less value if sold for some other purpose. As far as we know, there will always be a large stock exchange in New York, since the present one does not contemplate going out of business. But one stock exchange seems all that is likely to develop. If the present exchange should undertake to sell its building, it presumably would have to sell it to some other kind of buyer.

A more common case of a similar nature is that of a very expensive home built by a very wealthy resident in a small city. Were such a residence offered for sale, it would probably go at a great sacrifice because no equally wealthy buyer would be present to bid for it. Yet, in the hands of the person who built it, the home may be filling its purpose quite satisfactorily.

An interesting case involving this problem is that of *Northwestern Mutual Life Insurance Co. v. Weiher,*[11] in which a large insurance company in a moderate-sized city of Wisconsin sought a reduction in assessment on the ground that the home office building, designed for a specific purpose, could not be sold on the market for either its original or replacement cost. The court in this case upheld the contention of the insurance company. However, a New York State court sustained the assessment of the New York Stock Exchange building by the City of New York at far above its market value.[12]

On the supposition that property assessment is a measure of ability to pay, it would appear that assessors should have discretion in cases of this kind to depart from market value in its strict and literal sense and to assess the property on its value for the purpose for which it is being used. It has been pointed out that insurance companies, in appraising such property for insurance purposes, do not hesitate to depart from the market-value standard. Since the decision in the insurance company case,

---

[11] 177 Wis. 445 (1922).
[12] *People ex rel. New York Stock Exchange Building Co. v. Cantor et al.,* 223 N.Y. Supplement, 64 (1927).

several attempts have been made to liberalize the standard in Wisconsin, but without success. However, the courts have qualified their decision concerning the matter by developing the doctrine that in the case of property that rarely sells, evidence of "intrinsic value is acceptable." [13]

The suggestion is made that we should distinguish between "white," "gray," and "brown" elephants in property tax administration. A white elephant is genuinely obsolescent, and this fact should be recognized with assessments that discount cost of reproduction. A gray elephant (the Stock Exchange) is not obsolescent but only so specialized that no one would buy it except for an inferior use and at a reduced price. The brown elephant (factory buildings) is marketable without loss perhaps, but so seldom exchanges that no information as to exchange value is available. Special standards or procedures seem to be required for the second and third of these classes.

Obviously there are very large numbers of important properties for which there is little or no sales data—that is, recent exchange prices for these or similar properties. This forces the assessor to fall back on either (or both) a replacement-cost figure or a capitalization of net income (division of income by the prevailing rate of interest). The former has the limitations previously mentioned. The latter runs into difficulty in that the income associated with the property may be influenced by management (nontransferable) and may be a function of the business conducted on the premises as well as of the property. The assessor aims to assess a "going plant," exclusive of a "going business." Thus when an assessor assesses a bank building, he can assume perhaps that the building will continue to be used as a bank, but he is not entitled to attribute to the premises the good will or earning power of any specified banking business as such. Moreover, in ordinary circumstances a building should not be worth more than its cost of replacement. This follows from the principle of substitution; why pay more for an existing structure than the brick, mortar, and labor that can be had (it is assumed) to replace it? The problem differs in the case of land, which is ordinarily nonreproducible. Here the two relevant sources of evidence are the sales price of similar land and income, and it is not easy to separate income attributable to the land from that attributable to the improvement and the business. The problem is especially important where a classified property tax metes different treatment to land and improvement values.

It has been argued that, in property taxation, the standard of value should give greater weight to current earnings or earning capacity than it does at present. One way to do this would be to substitute the annual or rental value of property for the sales value. This might seem to create a tax on income rather than on property. The distinction is that the in-

---

[13] *Flambeau Paper Co. v. Windus,* 208 Wis. 583 (1932).

come tax is personal in character; it looks at what *A* actually makes from
his land during the year. Annual value, on the other hand, is an *appraisal*
of what a year's use of *A*'s land is worth. Thus, if *A* drives a particularly
hard bargain with his tenants, his income may be greater than his property would ordinarily yield; yet annual value assessment takes no account of this. *A*'s land will be assessed the same as other property with
similar physical characteristics or income potentialities. Annual value is
the basis of the property tax in Great Britain and other European countries. Under this system there is no attempt to tax anticipated increases
in the productivity of land or other property in advance of their appearance. It tends to reduce the taxpayers' difficulty in meeting taxes dis-
proportionate to current income. And finally, it avoids the injustices that
are said to arise from property income being capitalized into property
values at different rates for different kinds of property.[14]

On the other hand, annual value as the basis of property assessment
tends to favor increments to land value, thought by some to be especially
suited for heavy taxation. Moreover, few people in the United States
think of value as an annual affair, even though more property is rented
than is operated by the owner.

It would be possible to give more weight to capitalized income even
in the traditional American type of assessment. For instance, it has been
suggested that slum properties should be valued on their earnings and
without the usual restraint against evaluation of reproducibles above their
replacement cost.

THE CENTRAL ASSESSMENT AND EQUALIZATION
OF PROPERTY [15]

Purpose and Nature of Central Assessment. It has been observed
that the property tax is used to support the larger units of government
as well as the local towns, villages, and cities, and that it is necessary or
at least highly important for these central units to make an independent
mass appraisal of the taxable property in the smaller units. This needs to
be done in order to defeat competitive undervaluation, which may be
deliberately practiced by local units to reduce their share of taxes for the
support of central units. The consequences of competitive undervalua-

---

[14] The market, for instance, has been known to capitalize farm land at thirty
times its income and urban land at fifteen times its productive power. This may
be due to a number of factors including, for instance, the desire to own farm
land to continue an agricultural "way of life."

[15] The first three subsections of this section may be omitted by students who
wish to shorten their study of this subject.

tion and the effect of proper central assessment may be illustrated as follows:

Assume that *A* and *B* are two assessment districts (say, two towns) which together make up a county. Within their borders are $1 million and $2 million worth of property respectively. Assume further that *A* district is assessed on the average of 100 percent of true value, whereas *B* district is assessed on the average at only 50 percent of true value. Assume now that for *A* $10,000 and for *B* $20,000 must be raised for local purposes, and that an additional $10,000 for county purposes must somehow be divided between the two districts. Assume that *a* is a resident of *A* district with $10,000 worth of property assessed at true value, and that *b* and *b'* are residents of *B* district, each with $10,000 worth of property, but with *b* assessed at true value and *b'* assessed at 50 percent of true value. It is apparent from the assumptions that *a, b,* and *b'* should pay the same amount of tax since each has an equal amount of property and local tax levies are proportional to local wealth.

With no central assessment, the county taxes should be apportioned between the districts on the basis of their assessed valuation, and in this case each district would be required to raise $5000 for the county in addition to its local taxes. The tax rate would then be as follows:

District	Total levy required	÷	Assessed valuation	=	Total tax rate in percent
A	$15,000		$1,000,000		1.5
B	25,000		1,000,000		2.5

The tax bill for each of the property owners would then be calculated as follows:

Owner	Tax rate in percent	×	Assessed valuation	=	Tax bill
a	1.5		$10,000		$150
b	2.5		10,000		250
b'	2.5		5,000		125

Where there is no central assessment, *A* district bears an undue share of the county tax and this makes *a*'s tax bill too high. By the same token, *B* district escapes with an unfair advantage, and *b'*'s tax bill is lower than it should be. On the other hand, *b* is the victim of a bad error in the local assessment, having been assessed at twice the average rate of assessed to true value in his district. The lack of a proper central assessment that favored his district compensates somewhat for the local discrimination against him, but certainly there is no excuse for him to pay twice as much taxes as *b'*, his next-door neighbor.

Now suppose a system of central assessment is in operation. Instead of apportioning the county tax on the basis of total assessed valuation, the county would use true value in apportioning the taxes to each district. Since *B* district has twice as much true value, it would be required to raise twice as much county tax as *A* district. *B* district then would have to raise two thirds of the county taxes in addition to its local levies, and *A* district would raise one third of the county taxes in addition to its local taxes. The tax rate would then be as follows:

District	Total levy required ÷	Assessed valuation =	Tax rate in percent
A	$13,333	$1,000,000	1.33
B	26,666	1,000,000	2.66

One will notice that, although the allocation of the county tax was based on true value, in calculating the tax rate for the district the assessed valuation is used. Why? Mere introduction of central assessment does not change the assessed valuation of property within the district. It is necessary to base the tax rate on assessed value so that when it is applied to individual taxpayers enough taxes will be forthcoming to equal the sum sought. Applying a lower rate to true values would not change relative burdens.

The tax bill for each of the property owners would then be calculated as follows:

Owner	Tax rate in percent ×	Assessed valuation =	Tax bill
a	1.33	$10,000	$133
b	2.66	10,000	266
b'	2.66	5,000	133

With proper central assessment and the county tax equitably distributed between districts, *a* bears his correct share of the total taxes. It will be noticed that *b'*, who is assessed at the average rate of assessed to true value for his district (50 percent), pays the same tax as *a*, which is as it should be since his true value is the same as *a*'s. But *b*, who is assessed far above the average of his district, now pays twice as much as he should (since his true value is no more than the others, he should pay no more taxes than they do).

The remedy for *b* is review rather than central assessment—that is, the local board of review should adjust *b*'s assessed valuation to the level of other property in the district, which in this case is 50 percent. Thus a proper central assessment does not correct a bad local assessment. Central assessment merely assures a proper division of county taxes among the local units of government. With proper central assessment and review of local assessments, the tax burden on each one of the owners used in our illustration would have been the same.

Methods of Central Assessment. How is a proper central assessment made? Several methods have been tried. One of the older is that of using local assessments as a base and making corrections in the light of statistics on wealth, population, and so forth. This method involves a great deal of guesswork and is highly unscientific. A second method is to hear evidence presented by local districts. This has been called ordeal by oratory, and has proved very unsatisfactory. The sales-sampling method has been developed in several states. This consists of selecting in each district certain properties which have recently been sold, using these as a sample, comparing the aggregate sales price of the sample with the assessment of the same, determining a ratio of assessed to sales value for the sample, and applying the ratio to the assessed value of the district as a whole to arrive at a true value. In terms of a formula, the assessed value of the sample is to the sales value of the sample as the assessed value of the village (for instance) is to its true value. If ten properties constituting the sample were recently exchanged for $100,000 and the assessor listed these properties at an aggregate figure of $80,000, then the assessment ratio of the sample is 80 percent. If the district is assessed at $8 million, by the application of the formula the true value of the district would be calculated at $10 million.

The sales-sampling method appears to be a sound and scientific way to correct local assessments. However, it is not without limitations and difficulties. One of the most obvious is that not all sales are good indications of market value. Sales of this nature include forced sales, distress sales, sales to relatives, and so on. A program of investigating the sales (sometimes called fielding) to exclude sales of this type is a refinement which can be used to meet this defect.

Another difficulty is that the property sold may not be representative of all property in the district. A good sample must be representative, as every farmer who has tested milk well knows; it is for this reason that the farmer stirs the milk well before taking his sample. In the case of the properties, it may be that most of the sales are small or residential properties, or the assessor's bias may have appeared in his assessment of large properties of mercantile and manufacturing properties, as was shown in the preceding chapter. This difficulty has been met by a classification of properties and by sampling each class separately. A third difficulty may result from an insufficient number of sales, at least among certain classes of property. This has been met by the substitution of expert appraisals where the good sales are insufficient.

Equalization and Central Assessment Practice.   Equalization and central assessment are probably the weakest stage in the property tax procedure of most states. In many, the functions are confused with that of review, and central agencies attempt to correct individual local assessments. In others, equalization, as the name implies, consists of superficial modifications of the total assessments of subdivisions. These modifications are often based on inadequate knowledge. In some states, nothing that can be dignified with the title of central assessment, equalization, or review is provided. Local assessors are required to assess property with full knowledge that the better they perform their task (and the more in conformity to law), the more their districts will be penalized.

Agencies of Central Assessment.   The state tax department ordinarily has the responsibility of making the state central assessment of counties. It may delegate this task very largely to its agents, the supervisors of assessment. The county central assessment may be made by a committee of the county board, subject to the approval of the board itself. The committee may have available the evidence of the supervisors of assessment, and if the latter's recommendations are well supported, they will usually be accepted without modification. In many states with no supervisors, or where their work is little respected, the county central assessment is a rough and unscientific procedure.

Value of Good Central Assessment.   The importance of adequate central assessment in good property tax administration is often underestimated and can hardly be overstated. With competent central assessment it is possible to convince an assessor that assessment of property at true value does not mean high taxes for his district. Experience shows that undervaluation makes for unequal valuation. Assessors make their most accurate calculation when they aim at true value. Undervaluation creates difficulty for a taxpayer when he seeks to ascertain whether or not he is a victim of discrimination; he must compare his assessment not with the statutory standard but with his neighbors' assessments. If the assessors' work is to be reviewed by some outside agency with unrestricted powers to alter the local assessment, responsibility is divided. A good central assessment will do much to sustain the morale of the whole assessment process. With a proper integration of the entire assessment procedure, values can be kept very near the true value—that is, at one common level. Uncoordinated assessment can lead only to lower levels of assessment and greater inequalities among districts. Moreover, under weak central assessment, dissension between rural and urban areas is accentuated. Prolonged contests over the division of county support have featured county proceedings in some jurisdictions for years. Basing the division on facts rather than politics would be a relief to all concerned.

In addition, the assessment of railroads and other properties, when directly made by the state, is legally and morally difficult to defend without definite and scientific knowledge of the true value of taxable property in the state. Moreover, state aids are frequently distributed inversely according to the property valuation of districts, and for this reason alone such value should not be subject to the eccentricities of local assessment. Use of assessed value as a basis of distributing aids inversely to such value encourages lower and lower assessments.

Some states have been able to relieve themselves of the responsibility of central assessment by the separation of sources of state and local revenue. By separation is meant that the state levies no property tax but depends on other independent revenue. The hope of those who have supported separation was that it would automatically eliminate competitive undervaluation and the necessity for an elaborate central assessment. The experience with separation, as far as these objectives are concerned, has been disappointing. Where the county exists as an intermediate government between the local units and the state, the problem of county central assessment still remains. If the state is to forget all about the property tax and leave the municipalities to their own devices, the assistance of the state in supervision will be missed. Experience has clearly indicated that separation is not a successful means of circumventing the problems of property tax administration.[16]

The reaction of some critics to the entire process of central assessment has been that it is all very stupid; why not let the state assess property in the first place and avoid all this duplication of work? On paper this would seem to be a legitimate criticism and a logical conclusion. Actually, however, popular opinion is opposed to so much centralization of administration. Beyond a rather indefinite point varying from state to state, centralized machinery of assessment is likely to encounter the impediments of local suspicion and hostility.

---

[16] "The separation of sources has eliminated the necessity for centralized equalization of assessments in so far as inequalities in the amounts of state taxes are concerned, but the necessity still exists for such equalization whenever subventions are made to the localities on any basis of need"—T. R. Snavely, D. C. Hyde, and A. B. Biscoe, *State Grants-in-aid in Virginia* (New York: Appleton-Century-Crofts, 1933), p. 87. See also James W. Martin and C. M. Stephenson, "Aspects of the Movement Toward Separation of the Sources of State and Local Revenue," *Tax Magazine*, XI: 2 (February 1933), pp. 58–64; 80–81.

FUNCTIONS OF THE STATE TAX DEPARTMENT
IN PROPERTY TAX ADMINISTRATION

From what has been said, it can be concluded that the state tax department or some similar central agency is a very important element in efficient property tax administration. Its principal functions are (1) supervision of local assessment, (2) central assessment of districts, (3) direct assessment of railways and other property particularly ill adapted to local assessment, and (4) acting as an administrative "court of appeals" for aggrieved property owners and districts.

The third function—the direct assessment of certain properties—has not been discussed and will be reserved for later chapters dealing with taxes upon public utilities and mines.

In very few states, if any, is the tax department or commission equipped with powers, personnel, and finances to perform its property tax functions adequately. It can be said with assurance, however, that the quality of property tax administration will correspond quite regularly with the alertness and adequacy of the state tax department or that of some corresponding state agency.

Given a tolerably intelligent and public-spirited electorate and the exemption of property that it is impossible or unjust to assess, and given good supervision and intelligent central assessment, it is possible to administer the general property tax with a high degree of efficiency and success, even with a locally elected assessor.[17]

------

[17] Supplementary Note on State Tax Departments. Most of the states have some central tax administering agency variously known as a tax commission, tax board, tax department, department of finance, department of treasury, or board of equalization. In the past, the most common form of agency consisted of a tax commission of three members, but in recent years the trend has been toward a single-head administration. Originally the tax commission functioned mainly in the property tax field, but as state revenue systems were diversified, the administration of other state taxes (such as income or sales tax) was delegated to commissions. Formerly the commissions had judicial and research functions as well as administrative ones. Some of them provided excellent research reports recommending changes in the tax system. Now most judicial tax functions are exercised by an independent board of tax appeals, and the research function is delegated to legislative committees. The commissions were originally designed to represent an independent nonpolitical or bipartisan committee. More recently the idea has been to appoint either a political subordinate to the governor or else a professional administrator.

In addition to publications mentioned in the footnotes, the following recent sources are recommended: Lawrence Lee Pelletier, *Financing Local Government,* Brunswick, Maine, 1948; *Report of the Governor's Minnesota Tax Study Committee,* Harvey Brazer, director, 1956, chaps. V–VI; *Michigan Tax Study,* Staff

PROBLEMS

1. In a county composed of one city and a considerable hinterland of rural territory, the county is so assessed that the assessed value of the city constitutes half of the assessed value of the county. Actually, the value of the taxable property in the city is one third of that in the county.

   A manufacturing company in the city owns 20 percent of the taxable property in the city, but its assessment is only 10 percent of the assessed value of the city. If the city and county property tax levies are each $1 million, what difference in total taxes will a good central assessment (equalization) make for the manufacturing company?

2. Whitley is a city in Kingston County. In 1948 its assessed value was $1 million. This was one tenth of the assessed valuation of the county.

   The county board of Kingston County has evidence to show that all of the districts of the county except Whitley have been assessed at 100 percent of true value. Evidence concerning Whitley shows that ten pieces of property located in that city exchanged hands during the preceding year. These ten pieces of property exchanged for $100,000 but were assessed at $33,333.33. Among the ten was the property of John Wilcox, for which he paid $10,000 but which was assessed at $3333.33.

   The city of Whitley in 1948 had $50,000 to raise from the general property tax for local purposes; the county had $100,000 to raise for its purposes.

   What difference will equalization make to the tax bill of John Wilcox?

3. In a certain district ten items of property assessed at a total value of $750,000 recently sold for $1 million. The items were assessed at various ratios of assessed to sales value, the average divergence from the average ratio being 15 percent. Compute the coefficient of dispersion and appraise the quality of the assessment in the district.

4. The following data applies to Fitchberg:
   a. It is assessed at 75 percent of true value;
   b. It has three quarters of the assessed value and four fifths of the true value of the county in which it is located;
   c. Its assessed value is $75 million;
   d. County levy is $1 million; local levy (for municipal and school purposes) is $1.5 million.

Papers (Lansing, 1958), chap. 5. Excellent symposia on property tax administration and other property tax problems can be found in the annual volumes of *Proceedings of the National Tax Association Conference,* 1956–1960.

(1) Calculate the assessed value tax rate and the true value tax rate for the city.
  (a) Assuming no equalization.
  (b) Assuming equalization.
(2) Indicate the main purpose and consequence of equalization in this situation.

5. Assume that the City of Wyville has an assessed-value property tax base of $100 million and the local tax for local purposes of $2 million; that its proportionate share of the county tax as equalized is 50 percent and that the total county tax for county purposes is also $2 million; that the city is assessed at two thirds of full value; that all other districts in the county are assessed at 100 percent; that Wyville has a coefficient of dispersion of 25 percent.
  a. What would be the true value property tax rate in Wyville?
  b. What inequities, if any, do you perceive in this situation?

6. A student in public finance while making a study of his home city encounters these facts about it and a neighboring city:

	X (*home city*)	Y (*neighboring city*)
Population	7000	7000
Assessed value	$5,000,000	$7,000,000
True value	15,000,000	$10,000,000
Levy (all purposes)	$250,000	$280,000
Tax rate (percent)	5	4
Ratio of assessed to full value:		
On residential property (percent)	33	80
Industrial	33	50
Coefficient of Dispersion	10	25

On the basis of these facts what conclusion can be drawn as to:
  a. Which of the two cities has the higher tax burden? Why?
  b. One reason why property taxes are higher in the city selected in (a).
  c. Which of the two cities has the better assessment? Why?
  d. What has equalization done (or what might it do) to change the relative burden in the two cities?
  e. What difference in policy is apparent with regard to industrial development?
  f. What recourse do relatively overassessed property owners in either city have?
  g. What would be the effect of raising assessments in X?

7. Why is it that small cities and villages are usually the weakest link in property tax administration?

8. Distinguish different kinds of so-called obsolescent property and indicate how each creates problems for property tax administration.

9. In what important respect does the British property tax differ from our own?
10. Consider the arguments for and against election of local assessors as contrasted to their being appointed.
11. Comment on the proposition that property is always worth what could be had for it on the market.
12. Comment on the proposition that a low assessment need not mean a low tax burden.
13. The property tax is said to be a "locally collected–centrally shared tax." What is the minimum of central responsibility required to make such a tax work satisfactorily?
14. Distinguish between central assessment and review.
15. In the postwar period, many cities were said to have three property tax values; assessed value, equalized value, and sales value. Explain the meaning of these terms and why the figures representing them did not correspond.
16. Explain the problems of tax equity which arise when a city and the surrounding township consolidate for school purposes.
17. In 1949, property in the various assessment districts of Wisconsin was assessed at average percentages of true value ranging from 26.70 to 129.98 percent. Consider what these percentages establish with regard to inequity in property tax administration.

5

PROPERTY TAX MODIFICATIONS AND OTHER PROBLEMS

In a previous chapter it was suggested that the general property tax is not an immutable institution and that it has undergone considerable adaptation in recent years. It will now be considered from the standpoint of the modifications which it has been and is undergoing. Probably the most important of these modifications fall under four headings: improvement in administration; classification; exemption; and supplementation or diversification of the tax system. The first of these was treated in the preceding chapter and the last is treated indirectly in several subsequent chapters. Special attention is here given to the other two—that is, to classification and exemption. State tax limitation has also had important effects on the property tax institution and will be considered. In addition to modifications, certain problems of property taxation, hitherto not considered, are treated.

CLASSIFICATION OF PROPERTY

The classified property tax is designed to treat different types of taxable property differently. This may be done by applying either varying tax rates or varying ratios of assessment to true value to the different classes of property. As previously stated, some state constitutions prohibit classi-

94

fication (uniformity clauses) either by express provision or by interpretation. However, the majority allow some classification.

Classification of property has made considerable progress in the United States. About one third of the states now have a low flat-rate tax on money and credits, and several states, such as Montana and Minnesota, have more comprehensive classified property taxes, applying the principle to almost all forms of property.

Example. The application of tax classification is illustrated in the state of Minnesota. Following the constitutional amendment of 1906 permitting classification of property, Minnesota developed an elaborate system of classification. In the main, this has taken the form of varying ratios of assessment to true value. The proliferation of personal property classification extends to some thirteen classes with ratios ranging from 5 to 50 percent.

Thus, iron ore, mined or unmined, is assessed at 50 percent of true value, platted urban real estate at 40 percent, rural real estate and much urban personal property at 33⅓ percent, household goods at 25 percent, and certain rural personal property at 10–20 percent. Urban homesteads up to $4000 in value are assessed at 25 percent of true value; rural homesteads at 20 percent. The first $4000 of the full and true value of these homesteads is exempt from the state property tax. Until 1943 money and credits were assessed in full but taxed at a special low flat rate of 3 mills. Mortgages were subject to a registry tax only. The special treatment of intangibles was abandoned in 1943 in favor of exemption. However, the special treatment formerly applied in Minnesota is in vogue in many states, including some that, like Minnesota, have adopted a general income tax. Iowa, for instance, confines special classification to intangibles and applies a low flat rate of 6 mills to such property. Ohio confines classification to personal property, allowing reduced ratios of assessment to merchants' stock, livestock, and manufacturers' machinery.

Reasons for Classification. The proponents of the classified property tax feel that carefully adjusted differential tax burdens will alleviate many of the distributional inequities of the general property tax. Classification also is advocated on the grounds of expediency; it is said that certain forms of property, particularly intangibles, tend to evade the high rates of the general property tax but will be listed if only a low rate is applied to them. Finally, variations may be urged for purposes of furthering desirable social objectives.

The development of classification in Minnesota, however, is attributable more to historical and political forces than to considerations of logic. When the constitution was amended, the practices that then existed were more or less transposed into law. Since then modifications have de-

pended considerably upon the balance of power in the Minnesota legislature, a balance that usually has favored the rural interests. Nevertheless,
reasonable arguments can be advanced to support the classification system. The high rate of assessment that is applied to iron ore can be defended on the ground that this property represents gifts of nature which
are subject to depletion. The low rate on household goods, and that
formerly applied to money and credits, may be justified on the ground
that these forms of property tend to evade assessment if heavily taxed.
Finally, the differentials in favor of agriculture can be defended on the
score that agriculture is or was the victim of chronic depression.

Evaluation of Classification.   Special interest attends the low flat-
rate taxation of intangibles, since it constitutes the most widespread
attempt to apply property tax classification. The evidence indicates that
this innovation has usually resulted in a substantial increase in the
amount of such property placed upon the assessment rolls. However,
nowhere has the increase been sufficient to constitute a good assessment.[1] And, in some cases, the receipts from property taxes on this
class of property have been less under the classification than without it.
A few states, of which Ohio is an example, have combined special low
rates with central assessment. It is the practice of several states also to
assess certain intangibles under a special income tax. This special income
tax has the advantage of not driving intangibles into hiding before the
assessment date.

Classification of property such as is practiced in Minnesota has
been criticized on the ground that it opens the gate to political pressure
and abuse. But to some extent such classification is practiced anyhow
either by exemption or by administrative deviation from the statutes.
Nevertheless most critics would probably agree that the Minnesota experiment has been short of successful. It complicates the role of the
assessor; proliferates fractionalization of assessments leading to astro-
nomical rates; and lends itself to political pressures reflecting the efforts
of some groups to gain tax relief at the expense of others.[2]

Possible Improvements.   One might devise a far more rational classification system than any thus far applied. Land (especially urban land)
and natural resources would be assessed or taxed at the highest rate in
recognition of their nonreproducible character. The values associated
with such property are scarcity values; they are community-created and
unnecessary as incentives for private endeavor. Special concessions
might be given to some or all tangible personal property on the score

---

[1] Simeon E. Leland, *The Classified Property Tax in the United States* (Boston:
Houghton Mifflin Company, 1928), p. 403.
[2] See *Report of the Governor's Minnesota Tax Study.*

that this is most difficult to assess and taxes thereon are often passed on to consumers. Intangibles and household goods should probably be entirely exempt. Certain property that is usually exempt, such as the real estate of lodges, should be taxed at a low rate in recognition of the services received from government. Finally, it may be suggested that if municipalities wish to extend tax favors to new industries, they had better do it through reasonable classification than through outright exemption or assessment manipulation.

PROPERTY TAX EXEMPTIONS

Large and increasing amounts of property are excluded from the tax rolls. Some years ago it was estimated that about one eighth of the real estate in the United States was exempt from property tax.[3] The exceptions thus made to the general property tax rule are so for a variety of reasons. Included among the exempt property is much publicly owned real estate that is kept off the tax roll either because of certain rules of constitutional law or on the theory that taxing public property is taking money out of one pocket and putting it into another. The trend toward public housing and other public works has increased the amount of public property. Much debate has attended the exemption of defense plants particularly when it extends to the use of inventory and equipment by a private lessee for profit. Some states have taxed such property and have been sustained by the Supreme Court in doing so. Some property is exempt for social reasons—such as homesteads, churches, lodges, private schools; some for developmental purposes—as new industries; some for fiscal or administrative reasons—as household furniture; some to avoid double taxation—as credits.

Exemptions create a problem because they reduce the tax base and thus necessitate higher tax rates on the remaining taxable property. Often, it is very difficult to draw the line between property that is entitled to exemption and that which is not.

Great Britain is an example of a country that has greatly narrowed its property tax base: not only is its property tax confined to real estate; in addition, agricultural, manufacturing, and public utility property has been either partially or entirely "derated." This leaves the property tax confined largely to residential property and shops. Much reliance on centralized support for municipalities has followed.

The exemption of intangibles and certain types of tangible property

---

[3] Jensen, *Property Taxation in the United States,* p. 126.

has been discussed, and the subject of exemption of public property will be reserved for a later chapter on intergovernmental fiscal relations. Here we may discuss briefly the other classes of exemption mentioned above.

HOMESTEAD EXEMPTION

A form of exemption or partial exemption now allowed in about one quarter of the states (though with many variations) is that of so-called homesteads. Much of the legislation creating these exemptions took root during the foreclosure period of the depressed 1930s. As used in taxation, the term *homestead* includes any dwelling occupied by the owner as a residence, the site upon which the dwelling is located, and varying amounts of surrounding land. For rural land the maximum area may run as high as 200 acres, and for urban land it may include as much as an acre. Thus the exemption may include not only the land and improvements used as a place to live but also considerable property used to make a living.[4] In value, the exemptions range from $500 in Wyoming to $5000 in Florida and Mississippi.

The fiscal effects of homestead exemption depend on a number of variables, such as the degree of home ownership, area and value of homesteads, and the ratio of residential property to total property. A district which finds a large part of its property tax base exempt from taxation has cause for both sorrow and jubilation—the former because of the greater difficulty in meeting local expenses, the latter because its share of county and state property taxes will be definitely reduced. A district with a small amount of property exempt may also have occasion both to complain and rejoice, but for the opposite reason in each case. In general, a loss from the tax base in a district means a severe increase in local property taxes upon the remaining base, curtailment of expenditures, or increased aid from the state. The latter will probably involve adding a new tax to the state's system to provide relief for municipalities.

Pros and Cons of Homestead Exemption.   Homestead exemption is defended mainly on the ground that home ownership is a community asset and needs to be encouraged. Excessive tenancy has always been regarded as inimical to the public interest. For one thing, tenancy is less conducive to the proper care of property (good conservation, for instance) than home ownership. On the other hand, there are those who doubt the wisdom of encouraging the recipients of low and uncertain

---

[4] Logically, it should include a mercantile establishment above which the owner lives in a flat. The merchant's situation is not very different from that of the farmer, who claims exemption not only for his home but also for his contiguous income-earning property. But actually the laws do not appear to extend the merchant this privilege.

income to acquire residential property. These people may incur heavy loss of savings if they are unable to meet obligations or are obliged to migrate. The exemption of a specific minimum amount of value on all homesteads supplies a progressive element in the property tax *among homeowners;* it constitutes a larger proportion of cheap than of expensive homes.

On the negative side it is contended that the homestead exemption program offers nothing to those least able to pay, namely, the tenants; that indeed the program is likely to increase their burden in so far as higher taxes will be levied on nonexempt property and passed on to them by their landlords. Or, if no increases in property taxes are contemplated to replace lost revenue, then the effect of substitute taxes— particularly the sales tax—may be to increase the burdens not only on the tenants but also on the poor generally, including small home owners. People who own homes are presumably the more well-to-do citizens in the community, the very ones to whom the government might be expected to look for taxes. Here we have one example of many we shall encounter where the incentive approach to taxation runs head-on into the ability-to-pay approach. The latter would support a preference for an exemption or partial exemption of low-value housing as such. Moreover, the exemption is unnecessarily prodigal with the local tax base; not all homeowners need relief, and an exemption confined to some specific class such as old people and related to income would perhaps be more appropriate.

EXEMPTION OF PROPERTY USED FOR RELIGIOUS AND PHILANTHROPIC PURPOSES

Most states exempt educational, charitable, benevolent, and religious institutions from property taxation and also allow deduction of contributions to these institutions in calculating income for income taxes. The exemptions are defended on the ground that these undertakings are non-profit-making and that they perform services which the state would have to perform were they not in existence.

In the case of religious organizations, some objections to exemption have been raised on the score that they are a contravention of the rule that church and state shall remain separate. A nonbeliever is likely to ask why he should pay taxes to support other peoples' "pet religious propaganda." Some have ventured to doubt that church members are any better citizens than nonparticipants. Periodically bills are introduced in most legislatures to do away with the exemption of church property. Once in Wisconsin a bill was introduced to discontinue exemption of churches where ministers preach political sermons. But these bills are never taken very seriously. The exemption rests securely on the fact that most people believe churches should be encouraged indirectly if not directly.

The exemption of parochial (and other private) schools is also contentious. However, parents who send their children to these schools also pay taxes to support the public schools.

The rather prevalent exemption of lodges may be cited to exemplify the liberality with which the term *benevolent institution* is sometimes interpreted. It is true that the lodge building may be nonprofit-making—so are the homes that serve as shelter for millions of citizens. It may be true that lodges perform a good and useful function—so do country clubs and grocery stores. It is true that lodges which are mainly social perform some incidental charities—but so do the homes, for that matter.[5]

At one time the courts in Wisconsin drew a line between the Masons and the Elks, holding the former to be a charitable institution and the latter not.[6] More recently all fraternal societies operating under the lodge system in that state have been specifically exempted. Members of college fraternities and sororities may doubt the fairness of the classification that denied them a similar privilege. Perhaps the realistic answer is that there are more Masons in the legislature than Sigma Chis.[7]

Statutes and court decisions on exemptions present as many as five tests or conditions for the inclusion of institutions in an exemtpt class: ownership, use, occupancy, private gains, and profits. States usually use one or a combination of several of these in determining exemptions, but there is a twilight zone in any event. Is an office building in a downtown metropolis, valued at $200,000, owned by a denominational group, with the income from the property applied to a union college some 200 miles away, entitled to exemption?[8] Is a college entitled to exemption on en-

---

[5] In denying an exemption to the Benevolent and Protective Order of Elks, the Missouri Supreme Court in a classic decision said: "Charity is not a promiscuous mixer. Here she modestly stands outside or goes her way and waits; waits until the plaintiff [Elk's lodge] has finished using the spacious and comfortable rooms for the pleasure of its members; waits until the curtain has fallen upon the last scene of the vaudeville performance on the stage; until the dancers have tired and gone home; until the billiard rooms have been deserted to the markers; until the plaintiff has paid the cost of its own entertainment, and goes out and finds her, and hands her whatever it may have left in its own pocket. She gets not the use of the premises, but what remains of income to the owners after they have used it in carrying out the injunction of their organic law, by promoting their own welfare, enhancing their own happiness and cultivating their own good fellowship among themselves"—*St. Louis Lodge No. 9, B.P.O.E. v. Koeln,* 262 Mo. 444, 448 (1914).

[6] *Trustees v. Green Bay,* 122 Wis. 452 (1904).

[7] Other property of this character frequently exempted includes that of temperance associations, bar associations, labor and farm organizations, YMCA's, and parsonages.

[8] So held in *Commonwealth v. Board of Education of the Methodist Episcopal Church,* 166 Ky. 610 (1915).

dowment funds invested in a piston-ring factory? Does a publishing company, doing work exclusively for students, lose its exempt status when it contracts outside work though using the gains to help support the college paper? [9] Will it make a difference if no one connected with the company draws pay? These and many similar questions are a source of frequent arguments, conflicting statutes, and court decisions.

EXEMPTION TO ENCOURAGE ECONOMIC ACTIVITY

One of the most prevalent forms of tax exemption in the United States is that accorded to new industries. These are exempt in order to attract them to a particular city or state. States and cities are not allowed to adopt tariffs in order to preserve the home market for their own producers, but they may offer special favors to industry as an inducement for its location or expansion. Other inducements may include cash bonuses, loans, donations of site and building or their provision at nominal rentals, guarantees of favorable labor conditions, and so on. Encouragement of this sort is sometimes authorized by state statutes particularly in the southern states. Puerto Rico has a very ambitious program offering to certain qualified classes of industry relief from all major taxes, including the national net income tax, for twelve years. Not infrequently these inducements are offered by municipal governments without legal authorization; this makes municipal officials personally liable for misappropriation of funds, but usually no great hazard is involved if the action has strong sanction from local public opinion. Not infrequently also the assessor gives established industries "a break" (concession in assessment) in order to keep them.

These special inducements are an example of the weakness of the states and municipalities in applying taxes to industries able to migrate or threaten migration. The author knows of one case where a firm employing many people threatened to move out if the municipality raised its tax rate. The city, though hard pressed, decided not to take a chance. On the other hand, businesses on their own initiative often contribute very generously to municipal projects.

Motives of Tax Exemption for Industry. The motive behind tax exemption and other special inducements to industry may be defensive or expansionist. The defensive motive may appear in a small city with an industrial population that is left in desperate straits by the failure or removal of an important factory. Without the factory in operation, the city is badly demoralized, with hundreds or thousands of workmen seeking private or public relief, the real estate market collapsing as people leave town or lose their homes, the tax rolls suffering from delinquency,

---

[9] Held not exempt in *Cardinal Publishing Co. v. City of Madison,* 208 Wis. 517 (1932).

and so on. In such circumstances, a subsidy—whether or not legal—that would bring in an industry or keep the present one operating would likely appeal to the city fathers as a good investment of public money.

The expansionist motives are more complex. A community may desire new industries as a matter of pride, in order to raise local business and real estate values, to increase the local tax base, or to improve the balance between rural and urban population and offer more diversified employment opportunities to the people. The Supreme Court of the United States in a famous case [10] decided that direct subsidies for industry involved expenditure of public money for a private purpose and, therefore, were illegal. However, in some industrial cities the retention or recruitment of a local factory may seem a public purpose of the first order.

STATE AND MUNICIPAL EXEMPTION POLICIES

Is it sound policy for states and municipalities to grant tax exemptions to industry? Certainly something will depend here upon the universality of the exemption practice. If one merchant keeps his store open on Sundays while others are closed, he can make money by so doing. But if all merchants follow the same policy, none of them are benefited. Similarly, if only one municipality were to offer special favors, perhaps it could attract a considerable number of desirable industries. But when favors are universalized, they cease to be effective. The question then arises as to when and where the competition in subsidies will stop. One proposal is to let the state levy and collect the property tax on industry (as it now usually does on railroads) and distribute to all municipalities according to a formula. However, the derivation of a suitable formula would not be easy.

Questionable Effectiveness of Exemptions.   There is considerable dispute as to how effective tax exemptions and other concessions are in developing industry. Instances can be cited where a municipality showed bad judgment in its choice of a firm or made concessions entirely out of proportion to the prospective gains.[11] There are others where "mercantilism" appears to have paid off very well indeed.[12] The competition between New England and the South for the location of the textile industry

---

[10] *Citizens Savings and Loan Association v. Topeka,* 20 Wall. 655 (1874).

[11] A tax promotion program in Louisiana has been in operation since 1946 but its effectiveness has been seriously questioned—William D. Ross, *Louisiana's Industrial Exemption Program,* Division of Research, College of Commerce (Baton Rouge: Louisiana State University, 1953).

[12] W. D. Knight, *Subsidization of Industry in Forty Selected Cities in Wisconsin,* Bureau of Business Research and Science, School of Commerce (Madison: University of Wisconsin, 1947).

has turned on many factors of which the financial concessions of government is one of considerable importance. In some situations it is evidently quite possible for a community to buy an industry.[13]

It is not always realized that tax concessions and other inducements are at the expense of taxpayers who do not receive them. Tax exemption means a subsidy paid by the entire community, and it is very doubtful if all taxpayers have a proportionate stake in the benefits. Concessions might conceivably be supported by the infant-industries argument, but they are rarely confined to a nice calculation of the expense of moving and restarting. And where the conditions were favorable to its growth, industry in this country has had no trouble in getting started in new territory.

Conclusion. From the over-all point of view, it can be said that tax concessions to industry are demoralizing to fair competition both among industries and localities. From the municipalities' point of view this conclusion does not always hold. But if the municipalities are to follow a policy of tax exemption, the situation calls for careful permissive legislation (including the requirement of a local referendum), perhaps some state supervision, some intermunicipal cooperation, and a good deal of wisdom and restraint on the part of municipal officials. Further exploration of the broader aspects of this difficult problem would carry us beyond the objectives of this chapter.

STATE TAX LIMITATION

Although municipalities are in a subordinate position to the state and owe all their powers to it, they have usually been allowed to levy upon taxable property at their own discretion, both as to rates and purpose of the tax. They have been limited, if at all, by maximum statutory or constitutional limits which were too high or too loosely drawn to be effective. Within recent years, however, there has been a widespread movement in the United States to place an effective top limit upon property tax rates, one which falls well below the range of rates customarily levied in many municipalities, and this movement has been successful in a few states. The property tax has been a highly elastic source of revenue in most municipalities, and the attempt to make it more inflexible, where successful, is likely to have a profound effect on the problem of municipal finance.

---

[13] Seymour Harris, *The Economics of New England* (Cambridge, Mass.: Harvard University Press, 1952); Joe Summers Floyd, Jr., *Effects of Taxation on Industrial Location* (Chapel Hill: University of North Carolina Press, 1952).

KINDS OF TAX LIMITATION

An over-all tax limitation is an entirely different species from a specific limitation. Where the property tax is used by two or more layers of government (which is almost, if not universally, true throughout the United States), an over-all limit requires rationing—that is, the establishment of an agency [14] of some sort which allots to the various competing units a specified portion of the maximum rate. A specific limitation specifies a maximum for each levying unit and does not require rationing. The former in particular is likely to have a profound effect on local government; it means that local citizens can no longer determine whether to spend more of their own money on public services.

Tax limitation laws are not always quite so inflexible as the above explanation might lead one to believe. Frequently they provide that the ceiling may be exceeded on authority of referendum with a favorable vote of some proportion of the electorate [15] (sometimes including those not voting). Quite commonly, taxes required to pay interest and principal upon the public debt, or at least that portion of the public debt incurred before passage of the act, are excepted.

CRITICISM OF TAX LIMITATIONS

Some critics object to property tax limitations on the ground that they do not limit. Others believe that they are less intolerable, perhaps, for the reason that they are not always entirely effective. One loophole is the exemption of levies to finance debt. Where levies to service all debts are exempt from the limit, a municipality can circumvent the limitation by borrowing freely even for operating expenses. It can levy such property taxes as it chooses, provided it uses them to pay last year's bills. Where levies to service only those debts incurred before passage of the law are exempt, reduced expenditure may still be avoided by borrowing, but the difficulty of maintaining services within a balanced budget steadily increases under this program. Circumvention by resort to special assessment in lieu of property taxes is a common device, as is the levy of special charges for specific services such as sewage disposal. As previously mentioned, most tax limitation provisions permit levies in excess of spec-

---

[14] In Ohio, for instance, state statutes provide for each county a budget commission consisting of the county auditor, treasurer, and prosecutor. Dissatisfied districts may appeal to the board of appeals.

[15] In Ohio a simple majority is required to exceed the 10 mill limit if the issue is presented at a general (November) election or at a May primary in the even-numbered years. A 55-percent majority is required at a special election held on any other day.

ified limits by referendum, though how freely these referendums are used does not appear in the record. There can be little doubt that property tax limitation exerts a very decided restraint on the upward trend of property tax rates.

Adjustment to loss of revenue resulting from effective property tax limitation may involve the cutting of services or the levying of substitute taxes to replace the revenue. Since municipalities are usually strictly limited in their powers of taxation, the substitute taxes are generally enacted by the state and reach the municipalities via state aids. The substitute tax that has found most ready adoption, as in the case of homestead exemptions, is the sales tax, usually levied by the state and involving a distribution problem. Pending state assistance, municipalities in some states have found themselves in dire financial straits, extending to the point where fire and police protection were discontinued.

Many states have developed a measure of home rule for their municipalities—that is, the latter are guaranteed the right to make their own decisions in their own way on matters of local interest. The proponents of home rule deeply resent tax limitation. They contend that local communities have the right to spend their own money as they see fit and that interference by the state in this freedom is undemocratic. As previously stated, the state usually increases its support of tax-limited municipalities. But this again compromises their independence and self-reliance. It also raises the question whether state collection of taxes with local expenditure of revenue will contribute in the long run to the most economical and judicious spending of public funds on the part of the municipalities.

It is also contended that much of the property tax is capitalized and that consequently a reduction will serve only as a bonanza to present owners; future owners will get no relief. The capitalization theory, as discussed in the following chapter, holds that the value of property is related to the net income that can be earned from it; when the net income is increased, the capital value rises. Relief from a property tax burden results in a greater net income, which in turn is reflected in the selling value of the property. Thus present owners pocket all the benefit that property tax relief may bring; the position of future buyers will not be changed by the program except for one point to their disadvantage, namely, that they will have to make a greater outlay to purchase the property. The capitalization phenomenon is thought by economists to apply mainly in the case of land. Even here, however, the theory that all land taxes are immediately capitalized needs many qualifications. Nevertheless, the capitalization theory is entitled to a great deal of weight in considering the proposal for a blanket reduction in the property tax.

It is also argued against property tax limitations that they should wait upon the availability of a better tax as a substitute. Experience has shown that the most available and readily accepted state source to substitute for the property tax is the sales tax. We are not prepared in this chapter to consider the merits and demerits of the sales tax. It may have the advantage that it reaches a somewhat different set of taxpayers from those who pay the property tax. But the sales tax is vigorously opposed by many critics on the score that it is more regressive and certainly more capricious in its incidence than the property tax.

The limitation movement brings sharply into focus the merits and demerits of property taxation. That the property tax has many shortcomings and that it may be overworked is conceded, but fear may still be entertained less municipalities be manuevered into a position where their main alternative is to pull the leg of the state.

SPECIAL PROBLEMS IN TAXING INVENTORIES

ANNUAL INVENTORY VERSUS AVERAGE INVENTORY

One of the principal kinds of taxable tangible personal property is merchants' inventories. The present system of property taxation as it applies to merchants is criticized on a number of grounds. It is alleged that the assessment as of a specific day is unfair. The theory of the assessment as of a single day seems to be that much capital is constantly in motion and, as in the game of musical chairs, someone will halt the procession for a moment and take account of the situation. At that moment, the usual amount of inventory will be in existence and in somebody's hands. Since the property tax is an impersonal tax, it makes little difference in whose hands it is found. If a livestock shipper happens to have on hand a large consignment of stock, even for only a day—assessment day—he can be assessed upon this property. The merchant who sells agricultural machinery may be heavily stocked on May 1, whereas the merchant who sells coal may be virtually "cleaned out" at that time. This does not mean that one has more business or capital than the other or that one has more ability to pay or benefits received than the other. It is thus alleged that a snapshot picture of all businesses on a given day gives no fair evidence of their taxpaying power. The contention is that a time exposure might give a very different picture. In view of the fact that the day of the snapshot is advertised in advance, some merchants, if they are able, try to have as little on hand as possible. When and where automobiles in the hands of merchants are assessed as merchants' stocks, active selling campaigns are postponed until after assessment day so as to avoid large inventories on that day. Commercial storage warehouses, when their contents are assessable, experience a rapid falling off in business about assessment time, particularly when they are in competition with warehouses in states which exempt such property from taxation.

As a partial remedy for some of these difficulties, certain states now attempt to assess merchants on the basis of their average inventories for the year. This appears to be a sound innovation but is dependent, of course, upon the keeping of accurate books. Moreover, the average inventory is not very easy to calculate. If it is interpreted to mean the average of the inventories on hand during the first day of each month, merchants can still manipulate their stock to some extent, if they take the trouble to watch twelve days instead of one. Some states attempt to secure and average the high and low points of inventory during a year. No easy method of calculating an average for all 365 days of the year has yet been devised.

There is also an interesting legal question as to whether merchants' inventories should be assessed at their wholesale cost, at their retail value, or at what the stock would sell for as a whole to a new proprietor. Practice favors the first of these standards, but it can be argued that real estate values are based on what is paid by the ultimate consumer and that the same rule should apply to merchants' stock.

RAPID TURNOVER VERSUS SLOW TURNOVER

Merchants with large capital and a slow turnover complain that they are highly penalized by the general property tax. For example, assume a situation as shown in the accompanying table:

Store	Operating capital	Gross sales	Profit
A	$30,000	$ 30,000	$3,000
B	2,000	100,000	4,000

Store *A* is engaged in a trade which has a very slow turnover, such as the furniture business; store *B* in one with a rapid turnover, perhaps a meat shop. The property tax, which is gauged by the first column, gathers many times as much from *A* as from *B*. However, *B* has a much larger volume of business than *A* and under the sales tax would pay more. Thus far nothing has been said about net income or profit. *B* has the advantage here, and this fact would be taken cognizance of only through a net income tax. Those interested in the *A* store are likely to feel that a merchant's personal property is a poor measure of ability to pay or benefits received. The property tax on inventories, as a business tax, takes account of only one aspect of a business and other aspects seem as relevant in gauging tax obligations.

THE CHAIN STORE

The independent merchant often complains of the property tax upon inventories on the ground that it favors the chain store. Chain stores are said to enjoy the following advantages under the property tax:

1. The chain store as a rule operates with a relatively small stock and a rapid rate of turnover. There may not be very much in such a store at any one time but, like snow in Montana, "a great deal passes through." At the very time when the assessor is getting his information, huge trucks on the highways may be bringing a fresh stock of supplies to the chain store.

2. The chain store offers little or no information to the assessor who, when compelled to guess, does so conservatively. The independent merchant has books which the assessor can force him to disclose, and in some states income tax returns show facts concerning his inventory. Neither of these sources of information is available in the case of the chain store. Most of the bookkeeping is done in some distant city, and the income tax returns are submitted by the chain as a whole rather than by individual units.

3. The chain-store system has a considerable portion of its investment in intangible property, such as "organization value," which does not show up in assessments of unit stores.

4. Assessors frequently assess goods at the cost to their owners. Any advantage which the chain may have in buying may be reflected in a lower assessment, whereas the independent merchant, compelled to buy in smaller lots, must pay a higher price and be taxed on this disadvantage. Cost of wholesaling which enters the inventory value of independent merchants may be omitted in assessing the inventory of chain stores.

5. Chain stores have an opportunity to manipulate their stocks between one store and another and between stores and warehouses. Differences in assessment dates (as between states) or in tax rates (as between cities) can thus be used to a certain extent to reduce burdens.

The contention that the chain store obtains an unfair advantage under the property tax has been one of the grounds, and perhaps the most plausible, upon which special taxes on chain stores are based. These special taxes will be discussed in a later chapter. Here it can be said that vigorous supervision by the tax department, and assistance in securing information from the central office of chain stores and checking such information at least occasionally by means of auditors, may greatly facilitate a fair assessment.

SUBSTITUTES FOR THE PERSONAL PROPERTY TAX

Although we have considered the personal property tax mainly as applied to merchants, many of the same problems are encountered in its application to manufacturers and in this latter case the tax is also an important factor in intrastate and interstate competition. As we move toward the abandonment of the intangibles tax, the element in the property tax remaining as the most difficult to administer is the levy on tangible personal property. Obviously, few assessors can make even a pretense of assessing such property "on view." They are neither qualified nor financed to take inventory in all the stores about town. They can get some information sometimes from company books and income tax returns, and they can, if the law so provides, make use of a sworn statement from the taxpayer. At best, however, the tax is very troublesome to administer. Add to this the objections that the tax is readily shifted forward in higher prices, ignores turnover, favors chain stores, and penalizes the concern that attempts to stabilize employment by building up inventory, and a fair case is made against the continuance of this levy. Ohio has compromised with a classification system confined to personal property and providing a lower rate for it than for real estate. On the other hand, personal property frequently supplies a substantial part of the local tax base (15 or 20 percent, perhaps) and is as able to support government as other types of property. Most municipalities are even now looking for new sources of revenue and are not likely to entertain enthusiastically a prospect of losing old ones. The case for exempting or allowing special treatment for inventories does not apply in most respects to the taxation of machinery. Accordingly, there is strong support for confining the property tax to real estate and other business property subject to depreciation. However, to go even this far in reducing the local tax base involves sizable revenue losses or substitute sources; taking account of alternative difficulties, the decision may be for retention with an all-out effort to improve administration.[16] In states that exempt motor

---

[16] For a substantial analysis of the problems associated with the taxation of personal property and particularly inventory, see "Interim Report of the Committee in Personal Property Taxation on the Taxation of Tangible Personal Property Used in Business" (E. Emory Glander, chairman), *Proceedings of the National Tax Association Conference*, 1952, pp. 76–106; see also Morris Beck, "Exemption of Business Tangibles from Property Taxation," *ibid.*, 1959, pp. 150–161.

vehicles from personal property taxation there is often support for broadening the local tax base by including this considerable volume of wealth.

Four states exempt personal property entirely and a large number of others give some classes of personal property a favorable classification. The favorable treatment of industrial personal property provides a favorite device for improving the so-called business climate via the tax system.

THE PROPERTY TAX AND MUNICIPAL REVENUES

PLIGHT OF THE CITIES

Many American cities have found themselves hard pressed for revenues in the postwar period. For one thing, they have found their expenses rising with inflation while they have hesitated to raise assessments accordingly, partly because of uncertainties as to the trend in values, and partly because of consideration for the small home owner. Then, too, central cities have suffered from the migration to suburbs previously discussed. Finally, while welfare expenses have been generally less than during the 1930s, there has been a sharp new demand for public works and the acceleration in educational requirements has been formidable.

Municipalities have relied for revenue to some extent on state and federal aids and on shared taxes. Usually they have not fared too well in these programs. It is a well-known fact that municipalities are underrepresented in state and federal legislative bodies and that this abuse yields slowly, if at all, to attack. State and federal assistance involves a sacrifice in financial independence and self-reliance for cities. It involves going "hat in hand" to the central units of government when municipalities wish to expand their programs of public services.

An alternative way out for municipalities is to seek and obtain an enlargement of their taxing powers, so that they can supplement the property tax and spend their own money as their citizens wish. Outstanding developments in this direction include recent action of the Pennsylvania legislature permitting local governments, except rural townships, to tax anything that the state could tax but is not currently taxing. It is reported that municipalities have responded avidly with capitation (poll) taxes, amusement taxes, severance taxes, income taxes, mercantile license taxes, and miscellaneous levies.

Of these taxes, the income tax proved the most lucrative, but the per capita and amusement taxes were most widely adopted. Revenues from these taxes have proved substantial and are growing. Experience seems to establish that many municipalities (particularly the larger ones) can administer one or several of these taxes with a reasonable degree of success, though not without the services of a professional administrator and a small staff.[17] The local income tax has attracted particular attention. Although not easily administered, it scores in its recognition that jobs as well as property are a substantial source of urban income.

The New York legislature has also granted wide powers to permit municipalities to broaden and diversify their tax systems, but in specified fields only and not to exceed maximum limits. In other states, this movement has taken place largely without statutory empowerment and includes the development of city amusement taxes, retail sales taxes, gross receipt taxes, motor vehicle taxes, cigarette taxes, and even, in a few cases, net income taxes. Here it may be observed that the solution of the municipal tax problem along lines which will revive the vitality of local government is a matter of general and first-rate public concern.

Problem of Rural Governments.   The impression should not be conveyed that the revenue problem of municipalities is confined to cities. Rural property owners complained bitterly (and with reason) about their tax burdens during the 1920s and even more so during the early 1930s. This was a period in which farm income was trending downward and farm taxes were mounting. State aids and shared taxes and the assumption of highway costs by larger units of government have, in many cases, substantially relieved the rural tax burden. The problem has returned, however, with the drop in farm income during the 1950s. Farmers, it is believed, also have special difficulty in shifting their taxes.

Depleted and underendowed areas also have a place in the property tax problem. These communities have usually been the recipients of large amounts of state and federal aids, without which they could not have maintained even a semblance of decent standards of public services. These areas are a problem to the state with respect to land use, reorganization of local government, and avoidance of perpetuating obsolete communities.

The property tax problem of depleted and underendowed areas is fundamentally different from that of the cities. The former suffer because of inadequacy of the resources with which to support government; the latter because of inability to tax usually ample resources. The fiscally weak communities can be assisted by central governments primarily through grants-in-aid. Some reorganization of governmental machinery,

---

[17] *Report of the Governor's Minnesota Tax Study Committee,* chap. XIX; Robert A. Sigafoos, *The Municipal Income Tax: Its History and Problems* (Chicago: Public Administration Service, 1955).

attending or preceding the grant program, would reduce the size of the problem.

SUMMARY OF CHAPTERS 3, 4, AND 5

The general property tax, though until recently declining in relative importance, remains the outstanding and frequently the sole support for the local units of government in the United States. In its broadest form, it seeks to tax all goods owned that have exchange value and to tax them universally and uniformly. Other characteristics are its impersonality, its proportional rate structure, and its use as a locally collected, centrally shared tax.

The property tax is criticized on theoretical grounds, because it is said to correlate badly with both benefits received and ability to pay. The latter contention is supported by many arguments, perhaps chief of which are that the taxation of tangible property and equitable rights in such property is double taxation (when modified, the criticism usually is that the creditor is favored over the debtor), that the tax is inconvenient in timing and form, and that it creates a heavy burden and a high fixed charge upon shelter. In practice the property tax as administered is often regressive, shows other inequalities, and is characterized (particularly in its application to personal property) by a high degree of evasion. In spite of these criticisms the property tax is retained, a fact that can be explained in many ways, among which are that the tax is well suited to local governments and decentralized decision making, is considerably capitalized, and is less unfair than some of its principal alternatives.

Analyzing the problem of property tax administration in more detail, we find quite a complicated pattern. First, there are many units of government that rely simultaneously upon the same tax base. Second, there are a considerable number of steps from the levy to the collection of delinquent taxes and appeal to state administrative bodies and courts. Third, many problems are encountered in the local assessment of property, including the part-time, poorly paid, politically chosen assessor, multitudinous forms of personal property and real estate, and imperfect standards of value. In the local-assessment process many helpful aids may be provided, among the most important of which is adequate supervision by a central agency.

A highly important and badly neglected feature of property tax administration is the central assessment and equalization of property values. This is necessary to defeat competitive undervaluation among districts, to preserve the morale of those engaged in the assessment process, and so on. Preferably, it involves only the assessment of districts by a central agency and does not disturb local assessments of individuals. The central assessment can be based on scientific information through a process of comparing a sample of recently sold or appraised property with local assessments of the same property. In supervision of local assessments and the central assessment process, the state tax department plays a vital role in property tax administration.

The property tax has undergone considerable modification in recent years, including improvements in administration, limitation of rates, exemptions, and classification. The latter may take the form of applying different rates or ratios of assessment to different kinds of property and is particularly common in its application to intangible property. Among the exemptions that have gained considerable foothold in recent years is that of homesteads. This form of exemption relieves one class of shelter of a high fixed charge and favors home owners over tenants (usually poorer). Other important exemptions include philanthropic, fraternal, and religious institutions. These are exempt (though not always without plausible objection) principally on the score that they relieve the state of certain responsibilities. New industries are also frequently favored, a policy that presents serious problems in intermunicipal relations and in the maintenance of neutrality among taxpayers.

Tax limitations, especially those of the "over-all" type, have reduced property taxes, but they are criticized because they violate home rule, result in precipitous curtailment of services or the adoption of inequitable replacement taxes, and (through capitalization) provide present owners with an undue share of the benefits from reduced taxes.

As applied to merchants, the personal property tax is usually erratic in gauging inventory values (due to assessment as of a given day), is prejudicial to the taxpayer with a slow turnover, and discriminates against the independent merchant as compared with the chain store. The personal property tax has other limitations; some attention and experimentation have been devoted to finding a substitute.

Many units of government, particularly cities, have been hard pressed for revenue in recent years, largely because of the growing inelasticity of the property tax. The problem of the cities has been aggravated by suburban development. The cities need new supplemental sources of revenue through which they can tax their own ample resources without relying on aids and shared taxes from central units of government.

In conclusion, although constantly under attack and although cracking badly in places, the general property tax is probably destined to continue for many years as a major source of support for important public services. While the search for other and better sources of public revenue should go on, we should also continue improving this source so that it may work with that degree of equity and efficiency that a modern revenue system requires.

PROBLEMS

1. Starting with a present constitutional requirement that property taxes be imposed uniformly, how would you change the constitution and the statutes (in your state) to inaugurate an intelligent system of property classification for taxation purposes?
2. Churches are usually exempt from property taxation, partly on the ground that they save the state money because of their character-building activities. Does your experience confirm the alleged fact that church members "behave better" than other people?
3. The dormitories of a state university operate a cooperative store in a dormitory building selling supplies to students at cost (no profit). Consider critically the various grounds on which it might be contended that the *premises* and *inventory* are or should be exempt from property taxation.
4. Is it a violation of the rule that classification must be reasonable when a legislature exempts a Masonic temple from taxation but insists on taxing college fraternity houses?
5. An educational institution, fearing inflation, invests its endowment funds in factory property which is leased to independent operators. The rent received is used to operate the college. Should the factory property be taxed?
6. Consider the proposition that the homestead exemption adds a progressive element to the property tax.
7. A homestead exemption is said to be an incentive feature to a property tax law. It is criticized on the ground that it is contrary to the ability-to-pay principle. Is the incentive approach to taxation seldom, usually, or always in conflict with the ability approach?
8. New England is alleged to have lost heavily through the migration of its textile industry to the south. What considerations are involved in judging whether this is in the national interest? If your judgment is negative, what, if anything, can be done about the problem?
9. Industries are said to need a high level of municipal public services. Is this view inconsistent with the contention that they locate and expand where their taxes will be low?
10. On what ground is it alleged that a property tax limitation benefits present owners exclusively?
11. Is a property tax limitation properly described as a check on a community's right to spend its own money, or is it more accurate to de-

scribe it as a check on some people's penchant to spend other people's money?

12. Criticize the tangible personal property tax and explain alternatives.

13. The personal property tax is said to be unneutral in gauging inventory values. Why?

14. Is there any technique by which an average-inventory calculation of personal property can accurately gauge the average personal property that a firm had on hand each day and hour of a given year?

15. Differentiate four distinct ways of treating intangibles in property tax practice in the United States.

16. Compare and criticize movements in New York and Pennsylvania toward diversified local revenue systems.

17. Explain the difference between a specific and an over-all property tax limitation; explain the special implications for home rule where the latter type of limitation attends a locally collected, centrally shared tax.

6

SHIFTING AND INCIDENCE

One cannot probe very far into either the theoretical or the practical problems of taxation without running head-on into the problem of incidence. For instance, it is commonly believed that a cigarette tax paid directly by a manufacturer in North Carolina ends as a burden on the smoker, perhaps in Oregon. In fact, we are so confident of the shifting in this case that we label the tax a *consumption tax*. How do we know (if indeed we do know) that the tax becomes mingled with the price of tobacco and enhances the charge on the final consumer? Does the same happen to any tax imposed upon a producer, say, the personal property tax or the corporate net income tax? Verily there is more to taxation than meets the eye.

In the Soviet Union, where the major taxes in the tax system are sales taxes imposed on goods produced by governmental agencies, the distinction between prices and taxes (or between taxes and the profits of public undertakings) is thin indeed. But even under private enterprise and diversified taxation, prices and taxes can become closely entwined.

As previously observed, the subject of taxation involves usually a mixture of political and economic considerations. But this chapter on shifting will deal almost exclusively with the economic considerations. A legislative expression of intent regarding the incidence of taxation would ordinarily count for very little; it is economic, not legislative, law that rules this domain. Legislative bodies could hardly repeal the law of supply and demand even if they had the temerity to try.

Shifting is a form of tax avoidance, but it differs from other forms of avoidance in that, as a rule, it is not a deliberate process. One does not often feel the urge to blame the taxpayer when he shifts taxes. The shifting happened; it was not designed.[1] The businessman merely attempts to adjust production to the new conditions imposed by the tax and to do this in such a way as to maximize profits.

Definitions. Following Seligman,[2] students of the subject have usually distinguished three stages in, or aspects of, the process of shifting. They distinguish first between *impact* and *incidence,* the first being the initial and the latter the ultimate burden of a tax. They add the category of *effects,* which they conceive as either an economic consequence collateral to the incidence or too remote from the imposition to be rated as part of the money burden of a tax. Thus the impact of a tax is usually on the person who makes out the check to the government. If as a result of a tax, the prices charged by the person bearing the impact rise, the ultimate victim of these higher prices bears the incidence. The tax may cause a reduction in the quantity of goods exchanged, and this may mean unemployment for labor. These consequences are collateral and are classed as effects.

An alternative definition, suggested by Musgrave, is that incidence should cover all the distributive effects of a tax, that is, the changes in real income which the tax induces. There may be price, income, welfare, incentive and distributive effects of taxes. The term incidence is reserved for the last of these consequences. The two definitions do not differ widely but they can give different answers. For instance, a prohibitive protective tariff raises no revenue and on the first definition could have no incidence. No doubt such measure does have distributive effects that under the second definition would constitute incidence. While neither definition is free from difficulties the second appears in general to suffer less from ambiguities.

Of greater importance is the question of whether or not the price and distributive effects of a tax are to be considered apart and distinct from

---

[1] Not all critics agree with this position. Years ago, Lavid Hume sized up the problem of shifting as follows: "Every man, to be sure, is desirous of pushing off from himself the burthen of any tax, which is imposed, and laying it upon others. But as every man has the same inclination, and is upon the defensive; no set of men can be suppos'd to prevail altogether in this contest."—*Political Discourses,* Edinburgh, 1752, chap. VII. Hume's explanation seems to this author to greatly overstress the subjective element in the process.

[2] E. R. A. Seligman, *Shifting and Incidence of Taxation* (4th ed., New York: Columbia University Press, 1921); Musgrave, *The Theory of Public Finance,* chap. 10.

those of the expenditure of the revenue which usually but not necessarily follows the imposition of a tax. Governments may dispose of revenue by retiring public debt or by making other transfers. The separation of a tax from its disposition seems artificial yet unless this is done we might have to deal with several sets of effects depending on several possible dispositions. New and more taxes of any kind may have some effect on the general price level (inflationary or deflationary) apart from what is usually conceived as incidence. Musgrave seeks to abstract from this problem by analyzing incidence in terms of the substitution of one tax for another of the same yield. Our own analysis is simpler but less rigorous in that it follows the classical assumption that the diversion of resources from taxed to untaxed areas does not appreciably effect factor costs or prices in the latter. This would be strictly true only if the government itself enlarged its outlay and absorbed the diverted factors.

Directions and Forms of Shifting. Shifting takes place through a change in prices. The shift may be *forward,* in which case the taxpayer bearing the impact adds the tax to the price of the goods he sells. Thus, a tax imposed upon the manufacturer of cigarettes may be shifted to the wholesaler, by the wholesaler to the retailer, and from the retailer to the consumer, all in the form of prices higher than those prevailing before the tax.

Shifting is thought to take place most commonly along the line of exchanges by which a commodity is moved from the producer of raw materials to the final consumer. But shifting may also be *backward* in the form of a reduction in the price of raw materials purchased by the processor. A processing tax imposed on butter or pork may thus result in lower prices paid for milk and hogs by the processor to the farmer. In fact, it may even occur by passing a tax on to factors of production other than raw materials. For example, it is conceivable that an employer may relieve himself of his taxes by cutting wages. Ordinarily the employer can do this only to the extent that the tax gives him an excuse for driving a harder bargain. (Occasionally, however, as in the case of certain taxes imposed by the Social Security Act, the demand for labor may be reduced as a result of taxation, so that unemployment and lower wages may follow as a fairly likely consequence.) The factors of production are in some degree substitutes for each other and a partial tax changes the mix of the factors employed. In certain circumstances the present owner of a good absorbs the taxes that its future owner must pay. When the good is sold, all the predictable taxes on it are discounted by the purchaser. This phenomenon is known as *tax capitalization* or *tax amortization* and is discussed more fully and compared with shifting in a later section of this chapter.

HISTORICAL THEORIES OF SHIFTING

THE DIFFUSION THEORY

Nicholas François Canard stated in 1801 what has come to be known as the diffusion theory of taxation or shifting. Canard contended that the imposition of a tax is like extracting a bit of blood from one of the veins of a human being—although taken from a single vein, the loss is carried throughout the body by the circulation of the blood. Similarly, taxes are diffused throughout the economic system by economic transactions such as buying and selling.[3]

An American economist, David Wells, phrased this theory as follows:

> [Thus] taxes levied uniformly on things of the same class, by the laws of competition, supply, and demand, and ᵗhe all-pervading mediums of labor, will be distributed, percussed, and repercussed to a remote degree, until they finally fall upon every person, not in proportion to his consumption of a given article, but in the propor- tion his consumption bears to the aggregate consumption of the taxed community.

According to this theory, as Wells pointed out, a great capitalist such as John Jacob Astor, bears no greater burden of taxation than anyone else except as his consumption may be somewhat greater. Mr. Astor may seem to bear more taxes, but actually he is only a tax collector or conduit for the government.[4] By this theory, "every old tax is good, every new tax is bad," because any change in the tax system tends to upset the estab- lished equilibrium and causes friction and hardship until the equilibrium is reestablished. If this sweeping theory were accepted, there would be no point in discussing the principles of shifting or, indeed, little point in dis- cussing many of the other intricate and difficult problems of taxation. Most of the extensive class conflict that is apparent in taxation would have to be charged up to ignorance of economic principles. Few people, expert or otherwise, accept this interpretation at present.

Nevertheless, like most time-honored theories the diffusion theory does carry an important element of truth. Anyone who knows the tax system in practice must observe that taxes are never "so hard to take"

---

[3] *Principes d'économie politique*, Paris, 1801, cited by E. R. A. Seligman, *Shifting and Incidence of Taxation* (4th ed., New York: Columbia University Press,) pp. 159–163.

[4] David Wells, *Theory and Practice of Taxation* (New York: Appleton-Century-Croft, 1911), p. 584.

after the taxpayers have become accustomed to them. The adjustment is psychological as well as economic. Businessmen frequently complain as much about the uncertainty of future tax liabilities as of their present burdens. Tax burdens that to early writers on public finance would have seemed quite beyond the capacity of any nation are now borne with fair composure by the taxpayers, since they have gradually adjusted their affairs accordingly.

HOBSONIAN THEORY

A more persuasive view of the problem of incidence was presented by John A. Hobson,[5] a British economist, in 1920. He divided economic rewards into two classes: social costs and social surplus. The former he defined as the payments for goods and services necessary to draw forth the required supply; the latter, as payments beyond these necessary maintenance costs and incentives. To tax the former is impossible and the attempt is ill advised. The tax dries up the source (the supply is not completely inelastic) until shortages raise the prices of the taxed factors and thus readmit them to restore the requisite supply. Whether directly or indirectly, all taxes must come out of economic surplus.

The Hobsonian approach is sound enough but of only limited helpfulness. It leaves us the problem of distinguishing cost from surplus. It has long been recognized that nonreproducible resources have a highly inelastic supply and that their services would not disappear if their owners' rent were taxed away. Hobson thought that there is a large element of surplus also in inheritances and that there is some in most other forms of income, at least where they are distributed to individuals in large amounts. To say that taxes must come out of surplus is thus only a preliminary step in the analysis of shifting.

ANALYSIS OF SHIFTING

GENERAL PROCESS

As previously stated, incidence is a price phenomenon. Broadly speaking, the factors determining price are supply and demand. Taxes are usually imposed upon producers or suppliers who, consequently, must make the first move. The demanders are not as yet concerned. If the tax

---

[5] J. A. Hobson, *Taxation in the New State* (New York: Harcourt, Brace & World, 1920).

appears as an increase in the cost of production, the suppliers can go on strike, so to speak—that is, they can curtail the supply, and this will tend to raise the price. The decrease in supply can come about in several ways. First of all, each producer tends to produce less when the cost of production rises. Secondly, producers may find that they can no longer cover all their costs; when the time comes to replace the capital in the taxed industry, these producers may prefer to transfer their capital and invest it in some untaxed and, therefore, more profitable industry. The simplest way to conceive the more elementary problems in shifting is that some of the supply moves from a taxed to an untaxed area, thus relieving the pressure on the former. For example, if the furniture business is singled out for taxation, some of the furniture merchants may go into the grocery business.

A simple graphic presentation of what occurs can be seen in Figure 4. It will be recalled that quantities demanded and supplied vary with price, and this can be shown on a graph with quantities measured on one axis and prices on the other. Where the supply and demand curves cross, an equilibrium will be established—that is, at a certain price the quantity demanded will be exactly equal to the quantity supplied. In Figure 4 the original price was at point P_1. As a result of the imposition of the tax on cost, suppliers will supply less at any of the possible prices indicated on the vertical axis. In other words, the supply curve jogs to the left. A new intersection of the curves at point P_2 indicates that a higher price will prevail after the tax. The higher price constitutes the shifting of the tax. The vertical distance between the two supply lines indicates the amount of the tax.

If a tax is levied on the surplus above costs, it is less likely to be shifted. A cost of production may be defined as a payment necessary to secure enough of the factors of production to produce some desired output. If a tax is levied only on what remains after these payments have been made, the tax obviously does not affect these payments; hence, it does not change the quantity of factors that will be hired. Therefore, such a tax does not cause a change in supply and consequently not in price.

The situation described above is simple enough to be readily understood and constitutes the ABC of shifting. However, there are many complicating factors that determine shifting or the degree of shifting. Before undertaking an explanation of these factors, it is desirable to explore briefly the assumptions of traditional incidence theory.

The basic characteristics of incidence theory can be outlined as follows: first, since it deals with changes in price, incidence theory is but the application to taxation of general price theory; secondly, incidence theory employs the method of partial equilibrium analysis—that is, it considers the change in the price of the taxed good assuming all other

FIGURE 4

Simple Case of Shifting

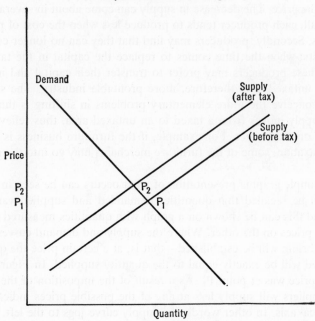

prices and incomes to remain constant; finally, incidence theory is concerned primarily with the effect of a tax on supply.[6]

---

[6] Some economists, such as de Marco, are exceptional in this respect, considering the effect of a tax on demand as a part of incidence theory. See Antonio de Viti de Marco, *First Principles of Public Finance,* English translation (New York: Harcourt, Brace & World, 1936), Book III, Chap. 4. The partial equilibrium analysis precludes any change in the demand for the taxed product arising out of the imposition of the tax.

Elaborating these characteristics, we may begin with the assumptions involved in partial equilibrium theory. These imply that:

1. The general level of income remains constant. This, in turn, is based on the assumption that the taxed market is such an insignificant part of the total economy that a change in expenditure on the taxed good (as a result of the tax) will not affect income and expenditure in the economy as a whole.

2. The demand (schedule) for the taxed good does not change as a result of the tax.

3. The relative prices of goods other than the taxed good do not change. This will occur if neither the demand schedules nor the supply schedules of other goods change. The demand schedules for other goods will not change if:

  (a) the change in expenditure on the taxed good as a result of the tax does not result in a significant change in the amount available for other goods. This will occur when the taxed good is an insignificant part of total expenditure, and

  (b) the effects of the change in amount available for expenditure on other goods as a result of the tax are distributed among so many

SHIFTING UNDER PERFECT COMPETITION

More detailed attention may now be given to the shifting of a tax on costs (such as a levy of so much per unit of production) under conditions of perfect competition. In general, perfect competition assumes enough

other goods that no one good feels a significant change in its demand. This means that the taxed good has no close complements or substitutes, or

(c) the elasticity of demand for the taxed good is one.

The supply schedules of other goods will remain constant, if the change in output resulting from the tax does not affect the prices of those factors which the taxed industry uses in common with other industries. If, as a result of the tax, the output of the industry changes, the quantity of the factors of production employed by the industry will change. There are two conditions, however, in which this will not alter the prices which other industries must pay for those factors:

(a) The price of the factor to the taxed industry itself does not change when the quantity hired by the industry changes. This will occur if the demand of the taxed industry for the factor of production is an insignificant portion of the total demand for the factor—that is, if the supply of the factor of production to the taxed industry is infinitely elastic.

(b) The price which the taxed industry pays for the factor changes, but its price to all other users remains constant. This could occur in the following circumstances: Assume the supply curve of the factor of production to the industry to be positively sloped. As a result of the tax, a smaller quantity of the product is produced, and the demand for the factors of production, therefore, falls; a smaller amount is bought and at a lower price. In order that total employment remain the same, that quantity of the factor no longer hired by the taxed industry must be absorbed by other industries. Therefore, the supply schedule facing each of the other industries increases. In order that this may not result in a factor price decline to the other industries, the increase in supply must be so widely distributed that the supply curve facing each industry rises by an insignificant amount. Assuming that equilibrium existed in the economy before imposition of the tax—that is, identical factors of production were paid the same in all their uses—it should be noted that the situation now has become one of disequilibrium, since the return to the factor in the taxed industry differs from the return to it in its other uses.

Let us now return to the first characteristic of incidence theory, namely that it is an application of general price theory, and let us note some of the major assumptions of that general price theory:

1. It is assumed that the entrepreneur tries to maximize money profits in both the long and the short run (within the limitations imposed by each period). However, he will not take any action which, although enabling him to maximize profits in the short run, will prevent him from maximizing profits in the long run.

2. Price theory studies the allocation of resources and the adjustment of prices in an economy in which tastes, resources, and technology are held constant: for example, the preferences of individuals for commodities and services are fixed; the laboring population will not change in size, age, or sex distribution; no new inventions will be developed.

producers so that no one of them is in a position to influence appreciably the market price; it also implies freedom to leave and enter the industry.[7]

Market Period. It is evident that adjustments in supply among producers will depend substantially upon the time allowed for the adjustments to occur. In the very short, or market period, supply may refer to the marketing of what has already been produced. If the stock on hand is perishable (as for example, strawberries), there is no recourse but to unload the entire stock at any price that will move it off the producers' hands. If a tax is levied in these circumstances, it cannot be shifted. The tax, therefore, constitutes a loss to the producers, but it will be better for them to take this punishment than to lose a larger amount by withholding the perishable supply. If the commodity is not perishable and therefore can be withheld for a time, the producer may hold back to some degree, hoping for a better market—that is, he may put less on the market when prices are lower and more on the market when prices are higher. If a tax is imposed under these conditions, the producer, anticipating a rise in price because of the tax, may withhold more of his current output than he otherwise would. This will tend to result in a decreased supply and increased price in the market period.

Short-run Period. The short run may be defined as a period "long enough to permit of any desired change of output technologically possible without altering the scale of plant, but which is not long enough to permit of any adjustments of scale of plant." [8] In the short run, as in the instantaneous period, firms may continue to supply the market (in this case they continue to produce a new supply) rather than suffer a greater loss—that is, they will produce at prices which will cover their variable costs (such as the cost of labor and the costs of raw materials). Other costs of operation, usually called fixed costs, need not be covered. The imposition of a tax, however, will cause some curtailment of output and

---

[7] In more detail the characteristics of a competitive industry are as follows:

1. Buyers and sellers have knowledge of one another's price offers.
2. All firms in the industry produce identical products.
3. Each firm produces such a small part of total supply that if it were to change its output, market supply would not be changed sufficiently to cause a change in market price.
4. As a result of (2) and (3), the demand curve facing the individual firm is infinitely elastic—that is, any output which the firm can produce can be sold at market price.
5. The demand of the firm for any factor of production is so small relative to total demand for the factor of production, that a change in the firm's demand does not cause a significant enough change in total demand to cause a change in market price. The supply curve of the factor of production to the individual firm is thus infinitely elastic—the firm can buy varying amounts at the market price.
6. In the long run, factors of production and firms are free to enter and leave the industry.

[8] Jacob Viner, "Cost Curves and Supply Curves," *Zeitschrift Für National-ökonomie*, III: 1 (1931), p. 26.

a decreased supply from each firm and therefore from industry as a whole. This is explained as follows.

In attempting to maximize net profits in the short run, the firm will produce to the point where marginal revenue equals marginal cost.[9] Marginal revenue is the addition to total revenue obtained by selling an additional unit of the product. However, it is one of the assumptions of a competitive industry that a firm can sell as much as it wishes at the market price. Therefore, the addition to total revenue gained by selling one more unit equals the price of the product, and the firm will maximize net revenue when it produces to the point where average revenue (price) equals marginal cost. Consequently, the amount that each firm will supply at alternative prices is that quantity at which marginal cost of production equals price: the firm's supply schedule is its marginal cost schedule, and the supply schedule for the industry is derived by adding together the supply schedules (that is, the marginal cost schedules) of the individual firms. The shape of the industry supply schedule will, therefore, depend upon the shape of the marginal cost schedules of the individual firms. Within the relevant range of operations of the competitive firm, marginal cost rises as output increases. The result of adding rising short-run marginal-cost schedules is, of course, a supply schedule for the industry that has a positive slope—that is, as price increases, more will be placed on the market by the industry as a whole.[10]

Let us now consider the actual shifting of a tax. Assume the price at which a firm is selling to be OP and the output of the firm to be OQ (Figure 5).

Let us consider a tax on cost, using the simplest tax of this type, a levy of so much per unit of output. The marginal cost of producing each output is raised by the amount of the tax, from MC to MC_1, and the producer, equating marginal cost and average revenue, will curtail output from OQ to OQ_1. Thus far no change in price has taken place. However,

---

[9] Marginal revenue is the addition to total revenue derived by selling an additional unit of the product. Marginal cost is the addition to total cost caused by producing an additional unit of the product. As long as marginal revenue exceeds marginal cost, the addition to total revenue exceeds the addition to total cost, net profit increases, and the entrepreneur will expand production. When marginal cost exceeds marginal revenue, the addition to total cost exceeds the addition to total revenue, a loss is incurred, and the entrepreneur will curtail production. Net profits will, therefore, be at a maximum when marginal revenue just equals marginal cost.

[10] It can be shown for the individual firm that when average costs are decreasing, marginal costs lie below them; when average costs are increasing, marginal costs lie above them; therefore, marginal costs intersect average costs at the minimum point of the latter. This statement is true for both average variable costs and average total unit costs. For a proof of the relationship between average and marginal costs and the fact that the relationship holds true for both variable and total costs, see Viner, *loc. cit.,* p. 28, n. 1 and p. 27, n. 3 respectively.

it will be noted that an increase in the cost of producing each quantity is equivalent to a reduction in the amount that will be produced at any given marginal cost, or at any given price, since production is carried to the point where marginal cost equals price. As the supply schedule of the individual firm shifts, the industry supply schedule, being but the aggregate of firm supply schedules, shifts as well, and by such an amount that the new price at which any output will be supplied (corresponding to the new marginal cost at which any output can be produced) exceeds the old price (and the old marginal cost) by the amount of the tax. Short-

FIGURE 5

Shifting in the Short Run

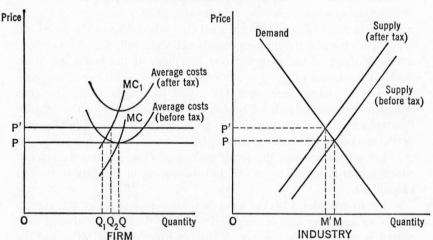

run output of the industry falls from OM to OM′, and price rises from OP to OP′. The new short-run equilibrium for the firm involves an output of OQ_2 and a price of OP′. It can be seen that the rise in price is less than the tax. This may be explained in the following manner: the cost of production exclusive of tax of the new output, OM′, is less than the cost of production exclusive of tax of the old output, OM. Therefore, the new cost of production plus tax is less than the old cost of production (old price) plus tax. It will be noted that total costs are not covered by the short-run increase in price. In the long run, therefore, firms will tend to migrate from the taxed to untaxed areas.

Long-run Period. In the long run, supply is likely to be much more elastic than in the short run. It will be recalled that the long run allows sufficient time for firms to change their scale of operation and to migrate from a taxed area. The producer can select his scale of plant, and he will, in producing any given output, select that scale of plant which can most cheaply produce the output in question. The firm will have a long-run average cost curve based upon this possible variation in scale.[11]

The industry will be in long-run equilibrium—that is, there will be no tendency toward a change in output—if

1. Each firm is in equilibrium so that there is no tendency for any firm to alter its output. This will occur at the point of maximum net revenue—that is, where average revenue equals marginal cost.
2. There is no tendency for firms to enter or leave the industry. This will occur when neither profits nor losses are being made—that is, when for each firm average revenue equals average cost.

The long-run industry supply curve, therefore, will show how much will be produced at any given price assuming that the long-run adjustment has been made to that price—that is, assuming that the industry is in equilibrium at that price, each firm operating where marginal revenue equals marginal cost equals average revenue equals average cost. A glance at the U-shaped average cost curve of the firm will show that average cost, marginal cost, average revenue, and marginal revenue can be equal only at the minimum average cost. The output represented by this point may be called the *least-cost output*. The long-run industry supply curve is therefore obtained by adding the least-cost outputs of varying numbers of firms. At any price, the number of firms will be such that no firm is making either profits or losses.[12]

As more firms enter the industry, the average-cost curve of each firm may rise. This may occur because as the industry expands, it must draw factors of production away from other industries by offering increased factor prices. Such an industry is known as an increasing-cost industry, and its supply curve will slope upward to the right—at higher prices, more will be put on the market because to put more on the market, a higher cost must be incurred.

If, as more firms enter the industry, the average-cost curve of the individual firm does not rise, the industry is one of constant costs. The industry supply curve is a horizontal line at some price—that is, the in-

---

[11] The long-run cost curve of the firm is an envelope of short-run cost curves, each of the latter representing a different scale of plant. The long-run cost curve is composed of those points on various short-run curves which represent the lowest cost of producing any given output. For a more detailed explanation, see Albert L. Meyers, *Modern Economics, Elements and Problems* (Englewood Cliffs, N.J.: Prentice-Hall, Inc., 1942), pp. 212–213.

[12] The concept of profit here used excludes such elements as necessary return to the entrepreneur; the latter is included in costs.

dustry can expand without causing the level of the least-cost output of the firm to rise.[13]

The long-run incidence of a cost tax depends greatly on the cost pattern of the industry. Assume the industry to be in equilibrium before the tax at a price of OP (Figure 6). The firm we are considering produces OQ. A cost tax is imposed raising the average and marginal costs to AC′ and MC′ respectively. Short-run equilibrium is reached at a price of OP′. However, total costs are not covered by OP′ and, therefore, firms will, in the long run, move out of the industry, supply will fall, and price will rise. If the industry is one of constant costs, the exodus of firms will not affect the level of AC′ and, therefore, before a new equilibrium can be established, price must rise by the full amount of the tax—that is, to OP″.

If, however, the industry is one of increasing costs, the exodus of firms will cause the average costs of the firm to fall—that is, average

---

[13] A third category known as decreasing-cost industries, is sometimes included. The conventional treatment of this type of industry involves an industry cost curve which slopes downward to the right and is less steeply-sloped than the demand curve at the point of intersection. A per-unit tax is treated as an increase in the industry cost curve—that is, the new cost curve is drawn to the right of and above the old one. Price rises by an amount greater than the tax. The decreasing-cost curve has been treated as a conventional supply curve. There are some difficulties, however, in the approach. It is very doubtful that a decreasing-cost curve can be considered a static supply curve of the type commonly em-

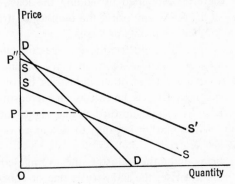

ployed in pure theory. Such a decreasing-cost curve usually represents changes in population, technology, or resources—that is, changes in the data usually held constant in price theory. Even if such changes are a function of the output of the industry, it is doubtful that the entire cost curve can be raised by the tax as is done with a conventional supply curve, but an alternative and perhaps preferable approach will be found to yield the same final result. More frequently, probably, such decreases in costs are not a function of the output of the industry in question, but are a result of innovations or a higher level of demand resulting from increased population or purchasing power. These causes of decreasing cost and, therefore, the lower cost levels themselves, do not disappear because of the tax. In such cases the incidence of the tax is not affected by the downward sloping cost curve of the industry.

FIGURE 6

Shifting under Conditions of Varying Costs

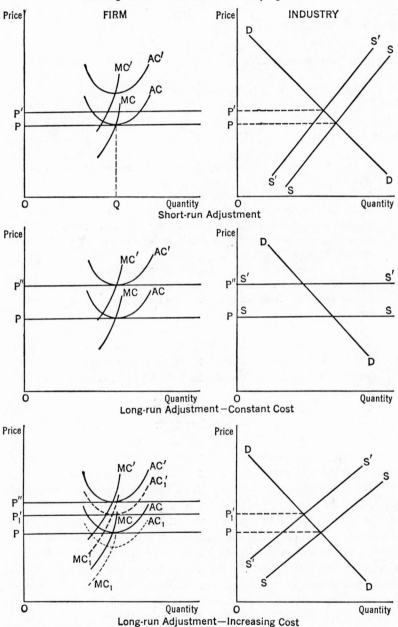

FIRM — Price

Price — INDUSTRY

Short-run Adjustment

Long-run Adjustment—Constant Cost

Long-run Adjustment—Increasing Cost

costs exclusive of tax will fall from AC to AC_1; therefore average costs plus tax will fall from AC' to AC'_1. Equilibrium will be reestablished by a price rise less than the amount of the tax—that is, from OP to OP'_1 instead of from OP to OP''.

SHIFTING UNDER MONOPOLY

In order to analyze the incidence of taxation under monopolistic conditions, it is necessary first to define a monopoly. A pure monopoly exists when a single firm is identical with the industry. The following conditions are implied:

1. One firm produces a product for which there are no close substitutes.
2. Other firms cannot enter the industry.
3. The market demand curve for the entire industry thus becomes the demand curve facing the firm, and since the firm has no rivals, the slope and level of the demand curve will not change with changes in price or output.
4. The industry supply curve of the factors of production is identical with the supply curve facing the firm and may be positively sloped. If so, as the firm buys more, the factor price which it must pay rises.

Like any other entrepreneur, the monopolist seeks to maximize profit and will do so by producing to the point where marginal revenue equals marginal cost. Figure 7 illustrates price determination in a monopolistic industry.

Cost and Revenue Curves. In dealing with price problems of monopoly, one should first familiarize himself with the nature of cost and revenue curves. As previously indicated, marginal costs and marginal revenue are distinguished from average costs and average revenue; the former are the additional costs and revenues resulting from the addition of another unit of output; the latter designate the total cost and revenue divided by the number of units. Thus if at 10 cents, one unit can be sold and at 9 cents two units can be moved, the average revenue with a volume of 2 is 9 cents, and the marginal revenue is 8 cents. Monopoly revenue curves will ordinarily start at the extreme upper lefthand corner of a graph and move downward to the right, the marginal curve falling more rapidly than the average curve. The cost curves will depend upon the prevailing cost conditions: increasing, constant, or decreasing. In Figure 7, costs are increasing with output, and the marginal cost is rising more rapidly than average cost. Volume is determined where marginal cost corresponds to marginal revenue—that is, the point of maximum

FIGURE 7

Monopoly Price Determination

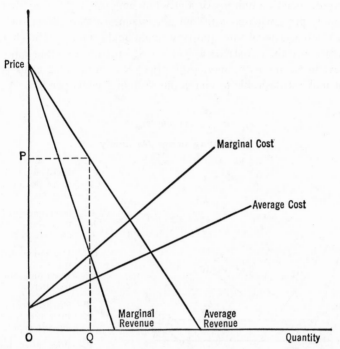

profit; the price is read on the diagram at a point on the average-revenue (price) curve directly above the intersection of the marginal cost and marginal revenue (price at this volume).[14]

---

[14] The entire cost curve of a monopoly follows roughly the familiar U-shape of the cost curve of the competitive firm. However, it is one of the characteristics of the monopolist that the decreasing part of his cost curve may extend for very great ranges of output. There may also be a long range of output for which costs are constant. The ranges through which costs may be decreasing or constant may be so great that market demand is satisfied when production is still in the range of decreasing or constant costs. Hence, the monopolist may produce on the falling, the flat, or the rising part of his cost curve. The cost curve of the competitive producer begins to turn up at an output so small that the firm satisfies only an insignificant portion of market demand. The competitive firm does not operate in the decreasing part of the cost curve, because if it did so, it could increase profits by expanding output. Price would not fall as would be the case if the monopolist were to expand output, because the competitive firm is such a small part of the entire industry. Since the range of constant costs is small for a competitive firm (if it were considerable, the firm would expand along it and might produce so much that it would no longer be a minute part of the industry; in that case the industry would no longer be competitive); the firm in competition operates on the rising part of the cost curve or, in the long run, at the lowest average-cost point.

Tax Incidence. The monopolist sets his price where his total net profit will be largest. Any tax which increases directly with the volume of output, such as a unit tax or a gross income tax, is likely to change the monopoly price whereas a tax on net income will not affect such price. For example, a local bus company might make more profit charging 7 cents per fare than charging 6 cents or 8 cents or any other amount. In that event 7 cents is the monopoly price. Now a tax of 2 cents per fare might make it desirable to charge more than 7 cents per fare. A net in-

FIGURE 8

Shifting under Monopoly

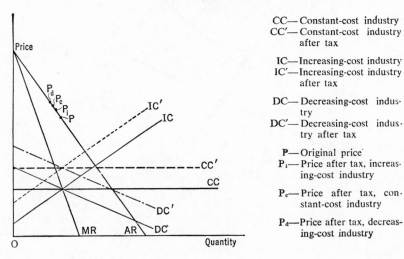

CC—Constant-cost industry
CC′—Constant-cost industry after tax

IC—Increasing-cost industry
IC′—Increasing-cost industry after tax

DC—Decreasing-cost industry
DC′—Decreasing-cost industry after tax

P—Original price
P_i—Price after tax, increasing-cost industry

P_c—Price after tax, constant-cost industry

P_d—Price after tax, decreasing-cost industry

come tax, on the other hand, if it affects surplus only, could not change the point of maximum profit. One half of a greater profit is still better than one half of a lesser one.

The long-run incidence of a cost tax on a monopolist will depend in considerable degree upon the cost condition of the firm. (See Figure 8.)

The greatest price rise occurs with decreasing costs, the next to greatest price rise with constant costs, and the smallest price rise with increasing costs.

Short-run shifting will differ from long-run shifting in that the supply adjustment in the former case cannot involve changes in scale of plant. Entrance of firms into the industry, which is one of the characteristics of the *competitive* long run, is here precluded by the definition of monopoly.

In general, shifting under conditions of monopoly tends to be less than under competition. One reason for this is that the monopoly has a cushion (surplus profit) that enables it to absorb part of the tax (average revenue is above average cost).

THE EFFECT ON SHIFTING OF VARYING ELASTICITIES OF DEMAND AND SUPPLY

Thus far the incidence of a cost tax has been discussed with reference to the nature of the industry (monopolistic or competitive) and the nature of the industry supply curve (increasing cost, constant cost, or, in the case of the monopoly, decreasing cost). Shifting is affected also by the elasticities of supply and demand.

The demand for different commodities is not equally sensitive to changes in price. The demand for cigarettes is relatively inelastic because cigarette consumption is a matter of habit. And the demand for salt or bread is much more inelastic because these are necessities of life; people will have their salt even if they must pay more for it. The demand for gasoline is more elastic, but experience seems to indicate that within reasonable limits people will not drive automobiles much less, as the higher price of fuel increases only slightly the cost of operation. On the other hand, the demand for butter and pork is elastic. This is due to the fact that substitutes for these foods can be readily found, and the consumer does not regard them as very essential.

In the perhaps typical case of positively sloped supply curves, an inelastic demand is favorable to shifting. In the case of horizontal supply curves (constant cost), the elasticity of demand makes no difference; the same proportion of the tax will be shifted in any event. In the case of decreasing cost, which we have discussed only in connection with monopoly, the greater shift will occur if demand is elastic.

Supply may also show various degrees of elasticity. When the supply curve has a positive slope, the greater the elasticity of supply, the greater the proportion of the tax which will be shifted. When, as is possible in the case of a monopoly, the supply curve has a negative slope, a larger proportion of the tax will be shifted when the supply curve is less elastic.

In general, the above relationships apply in both competition and monopoly. Some of them are shown graphically in Figure 9.

In monopoly demand is a matter of consumers' preferences among products with changing prices. We now turn to the area midway between monopoly and competition where demand (for the firm) may also involve gain or loss in business to other firms producing the same or very similar products.

FIGURE 9

Elasticities and Incidence

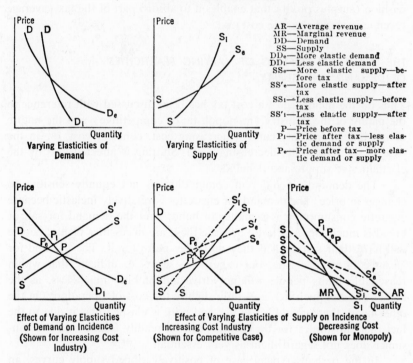

AR—Average revenue
MR—Marginal revenue
DD—Demand
SS—Supply
DD_e—More elastic demand
DD_l—Less elastic demand
SS_e—More elastic supply—before tax
SS'_e—More elastic supply—after tax
SS_l—Less elastic supply—before tax
SS'_l—Less elastic supply—after tax
P—Price before tax
P_l—Price after tax—less elastic demand or supply
P_e—Price after tax—more elastic demand or supply

Varying Elasticities of
Demand

Varying Elasticities of
Supply

Effect of Varying Elasticities
of Demand on Incidence
(Shown for Increasing Cost
Industry)

Effect of Varying Elasticities of Supply on Incidence
Increasing Cost Industry
(Shown for Competitive Case)

Decreasing Cost
(Shown for Monopoly)

SHIFTING IN IMPERFECT MARKETS

Thus far we have considered shifting under perfect competition and perfect monopoly. There is a third group of market situations, however, which contains some of the elements of both.

Differences between Competition and Monopoly. The essential characteristics in which monopoly and competition differ are the three discussed below:

> 1. Number of producers in the industry. Competition is marked by the fact that there are so many firms in the industry that the output of each is an insignificant part of the total output. Consequently, market price is not changed by a change in the output of any one firm. Therefore if a firm increases its output, it will not spoil the market for the other firms and will, therefore, not provoke retaliatory action by the other firms. Also, since the firm can sell all it wishes at the market price, it has no incentive to lower its price in

order to increase sales. At the other extreme, monopoly is characterized by the identity of the firm and the industry. There is only one firm in the industry.

2. Homogeneity of the product put out by the firms in the industry. In a competitive industry, all firms produce identical products. The output of any one firm is a perfect substitute for the output of any other. The monopoly situation again is the complete opposite. Since the monopolistic firm is also the industry, and the concept of an industry involves a product differentiated from other products, the monopolistic firm may be said to produce a product for which there are no close substitutes.

3. Ease of entry into the industry. Competition is marked by great ease of entry into the industry, so that in the long run no firm makes pure profits. Monopoly, on the contrary, is characterized by the fact that no other firm can enter the industry and hence, pure profits may persist indefinitely.

It is possible now to consider a group of market situations characterized by varying combinations of the above elements of monopoly and competition. Having briefly outlined these situations, we shall discuss their relationship to the problem of tax incidence.

Monopolistic Competition. Let us consider first a market characterized by the following:

1. A great number of firms—so many that if one increased its sales at the expense of others, there are enough firms so that each could lose only an insignificant amount of business and would not retaliate.

2. The output of each firm in the "industry" is somewhat differentiated from the output of any other firm. The outputs of different firms are but imperfect substitutes for one another. It must be recognized that as soon as differentiation of product exists, the concept of an industry is no longer clear. If a homogeneous product is produced, then it can be clearly said that this is an industry. However, in the case of imperfect substitutes, we encounter the problem that, to some degree, all products are imperfect substitutes for one another. When are products close enough substitutes that they may be called the output of a single industry? One method of avoiding this difficulty would be to use the term *industry* only in its strictest sense—to denote a group of products that are perfect substitutes for one another. Then, for example, instead of the passenger automobile industry, there would be the Chevrolet industry, the Cadillac industry, and so forth. This method has the advantage of greater rigor and clarity, but it encounters the difficulty that both consumers and businessmen act and think as if there were an industry, nebulous though their ideas may be as to the boundaries of such indus-

try. For this reason, therefore, we shall accept the concept of an industry and define it (admittedly somewhat arbitrarily) as a group of firms producing products which are close substitutes for one another and around which there exists a gap in the chain of substitutes. Since the product of any firm in the industry is somewhat differentiated from the product of other firms in the industry, the single firm can no longer assume a completely elastic demand curve for its output. If price is raised, the firm will lose some customers, but not all, since the unique characteristic of the product will retain some buyers. If the firm lowers its price, it will increase sales by attracting those for whom the unique quality was not worth the former higher price but is worth the present lower price. In short, the demand curve for the individual firm has a negative slope.

3. With regard to ease of entry into this industry, let us assume that there are no important barriers, so that in the long run equilibrium is marked by an absence of pure profit on the part of the firm. If now we combine the negative slope of the demand curve with the U-shaped average-cost curve of the firm, we can see that the no-profit condition can be satisfied only when the demand curve is tangent to the downward sloping part of the cost curve. Production on the downward part of the curve is also indicative of excessive capacity and malallocation of resources, characteristics of monopolistic competition.

For reason of brevity, attention may be confined to the long-run shifting of a unit tax only. The probable result of the tax is shown in Figure 10. The tax causes the cost curves to rise by the amount of the tax. At an intermediate stage, the firm continues to produce where the original marginal-revenue curve crosses the new marginal-cost curve. But this leaves the firm with a loss (the price is below average cost). The result is a migration of firms, and this, *from the firm's viewpoint,* increases the demand for its product as shown in the AR′ and MR′ curves. Equilibrium will be reestablished when the demand curve has risen enough to be tangent to the new long-run average-cost curve. If there has been no change in elasticity of demand, this new equilibrium price will exceed the old price by the amount of the tax,[15] and the new output for the firm remaining in the industry will be the same as the old output.

There are at least two circumstances, however, that modify the principles stated above with respect to the incidence of a cost tax. Both stem

---

[15] More accurately, the incidence will be the same as under perfect competition, since there are no pure profits to absorb part of the tax. If the concept of an increasing- or constant-cost industry can be applied to monopolistic competition (where the meaning of *industry* is vague) then, as in competition, if the industry is one of increasing costs, price will rise by less than the full amount of the tax.

from the fact that we are dealing here with a market of differentiated products. As firms leave the market and consumers switch to remaining firms, not all of the latter may be affected in the same way. The new patrons of existing firms may become more or less firmly attached to their suppliers than was true of the old customers, and this will decrease or increase the elasticity of the demand curve for the individual firm and cause more or less shifting than the above explanation dictates. Moreover, with differentiated products it is possible to alter the demand by

FIGURE 10

Shifting under Monopolistic Competition

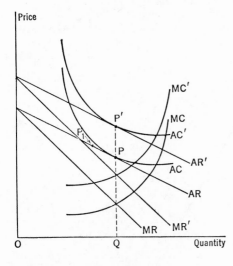

AC—Average costs before tax
MC—Marginal costs before tax
AR—Average revenue before tax
MR—Marginal revenue before tax
AC′—Average costs after tax
MC′—Marginal costs after tax
AR′—Average revenue consistent with long-run equilibrium after tax
MR′—Marginal revenue consistent with long-run equilibrium after tax
P—Price before tax
P_1—Intermediate price—inconsistent with long-run equilibrium
P′—Price after tax—consistent with long-run equilibrium
OQ—Output

advertising. It is possible that some of the rise in cost due to the tax may be absorbed by reduced advertising expense. It is also possible that increased advertising expense will make demand more inelastic and favor a greater increase in price than that anticipated from the above explanation.

Oligopoly. The second type of market situation in this group lying somewhere between perfect competition and perfect monopoly is a situation that may be called perfect oligopoly. Its characteristics [16] are:

---

[16] The characteristics of oligopoly were derived principally from Kenneth E. Boulding, *Economic Analysis* (rev. ed., New York: Harper and Rowe Publishers, 1948), chaps. 27, 37; Paul M. Sweezy, "Demand under Conditions of Oligopoly," *Journal of Political Economy,* 47 (August 1939), pp. 568–573; Martin Bronfenbrenner, "Applications of the Discontinuous Oligopoly Demand Curve," *ibid.,* 48 (June 1940), pp. 420–427.

1. There are so few firms in the industry that the output and price policies of each firm can affect the market price as a whole. Therefore, if a firm were to lower its price, it would draw away such a significant portion of the business from other firms that retaliation would be probable.

FIGURE 11

The Oligopoly Gap

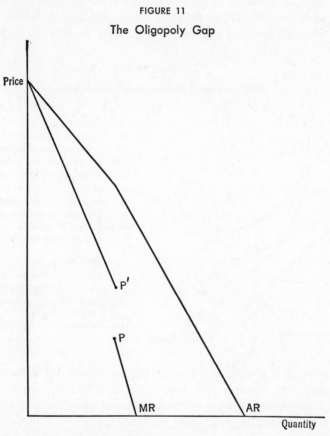

2. Each firm produces an identical product, so that only one price can reign in the market at a time.

3. There is no ease of entry—that is, new firms cannot enter the industry—and, therefore, pure profits may persist even in the long run. This may be due, for example, to control of some vital resource by firms already in the industry or to the fact that the optimum-size firm is so large that, while all firms already in the industry may be making a profit, the additional output that would result from an additional optimum-size plant would be so great that price would fall far enough to plunge all the firms into losses.[17]

---

[17] A list of the factors which might lead to the fact that, although firms already

If in this situation, we add the marginal-cost curves of the various firms, we derive the market supply curve. This interacts with the market demand curve to determine price. However, once price is determined, the following phenomenon occurs: if each firm could lower its price without retaliation, it could gain substantial numbers of sales. However, because there are so few firms in the industry, each is a significant part of the market; if one firm lowers price, others will follow and there will be very little gain in sales by the first firm. Therefore, the demand curve as seen by the firm is very inelastic for price decreases. On the other hand, if the firm were to raise its price, other firms would not follow, and the first firm would lose greatly in sales. Therefore, the "demand curve" facing the firm is very elastic for price increases and thus develops a kink at the market price.[18] The effect of this kink in the average-revenue curve is to cause a gap in the marginal-revenue curve at the current output.[19]

The effect of this oligopoly gap is to make the price rigid in the sense that, using the marginal revenue-marginal cost system of pricing, there is a range in which marginal cost may change without a change in price. Cost can move between P and P' without causing any change in price. Hence a per-unit tax may be imposed, and if it is not great enough

---

in the industry are making profits, outsiders do not contemplate profits for themselves if they enter, can be found in Fritz Machlup, "Competition, Pliopoly and Profit," *Economica,* 9 (1942), pp. 1–23, 153–173.

[18] The word *demand* is enclosed in quotation marks, because, as Bronfenbrenner points out, demand curves usually assume that rival reactions are ignored. Bronfenbrenner, *loc. cit.,* p. 420.

[19] The construction of an oligopoly gap can be done as follows: Given an oligopoly demand curve *ABC*. Continue *AB* to form a straight-line demand curve, *ABD;* continue *BC* to form a straight-line demand curve, *EBC*. Construct the marginal-revenue curves for *ABD* and *EBC*. The marginal-revenue curve for *ABC* is *AFGH*.

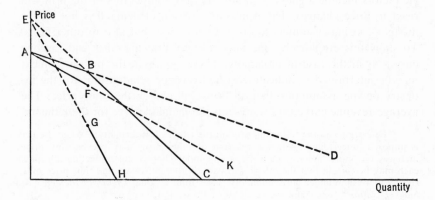

to cause marginal cost to move out of the oligopoly gap, there may be no change in price.[20]

The common case of imperfect oligopoly involves both a differentiated product and barriers to entry into the field. An example is the present automobile industry in the United States, a field of differentiated product and one that is notoriously difficult to enter. The oligopolist, in selecting a price, before and after taxes, has certain strategic factors to consider that play no part in strictly competitive situations. These strate-

FIGURE 12

Shifting under Oligopoly

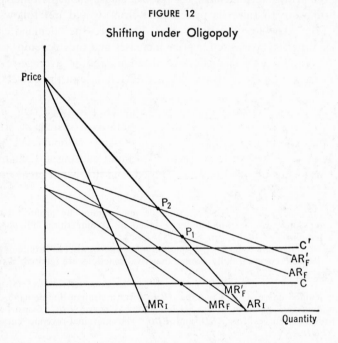

gic factors include a guess as to how the few competitors of the firm will react to price changes. The firm's anticipation of demand is not only a matter of losing customers to other commodities but also to other firms. To show this graphically, one may start by drawing costs and revenue curves as in the case of monopoly. These curves in the present context may be interpreted to indicate cost and revenue relationships for the industry on the assumption that all firms will charge the same price. The average-revenue curve thus represents the demand curve for the industry.

---

[20] Due argues in the following way on the effect of uncertainty: "When the tax is imposed, uncertainty as to the reaction of other firms may prevent any price increase. Or, more likely, since a tax is a definitely known cost, affecting all alike, each may be certain that the others will pass on the entire tax, and thus price may rise by more than under pure monopoly . . ." John F. Due, *Theory of Incidence of Sales Taxation* (New York: King's Crown Press, 1942), p. 63.

Now, superimposed upon this background, revenue curves representing the prospects of the particular firm may be added. They will be more elastic than the industry curves. The curves should be so drawn that the intersection points of the marginals will be directly below the intersection of the average-revenue curves (for firm and industry). The price must be one at which the market can be cleared if other firms follow the same price policy. A price rise greater than that of full monopoly but not by the full amount of the tax is indicated (Figure 12).[21]

THE UNIVERSALITY OF A TAX AMONG INDUSTRIES

The consequences of any tax may be divided into two major groups: effects on price and effects on income. As was pointed out earlier in this chapter, incidence theory sets aside considerations of income effects by assuming total income to remain constant. It then considers price effects by noting the effect of a tax on the supply of the taxed good.

FIGURE 13

Special versus Universal Tax

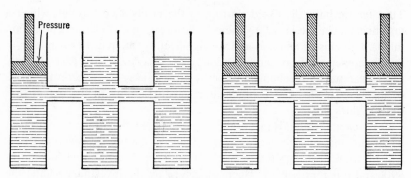

As far as a special tax is concerned, the change in supply is effected by a migration of firms and factors of production from taxed to untaxed areas. When a general tax is levied, there is no place to go to escape the tax. The difference in the two situations may be shown by depicting the different result of two experiments in physics: the first in which pressure is applied to a fluid in one of several connected vessels, and the second where it is applied to all the vessels.

Although there is little room for the migration of factors within the productive process when a general tax is levied, the supply of factors of production (and therefore of goods and services) can still be altered.

---

[21] The graph is an adaptation from one used by Due, *op. cit.,* Fig. 15.

For example, a tax may cause leisure to be substituted for labor, and cash hoards to be substituted for invested savings. If the income effects of a general tax could be ignored, then to the extent to which the tax caused a withdrawal of firms and factors of production from the productive process, output would decrease and prices would rise. On one definition this would be the incidence of the tax. However, a completely general rise in prices would not have any distributional effects. Moreover, income and expenditures are opposite sides of the same coin and it hardly matters whether the flow is taxed coming or going. Thus in terms of distribution, the incidence of the tax would be equivalent to that of a proportional income tax.

It should be added that to develop a tax with any such general coverage would be a formidable undertaking. So-called general sales taxes fall far short of filling the bill. And even a general tax could have differential effects due to differing elasticities of factors. Some factor prices (supported, for instance, by trade unions) could offer high resistance to cutting.[22]

TAX CAPITALIZATION

Thus far we have discussed shifting as the mechanism through which a tax effects a change in price. There is, however, another tax phenomenon that is both closely allied to and yet significantly different from shifting—the phenomenon of tax capitalization or tax amortization.[23] Like shifting, capitalization is a mechanism whereby a tax causes a change in the price of the taxed good. Yet capitalization can exist only to the extent that shifting does not.

By capitalization is meant the change in the value of the taxed object by an amount equal to the capitalized value of the tax. A simple example will illustrate this. Assume a piece of land yields an annual income of $90, and this represents a 3-percent return on the investment. Then the value of the investment is 90/.03 or $3000.[24] If a 1-percent tax on capital value is levied, the return falls to $60. The annual return is permanently lowered by $30. Therefore, the capital value is lowered by the capitalized value of $30—that is, by $30/.03 or $1000. The land is now worth $2000. Another way of expressing this would be to say that in

---

[22] See John F. Due, "Toward a General Theory of Sales Tax Incidence," *Quarterly Journal of Economics*, LXVII: 2 (May 1953), pp. 253–266.

[23] According to Seligman, amortization occurs when a tax is raised, capitalization when it is lowered.—Seligman, *The Shifting and Incidence of Taxation*, p. 222. However, frequently the words are used interchangeably to refer to the effects of a change in taxes, and we shall use them that way here.

[24] This follows from the formula: Value × Rate of Return = Earnings.

order for $60 to constitute a 3-percent return on investment, the amount to be invested must be equal to $60/.03 or $2000.

The phenomenon of tax capitalization may be explained with the aid of Figure 14.

New investment funds are treated as a stream that may flow into areas *A*, *B*, and *C*. If a tax is imposed at point *A*, reducing the yield at this point by half, funds will no longer flow into the area until owners adjust their asking prices downward, so that the yield is again equivalent to that available to untaxed alternatives. The burden of the tax thus falls upon the present owner of the good. Future owners, by paying a lower price, will secure the original rate of return on their investment.

FIGURE 14

Tax Capitalization

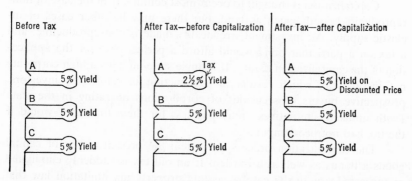

Capitalization occurs only under certain conditions, among them the following: (1) the tax falls on an income-producing good; (2) the pattern of future taxes is foreseeable and anticipated; (3) the total supply of the taxed good for the period under consideration is completely inelastic; (4) the tax (among investment alternatives) is unequal.

Several further generalizations about capitalization are possible. First of all, the tax may lower the general rate of return upon investments. (In the diagram above, the imposition of a tax at point *A* may reduce the ultimate yield at all these points. The increased competition at *B* and *C* while the gate is closed at *A* may reduce the yield at the former points below that prevailing before the tax, and Gate *A* can open as soon as yields there are equivalent to those received elsewhere.) Secondly, although only a differential tax is capitalized, a tax which is ostensibly uniform may have a differential effect if some areas can gain relief by shifting and others cannot. An ostensibly equal tax may also have a differential effect if it alters existing relative differentials in yield (due to different degrees of risk).[25] The points at which shifting and capitalization differ may be summarized as follows:

Shifting	*Capitalization*
Burden of the tax rests on future owners (of commodities).	Burden of the tax rests on present owners (of income-producing goods).
Price changes to compensate for one levying of the tax.	Price changes to offset all anticipated levyings of the tax.
Price rises.	Price falls.
Occurs through curtailment of supply.	Occurs when supply cannot be curtailed.

Capitalization is thought to occur most commonly in the case of nonreproducible goods, such as land, but there may be other cases of inelastic supply. An investment irrevocably made is nonreproducible, and a tax on a particular bond would afford a perfect case for the application of the capitalization theory. If a single state imposes a high corporate net income tax which results in a reduction in returns to investors, prospective buyers of securities of corporations operating in the state (with untaxed alternatives) may pay less for them than they would if the tax had not been imposed.

The capitalization process may yield the present owner of capital goods a bonus as well as a burden. If an old tax is suddenly eliminated or mitigated—as in the case of a state property tax limitation law that sets a maximum rate for the general property tax substantially below what many properties have been paying—the present owner may receive a substantial benefit in an increase in the value of his land. By the same token, of course, a future buyer will secure no benefit at all from lightening the property-tax burden, since he will have to pay a higher price.

Application of Capitalization to a Tax on Land and One on Buildings. Application of capitalization theory to a tax on land and one on buildings is revealing. A tax on buildings, which are reproducible, will tend to be shifted. Since buildings are reproducible, their supply is somewhat elastic; a tax, by raising the cost of production, will decrease the quantity produced at each price, and equilibrium will be reached at a smaller output and a higher price than before.

---

[25] It is possible that even when a general tax is laid on all income-earning goods, so that all are affected equally, there may occur a phenomenon very closely akin to capitalization. If the return on all existing investments is reduced, then the demand for all existing investments may fall; their prices may then also drop, and rates of return may then rise to the original level.

In the case of land, on the other hand, the supply is relatively fixed. With some qualifications and exceptions, no new land is being manufactured and no old land allowed to go into discard. In so far as this is true, the purchaser of land buys a nonreproducible good. He will pay for it according to its anticipated future income, and, if heavy taxes detract from the prospects, he will pay less on that account.

It should be emphasized with some haste that the supply of land is only relatively fixed. Rural land, especially, is subject to depreciation and may be reclaimed through the replenishment of its fertility. Farm and range land depreciates when it is damaged by erosion. However, in so far as land represents mere space, as is generally true of city sites, it is genuinely nonreproducible. But, in fact, even in this case it may to some extent be supplied or, rather, made available by grading, draining, and so on.

A further qualification to the general rule regarding the incidence of land and building taxes is in order. Although buildings are reproducible goods, they are not produced with the same rapidity as, for example, shoes. Monthly or even yearly additions to the stock of buildings are not often a significant addition to the total stock. Consequently, over a considerable period the supply of buildings may be largely inelastic and very little of the tax on buildings shifted. Instead it will be capitalized.

MODIFICATIONS IN ASSUMPTIONS AND APPLICATION OF INCIDENCE THEORY

To explain the probable effect of taxes when they are imposed within a complex institutional setting, some modifications of the assumptions of incidence theory are necessary. Here only a few of the most prominent of these modifications can be mentioned.

1. *Taxes on Public Utilities.* In the case of monopoly we encounter the political factor of public utility regulation. Here the possibility of shifting taxes is greatly affected by the decisions of the United States Supreme Court, under which all taxes—including income and profits taxes—may be reckoned as expenses of doing business when the net earnings of such utilities are compared with their capital by public utility commissions in the determination of utility rates.[26] This means that all public utility taxes tend to be passed on to the consumer. Undoubtedly, this process takes time and is subject to some uncertainties as to the effectiveness of regulation. In addition, utilities like other monopolies have to consider the monopoly price as well as the regulation price. If the former is below the latter, and if the tax is one that will not disturb the monopoly price (net income tax, for instance), the tax will not be

[26] *Galveston Electric Company v. Galveston,* 258 U.S. 388 (1922).

shifted. Economic law may take precedence over governmental law, in which case the company will continue to charge what the traffic will bear regardless of the fact that it is permitted to charge more. If a bus company finds it most economical to charge 5 cents per fare, even though permitted to charge 10 cents, then a net income tax on the company will not affect its price policy. A different answer would be in order if the tax were a fare tax.

2. *Political Considerations.* Again, in the case of monopoly and oligopoly, the businessman may not always seek to maximize immediate profits. Taking political factors into account, he may set his prices not at what the traffic will bear economically speaking but at what it will bear politically speaking. He may charge less than he could because he is sensitive to adverse public reaction to conspicuous profits. This adverse public reaction might carry a threat of a peacetime excess profits tax.

A monopolist may consider his rival economic force—the labor union. He may wish to avoid giving the union an incentive to present new wage demands and perhaps strike.

A monopolist may consider the effect of his particular price policy upon the general economic situation. He may have an interest in stabilizing prices over a long period of time.

The existence of so-called "gray markets" in automobiles and steel following World War II is evidence that oligopolists did not then charge all that customers were willing to pay. In these circumstances the imposition of a tax, even one on surplus, may change corporate price policy and lead to shifting that would not be dictated by the principles heretofore cited.

3. *Effect of Taxes on Demand.* A tax is very likely to have important effects on demand, notwithstanding the assumption in incidence analysis that demand schedules remain constant. Among these important effects on demand are the following:

Certain taxes, such as income taxes, may radically affect the distribution of income which in turn may reduce the demand for luxuries (such as yachts) and raise the relative demand for essentials (such as bread). The immediate effect on the luxury trades will be adverse, causing a drop in the output and price, though the latter may recover its former position as firms leave the industry. The opposite will occur for the essential goods.

Government expenditures may alter demand. A tax upon soft drinks, the proceeds from which are applied to vocational education, will at least increase the demand for vocational-school teachers.

A tax on a good that is a close substitute for another good will not (as assumed) leave the demand for the other good unaffected. Thus, a tax on coal will definitely improve the market for fuel oil. On the other hand, where the relationship between the two goods is complementary, a tax on the one will injure the market for the other (fuel oil and oil burners).[27]

Taxes may affect over-all spending (consumption plus investment) adversely and intensify a deflationary situation with resulting unemployment, general loss in income, and even a general fall in prices.

4. Effects of Expenditures on Costs. Government expenditures may also provide cost-saving benefits to businessmen. Thus, an output tax on potato growers to advertise potatoes or provide research in potato growing need not raise costs of production at all. If all taxes were attended by equivalent specific benefits to taxpayers, there would be no shifting. Of course, it can be argued that these expenditures would have been forthcoming without the tax (financed by borrowing or some other tax), but this may not be so realistic as the contrary assumption. All taxes probably yield some offsetting benefits that lower costs.

5. What Is Net Income? Taxes on what appears to be surplus as defined by the accountant may not be confined to surplus as defined by the economist. A corporate net income tax is at least partially a cost tax, notwithstanding the impression to the contrary. It is a cost tax because it is based on a definition of profits that includes imputed wages, interest, and rent on owned, in contrast to borrowed or hired, capital, and perhaps a necessary reward for risk taking—that is, it includes the return which is necessary to induce stockholders to invest their funds and perhaps their services in this corporation rather than in any other. Necessary profits on capital are not a part of the marginal cost that is equated with marginal revenue to determine optimum volume, but they are part of the cost that determines the long-run size and/or number of plants.

6. State of the Market. Other strategic factors may have a bearing. Taxes may be more easily shifted in a sellers' than in a buyers' market. The existence of trade unions may have an important bearing on the incidence of some taxes, such as social security taxes.

7. Effect on Untaxed Industries. Regarding costs, traditional theory assumes that the untaxed industries do not enjoy a reduction in factor costs as a result of the decrease in output in the taxed industry. However, if the decrease in output is significant and/or the unemployed factors tend to concentrate in a few untaxed industries, absorption of these unemployed resources can occur only by a reduction in their prices. Thus a lower cost of production (and to some extent, therefore, a lower price) in untaxed industries may offset the price rise in taxed industries.

Thus it has been argued that even a special excise affects only rela-

---

[27] A very large array of complications in shifting theory arises in cases of inferior-superior good relationships (margarine and butter), particularly when they are produced under monopoly.

tive prices of consumption goods and that its real incidence is a reduction in all factor rewards. On the assumption that incidence theory should abstract from governmental disposition of tax revenue (ignoring the fact that the government usually absorbs displaced factors by enlarging its demand for goods and services) proponents make a plausible case for this conclusion. Even granting all this, it still remains true that one who consumes more than the average of a taxed good bears a burden. One who consumes according to average proportions is compensated for his loss by the gain from the decreased prices of other goods.[28]

8. Difficulty of Empirical Verification. Shifting analysis is based almost entirely on deductive reasoning—that is, it is based on pure logic and never has been proved or disproved by observation or experimentation. The price changes that follow in the wake of new taxes may be due either to taxation or to a variety of other causes. For this reason, inductive or experimental proof of incidence is hard to establish. It is probably more fruitful to use inductive evidence to explore some of the basic assumptions behind incidence theory—for example, the assumption that the firm tries to maximize profits.

It is an open question whether for immediate tax policy the exceptions to the general principles of shifting are or are not more important than the rule. And it is a striking fact that traditional incidence theory is based almost exclusively on partial equilibrium analysis, which is conceded to be inadequate for the more typical case of general taxes.

It is now in order to apply the analysis of incidence to specific taxes.

THE SHIFTING OF SPECIFIC TAXES

INCOME AND PROFITS TAXES

Analysis of the net income tax affords an excellent illustration of the institutional factors that must be considered in determining the effect of a tax. In so far as the tax strikes income above costs, it is a tax on surplus and therefore tends not to be shifted to the same extent as a cost tax. Even to the extent that the tax affects the cost of production, shifting is rendered difficult by the fact that the income tax is a general tax, and consequently the usual mechanism of shifting (migration of firms and factors of production to an untaxed field) is unavailable. The alternative faced by factors of production and firms, on whom an income tax has been imposed, is withdrawal from the productive process. However, the

---

[28] See Earl R. Rolph, *Theory of Fiscal Economics* (Berkeley: University of California Press, 1954), chaps. 6–7; Musgrave, *The Theory of Public Finance.*

reactions of workers to decreased disposable income and of savers to a lower return on their investment is largely a matter of cultural conditioning and will vary from country to country and from era to era. Consequently, it is extremely difficult to decide once and for all the final incidence of the income tax; we can but point up some of the factors which must be considered.

Personal Net Income Tax. Let us consider first the personal net income tax. There seem to be equally valid arguments for saying that the supply of labor is increased or decreased by a net income tax. If the supply of labor is decreased, there will, of course, be a tendency for higher factor prices, and therefore product prices may tend to rise also.[29] The tax could discourage the labor supply because it reduces the incentive for effort and makes leisure more attractive. The opposite is sometimes asserted on the ground that once the workingman attains a standard he will not suffer it to be impaired without a struggle. As a matter of institutional circumstances, many people may have little choice in the matter; they have to work the hours prescribed by the factory schedule in order to retain a job.[30] As indicated in Chapter 2, empirical evidence, such as there is, lends little support for the view that work and investment habits in the United States have been radically changed by heavy income taxes.[31]

One can say in conclusion that because of its differentiation and general coverage, the graduated personal income tax is probably least susceptible to shifting of the major taxes that constitute the tax system. The point is often used as an argument for this mode of taxation.

Corporate Taxes. Opinions on the incidence of the corporate net in-

---

[29] As was pointed out in the analysis of a universal tax, the incidence of a tax explains mainly the price effects rather than the income effects of a tax. Therefore, the incidence of the income tax as analyzed here assumes a constant national income. The income effects involve the large field of aggregative economics discussed in later chapters.

[30] H. A. Silverman, *Taxation—Its Incidence and Effects* (London: Macmillan and Co., Ltd., 1931), p. 177; George F. Break, "Income Taxes, Wage Rates, and the Incentive to Supply Labor Services," *National Tax Journal,* VI: 4 (December 1953), pp. 333–352; Earl R. Rolph, *Theory of Fiscal Economics,* chap. 10.

[31] With respect to the supply of savings, it is contended that a personal net income tax has the following effects:

1. By reducing disposable income, the amount which can be saved is decreased. However, this assumes that the tax is paid out of savings. Silverman (p. 170) argues that lower income groups who save for security reasons or who use the savings to increase their stock of such personal durables as houses, are more likely to curtail expenditure for current consumption.

2. By reducing the return on investments, a net income tax strengthens the preference for cash hoards. Thus the propensity to save for investment falls.

3. By reducing the return on investments, the net income tax causes a shift from more risky to less risky ventures. However, if the more risky ventures consisted merely of bidding for already existing securities, this shift may not decrease production.

come tax are much more varied. There are some fairly strong grounds to support the view that the burden remains with the stockholders. The tax does not affect all competitors, and a graduated tax may place a different relative burden on each of them. The marginal competitors (of great importance in classical incidence theory) are not affected by the tax. In addition, the general character of the net income tax makes escape by migration impossible. The tax is on surplus rather than cost, and the levy will not affect the optimum volume for maximizing profits.

On the other hand, there are also grounds for the view that the corporate net income tax is shifted forward to consumers or backward to wage earners. Some businessmen have referred to the corporate tax as "a sales tax in disguise." Empirical studies of corporate profits under radically different rates of tax (1927–1954) have shown a persistency of return on assets that is difficult to explain except on the premise that much shifting does in fact occur at least in the long run.[32] The period covered by these studies provided rates in different years ranging from 12½ to 52 percent (not to mention the excess profits tax during part of the period). The stability of corporate earnings (after tax) in the face of these radical changes in the tax laws creates a strong presumption that the tax was not paid out of profits. On the other hand it should be said that this type of evidence is not conclusive: many variables beside taxes affect profit ratios.

As previously observed, an income tax might cause monopolies and oligopolies to raise prices where these businesses determine volume according to political rather than economic factors. It is argued that some corporations determine their price levels on the basis of what capital they may need for expansion (plus adequate dividends). The consumer thus provides the capital for expansion and presumably must provide more if taxes cut into the surplus that would otherwise have been available for construction.

Net business income often includes elements of imputed interest and rent; these are clearly cost factors and are recognized as such when the business employs them contractually. Economists have often argued that entrepreneurial services have a "supply price" like any other factor of production; that some part of business income is properly designated "necessary profits"; that this is a social cost rather than a surplus; and that a tax imposed on this element of profits must be recouped in higher prices or reduced costs in order to maintain the supply of "enterprise." Alfred Marshall was of the opinion that the costs of a "representative

[32] Eugene M. Lerner and Eldon S. Hendricksen, "Federal Taxes on Corporate Income and the Rate of Return on Investment in Manufacturing, 1927 to 1952," *National Tax Journal*, IX: 3 (September 1956), pp. 193–202; John C. Clendenin, "Effect of Corporate Income Taxes on Corporate Earnings," *Taxes*, 34: 6 (June 1956), pp. 391–398.

firm" rather than a marginal concern are most significant in price analysis.[33] Professor Seligman at least conceded that "If the government . . . demands too large a percentage of . . . anticipated profits, the individual may prefer not to subject himself to the risk and may decide to be content with a smaller but a surer return." [34] Under modern conditions, with a highly organized labor market, it seems quite probable that wages are affected in some degree by the level of corporate profits, which in turn is affected directly by taxes.

Taxes which burden one kind of investment more than another (investment in stocks more than investment in bonds, for instance) may, by changing the flow of capital from one line to another, end in a diffusion of the differential burden over all the investment field.

Excess profits taxes fall more largely on surplus than do corporate income taxes, and the former are probably less likely to be passed on to consumers. On the other hand, there is some support for the view that even levies of this type are shifted, particularly in a "sellers' " market and in the absence of price controls.[35]

The difference between a gross income tax, a net income tax, and an excess profits tax may be illustrated graphically as in Figure 15.

FIGURE 15

Areas of Corporate Taxes

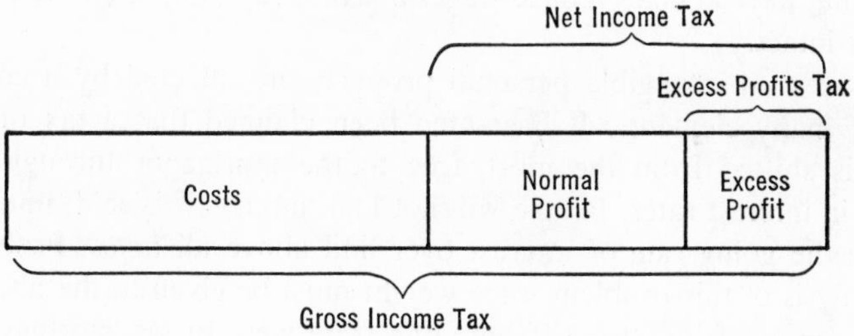

PROPERTY TAXES

The general property tax is a complex phenomenon and affords a great variety of possibilities of shifting. In its application to land, the important

---

[33] Alfred Marshall, *Principles of Economics* (7th ed., London: Macmillan and Co., Ltd., 1916), p. 317. See also Dennis H. Robertson, *Economic Fragments* (London: P. S. King & Son, Ltd., 1931), pp. 23–41.

[34] E. R. A. Seligman, "Income Taxes and the Price Level," *Academy of Political Science Proceedings,* II (1926), pp. 19–20.

[35] K. E. Boulding, "The Incidence of a Profits Tax," *American Economic Review,* XXXIV: 3 (September 1944), pp. 567–572. Boulding points that a tax on surplus may be shifted, if the entrepreneur is interested not in maximum money profits only but in the most desirable combination of size of plant and money profit.

fact is that the supply of land is relatively fixed. Except in the form of tax capitalization, shifting is not likely to occur here. Even the tendency toward tax capitalization may be defeated if all investments bear an equal tax burden. However, other investments are not usually taxed equally, at least in practice, and some relieve themselves of the taxes through other forms of shifting.

Taxes on buildings are thought to decrease the supply of buildings and thus to become a factor in rent, the purchase price of buildings, and the cost of doing business. Personal property taxes on consumers' goods are not easy to shift because these goods are held for use and not for sale. Personal property taxes on goods in the process of manufacture and sale would appear to be readily shiftable in so far as such taxes are universal among competitors. In such a case, like wages and interest, they constitute a part of the regular costs of production. Of course, if universality and equality in the general property tax are assumed—that is, if all producers pay at the same rate on all business capital—shifting cannot take place by migration from a point of high to one of low pressure. But if prices in the long run tend to cover all costs of production, at least of a reasonably efficient firm, then there is no reason to believe that the inventory tax is an exception. Business property taxes are on a single factor of production (capital), and this (by substitution) might mean lower capital returns and higher wages. It seems incongruous to argue that payroll taxes reduce wages but that capital taxes leave property returns intact.

Taxes on intangible personal property are affected by a combination of many elements. It has often been claimed that a tax on mortgages is shifted from the mortgagee to the mortgagor through an increase in interest rates. People will not loan money, it is said, unless they receive the going rate of interest over and above all taxes. Probably in the analysis of this problem some weight must be given to the alternative opportunities of investors. If only one state were to tax mortgages, and the tax were to follow the domicile of the mortgagee, lenders within that state would be at a disadvantage because borrowers could obtain credit from untaxed sources outside the state. In these circumstances the creditor might have to bear the tax. If one state alone exempted mortgages from taxation, the reverse would be true, and the creditors could probably retain their advantage. If the tax were universal both as to territory and all other investments, the lender could recoup himself only through the roundabout and uncertain process of more spending and less saving.

Traditional theory supports the view that heavy taxes on farmers would cause the latter to migrate from the farm, thus reducing the supply of farm products and raising prices. Some migration is occurring, but it rarely takes farmland out of production and many farmers claim that any economic adversity augments, rather than diminishes, the supply of farm produce.

INHERITANCE TAXES

Death taxes are generally thought to offer great resistance to shifting. They are not levied in the course of business and the principal way in which their shifting might occur would be through reduced saving and the higher rates of interest which might follow therefrom. The factors here involved are remote and uncertain in their operation and effects.

CONSUMPTION TAXES

The consumption taxes, including excises, tariffs, special and general sales taxes (possibly also gross income taxes), are regarded as the most easily shifted of all taxes. Indeed, they are called consumption taxes not because they are levied upon the consumer—the impact is usually on the merchant or manufacturer—but because it is thought that he will bear the ultimate burden. For the same reason they are also called *indirect,* though the term is not a very happy one since the taxes covered by this name are probably not the only ones that can be shifted.

Sales Taxes. One should not jump to the conclusion, however, that all taxes classed as sales taxes are always immediately shifted in full to the consumer. Most of the many factors bearing on incidence cited in this chapter are relevant to a problem of shifting in the sales tax field. Thus, for instance, shifting is likely to be greater in degree under competition than under monopoly, where demand is inelastic rather than where it is elastic, and under decreasing-cost rather than under increasing-cost conditions.

In the case of a state retail sales tax, merchants in borderline cities may have to compete with untaxed sales across the border. Even farther within the states, merchants may have to compete with untaxed mail-order business. These factors are impediments to shifting.

A merchant selling many goods may place the burden of a general tax upon the items that have the least elastic demand. He may not be able to do this, however, if he is obliged to compete with specialty stores that sell only items of inelastic demand.

In the case of a general retail sales tax, where the legislature expresses an intent that the tax be shifted and further requires merchants to bill the customer for the tax as a separate item on each bill of sale, the merchant may take the attitude that he is merely an agent to collect the tax at the source. Moreover, he may expect that all his competitors will take a similar attitude. The readiness with which merchants often succumb to state sales taxes suggests that this may be the prevailing view. Obviously, it will greatly facilitate tax shifting.

A truly general expenditure tax including capital outlay might, as previously explained, end as a proportionate burden on production factors. A general rise in prices, were it to occur, would have no distributive effects except those associated with inflation.

The Tariff.   The tariff is a tax upon the foreign supply of the domestic market, and it is often concluded that the domestic consumer has to pay the tax in full along with the other costs of the foreign producer. But the matter is not so simple as this. To mention one complication only, the commodity taxed may be one that can be produced at home for less than the former price plus the tariff. In that case, the foreign producer must either absorb part of the tax or expect to lose his market to a domestic producer.

Professor Taussig's analysis [36] of the incidence of the tariff, or the effect of the tariff upon domestic prices, divides the problem according to three different conditions of trade. The first condition prevails when a tariff is imposed upon a commodity that can be produced in sufficient supply as cheaply at home as abroad. The commodity may or may not be upon an export basis, but in any event the tariff should have small, if any, effect upon domestic prices of the commodity taxed. If the United States can produce enough of Commodity X to supply the domestic market at the world price, the domestic price will remain the same as the world price regardless of how much tariff is imposed. The world price itself may be somewhat affected by the new source of supply encouraged by the tariff.

The second condition exists when a considerable volume of imports of a taxed commodity continues to come in over the tariff wall. This is usual when the tariff is levied for revenue upon a commodity that cannot (at least within reasonable limits of practicality) be produced at home. The British tax on tea is a familiar example. In this case, the tariff does not differ very greatly from an excise tax imposed upon the domestic producer. As in the case of an excise tax—let us say, a processing tax— the burden may be shifted backward, but it is usually shifted forward to the consumer. Because of the conditions of increasing and decreasing costs in some industries, the cost and price may rise less or more than the tax. And, of course, the elasticity of domestic demand may also have a bearing on prices.

Imports in considerable quantity may continue even though do-

---

[36] F. W. Taussig, *Some Aspects of the Tariff Question* (Cambridge, Mass.: Harvard University Press, 1929), pp. 3–17.

mestic production contributes part and, under the influence of the duty, an increasing part of the supply. As a rule,[37] this means that the domestic price is maintained at a figure equal to foreign price plus the tariff. Importers would not forsake the alternative of disposition on the world market unless they could command a price in the taxing country equal to world price plus the tariff which must be paid. On the other hand, if one of the effects of a tariff is to influence foreign suppliers to sell part of their products upon the world market rather than in the taxing country, the world price itself will be affected.

Finally, there is the case where a duty keeps out all imports. Here, of course, no tax is paid at all, but prices may still be affected. A 100-percent tariff will not affect domestic prices more than a 50-percent tax, providing the latter is sufficient to exclude all imports. How much the prices will rise depends entirely on the conditions in the country imposing the tax—particularly on the cost which must be covered in order to meet the demand.

Conceiving trade as bilateral necessitates considerations of relative elasticities of demand in the trading countries. If one sells to the other a commodity that the other must have (no substitutes and very important) and accepts in return a commodity that can be readily dispensed with, the situation favors the country with the indispensable export. Fortunately exclusive supply of indispensible commodities rarely if ever occurs.

That a tariff may affect exporters as well as importers has long been recognized, and there is support for the view that exporters bear the incidence of such levies. On the well-accepted assumption that we cannot sell where we do not buy, a tariff that decreases imports will also lower the value of exports, and this may have a depressing effect upon the income of the export industries. If resources are shifted from the export line to create new competition in lines where the nation has been self-sufficient, a considerable diffusion of the burden of the tax may occur. One of the collateral effects will be a reduction of the national income. According to this view, it is only in certain circumstances that the price of the good upon which a tariff has been laid will raise.[38]

---

[37] There are important exceptions, see *ibid.,* chap. I.

[38] Earl R. Rolph, "The Burden of Import Duties," *American Economic Review,* XXXVI (December 1946), pp. 788–812. The author there argues that imports of America from England yield dollars that are traded for pounds, since the English exporters acquire dollars and want to trade them for pounds. The effect of an American tariff on British whiskey will be to reduce the number of dollars which English exporters offer in exchange for pounds. With a freely fluctuating exchange rate, this will cause a fall in the dollar value of the pound and hence a decreased dollar income available for those engaged in exporting to England. The primary effect of the tariff, then, is to decrease the income of those engaged in producing for export to that country upon whose products the tariff has been laid.

SOCIAL SECURITY TAXES

Many interesting problems of shifting are raised by federal and state social security legislation. These laws currently impose several taxes on payrolls, of which the employer pays all but one which is deducted from the pay of employees. One of the taxes is so administered as to induce the states to enact unemployment compensation laws—that is, taxes imposed by the states and used therein for unemployment compensation are allowed as a credit against the federal tax.

There has been much argument as to whether these payroll taxes are shifted to the consumer or (in the case of the employer's tax) to the employees, or whether they remain as a burden upon the parties who pay them in the first instance. The much published consensus favors the conclusion that the wage earner bears most of these taxes, but this view is by no means unanimous. Some of the factors which have a bearing on the conclusion may be mentioned. State unemployment compensation laws which are acceptable for credit may provide for a reduction in tax to employers who operate with little or no unemployment. Under the situation thus created, it is likely that the tax will be borne by the employer who is unwilling or unable to give steady work, in so far as his contribution is greater than that of his more efficient competitor. State laws may exclude employers of less than four employees, which again introduces an element of untaxed competition in certain cases. The employer may use more machinery and less labor as a result of the law, since the latter makes the employment of labor more hazardous and costly than theretofore. Here the decreased demand for labor (in so far as it does not merely shift to the machinery industry) may force wages down. On the other hand, wages may offer some inertia due to the resistance of employees who have become accustomed to a given wage scale and a standard of living based thereon. Moreover, something may depend upon the degree to which labor is organized to resist a wage cut. The fact that labor is more important as a cost in some lines than in others, and that mechanization is feasible in some cases and not in others, may result in shifts of labor and capital that diffuse the effects of the tax considerably. The above factors apply particularly to the payroll taxes for unemployment compensation, but they also apply to the payroll taxes for old-age annuities, except that in the latter case the employer cannot reduce his burden by providing regular, as well as less, employment. Furthermore, the old-age taxes apply to all employers and not only to those with four or more employees.

When the tax falls on the employees (as is true of half the old-age insurance tax), the probability that the ultimate burden will be borne by the wage earner is greater than when the impact is on the employer. This is especially true if the employee regards the payment as insurance rather than as a cut in wages.

The incidence of these taxes cannot be predicted with any great degree of assurance. On the whole, the safe conclusion would seem to be that it is divided among employers, labor, and consumer; but in what proportion cannot definitely be said.[39]

Some controversy has centered upon what becomes of the incentives in experience rating if the payroll tax is shifted. (Experience rating adjusts the tax to employers' records in achieving a stabilized labor force.) On the assumption that wages and prices will be the same for all competitors, any differential advantage in production will still redound to the benefit of the successful employer.

Like other general taxes, the most important consequences of the social security taxes lie in the direction of changes in national income. The single act of tax collection reduces purchasing power in the hands of the taxpayer and would, by itself, tend to have a deflationary effect. If, as the funds are collected, they are simultaneously used to purchase new government bonds, and then, in turn, are immediately used for increased purchases of goods and services, the effect is similar to that achieved by simultaneous increase of tax collections and expenditures— that is, the national income tends to rise (in a time of less than full employment) by the amount of the expenditures. If, as the funds are collected, they are used to buy up outstanding government debt, then the national income will change only to the extent that those from whom taxes are collected have a higher marginal propensity to consume than those from whom the debt is bought.

INCIDENCE OF REGIONAL TAXES

The problem of incidence at the regional level differs substantially from that at the national level where considerations of competition play less part. National taxes are likely to cover all competitors, and common burdens are relatively easy to shift to consumers. Taxes among competitors at the state level may develop differential burdens and present a unique problem in incidence.

---

[39] James K. Hall, "Incidence of Federal Social Security Pay Roll Taxes," *Quarterly Journal of Economics,* 53 (November 1938), pp. 38–63; Russell Bauder, "The Probable Incidence of Social Security Taxes," *American Economic Review* XXVI: 3 (September 1936), pp. 463–465; Herbert D. Simpson, *Compulsory Health Insurance in the United States,* Northwestern University, Chicago, 1943, Ch. IV; Eveline M. Burns, "Financial Aspects of the Social Security Act," *American Economic Review,* XXVI: 1 (March 1936), pp. 12–22, and her *The Economics of Social Security* (New York: McGraw-Hill Book Company, 1949).

If the in-state firm is subject to a special tax that its competitors do not pay, and the firm is the high-cost competitor, the tax might conceivably raise prices on the national market. However, it would appear that the firm must ordinarily absorb unilateral taxes. If it has been favored with a light burden it enjoys a rental element in profits that can and must absorb the tax. Presumably it has already capitalized its advantage and is charging what the traffic will bear when the tax is imposed. However, the conclusion need not hold in the case of oligopolies that do not follow the economics of pricing. And of course a tax now imposed by one state may later become general, in which case the problem disappears.[40]

The incidence of municipal income taxes also affords interesting problems. Based largely on payroll, such taxes could come out of business profits since business may have to bid for employees who are located outside the municipality and have no tax deducted from their pay. Whether business could then pass the tax on to consumers would involve some of the considerations outlined in the paragraph above. But payroll taxes may be in lieu of higher property taxes which employees who live elsewhere have to pay. On the whole it seems best to conclude that such taxes generally stay where they fall.

SUMMARY

Shifting is a price phenomenon and consequently, is affected by the type of market in which the tax is imposed. In pure competition, the firm is an insignificant part of the industry and accepts the price set by the market. At the other extreme, in monopoly, the firm is the industry and produces a product for which there are no close substitutes. In between these two market situations lie monopolistic competition and oligopoly, in which the firm has varying degrees of control over price and need fear varying amounts of retaliation from rivals.

Shifting usually takes the form of a decrease in volume and a consequent rise in price. Producers, seeking to maximize profits, produce to the point where marginal revenue equals marginal cost. When a tax is imposed on cost, each producer tends to curtail output, and, in the long run, producers will migrate from taxed to untaxed areas of the economy. A tax on surplus is less likely to be shifted, but such may be the case if

---

[40] Richard A. Musgrave and Darwin W. Daicoff, "Who Pays the Michigan Taxes?" *Michigan Tax Study* (Lansing, 1958), chap. 4; University of Wisconsin Tax Study Committee, *Wisconsin State and Local Tax Burden* (Madison, 1959).

the profits include interest on owned capital and wages of management. Some of the factors favorable to shifting are:

1. A longer period of time;
2. A less elastic demand;
3. A more elastic supply if the supply curve slopes upward and a less elastic supply if the supply curve slopes downward; and
4. The absence of monopoly profits.

Traditional incidence theory is particularly well adapted to the analysis of special taxes. A general tax poses a problem in shifting fundamentally different from that which arises from a special tax; in the former there is no escape from the levy through migration to an untaxed field, although some migration may occur from more heavily to less heavily burdened lines. A special tax need affect relative prices only; a general tax to be shifted forward must raise the general price level. There is considerable conflict of authority concerning the incidence of a general cost tax such as a general sales tax. On certain assumptions, a case can be made for the view that such a tax comes proportionately out of factor payments. However, a completely general expenditure tax is difficult to conceive and still more difficult to apply. There is also support for the view that all consumption taxes—general and special—rest proportionately on factor payments, a view that can be rebutted securely and completely only on the assumption that governments expand to absorb the displaced factors that attend a new tax.

Tax capitalization occurs when a purchaser discounts the special tax burden attached to an investment. This usually happens in the case of income-earning goods whose supply is perfectly inelastic; land is sometimes cited as an example of such a factor.

Application of incidence theory to actual situations involves some modifications in accordance with certain institutional factors. Four of these factors are:

1. Political considerations persuading entrepreneurs to prefer a volume of output that does not maximize profits;
2. The existence of close substitutes or complements for the taxed good;
3. The effect of government use of the tax revenue; and
4. The effect of the tax on demand through changes in the distribution of income.

Applying theories of incidence to the major sources of the tax system, one observes that net income taxes and inheritance taxes offer

the most, and sales taxes and other consumption taxes the least resistance to shifting. Business income taxes are more easily shifted than
personal income taxes. Property taxes are made up of many elements,
some shifted in higher prices to consumers, some capitalized, and some
remaining on the taxpayer. The social security taxes present a very complex problem of incidence; very probably the burden is divided among
the interested parties, though in what proportion this author does not
venture to estimate. The incidence of regional taxes, where one firm out
of many may be singled out for special burden, presents unique problems; unless the taxed competitor is the high-cost firm, the tax burden
may stay where it falls.

PROBLEMS

1. According to a diffusionist, where would the incidence of an inheritance tax lie? What would be its effect on the distribution of
   wealth?
2. Which is more likely to be shifted in greater degree, a tax on
   cigarettes or one on soft drinks? Why? Make a graphic presentation of your argument.
3. Explain and show graphically why shifting is likely to be more
   complete in the long run than in the short run.
4. Explain and show graphically the difference between an industry of
   increasing and one of constant cost and how the difference may
   affect shifting.
5. Explain and illustrate graphically the concepts of average revenue
   and marginal revenue involved in the calculation of monopoly price.
6. Discuss and illustrate graphically the shifting of a tax under conditions of monopoly.
7. The conventional diagram that is used to explain shifting in a competitive situation shows only a partial shifting of the tax. What becomes of the remaining portion of the tax?
8. Distinguish between competition, monopoly, oligopoly, and monopolistic competition. What are the distinctive characteristics of shifting under each of these conditions?
9. Explain the difference in analysis required where a problem in
   shifting involves a general rather than a special tax.
10. Does a special cost tax raise the general level of prices? Change
    relative prices? What is meant when it is said that such a tax is
    borne by the consumer?
11. Comment on the proposition: If a special tax is imposed upon the
    land owned by a landlord, he will raise the rent.
12. Comment on the proposition that a monopolist always chooses that
    volume of production which will yield him the highest immediate
    profit.

13. How might a tax on personal income reduce the supply of labor and raise wages, or (in effect) increase the supply of labor and reduce wages?

14. Which of the following propositions concerning the incidence of the corporate net income tax can be supported?
    a. Prices are often determined by political rather than economic factors;
    b. The tax raises the monopoly price;
    c. The businessman can shift any tax if he wants to;
    d. The tax includes elements of cost that might affect future expansion.

15. On what ground is it alleged that all labor legislation is at the expense of the workers?

16. Comment on the proposition: A tax on an industry of increasing costs causes the industry to shrink, and the increasing costs of producing each unit resulting from this shrinkage must be added to the tax to create a large increase in price.

17. Under what circumstances might a net income tax imposed on a public utility not be shifted?

18. It has been said that the ultimate incidence of social security would be the same whether the payroll taxes were levied on employees, employers, or both. Do you agree?

19. Comment on the proposition: Even though the property tax rests much more heavily on furniture merchants than on meat merchants, this does not affect the relative profitability of doing business in these lines.

20. An old idea suggests that society could lift itself by its own bootstraps so to speak by taxing industries of increasing costs to pay subsidies to those of decreasing costs. The tax would raise prices by less than the tax and the subsidy would reduce them by more than the subsidy. Is this idea valid?

21. Analyze the effects of a tax on industry in one state or city.

7

THE INCOME TAX—BACKGROUND AND PROCEDURE

The income tax occupies a place in the finance of central governments similar to that of the property tax in the finance of local governments. Consideration of the revenue system as a whole shows that the income tax is by all odds the predominant tax.

HISTORICAL AND LEGAL BACKGROUND

THE FEDERAL INCOME TAX

The income tax as a regular and important source of revenue in the United States is a recent development. Until the Civil War, the federal government subsisted largely upon receipts from the tariff and the sale of public lands. During the Civil War, under the pressure of sudden necessity, it resorted to income, inheritance, and a series of excise taxes. Several of the latter, particularly those on alcoholic beverages and tobacco, were retained after the war and continued to provide substantial revenue. Nevertheless, the tariff still held the leading position as a federal revenue source. In 1894 an unsuccessful attempt to reintroduce the income tax and make it a permanent feature of the federal revenue system was due not so much to the need of funds as to the tariff controversy between the two major political parties; the antiprotectionists promoted the income tax as a substitute for the tariff. But it was not until 1913 that the country finally accepted the net income tax—through a constitutional amendment. Before the tax had a chance to get properly under way, it was put to a rigorous test by the financial emergency of World War I. It proved successful, even beyond expectation, and since then has remained the backbone of the federal revenue system.

The Civil War Income Tax.   Although a new source of revenue to the federal government, the income tax of 1861 was by no means a novel device in the fiscal history of the American people. At the time of its enactment, there were six states with such legislation on their statute books and four others where the experience was still fresh in mind.[1] In none of these states was the tax popular or successful, a fate that, as will soon be seen, was to some extent to befall also the federal government's first attempt at drawing upon this source. The income tax of 1861, along with much other fiscal legislation included in the same law, was an emergency measure to finance the Civil War. It was adopted as a lesser of two evils and only after long bickering over a proposed bill to levy a direct tax on real property alone. A tax on real property would have required apportionment among the states according to their population. This would have been a time-consuming process and also was thought to involve special burdens upon the agricultural states of the west and southwest.[2] On the other hand, the "indirect tax" levied upon income would be speedier, requiring no apportionment among the states and, further, would fall upon those best able to bear it.[3]

---

[1] K. K. Kennan, *Income Taxation* (Milwaukee: Burdick & Allen, 1910), p. 210.

[2] Actually, in addition to the income tax, there was also a property tax levy of $20,000,000, to be apportioned among the several states and territories, including the states in secession. Only about two thirds of this sum was ever collected, and almost thirty years were consumed in the attempt. Eventually, however, even this sum was refunded.—H. E. Smith, *The United States Federal Internal Tax History from 1861 to 1871* (Boston: Houghton Mifflin Company, 1914), pp. 23, 38–44.

[3] This income tax law expressed the great haste in which it was drawn. No provision was made in it for exemptions above $800, or for credits and deductions other than certain specified taxes, with the result that its enforcement would have amounted to a levy on gross receipts rather than net income. The Secretary of Treasury, aware of the great confusion which would accompany its execution, made no attempt to place the law in operation, and in the following year it was succeeded by a new act. The income tax of 1862 was a revised version of the former law, with some refinement in the definition of taxable income; in estimating the latter, it allowed the deduction of all national, state, and local taxes paid upon property or the source of income; further, it allowed for the deduction of gains derived from manufactured goods upon which a stamp tax had been levied; and finally, it allowed a deduction of all gains for which a tax had been collected at the source. The latter feature followed the British practice of collection at the

The Civil War income tax went through many changes in the course of its duration. Between its enactment in 1861 and its expiration in 1872 it was amended six times. However, the basic features of the 1862 act remained predominant throughout the period. This act allowed a personal exemption of $600 and had a slightly progressive rate structure with a 5-percent top rate applying to incomes exceeding $10,000. This 5-percent top rate was exceeded only in the acts of 1864 and 1865, of which the latter imposed a 10-percent levy on incomes above $5000.[4]

In general, the administration of this tax was an arduous task for which the federal government was ill equipped both in experience and in organization. The law abounded in confusing provisions, the application of which was somewhat tempered by the rulings of the Commissioner of Internal Revenue.[5] These features helped to make the tax onerous and unpopular. Antagonism against it was strong even while the war was on,

---

source. This, however, applied only to salaries paid by the United States to its employees, including members of Congress, and to dividends and interest of certain specified corporations.

[4] Kennan, *op. cit.*

Certain other notable features of these taxes were: income from United States securities was taxed 1.5 percent under the 1862 law and at full rate under the later acts; various types of corporations paid on gross receipts and at different rates— for instance, under the 1864 act insurance companies were subject to a gross receipts tax of 1.5 percent, express companies to 3 percent, and telegraph companies to 5 percent.

Notwithstanding certain gross receipts levies on corporations, the Civil War income taxes applied mainly to personal incomes. Both corporate and partnership earnings were regarded as taxable income to the stockholder in the year the income accrued, regardless of whether or not such earnings were distributed. A similar provision applied to accrued interest, even when not realized. These features of the law resulted in the taxation of both realized and accrued income and thus involved considerable double taxation—see W. W. Hewitt, "The Concept of Income in Federal Taxation," *Journal of Political Economy,* XXXIII (April 1925), pp. 159–160. It is interesting to observe that after a long period of trial with the taxation of corporate income, there has recently been some support for a return to the Civil War practice of disregarding the corporate entity and taxing the stockholder upon his share of corporate earnings, whether or not distributed.

[5] Thus, although the statutes were at first silent on the subject of deductions for losses, repairs, depreciation and other business expenses incurred in the course of carrying on one's business or vocation, they were nevertheless deductible (Hewitt, *loc. cit.,* p. 158). However, no administrative measures could eliminate the many loopholes and annoyances which characterized these laws. Among the annoyances was one requiring the farmer to list his produce sold or on hand for the purpose of computing his income. Congress allowed house rent paid as a deduction, to put the tenant on a par with the home owner whose taxable income did not include the rental value of his house; but this turned out to be a source of abuse in the administration of the tax. These provisions illustrate the crudity of these early laws. Logically, rent paid on a house is a personal expense or utilization of income, not properly deductible in computing income. And by the same token, rent saved on the ownership of a house might properly be counted as positive income. (See discussion later in this chapter.)

but it became still stronger after the war. This public sentiment against the tax lingered long after its repeal and was a large factor in retarding the development of a permanent federal income tax. But, in spite of its defects and with only moderate and mildly progressive rates, it aided materially in financing what was then thought to be a very expensive war.

The Ill-fated Income Tax of 1894. In 1894, some thirty years after the Civil War experiment, an attempt was made to reinstate the income tax into the federal revenue system. During this interval, the nation had been following a policy of high protection, which incidentally provided the federal government with ample funds for its needs. President Cleveland, who had been elected in 1892 on a tariff-for-revenue-only platform, proposed to lessen the tariff's fiscal role and substitute an income tax to make up the difference. He was aided in this effort by the depression of 1893, which caused a temporary decline in governmental receipts. Essentially, however, the income tax grew out of the tariff controversy of the period. It was at this time that the antimonopoly movement was becoming powerful. Along with resentment of concentration in business went resentment of concentration in wealth. It was alleged that the tariff was the mother of trusts and millionaires, and the income tax was advocated, particularly in the south and west, as a preferable source of revenue. After long and bitter debates in Congress over questions of class and sectional interests, the Wilson Tariff Bill, of which the income tax was a part, finally passed both houses. But it was no longer the bill originally introduced; it was badly mutilated, especially in the Senate, and President Cleveland allowed it to become law without his signature.[6]

The actual features of the income tax of 1894 need not long detain us, as an early Supreme Court decision declared it void before it was put into operation. In general, it was patterned after the law of 1867, and such innovations as it showed indicated no great advance in the understanding of income tax techniques and principles.[7] It applied to both personal and corporate income, with a $4000 exemption for the former. Gifts and inheritances were included in the base.[8]

Unconstitutionality of the 1894 Act. The income tax statute of 1894 was speedily tested and found unconstitutional by the United States

[6] E. R. A. Seligman, *The Income Tax* (2d ed., New York: The Macmillan Company, 1914), pp. 499–505.

[7] Kennan, *op. cit.,* p. 259.

[8] Under income was also included interest, both realized and accrued, on all securities except those specifically exempt by law and on gains from real estate sold within two years of its purchase; deductions for certain taxes, interest on indebtedness, losses, worthless debts, and other necessary expenses incurred in carrying on one's business; collection at source was also provided, but only for salaries of United States employees.—Seligman, *op. cit.,* pp. 508–518.

Supreme Court in the case of *Pollock v. Farmers' Loan and Trust Company*.[9] The Constitution provides that representatives and direct taxes shall be apportioned among the several states according to their population. In this case it was contended that an income tax, at least in so far as it applied to the income from real estate and personal property, was a direct tax. If this contention were established, it would follow in effect that a federal income tax could not be levied.

A prolonged argument took place among the attorneys and judges as to what the Founding Fathers had meant by the phrase "direct tax" as used in the Constitution. One side quoted at great length the economic literature of the time to prove that income taxes were generally regarded in 1787 as direct taxes. The other side relied more heavily upon a long line of precedents reaching back to Washington's administration, when a levy on carriages was accepted by the Supreme Court as an indirect tax.[10] Many legal statements and decisions were marshaled to support the view that only land and capitation taxes were *direct* as the term is used in the Constitution.

It appears fairly clear that the final outcome of this dispute turned in large measure upon the economic rather than the legal opinions of the justices. Thus, Chief Justice Fuller expressed the conservative view of his time when he said: "The original expectation was that the power of direct taxation would be exercised only in extraordinary exigencies, and down to August 15, 1894, this expectation has been realized." [11] The attempt, he added, to use the income tax in time of peace created reason for circumspection and care. Justice Field went further and said: [12]

> The income tax law under consideration is marked by discriminating features which affect the whole law. It discriminates between those who receive an income of four thousand dollars and those who do not. . . . The legislation in the discrimination it makes, is class legislation. Whenever a distinction is made in the burdens a law imposes or in the benefits it confers on any citizens by reason of their birth, or wealth, or religion, it is class legislation, and leads inevitably to oppression and abuses, and to general unrest and disturbance in society. It was hoped and believed that the great amendments to the Constitution which followed the late civil war had rendered such legislation impossible for all future time. But the objectionable legislation reappears in the act under consideration. It is the same in essential character as that of the English income statute of 1691, which taxed Protestants at a certain rate, Catholics, as

---

[9] 157 U.S. 429 (1895); on rehearing 158 U.S. 601 (1895).
[10] *Hylton v. United States,* 3 Dall. 171 (1796).
[11] *Pollock v. Farmers' Loan and Trust Co.,* 157 U.S. 429, 574 (1895).
[12] *Ibid.,* p. 596.

a class, at double the rate of Protestants, and Jews at another and separate rate.

Justice Harlan, in an equally vigorous statement for the dissent, showed the influence of a different economic philosophy upon his legal opinion. He said: [13]

> The practical effect of the decision today is to give certain kinds of property a position of favoritism and advantage inconsistent with the fundamental principles of our social organization, and to invest them with power and influence that may be perilous to that portion of the American people upon whom rests the larger part of the burdens of the government, and who ought not to be subjected to the dominion of aggregated wealth any more than the property of the country should be at the mercy of the lawless.

The Corporation Excise Tax of 1909. Fifteen years after the 1894 income tax was declared unconstitutional, Congress passed a law providing for a corporate income tax of 1 percent on income in excess of $5000. This was not called an income tax, but an excise on the privilege of doing corporate business, the privilege to be measured by net income. This act was sustained by the United States Supreme Court.[14] Fifteen years' change in public opinion since the 1894 decision may have had a bearing upon the outcome. The Court, in order to sustain the measure, had to resort to the doctrine that there is a distinction between the subject and the measure of the tax and that, if the former clearly conforms to constitutional requirements, the Court will be more lenient in judging the latter.[15] Thus, Congress might do indirectly what it could not do directly. Although the Court probably reached a desirable conclusion in this case, it resorted to exceedingly fine distinctions and doubtful reasoning.

Constitutional Amendment and the Statute of 1913. When in 1909 Congress passed the corporation tax bill, it also proposed a constitutional amendment to enable Congress to levy an income tax unhampered by the apportionment provision of the Constitution. With its adoption in March 1913, this amendment brought to a close one of the longest chapters in the constitutional history of the income tax. The amendment provides that: [16]

---

[13] *Ibid.,* 158 U.S. 601, 685 (1895). A further discussion of the legal aspects of this case will be found in Chapter 19.

[14] *Flint v. Stone Tracy Co.,* 220 U.S. 107 (1911).

[15] A tax on the franchise was indirect and legal even if the value of the franchise were measured by net income.

[16] *United States Constitution,* Art. XVI.

Congress shall have power to lay and collect taxes on incomes, from
whatever source derived, without apportionment among the several
States, and without regard to any census or enumeration.

It was not known at the time this amendment was adopted that
within the next few years an emergency would arise that would stretch
all the revenue-raising resources of the government to the limit. Only
seven months after the power was granted to Congress, a levy was imposed on both personal and corporate incomes. This first federal income
tax under the amendment now seems like a very mild affair with its
normal rate of 1 percent upon personal incomes in excess of $3000
($4000 for a married person or head of family) and a top surtax rate of
6 percent upon incomes in excess of $500,000. During World War I,
however, the income tax was heavily relied upon to yield a large part
of a very large revenue, and it has never since returned to anything like
its pre–World War I level of rates.

STATE AND MUNICIPAL INCOME TAXES

In 1911 Professor Seligman, a national authority on taxation, wrote:
"More and more it has been realized by state officials and commissions
that any hope of a satisfactory state income tax is illusory." [17] He further
pointed out that where state income taxes had been tried in the United
States, they had proved a failure. A state income tax in Virginia yielded
only slightly more than $100,000 in 1909 and 1910, and in over 30
percent of the counties of the state no tax was collected at all. Undaunted
by this experience, Wisconsin adopted an income tax law in 1911, the
year in which Professor Seligman drew his conclusions. It attempted to
profit by the mistakes of other states and, therefore, framed the administrative provisions of its new income tax law with great care. Early state
income tax laws had relied for assessment of income upon local assessors,
usually the same assessors who assessed property. The Wisconsin income
tax law of 1911 inaugurated central administration of the income tax
through a state tax commission with civil service employees. Thus, as
early as 1912 the Minnesota Tax Commission was impelled to observe: [18]

That the Wisconsin income tax law has been a remarkable success
for the first year is now generally admitted. Not only has it resulted
in a large increase in revenue, but it has unquestionably distributed
the tax burdens more equitably among those able to bear them than
ever before in the history of the state.

[17] E. R. A. Seligman, *The Income Tax* (1st ed., New York: The Macmillan
Company, 1911), p. 419.
[18] *Third Biennial Report of the Minnesota Tax Commission* (Minneapolis,
1912), p. 164.

The success of the Wisconsin income tax law started a new movement in state taxation. In 1917 four states, Delaware, Massachusetts, Mississippi, and Missouri, and, two years later, New York and North Dakota, followed Wisconsin's example. At present about two thirds of the states have a state income tax applicable to either individuals or corporations or both. However the trend toward state utilization of this source is now largely halted; beginning with the depression of the 1930s, states (and municipalities) in seeking new revenue sources have shown a decided preference for retail sales taxes.

Faced with serious budgetary problems and a reduced property-tax base as a result of depression, Philadelphia (along with the District of Columbia) inaugurated the first local income tax in the United States in 1939. For legal and administrative reasons, the species of tax selected differed considerably from that in vogue in federal and state systems. It was levied at a flat rate and confined to wages, salaries, and net profits arising from unincorporated business and professional activities. Presently, several hundred municipalities, including many school districts, have such a levy though some of them include corporate income and provide a personal exemption. While the development has been confined to relatively few states (particularly Pennsylvania and Ohio), most of which have no state income taxes, it has attracted widespread attention as a possible supplement for the general property tax and a much-needed solution of the revenue needs of hard-pressed cities.[19]

INCOME TAX ACCOUNTING

THE INDIVIDUAL INCOME TAX

Some knowledge of the fundamentals of income tax accounting is essential for an understanding of the nature and objectives of the income tax.

Refining Gross Income to Net Income. The net income tax, as its name suggests, is based upon net income, a quantity obtained by starting with all that a taxpayer receives between two points of time (for example, January 1–December 31) and making certain refinements or subtractions therefrom. There are three main classes or kinds of subtractions. The first might be called "income not taxed." It consists of certain receipts that are ignored for purposes of income taxation. Congress pre-

---

[19] Leon Jay Quinto, *Municipal Income Taxation in the United States,* Mayor's Committee on Management Survey of the City of New York (New York, 1952), pp. 1–30; Robert A. Sigafoos, *The Municipal Income Tax: Its History and Problems* (Chicago: Public Administration Service, 1955).

scribes that they shall be excluded for certain legal, social, or other reasons. Within this category, one of the most important items is interest on state and municipal bonds.[20] The interest on some of the older federal bonds is also partially or entirely exempt. The policy of issuing federal bonds with a tax-exempt feature was discontinued in 1940. Other income not taxed includes life insurance received by a beneficiary, inheritances and gifts, pensions paid by the United States, and damages received in action for personal injury.

Considerable problems are associated with the treatment of gifts. Gratuities are not deductible to the donor nor taxable as income to the donee. It has been argued that they should be counted as income to the donee rather than, or perhaps in addition to, income to the donor. The donor exercises the power of disposition and the donee enjoys the benefit of the gift. Of course, the transaction involves no new creation of goods —it is rather a transfer of income or the passing of income from one person to another. Difficulty also arises in distinguishing gifts from *compensation, contributions,* and *support.* For example, tips appear to be gratuities but they are treated for income tax purposes as a reward for services (like wages). The same is true of most prizes. However, an award such as a university scholarship, requiring no service from the recipient is classed as a genuine gratuity. Sums received for correct answers in a radio quiz have in some cases been held gifts rather than compensation; those paid by corporations to widows of deceased executives are generally treated as gifts at least so far as the donee is concerned. Contributions are gifts to organized charities (or the like) and are deductible within limits and under certain conditions as indicated below. Support consists of maintenance for near relatives and is covered by a flat allowance for dependents.

Deductions. The second set of subtractions from gross income is the deductions. There are two kinds of deductions. The first consists of the expenses incurred in creating the income—the negative items that must be offset against the positive ones to give an algebraic total. As a rule, all business and professional expenses are deductible. These include wages paid out, depreciation on capital, business insurance, interest, taxes, rent, bad debts written off, and so on. Professional expenses include cost of operating automobiles necessary for professional use, subscriptions to professional magazines and books, expenses of attending professional conventions, and so on. As a rule, the living expenses of the taxpayer and his family are not deductible. These include such items as

---

[20] The exemption of the interest on state and municipal bonds is based in part on a long line of court decisions extending back to the case of *McCulloch v. Maryland* in 1819. Because of the divided sovereignty of federal and state governments, both have been precluded (with qualifications) from taxing the instrumentalities of the other (see Chapter 19).

wages to chauffeur, caretaker, maid, most medical expenses, life insurance premiums, household costs, commutation expenses, expenses of sons and daughters at college, dues to a lodge (as distinguished from a business association), and the like.

Business and professional expenses to be deductible must meet three tests. They must be an outlay in the creation of income (professional) rather than the utilization of income (personal). The distinction is not always obvious; it could be argued that the line between food for a cow (business) and food for the workingman (consumption) is arbitrary. They must be "ordinary and necessary" expenses. Outlays of a university professor to employ privately a research assistant would probably not meet the test. They must be operating rather than capital outlay, though the latter may be deducted in installments as depreciation. Thus, the expense of a new truck would not be deductible in the year of the outlay but it could be deducted over the years as the capital depreciated. Capital expenses is distinguished from maintenance and repair (sometimes with difficulty); the latter are deductible annually.

The second class of deductions might be called privileged personal expenses. These items are not logically deductible in calculating net income; they are certain dispositions of net income that are privileged by statute. In some countries they are largely disallowed. Logically, interest on a loan acquired to purchase a home or a family automobile is disposition of income rather than expense in creating income. Nevertheless, it is a deductible expense, as are state and local taxes on these consumption goods. The federal government permits the deduction of all taxes except death, gift, federal income and excise taxes, and taxes assessed against local benefits (special assessments). Medical expenses within lower and upper limits are deductible. The objective here apparently is to confine the benefit to cases of catastrophic illness.[21] Minnesota allows the deduction without limits.

Included among deductions of the second class are contributions to educational, religious, charitable, and other similar organizations. These contributions, however, may not exceed a certain percentage of the taxpayer's income. Moreover, the philanthropic organization must not devote its resources substantially to influence legislation. The rule has been that outlays to influence legislation were not deductible and that they rendered an organization ineligible for tax-exempt contributions. (However, the Revenue Act of 1962 made direct lobbying expense deductible). Thus outlays of public utilities designed to influence public opinion

---

[21] Medical expenses in excess of 3 percent of adjusted gross income and not to exceed $5000 on a separate return, $10,000 on a joint return, additional $5000 for dependents, over-all $20,000. Deduction for drugs and medicine is limited to the excess above 1 percent of income.

against public power is not deductible. Income of trusts and corporations dedicated exclusively to exempt purposes is ordinarily not taxable, but an exception is made where such organizations carry on business unrelated to their purposes (as a college operating a factory for income). Donations to college fraternities are in the twilight zone; the regulations hold that these organizations are principally social and that donations to them are not deductible. Contributions to the League of Women Voters are now held deductible.

In lieu of itemized deductions of the second class the taxpayer may take what is known as the standard deduction. It allows an arbitrary 10 percent of income limited to $500 deductible on a separate and $1000 on a joint return. This simplified procedure designed to accommodate a mass tax has obvious advantages, but it does cover up certain real differences among taxpayers that were formerly recognized.

Some of the most interesting cases of income tax accounting arise on the farm. Thus, for instance, the pay of a "hired man" is obviously deductible but the pay of a "hired girl" might be a mixed business and personal outlay requiring a proration. In so far as the hired girl contributes to the farm work (including the portion of her time given to take care of the hired man), her pay is deductible. Much the same problem arises in connection with the farm house.

MISCELLANEOUS OTHER PROVISIONS

Losses not in excess of positive items are ordinarily deductible, and some net losses may be carried forward and backward to the account of other years. Losses of several varieties, each with its own rules, are recognized; they include business losses, capital losses (from a sale of capital assets), bad debts written off, and casualty losses as from collision, theft, fire, or flood. A first-rate flood may create a substantial loss to the government as well as to private parties. Theft cases frequently involve difficulty with respect to adequacy of evidence.

Taxpayers are allowed to use either accrual or cash accounting in calculating annual income. The former allots expenses and income to time periods in which they were incurred; the latter to the time period when payment is made. Thus, under accrual accounting, wages that were earned in one year and paid in the next may be attributed both as expense and income to the first year. Also, accounts receivable are income in the year when they arise. However, under a principle which is known as *constructive receipt of income,* certain accruals such as uncashed bond coupons are always treated as income when due.

Personal Allowances and Other Credits. Gross income minus these various subtractions give the taxpayer's net income (for tax purposes).

However, additional credits for the taxpayer, his spouse, and dependents are allowed before the actual base is reached. These are presently $600 for each such allowance. Dependents as now defined include any close relative earning less than $600 and relying mainly on the taxpayer for support. In the case of children under 19 years of age (or older, if a student) the exemption is allowed on the sole criterion of major support.

Calculation of the Tax.   After credits are subtracted, the sum remaining is called net taxable income and is the tax base. If Mr. Smith has a gross income of $16,000, of which $1000 is not subject to tax, and if he has deductible business expenses of $5000, privileged personal expenses of $1000, and credits of $2000, his tax base will be derived as follows:

Gross income	$16,000
Income not taxed	1,000
Gross income for tax purposes	$15,000
Deductible business expenses	5,000
Deductible personal expenses	1,000
Net income for tax purposes	$9,000
Personal allowance (credit)	2,000
Tax base	$7,000

If this base is subject to a tax of 20 percent on the first $2000 of taxable income, 22 percent on the second $2000, 26 percent on the third $2000, and 30 percent on the fourth $2000 [22] the tax would be computed as follows:

$2000 × 20%	$400
2000 × 22%	440
2000 × 26%	520
1000 × 30%	300
Total	$1660

CORPORATE TAXES

By far the greater part of American business is now carried on by corporations. For taxation purposes these corporations are treated as entities separate from their stockholders. However, most of the procedure in calculating income taxes, as described above, applies also to corporate income taxes.

---

[22] The law also allows a married taxpayer or head of a household the privilege of attributing part of his income to his spouse or dependent. This will be explained in more detail later.

For many years corporations were taxed at a flat rate, but in 1935 a graduated rate scale was introduced. The 1936 law added another innovation in the imposition of a special surtax on undistributed corporate income, graduated according to the ratio of such income to total income. This feature proved highly controversial and was first mitigated and then dropped. Currently the corporate income tax is graduated; a rate of 30 percent applies to income up to $25,000; income in excess of this amount pays 52 percent. During the Korean war, an excess profits tax (now repealed)—with a rate of 30 percent of the "excess" as defined—was added to the corporate income tax. This made possible a marginal rate of 82 percent, but the effective over-all rate was limited by a ceiling to approximately 70 percent. Corporate taxes are in addition to personal taxes on dividends except for a small dividend-received credit (explained later). An excess profits tax was also imposed during World Wars I and II.[23]

PRESENT STATE AND MUNICIPAL INCOME TAXES

The character and procedure of state income taxes are similar in many respects to those of the federal tax, although the rates of the former are much lower (seldom exceeding 10 percent) and the personal exemptions are generally higher. Many of the prominent industrial states such as Illinois, Michigan, Indiana, and Ohio do not tax net income at all. Most states having a tax on personal income also levy a corporate income tax either with flat or graduated rates, predominantly the former.

As previously mentioned, the inauguration in 1939 of the Philadelphia net income tax marked the first use in the United States of this revenue source by a municipality. Pennsylvania has no state personal income tax and permits its municipalities to tax (with some limitations) any subject not taxed by the state. The rates applied have varied from 1 to 1.5 percent; no exemptions are allowed and deductions are confined to expenses involved in making the income. The tax applies to residents and nonresidents, and much is made of the fact that the levy enables the city to collect from those who earn in the city but live in the suburbs. Much of the tax is collected at the source. Receipts have been substantial and have relieved the city of extreme financial difficulties. The passage of enabling legislation in 1947 led to the use of the local income tax by many municipalities in Pennsylvania. A considerable number of municipalities outside Pennsylvania, such as Toledo, have also experimented with this levy using a somewhat broader base (including corporate income) and in some cases a personal exemption.

---

[23] These taxes and other levies which apply in certain circumstances will be explained in more detail later.

CONCEPTS OF NET INCOME

Although the authors of the Civil War income tax laws, the statutes of 1894, of 1913, and of subsequent years have all sought to tax net income as it represents ability to pay, the measures have differed considerably in their concepts and definitions of a proper income tax base. The failure of the legislators to follow a consistent rule has been due partly to the difficulty of deciding what constitutes net income. This is not surprising since even specialists on the subject cannot come to an agreement. The following paragraphs will be devoted to a discussion of some of the problems which must be faced in deciding what constitutes net income.

Receipts in Kind. Need receipts be money to constitute net income? The answer is clearly no. Receipts in the form of house use, services, produce, or securities are quite as much net income as money. Money's worth is equivalent to cash as far as net income is concerned.

However, there are two exceptions to the general rule. Advantages of employment not customarily reckoned in money are disregarded. Thus, the fact that a position may provide its holder with much prestige and offer a beautiful city in which to work are not matters of significance for the income tax. However, there is a large and growing area of so-called fringe benefits that are closely related to, if not in fact, income in kind. These include such features of the labor contract as medical care and life insurance. These are occasionally taxable but usually exempt as "conditions of employment." This type of allowance is now estimated to constitute 17 percent of all wages paid.[24] Further, there are "perquisites for the benefit of the employer" that are disregarded. Lodging for an attendant at a hospital and uniforms for a professional baseball player would qualify for this classification. The recipient probably does benefit from these allowances, but he has no choice in their disposition.

Irregular Receipts. Need receipts be regular in order to constitute income, or does income include such sporadic acquisitions as prizes won, gain from the sale of investment, and so forth? In the United States it has always been held that irregularity is no "defense" in determining net income. Receipts appear to be no less income merely because they occur in one splash rather than a regular flow though, as we shall see, the former causes some special problems in the application of a graduated rate. In Great Britain the opposite rule prevailed for many years but no longer survives.

---

[24] Chamber of Commerce, *Fringe Benefits—1955* (Washington, D.C., 1956), p. 34.

Illegitimate Receipts.   Must receipts be legitimate in order to constitute income? Again the answer is no. On one occasion, the Supreme Court was asked to pass on the question of whether a bootlegger must report his "bootleg" income. It was argued in defense of the taxpayer that no one is required under our law to incriminate himself. Justice Holmes, in delivering the opinion of the Court, stated that the income must be reported, but that the taxpayer, to avoid incrimination, might object to labeling its source in the return.[25] The rule is that illegal expenses are not deductible. Thus, money spent in the bribery of public officials would be disallowed as a deduction for the "bribor," but it would be taxable to the "bribee." Close questions have arisen in connection with black-market operations and some decisions have allowed illegal costs as a deduction against illegal receipts. The issue seems to turn on whether the expense as such is illegal or only an offset to an illegal gain. Gambling losses may be offset against gambling gains.[26] There is also a question of whether the nondeductibility feature covers illegitimate as well as illegal outlay (for example, medical "kickbacks" condemned by professional codes of ethics). Of course, the problem of taxing illegitimate income is more administrative than conceptual. However, many recipients of illegitimate income are quite willing to "play square with the revenue" providing collectors will not disclose information to police and prosecuting attorneys. But this raises a difficult question of cooperation among government officials.

Services without Exchange.   Must there be an exchange to create an income? The answer in this case is mixed and confused. One phase of the problem concerns the value of produce raised in the taxpayer's own garden and consumed by him and his family. Under the federal law this need not be reported.

In the United States, as contrasted with England, the rental value of a house occupied by its owner is not included as income. This creates inequality between the person who has invested in a home and one who has invested in other property and lives in rented apartments. The first need not report the rent saved as income, whereas the latter must include the rent or interest received as positive income and cannot deduct rent paid out as an expense. Thus, one way to "beat" the income tax in the United States is to own one's home. The services of the housewife to her family are nowhere counted as income, to the author's knowledge, but ignoring them produces the anomalous situation that were housewives to

---

[25] *United States v. Sullivan,* 274 U.S. 259 (1927).

[26] In certain countries, such as Australia and New Zealand, gambling gains are not considered income; this is perhaps dubious policy considering the penalties placed on legitimate acquisition.

keep each other's houses for pay, the national income (for taxation and statistical purposes) would rise sharply.

Obviously, a line must be drawn somewhere in reckoning as income the services of consumption goods used by their owners. The services of one's own automobile, clothing, and furniture are income in the broadest sense. One writer has suggested that we should consider the use of leisure time as income.[27] If *A* and *B* receive the same amount of money each year but *A* gets a week's vacation, does not *A* receive more than *B*? Similarly, if *A* is able to earn in 8 hours what *B* earns in 10 hours, does not *A* receive a larger income?

Probably practical considerations make it inadvisable to refine the income tax base to include many of the services that the taxpayer receives without exchange. The British rule with regard to houses, however, seems much better than that of the United States and worth its extra administrative difficulty.

Receipts of Cooperatives. An interesting problem of definition arises in the application of income taxes to cooperative business. Under the cooperative system of doing business, a group of consumers may unite to buy or manufacture goods at cost. Frequently the prices of these goods are so adjusted that a surplus remains, the disposition of which is within the discretion of the board of directors. It may be distributed to consumers in proportion to their purchases; it may be distributed to stockholders in proportion to their stock (not exceeding, in some cases, a top rate); or the board may retain the surplus as a reserve, to be used for expansion of the business or to dispense free services of a social or educational character. Cooperatives contend that when business is carried on by and for consumers there can be no profit or net income in any true sense. They say that this is particularly true of patronage dividends, which are the cooperative way of buying at a bargain. Competitors of cooperatives are likely to feel that acceptance of this view in income taxation would give cooperatives an unfair advantage; that the latter produce the same kind of services which give rise to taxable income when produced by ordinary businesses. However, even the competitors of cooperatives and their customers pay no tax on refunds similar to patronage dividends, such as those occurring through the use of trading stamps. Moreover, were cooperatives subject to tax on retroactive price cutting, they would be in position to avoid an income tax by cutting prices directly. This, however, would involve inconvenience and risk for the cooperatives.

Under the present federal income tax (and most other income taxes

---

[27] Henry C. Simons, *Personal Income Taxation* (Chicago: University of Chicago Press, 1938), p. 111.

in other countries), patronage dividends and reserves allotted to patrons are deductible to the cooperative, and they are taxable to the recipient only if they are incident to production. Thus, a farmer pays on patronage dividends arising out of the purchase of farm supplies but not on those due to the purchase of groceries. Dividends on cooperative stock (ordinary dividends) are neither deductible to the corporation nor exempt to the recipient.

The income tax, as can be seen, is primarily adapted to a market economy. As applied to a self-sufficing economy or cooperative economy, it works rather imperfectly.

Impairment of Capital. Most income tax laws accept the proposition that receipts may not be considered as income until allowance has been made for maintenance, depreciation, depletion, and obsolescence. These allowances are based on the theory that the tax is not to be levied on capital but only on the income produced by that capital; and that, therefore, all impairment of capital must be considered as negative income. *A* starts in business with $100,000 of capital and makes $10,000, but at the expense of a reduction in the value of his capital to the extent of $5000. He is less fortunate than *B,* who, with the same capital and the same receipts, suffers no impairment of capital. Now, capital may be impaired in a number of ways. One is that it may wear out as a result of service. This is called *depreciation.* Another way in which impairment occurs is through the sale of capital, piece by piece. This is called *depletion;* it occurs in the case of mineral and forest resources. A third cause of impairment presents itself when capital gradually becomes antiquated, or out of date. This is called *obsolescence.*

The income tax makes allowance for all these impairments. Reasonable maintenance and depreciation are legitimate deductions before arriving at net income. This is also true of obsolescence, although as an administrative matter the law may require that it must be realized (rather than anticipated) before a deduction will be allowed.

Depreciation accounting involves many questions of policy and definition that are troublesome for income tax legislation and administration. The method and timing of the deductions is sure to be a source of considerable argument. For example, two alternative methods employed are *straight-line* depreciation and the *diminishing-balances* method. The first simply amortizes cost in even per annum amounts over the expected life of the asset. The second applies a constant percentage deduction to the original value of the asset minus previous deductions. (Thus with cost at $100 and depreciation at 5 percent, the allowance for the first year would be 5 percent of $100 and that for the second year, 5 percent of $95). The second method writes off more than a proportionate share of value in the early years.

This introduces *accelerated depreciation* which is a term applied to any scheme that aims to telescope the write-off. Before 1954 this procedure had been allowed for new capital of military significance. Since 1954, all business taxpayers have been allowed to use various depreciation devices (including the diminishing-balances method) in a manner which would write off about two thirds of the value of new assets during the first half of the expected life of such equipment. The mortality table for different assets is a highly important aspect of the problem. The Treasury revised its standards in 1962 and the liberalization was estimated to cost the revenue well over $1 billion.

This new privilege of so-called accelerated depreciation is most plausibly defended on the ground that new equiment does, as an economic fact, lose value most rapidly in the early years. Empirical evidence from second-hand markets is submitted to support this allegation. An early write-off is also said to promote modernization of plant, thus keeping the economy dynamic. It encourages investment by reducing risk and providing more capital from internal sources (especially important for young and growing companies). Finally, it is said that the program involves no permanent loss of revenue since value written off can never exceed 100 percent.

Critics of the new privileges with regard to depreciation deny that the latter involve no loss to the revenue; there might be no loss in the case of a particular asset, but the point does not hold for a firm or the economy as a whole. In the case of a continuing business the revenue never catches up, so to speak, with its loss. Confining the program to new assets is said to discriminate unfairly among competitors. Investment might better be encouraged by reducing rates and perhaps needs no encouragement during a period of inflation.

Investment allowances differ from accelerated depreciation in that they provide for a percentage write-off at the time an asset is purchased in addition to full depreciation over the years. In effect they constitute an overt subsidy, and they aim at stimulating investment, especially in new equipment at a strategic time. They were introduced in the United States by the Revenue Act of 1962, which provided a tax credit for new equipment amounting to 7 percent of the outlay. (Since the basis for subsequent depreciation was to be 93 percent of purchase price, the subsidy in effect amounted to $3\frac{1}{2}$ percent). Much was made of the contention that the credit would help firms meet foreign competition and provide the incentive to keep abreast with technological progress. Objection contended that free enterprise should need no prodding to make replacements that are economically sound.

Replacement depreciation differs from accelerated depreciation in that it aims to allow deductions not only sufficient to return the taxpayer's capital in money but also in purchasing power. In times of severe inflation, ordinary depreciation will prove insufficient to cover replacement at a new level of prices. Replacement depreciation encounters many practical difficulties, among them the fact that new equipment may not be strictly comparable to the old in terms of efficiency.

Theoretically, *depletion* should be calculated at cost to the taxpayer of capital units sold. Actually, it is sometimes calculated on the basis of value at the time of discovery or as an arbitrary percentage of gross income. Percentage depletion in the United States is a very controversial area; it is criticized as arbitrary and overgenerous (frequently many times the actual cost). It is defended as a necessary incentive for the rapid exploitation of natural resources that are highly strategic for economic growth and the war effort. Opponents answer that military strategy would be served by conservation of these resources (more taxes, more imports, and less consumption attending higher prices). Proponents claim that the extractive businesses are unique in many ways including a high element of risk; opponents answer that the oil stocks of large companies qualify as a conservative investment and anyway the free market has its own method of adjusting prices and values to the special difficulties of doing business.[28]

Inventory Valuation.   Inventory profits are an unstable and speculative source of business profits, and some businesses have sought to reduce them to a minimum by last-in-first-out accounting (*lifo*). Inventory profits arise because of a rise in prices during the time businesses are processing or moving merchandise. They are unreal in the sense that they provide only the capital needed to maintain a stock of goods no larger than normal. Under *lifo,* the cost of each unit sold is considered to be the cost of a new unit presently added to the chain of units going through the plant. Thus, in Figure 16, if historical costing is used (first-in-first-out, or *fifo*) the inventory profit of Unit *A* is $1, but if replacement cost is used the profit is eliminated. If the unit sold is considered to be the one most recently purchased, much the same result is achieved. The process in effect creates a reserve out of inventory profits when prices are rising and uses it to offset losses when prices are falling. The system was originally used only by concerns producing homogeneous units but, with the aid of a price index, it is now used by department stores (though by no means universally).

The authorization to use *lifo* accounting for income tax purposes is criticized [29] on the score that it favors large concerns that are in the best

[28] See *Federal Tax Policy for Economic Growth and Stability*, Joint Committee on the Economic Report, 84th Cong., 1st Sess., 1955, pp. 419–504.

[29] Richard Goode, *The Corporation Income Tax* (New York: John Wiley & Sons, Inc., 1951), pp. 169–171.

position to take advantage of its complicated procedure. It is also argued that it postpones taxes during the upswing of the business cycle, thus tending to aggravate the swing. But in rebuttal to these contentions it may be replied that *lifo* only postpones (does not forgive) taxes and that accounting practices which avoid fictitious profits during upswings prevent undue optimism at the stock exchange.

FIGURE 16

Flow of Goods through a Plant's Inventory Pipeline

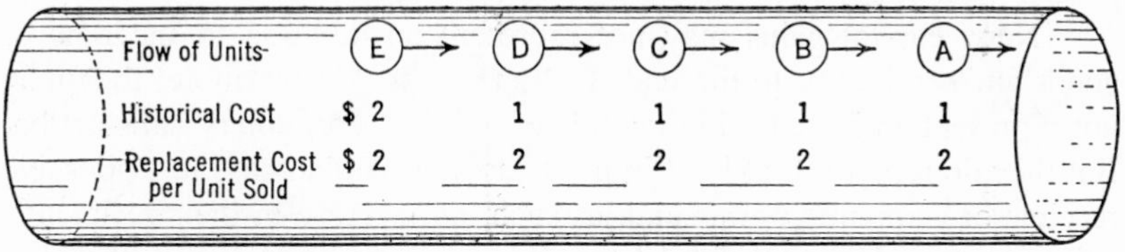

Flow of Units	E	D	C	B	A
Historical Cost	$ 2	1	1	1	1
Replacement Cost per Unit Sold	$ 2	2	2	2	2

Inventory Profits:

Under	f-i-f-o	$ 0	1	1	1	1
	l-i-f-o	$ 0	0	0	0	0

Capital Gains and Losses. There has been considerable discussion of whether capital gains and losses should be included in income for taxation and other purposes. Capital gains and losses occur when an individual sells for a profit or loss what is ordinarily retained as a source of income. They arise not as a flow of income from the fountain, but from the sales of the fountain itself. More specifically, they arise as a rule when an owner sells real estate or securities. They may also arise when the owner sells a factory or a machine. If the owner of a shoe factory sells shoes, his receipts are ordinary income, but if he sells a shoe machine he may have a capital gain or loss. On the other hand, a factory that manufactures shoe machines makes ordinary income rather than a capital gain or loss from their sale.

It is contended by some that a capital gain is not income. Before discussing this matter it must be pointed out that there are many definitions of income, but that most of them fall under three classes. First, there are the definitions that contemplate income as a flow of goods and services from a stock of capital, measured in monetary terms. This is the statistical concept used by economists who attempt to measure the national income from year to year. More precisely, it is that amount of production which the community can consume without impairing its stock of capital.[30] Second, there are the definitions that regard income as the money value of the goods and services that represent the realiza-

---

[30] *Survey of Current Business,* National Income Supplement, July 1947, p. 11.

tion of consumers' satisfaction. According to this view, frequently associated with Professor Irving Fisher,[31] savings are not income. Third,
there are the definitions that view income as the amount of money received by an individual to be allocated by him between consumption and
saving—that is, as that amount that is available for disposal by him between two points of time without his being worse off at the end of the
period than he was at the beginning. We assume that he disposes of his
income with a view to maximizing his satisfaction, whether it be through
consumption or saving. It is this latter concept upon which taxation is
generally based.

Now, capital gains may not represent an addition to the flow of
goods and services or to the real stock of wealth. Furthermore, they may
not represent an increase in the scale of living or consumers' satisfaction.
But they do represent, at least in most cases, a real increase in disposable
receipts or economic power and, as such, an increase in their recipient's
ability to pay. Under the third type of definition cited above, they are
most assuredly income.

Approaching the matter from another angle, it is possible to conceive income from either of two viewpoints—the social or the individual.
There may be considerable doubt as to whether capital gains should be
reckoned as income from the social point of view. There is, however,
far less question about including such gains as income from the individual
point of view.

Exclusion of "Unrealized" Gains and Losses. Viewing income as economic power, capital gains should theoretically be included as income,
whether they are "realized" or not—that is, whether or not there has
been an exchange. This would necessitate an inventory of all one's capital
goods each year and the change in inventory values from one year to another would be reckoned as income. Such procedure may now be followed in the case of merchandise inventories, but it would involve very
great (not to say insuperable) difficulties of appraisal in so far as capital
goods are concerned. Thus, because of the practical difficulties, only
realized capital gains, as appraised by an exchange, are considered as
income. Some economists have recommended that capital gains, whether
or not realized, should be included as income, but the consensus would
probably hold the suggestion impractical.

Contention That Capital Gains Are Illusory Income. Those who argue
that capital gains are not income may contend that these receipts do not
represent real increases in the national wealth or welfare. It is argued that

---

[31] Irving Fisher, "Income in Theory and Income Taxation in Practice," *Econometrica*, V (January 1937), pp. 47–48. For a counterargument, see Philip E.
Taylor, *The Economics of Public Finance* (New York: The Macmillan Company,
1948), pp. 397–401.

capital gains represent the present value of expected future income and that to tax both them and the future income is most assuredly double counting. If an owner's real estate doubles in value, it is probably because a prospect for higher future rents has developed. It would be double counting to consider both the anticipation and the realization as income.

Suppose that Mr. Smith goes into business and invests $100,000 in the venture. Suppose he loses money steadily for five years, say $20,000 each year, but that at the end of this period he has built up such fine prospects for the future that he is able to sell his business to Jones for $100,000 more than he originally invested. The layman would certainly conclude that Smith had come out even on his five-years' venture and that at the moment of sale neither he nor Jones, nor the country, were any poorer as a result of the venture. Yet some would consider it double counting to offset Smith's capital gain against his operating loss. This is the same double counting that some economists object to in treating saving as income. A $100,000 saving and investment adds to economic power only because it offers prospects for the future. However, if we accept power as the criterion of income, we need not be concerned about double counting in either case.

It is true, of course, that capital gains may be due to changes in the general price level and that in this case they are illusory gains. For example, a building may rise in value for no reason other than that the measuring stick has changed—that is, that the value of money itself has fallen. The building may represent the same purchasing power in terms of all other goods (except money) that it did previously. In this case the owner of the building has really gained nothing in terms of economic power. But there are many real changes in economic power that result from changes in the general price level. Unfortunately, it does not seem possible to segregate the real gains from the illusory ones.

INCOME TAX ADMINISTRATION

Many nineteenth- and early twentieth-century critics of the income tax recognized its theoretical virtues, but opposed it on practical grounds that the facts of income could not be ascertained with a suitable score of precision; that it would require a repugnant system of inquisition and espionage; and that after creating a nation of liars, it would end as a heavy and unequal burden on the conscientious. Although these concerns have been mitigated by what appears to be years of successful experience, they are not entirely dissolved even today. Studies of income reported on income tax returns matched with that estimated by the Department of Commerce have suggested that compliance may range from less than 50 percent in the case of farm income, interest, and rent to about 95 percent in the case of wages.[32] However, it should be said that these data are not entirely conclusive nor do they suggest an overall leakage of more than some 10 percent.

Collection at the Source. The phrase "collection at the source" (withholding) is used to describe the method of collecting taxes from the payers of income rather than from the payees. For example, in the case of wages, taxes are collected from the employer rather than the employee; in the case of rent, from the tenant rather than the landlord; in the case of interest, from the debtor rather than the creditor; and in the case of dividends, from the corporation rather than the stockholder. Instead of paying a workman his full wages, the employer may pay him wages minus the tax, which goes to the government.

Collection at the source offers the advantages of convenient payment, minimum delinquency, and minimum avoidance. Third parties usually have no interest in defeating the claims of the government. The disadvantages are the complications of applying a scale of exemptions and graduated rates to payments by third parties in such a way as to collect the proper tax without supplementary returns or refunds. The latter can be avoided by confining the collection to only part of the expected tax. A further disadvantage is that a substantial compliance cost is created for those who collect at the source.

For many years after the adoption of the American income tax, collection at the source was not applied, although precedent for its successful application had long existed in Europe. During World War II the federal government inaugurated the use of the system in the taxation of wages and salaries. This is called a *withholding levy*. Currently there is substantial support for the extension of withholding to interest and dividends where evasion of tax appears to be considerable. The states now predominately use withholding as to wages, and this technique is regarded as the backbone of administration at the municipal level. Most states that have adopted withholding have reported reduced evasion and collection problems.

World War II also inaugurated "current payment" of the tax. Under the former practice income earned in January 1940 was not reported until fifteen months later (March 1941), and the tax could be paid in installments after reporting. This permitted ability to pay to become "cold" before it was "tapped" by the tax system, and it impeded the use of the income tax as an anti-inflation device to draw off excess purchasing

---

[32] Selma F. Goldsmith, "Appraisal of Basic Data Available for Constructing Income Size Distributions," *Conference on Research in Income and Wealth* (New York: National Bureau of Economic Research, 1951), vol. 13, pp. 267–377.

power. The present system collects currently from wage and salary earners through withholding and from others by advance estimates and quarterly payment of taxes as they accrue.

Information at the Source. In lieu of collection at the source, income tax statutes may employ what is known as "information at the source." Taxpayers who pay out interest, wages, or rents to others are required to report such payments, together with the names and addresses of the payees. This would seem to be an effective substitute for collection at the source, at least as far as the ascertainment of income is concerned. Sometimes, however, a vast amount of information is collected and not utilized. Where the information-at-the-source reports are filed with the individual's reports, which is now the rule in the case of the federal and some state administrations, they are a very great aid to income tax administration.

Information returns can be processed economically by improved office machinery. In a day when federal and state taxes have mass application, mass techniques of enforcement have become a practical necessity. Much more information might be sought and matched than is now available. For instance, it would not seem impossible to secure complete information on the payment of interest by corporations to their bondholders. The owners of bonds are now cloaked with anonymity; this is not true of stockholders, however, though in some countries (for example, France), the latter also hold "bearer" securities.

Audits. Neither collection at the source nor information at the source can be applied to all income. It cannot be applied, for example, to business and professional income because to do so would decentralize rather than centralize collection. Objective information concerning such income is usually sought by auditing. Two kinds of audits occur: office audits and field audits. The first consists of checking the taxpayer's return for errors on its face; the second consists of checking the taxpayer's books. The chief difficulty with auditing is that it is expensive. Thus far only a small proportion of individual returns have been thoroughly examined and a still smaller proportion have been subjected to field audit. Income tax administrators are able to demonstrate that additional outlay for auditing pays handsome returns and improves the morale of *all* taxpayers, not only those audited. Nevertheless, federal income tax administration has been persistently undermanned partly because of inadequate appropriations and partly because of inability to recruit needed personnel. Taxpayers are obliged at their peril to maintain adequate records, but some—particularly farmers, professional and unincorporated businesses—frequently keep very informal books, and there is not always an adequate check as to what is and is not entered.

Some years ago the Internal Revenue Service initiated an extremely useful and sensible project to aid in directing and appraising auditing effort. This was called the audit control program, an intensive examination of a small, representative sample of returns to indicate the magnitude of determinable income tax errors and the relative gain in employing auditors' time at various possible points.[33]

Income tax administration in certain countries such as France has proved a grievous problem; bookkeeping is exceptional, most transactions are by cash payment rather than by check; and attitudes toward the revenue are notoriously negative.

Penalties. An administrative feature which is at least necessary and sometimes also effective is the penalties prescribed by law and enforced by administrators with the aid of the courts. Two types of penalties are distinguished: civil and criminal. Both include and the latter exclusively deals with fraud, which implies an evil state of mind, "a wilful attempt to evade tax." Criminal penalties in the federal law extend to a fine of not more than $10,000 or imprisonment not to exceed five years or both. Civil action for fraud is similar but requires less substantial evidence. Civil action also includes the lesser offense of negligence which covers evasion without intent to defraud but with oversights that would not be expected of a reasonably prudent person. Federal civil penalty for negligence is 5 percent of deficient tax to which may be added 5 percent per month of delay not exceeding a total of 25 percent if the evader was delinquent in filing a return. Civil penalty for fraud is 50 percent of deficient tax, and none of these penalties are exclusive of others. An interesting question of litigation arises where the taxpayer relies upon qualified counsel; usually this is an adequate defense. The criminal statute permits action against other persons than the taxpayer, including husbands, corporate officials, and counselors who abet others in evading taxes.

Net Worth Assessment: Doomage Power. Another device used to obtain an objective check upon income is the net worth assessment. Anyone who is suspected of failure to report income may be audited as to net worth at two different points of time. The net increase plus estimated living expenses afford a basis for estimating his income. Books and bank deposit accounts must be made available for such an audit.

Taxpayers sometimes attempt to explain augmented wealth without income on the ground that they received a gift from a dying parent or found a hidden treasure. The evidence in these cases is circumstantial,

---

[33] Marius Farioletti, "Some Results From the First Year's Audit Control Program of the Bureau of Internal Revenue," *National Tax Journal,* V: I (March 1952), pp. 65–78; *The Audit Control Program, A Summary of Preliminary Results,* Bureau of Internal Revenue, 1951.

but it will be accepted to maintain the tax if the fundamental facts and a plausible source of the increment can be established.

Taxpayers who refuse to cooperate in providing information are subject to the doomage power under which an assessment based on the assessor's "best guess" is valid.

Public Inspection. Much argument has surrounded the question of whether tax return should be available to public inspection. The rule is to hold income tax information strictly confidential, available at most to various government officials. This is thought to promote a full disclosure of facts by the taxpayer. On the other hand, the opposite course tends to promote public confidence in the integrity of the administration. Recent disclosures of graft and indiscretion in Washington brought proposals that all public officials make full disclosure of their incomes. Publicity is not to be underrated for its therapeutic value. Wisconsin allowed free inspection of its state income tax returns for many years, then required a modest fee, and now allows no inspection except by public officials.

Self-reporting: Attitude of Taxpayer. It will be observed that there is very little income for which there is no objective information and for which complete reliance must be placed upon the honesty of the taxpayer. It should be said, however, that in practice much reliance is placed upon self-reporting since there are many returns of small business-men, professional men, and farmers that are never supplemented with a personal audit.

Two attitudes toward the payment of taxes are common, and one or the other is likely to predominate in a given country with very great effect on income tax administration. One attitude regards taxation as a manifestation of tyranny and the revenue as an abstraction that may be robbed with good conscience. Taxation is a sort of game like that which sometimes goes on between a stupid pupil and a poor teacher. The other attitude regards taxation as a self-imposed discipline and cheating the revenue on a par with cheating one's neighbors. Were there no private acquiescence in the income tax, this type of levy would hardly be practical.

The British system of income-tax administration—said to be the envy of the world—owes its success to the following factors: (1) use of a law especially designed to be administrable, with its flat rate on the great mass of small and moderate-sized incomes; (2) the wide use of withholding; (3) decentralized administration (there are some 140 offices and districts in London alone); and (4) the quantity and quality of its civil service.[34]

---

[34] Administrative Machinery. Federal income tax administration, originally highly centralized, has now moved into the field partly to meet the convenience

PROBLEMS

1. In a certain year Mr. Jones has a net income from the following sources in the amounts specified:

Interest of federal World War savings bonds	$ 100.00
Interest on City of Los Angeles bonds	100.00
Dividends from the Burlington Railroad	100.00
Gross income from grocery business	5000.00

Mr. Jones has the following expenses:

Automobile expense and depreciation		$ 500.00
Addition to the store building		1000.00
Fuel, light, and water for the store		200.00
Depreciation on store building		400.00
Dues to the Rotary Club		20.00
Subscription to magazines:		
Fortune	$10.00	
Retail Grocers' Review	3.00	13.00
Expenses of unsuccessful candidacy for mayor		25.00
Property tax on his residence		200.00
Expenses of son at college		200.00

Mr. Jones is married and has a dependent son. If personal credits of $600 for himself and each dependent are allowed and if the tax rates are 10 percent on the first $2000 of taxable income and 15 percent on the second $2000 of taxable income, what tax will Mr. Jones have to pay?

2. A businessman has gross receipts from his business of $10,000, cost of goods sold of $3000, wages paid of $1000, and other ordinary and necessary business expenses of $1000. He has contributions of $200 and taxes on his home of $200. If he decides to use the standard deduction (short form) what will be his net income tax base?

3. Distinguish gifts, contributions, and compensation. What are the policy problems in treating gifts?

4. Comment on the proposition: The value of clean toilets at a place of work need not be included in gross income for income tax purposes.

---

of millions of taxpayers under a mass tax. Most responsibility is now centered in sixty-four districts with a district director in charge of collecting, auditing, intelligence, and the other main functions of income tax administration. The districts are under the supervision of nine regional offices whose function is largely supervisory. The national office in Washington develops the broad program and coordinates operations; it has charge of editing the Regulations and Statistics of Income; it deals with Congress. By any standards, the Federal Internal Revenue Service is an immense undertaking.

5. Mr. Smith, a farmer, provides a new roof for both his barn and his house. Is this expense deductible on his income tax return?

6. On what ground is it said that to be your own landlord is an innocent form of tax avoidance?

7. An heir to a sum of money invests it in a home. The money is insufficient to pay for the full cost of the home, and the heir borrows on a mortgage for the remainder. He pays interest on the mortgage and also property taxes on the home. Later he sells the property for substantially more than he paid for it, but buys another home at the same time of a similar character and costing as much as he received on the first sale. Consider the tax issues involved in this case.

8. Is the permission to use *lifo* accounting for income tax determination in the public interest?

9. It is said that a net income tax is levied on gross receipts minus expenses involved in creating the income. Cite two deductions from gross income allowed in federal personal net income taxation that do not follow this rule, that is, they are not expenses involved in creating the income.

10. Cooperatives argue that they really make little profit since they give away most of what they make to their customers. Why don't other (non-cooperative) businesses use the same technique to avoid taxes?

11. Distinguish among accelerated depreciation, replacement depreciation, calculation of depreciation by diminishing balances, and percentage depletion. What social objectives may be served by wise policy in depreciation allowance?

12. Comment on the proposition: Percentage depletion at present rates is a plausible recognition of the high risks encountered by the major oil companies.

13. Comment on the proposition: Neither accelerated depreciation nor percentage depletion allow the recovery of wasting assets beyond the cost of the assets.

14. Accelerated depreciation is a matter of timing a deduction rather than its cumulative amount; it follows that the Treasury will experience only a postponement and no ultimate loss of receipts. Comment.

15. Comment on the proposition: Free enterprise under conditions of adequate competition should need no special incentives in the form of investment allowances to keep abreast of technological progress.

16. Comment on the proposition: Investment allowances by stimulating investment in new equipment will cause unemployment.

17. Under what circumstances might capital gains be regarded as fictitious income?

18. Distinguish between collection at the source and current payment. Why are these techniques of administration regarded as important in the control of the business cycle?

19. It is often argued that the income tax is fair enough in principle but grossly unfair in practice because of evasion. Could the validity of this contention be tested and if so, how?

8

APPLICATIONS OF THE INCOME TAX TO CAPITAL GAINS, CORPORATIONS, AND THEIR SECURITYHOLDERS

The previous chapter introduced the income tax and treated some of its problems of definition and administration. The present chapter will be devoted principally to the application of the income tax to capital gains and losses, to corporations and their stockholders.

CAPITAL GAINS AND LOSSES

TREATMENT OF CAPITAL GAINS AND LOSSES IN THE TAX LAWS

The treatment of capital gains and losses (usually gains or losses incidental to the sale of securities or real estate) is one of the most difficult issues in personal income taxation. The canons of simplicity and stability have been violated frequently, and often severely, in laws covering capital gains and losses. The main methods for the taxation of capital gains include treatment of such gains like other income with no deduction for losses, taxation with full allowance for losses, and classified taxation of gains with losses deductible only against gains of a similar class. The reduction of gains and losses by percentages dependent upon the length of time the assets have been held by the taxpayer, the application of maximum rates, and the various provisions for the carry-over of losses not currently usable to offset gains have provided additional refinements. These features have been used in various combinations during the past forty years. The present law classifies gains and losses as short-term when the assets to which they pertain have been held six months or less. Short-term gains are taxed like other income. Long-term gains may be reduced to 50 percent of their amount in reckoning income subject to the regular tax, or they may be taxed separately at a maximum rate of 25 percent. The treatment of losses is parallel, except that they (whether long-term or short-term) can be deducted from capital gains in full and from other income up to a maximum of $1000. Moreover, a five-year carry-over of unused losses is permitted. The treatment of capital gains and losses for corporations is generally similar (including the provision of a 25-percent maximum rate on long-term gains), but there are some differences, such as the absence of the percentage reduction.

Capital gains are measured by the difference between the sales price of an asset and its "basis"; the latter is usually the acquisition price of the asset minus net allowances, if any, during the interim for depreciation.

A controversial point in present practice is that capital gains are wiped out or "forgiven" by a death transfer. Thus, if A buys securities for $2000, and they rise in value to $3000 before A dies, and they are later sold for $4000 by A Junior, the heir, the capital gain for income tax purposes will be $1000—not $2000. This combined with the fact that unrealized gains are not taxed means that very large amounts of such gains are never reached by the income tax. And the tax is contingent on the fortuitous factor of a sale. All that is necessary to avoid the capital gains tax entirely is to choose the right investment to begin with and hang on to it. A family fortune invested in a family business or in city real estate can grow indefinitely in value and never encounter the capital gains tax at all.

Traditionally the British and British Dominions have ignored both capital gains and losses in their income taxes. In recent years, however, the definition of a capital gain or loss has been restricted to exclude profits arising from transactions of a trading and speculative nature. Moreover, gains on securities held less than six months and real estate less than three years are now taxed (in Britain) as speculative. Critics argue that the distinction between speculative and investment gain is a dubious one.

It would also be possible to tax capital gains and allow losses through an independent tax not integrated at all with the income tax. Finally, one might apply a so-called roll-over technique, carrying forward gains where there is an exchange of investments as is now done where the taxpayer exchanges personal residences.

CHARACTERISTICS OF CAPITAL GAINS AND LOSSES

Capital gains provide a minor source of income in the economy, and they are received by relatively few taxpayers. They, however, are often a major source of income for particular individuals, and the total income derived from them is by no means negligible. Capital gains tend to be concentrated in the upper brackets of income, but capital losses are more prominent in the lower brackets.[1]

Realized capital gains and losses often have a longer periodicity than one year; they may have been accruing over a decade or more.

Realized capital gains and losses are not regularly recurrent, as is most other income. One may have a substantial gain or loss this year and never again in a lifetime. Without any averaging feature this means that capital gains may be bunched over time and treated with undue severity by the progressive tax. In the case of a group of people or that of an owner of many securities there is some degree of recurrence, but the pattern is far from regular.

Realized gains are frequently converted into new investments, whereas realized losses often result in new investment of a lesser value than the original; quite often neither is reflected in the recipient's scale or standard of living.

Realized capital gains and losses may be manipulated (to some extent) to suit the taxpaying interest of the recipients.

PROBLEMS OF CONVERSION AND DEFINITION

It is said that much of the time of a very well-paid tax bar is spent in converting ordinary income into capital gains. It is also said that the only two ways to get rich in the face of a high-powered progressive-tax system are to become the recipient of capital gains or to invest in an oil well and become the beneficiary of percentage depletion.

Most forms of conventional income can with some ingenuity and in some circumstances be converted into capital gains. Thus, the manager and principal owner of a closely held corporation can reinvest earnings rather than pay them out in salary or dividends. The sums will appear in personal account (if at all) as capital gains. A corporation may be organized to develop a property (such as a contractor building an hotel);

---

[1] Lawrence H. Seltzer, *The Nature and Tax Treatment of Capital Gains and Losses* (New York: National Bureau of Economic Research, 1951), chap. 8.

when it is completed the corporation may be liquidated, distributing the specific property (rather than cash) to the stockholders; the difference in value between the property and the original investment may be treated as a capital gain. Had the building been sold and dividends distributed, the profit would have been taxable at ordinary rates both to the company and the stockholders. This conversion device is known as the collapsible corporation; recent legislative restrictions have sought to curb its worst abuses.

A simple conversion device is the purchase below par of bonds due to mature in the near future. With a current market rate of interest at 4 percent, an old bond carrying a contract rate of interest at 3 percent and due to mature in five years, may be a better buy at a purchase price of $95 than a new 4-percent bond purchased at $100.

Among the most attractive means of converting wages to capital gains is the use of stock options in the remuneration of business executives. The options are to purchase stock at favorable prices and are usually exercisable (at the option price) over a considerable period. Stock thus acquired, when subsequently sold at a profit, yields a capital gain rather than an addition to the employee's salary. The code provides complicated boundary lines within which this conversion device may be exercised successfully.[2]

If a real estate broker has property that he customarily rents, his gain on the sale of such property is capital gain; if the property were held for sale (without renting), the gain would be business income. On the other hand, an investor in stock can count the increment on his holdings as capital gains regardless of his purpose in acquiring and holding them. If the taxpayer invents a new device and sells the patent, he may claim that his profit is a capital gain; the same rule curiously does not apply to copyrights. At one time an author could claim that he was not in the business of writing books if he wrote and expected to write only one book; in that event his royalties could be counted as capital gains.

ISSUES IN THE TAXATION OF CAPITAL GAINS

Several outstanding issues in the taxation of capital gains and losses may now be discussed.

Equity. On the grounds of equity, the case for including capital gains with other income is very strong. Most capital gains are as potent

---

[2] See Emmett Wallace, "Should We Continue to Encourage the Use of Restricted Stock Options?" *Taxes,* 39: 10 (November 1961), pp. 785–796; George E. Lent and John A. Menge, *The Importance of Restricted Stock Options in Executive Compensation,* Graduate School of Business Administration, Dartmouth College (Hanover, 1962).

as any other receipts in consumption or reinvestment. Moreover, as long as depreciation and obsolescence are recognized as (negative) income, appreciation would seem to warrant the same treatment.

To be sure, capital gains are often, as the British would say, "casual income." This means that they are often quite irregular in their realization. But most income is casual to some degree. The main objection to taxing casual income is that since it occurs irregularly, it is punished by the application of the higher rates in a progressive scale. Perhaps we need some new techniques in our income tax to permit refunds or credits where the tax on annual income over a period of years exceeds what the tax would have been on average income.[3] The development and adoption of such techniques are primary prerequisites for any reasonable and satisfactory solution to the problem of taxing capital gains.

The question arises as to whether classification according to the time factor makes sense. A rational defense may be attempted on the ground that short-term gains are likely to be more speculative than long-term ones, but this involves the issue of whether speculation is less useful than investment. Of course, gains on assets held more than a year involve bunching of income in the face of the progressive scale. The Swedes give the time factor more weight even than we do; they treat gains and losses on real estates held less than ten years (other assets, five years) as ordinary income and otherwise ignore these receipts entirely.

Discouragement of Exchanges.   Would the taxation of capital gains at full personal income tax rates greatly reduce the exchanges of investment capital and destroy the liquidity of such capital? Many have answered this question in the affirmative and have based thereon the conclusion that capital gains should be treated with care by the tax system. Why should a taxpayer exchange investments if, by so doing, he must forfeit a substantial part of his income-earning assets to the government?

This appears to be the strongest and soundest argument for low-rate taxation of capital gains. But it is by no means conclusive. Account must be taken of the fact that at present it is not so much the tax on capital gains which discourages exchanges as it is the loopholes in the tax. If one were to be taxed on his gains eventually anyhow and a favorable opportunity for an exchange now presents itself, the transaction might appear desirable in spite of a tax on the capital gains. If the taxpayer contemplates the exchange of one growth stock for another and slightly better prospect, the tax may constitute a deterrent. If he contemplates the exchange of a high-dividend stock for a growth stock, the tax advantages of gains over dividends is so great (even without rate limitation) that no tax deterrent is likely to "lock the taxpayer in." [4]

---

[3] This is discussed more fully in the next chapter.

[4] For a recent discussion of this and other economic effects of the capital-gains

Thinking about capital gains still follows the antiquated assumption that they are mostly due to fortuitous fluctuations in the prices of capital goods. Actually such gains are mainly the stockholders' realization of the reinvested earnings of corporations. Thus the solution of the problem is an integral part of the larger one of taxing corporations and their undistributed profits.

There is a question as to how much the social interest is involved in the matter of liquidity of investments. It has not been demonstrated that some restraint upon the willingness to exchange securities would be disastrous.

Perverse Effect on the Stock Market. It has been claimed that the taxation of capital gains has a perverse effect upon the stock market. When times are good and the stock market is booming, taxpayers retain stocks that they might otherwise sell. This tends to create an artificial scarcity of stocks, which aggravates the boom. The opposite influence in times of depression tends to aggravate an already demoralized market. But if some persons hesitate to sell stocks because of an anticipated tax, it is equally plausible to assume that others will be deterred from demanding stocks that promise a quick speculative profit. Were the owners to sell one kind of stock, they would probably use the funds derived from the sale to purchase and therefore increase the demand for other stocks. Thus the supply of and demand for stocks may not be greatly disturbed by a heavy tax on capital gains.

Capital Gains Taxation and Enterprise Incentives. Capital gains, along with dividends, are the principal return for risk taking which is of great strategic importance in a dynamic economy. Moreover, new enterprises might obtain new capital were it not for the unwillingness of investors in established enterprises to exchange investments and thus realize capital gains and pay taxes.

The present differential between the tax on capital gains and that on dividends affords a positive incentive to invest in new enterprises with a strong but uncertain potential for growth and financial improvement. These enterprises are highly significant in a dynamic economy. Were these gains to be taxed in full, it might be necessary to compensate by other tax measures that would insure adequate equity capital at strategic points. One such possibility is a more generous treatment of capital losses. Another is more moderate rates in the upper and middle brackets of income. A third is less punitive tax provisions applicable to distributed corporate income (discussed later).

<hr>

feature of the net income tax see *Federal Tax Policy for Growth and Stability,* Joint Committee on the Economic Report, 84th Cong., 1st Sess., 1955, pp. 367–418. Committee on Ways and Means, *Tax Revision Compendium,* 1959, pp. 1193–1300.

EXCHANGE WITHOUT REALIZATION

For capital gains taxation, there is no realization and no taxation without an exchange, but not every exchange provides a realization. Some exchanges are treated as only a formality and no gain is recognized; however, the taxpayer retains his former "basis" and may be taxed on a realized gain from a later transaction. The exchange of essentially similar goods by barter is a case of this kind. If a taxpayer buys a new residence within a year before or after selling his old residence, no gain is recognized under certain conditions. It has been argued that the same rule should apply to the sale of stocks, but if this were done very little of the capital gains tax would remain.

Only passing attention can be given here to a very technical subject known as corporate reorganization. This may involve a merger, which is the acquisition by one corporation of the assets of another, or a comprehensive recasting of the entire financial structure of a single corporation. The change usually involves an exchange of securities, but if it is consummated according to prescribed rules, it imposes no tax liability for capital gains.

THE CORPORATE NET INCOME TAX

The corporate net income tax as used for many years in Great Britain has been mainly a device for collection at the source. Stockholders are credited with the taxes collected from the corporation in their behalf. Where, as under our recent federal laws, the stockholder is allowed no credit for the corporate tax, the latter must be regarded as a business tax as such. Is this procedure warranted?

ARGUMENTS CONCERNING THE JUSTIFICATION OF A CORPORATE INCOME TAX

Application of the Ability Principle; Graduated Rates. The ability-to-pay principle is most readily applied to natural persons and, when it is employed to justify taxes on the corporate entity as such, many difficulties arise. Thus the phenomenon found in Mexico where a graduated business income tax is applied to all businesses alike, whether incorporated or unincorporated, impresses many as a strange procedure. Whether corporations have or do not have a soul has been frequently debated. Probably they would be the first to proclaim their capacity to suffer. But, in the last analysis, only natural persons pay taxes. The equity doctrine seems more logically applied to the corporation as an association of individual stockholders than as an entity in its own right.

The difficulty in the application of the ability principle to the corporate entity can be seen in the use of a graduated rate for the corporate tax.

Corporate net income as such tells us nothing about the rate of return on capital. A concern with $50,000 income may have a 100-percent return upon investment, whereas one with a $1 million income may be earning a mere 1 percent. That there is a necessary correlation between the size of corporate business and its profitableness has not been established. Looked at from the viewpoint of the owners, taxing a corporation on its net income affects them unequally because their equities vary in size. A $50,000 corporate income received by a corporation virtually owned by one stockholder represents more ability to pay per dollar of income than a $150,000 corporate income received by a corporation owned by 1500 widows and orphans.

The principal way in which the ability doctrine finds logical application in the taxation of the corporate entity is through recognition of the fact that corporate earnings represent the potential income of (in most cases) relatively well-to-do stockholders. Most dividends are received by those in relatively high brackets of income. But the application, to say the least, is highly rough and haphazard.

A case can and has been made for graduation according to the rate of return on corporate capital. For example, on the portion of income representing a 0–5 percent yield on investment, the rate might be 30 percent, with a higher tax rate on higher yields. With some qualifications, this was the basis of graduation in our wartime excess profits taxes. A major difficulty here is that no clearly valid method has been developed for evaluating assets. Obviously capitalizing income will not do and actual investment, historically determined, is also open to some objections. Moreover, no method of allowing for differential risk in the rate of return has developed. The conclusion has usually been to stick with net income as the basis of the corporate tax even though the rationale of such procedure is not very plausible.

Benefit and Special Privilege. A case for a corporate income tax can be made by approaching the matter from the angle of benefits received, or, perhaps more accurately, the cost of the corporation to the government. Governmental services are a factor of production, and it can be argued that business should pay for these services accordingly. However, it is not very logical to apply a cost doctrine only to corporations that make a net profit. Moreover, if part of the cost tax is shifted to the consumers, the business tax takes on the aspect of a consumption tax.

Sometimes it is contended that corporations receive special benefits from government in such legal privileges as limited liability (by which is meant that stockholders are not liable for debts of corporations, as are partners for debts of partnerships) and that these special benefits justify a special corporate tax. However, these legal privileges are available to all for the asking, and, under free competition, their monetary value should be nothing. It is true that competition is not that efficient, but business income taxes make no pretense of measuring the results of monopolistic competition.

Social Control.   Some defense for the taxation of corporations can be made on the score that such taxation provides a desirable tool for social control. One such use (which does not, however, require a general corporate income tax) is attempted through the taxation of intercorporate dividends. Formerly, intercorporate dividends were entirely exempt from taxation. Now they are included in the base of the recipient corporation to the extent of 15 percent of their amount. This feature of the law is designed partly with the objective of discouraging holding companies. The holding company device probably has legitimate uses, but it greatly complicates the financial structure of American business and makes for concentration of control. Probably adequate regulation would be a more suitable tool for controlling the abuses of intercorporate ownership. (The powers of the Security and Exchange Commission are largely confined to the public utility field.) But until such control is developed, these taxation devices may fill a useful function.[5]

The corporate net income tax with graduated rates or a specific exemption can also be used to favor small corporations and unincorporated business.

Economic Effects.   The revenue needs of the modern state are too demanding to confine taxes to levies that do a precise job of equitable distribution among individuals. Thus, we are forced to consider priorities among second-best or least-bad taxes. Important weight here must be given to economic effects. The corporate income tax (on the assumption that its incidence is largely on stockholders) does tend to reduce inequality among classes of income recipients. It probably reduces saving more than most alternative levies, and this may more than offset its restraining influence upon investment. On the assumption that the economy

---

[5] In present corporate tax procedure, corporations that have a high degree of overlapping ownership are permitted to file a consolidated return. This type of return facilitates administration and is defended on the ground that several very closely related companies really operate as one unit. And it allows losses to be offset within the family of companies when they could not be thus utilized in the case of independent concerns. In compensation for this advantage, concerns using a consolidated return are required to pay an additional tax of 2 percent on their combined net income.

tends to limitation from a chronic shortage of aggregate demand, the economic effects of this levy may be more favorable or less unfavorable than those of alternative levies. And on the assumption that less inequality among classes is better distribution, the same may be said of its consequences in terms of equity.[6]

BOND INTEREST AND THE CORPORATE TAX

There is also the question of whether bond interest should be a deductible expense if corporations are to be taxed under the net income tax. Legally, there is a difference between a bondholder and a stockholder in that the former is a creditor of the corporation whereas the latter is its proprietor. Actually, there is not very much difference between many stockholders, particularly those who have no voting power (or do not exercise it), and bondholders. Nevertheless, the differences between creditor and entrepreneurial interests are important in taxation; security classification is especially scrutinized in the case of so-called thin corporations (usually closely held) where the debt-stock ratio is conspicuously high. If the debt is not evidenced by a definite obligation with a fixed rate of interest and maturity date, the arrangement is likely to be treated as "phoney." However, corporations are not obliged to maintain any specific stock-debt ratio. If bond interest were not deductible, the tax burden upon corporations financed by stock and those financed in large part by bonds would be more equal. On the other hand, a tax on "operating income" (with no deduction for interest) could force a business into bankruptcy. Inclusion of cost elements in the income base would make the tax easier to shift. Bonds are long-term contracts, and the change to a tax on operating income would involve grave problems of transition. The opposite alternative, allowing dividends paid as a deduction in calculating the base of the corporate tax, looks more promising.

A GENERAL BUSINESS INCOME TAX

Another issue is whether corporations should be singled out for special taxes when partnerships and individual entrepreneurs are not.[7] One difficulty here is that there is no clear definition of what constitutes a business. Is farming a business? Should the professions be included? If an arbitrary line must be drawn somewhere, the point between corporations and other businesses may be as reasonable as any. It is this writer's opinion that, as a practical matter, little but confusion is accomplished

---

[6] Richard Goode, *The Corporation Income Tax* (New York: John Wiley & Sons, Inc., 1951).

[7] This will be given further consideration in Chapter 16.

by attempting to include businesses other than corporations in a business tax.

CONCLUSION

The taxation of business as such, like the taxation of most property under the property tax, finds little logical support except on opportunistic grounds. It does provide substantial revenue. Its economic effects may be less alarming than those of alternative levies. Also, it can be added that ways and means must be found to prevent avoidance of personal taxes through the use of corporations as savings banks. This is the problem of taxing undistributed earnings, of which more will be said later. Here it can be added that our present unwillingness or inability to apply personal taxes to the impersonal corporation creates no end of confusion.

DIVIDENDS

CASH DIVIDENDS

The complications that beset any attempt at just taxation of income earned through the corporate institution become especially apparent when the corporation, stockholders, and the various ways of disposing corporate income are all brought into the picture. The problems arising here vary with the disposition that is made of the corporate income—that is, whether it is distributed to shareholders in cash or its equivalent (in stock dividends) or not distributed at all. Attention will now be given to these problems.

Treatment under the Personal Income Tax. One of the questions of policy in taxing corporations and stockholders is the treatment of cash dividends under the individual net income tax. It is argued by some that, since the corporation pays a tax on its earnings, the stockholders should not be subject to an additional tax (or at least not a full tax) on these same earnings when they are distributed to him as dividends. To tax these earnings twice, it is claimed, is discriminatory double taxation. The corporate tax is merely a device for collecting at the source and, once the tax is collected in this manner, it should absolve the stockholder from all or at least part of his personal responsibility. However, the combination of corporate and personal tax may also undertax large stockholders who gain by the fact that undistributed earnings are taxed less than the upper-bracket personal rates. Moreover, to tax both the stockholder and the corporation is to discriminate in favor of the corporation which is partly financed through bonds, since the latter is not taxed on what it distributes to its bondholders.

On the other side of the argument, it is contended that the corporation is very definitely a legal entity separate and distinct from its stockholders; and this distinct-entity doctrine is often used to the advantage of the corporation, as, for example, in the matter of limited liability. Why should not this same doctrine now be applied to the disadvantage of the corporation? Furthermore, the corporation's tax may be regarded as a business tax and justified by the benefits business as such receives from the government. In that event, it is not illogical to include dividends in the measure of the personal tax paid by stockholders. To the layman, dividends are certain to appear like any other income and to afford the same ability to pay as any other income.

Moreover, in some cases, notably in the public utility field, corporations largely pass on their taxes to the consumer. In this case, the stockholder escapes both the direct and indirect burden unless dividends are included in his taxable income. The same may be true of a preferred stockholder of any prosperous corporation; his dividends are not directly affected by the tax which the corporation pays. And finally, since the corporate tax treats all stockholders alike in the indirect burden it imposes upon them, it is only by taxing the individual that a suitable differentiation may be made in making the progressive rates applicable to them.

Present Practice. The federal government formerly taxed cash dividends only under the surtax and exempted them from the normal tax. Since 1936 they have been subject to both taxes; however, in 1954 a partial credit on dividends was allowed the taxpayer (explained later). Some of the states that tax corporations under the net income tax do not tax the recipient of dividends from those same corporations. Treatment of cash dividends throughout the states ranges from exemption (which may take the form of an exclusion, a deduction, or a credit) to additional taxation.

Summary: Alternative Procedures and Unneutralities. Alternative procedures in the treatment of corporate income and dividends may be summarized as follows: (1) both corporate income and dividends might be taxed but this is criticized as double taxation; (2) dividends only might be taxed, but this would invite the use of the corporation as a savings bank; (3) corporations only might be taxed but this would not differentiate between the large and small stockholder; (4) dividends might be taxed to the stockholder and undistributed earnings to the corporation. This latter seems the most rational alternative, but it encounters the objection that it would discourage socially desirable reinvestment.

The present federal procedure is said to be unneutral as between (1) corporations and partnerships; (2) equity- and debt-financed corporations; (3) distributed and undistributed profits; and (4) corporate profits and other income.

STOCK DIVIDENDS

Much more difficult than the taxation of cash dividends is the problem of taxing stock dividends. Figure 17 shows the course of income earned by a corporation and the various points at which it may be taxed. It will be

FIGURE 17

Stream of Income to and from a Corporation and Points at Which Such Income Is Taxed

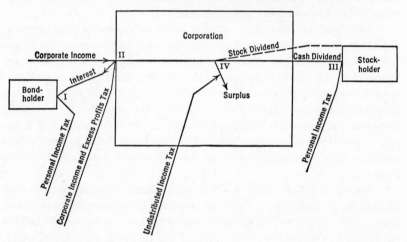

noticed that corporate receipts paid out to the bondholder are not regarded as income to the corporation, but are taxed at point I to the bondholder as part of his individual income. Point II is where the net income of the corporation is subjected to the corporate net income tax and the excess profits tax. Once income has passed by point II, it may go through the corporation and be declared as cash dividends or it may stay in the corporation. If the former is the case, the income will be subject to a personal tax at point III. If the latter is true, then the undistributed corporate income (addition to surplus) may be taxed at point IV. The corporation may also declare a stock dividend but, as will be observed presently, this distribution is not ordinarily taxed to the stockholder.[8]

---

[8] This says nothing about a liquidating dividend which is a return of capital to the stockholders pursuant to closing out a corporation. Liquidation in full, where a surplus is distributed, clearly gives rise to capital gains. A partial liquidation is sometimes interpreted as the equivalent of the distribution of an ordinary dividend out of surplus.

The Nature of Stock Dividends. There are several kinds of dividends which may be declared by a corporation and received by a stockholder. The first is a cash dividend, which consists of a payment by check or cash. The second is a stock dividend, which consists of a payment in stock issued by the corporation. And the third is a "dividend-in-stock," which consists of a payment in the stock of some other corporation. Perhaps it will help to clarify the nature of these distributions if their effects are illustrated in accounting terms. Taking cash dividends first, assume that corporation *A* has recently been organized, that it has raised $1 million by the sale of capital stock, and that this sum has been invested in plant and equipment. This is Stage 1. Stage 2 is at the end of a year's operation, after $200,000 of undivided profits have been accumulated. Stage 3 is immediately after a declaration of a cash dividend. It is apparent that what takes place in the case of a cash dividend is a transfer to the stockholders of those assets of the corporation which were acquired as earnings. Now the corporation is just where it started; it has no surplus or undivided profits, having transferred them to the stockholders. But the profits so transferred are subject to the personal income tax as part of the stockholders' income.

Stage	Capital *	Capitalization †	Assets	Liabilities
1	$1,000,000	$1,000,000	$1,000,000	$1,000,000
2	1,200,000	1,000,000	1,200,000	1,000,000 in stocks 200,000 in surplus or undivided profits
3	1,000,000	1,000,000	1,000,000	1,000,000 in stocks

* Income-earning assets of the company.
† Par value of outstanding stocks and bonds of the company.

The nature of stock dividends may be illustrated as follows:

Stage	Capital	Capitalization	Assets	Liabilities
1	$1,000,000	$1,000,000	$1,000,000	$1,000,000
2	1,200,000	1,000,000	1,200,000	1,000,000 in stocks 200,000 in surplus or undivided profits
3	1,200,000	1,200,000	1,200,000	1,200,000 in stocks

Assume that corporation A, starting with $1 million of capital (Stage 1), earns $200,000 by the end of its first year of business operation. This is depicted in accounting terms at Stage 2. Let us now assume that the earnings are reinvested in the corporation's plant and that stock dividends have been declared, each stockholder receiving his proportionate share of reinvested earnings in the form of new stocks. The result is shown in the illustration as Stage 3. It will be noted that the corporation has lost none of its capital, and also that the capitalization has been increased and that the surplus or undivided profits have been converted into additional stocks. Aside from the taxation of corporate income as such, unless there is some form of undistributed profits tax, these profits are ordinarily subject to no further tax [9]—quite in contrast to their fate had they been distributed in cash.

The nature of a dividend-in-stock may be illustrated as follows:

Stage	Capital	Capitalization	Assets	Liabilities	
1	$1,000,000	$1,000,000	$1,000,000	$1,000,000	
				1,000,000	in stocks
2	1,200,000	1,000,000	1,200,000	200,000	in surplus or undivided profits
3	1,000,000	1,000,000	1,000,000	1,000,000	in stocks

Assume that corporation *A*, after accumulating $200,000 of undivided profits, invested this money in the stocks of corporation *B*. These stocks are now a part of corporation *A*'s capital and must be listed among its assets (Stage 2). At Stage 3 a dividend-in-stock is declared, after which the company is in the same position it would have been in had it never purchased corporation *B*'s stocks but had declared a cash dividend. And like the latter, this income (dividends-in-stock) is taxable in the hands of the stockholders.

Are Stock Dividends Income?   The question whether stock dividends may be regarded as income has come before the United States Supreme Court on several occasions, and its answers have been mainly in the negative.[10] Its decisions, as well as the considerable supporting com-

---

[9] Except as reflected in realized capital gains.

[10] *Eisner v. Macomber,* 252 U.S. 189 (1920). Although it is here held that stock dividends are not income and may not be taxed as such, they may afford the taxpayer a taxable capital gain if and when he sells his stock. The Supreme Court has since substantially qualified the doctrine enunciated in this case, as will be later explained.

ments by students of the subject, are based mainly on the following grounds.

No Value to Stockholder. It is argued that when a stock dividend is declared the stockholder receives nothing of value. He obtains a piece of paper which is evidence of the fact that he now owns, let us say, two sixteenths of the corporation instead of one eighth. This argument may be plausibly answered by stating that it is not the mere act of declaring dividends that gives the stockholder advantage, but the accumulation of the profits over the months preceding the division. As a matter of fact, the mere declaration of a *cash* dividend gives the stockholder little if any advantage. The stockholder is "in" some cash, but he is "out" the expectation that he is about to be paid cash. Or to put it another way, what he gains personally, he is out in the decreased equity which the corporation has to divide. Why is a stock dividend not quite as much an advantage to the stockholder as a dividend-in-stock? [11] Both can be sold on the market for cash; and when either is sold it leaves the stockholder with the same absolute equity in the corporation that he held when it started business.

No Realization of Stock Dividend. A further contention is that an advantage must be *realized* to constitute income and that nothing has been realized in the case of a stock dividend declaration. Realization would seem to be a matter of having "a bird in the hand" instead of one "in the bush." There are contingencies which might intervene between the stock which is received as a stock dividend and the stockholder's enjoyment of his gain. But is this not true also in the case of a dividend-in-stock?

No Separation of Stock Dividend from Capital. It is also argued that there must be a separation from the corporation before the stockholder can realize an income. If the corporation and the stockholders are separate entities, how can the stockholder receive anything if nothing is severed from the corporation? In the case of a dividend-in-stock, it is clear that certain assets of the corporation are plucked off and handed to the taxpayer. In the case of a stock dividend, however, there is no plucking and the corporation loses nothing at all so far as its assets are concerned. The stock dividend constitutes a mere memorandum of the accumulated equity in the corporation which the stockholder's shares represent.

The Supreme Court could logically base a decision that stock dividends are not income on the ground that no separation from the corporation's capital takes place when such a dividend is declared. This,

---

[11] A dividend-in-stock has been held by the United States Supreme Court to be income.

at least, is one aspect in which a stock dividend differs from a cash dividend or a dividend-in-stock. However, the Supreme Court itself has been unwilling to follow this logic. In the case of *Koshland v. Helvering,*[12] subsequent to that of *Eisner v. Macomber,* it decided that stock dividends declared in preferred stock to a common stockholder are income when they disturb the previous proportionate holdings in the company. Obviously, no more separation from a corporation's assets takes place when a surplus is capitalized and issued in a way that changes proportionate holdings than when it does not.

Stock Dividends and the Assets of a Corporation. The final contention is that stock dividends are not income because the issuance of common stock to common stockholders does not change their proportionate claims upon the company. A stockholder who owned one tenth of the corporation's stocks hitherto will now own two twentieths. This does not hold, it is said, when a company that has preferred stock issues preferred stock to common stockholders, or presumably when common stock is issued to preferred stockholders. By the issuance of different types of claims to the existing security holders, the company may disturb their relative proportionate shares in itself. The Supreme Court's latest decisions apparently rest upon this distinction between two classes of stock dividends. The distinction is a true one, but is it significant? A curious problem arises when a corporation is forced to divulge stock (surrender to stockholders) as a result of antitrust decisions. Under the current law these are dividends in stock and fully taxable.

We have already mentioned that certain exchanges are privileged in that they are deemed not to give rise to income. In these cases the exchange is regarded as more formal than real. Of course, the tax that might be involved is postponed rather than forgiven (that is, the "basis" of the old assets is transferred to the new ones). This is the rationale behind the Court's approach to the stock-dividend problem.

Legal matters aside, should stock dividends be taxed? Are stock dividends a useful device in corporate financing? What of the undistributed earnings that are left uncapitalized? As the last question suggests, the problem overlaps heavily that of taxing undistributed earnings as such, a matter which will be considered presently. Stock dividends add to the attractiveness of undistributed profits giving to the individual an option (in effect) to convert them to cash all within the protected zone of capital gains treatment. Once used as a device for capitalizing accumulated surplus, they are now more and more regarded as a substitute for ordinary dividends.[13] As to present federal practice in this

---

[12] 298 U.S. 441 (1936).
[13] Dan Throop Smith, *Federal Tax Reform* (New York: McGraw-Hill Book Company, Inc., 1961), pp. 234–244.

area the act of 1954 clearly provides that all stock dividends, with very minor exceptions, do not give rise to income when they are received. One exception occurs when stockholders are given an option to receive cash. A question arises as to whether this covers the case where the board of directors has discretion over dividends as to two classes of common stock and declares cash dividends to one and stock dividends to the other.

THE EXCESS PROFITS TAX

The excess profits tax, as we usually think of it, is a business tax rather than a part of the income tax system. However, it figures in the picture of the income tax as applied to corporations and stockholders. For that reason a brief consideration will here be given to the nature and problems of this type of tax and the recent federal application of it.[14]

Explanation of Machinery of Operation. The excess profits tax in the United States has been used chiefly in times of emergency. It was first introduced during World War I, reintroduced during World War II, and again reintroduced during the defense mobilization which followed the outbreak of hostilities in Korea. The law has been repealed in each case after the emergency passed. The last two models of the excess profits tax have been very similar and our attention here can be largely confined to the system in force in 1953.

There are two main ways to separate excess from normal profits: one is to draw the line at a certain ratio of profits to invested capital; the other is to draw it at profits equal to those of some bench-mark period. The first indicates what may be called high profits; the second what may be called extraordinary profits. Our two recent laws have given the taxpayer the choice of these two, which means in effect that profits to be subject to the excess profits tax have to be both high and extraordinary. Our latest law reckoned "excess" on the invested-capital method as amounts above 12 and 10 percent on capital ranging to $5 and $10 million respectively and 8 percent on amounts above $10 million. It reckoned "excess" on the base-period method as amounts exceeding 83 percent of the average earnings of the three best years of 1946–1949 (losses counted as zero). Each of these methods has its difficulties. In-

---

[14] The literature on the excess profits tax is very abundant and includes many articles, hearings, and symposia. Special mention may be made of the following: Carl Shoup, "The Taxation of Excess Profits," *Political Science Quarterly,* LV (1940), pp. 535–555; LVI (1941), pp. 84–106, 226–294; *Law and Contemporary Problems,* X: 1 (1943); George Lent, "Excess Profits Taxation in the United States," *Journal of Political Economy,* 59: 6 (December 1951), pp. 481–497.

vested capital takes no account of uncapitalized price changes; two plants exactly alike except that one had been built (or purchased) during a period of higher prices would be given quite different bases. Base-period earnings take no account of the hundred and one reasons why one firm may have fallen behind others in the base years. The fact that Congress chose 83 percent of base-period earnings as a standard suggests that the period itself was anything but normal.

The rates of the tax in 1953 were 30 percent of excess with a ceiling effective rate on all profit of 18 percent. Thus, the combined corporate net income and excess profits tax might reach 82 percent at the margin but could not exceed 70 percent on the average.

Special Features and Problems. Some account of fluctuations in corporate income is deemed essential in applying an excess profits tax. In our latest experience, a carry-forward of five years and a carry-back of one year was provided, and this covered unused normal tax allowance as well as losses. Thus, if a corporation had normal earnings of $2 million and earned $1 million, $4 million, and $1 million in successive years it would have no excess profits on which to pay tax.

A major problem in framing an excess profits tax is the treatment of credit capital and interest. If only equity capital were taken into account, two concerns exactly alike except that one were financed in large part by credit would pay substantially different taxes. Assume that the *A* and *B* corporations each earns 10 percent (normal) on its capital; assume further that the *B* corporation is financed in half by credit capital on which it pays 5-percent interest. By "trading on the equity" it is in position to pay dividends of 15 percent on its stock. The *A* corporation is in position to pay only 10 percent since all of its capital is in stock. Should the *B* company pay an excess profits tax? The Congress has resolved this issue by compromise; during World War II half of credit capital (and interest) was included in the excess-profits-tax reckoning; in the later model the figure was set at 75 percent. Counting bonds and interest in the calculation is favorable to the company that borrows. Indeed, under the last law as applied, circumstances arose where it would pay a company to borrow and leave the proceeds idle in the company treasury.

The weaknesses of excess profits standards are all too apparent in the measures sought and provided for the relief of particular companies in particular circumstances, especially an abnormal or atypical experience during the base period. Thus, if a company had a disastrous fire or strike during the test years, it has a plausible claim for special consideration. The notorious Section 722 of the World War II law provided that if there were certain abnormalities of this sort in the base-period experience, the firm might construct a hypothetical experience to use as a substitute base. This proved all but unmanageable, and the postwar edition of the law provided that the firms with abnormalities might substitute the industry's experience instead of their own. The industry's experience would be provided by the Treasury in statistics indicating ratios of earnings to capital by groups of firms in the same general line of business. While this was no doubt an improvement, it involved difficulties of classification in the case of firms with more than one line of business. Industries which claimed abnormal experience as a whole might use experience from 1938 to 1949 (with qualifications) in lieu of that of the base period. Other relief included a "growth formula" (as a concession for rapidly growing industries such as television); and other specific concessions were made to certain taxpayers such as new companies, public utilities, and firms producing strategic metals.

Argument concerning Excess Profits Taxation. There is a strong consensus supporting the view that profits should not be rationed in ordinary times whether by taxation or other means. This is based in part on the view that profit differentials fulfill an economic function, directing new capital and resources into profitable areas. Monopoly profits do exist, but they are perhaps best commended to the attention of the antitrust division. Profits also vary with risk, and no excess profits tax has been framed that makes any allowance for this fact.

In extraordinary periods this logic appears not to hold; under the stimulus of inflation, full utilization of capital, and government orders, profits greatly exceed their usual portion of the national income. If men are being drafted and subjected to the casualties of war, the case for an excess profits tax, no matter the difficulties of application, seems irresistible. A higher corporate income tax might serve the purpose, but it does not differentiate between companies according to their benefits (windfalls) from the emergency. Graduation of the corporate tax according to size is logically weak.

Much interest has attended the issue of whether the excess profits tax helps prevent inflation. On the affirmative side, it can help to balance the budget and it may aid politically in persuading workers and farmers to support other controls. On the negative side, it may encourage waste (20-cent dollars). Particularly inviting to taxpayers are expenditures deductible now and likely to yield some return later: pension funds, advertising, and research outlay.

Conclusion. The excess profits tax is an example of failure of administrative and accounting techniques to achieve what is by definition a desirable goal. Profit trends are caused by a multitude of variables and to single out that portion that is attributable to one of them is all but impossible. Positive relief of one sort or another may appease the taxpayer, but it does not adjust relative burdens among competitors with an acceptable degree of precision.

TAXATION OF UNDISTRIBUTED PROFITS

In all countries where the income tax has been used, the tax treatment of undistributed profits has proved an embarrassing and difficult matter.[15]

Economics of the Problem.   Some mention has been made of the unneutralities in a corporate tax system which taxes both corporate earnings to the corporation and dividends received by the stockholder; this favors other income as compared with profits, credit financing as compared with stock financing, and undistributed as compared with distributed profits. Reinvestment may run to a large proportion of earnings—ranging to one half and more of corporate profits in good times. The decision to reinvest is largely that of corporate management and endows the inner circle of control with great power. Penalizing dividends may make it more difficult to sell new stock and thus to start new companies. On much the same reasoning, it may make for economic concentration—half of corporate America owning half of the other half of corporate America. On the other hand, it is urged that undistributed profits are an excellent source of capital; they are economically acquired and flow to points in the economic system where earnings probably justify new investment.

Attempts to Apply Special Taxes to Undistributed Profits.   Many critics have suggested that the most logical way to tax corporations is to apply a special levy to their undistributed profits only. This was tried in the undistributed profits tax of 1936. The experiment was not popular, and it was soon abandoned. But the test was hardly conclusive; it was designed more to force the declaration of dividends than to eliminate unneutralities; its rates accordingly were graduated according to the proportion of earnings retained, and it was superimposed upon an existing structure of corporate taxation rather than replacing it.

The undistributed-profits tax of 1936 left a memento in the celebrated Section 102 (now 531–537) which provides that when earnings are held to avoid personal surtax, they will incur certain penalty rates. The burden of proof, now carried by the Commissioner, is to show no legitimate business objective in withholding earnings from stockholders. A reinvestment of $60,000 is allowed regardless of objective. The section has been applied mainly in the case of closely held companies, but

---

[15] Goode, *op. cit.;* Harold M. Groves, *Postwar Taxation and Economic Progress* (New York: McGraw-Hill Book Company, 1946); J. Richards Petrie, *The Taxation of Corporate Income in Canada* (Toronto: University of Toronto Press, 1952); *Proceedings of the National Tax Association Conference,* 1950, pp. 54–73.

it creates an element of uncertainty for other companies. It has been widely criticized but its repeal would leave a wide-open invitation to use the corporation as a savings bank, thus avoiding very high surtaxes on personal income.[16]

Proposals. Suggestions for partial or complete integration of the personal and corporate tax have been much discussed in the postwar period. Several techniques have been proposed. One is the *partnership method;* this would assess stockholders on their prorata share of undistributed profits. It is the only method of achieving perfect integration, but it is regarded by most critics as impractical for several reasons. Among them is the fact that boards of directors are frequently in no position to make a final allotment of undistributed earnings particularly where there is cumulative preferred stock in the picture. Funds now available for common stock may be needed next year to supplement inadequate current earnings, all going to preferred. Moreover, an audit correcting corporate income some time after its earning might involve reopening large numbers of personal returns. Partial application of the partnership method, confining it to small and/or closely held companies, appears more feasible and indeed is applied in some countries such as Australia. But this procedure introduces difficulties of definition and unneutrality at the boundary line between those included and those excluded. A step in this direction was taken in 1958 when corporations with not more than eleven stockholders and meeting certain other qualifications were permitted to elect partnership treatment.

A technique which has had long application in Great Britain is called *withholding.* A corporate tax is levied at some appropriate rate in the personal rate schedule; it is collected from all corporate income; when dividends are paid and received the stockholder is allowed a credit for corporate taxes paid on his behalf. As applied to undistributed income, the corporate tax constitutes an advance payment for the stockholder. As in the case of withheld taxes generally, the advance collection is included in the personal tax base. A reverse type of credit has more following perhaps in the United States; it is called a *dividends-paid credit* and works as a deduction of dividends prior to the calculation of the corporate tax. This gives dividends the same status as bond interest and reduces the corporate levy to one on undistributed profits. A partial deduction for dividends has also been considered. Both the above techniques are distinguished from a so-called *dividends-received credit* which permits the stockholder to avoid the inclusion of all or part of his dividends in his personal tax base or a tax credit having the same effect.

---

[16] *The Taxation of Corporate Surplus Accumulations,* Joint Committee on the Economic Report, 82d Cong., 2d Sess., Washington, 1952; Tax Institute, *Economic Effects of Section 102,* New York, 1951.

The much mooted dividend credit in the Revenue Act of 1954 was of the latter type. It provided for an exclusion of the first $50 of dividends received by a stockholder and a 4 percent tax credit on additional dividends. This type of credit is criticized on the score that it excludes from the measure of the stockholder's tax what has been paid by the corporation on his behalf. Moreover, it disregards the fact that corporate taxes, at least those of public utilities, may be shifted forward to the consumer. Finally, it is said to favor large stockholders in the sense that in their case it closes a larger proportion of the gap between what was formerly paid and what should be paid (under perfect integration) than in the case of small stockholders. Taxpayers in the 90-percent income tax bracket cannot suffer greatly from double taxation.

Thus in a simple model, if *A* and *B* are large and small taxpayers (80-percent and 20-percent brackets respectively) each receiving $50 in dividends from a corporation that has earned $100 and paid $50 in taxes for each, the operation of the credit could be presented as follows:

	(1) corporate earnings	(2) corporate tax	(3) dividends paid	(4) personal tax	(5) total tax	(6) proper tax
A	$100	$50	$50	$40	$90	80%
B	$100	$50	$50	$10	$60	20%

	(7) double taxation factor (5–6)	(8) dividend credit [4% of (3)]	(9) double taxation factor relieved (8)/(7)
A	$10	$2	20%
B	$40	$2	5%

Apparently the last has not been heard of the double-taxation issue nor of dividend credits.

PROBLEMS

1. The *XYZ* corporation is financed by $1 million each of bonds, preferred stock, and common stock. It earns in 1956, $500,000 before any distribution to security holders and pays out $50,000 to bondholders, $50,000 to preferred stockholders and $100,000 to common stockholders. What is the base of the corporate tax? Why is it alleged that only common stockholders are double-taxed?

2. Peter Perkins has net receipts from his business amounting to

$20,000, one quarter of which can reasonably be regarded as a salary to himself as manager. He takes $5000 in profit from the business and reinvests $10,000 in his rapidly growing firm.

Assuming a corporate income tax rate of 30 percent, and an effective personal tax rate of 25 percent on $5000; 30 percent on $10,000; 35 percent on $15,000; and 40 percent on $20,000 of personal income: analyze the question of whether it would pay Perkins to incorporate.

3. A corporation starts business with $1 million invested in a building and $1 million of common stock. It then becomes prosperous and makes a very substantial profit and declares a stock dividend. Indicate what happens to its accounts.

4. If the *XYZ* corporation pays corporate taxes at the rate of 50 percent on corporate income and distributes the remainder of its earnings as dividends; and if *X*, a stockholder, pays personal taxes at an effective rate of 50 percent:
   a. How much tax will *X* pay per hundred dollars of earnings in this corporation?
   d. How much would he pay if the corporation were allowed a full withholding?
   c. How much would he pay if the stockholder were allowed a 10-percent dividend-received credit?
   d. How much would he pay if the corporation were allowed a full dividend-paid credit?
   e. How much ought he to pay if it be assumed that corporate and personal taxes should be fully integrated?

5. Peter Perkins owns a stock that over a two-year period has accumulated a 100-percent capital gain. He anticipates that the stock will not further appreciate in value but that it will pay an annual dividend henceforth of about 20 percent on its current market value. He can buy another stock which he calculates will double in value over the next ten years after which it will pay about the same dividends as the stock he now holds. His net income from other sources is about $100,000.

Will it pay him to sell his stock and buy the alternative one? Explain.

6. A real estate man buys a house and lot for $10,000 and rents it annually for $1000 for each of two years, charging off depreciation at the rate of $300 per year. He then sells the house for $11,000 to *B* who lives in it for a year and then passes it by inheritance to *B, Jr.* at which time it is worth $12,000. *B, Jr.* sells it to *C* a year later for $13,000. Who gets taxable capital gains here and how much?

7. A businessman buys a piece of land intending to use it as a parking lot. Five months later, because the city established a parking lot near his premises, he sells the land for a profit. Consider the tax problem here.

8. A corporation has $100 million of capitalization equally divided between Class A and Class B common stock. The board of directors has full discretion to allocate dividends between the two classes of stock and it regularly declares a cash dividend to one and a stock dividend to the other. Indicate the strategy of this arrangement and the tax problem involved.

9. Comment on the proposition: Some capital gains are taxed like ordinary income; some are taxed at special rates; and some are not taxed at all.

10. Comment on the proposition: Stock dividends give the stockholder something of value without costing the corporation anything.

11. Explain the nature and tax treatment of the following: stock dividends; patronage dividends; reinvestment to avoid surtax; liquidating dividends.

12. What are the difficulties in treating the corporate entity like any other person for tax purposes? Illustrate with the problem of graduating the tax.

13. Explain four possible ways of treating the corporate entity in income taxation and indicate objections to each.

14. Explain alleged unneutralities in our corporate tax structure. What are some of the possible economic effects of these unneutralities?

15. Consider critically the logic of the Supreme Court's position with regard to the taxability of stock dividends under the personal income tax.

16. What is meant when it is said that the last excess profits tax taxed profits only if they were both high and extraordinary?

17. Consider the difficulties in the measurement of extraordinary profits.

18. Comment on the proposition that a competitive economic system self-regulates profits, and rationing by taxation is therefore unnecessary and unwise.

19. Explain how the "partnership method" of taxing corporations might result in applying taxes to individuals on what they never have received or will receive.

20. Comment on the proposition that a dividend received credit does a rough job of integration, favors large stockholders, and discriminates against wages and salaries.

21. Explain how the problem of corporate income taxation is modified if it be assumed that the tax is shifted forward to consumers.

9

OTHER INCOME TAX PROBLEMS

PROPER ROLE OF EXEMPTIONS

The last two chapters have by no means exhausted the problems, both of structure and of policy, that abound in the income tax field. This chapter will consider the chief of these remaining problems.

Exemptions. We have noted before that it is not net income but some idea of "clear income" that is thought to constitute a prime measure of ability to pay. Long before progressive rates became fashionable in Great Britain, minimum exemptions were freely advocated and applied. There are several reasons for income tax exemptions and credits for dependents: (1) they protect a subsistence standard of living; (2) they provide a basis for differentiating among taxpayers according to need; (3) they avoid the administrative inconvenience of extending the personal tax to millions of small taxpayers; (4) they help to preserve the market for consumers' goods; and (5) they afford the political advantage of applying the direct tax system to relatively small numbers of taxpayers.

These reasons may be considered briefly in turn. The first—allowance of a subsistence standard—appeals quite properly to humanitarian impulses. But subsistence is a flexible standard depending on what a country can afford, what the economy produces, and the services a government provides its poorer citizens. Then, too, government is quite as much a necessity as any of the other elements of subsistence.

The second reason for exemption—differentiation—is undoubtedly valid, but it affords justification only of allowance for dependents. In judging credits for minor dependents, the effect on the birth rate may also warrant consideration.

The third ground for exemption—administrative convenience— probably is sufficient basis for some allowance. Much here depends upon the development of better techniques in administration.

As to the fourth reason, it is true that purchasing power can be protected by exemptions. However, where high exemptions lead to inadequate yields in the personal tax and the result is a shift from the personal tax to regressive substitutes, nothing is gained for purchasing power.

Finally, there is strong political opposition to low exemption. Very frequently a congressman is more interested in the number of people affected by a direct tax than in any other aspect of the tax. A high level of self-discipline is required for the citizenry to finance itself mainly by a direct levy.

Exemptions raise issues with political as well as economic implications. They exclude many recipients of income from the tax rolls. This results in "representation without taxation" and tends to undermine the morale of the large taxpayer who may be a very public-spirited citizen but who objects to being "shaken down" through what he regards as an unfair political advantage.

It is not always understood that the income tax base is frequently only a minor fraction of the national income. This is partly due to the fact that some income (such as tax-exempt interest) is privileged and some escapes as personal deductions. Of course there is also some leakage in reporting. But the principal subtraction is income not taxed— that is, personal exemptions. This runs to a very large figure and includes, of course, the allowance to persons taxed as well as to those not taxed. The personal exemptions also account in large part for the instability of the income tax base. If all taxpayers had a $1200 income, $1000 of which were exempt, a shrinkage of 10 percent in everybody's income would result in a more than 50-percent reduction in the tax base.

It is easy to demonstrate that $1200 a year for a married couple is insufficient to provide them with all the necessities, let alone the amenities, of life. But it is also easy to demonstrate that a minor fraction of the national income is insufficient to support, without confiscatory rates, a government that provides all the services we expect from ours. It is the author's view that, generally, income tax laws err on the side of excessive rather than inadequate exemptions.

Personal exemptions present problems both as to their absolute and as to their relative levels. Regarding the latter, some laws give a married couple more joint exemption than two single persons, some the same, and some less. American laws have usually granted less exemption for children than for adults, though the present federal law grants an equal allowance in each case. The exemption for children is of special significance because this allowance uniquely adjusts the tax base to the relative ability to pay of families. The exemption for children is required to indicate that a $3600 income for a family of six is equal in ability to pay to a $1200 income for a family of two.

On the other hand, some critics regard children as a choice of consumption; on such reasoning it is possible to support the conclusion that children are entitled to no allowance whatever in the calculation of taxable income. Sociological considerations can be brought into the argument. Exemptions support the birth rate, and this may or may not be desirable. Perhaps one answer might be indicated in a welfare state, another in a warfare state. The family-allowance programs of many countries carry support for children into positive allowances rather than negative credits. If exemption is to be regarded as a state subsidy, a case can be made for extending it to the families whose income is too low to be affected by a tax credit.

Techniques in Applying Exemptions. Several techniques of applying exemptions are exemplified in practice or in the literature of public finance. A case can be made for confining exemptions to the poorest taxpayers, sometimes called an *initial exemption*. This would conserve the tax base and support less severe marginal rates but it confronts a notch problem (see chapter 2) in applying the scale to those immediately above the exclusion limit. To avoid this a *vanishing exemption* might be attempted, the exemption allowance disappearing gradually as the base and scale move into higher brackets.

A *tax credit* may also be considered; it commutes the tax-saving value of the exemption to a common level regardless of bracket. It has the effect of taking the exemption out of the first bracket of taxable income instead of the highest one applicable to the taxpayer. In terms of the philosophy that would use clear income as the criterion for relative taxes, it makes little sense; one might as well commute business expenses to their tax value, allowing the latter as a deduction from taxes calculated on gross income. But on the view that the purpose of high taxes on upper and middle incomes is a matter of checking concentration of power which in turn is based on family aggregates, the credit can be approved as a partial vanishing exemption without a notch problem. On the other hand there is also support for more differentiation at all levels and this could be accomplished by allowing exemptions for taxpayers and dependents as a *percentage of income*. The present federal practice—the per capita flat sum allowance—is known as a *continuing exemption*.

PROPER ROLE OF PRIVILEGED DEDUCTIONS

It will be recalled that subtractions from gross income to arrive at a tax base are essentially of two different kinds. The first is the allowance for business expenses that are involved in the creation of income and that are required to arrive at an algebraic sum of the taxpayer's income and outgo. The second is the allowance for personal outlay—consumption expenses—which gives a privileged status to certain disposals of income. The four main deductions in the personal-privilege class are interest paid (on nonbusiness loans), state and local taxes (again nonbusiness), contributions, and medical expenses. Each of these is troublesome for income tax policy and administration; it can be regarded either as a refinement to derive ability to pay or as a concession to promote private outlay. For the latter purpose the procedure is perverse.

In the case of contributions for instance, the present deduction means that the government in effect assumes a very large share of the philanthropies of the rich and a very minor share or none in those of the poor. The medical-care deduction is said to be backdoor health insurance in which those who need it most get no benefit and others profit in inverse ratio to need. Such criticism invites the proposal that a flat tax credit be substituted for the deduction. The credit would peg the deduction to its value per dollar to some lower- or middle-income taxpayer. Thus a $100-deduction is worth $20 to a 20-percent bracket of income and this might be the maximum allowed any taxpayer.

Some of these deductions also add very substantially to the problem of income tax administration. The standard deduction was designed to help here but it takes away some of the refinement that these deductions are supposed to contribute. The proposal is now heard that the standard deduction should be built into the rate scale which could be done by allowing deductions of this sort only if they exceed 10 percent of adjusted gross income.[1]

---

[1] See C. Harry Kahn, *Personal Deductions in the Federal Income Tax*, National Bureau of Economic Research (Princeton: Princeton University Press, 1960), chap. 8.

APPLICATION OF THE INCOME TAX TO TRUSTS

The difficulties of applying the income tax to corporations is well known, but it is not so generally realized that a similar problem of hardly smaller proportion occurs in the case of trusts. The trust is a device by which a person or corporation is vested with title to certain property that he or it is to manage for the benefit of another person. Usually there are at least three parties to a trust: the settlor, or the one who creates the trust; the trustee, or the one who administers it; and the beneficiary, or the one for whose benefit it is created. Trusts may be established for various purposes. A familiar type is exemplified when a donor wishes a relative to have a certain income and, uncertain of the latter's ability to handle "money matters," leaves the administration of property from which the income is to be derived to a trust company or some other third party. Under this arrangement the latter obtains the legal title to the property, subject to certain conditions enumerated in the trust contract, while the beneficiary is accorded merely an equitable title to or interest in it.

Classification of Trusts. Trusts may be revocable or irrevocable— that is, the settlor may or may not reserve the right to change his mind. They also may contain a "reverter"—that is, they may provide that in event of certain contingencies such as the death of the beneficiary prior to that of the settlor, title may return to the settlor. The trust may be temporary only, granting equitable title to the beneficiary for a certain specified time, such as ten years. Various degrees of control may be reserved to the settlor, such as the right to vote the stock in trust, the right to borrow from the trust, and the right to modify disposition of benefits. The trust also may or may not provide support for some relative the settlor is obliged by law to support. The trust contract may call for the annual distribution of trust income to the beneficiary, or part or all may be left to accumulate for distribution at some later time.

In general, the rule is that distributed income from trust property is taxable to the beneficiary and the undistributed income to the trustee (or the trust itself, as a fiduciary return). The exceptions, of which there are many, occur when the settlor retains a substantial degree of control,[2] an uncertain reversionary interest, a certain reversionary interest to take effect within a relatively short period (ten or fifteen years), or when the trust is used to merely absolve the settlor of obligation to support dependants. In any of these exceptional cases the distributed or undis-

---

[2] *Helvering v. Clifford,* 309 U.S. 331 (1940).

tributed income of the trust may be [3] taxable to the settlor as though the trust had never been created.[4]

METHODS OF EVADING OR AVOIDING THE FEDERAL INCOME TAX

Ethics of Avoidance. Evasion and avoidance differ in that the former involves a breach of law whereas the latter does not. Avoidance, though within the law, may raise some interesting questions of ethics. Is a wealthy man morally justified in paying large sums to the proverbial Philadelphia lawyer in order that he may discover loopholes in the income tax law? Perhaps most people should regard their income tax as a contribution which they are privileged to make toward the joint enterprises of mankind. Actually, they are more likely to regard the tax as a game between the taxpayer and the government, with the taxpayer's goal the payment of the least possible amount of taxes. The good will of the taxpayer is an important and much neglected asset in the administration of all taxes. But with an economic system and distribution of wealth based primarily upon power, it is perhaps a little academic to expect taxpayers to contribute more in taxes than the law requires.[5] It is thus "up

---

[3] However, the state of the law is not clear or settled on many aspects concerning the taxability of trust income. Thus, it is argued with some support in the decisions that while the above conditions taken all together make a clear case for taxing the settlor, some one of them of and by itself would not. See E. Grady Paul, Jr., "Trusts and Federal Taxation," *Taxes,* 31: 8 (August 1953), pp. 608–619.

[4] But the trust is a highly flexible instrument and the problem of applying the income tax to trust situations is perennial. Thus a trust arrangement may provide for amendment of the trust by the settlor in conjunction with some other person. If the other person represents an interest adverse to that of the settlor, this will not leave tax liability with the settlor. Again the settlor may reserve power to "accelerate the benefits" provided this is in accordance with some objective standard rather than the settlor's whim. And the trustee may be given the power to select from a designated class of beneficiaries, again on some objective rule, those who from time to time shall receive benefits. This latter so-called "sprinkling trust" can prove very effective in minimizing taxes. See A. Mannheimer and J. I. Friedman, "Income Tax Aspects of Various Will and Trust Arrangements." *Taxes,* 30: 5 (May 1952), pp. 362–375.

[5] In England, where civic responsibility is highly developed, the courts have repeatedly recognized this tendency to use all available legal means to reduce taxes. This was very aptly expressed when the Lord President of the Court of Session, Edinburgh, remarked that "No man in this country is under the smallest obligation, moral or other, so to arrange his legal relations to his business or to his property as to enable the Inland Revenue to put the largest possible shovel into his stores. The Inland Revenue is not slow—and quite rightly—to take every advantage which is open to it under the taxing statutes for the purpose of depleting the taxpayer's pocket. And the taxpayer is, in like manner, entitled to be astute to prevent, so far as he honestly can, the depletion of his means by the Inland

to" the government to devise tax laws that are free from loopholes. This is not easy in a highly complicated economic order; certain time-honored institutions—notably, the corporation and the trust—aggravate the difficulty.

However, it should be added that avoidance is not always so innocent as the above paragraph suggests. Taxpayers also connive to amend the law in their own favor, and our legislative system with its development of legislation by committee is admirably adapted for their success in these maneuvers.

Methods of Avoidance Previously Discussed. Some of the more common guises of evasion and avoidance have already been mentioned. Except for the following four, which are treated quite extensively in other chapters, they will be discussed in more detail here.

1. Tax-exempt securities.[6] This is one of the most conspicuous and, in the author's opinion, one of the least defensible loopholes in the present law. However, it should be said that all these forms of avoidance are controversial, and some rational defense can be made for each of them. The term "loopholes" is resented by some critics; they prefer the word "windows."

2. Capital gains, especially on assets held until after the taxpaper's death.

3. Reinvestment of corporate earnings.

4. Percentage depletion.

The Personal Holding Company and Multiple Trusts. By the incorporation of an entity between the taxpayer and the sources of his income, the taxpayer can delegate his investment functions to an impersonal intermediary and thus escape high surtaxes. To illustrate how this device works, suppose Mr. *X,* who owns most of the stock in the *ABC* operating company, exchanges it for stock in the *IOU* investment company. By this means Mr. *X* is able to invest his earnings without receiving any dividend upon which he would be liable to high surtaxes. Recently, intercorporate dividends have been made partially taxable. Previously, the *IOU* investment company would not have been taxed at all. In one case a taxpayer as person contended that he had transferred property to taxpayer as corporation by verbal agreement. In court he was questioned as follows: "Will you give us full particulars of the discussion that took place between yourself as vendor and yourself as representing the new company?"

Revenue."—*Ayrshire Pullman Motor Services and D. M. Ritchie v. C.I.R.* (1929), 14 T.C. 754. Quoted from Findlay G. Shirras, *Science of Public Finance* (London: Macmillan and Co., Ltd., 1936), vol. I, p. 502.

[6] This loophole has been explained in Chapter 7 and is discussed in more detail in Chapters 19 and 20.

Recent federal statutes have attempted to plug the personal holding-company loophole in several ways. When a company falls under a statutory definition of a personal holding company, its income is taxed at high rates. The law now provides that when a corporation has 50 percent or more of its stock owned directly or indirectly by not more than five persons and when 80 percent or more of its income is from investments in other enterprises, it is a "personal holding company" and is singled out for especially heavy taxation (on reinvested earnings). Rents are included in the 80 percent, unless they constitute more than half of the total income of the company. The 1937 law also classed as a personal holding company the corporation receiving its income in large part from the services of one individual. Foreign personal holding companies are to be disregarded for income tax purposes—that is, their income shall be included in the accounts of the people who own them. In addition, since 1934 intercorporate dividends have been partially taxed.

It would seem that these new provisions of the federal law should prove an effective stopper against evasion through the personal holding-company device. Except for the application of the corporate income tax to undistributed profits and intercorporate dividends, avoidance through an investment corporation not so closely held as the personal holding company is still possible. And, because of the elaborate definitions and details of the new provisions, still other opportunities for loopholes may be found.

A taxpayer may create a trust for the benefit of his minor child, the income therefrom to accumulate within the trust until some future date. The income is not legally part of the father's income, for he has irrevocably parted with all legal claims to it. Yet it does not legally belong to the child. Legally it is the trust's income, and the law has included trusts among those required to pay personal income taxes. But if it is legally possible to create one trust, then it is legally possible to create 100 trusts. Until 1937 this would have meant 100 personal exemptions from the income tax. It still involves splitting a large income 100 different ways for purposes of avoiding the high rates of the graduated income tax. Thus, a man receiving and saving $1 million a year from investments may divide himself like an amoeba into 100 taxpayers, each receiving $10,000.

Family Partnership and Gifts of Property. A major problem for any progressive personal tax is the invitation it affords to divide the base. Sometimes the easy way to accomplish this is to convey income-earning assets to one's spouse or other members of his family. Often there is an urge to do this in such a way that the donor retains some control or reversionary interest in the property. This is the understandable desire to have one's cake and eat it too. For a man engaged in business, it may be feasible to make a partnership arrangement with his son. If the income thereafter legally belongs to the son, it is still in the family and may possibly be subject to a good deal of control by the parent. Of course, it is entirely possible for a father and son to be engaged in business together in a manner that raises no complaint about tax avoidance. But suppose the son is only an infant and his sole contribution to the partnership consists of capital which was placed in his name by his father, and suppose the whole scheme was admittedly devised for avoiding taxes. The Supreme Court in various decisions [7] held that such a partnership would be disregarded by the income tax and the earnings of the business would all, as before, be taxed to the parent. But Congress, in the Revenue Act of 1951, reversed the Supreme Court and specified that the family partnership as described above, whether for tax avoidance or not, is valid for income-splitting. The only limitation is that the return of earnings to the son must be properly apportioned to represent the real contribution of the son's (originally the father's) capital. It is expected that the influx of babies into the free enterprise system will be substantial. While a gift of income or property results in no direct change in income tax liability, it does result in a change of ownership; further income produced by the property is of course taxable to the donee. Thus gifts may have important income tax consequences.

Splitting to reduce the effect of graduated rates can also be accomplished by creating multiple corporations to do what might be done by a single firm. Thus a subdivider expecting to build 500 residences at a profit of $1000 per home can save substantially by using 10 corporations to build 50 residences each. By the additional stratagem of spreading the profit over two years, each corporation can be kept within the $25,000-annual profit that carries the low bracket rate of the federal income tax. However, this type of "gimmick" has not always passed the authorities; the latter may argue that the splitting was artificial and did not serve a business purpose.[8]

Splitting of Income among Spouses. Until 1948 the tax situation with regard to splitting of income among spouses was complicated by "community property" law in some ten of the states. Under this system of law the spouses are entitled to an equal share in what either earns after the marriage. Since the federal income tax followed local property law, a $100,000 salary in California might be assessed as two $50,000 incomes with resulting decrease in progression. The same was not true in most other states, and this resulted in grave territorial inequality. In

---

[7] *Commissioner v. Tower,* 327 U.S. 280 (1946); *Lusthaus v. Commissioner,* 327 U.S. 293 (1946); *Commissioner v. Culbertson,* 337 U.S. 733 (1949).

[8] See Ernest R. Mortenson, "Multiple Attack on Multiple Corporations," *Taxes,* 35: 9 (September 1957), pp. 647–658.

some cases a difference, 25- or 30-percent, in taxes depended solely on where the taxpayer lived.

This situation might have been relieved by requiring "mandatory joint returns" as is done in Britain. Under this system the income of the husband and wife is assessed as a unit. It was supported not only as a remedy for the territorial inequality and much of the avoidance discussed above but also on the score that ability to pay can be compared better by families than by individuals. On the other hand, it was argued that the proposal would discourage marriage, and some contended that it would even lead to illegitimate cohabitation! Two persons with independent incomes might hesitate to marry into higher brackets.

The 1948 law embraced a different approach to the solution, providing that the total income of spouses might be divided between them equally (on a joint return). At one stroke this law eliminated territorial inequalities and many opportunities for tax avoidance by gifts between spouses. In doing this, it gave substantial and rather spotty tax relief and it generally weakened the progressivity of the tax. The lowest bracket of income could gain nothing, of course, and the highest brackets very little. Single persons could gain nothing, and this was also true of married couples where each spouse had an independent income equal to that of his mate. This left the middle and upper-middle brackets and cases of one income for two spouses as the very substantial gainers.

The problem of income tax equity among family situations is subtle. Assume that Mr. and Mrs. White have an income of $10,000, all earned by Mr. White; that the Blacks have an income of $10,000, to which each contributes half; that Brown and Green, both single, have incomes respectively of $10,000 and $5000. Perhaps Brown should contribute at the highest rate because he has the highest per capita income. Should the Whites and Blacks contribute at a higher rate than Green on the ground that they have a higher family income adding to their power and security? And should there not be a distinction between the families on the ground that White has the higher-paying position and Mrs. White could seek employment if she chose?

Of course, it would also be possible to include children in the process of aggregation and division or perhaps to count each child as a fraction of an adult for purposes of division. This is the French practice. It is said to provide allowances for children in some degree proportionate to the standards of the income group into which they are born.

The 1951 act extended 50 percent of the benefit of income-splitting to heads of households (single persons with a dependent living in the same home). It was argued that many single persons have the responsibility of married persons and that the distinction between the two was artificial; a widow might have higher taxes after her husband died even though her income were substantially reduced. This line of argument suggests the conclusion that income-splitting may have created as many problems as it solved.

Expense Accounts. It has been suggested that our society should be labeled the expense-account society in which nobody dares have much of any income but many live like princes with virtually all consumption needs cared for on (deductible) company expense. The company executive gets about, entertains lavishly, and lives well (sometimes including his family) all in the name of business contacts, public relations, and the furtherance of trade. This may include theater and athletic events and (with some evasion) even the family vacation. There may be some exaggeration in the above picture, but that the ubiquitous expense account constitutes a considerable problem both in the definition of income and in administration, no one will deny. The Revenue Act of 1962 sought to eliminate a few of the worst abuses in the area.

IRREGULARITY OF INCOME

It has often been noted that our income tax system perpetrates an irrational and unintended discrimination against fluctuating income. It has also been observed that the necessity of fitting income into time periods such as calendar years may produce highly arbitrary results. Accounting, particularly as it deals with depreciation, inventories, and cash and accrual methods of keeping accounts, is heavily involved with the timing aspect of income. Fluctuating income may suffer because of unused personal exemptions or losses, progressive rates, and rate changes. The author of a successful novel may realize a million-dollar success on the basis of ten years of work. Were the income spread evenly over the period rather than concentrated in one year, his prospect for income after tax would be improved some 80 percent. If on a casual job an employee works from June to June, he may find his taxes less than half what they would have been had his job extended from January to January.

Principal Victims and Effects of Bad Timing. Those principally affected by the time factor involved in income accounting are: the recipients of casual income (such as prizes); authors and artists; those involved with capital gains and losses; athletes (because of short careers); unincorporated business; and corporations. Unfortunate results of bad timing may include adverse economic effects: risky business is more likely to experience fluctuating income than safe ventures; small business is more susceptible than large (the latter can offset losses from one venture against the gains of another); and capital-goods or equipment-producing industries are more involved than others.

A corporation that has large losses along with substantial gains will find, without a carry-over, that its effective rate of tax is very much higher than the nominal rate—indeed the former may be more than 100 percent. The case is even stronger with unincorporated business which confronts substantial progression in the personal tax scale. We have (in Chapter 8) considered the special problem of capital losses and observed that without a carry-over they are likely to afford the taxpayer no relief, especially if they are segregated and can be offset only against capital gains.

Concessions to Fluctuating Income.   Present relief to fluctuating business income permits a carry-over of losses for five years and a carry-back for three years. The greater emphasis on the carry-forward has been challenged, but it is defended on several grounds, the most persuasive of which is that it avoids refunds and allows many accounts to be closed without undue delay.

A relief section in the federal law allows compensation for services rendered over a period of thirty-six months or more, payment for which occurs largely in one year, to be spread over the earning period. Other averaging devices have been proposed and much discussed but never tried by our federal government. The British employed a moving average for many years, and in Wisconsin this device was tried during the late 1920s and early 1930s. These experiments encountered the objection, particularly in times of falling income, that the taxpayers were obliged to pay currently on ability to pay that had ceased to exist. Also there was trouble dealing with taxpayers when they first and last became taxable. The experience illustrates the fact that the interest in spreading income over time may conflict with another interest, namely, that of taxing income as it is currently received and in the taxpayer's possession. Canada at present permits five-year averaging for extractive industry only. But the system is optional with the taxpayer and in effect employs a "simple" rather than a moving average. Under this system the taxpayer is always paid up and averaging always works in his favor.[9]

The difficulties in averaging are impressive. For instance, all averaging proposals suffer from the fact that the income tax places no value on

---

[9] The taxpayer may figure his income over any five successive years, not employing any year more than once, and pay on the average annual income at terms prevailing in each year. See J. Richards Petrie, *The Taxation of Corporate Income in Canada* (Toronto: University of Toronto Press, 1952), pp. 193–195. For much the most ambitious and ingenious proposal for averaging including a life-time period and a cumulative base, see William Vickrey, *Agenda for Progressive Taxation* (New York: The Ronald Press Company, 1947), chap. 6.

leisure. A person who takes a sabbatical year without pay seems unduly favored if the income for that year is rated in a series at zero. But for reasons indicated above interest in the subject is persistent. Empirical evidence suggests that the cases of extreme inequity that occur in the absence of averaging are not many, and some remedy should be sought that would at least provide some relief in these instances. Particularly in the treatment of capital gains and losses, the failure to inaugurate some further averaging program may be regarded as an important limiting factor in the development of a rational tax system.

DIFFERENTIATION OF INCOME

In the typical net income tax system in this country, incomes are distinguished and classified mainly according to size, but it is also possible to differentiate them according to source. Such differentiation might be on ethical grounds, holding some income to be more legitimate and deserved than other income. For example, the income from rackets might be singled out for especially severe treatment. A second basis of differentiating income is according to the effects upon future production that taxing it might have. The thought here is that income is a necessary reward to draw forth the factors of production; these rewards should not be paid unless necessary, and they should be kept at the minimum required. Thus, it is alleged that the landlord is the recipient of rent for the services of land that he did not create and that would be forthcoming without such reward. Finally, differentiation may be based on the idea that income from property is more potent than income from services. This is the basis of the favors to "earned" as compared with "unearned" income found in many income tax laws, including the federal law during most of the period from 1924 to 1943. It is said that income from services is less able to pay taxes than that from investments because the former is dependent upon the short and uncertain tenure of the human faculties.[10] Any youth of reasonable prudence knows the difference between marrying a $100,000 income from services and one of like amount from property.

In the countries of Southern Europe, the income tax developed traditionally as a classified tax though more recently graduated surtaxes on an aggregate base have been added. The Mexican tax is graduated

---

[10] J. A. Hobson, *Taxation in the New State* (New York: Harcourt, Brace & World, 1920); R. H. Tawney, *The Acquisitive Society* (New York: Harcourt, Brace & World, 1920); John R. Commons, *Institutional Economics* (New York: The Macmillan Company, 1934).

and levied on seven different schedules with no attempt at aggregation. Thus a taxpayer with income from wages and from investments is taxed on two independent bases.

In spite of some valid defenses for the differentiation of income according to source, its wide application in the income tax structure does not seem advisable. Ethical distinctions are too subjective to serve as the basis of income classifications, and distinctions on the basis of effects on production are almost as difficult. Land rent and inheritances can be subject to special taxation outside the income tax field. Differentiation and graduated rates based upon quantitative measurement are not easily combined. The correlation between "earned" income and the size of income is not perfect, but it is sufficient to allow some recognition of the special claim of service incomes in the application of graduated rates.[11] The objective of including property in ability to pay can be achieved by an effective death tax or perhaps a net worth tax.

TREATMENT OF ANNUITIES AND INSURANCE

A very troublesome aspect of the income tax is its treatment of annuities and insurance. In case of an annuity, the annuitant deposits a sum with an insurance company (usually by installments over a period of years) and receives a return either as a lump sum or as an allowance during the annuitant's life or some combination of the two. An insurance policy differs from an annuity in that (with some exceptions) it provides a sum or an allowance for a beneficiary other than the insured at the latter's death.

The taxation of annuities has followed several rules over the years. Originally the annuitant paid nothing until his capital was returned and then he paid on all his receipts; later he was taxed on 3 percent of his capital during the period of capital replacement and then on all his receipts; since the 1954 Act the interest and capital factors are calculated over the years from the first payment to the taxpayer's expectancy and taxes are paid on the interest factor only; whether death occurs before or after expectancy does not matter. Thus, if a taxpayer at age 70 is expected to live ten years and receives $1200 per year on the capital sum of $10,000, taxes are and will continue to be due on the interest factor of $200 per year.[12]

---

[11] Harold M. Groves, "Commons' Theory of Reasonable Value as Applied to Taxation," *Property Taxes* (New York: Tax Policy League, 1939), pp. 174–186.

[12] See *The Taxation of Pensions and Annuities* (report), 79th Cong., 2d Sess., 1946. The 1948 revenue act inaugurated a double personal credit for taxpayers over 65 years of age and the 1954 act added an additional retirement credit for retirement income (other than social security) meeting certain qualifications.

Private and public retirement schemes are a large and growing problem for the income tax. Private pension plans have developed at a phenomenal rate, stimulated in part by high marginal levies on corporate income which cheapened the dollar invested in them by business taxpayers. Pension schemes to qualify fully for deduction and postponement of tax must meet certain specifications, including a requirement that the plan must not discriminate in favor of officers and another that it must cover 70 percent or more of regular employees. Plans may be integrated with social security protection. If the system qualifies, employers' contributions are deductible and not taxed to the employee until later received by the latter during retirement. Employees' contributions are not deductible, and they are treated during retirement as an annuity. There are other alternative ways of treating these deferments of income. So-called fringe benefits might be made taxable to the employee when they are incurred on his behalf. The employee's contribution could be regarded as deductible when it occurs and taxed when later enjoyed. Thus the tax-policy questions involved in the so-called pension-trust movement are substantial.

Professional groups in the United States, particularly doctors, have complained about alleged discrimination in the tax laws as they apply to pensions. They say that corporations regularly provide for executives' retirement by means of pension contributions but that there is no equivalent advantage for the self-employed. The Revenue Act of 1962 broke ground in this area providing that the self-employed (but not the employed who have no retirement system) might with qualifications deduct half of saving for retirement up to $2500 or 10 percent of income whichever was lower.

JURISDICTIONAL PROBLEMS AND TERRITORIAL MULTIPLE TAXATION

It sometimes proves quite as difficult to determine *where* this or that shall be taxed as to determine if it shall be taxed or *to whom*. Jurisdictional problems are especially acute when income taxes are employed by lower levels of government.

STATE PERSONAL INCOME TAXES IN THE UNITED STATES

What Income May the States Tax? One of the most difficult problems which the states are called upon to face in the administration of a state income tax is the determination of what income can and should be taxed as belonging within the state's jurisdiction. As applied to individuals, the question is which income shall follow the domicile of the tax-payer and which the source or situs of the income. The Constitution and the United States Supreme Court allow the states a wide latitude in this matter. The Court has held that it is not illegal for the state in which the taxpayer is domiciled to tax all of his income wherever earned; nor is it unconstitutional for a state which has no jurisdiction over the taxpayer as such to tax all of the income earned within the state, whether from property, business, or salary. It is clear that a state may not tax the interest and dividends *received* by a nonresident from a corporation within the state, but there is legal precedent for sustaining a tax upon the dividends *paid out* by such a corporation.

State Policies.   When it comes to the matter of policy, state statutes differ considerably in their rules on jurisdiction. Wisconsin traditionally taxed only income "earned within the state," by which was meant that income from property or business follows the location of such property or business, and income from services and intangibles follows the domicile of the taxpayer. With the inauguration of tax withholding, service income of nonresidents earned within the state was also covered. Some states (for example, Delaware) tax entirely on the domicile principle, taxing all income of individuals domiciled within the state regardless of where the income is earned. Many states (New York, for example) tax residents on all their income wherever earned, and, in addition, nonresidents on the income (including service income) earned within the state. New York also provides an arrangement under which it agrees to credit the tax paid by a nonresident to his own state against the New York tax, provided the other state reciprocates. New Jersey recently attempted to take advantage of this provision by taxing the earned income of commuters only. Whether this is constitutional has yet to be decided.

Gaps and Overlapping in the State Personal Taxation.   It will be observed that many chances for double taxation exist in the variety of state rules concerning jurisdiction. A taxpayer residing in Delaware and owning property in Wisconsin is taxed twice on the income from such property. On the other hand, if the individual lives in Wisconsin and owns property in Delaware, he pays no tax at all upon the income from that property.

The courts have been urged to set up strict rules of jurisdiction in the income tax field which would ensure that income can be taxed by one state and one state only. However, this raises the difficult question: If only one state is allowed to tax a certain income, should it be that of the taxpayer's domicile or that of the origin of the income? Faced with such problems, the present Supreme Court is likely to hold that these are matters for legislatures rather than the judiciary to decide. Credits to residents or nonresidents are sometimes allowed, but these also vary from state to state. On the merits, both states have a legitimate claim, and logic calls for an even division of tax on overlapping income. Progress toward uniformity in legislation can be made by interstate negotiation, agreement, and reciprocal action. But, in these jurisdictional matters, state interests often conflict, and each state is likely to follow its own advantage.

The multiple-taxation problem in the operation of state income taxes is aggravated by the application of different rules as to the domicile of the taxpayer. Some states provide that, if the taxpayer spends seven months or some other proportion of the year within their jurisdiction, this is sufficient to establish residence and personal jurisdiction over the taxpayer; others require a more permanent domicile; and the location of permanent domicile itself may be disputed by two or more states.[13]

Procedure in Dividing Income of Interstate Corporations. When it comes to corporations, the problem of jurisdiction is quite as troublesome as in the case of individuals. Here the problem arises in the apportionment of the income of interstate corporations doing business within and without the state. Sometimes such corporations keep separate accounts of their business by states. There are judicial decisions which permit them to be taxed on such division unless it can be shown to be unreasonable. But ordinarily no division is attempted by the corporation, and the states are compelled to establish rules of procedure for making such division themselves.

One of the fairest systems of apportionment is that applied in Massachusetts, where the law lays down the general rule [14] that income of interstate corporations shall be apportioned according to the average of three ratios: relative tangible property, wages and salaries paid, and gross receipts (sales and rentals or royalties) within and without the state. The Wisconsin law is similar, also using three elements in its apportionment formula: tangible property, cost of manufacture, and sales. Thus, if a corporation has 70 percent of its tangible property in Wisconsin, if 60 percent of its cost of manufacturing is incurred there, and if 20 percent of its sales are made from Wisconsin offices, 50 percent of the entire net income is apportioned to Wisconsin and is taxable under its law. In practice, tax departments find these formulas too general to be applicable to all interstate corporations and employ them as guiding principles rather than as hard and fast rules of measurement.

Territorial Multiple Taxation in Dividing Corporate Income. Application of the state income tax to corporate income creates serious problems

---

[13] The problem of double domicile is discussed in Chapter 10.

[14] The apportionment formula applies to certain business income only; income from securities, for instance, follows the domicile of the corporation.

of multiple taxation. If all states used the same standard for the division of corporate income, the problem would be unimportant. But the states employ a great variety of standards. If one were to use tangible property and another sales as their sole criteria, and were a company to own all its property in the first and make all its sales from the second, complete double taxation would occur. On the whole, the courts have shown little disposition to tackle this problem by compelling a uniform procedure.[15]

Further Problems in Allocating Income. It should be apparent from what has been said that the origin of income is no simple matter to determine, and actually it is much more difficult than has been indicated. For example, the sales activity of a business is usually allocated to the state and municipality in which its sales office is located and *from* which it makes its sales. Waiving a number of very troublesome matters of definition in the application of this rule, the question arises as to whether or not the area in which the company's customers are located or from which it draws its labor supply (the area in which it does business in the broadest sense) may not have some claim to its income. Corporate income from intangible property (securities) is thought to belong to the state of the corporation's domicile. This means the state which gave the corporation its charter; however, the state where it maintains its home office would seem to have a more legitimate claim. The issues of jurisdiction and apportionment of income from interstate business are now under study by a Congressional committee.[16]

JURISDICTIONAL PROBLEMS AMONG NATIONS

The problem of jurisdiction among nations is much the same as that among states. It is less acute in that the volume of international as compared with interstate transactions is less; but an additional source of confusion occurs, namely the citizenship of the taxpayer. Some progress in mitigating international multiple taxation has been made as a result of the efforts of the League of Nations, the United Nations, and other organizations. Agreements between nations have also been useful in attacking the problem.

---

[15] The courts have intervened to prevent the avoidance of the state corporate income tax by contracting away the income earned in one state to out-of-state subsidiaries. A Wisconsin corporation attempted to shift Wisconsin income beyond the jurisdiction of the state through the device of selling products manufactured in the state to an affiliated company outside of the state at a loss or not profit— *Palm Olive Co. v. Conway,* 43 Fed. (2d) 226 (1930). In this case, the Tax Commission computed what it considered to be a fair profit for the Wisconsin corporation, and its authority to do so was sustained by the federal court.

[16] Further discussion of some aspects of this problem will be found in Chapters 19 and 20.

With the advent of expanded investment abroad and the augmented concern about the balance of payments, new interest has attended the problem of applying the income tax to the foreign operations of American business. Long-standing rules have in general applied the corporate tax to the earnings of foreign branches (whether or not reinvested abroad) and to repatriated earnings of subsidiaries. In either case a credit against United States taxes for foreign taxes was allowed. The Revenue Act of 1962 attempted to apply the same rule to foreign subsidiaries (except manufacturing operations) that had been applied to branches.

The legislation was in response to considerable concern about so-called tax havens, a term applied to the organization of subsidiary companies in favorable tax areas which could take over certain operations formerly performed in, and taxable in, the United States. An administrative problem involves the fictitious transfer of profits by artificial arrangements such as selling to subsidiaries at less than would have been charged an independent company. An equity problem concerns the question of where business earnings should be taxed. An economic problem involves the effects of tax policy on international competition and the balance of payments. Encouraging foreign investment clearly involves an immediate strain on the balance because it requires the flow of cash abroad; in the long run, however, the augmented flow of repatriated funds might aid the balance.

PROBLEMS APPLICABLE TO STATE INCOME TAXES

Income Tax as a Centrally Collected—Locally Shared Tax. Some states distribute part of their income tax receipts to municipalities either on the basis of origin or some factor of need. The practice conforms to the logic that the income tax is in part a replacement for the property tax. But it confronts difficulties, among them the fact that origin is difficult to determine. Thus, when the taxpayer lives in a suburb and works in a central city, it is hard to say which municipality should receive the returned tax. Moreover, the income tax is largely an urban tax, and conflict between rural and urban communities is likely to develop over what should be done with the proceeds. The urban districts insist that taxes collected from income reported in their territory belong to them and that the use of a large portion of the receipts to finance the state or to provide state aids is unfair. They call attention to the rapidly mounting urban expenditures and the necessity for high urban taxes on real estate to meet these expenditures. Subventions and subsidies, they say, result in the continuation of homes, farms, and superfluous governments where it would be better if they were abandoned. The rural and depleted districts reply that economic areas are larger than a given city or county. The metropolis sells its goods and buys raw materials all over the state. Moreover, they claim that there is a common interest in many governmental services. For example, the metropolis is interested in rural education because, among other reasons, it draws heavily from the hinterland for its labor supply.

Widespread interest attended the innovation in New York in 1946 under which per capita payments to municipalities are substituted for taxes shared according to origin. The plan was made attractive by assuring regular payments from the state, the assurance to be backed by a reserve fund.

Migration of Industry and Wealth. One of the main arguments that has always confronted proponents of the state income tax is that this type of taxation drives industry and wealth from the state that employs it and thus tends to destroy not only its own base but that of the property tax as well. It is a well-known fact that interstate boundary lines impose limits upon state control (as well as trade union control) of industry. This is one reason why the federal government is pressed to widen its field of activities. Even where state control and state taxation might in the long run prove beneficial to industry and wealth itself, the fear of "killing the goose that lays the golden egg," or in this case the fear of causing the goose to fly to some more congenial social climate, is likely to be an effective barrier to social legislation and taxation. Industry is constantly moving about for a variety of reasons, and it is a simple matter to make it appear that it is adjusting itself to relative tax or other government-imposed burdens.

Of very great importance, though not generally understood, is the fact that state taxes are a deductible expense in calculating federal income taxes. This means that the federal government collects less federal taxes from both corporations and individuals in states that have an income tax, and this helps reduce differential total burdens among the states. Where state taxes are deductible against federal and the reverse, a combination of an 80-percent federal and a 15-percent state rate is not a 95-percent total, as might be supposed, but a total of 80.7 percent.

Legal Difficulties. In many states (including some of the wealthiest and most populous) there are impressive legal and constitutional barriers to income taxation. For example, Illinois passed an income tax law in 1932, but it was declared unconstitutional by the state supreme court. In the opinion of the court, income is property and, according to the constitution of that state, all property must be assessed at a "just and uniform rate." Similarly, in other states—among them Michigan and Indiana—the income tax has some very high constitutional hurdles to surmount.

Special Problems of Agricultural and Debtor States. It is reasonable, perhaps, to conceive of a state income tax strong enough to raise 20 or 25 percent of the revenue for state and local purposes in a state such as Illinois. But what about a state such as North Dakota, where there is very little corporate income to tax and where an individual with a $100,000 a year income is called a financial baron? North Dakota cannot expect to derive a substantial portion of its state and local revenues from its income tax unless it learns how to apply such a tax successfully to farmers and to people with small incomes.

North Dakota's problem is much aggravated, too, by the fact that it is a debtor state and much of its income is paid over its borders to creditors outside the state. The property tax is collected where the roots of income lie, but the income tax more often goes to the state in which income is enjoyed. Income tax reformers would unintentionally aggravate this problem with the proposal that all income should be taxed in the state of the recipient's domicile. In this connection it is important to remember that debtor states also require revenue.

Instability of Yield. The income tax is notoriously a "fair-weather tax," and its fluctuations in yield are likely to prove particularly embarrassing to states and municipalities, many of which can borrow for current expenses only with considerable difficulty, if at all. To meet this situation, these units of government could build up a reserve in good years for use during lean periods. But this involves the political difficulty associated with changing administrations. Probably more promising are the possibilities of developing the kind of an income tax which would be less "cycle sensitive." The position of the federal government is in striking contrast; in its case instability of revenue is now regarded as a virtue (described as built-in flexibility); the fluctuation is regarded as a compensating factor in checking the business cycle. Deficit financing is often not feasible for a government without monetary powers.[17]

The other side of the instability argument notes that taxes that do not accommodate the taxpayer's vicissitudes are onerous for him. Moreover, a tax that responds sharply to rising income is well adapted to recoup the gains from inflation and growth.

Should the States Tax Income? There is a long-standing argument as to whether the states and municipalities should (or should be allowed

---

[17] See Harold M. Groves and C. H. Kahn, "The Stability of State and Local Tax Yields," *American Economic Review*, XLII: 1 (March 1952), pp. 87–102; Harold M. Groves, "National Unity in Fiscal Policy—State and Local Aspects," *Proceedings of the National Tax Association Conference*, 1955, pp. 36–45.

to) "fish in the income tax stream" at all. Developments in Canada under which the income tax has been nationalized by agreement between the provinces and central government pose the question sharply. On the negative side, it is argued that multitudinous taxes on income will harass business and add confusion to an already complicated tax system. On the affirmative side, it is argued that income is the most rationally defensible of tax bases, that it supplements the property tax effectively, and that development in this area is essential to the maintenance of strong, independent local self-government.

MUNICIPAL INCOME TAXES

Mention has been made of the very considerable recent development of income taxation at the local level of government.[18] This raises many problems among them the following: (1) Should the local tax be a totally independent levy or should it be based on the state (or federal) tax or tax base with or without the assistance of state administration? (2) Should the tax extend to all income or only to certain kinds as in Philadelphia (payroll and unincorporated business earnings)? (3) Should the tax provide exemptions and progressive rates and if so in what degree? (4) What about jurisdictional disputes (as between suburbs and central cities) and the cumulation of levy by successive layers of government? (5) What is the incidence of a local levy on income?

Space does not permit an extensive discussion of these problems but the author may venture a few opinions concerning some of them. As to jurisdictional disputes, such conflicts at this level can be controlled by state legislation. In case taxpayers live in one district and work in another, the happiest solution would be a division of the tax. Elsewhere [19] the author has suggested that we might take a lesson in intergovernmental tax relations from the tax systems of the Scandinavian countries that allow municipalities to supplement the rates of the national taxes with semi-independent levies of their own. More conservative exemptions and little if any graduation are the rule at the local level, and very considerable local discretion is allowed in these matters without requiring dual administration. Local taxes must lean toward conservatism because they can be easily avoided by migration and because dependability of revenues

---

[18] Leon Jay Quinto, *Muncipal Income Taxation in the United States,* Technical Monograph No. 2, Finance Project, Mayor's Committee on Management Survey of the City of New York (New York, 1952); Robert Sigafoos, *The Municipal Income Tax* (Chicago: Public Administration Service, 1955).

[19] Harold M. Groves, "New Sources of Light on Intergovernmental Fiscal Relations," *National Tax Journal,* V: 3 (September 1952), pp. 234–238.

is of great concern to local governments. Municipal income taxes seek some middle alternative between regressive and progressive taxation, and they recognize the importance of jobs as a potential tax source. They are a means of recapturing some of the immense investment in education.

UNDERDEVELOPED AREAS

The income tax ranks very high among revenue sources in the opinion of most critics because of its relatively dependable incidence, its direct relation to ability to pay, and its availability to promote more equal distribution of wealth. But its important and successful application depends in high degree upon certain conditions that may not prevail in underdeveloped areas. Among these conditions are the following: (1) widespread literacy; (2) a reasonably high achievement in the arts of accounting; (3) willingness of taxpayers to accept direct taxation as a self-imposed discipline; (4) predominance of urban living or at least of agriculture that relies on exchange rather than subsistence farming; (5) abundance of capital and saving.

Thus it is one thing to recommend an income tax for a predominant role in the United States and another to do so for Mexico. A further development of the property tax and of certain consumption taxes might better suit the latter country.[20] The consensus among those who have studied the subject supports the view that an income tax with steeply graduated rates and ample exemptions can play a highly useful role, but the tax is not recommended for mass application. Special attention is needed to include speculative gains in the base of the tax or to reach them independently. This is to recognize the unfortunate propensity to invest in real estate and speculate in inventory especially if inflation attends a developmental program.[21] And of course, communist countries such as Russia present further factors to consider: there the distribution of income follows a planned pattern and sales taxes become hardly distinguishable from the profits on state industries. It is not an anomaly, as sometimes argued, that the sales tax in Russia overshadows the largely undeveloped income tax.[22]

---

[20] Richard Goode, "Reconstruction of Foreign Tax Systems," *Proceedings of the National Tax Association Conference,* 1951, pp. 212–221.

[21] *Taxes and Fiscal Policy in Under Developed Countries,* United Nations Report, United Nations Technical Assistance Administration (New York, 1954).

[22] In addition to the publications mentioned in the footnotes, the following sources are recommended to supplement the income tax chapters: William Vickrey, *Agenda for Progressive Taxation* (New York: The Ronald Press Company, 1947); Henry C. Simons, *Federal Tax Reform* (Chicago: University of Chicago Press,

SUMMARY OF CHAPTERS 7, 8, AND 9

Although there had been considerable experimentation with the net income tax in the United States in earlier years, the era of continual and important application of the tax by the federal government dates from the adoption of the 16th Amendment in 1913 and, by the states, from the discovery of a successful technique of administration in 1911.

The income tax base is arrived at by refining gross income, or, more specifically, by subtracting certain items classed as income not taxed, deductions, and credits. Deductions are of two classes: business and professional expenses, and items of personal expense designated by law as deductible. Once the base is determined, the tax is calculated by applying graduated rates to the brackets or sectors of income. The federal law applies to corporations as well as to individuals, and much the same procedure is applied to both. State income taxes, in operation in about two thirds of the states, follow the federal pattern with considerable variation, including higher exemptions and lower rates.

In choosing a concept of income for the tax base, many difficulties are encountered. For example, income consumed without an exchange ("imputed income") is a part of the national product but is not ordinarily counted in the tax base. Patronage dividends of cooperative associations are said to be nothing more than a "retroactive price cut." Impairments of capital by depreciation, depletion, and obsolescence are a recognized offset, but they offer many problems of proper timing and of public policy. Gains and losses on inventory constitute another problem area, particularly since *lifo* accounting has claimed recognition. More fundamental than any of the above is the long-standing question of whether capital gains constitute income.

Many techniques have been evolved to facilitate the administration of the net income tax. Collection at the source is one of these; it has been used in Europe for many years and was introduced in the United States as a withholding tax on wages and salaries during World War II. This method of collection has many advantages, particularly in the timeliness of payment and convenience for the taxpayer, but it is difficult to

1950); Roy Blough, *The Federal Taxing Process* (Englewood Cliffs, N.J.: Prentice-Hall, Inc., 1952); Committee on Ways and Means, *Tax Revision Compendium,* 3 vols. symposium, 1959. On legal aspects the magazine *Taxes,* Commerce Clearing House, Chicago, offers numerous articles of interest; an abbreviated tax service such as those supplied by Prentice-Hall, New York, and Commerce Clearing House, Chicago, can be highly useful.

adapt to the differentiation found in many income tax laws. Among other techniques used in the United States are information at the source, auditing, penalties, and self-reporting. The size of the administrative load and the inadequacy of appropriations for auditing, place a considerable premium on an attitude which regards taxes as a self-imposed discipline.

A moot point in American income tax policy is the treatment of capital gains and losses. This income, if so it may be called, has special characteristics, including its irregularity, long and indefinite periodicity, and amenability to manipulation. Possible alternatives of tax policy include the traditional British procedure of largely ignoring these receipts, treating them like other income, giving them a special classification with special treatment, use of a so-called roll-over (postponement), and taxing them under a levy entirely separate from the income tax. The problem is complicated by the fact that gains accrued on assets passing at death are wiped out for income tax purposes. Treatment like other income, except for ceiling rates and a certain segregation of losses, is the rule applied by our federal system. Plausible claim for special treatment is based on the idea that full taxation would unduly discourage exchange and have other undesirable consequences.

Probably the most troublesome problem in income tax policy concerns the treatment of corporations, corporate income, cash dividends, stock dividends, and particularly undistributed profits. Business income may be taxed at a flat or graduated rate, with or without the inclusion of income from nonincorporated business and with or without account of the ratio of income to capital. Stock dividends have been held by the United States Supreme Court not to be income, but the Court's decision is vulnerable on many points and has been substantially modified by the Court itself. Anyway a decision not to tax them (with qualifications) has been made by Congress. The excess profits tax is based on the rate of earnings in relation to capital or during a war, on the ratio of wartime to prewar earnings. Strong justification for such taxation during a war is afforded by the weakness of competitive controls, but the tax involves extraordinary difficulties of definition and administration. Extensive relief for corporations with abnormal experience has been found necessary but very difficult.

Undistributed corporate income was specially taxed under the income tax law of 1936, but this law was repealed in 1939. Undistributed profits are usually accepted as a desirable means of recruiting new equity capital, but the unequal application of taxes to this disposition of earnings as compared with dividends is criticized both on the ground of equity and that of economic effects. Many proposals for the special tax treatment of undistributed profits and the mitigation of double taxation of corporate earnings are currently entertained; among the most popular is the deductibility of part or all of dividends paid in applying the corporate tax.

Other income tax problems include a selection of a proper level and form of personal exemptions, the role of personal expense deductions including the standard deduction, avoidance associated with trusts, personal holding companies and family partnerships, income-splitting, pensions, and the more equitable treatment of irregular income. The latter may take the form of carry-overs or averaging. Equal division of income among spouses, introduced in 1948, solves some difficult problems but creates others.

The income tax presents many problems of multiple taxation. In the personal income tax this involves the question of which jurisdiction may claim the right to tax; whether it is where the recipient of income is domiciled or where he "earns" the income. In the case of interstate corporations, the income must be apportioned among the states in which the corporation is doing business. This is a difficult task. In the case of a foreign subsidiary corporations, the exemption of reinvested earnings is at issue.

State and municipal income taxes involve certain other problems such as instability of revenues and the migration of industry and wealth. Municipal taxes may be entirely independent levies or they may be attached to state or federal levies to avoid dual definition and administration. Considerations of revenue and migration avoidance indicate conservative exemptions and graduation. These taxes raise sharply the question of whether the important income tax instrument should not be reserved for the federal government.

Underdeveloped economies frequently lack certain prerequisites for the important application of the net income tax; but in a mature capitalistic economy the net income tax, in spite of its many difficulties and limitations, is usually accepted as the most rational method of raising revenue.

PROBLEMS

1. John Smith has a taxable income of $100,000, out of which he buys $50,000 worth of stock; he gives half the stock to his wife and the other half to his son. Will these transactons reduce his income tax liability now or in the future?

2. Jasper Jones has a $6200 gross income, deductions of $1000, and a family exemption of $1200. Mrs. Jones has no income of her own. Taking account of income-splitting, calculate how much tax

the Jones would pay. Would the Jones have to pay less if half the income were earned by Mrs. Jones?

3. Mr. and Mrs. White have an income of $10,000 all earned by Mr. White; Mr. and Mrs. Black have an income of $10,000 to which each contributes half; Mr. Brown and Mr. Green, both single, have incomes of $10,000 and $5000 respectively. Explain how these taxpayers would fare under mandatory joint returns, optional joint or separate returns, splitting. On what grounds might it be urged that any of these taxpaying units should pay at a higher rate than another?

4. A corporation with an income of $1 million does 51 percent of its business in an income tax state and declares dividends to X and Y, one domiciled in the taxing state and the other domiciled in an adjoining state. Consider the jurisdictional problems here involved.

5. Peter Perkins sets up a trust for the benefit of two sons with a trust company as trustee. The trust can be amended at any time by agreement between Perkins and the trustee. Perkins reserves the power to borrow from the trust without interest. Income from the trust is to accumulate for 20 years when the sons will receive it in equal portions along with the corpus of the trust. However, if either son should need money at any time, the trustee can distribute the necessary amounts at its discretion. Explain how this arrangement would be treated by the net income tax and why.

6. Labor leaders frequently take the position that the personal exemption for individuals is equivalent to the allowance for maintenance and depreciation for business. Is this position sound?

7. Would there be a gain for incentives if exemptions were confined to a minimum allowance for the poor and the standard deduction were built into the rate scale, thus broadening the base of the income tax and making possible the reduction of marginal rates?

8. Who is to blame for subtle forms of income tax avoidance?

9. Comment on the proposition: No splitting is allowed in the case of a father-and-son partnership where the son contributes only capital that his father has given to him.

10. It is said that the deduction for contributions means that the federal treasury matches individuals' gifts and at a much higher ratio in the case of wealthy than in that of poor givers. Is this in the public interest? It is also said that no adequate administrative check on contributions has been devised. What could be done about this problem?

11. What are the social considerations that support concessions to fluctuating income?

12. What are the fundamental difficulties in any system of averaging? Explain the difference between a simple and a moving average.

13. What is the logic of special concessions to so-called earned income? Is the case convincing under all circumstances?

14. Explain the present system of treating annuities for tax purposes.

15. The *XYZ* Corporation of the United States creates a marketing subsidiary in Luxemberg, and the subsidiary invests in industrial developments in other European countries. Some of these developments send exports to the United States. Consider the issues of public policy here involved.

16. State the argument for or against the tax-credit system of calculating income tax exemptions.

17. Contrast the difficulties of the federal government and the states because of unstable income tax revenues.

18. Minnesota taxes wage income according to situs, Wisconsin according to domicile. Does this mean that a person who lives in Minneapolis and works in Hudson, Wisconsin will be double taxed?

19. What is the bearing of income tax deductibility on migration to escape the state net income tax?

20. Contrast the type of income tax used by Philadelphia with that used by the federal government. Would a federal-type tax suit Philadelphia's needs?

21. Consider the proper role of an income tax in Iraq.

10

DEATH AND GIFT TAXES

INTRODUCTION

In the total revenue picture, the death tax is not very important (less than 2 percent) and it could be dropped with hardly a ripple in the treasury. Moreover, the tax does not affect many people or anybody very often. While the influence of war and inflation have brought the income tax to the crossroads, less than 2 percent of the adult population will meet the qualifications of the federal estate tax fraternity ($60,000 exempt). It is true that the state inheritance taxes are much broader, but they are also much less intensive as to rates. It is true that existing death tax institutions might produce much more revenue if their weaknesses were repaired. But their potential is limited by the fact that wealth is only a small multiple of annual income and turns over by death only once in a generation. Nevertheless, it is generally conceded that wealth as well as income is a factor in ability to pay; the death tax is the only personal tax on property in the American tax system. The social effects of the tax, moreover, go beyond its place in the revenue system. Finally, for those who contemplate a career in the legal profession, the estate tax cannot be overlooked lightly; it is a highly remunerative field of practice and one in which bad advice can cost clients heavily.

243

FORMS OF DEATH TAXES

Death taxes assume two major forms, one called the estate tax and the other, the inheritance tax. The term *estate tax* is used to describe a levy upon the entire estate left by the decedent, whereas the term *inheritance tax* is applied to a levy upon the separate shares of the estate transferred to the beneficiaries. Ordinarily, estate taxes provide for a single uniform exemption, although they may also allow specific exemptions according to number of dependents and relationship to decedent (similar to those provided in income taxes). In either case, if the rates are graduated, the brackets apply to the net estate as a whole. Inheritance taxes, on the other hand, usually carry an elaborate classification of heirs and provide a specific exemption and a special scale of rates for each class. Graduation in such laws is based upon two factors: *The size of the share* and the *degree of relationship between the heir and the decedent.* Table 3 presents a typical schedule of rates, exemptions, and classification by heirs and size of inheritance, as embodied in the California law (1963).

   Estate Tax versus the Inheritance Tax.   The estate tax is simpler and more productive than the inheritance tax. It avoids entirely the exceedingly complicated task of determining the value of shares where the transfer involves life estates, contingencies, and remainders.[1] The inheritance tax, on the other hand, gives special weight to the ability to pay of the heir, although if his circumstances apart from the inheritance are not taken into account, the measure of his ability to pay is incomplete. Inheritance tax rates are often deceptive; they may appear very high in the top brackets, yet the average effective rate of the tax on all transfers may be very low. The overwhelming majority of estates are left to near relatives, which means that most of them would fall under Class A in the schedule presented below. An analysis of inheritance tax transfers in Wisconsin in 1927 and 1928 showed an average effective rate of 3.1 percent.[2] The Wisconsin rates were somewhat more severe than those of the California tax now in effect.

   Refinements of the Inheritance Tax.   The inheritance tax is generally thought to be a refinement on the estate tax. Some further modifications have at times been suggested, and at least one has also been tried. Of

---

[1] A life estate is a grant of limited enjoyment of an estate during the life of the heir. A contingent estate is one in which enjoyment is conditioned upon the occurrence of some event which may or may not take place. A remainder is the underlying right to property which accompanies the grant of one or more life estates.

[2] *Report of the Wisconsin Tax Commission* (Madison, 1928), p. 208.

TABLE 3

Rates of the California Inheritance Tax, 1963

Relationship of beneficiary to deceased	Exemption	Rates (in percent) applicable to the fraction of the inheritance in excess of exemption from						
		0 to $25,000	$25,000 to $50,000	$50,000 to $100,000	$100,000 to $200,000	$200,000 to $300,000	$300,000 to $500,000	$500,000 and up
Class A								
Minor child	12,000	2	3	4	7	9	9	10
Husband,* wife,* other child, parents, grandparents, grandchildren	5,000	2	3	4	7	9	9	10
Class B								
Brother, sister, or descendant of either; son-in-law; daughter-in-law	2,000	6	10	13	15	15	17	18
Class C								
Uncle, aunt, or descendant of either	500	7	12	15	15	15	18	18
Class D								
All other †	50	10	15	18	18	18	22	24

* One half of the community property is also exempt.
† Does not include charitable bequests; these are entirely exempt.
SOURCE: Commerce Clearing House, *Inheritance Estate and Gift Tax Service*, 1963, ¶ 1300.

the suggestions, the best known is that of Rignano, the Italian economist, who proposed differentiating between what the deceased has added to his estate and what he himself had inherited and now passes on.[3] Another proposal is to vary the inheritance tax rates according to the wealth of the heirs at the time of the transfer. This was experimented with by Germany and Italy for a short time between 1919 and 1923, but the results were unsatisfactory because of administrative difficulties involved in valuing the prior wealth of the heirs.[4] A further proposal is to integrate the inheritance tax with the net income tax. But this ignores the fact that death transfers are in property rather than income. It may be better to proceed in this field on the supposition that death taxes fall upon the decedent and thus confine them to levies on the estate only. As in the case of the income tax, an estate tax may be conceived as a levy upon what the deceased has to dispose regardless of how he may choose to dispose of it. Differentiation among heirs may be expected in due course from the income tax and future estates tax.

This chapter includes an account of the gift tax; it is a member of the death tax family principally because its employment is largely to prevent avoidance of the death tax. For reasons that will become apparent presently, current proposals contemplate a merger of the estate and gift tax so that all transfers from one donor would be subject to one cumulative transfer tax. Integration could also be applied to the inheritance and gift taxes.[5] Either a death tax or gift tax might be refined to take more account of the time elapsing between successive transfers.

THE HISTORY OF DEATH TAXES

One of the earliest recorded taxes is the inheritance tax, which dates all the way back to antiquity. In the Middle Ages the inheritance tax appeared as one of the institutions of the feudal system.[6]

In modern times Great Britain is recognized as the country in which

---

[3] Eugenio Rignano, *The Social Significance of the Inheritance Tax,* tr. W. J. Shultz (New York: Alfred A. Knopf, 1924), part I, chap. I.

[4] W. J. Shultz, *The Taxation of Inheritance* (Boston: Houghton Mifflin Company, 1926), pp. 309–311.

[5] Recently a new species called an "accessions tax" has been proposed. It would accumulate all receipts by gift or death transfer to a given donee and in addition would appropriate to the government a prorata share of the earnings of property in trust. See Harry J. Rudick, "What Alternative to the State and Gift Taxes?" *California Law Review,* 38: 1 (March 1950), pp. 150–182.

[6] Under this system the ultimate title to all land was vested in the sovereign, and inheritance could take place more or less only at his sufferance. Property was usually allowed to pass freely from father to son, but there was no clearly recog-

death taxes have reached their highest development—at least from the standpoint of their relative place in the revenue system. British death taxes in modern form date back to 1894. The British system formerly consisted of several taxes: the legacy and succession duties (like our state inheritance taxes) and an estate tax. In 1949 the succession (inheritance) part of the dual system was dropped in favor of the single estate duty.

Although the federal government of the United States had used death taxes as emergency measures in previous periods, it was not until 1916, under the pressure of revenue needs for World War I, that an estate tax became a permanent addition to the federal revenue system. The early tax was very mild compared with present-day standards. It carried an exemption of $50,000 and rates ranging from 1 to 10 percent. In 1963, the exemption was $60,000, and rates ranged from 3 to 77 percent, the latter upon portions of taxable estates above $10 million.

State inheritance taxes date back to the Pennsylvania law of 1826, and there were some probate duties in even earlier periods. Early laws were characterized by weak administrations, proportional rates, and limited application (to collateral heirs and, in some cases, personal property only). The New York law of 1885 was carefully drawn and well administered, although it still applied only to collateral heirs and was a proportional tax. Direct heirs were included in 1891, but it was the earlier law which served as a model for the other states—that is, until Wisconsin enacted its progressive inheritance tax in 1903. The Wisconsin law was hailed as the first scientific inheritance tax act. In addition to the elimination of the objectionable features mentioned above, its rates were graduated both according to the amount of the transfer and the degree of relationship between the heir and the deceased. And the act broke precedent by including real estate along with personal property, even in its application to direct heirs.[7] The state inheritance tax (and occasionally,

---

nized right other than that of the ruler to give or take title. In case the deceased left no direct heirs, the property was supposed to escheat to the crown, although relatives might acquire good title if they paid the crown a "relief." This "relief" was what might be considered the feudal equivalent of the modern inheritance tax. In some countries, notably, France, Spain, and Portugal, direct lines of descent can be traced between these medieval feudal obligations and their modern inheritance taxes. Even when there is no apparent connection between the two exactions, the medieval principle of escheat is sometimes relied upon to justify the modern tax. It was the principal basis upon which the state and federal courts of the United States sustained the legality of the state inheritance tax.—Shultz, *op. cit.,* pp. 7–10. Two court cases discussing this principle are *Magoun v. Illinois Trust and Savings Bank,* 170 U.S. 283 (1898); *United States v. Perkins,* 163 U.S. 625 (1896).

[7] Solomon Huebner, "The Inheritance Tax in the American Commonwealths," *Quarterly Journal of Economics,* XVIII (August 1904), pp. 529–550; Max West, *The Inheritance Tax* (New York: Columbia University Press, 1908), pp. 97–155; Shultz, *op. cit.,* pp. 98–135.

estate tax) has gained much ground both extensively and intensively during the last four decades.[8] However, it is fair to say that, whether the test be in terms of the law, the administration of the tax, or the revenue need, state death taxes are not very impressive.

RELATION OF FEDERAL AND STATE DEATH TAXES

Whether the federal government, the states, or both should use the death tax field as a source of revenue has been a matter of some dispute. Some early attempts to inaugurate a federal estate tax in peacetime (as in 1909) were strongly opposed by state officials. One of the strongest opponents was the National Tax Association, an imposing organization consisting mainly of scholars and state tax administrators.[9] Sixteen years later this organization was still opposed to a federal death tax, and in 1925, in cooperation with a Special National Conference on Inheritance Taxation, it went on record for the repeal of the federal estate tax in order to leave this source of revenue to the states.[10] Another prominent representative of the opposition was Andrew Mellon who, while Secretary of the Treasury, appeared before the Ways and Means Committee of the House of Representatives and presented the view that "by tradition, legal theory, and revenue necessity" the death tax belongs to the states.[11] He stated that his conclusion was not based on opposition to death taxes, but on the theory that some taxes, of which the estate tax is one, can be more properly levied by the states than by the federal government.

---

[8] The enactment of the federal credit in 1924 and 1926 had a particularly stimulating and unifying effect. The credit provision of the federal law permits payment of part of the federal estate tax with state death tax receipts and thus alleviates some of the burden that might result from paying both state and federal taxes on the same estate. At present only Nevada fails to take advantage of this credit, and several states levy a tax which is just sufficient to cover it. Most of the other states, including those with some other form of death taxes, have also enacted special legislation (usually a minimum estate tax) which insures them full advantage of this provision of the federal law.

The predominant form of death tax among the states is that on inheritance. The California schedule given in Table 3 is fairly typical of most state inheritance taxes—that is, they are graduated according to both size of legacy and kinship between the decedent and the beneficiaries. Exemptions, although not usually as large as that allowed by the federal law, are fairly generous.—John Gronouski, "Inheritance, Estate and Gift Taxes," *Michigan Tax Studies*, 1958, pp. 470–471.

[9] Shultz, *op. cit.*, pp. 155–156.

[10] *Bulletin of the National Tax Association*, XI: 3 (December 1925), p. 70.

[11] *Hearings, Revenue Revision, 1927–28*, 69th and 70th Cong., House of Representatives, Committee on Ways and Means, p. 13.

FEDERAL VERSUS STATE DEATH TAXES

The legal-theory argument referred to above is based upon the proposition that the state has the ultimate title to land and other property. It is under state law that property at the time of death passes from the deceased to the heir, *and it is to the state that the property escheats in case there is no heir*. Possibly these facts give the state easier access to information concerning estates than is available to the federal government, but this hardly seems a weighty objection to the latter's remaining in the death tax field.

Revenue Necessity.   As to revenue necessity, it probably is true that the states have less financial resources and relatively more need for revenue than the federal government. But certainly a plausible case could be made for the reverse of this proposition, particularly since the recent federal deficits.

Relinquishment and Low Rates.   Although the proponents of federal abandonment of the death tax field to the states profess no opposition to death taxes as such, the fact remains that, were the federal government to step out of the picture, state competition would reduce death taxes to a bare minimum. States are sorely tempted to bid for wealthy residents, particularly for the aged ones, by setting up very lenient death taxes or by entirely eliminating such taxes. Any state which would refuse to enter this competition would be pressed to do so for fear of losing "the goose that lays the golden eggs." Florida in 1924 adopted a constitutional amendment expressly ruling out all inheritance taxation. This was done with the avowed purpose of inducing the wealthy to establish residence there. The state is said to have thought it good business to tax the wealth that might be brought within its borders before the owners died rather than after. Not to be outdone, Nevada repealed its inheritance tax law in 1925.

The Difficulty of Localizing Inheritances.   Another argument in favor of retaining the federal tax is that it makes for a *more equitable distribution of death tax revenues and the benefits resulting therefrom*. Were the federal government to withdraw from the field, certain states would secure an undue advantage in their share of revenue from this source. Some states, like New York, would procure a relatively large revenue from the tax, whereas others, like North Dakota and Montana, would derive but scant benefit from it. Huge fortunes in particular have frequently been derived from business profits which may have come from trade over an area far beyond the limits of any one state. For example, when a wealthy manufacturer of tobacco died not long ago, it was felt that, since his large estate had been built by contributions from tobacco farmers and consumers in many parts of the country, it should not be earmarked for one state just because he happened to have resided there. Similarly, a person might make a fortune harvesting the natural resources of a specific state and move to another shortly before his death. Through the use of death tax revenues by the federal government for central purposes, or for distribution in aids to the states, a broader benefit could be derived from the tax.

Multiple Taxation. There is still another argument for the retention of the federal death tax. It is contended that the use of the tax by the states must encounter the confusion and inequities of multiple taxation. The possibilities of multiple taxation in the death tax field as will be seen later are substantial.

FEDERAL CREDIT—THE 80-PERCENT-CREDIT CLAUSE

The federal government has devised and adopted a compromise solution of this issue of federal versus state death taxation. The compromise is called the federal credit and provides that, within limits, the taxpayer may pay his federal estate tax with state inheritance tax receipts. *The limit is 80 percent of the federal tax* computed according to the 1926 schedule of rates. The effect of the credit is to deprive a state which has no death tax of any revenue from this source, although its residents must pay quite as much tax as though they lived in a state which imposed such a tax. Suppose, for example, that the federal tax on a particular estate is $100,000 and that the state death taxes are $80,000. The estate would pay only a total of $100,000, 80 percent of which would go to the state. If the decedent had moved his domicile to a tax-free state shortly before his death, the estate would still have to pay $100,000, the only difference being that all of the money would be paid to the federal government.

Effect of Federal Credit upon State Legislation. Florida carried the federal credit law to the United States Supreme Court, contending that it was unconstitutional because it was not uniform in its effect and was an undue interference by the federal government with the freedom of the states in their choice of a revenue system. The Supreme Court, however, in a unanimous decision sustained the law.[12]

When the credit was adopted, some states with death tax laws hastened to advertise their advantage over the noninheritance-tax states as domiciles for wealthy taxpayers. With total death tax burdens no higher than those of the noninheritance-tax states, they could retain a large part of the revenue instead of sending it all to Washington and would thus need less from other taxes. This was too much for the State of Florida. By a substantial majority it voted in 1930 to amend its con-

---

[12] *Florida v. Mellon,* 273 U.S. 12 (1927).

stitution, repealing the prohibition of death taxes in that state. The amendment permitted an estate tax—but only for as long as the federal credit might be in force and only to the extent necessary to absorb the full credit allowed against the federal tax. Several other states have also enacted minimum estate tax laws in addition to their regular inheritance tax. The minimum estate tax, which empowers states to retain the difference between their own and 80 percent of the federal tax, ensures them the full benefit of the federal credit.

The federal credit has proved a useful instrument in the coordination of federal and state death taxes. But it now needs to be modernized and kept up to date. The present attachment of the credit to the now antiquated 1926 law is unfortunate. Also there is good reason to extend the crediting program to cover state and federal gift taxes.[13]

CASE FOR AND AGAINST DEATH TAXES

Death taxes are now generally accepted but there is still much debate concerning their justification and their proper role.

ARGUMENTS IN FAVOR OF DEATH TAXES

Inheritance as an Indication of Ability to Pay. Proponents of death taxes usually make much of the allegation that these levies are in accord with ability to pay. As previously stated, the view is held that property as well as income indicates ability and the death tax is a personal tax on property. Of course, the timing may be capricious depending as it does on the irregular factor of longevity. But death is a strategic time for the state to assert its claim when readjustment, reappraisal, and liquidation of property ordinarily occur. It is not too clear whether it is the ability of the deceased or that of the heir which is the target, but it does not matter too much; the ability is there to sustain the tax in either case.

Of course, the timing of the death taxes may not always seem opportune to the heir, particularly if the heir is the surviving widow. As a result of her husband's death, she may have been deprived of her main source of support. She may have difficult adjustments to make, including a financial one. It may seem to her that the government is choosing a most inopportune time to add to her cup of woe by imposing an inheri-

---

[13] Committee on Intergovernmental Fiscal Relations, *Federal, State, and Local Government Fiscal Relations,* U.S. Treasury Dept., Senate Document No. 69, 78th Congress, 1st Sess., 1943, pp. 14–16; Advisory Commission on Intergovernmental Relations, *Coordination of State and Federal Inheritance, Estate, and Gift Taxes* (Washington, 1961).

tance tax. Often, too, she may have been a partner in the amassing of the estate now left to her. These special circumstances have been widely recognized in inheritance tax laws by the grant of especially large exemptions in case of property left to a widow; the Revenue Act of 1948 extended these privileges through what is known as the marital deduction (explained later).[14]

At the other extreme among the beneficiaries is the collateral heir, or, in other words, one who is not a close relative. His ability to pay arises from being the recipient of a windfall. He finds himself suddenly possessed of wealth which he probably did not expect and which he is quite accustomed to do without. His receipt of an inheritance appears to be a very strategic occasion for the government to obtain a "contribution" to its treasury.[15]

Inheritance as "Unearned" Income. From the standpoint of the heir, the important fact in inheritance taxation is not so much the receipt of wealth as its source. To him the inheritance constitutes an unearned income. He seldom has rendered an equivalent to either society or the decedent which would ethically justify a future claim on his part upon the productivity of society. It may be necessary to allow the decedent some freedom in the disposition of his estate in order to induce him to produce and save—a point which will be considered presently. On the trusteeship theory of wealth, the decedent has earned his status as trustee in the ordeal of competition—not so the heir. Looking disinterestedly at the status of the heir and considering only the aspect of equity, one can say that he is entitled to adequate support and education to his maturity. Beyond that what he receives is special privilege and "inequality of opportunity."

Death Taxes and Equality of Opportunity. Another justification for the inheritance tax is that it serves to create equality of opportunity. This species of equality, sometimes referred to as "cradle equality," is not infrequently accepted as desirable by the most "rugged" of individualists. The idea is that we should all start at the same tape line and be allowed to go as fast and as far as our talents will carry us. Actually, of course, many are privileged to begin the race with a long financial lead, whereas others are burdened with the handicap of poverty. To the extent that death taxes tend to equalize the competition, they serve as a means whereby each generation is partially freed of the inequalities of the past.

---

[14] If a death tax could be devised which would exempt all interspouse transfers and postpone taxes on transfers to minor children until they reach their majority, this would segregate the ability to pay that is sought in this area of taxation.

[15] The importance of expectation in the psychology of sacrifice was described by Jeremy Bentham as follows: The heir would suffer no hardship, "for hardship depends on disappointment; disappointment upon expectation . . ." and if the law of succession leaves him nothing, he will not expect anything.—*The Works of Jeremy Bentham,* William Tait, ed. (Edinburgh, 1843), vol. II, p. 589.

Inheritance is generally accepted as an established feature of our economic society, but that it is a necessary part of our institution of private property and the capitalistic system, at least in its unrestricted form, has often been questioned. That there is nothing immutable about the institution is suggested by the fact that the forms, laws, and customs of which it is comprised differ very substantially both in time and space. No modern state, for instance, would give such a free hand to private owners that they could prescribe for generations ahead without limit how their property should be used. Jeremy Bentham and John Stuart Mill, among others, went so far as to question the usefulness of the institution in most cases, the former advocating its abolition for all except direct heirs and the latter proposing a severe limitation on the sum which any one individual should be allowed to inherit.[16]

Death Taxes and a Wider Distribution of Wealth. Some would justify death taxes on the theory that they tend to correct a bad distribution of wealth. This assumes, of course, that the present distribution is bad—a not uncontroversial assumption. Some aspects of this problem have been discussed in Chapter 2. It may be approached not only from the angle of equity, in which case the student asks himself what a fair distribution of wealth is, but also from the pragmatic angle which takes into consideration the adequacy of saving and spending, the wastefulness of possible extravagance and idleness on the part of heirs, and the social consequences of concentrated wealth and power. Among the social consequences that will need to be considered is the control of such institutions as the schools, churches, newspapers, radio, and cinema. Needless to say, a consideration of all these matters would carry us far afield. But it may be observed in passing that death taxes are an everready weapon for an attack on concentrated wealth and power.

Other Arguments for Death Taxes. Death taxes are relatively easy to assess and collect. Moreover, once levied, they probably cannot be shifted. They reach earnings from such securities and salaries as are exempt from the income tax,[17] and other property or income which may have avoided taxation during the owner's lifetime.[18]

---

[16] "The inequalities of property which arise from unequal industry, frugality, perseverance, talents, and to a certain extent even opportunities, are inseparable from the principle of private property, and if we accept the principle, we must bear with these consequences of it; but I see nothing objectionable in fixing a limit to what anyone may acquire by the mere favor of others, without any exercise of his faculties, and in requiring that if he desires any further accession of fortune he shall work for it." J. S. Mill, *Political Economy* (Ashley, ed.), book II, chap. II, p. 232.

[17] It is judicially well established that tax-exempt securities are not immune from death taxes. See, for instance, *Plummer v. Coler*, 178 U.S. 115 (1900).

[18] Early state inheritance taxes in some cases were confined to personal property and were based mainly upon the idea that much of such property escaped taxation during the owner's lifetime.

ARGUMENTS AGAINST DEATH TAXES

Death Taxes and the Incentive to Save. The most potent arguments against death taxes center on the allegation that they are a direct attack on the nation's capital. "We are now selling our seed grain," said one critic, referring to death taxes, "and will have nothing to sow when next spring comes." When the estate tax was introduced into the British revenue system in 1894, it was accomplished with much head-shaking on the part of capitalists, bankers, financiers, and economists, to whom it appeared as a tax on capital and a scandalous waste of the inheritance of the nation.[19] There are several respects in which an inheritance tax may be viewed as having a deleterious effect upon a nation's capital. The first is that the freedom to dispose of one's property is a necessary incentive to the accumulation of capital. Without this, it is argued that, after they have accumulated a certain amount of wealth, men will spend their time and money in idleness, waste, and riotous living.

The argument loses some of its force when one takes into account the futurity of the tax. Thus it is contended with plausibility that those who amass fortunes are congenital optimists not given to morbid thoughts and indisposed "to drop out of the game." It is likely that dollar for dollar death taxes are less inimical to incentives than income taxes. Indeed, death taxes are often supported on the ground that they strike the special privilege element in wealth while sparing the creative element.

Death Taxes and the Ability to Save. Nevertheless, it is commonly held and probably on sound ground that death taxes are peculiarly inimical to saving. It is clear that they cut into the ready-made saving that might otherwise have gone to the heir and also that they diminish the latter's capacity for future saving. Of course, income taxes and other taxes also impinge upon potential saving but they do not in the same sense come out of money that has already been saved. However, second-generation fortunes, were they not taxed, might give rise to lavish expenditure by heirs not only out of income but also out of capital. It can be contended that saving in a well-developed economy tends to be overdone, in which case the tendency of death taxes to cut savings would be salutary. And it can be noted that the government itself does some saving as when it invests a part of its taxes in durable goods.

Death Taxes and the Break-up of Effective Productive Units. One of the proper concerns of those who doubt the wisdom of death taxes is that they may destroy an effective combination of business capital and direction. Instances can be cited where small and independent businesses because of the tax are threatened with forced sale to large companies

---

[19] Henry Higgs, "Death Duties or Life Duties," *Quarterly Review*, CCLV (1930), p. 108.

(thus aggravating the monopoly problem). It may sometimes occur that a son will inherit his father's genius as well as his wealth, and in this case perhaps the social interest would be best served by preserving family continuity in the control of small firms. Moreover, efforts to keep estates liquid in preparation for death taxes may discourage their use in risk-taking enterprise.[20]

But the businessman who hopes to see his son eventually take over is not altogether defenseless in the face of the death tax. He can make use of life insurance, gifts before death, installment payment after death,[21] and the charitable trust to ease the transition of ownership. Moreover, in the more typical case where business is owned through share capital, a change of ownership may leave management unaffected.

Death Taxes and Philanthropy. In the arguments against death taxes the point is also made that only through the preservation and enlargement of private estates may we expect the institution of large-scale private philanthropy to continue. Gifts for educational and charitable purposes have been very large in the United States, probably larger than anywhere else. However, available evidence indicates that charitable bequests in recent years have amounted to only some 6 or 7 percent of total net economic estates.[22] Moreover, the short-run effect of death taxes is to encourage philanthropy; donations for most philanthropic purposes are exempt from tax and this means, in effect, that the government contributes heavily to donees specified by the taxpayer.

Other Economic Effects. Because of liquidations required by death, estate owners in later years tend to adjust their investments seeking to acquire greater liquidity. To take advantage of death tax loopholes, considerable wealth is entailed in trusts. Little is known about the creative aspects of wealth in trust but it is undoubtedly less suited for a venturesome role than wealth owned outright by individuals. The marital deduction (later explained) favors leaving property to women particularly elderly women. Thus death taxation can have some unwanted economic effects though some of the latter might be avoided with a more skillfully drawn statute.[23]

---

[20] C. Lowell Harriss, "Estate Taxes and the Family-Owned Business," *California Law Review*, 38: 1 (March 1950), pp. 117–149.

[21] The federal government allows the Commissioner to extend the time of payment not to exceed ten years. State laws are seldom so generous. On the contrary, many of them provide heavy penalties if the tax is not paid within a fairly short time.

[22] C. Lowell Harriss, "Federal Estate Taxes and Philanthropic Bequests," *Journal of Political Economy*, LVII: 4 (August 1949), pp. 337–344.

[23] For more elaborate consideration of the economic effects of death taxes consult C. Lowell Harriss, "Economic Effects of Estate and Gift Taxes," in *Federal Tax Policy for Economic Growth and Stability,* Joint Committee on the Economic Report, 84th Cong., 1st Sess., 1955, pp. 855–864.

PROBLEMS OF MULTIPLE TAXATION

Introduction. The possibilities of multiple levies in death taxation are numerous. The problem has been aggravated by a change in view by the Supreme Court, but it has been mitigated by state reciprocal legislation limiting taxation of intangibles in many states to the jurisdiction of domicile. Assume that Mr. Smith dies a resident of New York and leaves all his property to his son, Mr. Smith, Jr., of Philadelphia, Pennsylvania. The property consists of a house and lot in Toledo, Ohio, and several shares of stock in the *XYZ* Company, which stock at the time of the death is kept in a safety deposit box in Boston, Massachusetts. The *XYZ* Company is incorporated in New Jersey, owns property, manufactures, and sells goods in Michigan, Indiana, and Illinois, and has customers for its product in every state in the Union and several foreign countries. The question now is which states could and should tax what under the inheritance tax.

The possible claims of the states may be summarized as follows: New York might lay claim to part or all of the estate on the ground that the deceased was domiciled there; Pennsylvania might assert its right to tax the estate because it is the domicile of the heir; Ohio might claim the right to tax the house and lot on the ground that they are located there; Massachusetts might lay claim to the securities on similar ground; New Jersey might claim the securities as the domicile (or at all events the state of incorporation) of the company whose securities are involved; Michigan, Indiana, and Illinois might each claim part of the securities according to the relative value of the corporation's property located within each state because they are the territories in which the corporation's physical assets are located; finally, all states might make some claim on the ground that the corporation is doing business in their territory by selling to their inhabitants as customers.

Supreme Court and Multiple Taxation. Not all of these claims were ever good, and others have been outlawed by the United States Supreme Court, though of the latter some have recently been readmitted to validity. The "states at large" have never had a sound legal claim; the corporation legally does business only in the states "from" which it sells and not "to" which it sells. Logically it would seem that the state of Pennsylvania has a good claim since the ability to pay is perhaps as much the heir's as the decedent's. However, nowhere in this country, and rarely abroad, has the state of the heir's domicile asserted any claim.[24] The

---

[24] Shultz, *The Taxation of Inheritance,* pp. 239–240. This is strong evidence of the fact that death taxes are usually conceived as being taxes upon the decedent.

estate is administered in the state where the decedent was domiciled at the time of his death and which has been assumed to have exclusive rights, as far as such rights are based on domicile.

One of the most troublesome problems has been that of taxing intangible property under death taxes. Prior to 1932 there was authority for states to assess, under the inheritance tax, stocks and bonds kept within their borders even though the decedent was domiciled elsewhere. In that year, however, the Supreme Court became concerned over the possibilities of double taxation, once by the state of the domicile of the decedent and once by the state in which the securities might be kept. Therefore, it laid down the principle that, for inheritance tax purposes, intangibles follow the domicile of the owner.[25] For a number of years the Court asserted quite vigorously the unconstitutionality of the multiple taxation of intangibles. In 1939 the Court began to take a different view. In two companion cases [26] it held that both the state of the domicile and the state in which the intangibles are deposited could tax the transfer. It maintained that when a taxpayer avails himself of the benefit and protection of the laws of another state, he must pay for that protection.

Michigan, Indiana, and Illinois have a remote theoretical claim but, on the doctrine that the corporation and the stockholder are separate entities, the deceased possessed nothing over which these states have any jurisdiction. This is true because the legal title to all the corporate property is in the corporation and not the stockholder.[27]

New Jersey has a strong claim on legal grounds because, having created the corporation, it could presumably impose such conditions of incorporation as it sees fit. Until 1932 it was quite common for the state of incorporation to tax nonresidents upon the full value of their shares in the corporation. During that year the Supreme Court ruled out all rights of the states to tax merely because they had incorporated the company in which the decedent held shares.[28] This remained the law until 1942, when the Supreme Court again made it possible for states of

---

[25] *First National Bank of Boston v. Maine*, 284 U.S. 312 (1932).

[26] *Curry v. McCanless*, 307 U.S. 357 (1939); *Graves v. Elliott*, 307 U.S. 383 (1939).

[27] Judicial opinion on this matter has not been unanimous. In a Wisconsin case [*Estate of Shepard*, 184 Wis. 88 (1924)] a minority opinion held that the corporation might, through its relationship as agent for its stockholders, bring the latter under the jurisdiction of the states in which the corporation did business. The dissent also laid stress on the fact that the corporation is only a legal fiction and that stockholders could acquire a right to physical property by merely dissolving the corporation. At one time many states taxed nonresidents upon their shares of stock in corporations owning property in these states; this is no longer permissible under the decisions of the United States Supreme Court—*Rhode Island Hospital Trust Co. v. Doughton*, 270 U.S. 69 (1926). See also Nichols, *Taxation in Massachusetts*, pp. 97–100.

[28] *First National Bank of Boston v. Maine*, 284 U.S. 312 (1932).

incorporation to reassert their claims.[29] Thus at present, intangibles transferred under an inheritance tax may be assessed in the state of the domicile of the deceased, in the state where they are deposited, and in the state of incorporation.

The state of Ohio has a well-recognized and exclusive claim to tax the transfer of the real estate located within its borders.[30] Were there tangible personal property involved, it would follow the same rule.[31] Moreover, real estate and tangible personal property are taxable only in the state where they are located.

The present trend in Supreme Court opinion is toward the view that to rule out one plausible state jurisdictional claim in favor of another is arbitrary and beyond the prerogative of the Court. The dissenting view stresses the inequities and complications of multiple taxation as a practical matter. The conclusion apparently is that legislatures must shoulder some of the difficulties that courts have hitherto carried for them.

Problem of Domicile. It is perfectly legal for an individual to change his domicile in order to avoid taxation, or for any other reason. Considerable uncertainty arises, however, as to when a domicile is actually changed. Certainly, much more is required than a mere statement to the effect that one's domicile has been changed. It is clear in the law that every person has a domicile, and only one; it is the place of his birth, unless he later changes it. To change it, he must have had the intent to establish "a permanent abode" elsewhere and have made some overt act in the direction of moving there.

The main element in domicile is intent, and intent may be proved or disproved by a wide range of evidence. One of the most celebrated domicile cases in inheritance taxation is that of Dr. John T. Dorrance.[32] Until 1925 Dr. Dorrance was admittedly domiciled in Camden, New Jersey, where he lived with his family on a modest country estate. In the course of time, as sole owner of the stock of the Campbell Soup Company, also of Camden, he became very wealthy, and as a result he decided to move to an environment more in keeping with his station in life. In 1925 he moved to the suburbs of Philadelphia, where he purchased a sumptuous estate of 150 acres at a cost of over $1 million. Meanwhile, he also retained ownership of the New Jersey home, which he gave over for use to his mother and sister. Occasionally, however, he visited and

---

[29] *State Tax Commission of Utah v. Aldrich,* 316 U.S. 174 (1942).
[30] *Dana v. Treasurer and Receiver General,* 227 Mass. 562 (1917).
[31] *Frick v. Pennsylvania,* 268 U.S. 473 (1925).
[32] The following description of the Dorrance Case is adapted from 81 *U. of Pa. Law Review,* 177 (1932).

slept there, although most of the time he stayed with his family in Philadelphia.

The evidence concerning this case disclosed the fact that ten servants had been employed in New Jersey before and only two after the removal; more than twenty-five were regularly employed about the house and grounds in Philadelphia. The cost of running the New Jersey establishment decreased from $20,000 in 1924 to $6500 in 1929, in which year expenses at the Pennsylvania establishment aggregated $90,000. The Dorrances entertained exclusively in Pennsylvania, and the children attended school and church there. On the other hand, Dr. Dorrance voted, paid taxes, and held a vestrymanship in New Jersey. He drew his will according to New Jersey laws, and it was disclosed that he had been assured by legal advisors that he would not have to surrender his New Jersey domicile by acquiring his Pennsylvania home.

The Pennsylvania supreme court, in sustaining the inheritance tax of that state upon the Dorrance estate, reaffirmed the oft-enunciated principle of domicile: "A man's home is where he makes it, not where he would like to have it." Physical characteristics, time he spends in it, things he does therein, the persons and things therein, his mental attitude toward the place, the elements of his other dwelling places, if any—all have a bearing on the question. On the other hand, the New Jersey courts held that, "Where a person domiciled at one place moves to a new abode, his domicile will not be changed if he intends not to abandon the old home but to return to it, even though the particular time of such intended return be not definitely fixed."

The Dorrance case is interesting, not only because of the light it throws upon the problem of domicile but also because of the conflicting claims of two states. Both New Jersey and Pennsylvania claimed Dr. Dorrance, and both assessed and collected death taxes on his estate. In the former, the tax amounted to approximately $12 million, and in the latter, $14 million. An appeal to the United States Supreme Court failed to bring relief, as the Court refused to take jurisdiction. There is some doubt about the power of federal courts and Congress to force rules as to domicile upon the states. A number of states have filled this gap by agreements to arbitrate cases of disputed domicile.[33]

---

[33] The cases here discussed are: *Dorrance's Estate,* 309 Pa. 151 (1932); *In re Dorrance,* 115 N.J. Eq. 268 (1934); *Dorrance v. Pennsylvania,* 287 U.S. 660 (1932). See also an opinion holding that the Constitution does not require "uniformity in the decisions of the courts of different states as to the place of domicil, where the exertion of state power is dependent upon domicil within its boundaries." —*Worcester County Trust Co. v. Riley,* 302 U.S. 292 (1937). However, see also, *Texas v. State of Florida,* 306 U.S. 398 (1939). A committee of the National Tax Association has given the problem prolonged consideration; see *Proceedings,* 1936–1940.

In a subsequent case, a wealthy decedent had residences in both Delaware and Pennsylvania. Heirs sought to avoid the Pennsylvania tax because it was the higher of the two and would moreover cut into a residual bequest for charitable purposes which in turn would augment the federal tax (charitable grants are deductible and the state tax is not). Further issue involved the recognition by Pennsylvania of an out-of-state charity. The worst fate of all of course would be the obligation to pay both state taxes. In this case the Pennsylvania court surrendered.[34]

A domicile once acquired continues until it is really abandoned and until a new domicile is actually acquired. Thus, a resident of Iowa was held to be still domiciled in Iowa when he died en route to the land of his birth where he expected to remain indefinitely.[35] It was not enough to abandon his old domicile, which he did; he also had to acquire a new domicile, which he did not do since he died en route. There is a conflict of authority, however, in cases of this kind.

Of course, as previously explained, much of the incentive to migrate in order to escape the inheritance tax was eliminated by the "80-percent-credit" amendment to the federal estate tax.

EVASION AND AVOIDANCE

If loopholes are a major problem for the income tax, they all but cover the ground in the case of the death tax. It has been said of the estate tax that it constitutes an interesting game, played for high stakes, with heavy penalties on inadvertence and lack of foresight and high reward for cunning supplied by lawyers for high fees. This says nothing—no doubt advisedly—about the revenue.

HIDING

Some transfers of personal property take place without ever being revealed to the death tax administrators. Cash, jewelry, and unregistered bonds lend themselves to this direct form of evasion. However, escape of this sort is not easily accomplished under alert and competent administration.[36]

---

[34] Case of Pierre Samuel Du Pont, *New York Times,* April 3, 1955, p. 64; July 26, 1955, p. 40.

[35] *In re Estate of Jones,* 192 Iowa 78 (1921).

[36] If the administrator works in an income tax state, he may have access to the income tax records from which he can detect transfers of income-earning property. In addition, practically all states require that the death tax administrator be given first access to safety deposit boxes after the renter's death. The administrator usu-

MIGRATION

Another means of avoiding or reducing death taxes is to run away from them. It probably is much easier for an individual taxpayer to change his residence than it is for an industry to change its place of business. However, a change of domicile may be no small matter even for the individual, involving, as it often does, the severing of some long-established ties.

GIFTS

By far the most common method of avoiding death taxes is through gifts of property before death. Gifts are usually classified into four types: (1) gifts in contemplation of death, (2) gifts to take effect at death, (3) gifts *causa mortis* or "deathbed" gifts, and (4) gifts *inter vivos* (between living persons). A gift in contemplation of death is included by most death tax statutes as a part of the death tax base. But there is much confusion and argument concerning whether or not a gift is in contemplation of death or *inter vivos*.[37] A gift *causa mortis* needs no further discussion; it is in the nature of a distribution at death by a sort of oral will and is clearly included in the base taxable under death taxes.

Gifts in Contemplation of Death. Contemplation of death is a matter of degree. It is agreed that it does not include "that expectation of death generally entertained by every person." [38] Everyone expects to die, of course, and is always influenced by the thought that he cannot take his wealth along to the grave. To hold otherwise would rule out gifts *inter vivos* altogether. The courts generally take the view that mere old age is not sufficient in itself to establish contemplation of death. It seems plausible to hold that contemplation of death increases at least proportionately as one gets older. But there is no general agreement as to when one is old, and the argument that much of the great work of the world has been done by men over seventy is likely to meet with a warm reception by a court many of whose members are about that age. The usual ground for proving contemplation of death is illness.

---

ally has the power of placing the executor of the estate, or even the relatives of the deceased, under oath and taking testimony. Thus the sources of information are fairly adequate. It is true that some very small estates are probably missed entirely, particularly if there is nothing but a small life insurance policy and some personal property involved. An estate of this kind may not go through any court at all. But even in cases such as this it is possible for the administrative agency to require notice from insurance companies of all insurance payments. The latter could furnish a means of checking, quite effectively, evasion of insurance. The total amount of such evasion is probably not very large.

[37] More will be said later about gifts to take effect at death.

[38] *United States v. Wells*, 283 U.S. 102 (1931); *State v. Pabst*, 139 Wis. 561 (1909); *In re Case's Estate*, 191 Wash. 6 (1937).

The subtleties of contemplation-of-death litigation run all through the case law on the subject. In one case, a decedent at the age of 75 had made substantial gifts a short while before her death. She had cancer at the time of the gifts, but she had never been informed of this fact and had long-range plans for the future. The Court ruled that the gifts were in contemplation of death; a woman of her intelligence "must have suspected something" from the nature of her treatment. On the other hand, a taxpayer of advanced age made gifts to twenty nieces and nephews; should he desire, he could call on any of them for ten months' room and board. The Court held that this indicated that the decedent was preparing for a long life and concluded that contemplation of death was not a major motivation. Curiously, one may with immunity give away property to escape the income tax but not to escape the death tax; the latter raises the presumption that thoughts of death motivated the act.[39]

Unconstitutional Conclusive Presumption of Contemplation of Death. As the result of court decisions concerning age, the state of Wisconsin in 1915 enacted a statute providing that gifts of a material part of the donor's property in the nature of a final distribution made at any time during a six-year period prior to death were *conclusively presumed* to be in contemplation of death. The constitutionality of this measure was several times upheld by Wisconsin courts, but upon appeal to the United States Supreme Court in the case of *Schlesinger v. State of Wisconsin,*[40] the statute was overruled as contrary to the Fourteenth Amendment. The Court held that the conclusive presumption covers cases where gifts in fact *inter vivos* would be presumed in contemplation of death, and that this would constitute unreasonable classification and therefore deprivation of property without due process of law. The state, said the Court, cannot enforce an arbitrary tax in order to facilitate the collection of a lawful one.[41] A person who dies in an accident shortly after a gift cannot be presumed to have been motivated in his decision by the thought of impending death.

---

[39] For a discussion of these and other contemplation-of-death cases see Harry Rubin and David G. Schaff, "Gift Tax or Estate Tax Transfers," *Taxes,* 29: 3 (March 1951), pp. 207–214.

[40] 270 U.S. 230 (1926).

[41] A minority opinion by three justices cited precedents in which somewhat arbitrary provisions to facilitate administration of statutes had been sustained and held that the precedent should be followed here. The minority added that if the period of conclusive presumption had been six months instead of six years, it would have seemed quite clearly a reasonable administrative measure, and that "reasonable men might regard six years as not too remote." That the decision did not turn upon the length of the presumption period, however, was demonstrated when six years later the court overruled a clause in the federal statute which provided a conclusive presumption period of two years instead of six. *Heiner v. Donnan,* 285 U.S. 312 (1932).

Constitutional Prima Facie Presumption of Contemplation of Death.
Following the Court's ruling on the six-year presumption clause, the federal government and many states enacted legislation providing a two-
year period before death in which gifts would be *presumed—though not
conclusively*—to be in contemplation of death—that is, in cases of this
kind the burden of proving noncontemplation would rest with the estate.
At present, under the federal law, gifts made within three years of death
are presumed to be in contemplation of death, and gifts made before this
interval are conclusively presumed not to be so motivated. The courts
have generally held this phrasing of the law valid.[42] The presumption is
a considerable factor in establishing contemplation notwithstanding that
it "can not stand against ascertained and proven facts showing the contrary to be true." [43]

Gifts to Take Effect at Death—Trusts. The problem of gifts as a
means of avoiding the inheritance tax is very much complicated by the
existence of trusts. The nature of this device was explained in the previous chapter. For the present purposes it is important to note that trusts
may be revocable or irrevocable—that is, the settlor may or may not
reserve the right to change his mind and take back the property from
the trustee. For example, *A* may create a trust for the benefit of *B,* but
with the proviso that, if the latter proves unworthy, the trust will be
revoked. This is a case of a revocable trust. In an irrevocable trust there
are no such strings attached, *A* having decided "for better or for worse"
to permit the trust to stand.

Trusts may be created in such a way that the benefit, or the income
therefrom, goes immediately to the beneficiary, or they may be created
so that the benefit or income goes immediately to the settlor and to the
beneficiary only at the settlor's death.

Judicial Opinion concerning "at Death" Gifts. Death tax laws generally include a clause which makes "gifts to take effect at death" subject
to tax as part of the estate. Just what constitutes gifts to take effect at
death has been in some dispute but, in general, revocability of the trust
agreement or the reservation of a life estate to the settlor is sufficient to

---

[42] *Will of Harnischfeger,* 208 Wisconsin 317 (1932); *In re Button's Estate,* 190
Wash. 333 (1937). In the former case a donor had made substantial gifts within
two years of his death. He was in his seventies at the time he made the gifts but
was in good health and spirits. It was argued for the state that the donor had
made "an extensive re-arrangement of his affairs" at the time of the gifts and
that this was done "to put his house in order" for death. The rearrangement consisted, among other things, of retirement from active business, drawing a new
will, and creating a foundation for the benefit of his employees. The court accepted this as sufficient evidence of contemplation of death.
[43] *United States v. Wells,* 283 U.S. 102 (1931).

establish such status. Trusts or other transfers in any way "measured by the life of the donor" are taxable.[44]

Even though a gift in trust may not be taxable as a "gift to take effect at death," it may still be taxable as a gift "in contemplation of death" if the fact of contemplation is established, or, under the presumption clause, the fact of noncontemplation is not established. It is sometimes said that the entire dispute may in due time be relegated into history as the policy of taxing gifts *per se* becomes universal. However, this conclusion overlooks the fact that, even with a gift tax, an important advantage may still be gained by the taxpayer if he can establish that a transfer is a gift rather than a bequest. The advantage arises from the fact that the gift tax often carries a separate exemption and separate graduation. Occasionally, in addition, it may involve a lower rate schedule. The discussion above concerns only the inheritance and estate taxes, both of which differ from a gift tax in that the latter applies only to gifts *inter vivos*.

Use of Trusts and Powers of Appointment to "Skip" Taxes. Probably the most important source of avoidance in the estate tax field is the use of trusts and powers of appointment to skip one or more generations in handing down property. Thus X may leave his property as a life estate to his son and, thereafter, as a second life estate to his grandson and, finally, in remainder to his great-grandson. This is treated by the law as a single transfer, subject to only one tax; the creation of a life estate with a remainder constitutes one transfer, and the passage from life tenant to the remainderman is not taxable. Powers of appointment add a refinement by allowing the life tenant some discretion in naming his successors; but they do not make such transfers taxable as long as the powers are specific rather than general; that is, if they are limited to a choice among close relatives.

As far back as 1926, when estate tax exemptions were quite high and the rates relatively low, it was estimated that a full one quarter of inherited property was being transferred by way of life estates with remainders.[45] At present, with estate and gift taxes higher, the use of property settlements of various kinds—trusts, life estate-remainder, and powers of appointment—is apparently the common practice in most estates of $60,000 or more. Probably one half of inherited property was transferred to skip at least one death tax. The full fiscal effect of this practice will be felt more when the initial life tenants die and property worth millions of dollars will pass untaxed to later life tenants or remaindermen.

---

[44] Reversionary interests in trusts not so measured are taxed at their actuarial value like any other asset owned by the decedent.

[45] Shultz, *The Taxation of Inheritance,* p. 231.

The remedy for avoidance of the estate tax by use of the life-estate-remainder device is to make a transfer from the life tenant to the remainderman taxable. Precedent for such provision can be found in Great Britain. An equally fundamental remedy would be to adjust the estate tax to the differential in age of the donor and heir. A thirty- or forty-year differential would be regarded as standard. An age differential of zero might be sufficient ground for completely disregarding the transfer for death tax purposes. An age differential between zero and thirty or forty might allow a fractional weighting. For example, a ten-year differential would support an exemption of two thirds or three fourths of the estate. A differential of more than thirty or forty years would result in a weighting of more than 100 percent or an increase in the base over the amount actually transferred.

Time is one of the essential dimensions of an estate tax and one that is largely neglected. In some death tax statutes, provision is made for rapid successive transfers. Illustration may be given of automobile accidents in which greatgrandfather, grandfather, and father all die in the course of one day. This may involve three separate taxes within a few hours. To prevent an excessive burden on the estates, statutes commonly provide that a second transfer within five years, or some other period, will be exempt from tax.[46] No similar provision, however, applies to intervals between tax that are abnormally long.

Philanthropic Gifts. Congressional policy in allowing tax concessions for various kinds of gifts to charitable, educational and religious institutions has been very liberal. One theory supporting this policy is that if tax-favored institutions were not to perform certain services, the state would be obliged to undertake them. A gift to charity at the margin of a very large income or estate is mainly financed by the federal government. However, the creation of a charitable trust does not always divest the heirs of the deceased from control of the property so distributed. For example, Andrew Mellon left an estate of approximately $100 million almost entirely to the A. W. Mellon Educational and Charitable Trust. The charitable deduction granted to the estate practically wiped out an estate tax of about $67 million, and the property continued in the control of those nominated by Mr. Mellon: namely, his son, son-in-law, and attorney.[47] The element of control in modern economic life is often of greater strategic value than bare legal title. Possibly there should be some

---

[46] The federal law was amended in 1954 to allow a 10-year period during which a second transfer of the same property would not be fully taxed. Exemption decreases 20 percent with each successive two years of this period.

[47] Erwin Griswold, *Cases and Materials on Federal Taxation* (Chicago: Foundation Press, 1940), p. 263; Randolph E. Paul, *Federal Estate and Gift Taxation* (Boston: Little, Brown & Co., 1942), vol. I, p. 689.

top limit to the deductibility of charitable gifts for the estate tax as there is now a top limit in the case of the income tax.

THE MARITAL DEDUCTION

The Revenue Act of 1948 affords a married person the opportunity of leaving half of his estate to his spouse free of tax. This extends to death taxation privileges parallel to those now allowed in income taxation. It also recognizes the fact that the spouse may die soon after the deceased and has been a partner in the creation of the estate.

However, the marital deduction creates certain problems both for the government and the estate owner. It creates a wide-open avenue for minimizing taxes by dividing the base of the tax in the face of the progressive scale of rates. In fact, the estate can now be divided into quarters, exemplified as follows: one quarter may be given to a son directly and during life; another quarter may be given indirectly (as later explained) through the spouse; a third quarter may be left to the spouse by testamentary transfer (at death); and a fourth quarter may be left to the son again by testamentary transfer. This can cut deeply into the effectiveness of the tax.

As to the estate owner, he may be troubled by the fact that his spouse may be ill suited to manage his wealth and may disinherit the son in favor of a second spouse.[48] He may safeguard himself to some extent on the first point by a "marital-deduction" trust (with general power of appointment) but he cannot avoid the second difficulty and still qualify for the marital deduction. Moreover, it is now established that a marital deduction trust must give the surviving spouse full power to invade the principal of the trust fund established for his or her benefit.

A system which allowed free transfers to spouse and minor children, aggregating gifts to the latter from one donor and spouse to be taxable when the children reached their majority (if in their possession) or thereafter as received, might solve more problems than it creates and would be worth considering.

TAXATION OF GIFTS *INTER VIVOS*

Contemplation of death is extremely difficult to establish. The evidence involves the state of the donor's mind at the time of the giving, a condition which is not easy to determine or prove. To make matters worse for

---

[48] Charles Looker, "The Impact of Estate and Gift Taxes on Property Disposition," *California Law Review,* 38: 1 (March 1950), pp. 44–70.

the state, the family physician, who may be presumed to know something about the health of the deceased at the time the latter made the gifts, is usually "privileged" to withhold testimony. Friends and neighbors of the deceased and the heirs are frequently brought in to testify to such habits and characteristics of the deceased as that he chewed tobacco, drank strong whiskey, went swimming late in the fall, went on long fishing and hunting trips, and talked of living ten years or longer. These are evidences which are hard to controvert by strangers, and as a result the impression often prevails among those concerned in the administration of these laws that the inheritance and estate taxes strike mainly the estates of those who die unexpectedly and who have not had sufficient time to put their "house in order." And, of course, the difficulty of administering the inheritance and estate taxes has not been made any easier by the court decisions which ruled out the conclusive presumption statutes.

Justice Stone, in a dissenting opinion in a case declaring a conclusive presumption clause unconstitutional,[49] stated that up to 1932 the courts had decided 102 cases dealing with whether or not gifts had been in contemplation of death. In only twenty cases, involving $4 million, was the government successful in its efforts. In seventy-eight cases, involving gifts of $120 million, it was unsuccessful, and there is no evidence that it has done much better since.

Gift Taxes in Practice. It has been mainly for this reason, to prevent a wide loophole in the enforcement of the death taxes, that there has developed in recent years a demand for a gift tax—a tax which would reach those gifts that could not be proved to be in contemplation of death. The federal government and some dozen states now have gift taxes.[50] The federal gift tax at present carries rates three fourths as high as those of the federal estate tax, and the law in general parallels that of the estate tax. The gift tax provides for a special exemption of $30,000 during the donor's lifetime. He can also make use of an additional annual exemption of $3000 which he can give away, tax free, to each of any number of persons. The annual exemption is not cumulative; it cannot be carried over from one year to another. Gifts which exceed the exemption are taxed annually according to a progressive rate schedule applied to a base which is determined by the cumulation of taxable gifts made by the donor since 1932, when the act went into effect. For example, assume that in 1949 a donor makes taxable gifts of $25,000 over and above annual exemptions and that in previous years he has made taxable gifts

---

[49] *Meiner v. Donnan,* 285 U.S. 312 (1932).

[50] The first federal gift tax was enacted in 1924 but was repealed in 1926. The present tax was enacted in the Revenue Act of 1932 and has since been in effect. It has been modified several times through amendments.

totaling $60,000. Then his tax rate on this year's gift of $25,000 will be that which is applied to the bracket ranging from $60,000 to $100,000. However, since the passing of the new community property law of 1948, husband and wife can split a gift as well as income. Thus, a gift to a third person may be treated as coming half from the wife and half from the husband. This will reduce the taxable amount considerably, but the advantage applies only to married couples. State laws resemble the federal, though they parallel their own inheritance or estate taxes rather than the federal estate tax. These gift taxes are supplementary to death taxes and do not duplicate them; if a gift is taxed as a gift, it will not be included as a part of an estate or inheritance, and vice versa.

Occasionally, some difficulty arises in distinguishing gifts from ordinary support by a relative. The exemptions afford the taxpayer some defense against the taxation of such transfers. Moreover, they can usually be excluded by administration. It is not the purpose of the gift tax to tax "support" or "token" gifts. The tax is aimed at substantial transfers which are attempts to pass on property from one generation to another. There can be no reasonable doubt that a gift tax as a means of blocking a detour around the death taxes has a legitimate and permanent place in a modern revenue system.

Although the passage of gift tax legislation was a step in the right direction, it failed to recognize that gifts during life are not essentially different from gifts at death. Under existing law with two transfer taxes, the estate owner is free to use either or both, according to his particular advantage. It is quite convenient for him to make use of the exemptions and lower brackets of both and thereby escape the upper brackets of either. Thus the progressivity and revenue-raising capacity of both taxes are defeated. In the author's opinion, both levies should be replaced by a single, cumulative transfer tax. Here we might well follow the example of France which established an integrated transfer tax in 1942.

Gift of Life Insurance Premiums. The use of gifts is a highly available and inviting means of avoiding the death tax, but they are discouraged by the unwillingness to part with current resources and uncertainty as to their effect on children. The 1954 Revenue Act, however, made the gift of life insurance equivalent in all important tax consequences to that of other property. Theretofore, such gifts could not avoid death taxes if the premiums had been paid by the donor. A favored scheme now works as follows: *A Jr.* takes out an insurance policy on his father's life and the father annually provides Junior the wherewithal to meet the premium cost. These small gifts will incur little if any gift tax, and when *A* dies the insurance company will settle with Junior and there will be no death tax.

ESTATE PLANNING

In recent years a considerable occupation has developed in what is called estate planning. The planner is a professional advisor to people of wealth, aiding them to plan investments and wills in such manner as to serve family and business needs and to minimize taxes, current and future. Instrumentalities familiar to the planner are marital deductions, trusts, insurance, and *inter vivos* gifts. The planner is frequently confronted with a bewildering array of family relationships, property holdings, and possibilities of rearrangement. He can be of great service to his clients and fill a role for them similar to that of the family doctor and lawyer.

OTHER NET WORTH TAXES

It is perhaps logical to mention in a chapter on death taxes that there are certain alternative ways and times for the taxation of the net wealth or fortune of individuals. One is the net worth tax, which is like the estate tax, except that it falls at regular intervals of time rather than at death. This type of tax meets an important objection to the death taxes, namely, that their imposition is irregular. But the time chosen to levy death taxes has certain strategic advantages mentioned earlier in this chapter. Closely akin to the net worth tax is the capital levy. This tax is usually thought of as a graduated net worth tax, but one which is levied only in time of an emergency.

Net worth taxes entail grave valuation problems, but they have been levied in Scandinavian countries for many years. As compared with net income taxes they levy on the capacity to earn income rather than on income itself. Of course they do not reach the intangible "wealth" that takes the form of investment in people. The suggestion has been made that this omission could be avoided through capitalization of expected future earnings from services, but among other objections this might involve heavy taxes at an unstrategic time for young and promising students.[51]

---

[51] See Earl R. Rolph and George F. Break, *Public Finance* (New York: The Ronald Press Company, 1961), chap. 9.

Both the net worth tax and the capital levy would likely meet with constitutional objections if used by the federal government—unless levied on the basis of apportionment among the states according to population.

In addition to the publications cited in the footnotes, the following sources are

SUMMARY

Death taxes are usually levied in either one of two forms, as inheritance taxes or as estate taxes. The former are based on the individual shares transferred to the heirs, and the latter on the undivided estate. The estate tax is simpler and more productive; the inheritance tax is usually thought to be more equitable in that it has some correlation with the ability to pay of the heir. Other refinements to improve this correlation have been suggested and occasionally tried.

Death taxes have a long history behind them. In their modern form they have probably been used with the greatest fiscal success in Great Britain. As in the case of the income tax, United States experience with death taxes is rather recent. Use of the estate tax as a continuous feature of the federal tax system dates only from 1916.

Some dispute has persisted over the question of which unit of government has the better claim to death taxes, the federal or the state. At one time there was very substantial support for the proposition that the federal government should surrender this source to the states. This was objected to on the ground, among others, that interstate competition would reduce death taxes to negligible proportions. The issue was compromised by the adoption of a federal credit under which a considerable portion of federal taxes can be paid with state inheritance tax receipts.

Death taxes are supported mainly on the ground that they are in accord with ability to pay and have a salutary effect on the distribution of wealth and income. In opposition to this argument, however, is the contention that they consume the capital fund of the nation which uses them. There are many angles of approach to this argument. Probably most taxes are to some extent at the expense of potential saving. Because of their concentration upon accumulated funds, death taxes do probably reduce saving more than other taxes. But estate taxes are probably less injurious to enterprise incentives than is the income tax. These taxes, however, may create unfortunate consequences in their impact on small family-owned businesses.

Multiple taxation was at one time a very serious problem in the

recommended to supplement this chapter: William Vickrey, *Agenda for Progressive Taxation;* James A. Maxwell, *Tax Credits and Intergovernmental Relations* (Washington, D.C.: The Brookings Institution, 1962), chap. 2; *Federal Tax Policy for Growth and Stability,* Joint Committee on the Economic Report, 84th Cong., 1st Sess., 1955, pp. 817–870; recent articles in *Taxes,* particularly concerning recent developments in the taxation of trusts, estate planning, and so on; an abbreviated federal tax service.

application of state death taxes, and the trend of United States Supreme Court opinion has greatly enlarged the problem. The Court has recently espoused the view that where there is a plausible ground for tax jurisdiction the Court will not declare the exercise of the taxing power unconstitutional. Double domicile is another serious jurisdictional problem.

Evasion and avoidance of death taxes take place principally through gifts and the creation of limited interests in estates so as to skip taxable transfers. Gifts in contemplation of death or to take effect at death have long been taxable as part of estates and inheritances. However, it is difficult to establish just what gifts *are* in contemplation of death. The Supreme Court ruled invalid the conclusive presumption that gifts made within a certain period before death are in contemplation of death. Revocable trusts and trusts providing income to the settlor during his life are gifts to take effect at death. Gift taxes have been enacted to prevent avoidance of death taxes by large gifts. Integration of gift and death taxes has not yet developed but is strongly recommended. Another major source of avoiding the estate tax is by the use of life estates and powers of appointment. This results in skipping a generation or more in successive transfers. The remedy here is to tax the transfer from the life tenant to the remainderman, or to include the age differential between deceased and heir as one of the dimensions of the tax. The marital deduction now affords an opportunity to fragmentize an estate and thus defeat the progressive rate scale. Gifts of life insurance or premiums to provide it (with the donor the insured party and the donee the owner of the policy) furnish a highly effective means of minimizing taxes. The estate planner has appeared to help the estate owner order his investments so as to meet family and business needs and minimize taxes. Some bold thinking and courageous reform are required to give the estate tax the place in the revenue system that it deserves.

PROBLEMS

1. Mr. Smith at the age of 65 possesses a million-dollar estate. He has a wife of the same age, two daughters aged 30 and 35, and two grandsons aged 8 and 10. He has a slight heart ailment, but his wife is in perfect health. His wife is not a "good business woman." Taking account of marital deductions, gifts before death, gifts in contemplation of death, and life-estate trusts, explain the various ways in which Smith might lay his investment plans to minimize future death and gift taxes.
2. If a person owns real estate in a state where he is not domiciled, what would be the effect on inheritance tax jurisdiction were he to create a corporation to own the real estate?

3. Mr. Jones, 80 years old but in good health, sets up a trust. The trust is irrevocable and provides a life estate for a son with ultimate disposition among the grandsons. The son is given power to designate which of the grandsons shall inherit and how much. How will this transaction be taxed?

4. Consider the proposition: Federal surrender of the death tax to the states would weaken the tax and destroy its territorial equity.

5. Explain the purpose, mechanics, and effect of the "federal credit."

6. Mr. Jones and Mr. Smith are wealthy owners of estates. When Jones dies, he leaves $5 to each inhabitant of his home city (population 100,000). Smith leaves a $500,000 estate to his nearest of kin, a cousin. Explain how an estate tax and an inheritance tax will apply to these situations.

7. Explain what is meant by an "integrated transfer tax" with a "cumulative base."

8. Account for the fact that the yield of the death tax in this country is insignificant compared to the net income tax.

9. Comment on Andrew Carnegie's proposition: To leave large fortunes to children is a case of "misguided affection."

10. Consider the proposition: In a modern capitalistic economy the type of tax needed is one that will reduce saving and not discourage investment. Compare income and death taxes as candidates for this role.

11. Indicate the fallacies in the following proposition: An estate tax aggregates (adds together to form one base) all the gifts whether at death or otherwise made by one donor; an inheritance tax aggregates all of the gifts at death or in contemplation of death received by one donee.

12. Explain the difficulties confronted by a medium-sized, family-owned business under the death tax.

13. State three reasons why one may reduce his taxes by a gift *inter vivos* even though such gift is subject to a gift tax.

14. What facts about taxation should a young insurance salesman call to the attention of a rich client in an interview?

15. Explain the following features of the marital deduction:
    a. How it enables the taxpayer to quarter the base of his tax;
    b. How it partially solves the problem of caring for a widow without business sense but does not avoid disposition in favor of a second husband or his heirs.

16. What is meant by a skip-a-generation trust and how is this used to accomplish avoidance? How do the British attempt to block this so-called loophole?

11

TAXES ON CONSUMPTION

BACKGROUND OF CONSUMPTION TAXES

Consumption taxes are levies paid by the consumer in the price of the commodities that he purchases. These taxes vary with the consumer's expenditures, in contrast with property taxes, which vary with the value of goods owned, and income taxes, which vary with the receipts during a definite period of time. Consumption taxes also differ from property and income taxes in that the former are not as a rule directly imposed upon those who are expected to bear the ultimate burden. Their existence depends upon shifting. It has already been observed that there is no general agreement as to the incidence of taxation. Some hold that all taxes in the last analysis are paid by the consumer; many others believe that property taxes, not customarily thought of as consumption taxes, are nevertheless paid, in part at least, by the consumer. However, a fairly definite group of taxes are treated generally as consumption taxes, partly because they are intended to be paid by the consumer and partly because the probability of shifting is especially strong in their case.

Consumption taxes also differ from other taxes in terms of timing: they tax the consumer when he is dissaving while other taxes apply when he is saving.

EXTENT OF CONSUMPTION TAXES

Consumption Taxes in the Individual's Budget. Few people realize how much of their expenditure is absorbed by consumption taxes. If the average low-income family, with no taxable property or income, could be shown how much it is contributing to the government, it would be startled at the discovery. It would find, for instance, that 8 cents of the price paid for a standard package of cigarettes is federal tax alone; added to this are the usual state taxes of from 2 to 8 cents; assuming a 3-cent state levy and consumption of a package per day, this amounts to an annual tax of over $40 on this single item. The British tax is about four times our own and the Canadian levy also somewhat higher. The yield statistics indicate that liquor and tobacco taxes cost the American people about $37 per capita per year. To be sure, both cigarettes and liquor belong to a group of commodities that are singled out for especially heavy levies. But even under the 3-percent retail sales tax, which is quite common among the states, an individual pays $30 or more in taxes for every $1000 spent on taxable merchandise.

Consumption Taxes in Federal and State Tax Systems. During much of its history the federal government relied exclusively upon consumption taxes for its tax revenue and, although this has ceased to be true in recent years, these levies (tariffs and excises) still play an important role in the revenue system. In 1961 taxes roughly classed as consumption taxes amounted to about 14 percent of federal revenue. Federal liquor and tobacco taxes brought in about 38 percent of consumption tax revenue. A long list of items of popular consumption was included in the tax system among which were the following: automobiles, cameras and photographic equipment, electric, gas, and oil appliances, gasoline and lubricating oil, matches, musical instruments, phonographs, radio sets and parts, household refrigerators, sporting goods, television sets, air transportation, local telephone service, playing cards, admissions, cosmetics, handbags, and luggage. By no stretch of a definition could all of these items be classed as luxuries.

In the state revenue systems consumption taxes played a very minor role until the depression of the 1930s when the retail sales tax gained wide acceptance. In point of revenue it is now the leading state tax. Taxes on liquor in some form are collected at both state and local levels throughout the nation, and tobacco taxes are levied in most of the states. Municipalities have also entered the field with retail sales taxes (for example, New York City), cigarette taxes and, especially, admissions taxes.

Consumption Taxes in Other Countries and Eras. During the period between the two World Wars, most of the European countries inaugurated and came to rely heavily upon general "turnover" taxes. Great Britain is the classic example of a country depending mainly on direct taxation; but it has for many years relied on heavy liquor and tobacco taxes (much heavier than any known in the United States), and it accepted a "purchases" tax on a wide range of commodities at high rates during and after World War II. A similar measure is applied in Australia and New Zealand. These taxes are collected at the wholesale level. A 10-percent retail tax is accepted in Norway where its popularity is maintained in part by subsidizing food consumption.[1] The Canadian tax, inaugurated in 1920, is a manufacturers' sales tax. During or shortly after both World Wars, strong pressure for a federal general sales tax developed in the United States but proved unsuccessful. The fiscal monopoly (exclusive government distribution of certain commodities, such as tobacco or matches) is very common in Europe. In Soviet Russia sales taxes are scarcely distinguishable from profits on government enterprises and they hold a predominant place in the tax system.

Heavy as are consumption taxes of the present era, they are undoubtedly less burdensome on the necessities of life than those of the eighteenth and nineteenth centuries. Favorite sources of revenue in those periods were levies on salt, soap, candles, coal and other similar commodities. The levy on salt was very common and still survives in a number of countries. This commodity has a highly inelastic demand. British taxes of the Napoleonic era have been described as including levies on everything "which it is pleasant to see, hear, feel, smell, or taste."

SELECTIVE VERSUS GENERAL CONSUMPTION TAXES

Consumption taxes may be classified in many ways, one of the most fundamental of which is the division between special taxation of separate commodities or individual items of consumption and general taxation which aims to cover all or nearly all consumption. There are intermediate species, such as the Wisconsin tax of 1962, which cover a wide range of goods but which also exempt or ignore an equally wide list. The British purchase tax which is of this latter design has the additional distinction of varying rates among classes of goods, some class lines being based on the price of the good. Thus dress shirts might be taxed in some category and work clothes exempt.

Selective sales taxes have the advantage that they can avoid levies

---

[1] John F. Due, *Sales Taxation* (Urbana: University of Illinois Press, 1957), chap. XII.

on the necessities of life. Special taxes can (though they do not necessarily) achieve a "better" distribution of burden.

Special taxes, however, are said to be discriminatory and capricious
in two respects. The first and least serious is their discrimination against
specific lines of business. Those interested in the manufacture and distribution of furs, luggage, and jewelry, for instance, are likely to see no
adequate reason why the government should single out their businesses
for special punishment. The answer is made that given sufficient time
these businesses will not be less prosperous because of the tax. Factors
will have migrated to untaxed areas to even up the competition.

The second discrimination is against consumers whose burden is
said to depend upon varying taste that should be irrelevant in distributing tax burdens. Why should A contribute more to the government
than B merely because the former's innocent tastes run to photography
and the latter's, let us say, to antique furniture? Obviously the more general the tax the less it will depend on these allegedly irrelevant differences.

In the argument against special excises much is often made of the
fact that where consumption is diverted from taxed to untaxed goods the
government gains nothing while consumers are out nevertheless, because
they have foregone their first choice of goods. For this reason, goods with
inelastic demand are preferred for excising.[2] A special class of consumption taxes is those on the so-called vices such as liquor and tobacco. In
this case the government presumably is interested both in revenue and
curtailment of consumption. It wins either way, so to speak, no matter
how the consumer may respond to the taxation of his indulgences. However, in case the poor are heavy consumers of these goods and the demand for them is very inelastic, the persistent consumer may find himself with less to spend on the preferred amenities—the milk fund for the
children perhaps—because of the tax.

A trenchant criticism of the fiscal-sumptuary argument for consumption taxes has been made by Professor Henry C. Simons. He said: [3]

> Many liberal persons defend levies like the tobacco tax on the curi-
> ous grounds that tobacco is not a necessity—that poor people may
> or can avoid the burden by not consuming the commodity. This
> position invites two comments. First, it is hardly accurate to say
> that no burden is involved in getting along without the commod-
> ity. Second, it seems a little absurd to go around arguing that poor

---

[2] See Earl E. Rolph and George F. Break, "The Welfare Aspects of Excises,"
Journal of Political Economy, LVII: 1 (February 1949), pp. 46–54.
[3] *Personal Income Taxation*, pp. 39–40.

people could or ought to do without tobacco, especially if it is taxed, in the face of the facts that they simply do not do anything of the kind, that the commodity was selected for taxation because they are not expected to do so, and that the government would not get much revenue if they did. The plain fact, to one not confused by moralistic distinctions between necessities and luxuries, is simply that taxes like the tobacco taxes are the most effective means available for draining government revenues out from the very bottom of the income scale. The usual textbook discussions on these points hardly deserve less lampooning than their implied definition of luxuries (and semi-luxuries!) as commodities which poor people ought to do without and won't.

SPECIAL EXCISES

Nevertheless, special excise levies have the important moral advantage that they leave the taxpayer a choice, whether or not he accepts it, and they do not inevitably undermine the resources essential to human welfare.

Motor Fuel Tax. The motor fuel tax will be treated as one of the members of the motor vehicle tax family. It has some features in common with the consumption taxes but, were it considered as one of them, it would be quite unique in that the tax paid is closely correlated with the special benefit that the taxpayer receives from a government expenditure, namely, the use of the highways.

Liquor Taxes. The liquor tax field is a very lucrative source of revenue, yielding all units of government about $4 billion. These taxes, more than any other consumption tax, have a sumptuary purpose. Most people (especially the wealthy) accept the view that cheap whiskey would be "bad for the country." An additional and related argument for liquor taxation is the contention that the liquor business entails a large amount of social cost otherwise borne by society: automobile accidents, lost work time, institutional expense, and the like.[4]

However, in the United States it is generally agreed that a top limit to these taxes is set by the necessity of minimizing "bootlegging," which was so prevalent during the prohibition period. The problem is not important in the case of beer. It is taxed, as a rule, about 3 cents on a 10-cent glass, which is substantial but hardly excessive. It is claimed by the manufacturers that the present tax on hard liquor invites wholesale

---

[4] K. William Kapp, *The Social Cost of Private Enterprise* (Cambridge, Mass.: Harvard University Press, 1950).

evasion and that federal enforcement agencies, though fortified with ingenious techniques, are inadequate to keep the illicit traffic within reasonable bounds. In order the better to control the liquor business and retain all the profit from the distributive end of it, a number of states now have assumed a monopoly of the retailing business. These states receive profits from the business in lieu of taxes.

It is argued that to achieve the best results from a sumptuary standpoint, heavier taxes should be placed on hard liquor than on beer. Since this makes hard liquor relatively expensive compared with beer, it might induce people to change their drinking habits in favor of the latter. This is desirable from a social standpoint because the consumption of beer has fewer evil social consequences than the consumption of hard liquor. The British are said to have achieved substantial success with this social objective of liquor taxation.

In the consumption tax field, as in many others, one of the most disturbing problems is the invasion of the field by both the states and the federal government. It was hoped that with the end of prohibition in 1934 this conflict could be avoided, at least as to the liquor tax. It was suggested that the federal government should collect all the excises and that the states should confine themselves to license fees charged those engaged in the business. In order to persuade the states to stay out, the federal government was to distribute part of its collections to the states. However, as had been characteristic of all similar attempts, there was no clear agreement on how the money should be distributed. A complication arose from the insistence of the dry states that they were entitled to some of the proceeds. Thus the effort proved abortive, and we now have both levels of government in the field, with the consequent wide range of practices among the various states. Diversity may serve a useful purpose, however, in giving expression to a variety of opinion concerning liquor consumption. Moreover, the liquor tax field is one in which federal-state cooperation as to administration has been highly developed with quite salutary results. Efforts to hunt out the bootlegger have been characterized by joint use of facilities and information to a remarkable extent. In this respect the field furnishes an example of collaboration that might well be cultivated elsewhere.

The problem of liquor taxation is closely associated with the prohibition movement.[5] Proponents of prohibition object to liquor taxation on the ground that this creates a strong vested interest in the retention of the legalized distribution of liquors. Those favoring the liquor business

---

[5] For an account of the colorful history of liquor taxes in the United States see Tun Yuan Hu, *The Liquor Tax in the United States, 1791–1947,* Graduate School of Business, Columbia University (New York, 1950).

have sometimes succeeded in getting the receipts from liquor taxes earmarked for education. This would provide them with a good defensive argument should prohibition threaten to return.

The liquor tax at the state level is ordinarily levied on consumption rather than production. However, in Kentucky a heavy special tax is imposed on liquor produced in the state for consumption there or elsewhere. It seems probable that on account of untaxed competition, this tax is mainly absorbed by producers. They continue in business because of superior leadership and trade secrets—a most extraordinary phenomenon.[6]

Tobacco Taxes. The federal excise tax on tobacco products has long been a part of the United States revenue system and is usually regarded as one of the most productive, easily administered, and socially justified of the existing taxes. It is collected from the manufacturer with little expense and small chance of evasion.

State taxes on tobacco encounter more difficulties. These taxes must be collected from wholesalers and retailers of whom the number is very large. Direct purchase across state boundary lines has proved a troublesome source of evasion. Recently the federal government broke precedent and came to the relief of the states with its Jenkins Act under which out-of-state mail-order shipment must be accompanied by notice of consignment and consignee to the tax administrator of the recipient's state. This affords the administrator the opportunity to apply a "use tax" (explained later). With the aid of this law and much cooperation among collection officials, the problem of evasion by interstate shipment has been reduced to manageable proportions.

Outside its ease of collection, the tobacco tax has appeal the world over because the demand for tobacco is highly inelastic. This permits the taxmakers to hang a fantastic tax on an otherwise cheap product and keep the consumer coming back for more. Tobacco consumption falls in the area of compensatory psychology. One "needs a smoke" largely to favor himself in moments of boredom and fatigue. The more the favor costs the individual the greater favor it constitutes. The British, partly to conserve foreign exchange, have put this theory to its severest test and it has held up remarkably well. The British tobacco tax alone yields almost as much relative to total revenue as the entire excise tax system of the United States.

Liquor and tobacco taxes, unlike most sales taxes, apply chiefly to the consumption of adults. They do not affect the family group adversely as compared with childless couples or single individuals.

---

[6] Orba F. Traylor, *The Whiskey Production Tax in Kentucky, 1933–1947*, Bureau of Business Research, University of Kentucky (Lexington, 1949).

An interesting feature of tobacco taxation is the discrimination shown certain tobacco products in contrast with others. The federal government discriminates only in favor of pipe and chewing tobocco, which pay less than half as much tax ad valorem as cigarettes and cigars. Of the forty-seven states taxing tobacco products in 1962, all but eleven taxed cigarettes only. This favoritism toward the cigar smoker may be explained in two ways: first, the survival of a prejudice against the cigarette and, second, the fact that most politicians have a fondness for a cigar, either for their own consumption or as petty bribery before elections. The trend of demand away from cigars has also been used in support of favored treatment for this tobacco product. From the standpoint of ability to pay, the cigar smoker is at least as able as the cigarette smoker to support the government (and usually more so). Tobacco taxes are also made more regressive than they need be by virtue of the fact that as applied to cigarettes they are specific (based on number) rather than ad valorem (based on value). Probably poor consumers patronize cheaper cigarettes to a greater extent, relatively that is, than do the well-to-do.

The tobacco taxes, like the liquor taxes, yield well and the receipts from this source fall off very little even during years of intense depression.

Taxes on Miscellaneous Luxuries. It has already been indicated that the federal government and a few states tax a variety of "luxury" expenditures in addition to those just discussed. All levels of government have applied excises to admissions successfully. The states have not done too well in the taxation of soft drinks; a fairly elastic demand and the inaccessibility of the manufacturer have proved handicaps. New possibilities in the excise tax field are not as abundant as might be supposed. On the political side, industries such as fur and leather-goods protest bitterly the special character of their tax burden; if we must tax consumption, they say, why not be neutral about it and treat all goods and services alike. One experienced author lists the requirements of a suitable object for excise taxation as follows: large volume; inelastic demand; nonessential character; ready definability; no close substitutes (unless these also can be taxed).[7] He doubts that a tax as broad and as detailed as the British purchase tax would be successful under American conditions. The British have attempted to classify luxuries on the basis of selling price (a shirt selling for more than $4, for instance); this has encountered the objection that it creates a gap in pricing where no goods at the dividing line are available to the consumer.[8]

---

[7] Roy Blough, *The Federal Taxing Process* (Englewood Cliffs, N.J.: Prentice-Hall, Inc., 1952), p. 341.

[8] Due, *op. cit.*

SPECIES OF TAX

The consumption tax field presents a considerable variety of species which now may be briefly listed and distinguished:

1. Special excise tax: on individual goods and services.
2. Selective sales tax: (British Purchase Tax) like (1) above but broader.
3. Gross income tax: (Indiana) covers all exchanges with no distinction as to levels (retail, wholesale) or as to commodities and services.
4. Turnover tax: (Germany) much like (3) though less inclusive as to services.
5. Transactions tax: extends beyond exchanges to cover such transactions as bank deposits.
6. Manufacturers sales tax: (Canada) confined to sales of commodities at the manufacturers' level.
7. Retail sales tax: (Michigan) confined to sales at retail; may include some services; does include final sale of some capital goods (cash register to merchant).
8. Value-added tax: (Michigan) like a gross income tax except that an effort is made to eliminate duplication (cost of goods sold deductible).
9. Over-all spending tax: like a net income tax except that the levy is on total annual spending (saving and investment exempt).
10. Use tax: a supplementary levy on the use or possession of a commodity specially immune to taxation on its acquisition.
11. Net income tax without personal exemptions: (Philadelphia) frequently labeled a gross income tax though really on net income.
12. Tariff or customs: on goods bought or sold in foreign trade.

Comparative discussion of these many possible levies must be strictly limited here. The gross income tax and other multiple-stage sales taxes are objectionable because of their fortuitous duplication and favor to integrated firms (covered in more detail later). The manufacturers sales tax is relatively simple to administer because the number of firms involved is relatively small; it is criticized on the ground that it invites pyramiding (more later) and usually must exclude services; the retail sales tax does not encounter these limitations but it is harder (more decentralized) to administer.

The Retail Sales Tax. The single-stage tax on retail sales is the favored consumption tax of the American states. It is popularly conceived as a general tax on consumer purchases. Actually this conception is far from valid. Most sales taxes, like general property taxes, show a bias for the tangible and omit such service items as haircuts, repairs of various sorts, advertising, accounting, and banking. On the other hand they include so-called last sales to business of such items as fuel and equipment. Curiously, a locomotive purchased by a railroad is a retail sale as defined. Thus the retail sales tax is not a general consumption tax at all; it is a partial consumption tax combined with a partial business tax.

A survey of twenty-five sales tax statutes indicates that the typical tax base includes the exchange of all tangible property except the following: motor fuel; school lunches; feed seed and fertilizer; free meals; and newspapers. On the other hand all services are exempt except gas and electric service and admissions. The tax also does not apply to sales to federal, state, and local governments, or to charitable, educational, and similar organizations. With regard to sales to business consumers, the tax base includes all sales except ingredients of products destined for resale, with the term "ingredient" defined to include fuel and power used in industrial processing, and nonreturnable labels and containers.

Over-all Expenditure Tax. The over-all expenditure tax (proposed during World War II) would add a fifth page so to speak to the net income tax return; it would be based on spending for consumption goods and would provide personal exemptions and graduated rates. The principal objection to this tax is administrative; as a device for controlling inflation it has obvious merit; it is first cousin to "over-all rationing" under which the consumer may spend as he chooses but is fined, so to speak, if he exceeds a limit. The tax is now proposed in Great Britain [9] where it is supported to extend equalitarian taxation to those who live well off previously accumulated capital.

Allowing the taxpayer a ready means of avoidance (saving), it could be steeply graduated with rates that need not stop at 100 percent of the base. However, confining taxes to expenditure could have unwanted effects on accumulation. To prevent this, proponents would rely heavily on the death tax. Involved also is the question of whether the economy would profit by a considerable addition to saving. Redundant saving could cause unemployment but with a high rate of investment its redundancy might disappear in a high rate of economic growth. An alleged advantage is that the tax would relieve the double-taxation of saving and interest, the latter having been paid to compensate for a sacrifice associated with waiting for enjoyment. But it is not clear that

---

[9] See Nicholas Kaldor, *An Expenditure Tax* (London: George Allen and Unwin, Ltd., 1955).

imposing a tax on this sacrifice and reward involves any duplicity. The case seems to be parallel to that of additional sacrifice and more pay through additional economic effort of any kind.

PROBLEMS OF SALES TAXATION

Integrated Industry. Sales taxation involves many problems of administration and equity. One such problem arises in connection with the multiple-stage sales tax because the number of turnovers in an "integrated industry" is less than in one made up of independent units. By an integrated industry is meant one in which industrial combinations have proceeded in a vertical direction (as when the Ford Motor Company acquires iron mines, rubber plantations, and other factors used in the assembling of a Ford car). The multiple-stage sales tax gives an advantage to the integrated industry. If, as in the diagram below, the integrated firm X combines all steps in the processing and distribution of a commodity up to and including the sale to the final consumer, and if parallel to this integrated combination is a series of six independent processing and distributing concerns, *A, B, C,* etc., among which goods move by sale and exchange, there will be six levies on the commodities of the second system of manufacture and distribution, but only one on the first. In order to avoid this discrimination, Germany at one time at-

$$X \longrightarrow \text{CONSUMER}$$
$$A \rightarrow B \rightarrow C \rightarrow D \rightarrow E \rightarrow F \rightarrow \text{CONSUMER}$$

tempted to apply the turnover tax to the "exchanges" made between the branches or divisions of the integrated industry, an innovation described by Professor Buehler as "more interesting than helpful." [10] On the other hand, it can be argued that the gross sales tax is a tax on middlemen, which tends to discourage an expensive and overdeveloped feature of production.

Moreover, the fortuitous duplications of a multiple-stage sales tax involve unneutralities among products and consumers. One commodity may require more exchanges in production and distribution than another and bear a heavier tax accordingly. These difficulties are mainly avoided by a value-added tax which allows a deduction for cost of materials as goods move along in the productive process. But the value-added tax is more complicated to define and administer than a retail sales tax which

---

[10] A. G. Buehler, *General Sales Taxation* (New York: The Business Bourse, 1932), p. 101.

also avoids duplication. The latter, however, cannot be used effectively by a unit of government that has much manufacturing business and only a small amount of mercantile trade.

Michigan has broken new ground with its so-called business receipts or "value-added tax." The tax is in addition to and not a displacement of the older retail sales tax. It can be conceived of as a production rather a consumption levy; it is designed to reach goods produced to sell outside the state. It has long been thought that value-added might afford a broad and relatively neutral base of taxation but the Michigan version abounds with exceptions and arbitrary limits such as the one that limits value-added for tax purposes to 50 percent of gross income.[11] The idea of taxing value-added has also been entertained by Japan, and it is highly developed in France as a manufacturers' tax. The French model now has strong support for general application in the European Common Market. An important feature is that it refunds cumulated collections in the case of exports. This provides a competitive advantage in international trade. Partly on this account there is considerable support for its adoption in the United States as a partial substitute for the corporate income tax.

Interstate Commerce.   Another problem involved in the state sales taxes in the United States is that of the federal prohibition of state taxes on interstate commerce. As a result, sales made to the residents of the taxing state by mail-order houses, and borderline merchants outside the state are immune from taxation. However, recent decisions have widened the powers of the state to tax such transactions, and it is now allowed to do so if the seller maintains a place of business in the taxing state.[12] Sales made over state boundary lines by sellers inside the taxing state are also immune. Not only does this involve a loss of revenue, but it also creates an unfair disadvantage in trade. Determination of the volume of such sales may be difficult from an administrative point of view, and their exemption may cause considerable shrinkage in the tax base, particularly in the application of multiple-stage sales taxes.

This problem involves important legal questions as to what constitutes an interstate sale. If a New Jersey resident orders a rug by telephone from a New York store and has the rug delivered, would this be interstate commerce? Would it make any difference if the customer took

---

[11] Peter A. Firmin, *The Michigan Business Receipts Tax,* Michigan Business Reports, No. 24, Bureau of Business Research, University of Michigan (Ann Arbor, 1953).

[12] *McGoldrick v. Berwind White Coal Mining Co.,* 309 U.S. 33 (1940); *Nelson v. Sears, Roebuck & Co.,* 312 U.S. 359 (1941). That the Court will not extend the tax privilege to cover sales that are strictly interstate has been decided in *McLoed v. J. E. Dilworth Co.,* 322 U.S. 327 (1944). Here salesmen from a home office in Tennessee took orders from customers in Arkansas and delivered to the latter from Tennessee. The company had no outlet in Arkansas.

the rug himself instead of having it delivered, or if he ordered the rug in New York to have it delivered later in New Jersey? Apparently mere negotiation across boundary lines is insufficient to make a transaction interstate commerce; the latter term "extends to the transactions in which interstate shipment of goods is contemplated and perhaps required." [13]

Attempts have been made to circumvent the interstate commerce restriction. States applying the gross income tax may include out-of-state sales by calling the tax, as applied to manufacturing and the extractive industries, a production tax rather than a sales tax. Several states have now enacted a "use tax," which taxes storage or use of goods within a state even though they may have been purchased outside. It was thought by many that this law would not be sanctioned by the United States Supreme Court, but in a 7-to-2 decision the Washington use tax was sustained.[14] Justice Cardozo in the majority opinion made much of the fact that equality rather than discrimination was the purpose of the tax. However, administrative difficulties loom very large in any attempt to apply a use tax to the entire field of goods purchased over state boundary lines. In the case of automobiles, a check can be made when the vehicle is registered for its annual license. The tax cannot be collected at the source if the taxpayer maintains no place of business in the taxing state. It is questionable that the use tax can be effectively applied to goods purchased over state lines from borderline merchants. In general, the observation may be made that the use tax device and the Supreme Court's decision have transformed a difficult legal problem into an equally difficult administrative problem.[15]

Pyramiding. Although consumption tax shifting is not always perfect, it is sometimes more than perfect—that is, the tax is "pyramided." A tax imposed upon the manufacturer and added to his price increases the cost of goods when they reach the wholesaler, the jobber, and retailer; if each calculates his customary percentage of profit or markup on this augmented base, the ultimate consumers will pay considerably more in increased prices for goods than the government receives. It is the merchants who receive the difference, and, so to speak, make a profit on the tax. Of course, given time and perfect competition, pyramiding (except to pay for interest upon the capital advanced as taxes for the consumer) could not exist. But one or the other of these conditions is often absent.

Small Purchases. Treatment of the small purchase under the sales tax involves either discrimination or penny-splitting. In New York City

---

[13] Paul J. Hartman, *State Taxation of Interstate Commerce* (Buffalo: Dennis and Co., Inc., 1953), p. 58.

[14] *Henneford v. Silas Mason Co.,* 300 U.S. 577 (1937).

[15] Maurice Criz, *The Use Tax* (Chicago: Public Administration Service, 1941).

a purchase of 1–12 cents originally involved no tax; 13–62 cents, 1 cent; 63–100 cents, 2 cents. On more than a dollar of purchase the tax was 2 cents on every dollar plus the above rates according to the amount of excess over the even dollar. A 1-cent sales tax on a 13-cent package of cigarettes represented a tax of about 8 percent of the purchase price. A 50-cent purchase also called for a 1-cent tax, representing in this case exactly 2 percent of the purchase price. The problem may be only one of the relation of the merchant to his customer. This is true if the state collects its percentage regardless of the size of transactions; but even here, the situation may arise where the merchant collects more (or less) than he pays the state.

An alternative to the bracketing system, explained above, is provided where a state issues sales tax tokens.[16] The ones once in use in several states were small bits of metal or plastic, appropriately stamped as mills, which constitute change for a penny. The tokens eliminate most of the inequity in applying the sales tax to small purchases, but they are a source of annoyance and inconvenience to the taxpayer and create some danger of counterfeiting. If the tokens have more value as substance than as coin, they will disappear from circulation in accordance with monetary principles.

Problems of Definition and Exclusion.   No end of confusion in retail sales taxation arises from the necessity of defining a retail sale. Quite frequently the term is defined to include all sales except those for resale. This means that if the commodity being sold is a material ingredient in another that will be sold again presently, no tax applies. Thus, if copper is sold to a manufacturer for fabrication, the exchange will not be covered, but the fuel sold to the manufacturer to facilitate the fabrication will be taxed.[17] Farmers sometimes complain about the fact that they pay a retail sales tax not only on the goods that they buy for their households but also on the goods they purchase to operate their farms. Food sold to the farmer for his cows is for resale, but medicine sold to cure the cow's illness is a final sale. These distinctions appear arbitrary; moreover, on the assumption of forward shifting, the taxation of capital goods involves double taxation. Figure 18 shows the problem. Simple solution seems to be to tax only goods sold for consumption. But this creates the impossible administrative problem of separating sales (of fuel, for instance) made to consumers from those made to producers.

Other puzzling problems of policy are associated with trade-ins and sale of containers. If a merchant charges for beer bottles giving a refund

---

[16] The tokens are usually in mill denominations, which makes it possible to apply a 2-percent tax equitably to the nearest 5 cents of the purchase price.

[17] John F. Due, *The General Manufacturers Sales Tax in Canada* (Toronto: Canadian Tax Foundation, 1951); Milton C. Taylor, "Toward Rationality in a Retail Sales Tax," *National Tax Journal*, V: 1 (March 1952), pp. 79–85.

when the bottles are returned, are the bottles sold once or twice or not at all? If the consumer trades in an old car for a new one, is this a double sale or the sale of a new car with or without the offset?

Mention has been made of the fact that many services are frequently excluded from the base of the retail sales tax. On the merits there appears to be no good reason for confining the tax to tangibles. Moreover, if services are excluded, troublesome problems arise as to the separation of goods and services in case of such businesses as barber shops, shoe-repair establishments, restaurants, and garages.

FIGURE 18

Double Taxation

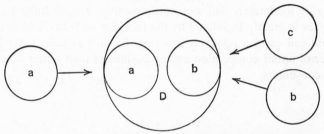

NOTE: *a* and *b* are commodities sold for resale and physical ingredients of the consumption good *D; c,* a catalyte, is not physically embodied in *D* though it is economically; a tax on *c* and *D* involves arbitrary distinctions and fortuitous double taxation.

Strong ground can be offered for excluding food and medicine from a retail sales tax. However, all such exclusions involve difficulties both of definition and administration. Salted peanuts are a food and sugar-coated ones are a (taxable) confection. Ice cream is a food and the topping placed on it doesn't change anything. Therefore sundaes are tax free. If soda water is added to ice cream to make a soda, then we have a taxable item. And so on.

In the case of a manufacturers' tax, special difficulty attends the determination of a fair price on which to base the tax. If the manufacturer does his own wholesaling and sells directly to retailers (or even consumers) his prices will be higher than those of his rivals who confine themselves to manufacturing. In this situation some concessions must be provided to preserve neutrality.

Difficulties of Administration. Ease of administration is said to be one of the virtues of a sales tax, but on close examination it will be found that its administration is far from simple. It is said that, even after the French "turnover" tax had been in effect for four years, 40 percent of the taxable turnover was still evading the tax. Contrary to expectations, it was found by the French authorities that "no levy known up to that time demanded from the tax agents more sustained vigilance, greater perspicacity, keener knowledge; none raised more delicate and even more difficult questions of interpretation; none necessitated such extensive and diverse information." [18] Similarly, one of the officials in charge of the New York retail sales tax law referred to the latter as "the most difficult and perplexing statute which we have ever tried to administer."

In sales tax administration, some states require reports and audits that involve many of the difficulties connected with the administration of the net income tax, except that here every "hole-in-the-wall" concern is involved in the problem. Some independent check can be made through examination of numbers of employees, size of establishment, and the like. Evidence as to the cost of administering sales taxes indicates that the expense is moderately but not conspicuously low. Administration of sales taxes is greatly facilitated by the fact that such taxes have a broad base and can carry a relatively low rate. Evasion of sales taxes is more a matter of unfair competition among businesses than unfair distribution among consumers.

ARGUMENT CONCERNING CONSUMPTION TAXES

The proponents of indirect taxes and those of direct taxes have long been engaged in debate, the former contending that consumption taxes are easiest to pay and least hard on incentives, the latter that they are irrational in design and unfair and capricious in incidence.

Ease and Convenience of Payment. Consumption taxes are often defended on the ground that they are generally painless—in other words, "easy to take." Taxes are onerous enough, it is said, and why "indulge in austerity" by requiring payment the hard way. The fact that consumption taxes are usually hidden in the prices of goods purchased means that people are seldom fully conscious of them. Moreover, consumption taxes are paid on an automatic installment plan, so to speak. There are many who can meet payments of 10 cents each day but would find themselves unable to cope with a bill of $36.50 once during the year. If a highwayman were to exact 1 cent from each student each time the latter came upon a university campus the ingenious thief would gather a substantial sum during the year, and no one would feel the loss keenly. Students might resent this less than their annual tuition fees. Perhaps in the

---

[18] Carl L. Nelson, Gladys C. Blakey, and Roy G. Blakey, *Sales Taxes* (Minneapolis: League of Minnesota Municipalities, 1935), p. 18.

course of present-day living people have become accustomed to being plundered in subtle ways and by installments. Convenience of payment was one of the four canons of taxation proposed by Adam Smith and has been universally recognized as an important consideration in choosing sources of revenue.

A tax or tax system which is easiest on the taxpayer psychologically is likely to provide most adequate revenue. Some argue that these taxes must be judged in part by the degree to which they help solve the problem of insuring the outlays that the government deems important. This connects taxation with public expenditures. Thus, many critics accept state sales taxes on the score that they make possible an adequate program of education. According to this view, a good expenditure might be said to justify a bad tax. On the other hand, there are also those who say that good taxes (meaning direct taxes) are the best defense against careless public spending. Moreover the use of withholding achieves for the income tax some of the psychological advantages of a sales tax.

A widely read book stated the argument for the sales tax as follows: [19] "The community is affluent in privately produced goods. It is poor in public services. The obvious solution is to tax the former to provide the latter—by making private goods more expensive public goods are made more abundant." Against this approach it is argued that with taxation taking so large a piece of everyone's earnings, we should insist on higher and not accede to lower standards of rationality in its distribution.

Fostering Industrial Development. Sales taxes are criticized for paying scant respect to ability to pay, and by the same token they preserve incentives (impose no discriminatory burdens upon the successful). At the state level, they probably offer less impediment to industrial location than alternative levies. The retail type of levy involves merchants, consumers, and farmers more than manufacturers and it is the latter who are most mobile. In terms of the domestic market, the sales tax reaches both imports and the in-state supply and it does not tax exports.

General Contribution to Government. Consumption taxes are also defended on the ground that they make everyone contribute to the government. This is said to be desirable because, first, everyone receives some benefit from government and, second, it tends to make everyone interested in the government and less inclined to support extravagant public expenditures. Where a few people pay all the taxes and the masses enjoy the benefits of government, the many are likely to exploit the few by voting for every new bond issue and public service. On the other hand, exemption of a minimum is a well-established principle and many will

---

[19] John Kenneth Galbraith, *The Affluent Society* (Boston: Houghton Mifflin Company, 1958), p. 315.

deplore a tax that reaches the first dollar even of the most meager retirement income.

It will be observed, of course, that the latter part of this argument is
inconsistent with the first argument presented above. If consumption taxes
are painless, they are poor protection against governmental extravagance.
A direct tax—like the poll tax, for instance—would be much more effective in making everybody tax conscious.

Reaching the Fluid Population.   One of the soundest arguments for a
sales tax, especially in some states such as California (heavy migration)
and some cities such as New York (shopping center), is that this is a
way to secure some contribution from the fluid population—that is, the
commuters, the tourists, the suburban shoppers, and others "passing
through." Unfortunately, the tax is not confined to these groups. Moreover, the transients, whose patronage may be the livelihood of the settled population, can sometimes be "scared away" by taxation they would
not encounter elsewhere.

Stability and Timing.   As previously observed consumption taxes
tend to fluctuate less than income taxes; people are likely to continue
their consumption expenditures at only a little less than normal standards even if they suffer a crop failure or incur unemployment. Thus in
some sense and some degree the sales tax is like a net income tax with a
built-in averaging feature. On the other hand, opponents allege that
this is but a case of bad timing: expenses are hard for the taxpayer to
meet during bad years and the sales tax only adds to the difficulty. Thus
critics insist that the income tax levies on taxpayers *when* they have
ability to pay; the sales tax hits them when they are down. Among others
who will bear the brunt of this bad timing are students and senior citizens.

Close Correlation with Progressive Income and Inheritance Taxes.   It is
often pointed out that consumption taxes, like income taxes, may be defended as a part of the tax system without attempting to justify their use
to the exclusion of all other taxes. Thus, it is said by many that the income tax is an effective means of reaching the ability to pay of the well-
to-do, but that it cannot be successfully applied to the larger number of
relatively poor people; these people, it is contended, enjoy benefits and
also have some ability to pay which can best be reached through consumption taxes. It may be added that partly because of exemptions the
income tax is often disappointing in its yield. Many have also favored the
sales tax as an alternative to part of the property tax, which is regarded
as excessive.

On the other hand, it may be answered that the techniques for applying the income tax to the great masses of people are slowly being per-
fected and that no sufficient effort in this direction has been made in the

United States. Also, the question may be asked: Why add another regressive tax to the tax system as a way of relieving the property taxpayer?
Actually, the poorest of small home owners might find themselves paying
more rather than less were the sales tax substituted for part of the
property tax. There is also dissent to the view that the employment of
many taxes is always better than the more intensive use of a few. The
latter has the advantage of greater simplicity, less confusion as to incidence, and reduced cost of administration and compliance.

Consumption Taxes as an Anti-inflation Measure. During war and
other inflationary periods, there are arguments both for and against consumption taxes that might not apply at other times. A general sales tax
during such periods, it is said, would check inflation in two respects:
first, it would drain excessive mass purchasing power into the treasury,
and, second, it would tax the act of spending and serve as a psychological
restraint upon extravagant outlays. Moreover, as a political matter, it
seems certain that a diversified revenue system can be pressed into higher
yields than a concentrated one. Adequacy of revenue, especially to meet
emergency needs, lies very close to the heart of the inflation problem.
On the other hand, inflation consists of pressure on prices, and consumption taxes might only add to the pressure. This would be true if enough
people had, through contract or otherwise, the means of converting the
tax into more pay—thus giving impetus to the inflation spiral. Consumption taxes, like any other, will be deflationary as compared with government borrowing; unless they lead to private borrowing which the banking system cannot or will not restrain, they will provide the means for
government expenditure without the enlargement of the money supply
or of aggregate demand.

No Minimum Free of Tax. A typical retail sales tax covers with no
exception the first dollar of unemployment compensation, social security
benefits, student maintenance, and even public relief. An income tax usually not only exempts a minimum but it adjusts the allowance for family
needs. The sales tax exempts savings, taxes, and services, outlays that are
the special prerogative of the well-to-do. Not only is there no allowance
for family needs—actually the sales tax usually imposes higher burdens
on large families than on small ones.

Regressivity. The typical sales tax is regressive, bearing with greater
relative weight on poor families than on rich ones. Typically for a family
of three a sales tax will usually collect about twice as much per thousand
dollars of income at the $1000–$2000 income level as at the level of
$10,000 and over. The larger the size of family (at equal income levels)
the less tax one has to pay under an income tax, but the opposite is true
under a sales tax.

It has been argued that annual data presenting ratios of tax to earnings overstate regressivity because the lower brackets of income are represented in part by people who are temporarily depressed and who continue spending according to normal or expected earnings. The point has some validity, but for some people and in some sense it is the year's accounts that are significant. Here the problem is the one of timing previously discussed.

Regressivity of sales taxes can be reduced by exempting food from the tax base. Critics argue that the exemption encounters too many difficulties of its own; they say that food is difficult to define; that omission intensifies administrative and compliance difficulties; that the food exemption cuts excessively into revenues; and that it creates arbitrary distinctions between families with different budgetary allocations.

Where the sales tax attends an income tax, regressivity might be mitigated by the use of a credit for a minimum of purchases. If a $15 per capita credit were combined with a 3 percent sales tax, the allowance would be equivalent to exempting $500 of taxable sales to each person. If the credit were greater than the income tax, a refund would be allowed; to do otherwise would defeat the purpose of the credit provision. This expedient has been advocated in the tax literature but has no precedent in practice. Critics argue that its administrative feasibility is uncertain and that if one is to make an income tax out of a sales tax, he might as well have used the former levy in the first place.

Capriciousness. Sales taxes are said to distribute burdens crudely even among those with the same size of income and family. Critics claim that this is the case because these taxes leave saving out of their measure and usually do not (probably cannot) tax all personal expenditure. This leaves the tax burden to be resolved by the capricious and irrelevant factor of differences in taste and other circumstances that dictate different budgetary patterns. Most published data indicate the average burden of families at different income levels and they tell us nothing of the dispersion of particular families about the average. If all consumption expenditure and only consumption expenditures were taxed, the dispersion factor would be confined largely to differences in saving and dissaving. As previously explained this is to some extent a difference in timing the burden.

Perhaps it is realistic to conclude that consumption taxes rest primarily upon the Machiavellian principle of taxation—"most feathers for the least squawking." The principle is time-honored, and there are few who think we could finance modern government without any application of it at all.[20]

---

[20] Daniel C. Morgan, Jr., "Reappraisal of Sales Taxation: Some Recent Arguments," *National Tax Journal* (March 1963), pp. 89–101.

MUNICIPAL SALES TAXES

Municipal sales taxes were first inaugurated in New York City in 1934 and since then they have spread to well over 1000 cities (and some counties), most of them in New York, California, Mississippi, and Illinois. The most outstanding objection to such taxes is that they tend to encourage the development of shopping centers in suburban areas. Cities have attempted to meet this problem by exempting sales for out-of-city delivery and taxing outside purchases by residents through a use tax. But this pattern involves an enforcement problem, encouragement of uneconomic delivery, and (where the tax is widely used) considerable confusion. California grappled with this problem by encouraging the counties to enact a standard tax, state collected, with provision of a credit for municipal taxes. Illinois permits municipalities to levy a small-percentage supplement to its state sales tax.[21]

The adoption of the sales tax in New York at about the time that Philadelphia enacted its municipal income tax posed two solutions to the municipal fiscal problem that have been of great interest to the critics.

THE TARIFF

Nature of Tariffs. For many centuries taxation upon territorial trade has been a major source of revenue for a large number of governments. Formerly such levies were often applied to internal trade (among the divisions of a country), but currently they are largely confined to international trade. Exports may be taxed as well as imports, but the latter is more common and the exclusive practice in the United States. Export taxes are of great importance in some of the tax systems of South America where they are used to recapture profits from the sale of natural resources and sometimes (with reserves) to stabilize an economy highly susceptible to fluctuations in the prices of raw materials. Tariffs may apply to all imports, but in practice they apply more commonly to specific items only. They may be entirely for revenue or entirely to protect domestic industry or a combination of the two. An examination of the tariff history of the United States suggests that our own tariffs have usually been highly selective, that the level of rates has usually been high, and that the objective has been one of protection more often and to a

---

[21] Due, *op. cit.*, chap. XV.

greater degree than to provide revenue. Nevertheless, during much of the financial history of the United States the tariff was the major source of revenue. Presently it provides less than 1 percent of total federal tax collections.

Tariff for Revenue.   It has often been pointed out that the protective and revenue aspects of the tariff are incompatible; a tariff may both yield revenue and protect at the same time, but to the extent that it performs one of these functions, it fails at the other. The best protection is provided by a tariff so high that it keeps out foreign goods entirely; this would be worthless as a revenue measure. The best revenue tariff is upon goods which must be produced entirely outside the country; such a tariff cannot defeat its own ends by encouraging a domestic source of supply but, of course, this kind of tariff is worthless for protection.

Tariffs are first cousins to excises, and most of what has been said about the latter applies to the former. As a consumption tax, tariffs on luxuries would be preferable to those on necessities. Something can be said, however, for maintaining as much neutrality as possible; a discriminatory tax disturbs the natural order of consumers' choices and creates unfair competition. When a consumer shifts from his first choice in consumption to his second, the government gains no revenue and the consumer loses the differential in satisfactions. A completely neutral tariff, however, could only be achieved by taxing all imports and supplementing this with a compensatory general domestic sales tax. Neutrality from the standpoint of competition could be achieved by taxing only commodities that cannot be produced competitively at home. In the United States this would include, for instance, coffee, tea, and chocolate. Significantly, these commodities are not, and seldom have been taxed.

In so far as the tariff raises domestic prices, it taxes the consumer and makes business more profitable for domestic producers. The rise in domestic prices may cost the consumer more than the government receives. The tariff may constitute a bounty, paid by domestic consumers directly to domestic producers.

Tariff for Protection.   The nonfiscal aspects of a nonfiscal tariff are largely outside the field of public finance. No useful purpose would be served by attempting to review the debate between the proponents of free trade and the supporters of protection. It is a well-known fact that most economists have been opposed to protection. Their case against the tariff is mainly that it is an impediment to the territorial division of labor, which, like other forms of specialization, adds to economic efficiency. If a tariff wall between nations is desirable, why would the same rule not hold as between states, counties, cities, wards, and even neighbors? Moreover, a country that professes concern about waning competition in enterprise should hardly be the one to exclude such competition from abroad.

Some recent trends in tariff making have been encouraging. One is the delegation of certain tariff-making powers by Congress to the President. This began in 1934 when President Roosevelt was given the power to negotiate trade agreements with other countries and to reduce the tariff by proclamation in accordance with these agreements. No tariff could be lowered or raised by this means more than one half. Although agreements were to be bilateral, reductions might be general, except for nations that discriminated against United States trade. This legislation, with some modifications, has been extended periodically, and numerous agreements have been negotiated under it. The legislation recognizes the oft-demonstrated fact that Congress is not properly constituted to pass a good tariff law. Territorial representation is too amenable to the pressure of special producer interests and too inattentive to the almost inarticulate interest of the consumer.

The innovation cited above also recognized the fact that the tariff is a bilateral matter. If it were to be conceded that one nation can gain by taxing another's exports, what shall we say of the situation when the other nation retaliates? The multilateral character of barriers to international trade has been further recognized by international conferences and agreements on the subject.

On the other hand, some recent developments are also an impediment to freer trade among nations. One of these is the propensity of nations to market commodities through governments rather than through individual buyers and sellers. Another is the development of very extensive internal controls that seem to require a counterpart in international trade. It may be fatuous to expect freer international trade in an economic order becoming constantly more mercantilistic in other respects.

Increasing recognition is also given to the fact that exporters have a vital stake in the tariff. In general, it is true that a nation which refuses to buy abroad cannot sell abroad; no means of payment will be available. While the United States is singularly independent of foreign trade, certain of its industries, including agriculture, rely substantially on foreign markets. Trade barriers can be viewed not as a case of making the foreigner pay but as an issue between exporters and producers for the domestic market.

Specific Tariffs. If space permitted a thorough presentation of the tariff problem, it would be necessary to examine in some detail the specific taxes on imports, each of which has its own problems and its own effects, even though all are lumped together in speaking of *the* tariff. Historically, the two items in most dispute have been the tariff on wool and that on sugar. But the intriguing problems in these areas must be left to the special investigation of the student who is interested in pursuing them further.

SUMMARY

Though consumption taxes are less important now than formerly, at least in the over-all tax system, they have some place at all levels of government and constitute a leading source of revenue for the American states.

Selective sales taxes are more controllable in terms of distribution than general sales taxes, but the former are discriminatory particularly as among consumers of different tastes. Moreover, where demand is elastic and the tax causes substitution of consumption goods, the tax may burden consumers without raising revenue.

Liquor and tobacco have been favorite objects of special taxation for a long time. The former lacks full social approval, and the latter is distinguished by its inelastic demand. Administration of tobacco taxes, particularly at the federal level, is impressively easy and inexpensive, but liquor taxes involve serious evasion problems.

Consumption taxes run to many species, of which three of the most common are the gross income tax, the manufacturers sales tax, and the retail sales tax. The first encounters the impressive objection that it involves fortuitous duplication and favors integrated industries. The manufacturers sales tax invites pyramiding and is not well adapted to include services in its base; the retail sales tax is less encumbered by these limitations but it is harder to administer.

Among the other problems of retail sales taxation at the state level are the legal obstacles to taxing interstate sales and the application of the law to small sales. Even more formidable is the problem of defining a retail sale. Present definitions are often arbitrary and include a more or less indiscriminate mixture of capital and consumption goods. There is little plausible reason for the exclusion of services; it involves unneutralities among consumers and special administrative difficulties. Municipal sales taxes encounter the danger of driving trade to outlying merchants.

In the extended argument concerning direct versus indirect taxes in general, and the retail sales tax in particular, the following points are noted: sales taxes are convenient; they are less inimical to incentives than direct taxes; they reach the fluid population; and they can be used to supplement direct taxes effectively. On the other hand they leave no

minimum free of tax, are badly timed in terms of the taxpayer's convenience, and are often regressive and capricious in their distribution. Favorite antidotes for regressivity are food exemption and a credit for minimum purchases.

A tariff is a consumption tax on the consumer of imported goods.
Many tariffs, including most of those in the United States, have been imposed largely for the nonfiscal purpose of encouraging domestic industry.
From the fiscal standpoint tariffs could be improved by concentrating
upon a few articles which are not among the necessities and which are
produced mainly abroad. Recent innovations giving the President power
to change tariffs, with limitations, and the increasing recognition of the
bilateral character of trade and of exporters' interests, are important mile-
stones in the history of the tariff as a nonfiscal device.

PROBLEMS

1. A manufacturer buys a good for $100, expends $100 on its cost of
   manufacture and sells it for $220 including profit. He passes the
   good on to a wholesaler and the later passes it on to a retailer, each
   of which adds 20 percent to the price to cover expenses and profits.
   a. If a 10-percent tax is imposed on the manufacturers' sale, show
      concretely how this might be pyramided.
   b. What would be the base here of a retail sales tax? value-added
      tax? gross income tax?
2. On what ground is it said that the imposition of a special excise,
   applied to a good with elastic demand, imposes a sacrifice on the
   taxpayer without benefit to the government? Compare merits of
   general and special excises.
3. Special excises on luxuries of highly inelastic demand will have
   the same influence upon consumption through their purchasing
   power effect as do taxes on necessities. Comment.
4. Comment on the proposition: Tobacco taxes are more regressive
   than they need to be.
5. What is meant by "social cost" and how is this a factor in liquor
   taxation?
6. X and Y are merchants and A and B are residents in adjoining
   states, each with a sales tax. A and B do all their shopping across
   the state line. In what circumstances, if at all, can the state tax
   the purchases of these individuals?
7. Distinguish among (a) pyramiding, (b) cumulative effect of a
   gross income tax, (c) incidence of a sales tax.
8. Distinguish between a final sale of a commodity and a sale to a
   consumer. Does taxing the former involve double taxation of the
   consumer?

9. In what circumstances might a ten-cent store collect more from the public through a sales tax than it pays to the government?

10. Distinguish among (a) net income tax, (b) net income tax without exemptions, (c) gross income tax, (d) value-added tax, (e) use tax, (f) retail sales tax, and (g) transactions tax.

11. What unneutralities are involved in a gross income tax? Are these avoided by a value-added tax and, if so, how?

12. Compare the merits of a manufacturers and a retail sales tax.

13. Consider the merits of an over-all expenditure tax with personal exemptions and graduated rates. How is it possible to graduate such a tax with rates exceeding 100 percent and still have a non-confiscatory tax?

14. To what extent and under what conditions, if at all, will a good public expenditure justify a bad tax? How can it also be argued that a good tax will prevent bad expenditures?

15. What is meant when it is argued that the sales tax is regressive? capricious? ill-timed? What could be done to mitigate these features?

16. Why might a production tax on the manufacture of beer in Milwaukee not be feasible?

17. Explain complications in applying a sales tax to an automobile "trade-in."

18. It is said that the trouble with a sales tax is not that it is wrong in principle but that it doesn't have any principle; that it is the equivalent of a flat income tax with a lot of irrational omissions, plus a business tax that covers some but not all business expenditures. Comment.

19. How is the domestic exporter involved in a tax on imports?

20. Is it possible to devise a tariff that would not interfere at all with international competition? How?

12

MOTOR VEHICLE TAXES

The highway plant and its use in an American state are truly impressive phenomena. Some states have enough surfaced roads to stretch three or four times around the globe. In 1920 there were 9 million motor vehicles in the United States; by 1965, according to conservative estimate, there will be 81 million and they will travel 800 trillion miles. The professional and business use of the highway system is substantial. Farmers depend upon the highway and the motor vehicle for their mail delivery service and the transportation of their children to a modern school. They deliver their produce both to the local and the central market in large part by truck. Truck and bus may be the only transportation service for a large number—of the smaller municipalities. The automobile along with food, clothing, and medical care is regarded as one of the necessities of life. Will Rogers described the United States in depression as the only nation to go to the poorhouse in an automobile. In the postwar era, more traffic, higher speed, and postponement of highway improvement have elevated the highway problem to a top position among the concerns of government at all levels. The ambitious federal aid program of 1956 authorized the expenditure of nearly $27 billion of federal money over 13 years; it especially emphasized the completion of a superhighway system to connect metropolitan centers.

This meteoric rise of the motor vehicle to almost universal use in the United States has created a demand for many large new governmental expenditures. Of these, foremost has been the demand for a vastly more expensive type of highway with a coordinated system of through routes. In addition, new needs have made their appearance in the forms of parking facilities, protection for pedestrians, traffic regulation, and so on. City planning boards now spend much of their time finding ways and means to prevent the automobile from strangling the cities; they regard the motorist as an uneconomic user of urban space and seek to substitute mass transportation, though not always with success. The expanding expenditures to meet these needs brought the problem of raising additional revenue. In solving the latter, a new family of taxes—which may be called the motor vehicle tax family—was developed. Although these levies are usually called "taxes," they have a high degree of correlation with special benefits to the taxpayer. Moreover, the receipts from them are usually set aside for the specific purpose of financing roads and streets.

Of course, these taxes do not cover all the expenditures on highways and streets; the rest of the needed funds comes from various sources such as special assessments, general property taxes, and borrowing. This chapter will be devoted particularly to motor vehicle taxes, but some attention will be given to alternative ways of financing highways. However, no consideration will be given to borrowing, as ordinarily it is but a postponement of one of the other revenue-raising alternatives.

Given the existence of a vast number of motor vehicles and the traffic they create, it becomes apparent that we cannot afford to be without a very expensive highway system. Under these conditions, we pay for good highways in increased operating expense whether we have them or not. Thus, the demand for highways is a derived demand. But the pattern of highway finance itself can alter the demand for motor vehicles. Had we followed the British practice with motor fuel taxes in the range of 30 cents per gallon, our motor-vehicle demand would have differed both in kind and numbers. In the last analysis, the problem is one of the proper allocation of resources.

THE BENEFIT PRINCIPLE IN HIGHWAY FINANCE

The theory that taxes should be distributed according to benefits received, as has been observed, encounters two important objections. One is that benefits cannot be measured, and the other is that society may prefer a wider consumption of certain public services than that which direct beneficiaries could afford. Neither objection is entirely applicable in the case of highway finance. Various instrumentalities such as the motor fuel tax are thought to do a tolerable job of measurement, and most of the beneficiaries of highway services are well able to pay for such services. Accordingly, it is in this area that accounting and charging on the benefit principle has its widest and most plausible application. Nevertheless, the benefit approach encounters important limitations even in highway finance. Among them are the following: (1) Benefit is divided in uncertain proportions between users and others. (2) User benefits are measurable but only roughly; all the alternative user-taxes have their limitations. Motor fuel taxes take inadequate account of weight and use of vehicles off the highways; licenses take inadequate account of distance and state boundary lines; even the ton-mile tax, which is difficult to administer, takes no account of actual as contrasted with capacity loads. (3) Funds collected from users may not (and perhaps should not) be distributed strictly according to use. Much of motor vehicle traffic (perhaps half) is in and about metropolitan areas, but the motorist is interested in the entire highway system any part of which may serve him if he so chooses. Some attention accordingly must be given to the benefits associated with readiness to serve. (4) Obligations for general government support get intermixed with those for special services.

THE FUNDAMENTAL QUESTIONS OF HIGHWAY FINANCE

The three fundamental questions of highway finance are these: (1) what part of the cost of highways should users pay? (2) what contribution to general government should highway users make? and (3) how should the highway users' share be allotted among the several types of users— motor vehicles of different values, sizes, and weights?

Should the Motorist Pay for the Roads? It is generally conceded that motor vehicle owners should contribute to the cost of constructing and maintaining highways, but to what extent is a highly controversial question. One view holds that all the costs of roads and streets should be met by special motor vehicle taxation. This is based on the assumption that provision of improved highways is essentially a business undertaking and should, therefore, be economically self-supporting. It is admitted that society as a whole derives many benefits from this business, but in this respect highways are in the same position as public utilities. The service rendered in the latter case, such as the supplying of water, gas, or electricity, may be of general as well as special benefit, but the special benefit is of such greater relative importance that it justifies a charge sufficient to pay for the entire service.

On the other hand, those who oppose this view maintain that highways serve other functions than those directly relating to motor vehicles and that to place the entire cost of highways upon motorists is unfair. They emphasize the benefit society as a whole derives from the free and rapid transportation of goods and services. A person who never drives a car may still benefit greatly from the highways, as, for instance, when he can procure a physician at his home without delay in case of sudden illness. The owner of a cluster of cabins on a main highway may have no automobile; it could hardly be argued that he received no benefit from the highway's improvement. This theory also distinguishes between the different components of the highway system. The main highways, serving primarily as arteries of motor vehicle travel, render more service to the majority of motorists than do local roads and streets. The cost of the latter is thought to be a "land service expenditure," since the land and those dwelling on it benefit more than does the general highway user. Consequently, it is alleged that, in an equitable allocation of highway costs, some payment for "land service" is rightly chargeable to the land served. Thus, the users, the property owners, and the community at large all benefit from highways; and, as usual, the benefit theory leaves us "up in the air" as to a proper division among beneficiaries.

Probably the most rational way to apply the benefit principle among different types of roads and different classes of beneficiaries is to start with a highway traffic count that will indicate the proportionate use of a given highway by residents and nonresidents of the district in which the highway is located. The proportion of nonresident use applied to the cost of the road will represent the minimum of contribution that should be expected from users. The remaining cost of the highway can be covered at the discretion of the public by any one of three alternative sources: general property tax; local vehicle tax; return of state-collected vehicle tax via state aids.

The following procedure is also sometimes recommended: (1) start with the arterial system and impose taxes at a level that will pay for this system by charges upon its users; (2) allot to other roads an "earnings credit" equal to the user-charges collected on these highways; (3) fill the remaining cost of the secondary and tertiary road systems in some manner from nonuser taxes.

Contributions to General Government. The above calculus ignores the contributions that owners of vehicles (and facilities maintained for their use, such as roads) should make to general government. For the view that these should be substantial it is urged that (1) vehicles and highways comprise a vast storehouse of wealth; (2) vehicles occasion much special governmental expense outside the outlay for roads and streets; and (3) competitors of commercial users of highways (railroads versus trucks) pay heavy taxes to support general governmental functions. It might be added that much automotive wealth is in the luxury class and that the motorist uses a natural resources (gasoline) that is in prospective short supply.

However, it can be argued plausibly that the questions of how much highway users should pay to general government and how much they should pay for highways are separable issues and that confusion arises if we attempt to resolve them at the same time.

Division of Charges among Highway Users. The division of charges among highway users is principally a matter of how much more heavily trucks and busses should pay as compared with lighter vehicles. Most of the analysis of this problem must wait for an examination of specific taxes. Some contend that the proper approach is one of "incremental costs." These include both the extra facilities that are added to support the heavier vehicles and the extra wear and tear on all facilities caused by heavy loads. What these incremental costs may be is a first-rate engineering problem; numerous tests have been and are being conducted to determine the correlation between heavy loads and costs, but definitive answers are elusive. Moreover, this analysis leaves unanswered the question of how to divide common costs—those of basic highways. These latter must be divided by some unit of use or service. Some argue that ton-miles are the appropriate unit; others, that vehicle miles should be used. Still others would abandon the incremental-cost approach entirely and divide costs by a use-unit only —probably ton-miles.

Some confusion between benefits and costs also beclouds the highway finance problem. Benefits are conceived of as savings to the motorist and costs as government outlay. But benefit among highway users is largely another name for demand. An investment is justified if the demand will be adequate under a proposed pattern of taxes to make the highway self-liquidating.

ALTERNATIVE METHODS OF FINANCING HIGHWAYS

SPECIAL ASSESSMENTS

Special assessments for highways are usually on a frontage basis and confined to the land abutting improvements. They are levied on the theory that the highway renders a special service to land, thereby adding to its value.

Special assessments are ill adapted for financing through rural highways. One reason for this is that such highways are likely to benefit the cities located on them much more than the abutting owners. The centers of large population gain because their trade areas expand, but the small villages along the highway may actually suffer a loss in trade due to the ease and economy with which their residents may now journey to the larger centers. Another factor to consider here is that the abutting property owners might be better served by a less costly road. Concrete highways, especially, may prove something of a nuisance to farmers. High-speed traffic drives the horse-drawn vehicles off the concrete and is a handicap in getting livestock to pasture. Fast-driven vehicles also endanger the lives of children and do some damage by killing the farmers' poultry. Other disadvantages to the farmers include noise and some loss from petty thievery. On the other hand, the road may give them a direct outlet for produce through sales to tourists as well as a better access to the urban markets.

Nevertheless, considerable interest is manifest in the effect on land values that will attend the new superhighways with their limited points of access. Whether excess condemnation or special assessment can be used to capture some of this increment and whether this can make a significant contribution to highway finance is an open question.

Actually, the use of special assessments is confined mainly to cities. Some of the objections to their use in financing rural highways apply also to their use in financing city streets. A through street, particularly, is likely to benefit those at either end more than those who live along it. Fewer objections are encountered when special assessments are used to finance streets that serve mainly those residing on them. Even in this case, however, their use is fraught with considerable difficulty. The special assessment is levied before actual benefit to property has occurred, and the estimation of benefit involves much guesswork.[1] Usefulness of this type of levy in financing streets associated with new subdivisions is conceded.

TOLL ROADS

Financing roads by means of tolls once had considerable vogue (in the turnpike era of the nineteenth century), and there has been a conspicuous revival of interest in this institution in recent years. Pennsylvania's famous turnpike, financed by tolls, was the pioneering venture; New Jersey, New York, and Ohio, among others, followed with ambitious projects. The success of the very expensive New Jersey project is reported to have far surpassed expectations. It was built and is being

---

[1] For a more extended discussion of the problems involved in special assessments, see Chapter 18.

operated by a semipublic authority with the promise that the property will be conveyed eventually to the state. The project was financed largely by 35-year bonds bearing interest at $3\frac{1}{4}$ percent and subscribed by insurance companies, trust funds, and savings banks. Considerable state legislation authorizing toll roads has recently been adopted. However, the consensus supports the view that only under special conditions is the toll road feasible. These conditions include an important advantage for traffic in the toll route, with few points of ingress and egress along the highway. Administrative costs are a formidable obstacle, and motorists are likely to object to the charge, along with existing levies, as double taxation. If local traffic is substantial, duplication of facilities is necessary. It is interesting to note that toll road charges are based on mileage with some classification for weight of load; thus they apply the benefit principle of collection with considerable precision.[2] Toll charges run to five or six times the usual motor fuel tax; that the demand stands up reasonably well in the face of these charges indicates the high value motorists give to time and safety in travel. Nevertheless, not all toll roads have met the expectations of their promoters and interest in new construction has waned since the federal government undertook its superhighway program.

GENERAL PROPERTY TAX

As a practical matter, most of the cost of highways not borne by highway users will fall upon the general property tax. Most people own both a home and a car, and it may seem a matter of indifference whether they pay for a highway through a levy on one or the other. But the correlation between automobile- and home-ownership is by no means perfect. And moreover, at stake in the division is the allocation of resources as between motor vehicles and other consumer goods.

MOTOR FUEL TAX

Once it is decided what the total highway bill shall be and what proportion of the total highway cost should be borne by motor vehicles, there still remains the problem of determining which of the several motor vehicle taxes should be used and to what extent. This problem will be considered along with others in the discussion of the various members of the vehicle-tax family which follows.

---

[2] Wilfred Owen and Charles L. Doering, *Toll Roads and the Problem of Highway Modernization* (Washington, D.C.: The Brookings Institution, 1951); D. Netzer, "Toll Roads and the Crisis in Highway Finance," *National Tax Journal*, 5: 2 (June 1952), pp. 107–119.

The two principal members of the motor vehicle tax family universally used in the United States are the motor fuel tax and the motor license tax. Although the motor fuel tax appeared upon the scene (1919) considerably later than the motor vehicle license tax, it swept the country in a decade and is now the most productive of the highway-user taxes. Currently, the modal rate is 6 cents per gallon and several states have pushed the levy to 7 cents. The trend, though now very gradual, is still upward.

In 1932 the federal government also entered the field and added its 1-cent levy (4 cents, 1962) to that of the states. The cities and counties in several states also levy a tax in addition to that of the state and federal government. Taxes on special fuel, the most important of which is diesel oil, are imposed in nearly all of the states. From the standpoint of productivity the levy on motor fuel has become second only to the general sales tax in significance among state taxes.

Advantages. Of all the taxes that have ever been employed in the United States, the motor fuel tax probably comes nearest to being a popular tax. From the governments' standpoint, its first virtue is ease and inexpensiveness of administration. When rates were low this was particularly true. Even today the cost of administering gasoline taxes is probably lower than that of any other major state or local tax. Another advantage to the states is that the gasoline tax exacts contributions from out-of-state tourists in rough proportion to their use of highway facilities. Finally, the tax has proved to be a consistent producer of substantial revenue. Its yield can be depended upon in poor as well as in good years. From the taxpayer's standpoint, the tax is readily accepted as the price for good highway service.

However, there is a growing realization that motor fuel consumption has some limitations as a measure of benefits received. The correlation between gasoline consumption and wear and tear upon the highways is particularly low for vehicles of different weights. This point will be further discussed later in this chapter.

The motor fuel tax is a specific tax (so much per gallon); and, as is the case with all taxes of this character, its yield tends to lag badly during inflation. Ad valorem taxes, in contrast, have a built-in escalator. Present inadequacy of highway revenues is attributable in no small part to this factor.

Administration. Motor fuel taxes were conspicuously free from administrative difficulties when the rates were low, but, with successive advances in the rates, a considerable problem of evasion appeared. With a 6- or 7-cent gasoline tax (9 or 10 cents including the federal tax), the levy may amount to a quarter or a third of gross sales and substantially more than the profit. Such a situation may be depended upon to strengthen the ingenuity and weaken the integrity of some dealers.

For many years the most prevalent form of motor-fuel-tax evasion consisted of smuggling across state boundary lines. By the cooperative efforts of honest dealers, exchange of information among states, and a strict licensing system, this leakage has largely been eliminated.

Many states exempt from tax all or most motor fuel not used on the highways. Since the tax is regarded as a toll for the use of the roads, it seems illogical to tax gasoline used in farm tractors, airplanes, stationary engines, or on railways. However, where the same taxpayer owns both a motor vehicle and a mechanism that consumes gasoline off the highways, it is exceedingly difficult to determine how much gasoline is used on and how much off the highways and thus how much should be taxed and how much not taxed.

In order to avoid taxing motor fuel not used in motor vehicles, a common procedure is to require the purchaser of such gasoline to pay the tax at time of purchase and then seek a refund. To qualify for the refund he must present to some state official an invoice of the purchase and an affidavit of use off the highways. The state has scant check upon the honesty of the affidavit. Beyond the assurance of purchase evidenced by the invoice, the possession of a mechanism using gasoline off the highway (which can be checked), and the plausibility of the amounts upon which the refund is demanded, the state must rely largely upon the honesty of the taxpayer.[3]

Exemptions and refunds are very important in a state such as North Dakota where the majority of the population are farmers, most of whom own tractors and automobiles. In such states the annual amount of refunds may range as high as 30 or even 40 percent of collections.

THE MOTOR VEHICLE LICENSE TAX

The most important member of the motor vehicle tax family other than the motor fuel tax is the motor vehicle license tax.[4] It is an annual payment for the privilege of using a motor vehicle on public highways and streets. The registration tax appeared first (New York, 1901) as a regulatory measure and consisted of low flat, nonrecurrent payments at the time a vehicle was purchased. During the first decade of experience with licensing cars, the practice of an annual charge for revenue became estab-

---

[3] An investigator appointed to check up on flagrant cases of abuse of the refund privilege in Oklahoma found many such cases, including use of untaxed gasoline in a school bus operated by the claimant under a contract with a school district, use in dairy delivery trucks, and reselling from a filling station operated on a farm. Not all of these abuses could be proved, but they were suspected upon plausible ground. (*Third Biennial Report* of the Oklahoma Tax Commission, 1938, pp. 25–26.)

[4] The license charge is sometimes called a fee, but since it is imposed primarily for revenue rather than as incident to and in payment for administrative services, it is more properly called a tax. See Chapter 18.

lished. With the advent of the gasoline tax, some states reverted to the low flat rate but most states retained a graduated charge as a major source of revenue. The tax is about half as productive of revenue as the motor fuel tax.

States have experimented with many bases for measuring license taxes, including horsepower, value of car, piston displacement, wheel base, gross weight, and net weight. Expert opinion generally favors gross weight (including the capacity load of the vehicle as well as its own weight) as the standard.

Advantages. If the gasoline tax is so popular and has as many advantages as the foregoing discussion has suggested, the question naturally arises: "Why have any other motor vehicle tax?" The place of the motor vehicle license tax in the tax system is defended on the following grounds:

1. It can be used to correct a low correlation between weight and gasoline consumption. A 6-ton truck may wear out the highway, or at least enjoy the benefit of highway service, twice as much as a 3-ton truck and use considerably less than twice as much gasoline. Figures compiled from surveys made by the Highway Cost Commission in the state of Washington show that the average fuel tax per gross ton-mile paid by private passenger cars under a 5-cent tax was 2.25 mills per ton-mile, whereas that paid by a 34,000-pound truck and a 68,000-pound truck-trailer combination was only 0.83 and 0.53 mills per ton-mile respectively.[5] In order to serve as a corrective for the low correlation between gasoline consumption and the weight of a vehicle, the license fees should be graduated so that rates advance more rapidly than weight. For example, if the license tax schedule imposes a $25 tax on a 3-ton truck, then it should impose a tax higher than $50 upon a 6-ton truck. The level of tax on the heavier truck may take account of the fact that large trucks frequently cover more mileage than small trucks and automobiles; that their frequent use of diesel fuel gives them more advantage than the above figures indicate; and that wear and tear on the highways may increase more than proportionately with the weight of the vehicle.

2. The license tax is justified as a sort of overhead charge on the ownership of a car, whether the owner uses it often or not. The contention is that public outlay for automobiles, such as that for highways, parking space, traffic officers, and so forth, must be geared to a peak load, and the more cars there are in the community the higher the peak

---

[5] *Supplemental Report of the Highway Cost Commission to the State Legislature,* State of Washington, January 1937, p. 64; a later study estimated that during 1948 passenger cars accounted for 51.57 percent of the gross ton miles operated on Washington's highways whereas they contributed 57.04 percent of highway-user taxes. Similar data indicated, however, that lighter trucks were favored as compared with heavy trucks. James C. Nelson, *Financing Washington's Highways, Roads and Streets* (Olympia, 1948), pp. XII–XIII.

load is likely to be. Miss *X* may use her automobile only on rare occasions, but these occasions may be when almost everyone else is on the road. Thus it is thought that the cost of motor vehicles to the public depends upon their ownership as well as use; as in the case of public utilities, there should be a minimum charge for readiness to serve. The license tax is such a charge.

Proponents of weight-distance or ton-mile taxes have raised serious question as to whether the license (except a nominal fee) fills any useful purpose where this third type of user-tax is in effect. The license admittedly has the fundamental defect that it takes no account of distance traveled. A case for retaining the license even under these conditions can be made. It may be a convenient way of taking some of the administrative load off a weight-distance tax. Moreover, it can be refined (as in Louisiana) to take some account of average distance by classes of vehicles. A higher rate can be charged, other things being equal, for a vehicle that is likely to be on the road constantly than for a dump truck.

The cost of administering the motor vehicle license tax is impressively high, particularly in contrast to that of the gasoline tax. On the other hand, it can be argued plausibly that much of this cost is inevitable in any event, since a licensing system is required in order to police the highways adequately.

FEDERAL SALES TAXES

For many years the federal government levied certain taxes on motor vehicles, but the revenue went into the general treasury and was not associated with federal aid which the government distributed to the states for highways. The new federal aid program, however, added substantially to the federal motor vehicle tax system and earmarked these revenues for a highway fund designed to cover the cost of the new program. Most of the federal taxes are sales taxes, and they include excises on the sale of new vehicles, tires, motor fuel, and lubricating oil. However, the federal government also inaugurated a special weight-distance tax on vehicles with a gross weight of more than 26,000 pounds.

TON-MILE TAX

Many states have experimented with special taxes designed "to make trucks and busses pay their share." One form which such legislation has taken is the ton-mile tax. As the name implies, the measure of this tax includes both factors, weight of the vehicle and distance traveled. This affords (except for administrative difficulties) an admirable correlation between taxes levied and wear and tear on the highways. However, the determination of a suitable rate level is not easy. The ton-mile tax may be in lieu of or in addition to a graduated license levy; in the latter case it is called a "third structure" tax. A refinement classifying ton-miles according to size of vehicle is called a weight-distance tax; it distinguishes between a 1-ton truck traveling 20 miles and a 20-ton truck traveling 1 mile.

There are three types of carriers in the trucking business: common carriers, which carry for hire and fulfill a regular schedule on a regular route; contract carriers, which carry for hire but have no regular schedule nor route; and private carriers, which do not offer their services to the general public at all. The ton-mile tax was first applied in many states to common carriers, but more recently it has been applied to cover all types of carriers.

The ton-mile tax as a means of collecting for road use by heavier trucks has impressive advantages. It is the only type of levy that can take adequate account of both the weight and mileage factors in the case of the heavier vehicles. One critic observes that "certainly some common unit of highway service is needed when we have vehicles ranging from 2,000 pounds to 76,000 pounds traveling from 5,000 to 100,000 miles per year on the highway." [6] Moreover, the tax applies a fair and automatic standard to out-of-state trucks that cannot be reached (under reciprocity) by a license tax.

On the other hand, ton-mile taxes have proved difficult and expensive to administer well, and they involve additional costs of compliance. Administration is a matter of detailed reporting subject to audit and reinforced by weighing trucks at stations and spot-checking truck movements. Truckers also complain that the system can take no account of the fact that trucks often move with less than capacity load or even empty (on return trips).

The experience of the states with weight-distance taxes has been marked by an important revival of interest. In New York a weight-distance tax was inaugurated after the usual intensive research given to most new legislation in that state. The Oregon experience is notable because of the well-supported claim that it has secured a 95-percent enforcement at an administrative cost of less than 5 percent. The Oregon law went before a popular referendum in 1952, and notwithstanding a lavish campaign to defeat the measure, it was sustained by a large majority. The well-organized trucking industry in many states wields a lobby of awesome potency.

---

[6] Richard M. Zettle, "Some Problems of Highway Cost Assignment, with Special Reference to the Truckers' Share," *Proceedings of the National Tax Association*, 1953, p. 115.

NEUTRALITY AMONG COMPETING TRANSPORTATION AGENCIES

The previous discussion involves only the problem of neutrality among highway users—how much should large trucks pay as compared with small ones and as compared with automobiles. But there is an equally important problem of neutrality involved, that is, the relative burden on competing forms of transportation. The trucking (and air) transportation business has been growing rapidly at the expense of railroads. It is now said to employ three and a half times as many employees as its rival, and its lobby is probably more powerful than the notorious one of the railroads in their palmiest days. Railroads have contended for a long time that they are being taxed to provide a roadbed for their competitors. Railroads as well as highways are essential to defense, and in view of the progressive shifting of traffic to the highways, we need to be doubly sure that competition in the transportation field is not weighted by the government in favor of the stronger competitor. The matter of tax neutrality among transportation agencies has been the subject of some research but the studies have not come to the same conclusion. The most recent and elaborate of these studies did conclude that the commercial users of highways have a substantial tax advantage over their railroad competitors.[7] The analysis preceding any sophisticated conclusion is necessarily elaborate; it involves all the fundamental questions we have discussed in this chapter and especially the question of the amount of taxes highway users should pay to general government. Some students contend that commercial users of highways should pay a "property tax equivalent" on their wealth, including the highways themselves which are regarded as equivalent to the railroads' roadbed. The debate is not one that is likely to be settled with any high degree of finality.

OTHER TAXES AFFECTING MOTOR VEHICLES

Although the principal taxes that affect the motor vehicle have been covered, there are numerous others which may be mentioned in passing. Within the motor vehicle tax family are the drivers' and chauffeurs' license fees imposed by most states. Usually they are unimportant as

[7] Ronald B. Welch, *Carrier Taxation,* report submitted to the Board of Investigation and Research (Washington, 1945).

revenue sources and are incidental to administration. Occasionally, however, they produce a fairly substantial revenue.

Among the taxes outside the motor vehicle tax family, but which affect motor vehicles in a considerable number of states is the personal property tax. The trend, however, is away from taxing motor vehicles as personal property. The sale of motor vehicles is usually subject to a sales tax (federal and in some cases state). Occasionally, filling-station sales of petroleum products are included in the general retail sales tax; more often they are exempt. The sales tax is objected to by petroleum retailers because it is said to be a tax upon a tax—that is, the selling price which is the base of the tax already includes the state and federal gasoline tax. However, there seems to be no good reason why the consumer of gasoline should not contribute to general government along with other consumers. Filling stations are sometimes subject to the chain store tax, and this may or may not be passed on to the motor vehicle owner and user. Finally, many cities have installed parking meters and collect substantial sums from motorists for the privilege of parking in certain areas (see Chapter 18).

DIVERSION OF MOTOR VEHICLE TAX FUNDS

Another problem which has come to the fore in recent years is diversion of gasoline and motor vehicle license tax revenues to other than highway purposes. During the lean years of the early 1930s, gasoline and motor vehicle taxes were among the few that produced a relatively constant flow of revenue. Many of the states were hard pressed for funds with which to meet relief and school expenditures and to balance their budgets. The result was a considerable diversion of gasoline taxes from highway to other purposes. Since the 1930s the trend in diversion has been downward, but it is still substantial in some states. A second type of diversion has been the use of state highway aids by localities for other purposes than that intended. This latter type of diversion might be checked, as a rule, by vigorous administration, but such has not always been provided.

The diversion policy has been vigorously criticized on the ground that the justification for the motor fuel tax is its use for the construction and maintenance of highways; that without this justification the tax becomes an ordinary sales tax and a very high sales tax at that. In the federal Hayden-Cartwright Act of 1934, the principle was laid down in a federal-aid statute that "it is unfair and unjust to tax motor vehicle transportation unless the proceeds of such taxation are applied to the construction, improvement, or maintenance of highways." [8] Considerable

---

[8] *U.S. Statutes at Large,* 48, Ch. 586, Sec. 12.

pressure, sometimes successful, has been exerted to procure the enactment of nondiversion provisions in state constitutions.

Concerning the diversion problem, it must be remembered that in
local expenditures for roads and streets there has been much diversion
of general property taxes for highway purposes. Since in few, if any,
states total expenditures for highways even in depression years have been
less than total motor vehicle taxes, it can be argued that there has been
no *net* diversion. This is on the assumption, of course, that the motor
vehicle owner should pay for the entire cost of roads and streets.

There has been considerable popular misunderstanding and abuse
of the term *diversion*. In the broadest and soundest sense, there is no
diversion of motor vehicle tax revenues until motor vehicles and the sale
of such vehicles and of motor fuel have paid the same taxes for the support of general government as other property or sales, in addition to paying for the entire cost of highways and streets. This heavy imposition
may not be advisable, but until it is made there is no diversion. The
automobile is associated with heavy public expense in addition to that of
highways (parking and traffic control, for instance), and it is sometimes
argued that even with some direct diversion, the motorist gets more from
the public than he supplies. The attempt to put an antidiversion clause
into state constitutions not only encounters difficulties of definition but
represents one more effort to put beyond legislative discretion a matter
that is clearly within the proper range of legislative policy. Here is another manifestation of the power of well-organized pressure groups to
fasten undesirable tax restrictions upon what should be "the sovereign
state."

Waiving the question of whether or not there is diversion, the legislature should have the right to levy an excise tax on gasoline if it sees fit.
Probably there are better ways of raising general revenue than the
gasoline tax, but there are also worse—for example, the retail sales tax
which includes in its base, as a rule, most of the necessities of life. Frequently the license fee includes a property tax component (levied in
lieu of the personal property tax), and this part of so-called user taxes
logically should go into the general funds.

RECIPROCITY

States do not require a special license for the use of their highways by
out-of-state passenger cars. This means in effect that reciprocity is practiced. Reciprocity, however, has not been the prevailing practice with
regard to trucks and busses. The extra levies imposed upon vehicles engaged in interstate traffic are strongly criticized as a trade barrier, and

an effort is being exerted to extend reciprocity to commercial vehicles. A considerable network of reciprocity legislation and agreements has been built up accordingly. The result is laudable in its elimination of a barrier to trade, but it is objected to by the so-called bridge states which provide an avenue of passage for vehicles between important cities in adjoining states. To make matters worse, the system affords the interstate transport companies the opportunity to shop around for the cheapest bidder in obtaining their licenses. Reciprocity built on a mileage tax so that contributions could be prorated seems to be the answer, but it will require more cooperation than the states have thus far developed.[9]

SUMMARY AND CONCLUSION

Highway finance is the area where the most pronounced application of benefit taxation is observed, but even here it encounters many difficulties and limitations. Highway finance raises the fundamental questions of who should pay for the highways, how much should highway users pay to general government, and how should the users' highway bill be divided. In striving for an answer to these questions, governments have employed many measures to finance highways, some of which are designed to reach users and some nonusers. Of the latter, the special assessment and general property tax are the most prominent; of the user-charges, the fuel tax, license, and ton-mile taxes have the widest use. Most popular is the motor fuel tax but it fails adequately to take into account the high ratio of tonnage to fuel consumption in the case of trucks; most controversial is the ton-mile levy which takes account of the significant factors but which is difficult to graduate properly and to administer. Additional complications are afforded by reciprocity agreements under which trucks may use highways of states other than those which license them without extra charge. Highway finance abounds with

---

[9] Numerous excellent state reports on highway finance are available. Among the recent ones in addition to those mentioned in footnotes are the following: Legislative Research Committee, Minnesota, *Motor Vehicle Taxation,* Publication No. 8, St. Paul, 1948; Bertram H. Lindman, *A Proposed System of Highway Finance for the State of California,* Sacramento, 1946; Richard M. Zettel, *An Analysis of Taxation for Highway Purposes in California, 1895–1946,* Sacramento, 1946; Herbert D. Simpson, *Highway Finance,* State of Ohio, Columbus, 1951; Wisconsin Legislative Council, *Interim Report on Highway Finance,* Madison, 1952; James C. Nelson, *Financing North Dakota's Roads,* Bismarck, 1952; Nebraska Legislative Council, Committee Report No. 37, Lincoln, 1952. See also O. H. Brownlee and Walter W. Heller, "Highway Development and Financing," *American Economic Review,* XLVI: 2 (May 1956), pp. 232–250; symposium of articles in *National Tax Journal,* X: 2 (June 1957); *Proceedings of the National Tax Association Conference,* 1961, pp. 675–691.

unneutrality problems, the most difficult of which is that of equal taxation among competing forms of transportation, particularly railroads and trucks.

PROBLEMS

1. Utilize the data given in the text that the average fuel tax paid by a passenger car under a 5-cent tax is 2.25 mills per ton-mile, while that for a 68,000 pound truck is .53 mills per ton-mile. Assuming 20,000 miles of travel in both cases and a $16 license fee for the automobile, calculate the license fee for the truck which will compensate for its advantage under the motor fuel tax.
2. By what analysis and procedure can a state or nation determine how much of its resources it can wisely devote to highways?
3. Appraise the application of the benefit principle in highway finance.
4. Why is it unfair to expect abutting property to pay for the cost of "through roads"?
5. What special circumstances are required to make a toll road feasible?
6. What is meant when it is said that trucks should pay the "incremental cost" of the highways they use? What additional problem is associated with so-called common costs?
7. It is said that automobiles are uneconomic users of urban space. How can such uneconomic use be curbed to solve a city's traffic problem?
8. On what ground do the railroads argue that the tax system favors their competitors? Can this argument be dismissed on the ground that the railroads constitute an antiquated mode of transportation?
9. What element of unfairness is eliminated and what created by the use of reciprocity in license fees among the states?
10. Consider the arguments for and against segregation of highway-user taxes for exclusive use on the highways.
11. Assuming that certain highways should be financed entirely by user-taxes and that taxes for these roads should be confined to their cost, how could one proceed to calculate the proportion of total highway costs that should be borne by users?
12. Motor fuel taxes take account of both weight and distance traveled by motor vehicles; as to weight, they differentiate inadequately, but this can be corrected by a graduated license tax. Comment.

13

THE POLL TAX

The poll tax is not an important source of revenue in the United States. The reason for presenting it as a separate chapter is mainly that the poll tax provides an introduction to the interesting subject of the relationship between taxes and ballots. Notwithstanding the statement that the tax is unimportant as a fiscal device, it is used in well over two thirds of the states as a source of either state or local revenue, or both. But in many instances today the political aspects have taken precedence over its financial significance. The rates in most cases are from $1 to $4. However, both historically and geographically there are many cases where the poll tax is much more important than in this country today.

The idea of collecting revenue on a per capita basis is a very old one. In the ancient civilizations of Greece and Rome, as well as in medieval England, the tax was used as a means of raising funds for the treasury. The term signified a tax on heads and had nothing to do with the right to vote. It was transplanted to America in the seventeenth century and constituted one of the major direct levies in some of the American colonies. Before the advent of the automobile and the central highway system, poll tax receipts were quite commonly used to pay for local roads; under this system the tax could ordinarily be rendered by direct service in improving the highways.

ARGUMENTS FOR THE POLL TAX

Universality. The principal argument for the poll tax is that it requires those who otherwise pay no direct taxes to contribute something to support the government. This argument rests upon the proposition that all *should* contribute something to the government. This is based on the theory that all receive benefits from government and that voters are less likely to be extravagant when aware that it is their money in part that governments are spending. The latter theory has never been supported with empirical evidence but it is plausible to assume at least that taxpayers in the higher brackets react less unkindly to tax burdens that are widely shared. The sales tax is similarly supported but, because of its indirect and hidden character, this tax is thought to be inferior to the poll tax in achieving these objectives. The argument would be more persuasive perhaps if poll taxes in practice were not featured by so many exemptions. Ordinarily they apply to adults only, and sometimes they are confined to able-bodied males between the ages of twenty-one and sixty. Of course, even this narrowed version of a per capita tax reaches most voting families.

Diversity. Poll taxes, along with others, might conceivably be supported also on the score that they add some diversity to the tax system. In taxation, it is said, one should not put all his eggs in one basket lest the basket break. Even the best tax becomes obnoxious if it is overworked. Moreover, the loopholes and irritations and administrative shortcomings of any one tax taken by itself lose significance as the particular tax is fitted into a mosaic of taxes, each with its own but different limitations. A skillful avoider might escape any one tax, but he could hardly escape a tax system with fifty or a hundred members. Only a moderate amount of ingenuity on the part of tax makers would be required to design a very diverse tax system. There are many aspects of life that might serve as the basis of a tax levy.

Other critics see little if any merit in this line of argument. They would concede, probably, that not all the legitimate objectives of taxation could be achieved with any one tax, however meritorious. But they would challenge the proposition that a tax system with fifteen taxes must be better than one with six. They ask for assurance that the errors in many bad taxes would be compensating rather than cumulative. They find only a few taxes that relate burdens to some legitimate measure or accomplish any other good purpose. To these critics the poll tax cannot be defended merely because it increases the size of the tax family.

RELATION OF THE POLL TAX TO VOTING

Until rather recently in terms of historical time, the voting franchise carried a property-ownership qualification. This rule survives to a considerable degree in most English-speaking countries (outside our own) for local elections and referenda. The rule also prevailed in this country during the early years of our national existence and was surrendered by conservative opinion with the greatest reluctance. Professor Edward Sait quotes the following from a speech concerning the proposed abolition of the property qualification for voting, delivered by Chancellor Kent at a New York State Constitutional Convention in 1821: [1]

> Such a proposition at the distance of ten years past, would have struck the public mind with astonishment and terror. The apprehended danger from the experiment of universal suffrage, applied to the whole legislative department, is no dream of the imagination. It is too mighty an excitement for the moral condition of men to endure. . . . There is a constant tendency in the poor to covet and to share the plunder of the rich; in the debtor to relax or to avoid the obligations of contract, in the indolent and profligate to cast the whole burthen of society upon the industrious and virtuous; and there is a tendency in ambitious and wicked men to inflame these combustible materials. . . . We stand therefore on the brink of fate, on the very edge of a precipice. If we let go of our hold on the Senate, we commit our proudest hopes and most precious interests to the waves.

Today this speech sounds like a voice from a bygone era. Little support, probably, could be mustered for the view that propertyless tenants and wage earners should have no voice in government. There might be more backing for the view that there should be some educational, intellectual, or informational qualification for voting, but even this would seem to most people highly undemocratic. In voting, each person represents his own interest and his own view of the general interest. We are skeptical of the disinterestedness of the so-called best people in serving as trustees for the folk "on the other side of the tracks."

Nevertheless, there may be some merit in the idea that there should be a close association between taxpaying and voting. Government necessarily involves a great deal of "spending other people's money." The process is likely to work better, and the morale of the taxpayer to be more readily retained, if the payment of direct taxes reaches a large part

---

[1] Edward M. Sait, *Political Institutions, A Preface* (New York: Appleton-Century-Croft, 1938), p. 427.

of the voting public. The feeling that most of those who direct the government should have a share in the consequences is not entirely unwarranted. As previously observed, this is one of the reasons for avoiding excessive personal income tax exemptions. But only with limitations and a graduated rate related to income would the poll tax become equivalent to a personal net income tax.

In several of our states, all in the south and decreasing in number, the poll tax payment is made a qualification for voting. This is criticized on the score that it unduly limits the franchise and discourages participation in government. This view is strengthened by the fact that in states that use the tax as a voting qualification little or no attempt is made directly to collect the poll tax. The situation may be contrasted with that in Australia where people are fined (or taxed) for not voting. The Australian measure is regarded in that country with some dissatisfaction because it is said that voting is a privilege as well as a duty. Paraphrasing an old proverb, one can say that "you can force a man to go to the polls but you cannot make him think." The situation in New Zealand is more ideal, perhaps; there a very large percentage of the eligible voters (sometimes as high as 95 percent) participate in national elections without compulsions.

The available information indicates that participation in elections in poll tax states is very limited.[2] In forty states where the poll tax was not a qualification for voting, 71 percent of the eligible voters participated in the election of 1940; the percentage in eight southern poll tax states was 22 percent. Rhode Island with a population of 687,000 cast more votes for two representatives in Congress than were cast for thirty-six representatives in southern states with nearly 11 million population. Representation in the south shows a much smaller degree of turnover than in the rest of the country. This frequently gives southern representatives a high seniority rating in Congress, which means that these representatives secure chairmanships of committees which, in turn, carry a great deal of power.

---

[2] It should be said that the poll tax is only one of several reasons for this fact; there are other legal restrictions, particularly for participation in primary elections; final elections may involve no closely contested issues. On the other hand, comparisons of primary election data in southern states with and without poll tax and of election data in some states before and after poll tax inauguration or repeal indicates that the poll tax is an important factor in voting—Donald S. Strong, "The Poll Tax: the Case of Texas." *American Political Science Review,* XXXVIII (1944), pp. 693–709. See also *Hearings before a Subcommittee of the Committee on the Judiciary,* 77th Cong., 2d Sess., 1942. Voting qualifications and practices were also extensively discussed in 1957 hearings on civil-rights legislation: *Hearings before Subcommittee N. 5 of the Committee on the Judiciary,* House of Representatives, 85th Cong., 1st Sess., 1957; *Hearings before Subcommittee on the Judiciary,* Senate, 85th Cong., 1st Sess., 1957.

Anti–Poll Tax Legislation in Congress. Much interest has attended
the attempts to pass federal legislation to outlaw the poll tax payment as
a condition of voting in federal elections. An important question here
concerns the constitutionality of this approach to the problem. The
federal Constitution states (Art. I, Sec. 2): "The House of Representatives shall be composed of Members chosen every second Year by the
People of the several States, and the Electors in each State shall have the
Qualifications requisite for Electors of the most numerous Branch of the
State Legislature." Moreover, it provides in Section 4 that "The Times,
Places and Manner of holding Elections for Senators and Representatives, shall be prescribed in each State by the Legislature thereof; but the
Congress may at any time by Law make or alter such Regulations. . . ."
The 14th Amendment adds that ". . . when the right to vote at any
election for the choice of . . . President . . . [and so forth] is denied
to any of the male inhabitants of such State, being twenty-one years of
age, and citizens of the United States . . . the basis of representation
therein shall be reduced in proportion. . . ." It can be seen that these
provisions leave some room for dispute concerning the power to determine qualifications for voting in national elections. It is argued, finally,
that the poll tax qualification for voting is a tax on a federal function
and thus, by long-standing judicial tradition, illegal. As for legal decisions, poll taxes as such (without act of Congress) have been sustained
but so also have federal corrupt practices acts.[3] There is evidence to support the contention that the poll tax fosters corruption in elections; it is
a constant invitation to buy votes.

The issue is complicated by the fact that many of the nonparticipants in southern elections are Negroes. As a tactical matter, the argument against federal legislation maintains that it is unwise and un-
feasible to force such legislation upon the poll tax states before public
opinion there is ready for the innovation. In support of this view it is
observed that several southern states have receded on their own from
the poll tax qualification. The issue has been before Congress at several
sessions, has passed the lower house with a substantial majority, but has
been defeated in the Senate sometimes by filibuster.[4] Currently an anti-
poll tax amendment giving Congress the clear power to bar the use of
the tax in restricting participation in federal elections has passed Congress and is in process of consideration by the state legislatures.

---

[3] See "Anti-Poll Tax Legislation—Constitutionality," *New York University
Law Quarterly Review,* 21 (1946), pp. 113–121; Ben F. Looney, "The Constitutionality of Anti-Poll Tax Measures," *Texas Bar Journal,* 7 (1944), pp. 70, 88–92.

[4] For a recent discussion of the subject see the debate in Congress (Senate)
on a proposed constitutional amendment to bar poll taxes as a condition for
voting: *Congressional Record,* Senate, March 16, 1962 and following.

DIFFICULTIES IN THE POLL TAX AS A FISCAL MEASURE

Administrative Difficulties. One of the main objections to the poll tax is its administrative difficulties. Administrative procedure that would ensure proper, prompt, and productive revenues from this tax has been almost impossible to design. Applied to persons with property or substantial incomes, the poll tax is reasonably easy to collect; levy on their property or attachment of part of their income is always possible. However, these people pay substantial taxes without the poll tax. Successful administration of the tax must be judged by the degree to which people with little or no property or income are reached. The grocer, the meat merchant, and the small-loan company have all learned how difficult and expensive it is to collect from these people. The government has generally been less skilled and less ruthless in collection than most of these private agencies. The small-loan companies are frequently authorized by law to collect up to 42 percent interest from small borrowers, most of which must go for collection costs. The government can hardly hope to do better.

Some poll taxes have been collected at the source from employers. In other cases, provisions have been made for imprisonment as a penalty for nonpayment. In some states the poll tax is collected by a house-to-house canvass. A commission for collection has been tried. Occasionally payment is made a voting prerequisite. In some states the poll tax must be paid before an automobile license can be obtained.

All of these methods have their difficulties or limitations. Collection at the source, of course, cannot be made universal. Imprisonment is sure to be expensive and smacks of imprisonment for debt. The house-to-house canvass finds many people not at home or without ready cash. Those with little property or income are in an advantageous position in dealing with collectors. Payment as a voting prerequisite does ensure that those who do not pay have no voice in spending "other people's money." But this is criticized as undemocratic and as likely to lead to political corruption and petty bribery. Making the poll tax a condition for granting an automobile license can be effective in reaching only those owning or operating automobiles.

Equity Shortcomings. The poll tax is also opposed because it is regressive, defining that term as a characteristic of a tax that increases inequalities. The flat-rate payment is obviously a larger percentage of the income of poor than of wealthy people. It is levied on individuals without regard to their ability to pay and thus violates the major aspects of the theory of equity in taxation discussed in Chapter 2. The poll tax is an example of pure mathematical equality in taxation, but legislators hesitate to carry this principle to its logical end. All poll tax laws in the United States fall short of universal application; instead they profess to apply the principle of reasonable classification, make exceptions, and yield only a very small amount of revenue.

Since classification and differentiation are thus recognized and sanctioned, the question may reasonably be asked: Why not go a step farther and inaugurate or broaden the personal income tax?

PROBLEMS

1. What would you suggest as reasonable and adequate qualifications for voting? Should poor people be encouraged to vote or be discouraged? Is the Australian policy of fining nonvoters a wise one?
2. Criticize the proposition that the poll tax is justified because everyone should contribute something to the cost of government.
3. Does your state levy or authorize municipalities to levy a poll tax? If so, with what success?
4. Comment on the following: There is too much discrimination in taxation; what we need is a tax system that will treat all people alike, that is, a system that will collect the same amount from every person.
5. Consider the proposition: A tax system with fifteen kinds of taxes is likely to be better than one with five.

14

SOCIAL SECURITY TAXES

INTRODUCTION

Largely during the past thirty years there has evolved in the United States (and to an even greater extent in other countries) a social security system embracing a vast new field of legislative detail, very large numbers of people, and impressive transfers of money. Much of this field for study cannot be covered here; as in the case of the tariff, its intensive study belongs to another discipline. But it cannot be ignored either, for its intake passes under the name of "taxes" and its financial aspects are important and of wide influence. Unfortunately, there is no clear line between the financial and other aspects of the field.

Our federal old-age and survivors' insurance system is said to be the world's largest insurance institution with over 80 million clients. Estimates have been made that place the total of "government insurance" at a larger volume than all private insurance combined. Fortunately, this is one sector of government that is very efficiently and economically administered; no taint of scandal has ever been associated with it.

Reasons for Development. Some of the reasons for embarking upon so extensive an undertaking may be briefly sketched. It is recognized that while a dynamic economy is very productive, it creates many individual casualties. Private insurance can mitigate the problem for the individual but only when there is the requisite purchasing power. Social security borrows from private insurance the idea that those who are lucky enough to escape certain hazards should contribute to ease the lot of the less fortunate.

The trend, particularly for older members of society, has been toward greater insecurity. Medical science has increased longevity; at age 65 the average person can look forward to more than 13 years before death. The gap between life expectancy and work-life expectancy is considerable and still widening, despite a reaction to the view that older people should make way for youth by retirement in the middle sixties. Private support for the retired usually takes the form of savings (including private insurance) or assistance by younger relatives. More than one half of American families have negligible savings. It takes a very substantial accumulation to provide a retirement income of $100 per month, and the inflationary tendencies of recent years have magnified the undertaking. Assistance from relatives is neither so popular nor so dependable as was once the case; geographic separation of relatives is now more common, and the maintenance of mutual living quarters less frequent. About 70 percent of aged couples own homes, 86 percent of these without mortgage; but general income outside of social security is very low and even including social security, two thirds receive less than $1500 per capita.

Hazards Involved. Concern for insecurity is not of course confined to old age. Other hazards include unemployment, dependency of children, industrial accident, illness (involving both unemployment and cost of medical care), and permanent disability. The term "social security" is extended to cover aid to the handicapped (such as the blind) and also family allowances (where the state shares the cost of maintaining and rearing children). The latter institution exists in many countries but not in the United States. Some social security systems attempt to cover all of these hazards in a universal and integrated system. Our own program is more diverse. It began with compensation for industrial accidents, initiated by the states and still under their auspices. The Great Depression brought great interest in unemployment; a system of compensation for it was inaugurated by Wisconsin in 1932, but it spread to the entire country only after the national government took account of this hazard in the Social Security Act of 1935. The act left the direct responsibility with the states, encouraging them to inaugurate and maintain unemployment compensation by means of a payroll tax and a credit (explained presently). The hazard of old age is treated under two programs: an all-federal contributory program, financed by a dual payroll tax (employer and employee) plus a net income tax on the self-employed; and state programs for old-age assistance financed by the states with federal aid. The former is an insurance program and carries no means test; the latter is available only for the needy (though with varying degrees of strictness in the interpretation of that term). The two programs are continued in operation largely because they cover different segments of the population. Other programs for federal grants-in-aid to the states include aid to the blind, aid to dependent children, child welfare and health service, rehabilitation, and, since 1950, permanent disability.

Governments have been drawn increasingly into the field of health services and currently provide between a fifth and a fourth of what is spent for medical care. Strong support has appeared for the extension of the social security system into this area. Failure of health may be related to occupation (occupational disease) in which capacity it is frequently covered in state workmen's compensation laws. Dissociated from industry, it may still cause unemployment and loss of wages. Several states have extended their unemployment compensation or workmen's compensation laws to include compensation for this loss of pay. Medical expenses are included in the allowance to relief- and old-age-assistance clients. The proposal to provide prepaid health insurance to cover cost of medical care financed by additional payroll taxes has been the center of recent controversy over health insurance—referred to by its enemies as "socialized medicine."

Private Developments. The social security program of the government has been accompanied by private developments that have influenced and in some cases stimulated public action. Welfare in general (and particularly retirement benefits) has become a widespread issue of collective bargaining in private industry. The remarkable growth of the pension movement has been to some extent a tax phenomenon, encouraged by the fact that contributions into pension funds are a deductible expense and in times of high taxes are largely "at the expense of the government." Pension systems are thus within the large area of quasi-public activities paid for in part indirectly by the general taxpayer (and perhaps to some extent by the consumer). Moreover, rivalry among unions has in some cases assumed the form of bidding and out-bidding for "fringe benefits." The result is a network of pension schemes that run to many thousands of funds and capital counted in billions.[1] This movement has influenced social security legislation in many ways. Many

---

[1] *Federal Tax Policy for Economic Growth and Stability,* Joint Committee on the Economic Report, 84th Cong., 1st Sess., 1955, pp. 763–797; Committee on Ways and Means, *Tax Revision Compendium,* 1959, vol. 1, pp. 539–578; vol. 2, pp. 1301–1536.

pension agreements provide for benefits to amount to a certain figure when added to social security allowances. This tends to enlist employers behind a more generous program of public benefits. The private programs have been criticized on various grounds, and an alternative public program has been advocated as a sounder development. Most private pension funds check the mobility of labor since employees have no vested rights that hold against a change of employment; all of them make it more difficult for older people to obtain employment (younger employees strain the fund less since most of them will not continue with the company until they reach retirement age). Most recent private addition to security institutions is the guaranteed annual wage (supplementary unemployment compensation) now being promoted with some success by American labor unions.

Tax Treatment of Retirement Income.   This may be the appropriate place to review the tax treatment of the many models of retirement plans and deferred compensation. Payments by the employer in ordinary life insurance or an annuity are income in kind and among the "fringe benefits" that are taxable. However deferred compensation, as where a firm agrees to pay an executive over 20 years for 10 years of work, is income to the recipient when received rather than when earned. Qualified pension plans permit current deductibility of the employer's contribution and taxability of the pension to the employee when the latter receives it. Old-age and survivors' insurance contributions made by the employer are deductible as made; employee's contributions are not deductible and the social security benefits paid during retirement are not taxable.

A considerable number of critics argue that the exclusion of social security benefits from income taxation was a mistake that should be corrected. They argue that it is unwise to exclude from the tax base such a large flow of personal income, a considerable part of which goes to well-to-do persons and the remainder of which would be protected by exemptions and graduated rates. Perhaps recognition must be given to the fact that current payments by employees are nondeductible and that thus to tax social security benefits in full without changing this feature would involve an element of double taxation. The simple way to avoid this is to make such contributions deductible. This would also give due consideration to those who contribute to the system but never become eligible for benefits. The alternative and much more complicated procedure would be to tax social security benefits like a private annuity and exclude an estimated proportion that was contributed by the beneficiary himself. In view of the fact that current recipients have contributed only a very small portion of what they are receiving, this latter plan would be most propitious for the revenue.

FINANCIAL STRUCTURE OF SOCIAL SECURITY PROGRAMS

Taxes. Briefly, the federal old-age and survivors' insurance system is financed by three specific taxes. One is called an income tax on wage earners, proportional to their wages. Beginning in 1937 with a rate of 1 percent, it now is levied at a rate of $3\frac{5}{8}$ percent and is scheduled to increase at specified intervals until it reaches $4\frac{5}{8}$ percent in 1968 and thereafter. It is collected by the employer who deducts it from wages. The second is a parallel levy, but it is called an excise tax and is applied to the employer and cannot be deducted from wages. The incidence of the tax is another matter and is generally thought to be borne in large part by the employee.[2] To these are now added a third levy to bring the self-employed into the system. Since in this case the employer and employee are combined so to speak and no equivalent of wages exists, deriving an appropriate levy for this group proved a considerable problem. The solution was a net income tax (with some qualifications and without credits) on employment income above $400 and at rates midway between that of each payroll tax and the two payroll taxes combined. The taxes are confined to a maximum of $4800 of wages paid to an employee during a year or equivalent earnings of the self-employed.

The fourth tax in the system is designed not to finance any program directly but to encourage the states to establish and finance unemployment compensation plans. This is an excise tax levied upon employers of four or more persons, at a nominal rate of 3 percent based on employees' wages. The federal government levies this tax but allows a 90-percent credit on contributions paid by employers under approved unemployment compensation plans. The federal tax is reduced to take account of experience rating in the states under which the latter's rates are adjusted to the varying incidence of unemployment among firms; in effect, the federal tax is .3 percent above the contributions paid to the states.[3] The funds collected by the states under their unemployment compensation laws are turned over to the federal government to be invested and held in trust for the several states (to which they belong) until they are requisitioned to be used for the payment of unemployment compensation.

---

[2] Shifting and incidence of social security taxes has been discussed in Chapter 6.

[3] During recent years federal legislation has augmented the total tax and the federal share by small percentages to aid the states in providing extended benefits during periods of high unemployment.

The employment tax which the federal government collects directly is paid into the general fund. However, the federal government grants aids to the states from the general fund to defray proper administrative costs of their unemployment compensation systems.

In addition to these four taxes and two systems of insurance, the social security act provides for extensive federal aids to the states for social assistance (old-age assistance, aid for dependent children, etc.). These funds come from the general treasury; the state and local funds with which they are mixed usually come from general taxes though there are a considerable number of cases where particular taxes (such as the sales tax in Colorado) are earmarked for welfare purposes.

Coverage. The old-age and survivors' insurance system instituted by the Social Security Act does not include all gainfully employed people either as to taxes or benefits. Originally, farmers, agricultural labor, domestics, operators of unincorporated business, professional persons, public employees, railway employees, and a few other classes were excluded. The exclusions added up to about 40 percent of the gainfully employed. Coverage has now been extended to include most of those originally omitted; among those added were regular farm help and many domestics, some state and local government employees, and most of the self-employed including farmers. This leaves some professional persons (notably doctors), as well as many public employees and seasonal agricultural workers, outside the system. As previously noted, doctors would prefer and hope to achieve special legislation that would allow for the self-employed an income tax deduction for a certain amount of saving to be taxed later during retirement. Railroad employees have an independent retirement system by federal legislation, and there are a great many independent retirement systems for different groups of public employees. Employees of nonprofit organizations and of state and local governments (except in some cases where the latter are under existing retirement systems) may at their and their employer's option participate in the social insurance system.

Benefits. The social security taxes are often described as special-benefit levies, the system is called contributory, and the program is defended on the score that it applies the insurance principle to the retirement hazard. But it is also said that *social* insurance departs more or less freely from the cost-benefit contracts that characterize contractual private insurance. Only the insured workers and their dependents who pay taxes are entitled to benefits (though even this statement needs qualification if one considers incidence as distinguished from the impact of these taxes). In our old-age and survivors' insurance system an account is kept for each individual participant. But there are also radical departures from the cost-service principle. There are those who pay and get no benefits and many who pay little and get much. In all retirement systems some favor is given to those who are near retirement when the program starts. Unless this is done much of the benefit of the program is long postponed. The contrast between social insurance and private annuity contracts in these respects is conspicuous, but that with private pension plans is not sharp.

Eligibility for retirement benefits is in terms of quarters worked in covered employment; the standard requirement is 40 quarters but older persons may become eligible with as little as 6 quarters covered. The amount of benefits is based on the wages on which taxes were paid by the taxpayer during a (varying) number of his later years. Benefits are to some degree weighted inversely according to wages; thus the maximum at $4800 of pay per year is slightly less than half the preretirement pay; this includes secondary benefits for the spouse at half those for the earner. Surviving spouses can claim benefits at three quarters of the primary allowances. Earnings after retirement up to $1200 per year are permitted without prejudice to benefits; beyond the age of 72 no limit is prescribed.

Whatever may be the application of the benefit principle in the American system, it is apparent that the ability principle has no wide or consistent application. To give it such application, the program would require financing under the progressive income tax. The issue is rendered somewhat academic perhaps by the high first mortgage on this latter tax pledged to military preparedness. However, more concession to ability to pay could be provided by raising or eliminating the $4800-limit on payroll tax contributions.

PROBLEMS OF OLD-AGE INSURANCE

THE FINANCIAL RESERVE

There are two versions of what constitutes paying-as-one-goes for old-age insurance. One is that we pay-as-we-go if current cash outlay is balanced by current receipts. The other observes that our system involves commitments for the future and claims that we are not paying-as-we-go unless we provide an "actuarial reserve" to meet costs as they accrue. Any retirement system is likely to find the going easy in the early years if only current outlays are met. Its obligations mushroom with time, because more and more of its clientele become beneficiaries and remain on the benefit rolls for a long time.

The subtleties of the social security reserve question can be better understood if we examine the difference between accrual and cash accounting in governmental budgets. Accrual accounting records as an expense items that require no cash outlay but which represent a future liability currently incurred (or at any rate foreseen). These items are cared for by setting up a reserve account. Reckoning actuarial costs of old-age insurance as an expense (accrual accounting) means that a budget cannot be balanced on an accrual basis unless it shows a surplus on a cash basis. Conversely, a budget balanced on a cash basis will show a deficit on an accrual basis.

The situation is complicated by the fact that when our government builds a social security reserve, it invests the money in its own securities (usually by giving its insurance trust fund a bond). Were the policy of investing in private obligations followed, the government might find itself with substantial interest in a large block of American industry. The present policy means that the addition to reserve is available for current spending. No end of conflict and confusion has developed around this fact. Critics have argued that the reserve involves double taxation: once to build the reserve and once to liquidate it for later social security requirements. The argument is neither true nor false; the answer is "it all depends." Whether the taxpayer will benefit from the reserve depends upon whether the government enlarges its expenditure over what it would have spent had there been no social security revenue it could borrow. If it does, then the program makes possible additional present services, but it can be of no help to the taxpayer later on. If it does not, then the interest earnings on the securities held by the fund reduces the total obligations that will have to be met in the future. Had there been no internal source of funds, external debt would have been augmented, and this debt would now have to be serviced in addition to taxes required to meet social security outlay.

As to the historical development of the reserve, the original plan contemplated a sizable fund to be built up in the first decades of the program. However, during the late years of the 1930s the objection was raised that the program was deflationary. Beginning in 1939 the plan was revised to confine the reserve to "contingency" proportions and to freeze tax rates with this end in view. The reserve now amounts to about $23 billions and is not growing.

Much argument, especially in the 1930s, centered on the allegation that the reserve is deflationary. Again the answer is, "it all depends." If the federal government were to take money from the taxpayer and set it aside in a corner, this would indeed be deflationary. On the other hand, if the government were to use the money paying for additional expenditures not otherwise contemplated, the result would certainly not be deflationary and would in fact be mildly inflationary. Were it to use the reserve fund to buy up (retire) debt held by nonbank owners, the result would probably be somewhat deflationary since bondholders are more likely to hold money (not spend it on consumption or investment) than taxpayers. Retirement of debt held by banks would probably be more deflationary. This reverses the process by which much inflation starts. On the other hand, the banks obtain a replenishment of reserves in the process (potential reserves are converted into actual reserves), and if they expand loans as a result of the payment, the deflationary effect will be counteracted. A fifth possibility is to purchase debt held by the federal reserve banks; this again would be clearly deflationary and much like the setting aside of cash.[4]

RELATION OF OLD-AGE INSURANCE TO OLD-AGE ASSISTANCE

The old-age assistance program carried on by the states with federal aid has continued to supplement the insurance program and until 1950 involved the larger expenditure of the two. It is financed to more than one half its cost by federal grants-in-aid. States differ widely both in the level of payments and in the percentage of population over 65 years that is receiving assistance. The latter is partially explained by the fact that some states, particularly the agricultural ones, have a much larger percentage of persons not covered by old-age insurance. State old-age assistance programs have been influenced in many cases by pressure politics. Because of organized pressure, expenditure for the aged has tended to be more generous than that for dependent children. In Colorado a liberal pension program for all qualified persons was incorporated by referendum vote into the state constitution in 1936. Other state services have been extremely cramped by this program. Moreover, in this state, the combination of an earmarked tax and the requirement that its receipts be devoted exclusively and annually to old-age assistance has deprived the legislature of adequate control and made beneficiaries the object of fortuitous bounties. In California a constitutional amendment passed by referendum (though later repealed) lowered the age requirement from 65 to 63, increased the minimum provision from $60 to $75 per month, made old-age expenditure a prime claim on state revenue, and made the administrator of the system an elective officer. The name of the first administrator was actually included in the constitution.[5] In

---

[4] Retirement of debt held by the public is of and by itself inflationary; it is the combination of tax imposition and debt retirement that is here considered.

[5] *Newsweek*, August 8, 1949, p. 72.

eleven parishes in Louisiana recipients of old-age assistance were found receiving average grants higher than the average per capita cash income in the parish.[6]

ECONOMIC EFFECTS OF OLD-AGE SECURITY

The old-age security program could hardly fail to have important economic effects. Arguments concerning some of these effects closely parallel those for and against the so-called welfare state. It is argued, for instance, that the program adversely affects incentives. The argument is countered with the proposition that free enterprise, sometimes on its own initiative, was first in the field (and for executives at that). Private savings could be discouraged by the system but such evidence as we have indicates that this criticism is ill founded. People visualizing the possibility of independence during retirement are likely to save more rather than less, and of course private savings are supplemented by public or institutional saving when programs are adding to reserves. The program is usually thought to afford some protection against economic instability; come hard times consumption will be maintained by dependable social security incomes. Sale of securities to liquidate reserve funds might however reduce the money supply. Social security and other pensions involve large transfers of income a considerable part of which is probably redistribution in favor of the poor. The program may be viewed as a means by which a youth saves for his old age, and it can also be viewed as a means by which the current generation of youth supports the current generation of old people. In either case, it indicates that more would be available to the active population if less were dedicated to the retired. And for the present at least most social security benefits go far beyond the past contributions of their recipients. In terms of the capital market, saving for social security involves no new source for risk capital, but private pension funds are utilized considerably though conservatively for this purpose.

Social security outlays in public budgets are usually described in national-income analysis as transfer payments. They involve a transfer of funds from one group of private citizens to another or from one group to the government with a return to the same group later. In a sense all taxes involve such a transfer, but in the usual case they are returned to the economy in exchange for commodities or services in the course of productive activity undertaken by the government. The economic effects of transfer payments differ from those of other outlays in that these payments do not create an inflationary demand for goods and services.

---

[6] Edward W. Stagg, "Louisiana Story," *Tax Outlook*, 9: 6 (June 1954), pp. 6–9.

FOREIGN SYSTEMS AND ALTERNATIVE PROPOSALS

To finance an elaborate scheme of social security benefits, New Zealand uses a 7.5 percent net income tax applicable to both business concerns and natural persons and without benefit of personal credits. Thus, the financial support is closely integrated with the net income tax. On the benefit side, their program contemplates a system in which allowances will be independent both of need and of contributions. The British system involves flat-sum taxes on wages though these direct payments are heavily supplemented from the national treasury. The Canadian system is financed by a tax of 3 percent on manufacturers' sales, a personal income tax of 3 percent (not to exceed $90), and a corporate income tax, which is also 3 percent. Neither the British system nor the Canadian system differentiate benefits on the basis of taxable earnings.

Critics of the American system point to its future commitments as irresponsible; however, they also dislike the reserve and say it is an invitation to abuse. Their preference apparently is for a system like that of old-age assistance plus a modest allowance free of a means test. Some would substitute a universal net income tax for the payroll taxes now in use. Other critics (on the left) argue that the system is alright except that its coverage is too narrow; they would prefer to see the scope of the system broadened to include all of the population and all of the major hazards. Although the contributory principle has been severely compromised, it still finds staunch support on the ground that it is a defense against inflationary excesses and much more than a gesture to the idea of individual responsibility. Some opinion supports the view that the application of the contributory principle should be strengthened.

UNEMPLOYMENT COMPENSATION

Space permits no elaborate account of the American system of unemployment compensation. One of the most controversial features is experience rating under which rates of tax are adjusted according to the incidence of unemployment in particular firms or industries. The system is defended on the score that it creates an incentive to stabilize the labor force and distributes the necessary overhead cost of unemployment to the firms, industries, and products with which it is associated. Critics argue that the feature makes employers unduly solicitous about eligibility in particular cases; that it unduly penalizes inherently unstable industries (such as the construction industry); and that it tends to aggravate the business cycle. The latter contention is based on the possibility that high unemployment will mean low reserves and initiate higher tax rates when times are bad; this point in the business cycle, according to the dispensation of compensatory economics, is when rates should be reduced. The issue is related to adequacy of reserves which in turn is related to the proposal to nationalize the entire program. Adequacy of state funds has been fortified to some extent by legislation that permits the states to borrow (in effect) from the federal pool. It is also contended that experience-rating formulas (which differ considerably from state to state) can be adjusted to avoid increases in taxes when a wave of unemployment strikes. Unemployment compensation under our system is a form of separation pay and is not calculated in any event to care for the unemployed during prolonged periods without work. There is much to be said for a dual system with the states compensating for some forms of unemployment and the federal government for others. But some critics argue that we should seek more positive remedies for chronic and cyclical unemployment.

Typically, our system provides compensation to wage earners while involuntarily unemployed (after a waiting period) of one-half working pay up to $30 or $35 per week for a maximum period of 26 weeks. Compensation is related not only to rates of pay but also to weeks of employment during the previous year. Eligibility is not extended to workers on strike or out of a job because of misconduct or unavailability for work (due for instance to illness).

HEALTH INSURANCE

The fields of medical care and preventive medicine are ones in which governments are quite deeply involved. Government participation is particularly important in public health, hospital construction, care for the indigent, and services for the military forces and veterans. There are several reasons why this participation is likely to be extended. One is that health care like education is to some degree an "unwanted necessity." This is another way of saying that the social judgment concerning the adequacy of medical care is likely to be considerably more generous than the private individual judgment. As in the case of education, there is a feeling that the social interest requires more outlay than private individuals can or will provide from their own funds. The same is less true of housing and food where the welfare interest is equally important. Medical care encounters not only limitations of purchasing power but also inhibitions associated with the futurity, irregular budgeting, and unpleasantness involved. However, the development of private insurance on a large and growing scale has somewhat diminished the difficulty of budgeting medical expenses. But there are inherent obstacles to the achievement of anything like universal coverage in such private institutions. While private insurance does to some extent require the well to pay for the ill, it cannot make use of the ability-to-pay principle in its financing.

Social security has entered this picture with proposals in Congress for the extension of payroll taxes and a benefit plan to cover the cost of most medical bills with a compulsory public universal insurance system. Precedent for such action can be found in many foreign countries. The proposal contemplates payment of doctors and dentists out of social security funds according to any one of three patterns decided by local option: (1) a fee schedule; (2) a salary; and (3) a per capita allowance (so much per patient.)

It is argued against the proposal that it would (1) so increase demand as to swamp our existing medical and dental facilities; (2) invite malingering (fancied ailments); (3) revolutionize the medical profession (which in the main has been very hostile to the idea); (4) encounter formidable administrative difficulties particularly in the allocation of funds. Moreover, it is contended that most people encounter no great problem in meeting ordinary medical bills; it is catastrophic illness and extraordinary outlay that is the core of the problem. Most recent controversy concerns the proposal to extend the social security system to cover medical expenses (mostly hospital expenses) to the aged only.

These objections are impressive and have encouraged proposals for some more modest piecemeal attack on the problem. One approach is to decentralize the administrative aspect of the problem by offering federal aid to the states for a considerable range of programs including prepaid medical care for those who are unable to purchase it from private sources.[7] Another approach starts with the observation that medical expenses within severely circumscribed limits are currently deductible on personal income tax returns. This means that the government in effect pays at least 20 percent of medical expenses that qualify for deduction. Working from this beginning, it might be possible to devise a more generous and universal credit for the expense of catastrophic illness—defined perhaps in terms of the size of family outlay for medical care and the ratio of such outlay to total family income. However, the income tax is a poorly designed instrument for the relief of the lowest stratum of taxpayers—already excluded by exemptions; it would strain the concept of the tax to graft an effective health insurance program onto it.

---

[7] *Building America's Health,* A Report to the President by The President's Commission on the Health Needs of the Nation, vol. 1 (Washington, D.C., 1953).

CONCLUSION

Recent years have witnessed widespread acceptance of the view that the business of government includes the protection of people against the hazards of an industrial society. There are many who regard this trend as undermining the economic virtues upon which a free and prosperous economy must rest. Others regard the trend as a wholesome economic development and a realization at long last that collectively "we must be our brothers' keeper." They also point to the fact that from the very beginning of English-speaking settlement in this country, it has been the responsibility of government to provide for the support of all people in need and without other means of support. From this point of view, the present social security programs are merely improved methods of meeting governmental obligations which have long been recognized.

SUMMARY

Social insurance in this country has developed rapidly since 1935, and in recent years it has been prodded forward by the common and tax-abetted practice of including private welfare programs in labor agreements. Benefits of private pension funds are with qualifications included in the income tax base, but this is not true of social security benefits, a feature of the income tax that is subject to much valid criticism. But if social security receipts were taxed, some antidote for double taxation of employees' contributions might be thought necessary. The federal government provides three specific taxes to support its old-age insurance program; an additional tax along with a credit is added to encourage the states to maintain unemployment compensation; and a program of old-age and other assistance is financed out of aids and general taxes (mainly). The special taxes are presumably special benefit levies on payroll and employment earnings, but the departures from the cost-service principle in the eligibility and benefit features of the old-age insurance system are pronounced.

Among the problems of old-age insurance, the accumulation of a financial reserve has proved most controversial. The reserve is alleged to involve double taxation, but this is valid only if the existence of the fund induces greater current expenditure than would otherwise occur. The reserve is also said to be deflationary, a point that turns on the disposition of the fund. The economic effects of the social security program are important; one of the most pronounced is the heavy burden that it casts on productive workers; but the burden can be minimized by lengthening the average age of retirement. Our system is under considerable criticism and contrasts at several points with a program recently enacted in Canada.

Unemployment compensation is criticized for its experience-rating feature and its mainly decentralized state control. The former feature is alleged to involve tax timing that will aggravate the business cycle. Public health insurance is an accepted feature of many social security systems abroad, but here its proposal has been the occasion of much controversy. It is criticized among other grounds on the score that its administration on a national scale would prove difficult and that it would demoralize the medical profession. Some would confine its application to catastrophic illness, cost of which the underprivileged citizen finds most difficult to budget and pay.

PROBLEMS

1. Assume that in 1957 the budgetary situation of the federal government was as follows:

Cash receipts (other than social security taxes)	$5,000,000,000
Social security tax receipts	1,000,000,000
Cash outlays (other than social security payments)	5,400,000,000
Cash outlays for social security payments	400,000,000
Required for actuarial social security reserve	400,000,000

Is the budget in balance, overbalanced, or short of balance? Why?

2. Making a speech in Congress on May 12, 1949, Senator McClellan of Arkansas cited figures to show that during the operation of the social security law the federal government had collected in social security taxes a total of $52 billion and had expended for benefits $12 billion. Said the Senator: "It is true that the Government has deposited, in trust, its bonds and certificates of indebtedness for the respective amounts of these special funds, which it has expended for other purposes. Such bonds and certificates of indebtedness, however, Mr. President, will have to be redeemed by the Federal Government from general taxes collected from the American people." Would you characterize the development of which the Senator speaks as proper, corrupt, extravagant, or inept? How should the program have been managed?

3. Mr. Stone, a business executive, is employed and nearing retirement. He has qualified for social security benefits. He now has

three offers from important firms. The first would pay him a salary
of $20,000 annually and ten years thereafter. The second would
pay him $20,000 annually plus a retirement annuity. The third
would make payments for him into a retirement fund enjoyed by
all employees of the firm.

Indicate how the social security payments and the various private
pension arrangements would be treated by the tax system.

4. Outline the argument for and against taxing social security income
   when it is realized.
5. Friends of old-age security legislation claim that it offers bargain
   insurance for all eligible persons. Why is the bargain much better
   in some cases than in others?
6. Is the payment of retirement allowances a burden? Upon whom?
   How can the load be reduced?
7. Consider the relation of the private-pension movement to the general tax system; to social security.
8. Compare the recent Canadian old-age insurance program with that
   of the United States, indicating advantages and disadvantages of
   each.
9. To what degree are social security taxes special-benefit taxes?
   Wherein lies the departures from the special-benefit principle? To
   what degree do they apply the ability principle? How might it be
   given greater weight?
10. What are the major criticisms of our present system of unemploy-
    ment compensation? What is the justification, if any, for unemploy-
    ment compensation financed without a contribution from employees?
11. Why do some states provide more old-age assistance than others?
    How is the pattern of state and local expenditures distorted by pres-
    sure politics in the social security field?
12. What in general is the proposal that has engendered the controversy
    over what its opponents call "socialized medicine"? What are some
    of the objections to this proposal? What more conservative alterna-
    tives are available?
13. On what grounds is it asserted that the social security system tends
    to reduce instability in the economic system?
14. The "health insurance" provided by the income tax deduction for
    medical expenses is one that gives special advantages to low-income
    families. Comment.

15

THE TAXATION OF NATURAL RESOURCES

Natural resources are the economically useful products of nature, the presence of which is not due to the expenditure of either labor or capital by man. They are usually of ancient origin and are frequently conceived as "the common heritage" of all. The term *natural resources* includes a wide field not easily classified. Some resources are both destructible and reproducible, as forests and soil fertility; others are destructible but not reproducible, as minerals and petroleum; still others are neither destructible nor reproducible, such as urban land sites. These peculiarities complicate the tax problem and warrant some special consideration for the taxation of natural resources.

In dealing with natural resources that are destructible and not reproducible, such as minerals, and to a lesser extent with resources that are destructible but also reproducible, such as forests, conservation is a major interest. The depletion of forests cannot soon be replaced, while the depletion of minerals means an irreparable loss. It is sometimes thought that certain taxes (particularly severance or yield taxes) imposed upon such resources tend to conserve them by decreasing their rate of exploitation. On the other hand certain other taxes (such as ad valorem taxes) are thought to have the opposite influence; the rate of exploitation is increased in order to sell out from under the tax.

Of course, the taxation of natural resources has as much to do with obtaining revenue as with preserving the resources. The state of Texas collects a major fraction of its state revenue from "severance" taxes. The revenue consideration is uppermost in the application of taxes to indestructible resources, such as urban land. High taxes on destructible resources are advocated on the ground that they are a common heritage and can be taxed but once. Where a single district or a few districts have a monopoly upon an important resource, large sums may be collected from outsiders by the imposition of taxes before materials are exported. From the administrative point of view, many natural resources have a further fiscal characteristic; they are uniquely difficult to appraise.

There are many kinds of so-called windfalls in economics, some of which are associated with nonreproducible goods. The economists have singled out the special term "rent" to distinguish the income from such goods. According to widely accepted theory, rent represents a surplus that can be taxed away without any repercussions on the supply. However, what is commonly called rent is by no means the only species of economic surplus. Some authors have argued for a tax system functionally designed: so-called earned income would be treated favorably to preserve incentives; windfalls would take the brunt of the tax system; and perhaps the income from transgression would be given roughest treatment of all. This approach to taxation may be contrasted with a quantitative approach that seeks to differentiate mainly on the basis of size of income or wealth.

TAXATION OF FORESTS

NATURE AND IMPORTANCE OF FOREST RESOURCES

Forests are a resource that is continually being built up by nature, a process that is both helped and hindered by human beings—helped through conservation work of various sorts and hindered by man-made fire and premature cutting. Because the development of forest resources in the United States is substantially less rapid than their depletion, an interest has been created in conserving and developing forests. Forest products have many important uses for consumers. In addition, forests reduce soil erosion, which does great damage to agriculture, and prevent floods, which destroy large amounts of property. There is both a social and an economic interest in the attractive scenery and recreational facilities that forests afford. Finally, and perhaps most important, forests constitute the best use of large quantities of land and offer hope of renewed economic independence to large sections of many states.

PROBLEMS CREATED BY DEFORESTATION

Decadent Communities. The rapid deforestation of the United States creates not only a problem of conservation but also a problem of territorial maladjustment. The industries and cities which were built because of the accessibility of forest raw materials become decadent when the supply of the latter is exhausted. In order to maintain an adequate standard of public services in these denuded areas, local taxes are often supplemented with state aids, which, if long continued, become a serious financial problem for the rest of the state.

Unproductive Land. A large part of the problem of these cutover regions is the uncertainty of their adaptability to other productive purposes. Until the early 1920s these regions faced the future with confidence in the tradition that "the plow follows the ax." It was supposed that agriculture would supersede lumbering as the major industry in most of the wooded areas. However, the market for farm products ceased to expand at the end of World War I. A general belief arose that too much land was being cultivated. Moreover, much first-rate forest land will never be good for agricultural purposes.

Tax Delinquency. The condition of the denuded areas has been reflected in huge amounts of tax delinquency, ending in the public acquisition of large tracts of land. This process has been described as the development of a new public domain.

Tax delinquency is both a cause and a result of the financial difficulties of these problem areas. As a cause, it reduces the tax base and thus makes the taxes higher on the property remaining in private hands. High taxes produce tax delinquency; and so it goes, in a vicious circle. The tax base is substantially reduced also, in many places, by the development of state and federal forests and the reservation of land for Indians. As a result of all these factors, in some counties less than 45 percent of the land is taxable.

Bad Assessment of Property. The financial problem of these communities is augmented by other causes as well. Usually they have the poorest property assessments to be found in the states. Property is often assessed according to what the traffic will bear. Cutover land is generally overassessed. This may be due to the fact that a certain value of land on the basis of its agricultural prospects still lingers. Much cutover land is owned by absentees who, lacking voting rights in the election of assessors, are often discriminated against by the latter. In Wisconsin, where the county credits the town with unpaid taxes, excessive assessments are occasionally deliberate—that is, they are imposed in order to reduce the town's share of cash payments to the county.

These developments and difficulties added impetus to the demand for reforestation programs. These programs, however, were confronted with, among other things, a system of taxation which was alleged to discourage conservation and forest development.

CRITICISM OF PROPERTY TAX AS APPLIED TO GROWING FORESTS

The tax receiving most criticism was the general property tax. As applied to forests and prospective forests, it was contended, first, that the tax was inconvenient for the forest owner as to time. The forest owner is expected to pay taxes for many years [1] before his ability to pay is realized. Forests may be regarded as similar to agricultural crops. The latter, however, are annual and are not usually included in property tax assessments. Forests, because of their slow maturity, are the exception. Farm crops bring an annual income to the landowner, whereas the owner of timberland receives no regular income except in the unusual case of rotation cutting. Forests involve substantial risk, particularly from fire; under the property tax this risk is practically all assumed by the owner and very little by the government. It is said that because of the slow maturity of the forest crop, the owner must pay interest and taxes upon taxes. Those paid in the early years are embodied in the forest property upon which taxes are paid in subsequent years.

A second objection to the property tax, closely related to the first, is that its future burden is unpredictable. The speculative element in a long investment is great enough without an additional uncertainty as to governmental obligations.

Finally, it is said that the property tax encourages the premature cutting of forests because the owner will harvest early in order to avoid further impositions of the tax. Good forestry may require two cuttings of a forest, the first to take out the mature trees only. If the first cutting is done with care, the smaller trees will have a better opportunity to develop rapidly to permit another cutting. The property tax encourages harvesting all at once to minimize taxes.

REQUISITES OF GOOD FOREST TAXATION

Critics of the general property tax as applied to forests have sought a forest tax which would meet the following conditions:

---

[1] In Minnesota a minimum of fifty years is required for jack pine or white spruce pulpwood and a maximum of one hundred years for good quality Norway pine saw logs.—Roy G. Blakey and Associates, *Taxation in Minnesota* (Minneapolis: The University of Minnesota Press, 1932), p. 147.

1. Impose a burden on the forest owner which involves neither subsidy nor discrimination;

2. Eliminate the uncertainty in future governmental burdens which a forest owner may be called upon to meet;

3. Provide local communities with the means that are necessary to maintain minimum standards in local government during the period of forest development;

4. Time the tax burden, as far as possible, to fall when the forest yields in income;

5. Impose no obstacles to the best use of, or to new investment in, forests.

SPECIAL FOREST TAXATION MEASURES

Wisconsin's Forest Crop Law. A large number of states now have legislation that puts forest property in a separate class for taxation purposes and gives it special treatment adapted to its peculiar characteristics. The Wisconsin Forest Crop Law will serve as an example of one type of special legislation. Under the Wisconsin law, a yield tax is combined with an annual levy and an annual contribution by the state to the local government in which the property is located. It should be observed, however, that the application of this law is optional with the owners of forestland. Before the law comes into operation with respect to his land, the owner makes application for its inclusion under the scheme, after which the relationship between him and the state is contractual. Once his land is listed, he pays to his local government 10 cents per acre, which the state matches with an equal amount. The latter, however, must be shared by the town with the county and the school districts. These contributions are designed to help municipalities maintain services while the forest crops are growing. In case the land listed is county-owned there is no local payment by the landowner, but the state contributes an additional 10 cents to the county to be used by it for forestry purposes only. The yield tax, all of which goes to the state, consists of 10 percent of the value of the products harvested from privately owned lands and 50 percent of that harvested from county-owned lands. Four fifths of the latter yield goes to the state forestry fund.

Summarizing these provisions one can list the major items as follows: (1) present and future taxes are set by contract; (2) taxes are limited by a specified ceiling; (3) a yield tax is substituted for a large part of the property tax; (4) local units of government receive compensatory payments from the state; and (5) county land as well as privately held land may be listed.[2]

---

[2] Other provisions of the law specify that land may be listed only in lots of at least forty acres and that it must be "suitable" for forestry. Moreover, the

Achievements and Limitations of the Wisconsin Law. While a very large area of land has been listed under the Wisconsin forest crop law, the overwhelming proportion of this land is not owned privately, as was originally contemplated, but is owned by the counties. Notwithstanding the improvement in the outlook for taxes, the prospective forest owner has regarded the distant future as too uncertain to warrant the venture. Private owners derive enough advantage from the plan so that most of those who anticipate the development of a forest crop prefer to have their land listed under the state law rather than subject to the property tax. However, except for corporations which can afford to develop raw materials as an assurance of an available supply for an established industry (such as the paper industry), the financial incentives of the law are usually insufficient to justify investment in forest development. The real advantages of the law are (1) better care of public forestland; (2) better rural planning and land use; (3) increased local interest in forestry; and (4) better prospects for a replenished resource that eventually will help to support the industries and government of the state. The successful operation of the law has been facilitated by rural zoning, which in turn has been greatly extended under the influence of the law. The law does nothing, of course, to promote the best care of submarginal land unfit for a commercial forest.

Other Forest Tax Laws. Over half of the states have special provisions in their statutes for the application of the property tax law to forests. Most of them make concessions to growing forests and recoup with a yield tax. In some of them, trees or land and trees meeting certain specifications are exempt for a certain number of years without any yield tax feature. The provision of a state payment to local communities is exceptional. Some states have special provisions to encourage the development of small woodlots on farms. Just how far these measures have been successful in "bringing back the forests" is not disclosed, though the rather meager acreage reported in most states suggests that these laws have had a fairly limited application.[3]

---

owner must make a reasonable indication that he is getting a forest under way and must, to a reasonable extent, practice the rules of forestry. The law provides for an inspection by the state both when the property is listed and five years thereafter. The property may be withdrawn from its forest-crop status on the initiative of the owner or of the state, the latter only in case of the owner's failure to practice forestry. When withdrawing, the individual is required to pay the property taxes (plus interest) which would have been levied upon it had the property not been listed. A supplementary law passed in 1953 provides that farm woodlots of less than 40 acres, properly managed, may be entered under contract with the state for 10 years with fixed tax liability of 20 cents per acre per year.

[3] For a recent authoritative and comparative treatment of the subject see Ellis T. Williams, "Trends in Forest Taxation," *National Tax Journal,* XIV: 2 (June 1961), pp. 113–144.

TAXATION OF MINES [4]

SPECIAL TAXATION OF MINES AND MINERALS

The question arises as to whether the mining industry may properly be singled out among the industries and occupations for special taxation. This matter has long been the subject of heated debate in Minnesota, where the iron mines are subjected to the top rate of assessment under the classified property tax and pay an occupational or severance tax besides. It is urged by those who defend exceptionally heavy taxation for the mines that the latter are a gift of nature to all the people of the state and that they represent a disappearing asset which will not always be available as a tax base. The fact that many of the mines are owned by absentees and that the mining interests have only a small representation in the legislature may also have a bearing on Minnesota's mine tax policy.

In opposition to the policy of exceptionally heavy taxation, it is alleged that mines are not the sole gift of nature, but that urban land, soil fertility, and even inherited talents must be placed in the same category. Even the fact that mines are a "gift" of nature is often belittled; rather, it is stressed that they are a business that requires investment and one in which the risks and hazards are exceedingly great.[5] In answer to the proposition that mines are a diminishing asset, it is said that their products are not destroyed (not immediately at least) but are converted into manufactured goods which, when added to the tax rolls, become a taxable asset of the state. Finally, and most important of all, it is alleged that excessive taxation kills the "goose which lays the golden [or the iron] egg"—that is, high taxation discourages investment in mines, prospecting for new mines, and development of old ones. This contention, offered by the mine owners, has been supported in Minnesota by the tax commission [6] and other highly competent critics.[7]

Deterrent Effects of Heavy Taxes on Mines. The question whether taxation has a deterrent effect upon mining depends in the last analysis on whether the tax is imposed on a cost or a surplus. A tax imposed on the mere ownership of nonreproducible gifts of nature has a different effect than one imposed on their exploitation and preparation for consumption.

---

[4] For comprehensive recent discussions of this subject, see *Proceedings of the National Tax Association Conference,* 1948, pp. 223–271; 1952, pp. 574–608; 1959, pp. 383–410.

[5] See next several paragraphs for a discussion of this point.

[6] *Eleventh Biennial Report of the Minnesota Tax Commission,* 1928, chap. XI.

[7] Blakey and Associates, *op. cit.,* chap. IX.

But these two aspects, ownership and exploitation, blend into each other in a very elusive way. Obviously, a tax on a clear find will not hinder anyone from making the find. If *A* finds a pocketbook containing valuable notes, as long as this windfall carries a tax less than 100 percent, he will not hesitate to pick it up. Nor will *B,* to whom he offers his find for sale, hesitate to invest in it because part of its contents will have to be turned over to the government. The tax simply will cause *B* to offer *A* less for his treasure.

However, suppose *A* is regularly engaged in the process of hunting lost pocketbooks but finds only one every six months and that one is only lightly stocked with valuables, may he not get discouraged if the government deprives him of half of his findings? And is not this latter supposition quite analogous to the situation in mining, where extensive outlays are often required to discover so-called gifts of nature and even more to uncover and bring them to the surface?

It is clear that in the mining business there is an element of "surplus value," "pure site value," or "scarcity value," whatever one may wish to call it, which is not capable of discouragement by any degree of taxation short of confiscation. If mining as a business is exempt from taxation, there is no danger of discouraging it as an ownership of the scarce gifts of nature. In practice, however, it may be quite difficult to separate the values that are created by nature and those that are created by man. Gross value of produce minus necessary costs of production, including necessary outlays for prospecting, should give "a true surplus." However, there may be some difficulty in determining what is necessary cost. The problem in mine taxation is one of framing and administering the law so that it is the surplus element which will be taxed and not the cost element.

Whether in practice it is possible to separate these two elements with tolerable accuracy is not a matter for dogmatic conclusion by one unfamiliar with the practice of mine taxation. The weight of authority seems to support the view that mine taxes discourage mining. Nevertheless, the common failure to recognize the element of surplus existing in mine property values and incomes makes one skeptical about the prevailing conclusion.

Relation of Mine Taxes to Conservation.   Instead of discouraging mining, it seems more plausible to conclude that an ad valorem property tax on the value of mines and minerals will have the opposite effect—that is, it will encourage the owners to mine out from under the tax. If this is the result, then the ad valorem tax is open to some objection from the standpoint of conservation. If the tax stimulates current production, it will tend to depress rather than increase prices. This in turn may stimulate demand, which again may be undesirable from the standpoint of conservation. The annual harvest of natural resources is kept in check to some extent by the inability of the public to buy more at tolerable prices. This check "puts the brakes" on any tendency to produce and market all available resources within a short period. A tax such as the gross production tax or one like the gasoline tax tends to be passed on to the consumer and thus cuts down demand, which in turn has advantages from a conservation standpoint.

Incidence of Mine Taxation. According to the commonly accepted rules of shifting, a gross production tax will be passed on to the consumer, at least in part. In so far as it is universally imposed by the governmental units in which production takes place, it applies to all mines and all production and thus meets one of the main conditions favorable to shifting. Net production taxes and ad valorem taxes, on the other hand, are aimed at a surplus: presumably they do not extend to mines that afford no profits above the cost of production. In so far as they accomplish in practice what they aim at in theory, they will not be shifted.

Mine Taxation and the Balance of Political Power. Mine taxation has often become a very intense political issue, with the result determined by the balance of power of interest groups.[8] Where a mining company is large, prosperous, and absentee-owned, it is especially vulnerable to political exploitation. Illustrations are cited of mining towns where the property tax base is largely mine property and where the majority of voters have no direct stake in the prosperity of the mines. This situation leads quite naturally to extravagance, a tendency that Minnesota has sought to check by a per capita limitation on local public expenditures. The clash of political forces often includes the rivalry between city and state for the public revenue from the mines. Oddly enough, the political weakness of mine owners in state legislatures is associated with exceptional strength in Congress. Income tax favors (depletion) for mine and oil companies have been maintained in the law despite the recommendations of the Treasury and repeated attacks of the critics. Congressional balance of power on this question is influenced by logrolling factors similar to those that appear in the tariff issue.

FORMS OF MINE TAXATION

The Ad Valorem Tax. The direct application of the general property tax to mines and minerals is called the ad valorem tax. It is the clearest means of equating the tax burden on mines with that on other property. It provides the state and local governments more stable revenue than any other form of mine taxation, and it is less arbitrary than its rivals.

---

[8] Warren A. Roberts, *State Taxation of Metallic Deposits* (Cambridge, Mass.: Harvard University Press, 1944).

The principal difficulty with the ad valorem tax is administrative. It is no simple task to evaluate a mine of any kind. The valuation must depend upon the thickness of the seams of ore, the quality of the mineral, the probable mining costs, transportation expense in marketing, and so on. Obviously this is too technical a task for local assessors. Nevertheless, there are still a few states in which local assessment prevails. The better practice is to turn the valuation over to the state tax department or some other state agency. In Minnesota, when mines were locally assessed, the mines themselves did most of the assessing; and in Michigan, when state assessment superseded local assessment, the value of mine property on the tax rolls increased over fourfold.[9]

It might seem to the layman that it would be impossible to appraise a mine with any accuracy in the most favorable circumstances. But such is not the case. The tax department, with the aid of experts to measure the quality and quantity of ore by drilling for samples, can sometimes assess a mine as accurately as it does most other property.

This is not to say that the ad valorem tax can be administered with tolerable success in the case of all types of mines. It can be successfully applied to coal, iron, copper, and zinc mines. On the other hand, deposits of gold and silver, and usually lead, are too inaccessible and unpredictable to permit their assessment with reasonable accuracy. The extent and value of deposits are frequently a mere speculation to the owners and equally so to appraisers.[10]

Other Types of Mine Taxation.   Where mines cannot be assessed efficiently on an ad valorem basis, and sometimes even where they can be so assessed, various types of income or production taxes have been levied. These may be in lieu of the ad valorem tax or supplementary to it, as in the case of the occupational tax on the net value of ore mined in Minnesota. Among the taxes so levied are tonnage taxes (sometimes called severance taxes), at so much per ton or other units of measurement. Of course these taxes collect nothing from nonproducing mines and mineral lands. A gross production tax based upon gross value of product is a simple tax to understand and administer and is the nearest equivalent in taxes of this type to the general property tax. Like all gross taxes, it is criticized on the ground that no account is taken of expenses of production. Net product taxes meet this difficulty but afford no revenue at all from mines which are not profitable. As a rule some of the mines are unprofitable all of the time and all of the mines are unprofitable some of the time, yet it is said that all should pay some taxes. Some of the states

---

[9] H. L. Lutz, *The State Tax Commission* (Cambridge, Mass.: Harvard University Press, 1918), pp. 315, 405–406.

[10] In the case of aluminum and manganese, the technology of mining and refining is undergoing such important and frequent changes that the valuation is, to say the least, exceedingly difficult.

have taken the net income from mines and doubled or tripled it in order to get a base for property taxation. Recently several states have enacted a developmental tax program with regard principally to investment in plant from the manufacture of iron ore from taconite (low-content raw material). This takes the form of a low production tax. Probably no conclusion can be drawn concerning the consensus as to the best system of mine taxation, particularly where the ad valorem system is impractical.

TAXATION OF OIL AND GAS RESOURCES

The administrative difficulties that the ad valorem system of taxation encounters in its application to certain mines are even greater in the case of its application to oil and gas resources. Not only are these latter properties unpredictable as to output, but in addition they are, in many cases, very short-lived and otherwise unadapted to ordinary property tax treatment. Nevertheless, some states still attempt to tax them under the general property tax. Most states apply to such properties the gross production tax.

Mines and Oil Wells under the Net Income Tax. Mention has been made of the fact that mines and oil wells cause much difficulty in the administration of net income taxes. Theoretically, depletion, or the reduction in capital value as a result of sale of assets, should be a deductible expense. It is allowed as such under the federal law, but administration is difficult, and the law now provides for depletion deduction in the case of some resources on the basis of certain percentages of gross income. The system is criticized as arbitrary and the percentages allowed as excessive. It is said that the one way "to make millions" and not run afoul of the federal revenue is to operate an oil well.

SPECIAL TAXATION OF NATURAL RESOURCES IN LAND

Of course, the principal natural resource in most countries is land. In some form it is necessary for practically all economic activity. Urban land is essential as a site for the location of labor and capital or for the location of homes; rural land is the ultimate source of most food and much clothing.

It has been contended for many years that land is an economic good especially well suited for taxation. The basis for this contention can be seen in the common analysis of the factors and functions of production which discloses the differences between capital and land.

LAND AMONG THE FACTORS OF PRODUCTION

Land, labor, capital, and entrepreneurial services are the elements that may be combined to produce economic goods. Each of these factors has a personal contributor—landlord, worker, capitalist, and entrepreneur. Each receives a reward—rent, wages, interest, and profits. Each—except perhaps the landlord—makes a contribution or renders an equivalent for his reward. The worker labors; the capitalist saves; the entrepreneur risks. But it is alleged that the landlord makes no contribution. This is not to say that natural resources are not essential for production. The contention is that the landlord merely appropriates natural resources and does not create them or their value.

FUNDAMENTAL TAX DIFFERENCES OF LAND AND CAPITAL

Many economists make no distinction between land and capital. According to the proponents of special land taxation, however, there are many fundamental differences between these two. Some of the alleged differences are as follows:

1. Natural resources are discovered and appropriated; capital is produced. Man makes the buildings on the earth, but he does not make the sites for them.
2. Land is not capable of reproduction; capital is. The value of capital cannot rise above its cost of reproduction; the value of land can rise indefinitely.
3. Income from capital involves a return from the recipient to the commonwealth; income from land does not.
4. Land cannot migrate; capital can.
5. To a very large extent, land is not reproducible and, therefore, taxes imposed on it are not shifted to the consumer, as are most taxes on capital; they tend to be capitalized and become a "burdenless" tax upon the purchasers. Taxes on cigarettes make them expensive; taxes on land make it cheap.

EXAMPLE OF LAND VALUE INCREMENT

Proponents of special land taxation have no difficulty in citing cases where landowners have profited immensely as a result of the growing population of a large city. For example, take the financial history of a lot on the southwest corner of State and Madison Streets in Chicago: [11]

---

[11] Fred R. Fairchild, Edgar S. Furniss, and Norman S. Buck, *Elementary Economics* (rev. ed., New York: The Macmillan Company, 1930), vol. II, p. 149

In 1830 when the population of Chicago numbered 50 people, the plot of ground was bought for $20. In 1845, when the city's population had increased to 12,000, the value of the land had risen to $5000. By 1860 when the population was 109,000, the lot was worth $28,000, or 1,400 times its original value. In 1875 the population of Chicago had increased to 400,000, and the land had risen in value to $92,500. In 1894, with the population at 1,500,000, this quarter acre of ground had a value of $1,250,000.

The author who compiled these impressive data concerning one case of land value increment topped off his figures with certain comparisons as follows: [12]

> Six hundred average Illinois farms would not now exchange for this quarter acre of raw prairie land, and nearly three thousand years of labor of one man would be required to buy it. If 500 years before the Christian era, some man had found employment at the equivalent of $1.50 a day; had, like some wandering Jew, been preserved through the vicissitudes of the centuries; had been miraculously sustained without expense for any of the necessities or luxuries of life; had done his work regularly from that day to this, 300 days in the year without losing a day, and had hoarded all his wages, his savings would not yet be enough to buy this quarter acre of prairie land at the mouth of the Chicago River.[13]

THE SINGLE TAX ON ECONOMIC RENT OF LAND

The most celebrated of all proposals for the special taxation of land is that which usually passes under the name of *The Single Tax*. At one time this proposal aroused considerable interest, and even today it has its strong adherents. The following section will be devoted to a discussion of

---

(quoted from the *Eighth Biennial Report of the Bureau of Labor Statistics of Illinois*, 1894, p. 279).

[12] *Ibid.*

[13] Criticizing ability to pay as a single canon of taxation, Professor John R. Commons has stated the theoretical case for special land taxation as follows:

"But if there is another canon of taxation that may properly be applied, namely, the effects of wealth production, guided by the public purpose of favoring wealth production, then the man who gets his wealth by the mere rise in site values should pay proportionately higher taxes than the one who gets his wealth by industry or agriculture. In the one case, he extracts wealth from the commonwealth without adding to it. In the other case, he contributes directly to an increase in both private wealth and commonwealth. Hence, looking at it from the commonwealth, or social utility, standpoint, there are two kinds of ability to pay: that ability which varies directly with one's additions to the commonwealth, and that which varies inversely with one's additions to the commonwealth. The first we shall name Ability to Serve, the second, Ability to Pay."—John R. Commons, *Institutional Economics* (New York: The Macmillan Company, 1934), p. 819.

what the proponents of this tax mean by it and how they propose to operate it.

Exposition of Single-tax Proposal.   The single-tax advocates propose to base their tax upon economic rent. By economic rent they mean the annual value of a parcel of land. Economic rent is not to be confused with net income from land. Idle land has no net income, but that does not mean that it has no annual value. A bad manager may get no net income from a parcel of land. This does not mean that such land has no economic rent.

What is meant by economic rent can be made clear by two illustrations. *A* and *B* are farmers and neighbors, and *A* offers to let *B* have a year's use of forty acres of land for $400. There is nothing on the land —not even fences. Assuming that this was a fair price for what was being offered, the $400 is economic rent.

Or, again, suppose *C* owns a city lot and building upon which he is able to make $4000 each year. Part of this net income must be attributed to the capital invested in the improvement on the lot and to the labor of *C* himself. The latter may be determined by appraising the value of *C*'s services were he to offer them on the market. The same applies to the value of the reproducibles or improvements—that is, how much he could earn on his investment in some other line of business. Finally, there is the value of the land, which may be calculated by reference to the market as in the case of labor. If the values of these three deductions do not add up to $4000, the residue is profits (not to be confused with economic rent). The economic rent, as indicated above, is the market value of the use of the land for one year.

The rate of the single tax according to its most orthodox followers would be 100 percent; some are willing to accept a rate sufficiently high to provide the revenue needed for government.

The tax would be levied annually. In this respect, Henry George's single tax is not to be confused with Lloyd George's land-value increment tax. The latter was to be collected not annually but only when an exchange of land took place.

The orthodox single-tax proponent urges his tax to the exclusion of all others. Again, some of the less orthodox followers have been willing to give ground and accept, along with heavy taxes on land, certain other taxes—perhaps income and inheritance taxes.

Unsound Criticisms of Single Tax.   Some of the superficial criticisms of the single tax are unsound. For example, it is said that a tax system that takes all that a person is able to make on a parcel of land deprives him of all incentive to own or improve the land or to use it to its best advantage. Those who make such assertion either have small understanding of single-tax theory or are claiming that the single tax does not work according to its theory.

No incentive to own? The incentive to own remains because land becomes less expensive—in fact, of nominal cost only.[14] Besides, one must have land as a situs for labor and capital from which one would still be allowed to acquire all economic rewards except rent.

No incentive to improve land? On the contrary, the incentive to improve land would be considerably strengthened by the fact that no taxes would be levied on improvements. One of the principal single-tax arguments is that the proposed tax system would stimulate improvements. The single tax is a developmental tax policy. Take the taxes off from labor and capital, it is said, and these necessary elements of progress will be forthcoming in more generous measure than ever before. Why should a man who paints his garage be penalized by an additional dose of taxes?

No incentive to operate land efficiently? Those who so argue confuse rent with profits. A single tax is not a tax on excess profits. Special efficiency would still be entitled to its reward. As a matter of fact, because of the necessity of paying the tax, the single tax might force some to raise their efficiency.

An old controversy relates to the question whether capitalized taxes of long-standing can be said to be burdenless. It is clear that taxes on land reduce wealth of those owning such property at the time levies are first imposed. But it is hard to conclude that the present generation must have inherited less because of ancient losses incurred by previous generations. Perhaps the forefathers would have consumed more and saved less or labored less had there been no tax.

Valid Criticisms of Single Tax. What seem to the writer to be valid and important criticisms of the single tax are the following:

1. It is too single. Granting it to be true that at least much income from land is unearned, it is also true that much income from many other sources is also frequently unearned. The notion that the landlord is a thief and that all the rest of us are "worthy of our hire" is one which has not and will not find support among most citizens, particularly the ones who have no taste for abstractions. Income in gifts, inheritances, and monopoly profits are commonly cited as examples of unearned income from other sources than land. A considerable part of wages and salaries is also thought by some to be unearned. Why is Mr. X able to command a $100,000 salary? As in the case of finance from a choice lot, it is probably due to a combination of circumstances over which he has had scant control. A fortunate endowment of qualities and the proper social environment may have had far more to do with X's success than industry and thrift. It is exceedingly difficult to isolate the unearned portion of the

---

[14] According to the theory under which land values are determined by capitalizing net income, if the net income from land is nothing, its capitalized value is nothing. Under the single tax, the government would have the equivalent of a 100-percent mortgage on all land which would be bought and sold as though it were subject to a 100-percent mortgage.

national income. It seems highly probable that most of it is in the higher brackets of income, an additional ground in support of a graduated net income tax.

2. The single tax is an attempt to mop up spilled milk. In a young and rapidly developing country, many profit by the social and economic changes taking place in the community. Before long, however, this unearned wealth becomes diffused by exchange, inheritance, and so forth. A working man may have spent his entire life laying up some savings to invest in a little land. Should he then, after his investment, be expropriated by the single tax?

3. The single tax flagrantly disregards the principle of ability to pay. The time was, perhaps, when concentrated wealth was mainly in real estate, but this has ceased to be true. Most of the largest estates show a relatively small percentage of real estate. Moreover, it will be found that land constitutes a larger proportion of rural than of urban property. In typical rural communities, as much as four fifths of real property values are made up of land values; in moderate-sized urban centers, well over half of real property values are in improvements. Thus, an exemption of improvements would reduce the farm tax base far less than the urban tax base. A very large amount of land is owned by relatively poor people, and it is probable that within certain ranges of income there is an inverse correlation between size of fortune and the proportion of it held in real estate.

4. It should be mentioned that in practice the distinctions drawn between land and capital can nowhere be as sharply defined as they are in theory. Agricultural land, for instance, includes fertility, which is an exhaustible and reproducible factor like capital. Fertility is not the only intangible "improvement" concealed in land values. At one time, Professor Commons devised legislation which sought to isolate "pure site values" from other elements of land value and single out the former for special taxation.[15] This objective is sound from a theoretical standpoint but not easily managed as a practical matter.

History of Single Tax.   Space will not permit an extended discussion of the history of the single tax. Although the idea of special taxes on land was not new with Henry George, he was the first to build a social and economic theory around it which became the basis of a great social reform movement. As editor of the San Francisco *Post* during the 1870s, George had the opportunity to observe the effects of what he regarded as a mistaken land policy in a young and rapidly developing country. In

---

[15] John R. Commons, "A Progressive Tax on Bare Land Value," *Political Science Quarterly*, XXXVII: 1 (March 1922), pp. 41–68; the Grimstad Bill introduced in the Wisconsin legislature in 1921 embodied Professor Commons' proposals.

his *Progress and Poverty,* published in 1879, he boldly and eloquently presented the philosophy of the single tax. The book was very widely read and captured considerable following. George ran for mayor of New York City in 1886; in his platform he asked, "Why should the people pay rent to private parties and taxes to the state rather than rent to the state and no taxes?" Since his death in 1897 a well-financed and ardent movement supporting his philosophy has survived, but it has not been too successful in enlarging its following. The single tax as a reform movement seems to have a very limited popular appeal in the American environment.

Experience with Special Land Taxation. The British Dominions— Canada, Australia, and New Zealand—have had considerable experience with special land taxation. In Canada the western provinces have for many years either exempted improvements from property taxation entirely or given them a very favorable classification. Rural improvements are ordinarily entirely eliminated from the assessment roll, and urban ones are rated according to local option with legal assessment ratios ranging all the way from 0 to 100 percent. The single-tax movement in western Canada reached its height during the western land boom (ending in 1913) which involved one of the greatest population movements in history. The collapse in the boom brought a heavy crop of land forfeitures for taxes and a demand for a broader base. Western Canada has been retreating from the single tax ever since, but the retreat has been gradual and apparently reluctant.

The application of special land taxes in the south Pacific countries has been more persistent and popular. The national land taxes of Australia and New Zealand, and the state taxes of the former, are not based on strictly Georgian principles (indeed they are sharply criticized by the Georgians). They are characterized predominantly by graduation, a minimum exemption, and other features, giving these levies the earmarks of "personal taxes." They aim not so much at government collection of economic rent as dismemberment of great estates and the development of widespread ownership of land. They go back in Australian history to the days when land-hungry settlers and erstwhile miners sought to wrest good holdings from those who had "come in on the ground floor." In several Australian states local taxes or rates are based exclusively on land values; in other states and New Zealand local option is generally allowed.

Local taxation confined to land encounters in Australia and New Zealand the very favorable circumstance that many public responsibilities (education, for instance) which are borne locally in the United States and Canada are there undertaken by the state or national governments. This frequently makes possible the combination of a narrow tax base and a moderate rate. With the rates moderate, a tax confined to land need not depress land values; indeed, it is argued that the stimulus to city growth resulting from "enlightened" taxation adds more to land values than the tax subtracts.

It is in Australia that the greatest effort has been made to isolate and tax "pure economic rent." This has afforded some very subtle problems of theory and administration. It may seem that land value can be derived by taking the total value of a property and subtracting the value of improvements. But this will often fail to give a defensible answer. The question arises as to whether land takes on value because it is the situs of a profitable business. The American practice of assessing utilities usually assumes that the value of the business carries over into the value of the premises. However, this is exceptional under our system. Ordinarily, two lots in equally good locations would seem to have the same value notwithstanding the fact that one is associated with a profitable and the other with a losing business. There have been cases in Australia where profit from business (as in using the land for a race course) was held to "run with the land." The improvements that administrators seek to subtract (or abstract) are, of course, the particular and not the general improvements of the community. It is recognized that improvements may be intangible as well as tangible. A tennis court is considered an improvement and not one of "the original and indestructible powers of the soil." But there is some skepticism in the case of ancient intangible improvements. Must two lots be assessed forever at different figures because several generations ago one of them was marked by a gully which required filling?

It is interesting to observe that the single-tax movement in Australia is not mainly a class movement and attracts many (including some real estate dealers!) who espouse no other form of radicalism (if this tax doctrine may be so designated). Many of the Georgians are well established and quite successful in "the free enterprise system." Many of them prefer the Liberal (conservative) to the Labour (socialist) party.

The city of Canberra, new capital of the Australian commonwealth, is engaged in a novel experiment in land management. The city was and is being built upon land that cost the government nothing or practically nothing. No part of the land is being sold but is leased instead on long contracts that call for periodic review of the rental.

The above does not exhaust by any means the many applications of special taxes to land. Mention was made earlier of the land-value increment tax which operates in a manner similar to the capital gains feature of our net income tax. It was tried in Great Britain and abandoned, but it still has some application in a few countries. Special assessments (treated in a later chapter) are also a member of the special-land-tax family. Fairhope, Alabama, sometimes described as a "single-tax colony," applies the Georgian doctrine through a private corporation that owns the land, collects the rent, and settles with the state as though it were paying the general property tax. Mention should also be made of movements, sometimes successful, in many parts of the world to induce the government to break up large estates (by confiscation) and redistribute the ownership of land in so-called functional units.

Conclusion. All things considered, it seems to the author that the case for the special taxation of land, particularly urban land, rests on sound ground. It is very doubtful whether cities ever should have allowed the sites within their boundaries to have passed entirely from public ownership. The main sound argument for private property in city sites is that city governments are too corrupt to manage a real estate business. Failing to follow the course taken by the city of Canberra, the next best program is to recapture a large amount of urban [16] economic rent through special taxes on land. The inequalities of such a program would be largely eliminated by the capitalization process over a period of time. Immediately, however, the inequalities resulting from a drastic increase in land taxation would be very important. Moreover, the strong theoretical basis for special land taxation is not generally understood by the lay public, to whom a dollar of income is a dollar of income whether from land or any other source. Consequently, special land taxation must wait upon economic education and, in any event, must proceed gradually.[17]

SUMMARY

Natural resources have distinctive characteristics which justify their special consideration for taxation. In some cases, they are to such an extent subject to depletion that a strong interest in conservation arises; in others, they are nonreproducible and relatively fixed in supply, factors which are conducive to a program of special taxation of such property.

Both the importance of forest resources and the problems created in certain areas by deforestation (such as tax delinquency) prompt a widespread interest in forest development. It is said that the general property tax is inimical to this program because it is inconvenient (as to time) for the forest owner to pay and leads to premature harvesting to avoid the tax. Special forest taxation of several varieties is being tried in

---

[16] Rural land involves somewhat different problems because of the element of soil fertility in land values. Moreover, the imposition of high fixed charges upon the productive assets of farmers may produce undesirable results.

[17] For a recent symposium on site-value taxation see Canadian Tax Foundation, *1961 Conference*, pp. 68–109.

many states. The Wisconsin Forest Crop Law, one of these experiments, combines a low flat acreage tax, a yield tax, and payment by the state to local communities where land is listed. County as well as private land may be entered. This program has been successful in enlisting widespread local interest in forestry. Over half the states now make some special provision for the application of property taxes to forests.

In the taxation of mines, a lively controversy is taking place concerning the question of whether mines should be taxed at a higher rate than other property or business. An important element in this controversy is the alleged deterrent effect of heavy taxes upon mining. Logically, mine values should contain an ingredient of surplus which should bear taxes without discouraging mine operation, but whether the surplus can be distinguished from necessary costs for taxation is not established. Certain mines can be successfully taxed ad valorem, but others require special taxation. Tonnage taxes, gross production taxes, net production taxes, and property taxes applied to multiples of net proceeds are other varieties of mine taxation in use. Oil wells offer taxation problems similar to those of mines, except that the former are less well adapted to ad valorem property taxation.

Natural resources in land are said to differ from most other property in several respects which make them a specially apt subject for taxation. One expression of this point of view is the single-tax proposal which advocates placing all taxes upon the economic rent of land. Many unsound criticisms are leveled at this proposal. However, it is open to valid objection in its singleness, its refusal to recognize the diffusion of past land values, its flagrant disregard for the ability-to-pay principle, and its assumption that site values can always be distinguished from other elements of value in land. Special taxes on land of various sorts have been applied quite extensively in other countries and to a more limited extent in the United States. Particularly at a time when property tax limitation, homestead exemption, and gross income and sales taxes are quite the vogue, the large element of truth in the old-fashioned notion that land values invite taxation should be emphasized.

PROBLEMS

1. "According to strict theory, no land tax on capital value, supported by current income, can ever be confiscatory. The tax decreases income, and this decreases the value of the property, which in turn checks the impact of the tax." Do you agree?
2. Consider the case of three adjacent lots, one of which supports a hotel while the other two are vacant. The three lots may be assigned equal value on the score that the hotel might with equal propriety

have been built on any one of them. Actually, the commitment has been made to use one of the lots for the hotel, and the others could be used in an identical way only by destroying the business value of all of them. It appears highly doubtful that an equally valuable use may be found for the idle lots. Should the lots as such be assessed at the same or at different values?

3. A baseball player commands a salary of $75,000. The cost of his service as measured by the incentive required to induce him to play baseball is a modest cost of maintenance. The value of his service as measured by the receipts he brings in at the "box office" runs to hundreds of thousands of dollars. Is the salary, in excess of maintenance, similar in all important respects to the rent on a city lot?

4. All the factors of production show differential advantages of position or of quality between the more fortunate and the marginal units. Does this establish the conclusion that there is nothing unique about land among the factors?

5. Land is not ordinarily produced, but it is made available for more profitable uses by the technological improvement in transportation. Do the latter invalidate the view that the supply of land is inelastic?

6. Comment on the proposition: The tax on mines that is most likely to achieve neutrality with other taxpayers is the ad valorem tax.

7. Comment on the proposition: Taxes on mines are especially prone to discourage enterprise in mining.

8. Comment on the proposition: Mine taxes are a hindrance to conservation.

9. Criticize the property tax as a levy on growing timber.

10. Consider legislation modeled on the Wisconsin Forest Crop Law as to a) security it gives present owners; b) allegation that it gives present owners a subsidy.

11. Consider the proposition: Long-standing land taxes are burdenless.

12. Why would the single tax be difficult to apply in the case of rural land? Wherein is it said to ignore the diffusion of past increments to land values?

13. Comment on the proposition: When taxes are imposed on land, what the landlord does forthwith is to raise the rent.

14. Distinguish the following: single tax; graduated tax on bare land values; unearned increment tax; classified property tax with heaviest weight on land values.

15. Consider each of the following arguments that may be applied to the single tax theory:
    a. That it would weaken incentive;
    b. That it is too single;
    c. That it would fail in practice to isolate nonreproducibles;
    d. That transportation improvements have reduced the problem it sought to solve.

16

TAXES ON GENERAL BUSINESS AND PUBLIC UTILITIES

The subject of business taxation falls quite distinctly into two divisions. The first concerns the nature and justification of special taxes upon business in general; the second deals with the application of general or special taxes to particular business. Of the latter, attention here will be confined to taxes upon public utilities. The taxation of banks, insurance companies, and chain stores will be treated in the next chapter. In addition, mention will also be made of the application of general taxes to business.

TAXES ON BUSINESS IN GENERAL

Directly or indirectly, many general taxes, not so aimed, nevertheless fall in part upon business. The general property tax must be paid on factories, store buildings, and goods in the process of manufacture or on hand for sale. The income from unincorporated business and the interest and dividends from incorporated business are taxed under the personal income tax. The income tax may also apply to corporations, as such, in the form of either a corporate net income tax or an excess profits tax.

360

The gross income tax includes business among the taxpayers; and a retail sales tax, although thought to rest ultimately upon the consumer, is paid in the first instance by merchants. Using the broadest possible concept of business (as all economic activity), we may say that all income arises from business. If the frequent assertion that all taxes come out of income is also accepted, the conclusion is inevitable that all taxes are business taxes.

Justification of Business Taxes. Many students of taxation have suggested that in addition to the general taxes paid by business, some special business tax should be imposed. This subject was discussed in connection with the corporate income tax, but a brief recapitulation may be in order here. The theoretical justification for a business tax is perhaps strongest when viewed from the point of benefits and costs. Business activity in a modern community is greatly facilitated by the orderliness, security, and general enlightenment prevailing, all of which are attributable in large part to government. Many of the problems that the government faces nowadays arise from the way modern business is conducted.

Whether the ability-to-pay concept can be applied to business is a matter of dispute. Certainly, business has what many have accepted as one attribute of ability to pay—namely, the power to meet tax bills.

Business taxes have much to recommend them on practical as well as theoretical grounds. For example, they afford a means whereby revenue from the same source may be shared between the jurisdictions of origin and domicile. The district in which the business is carried on may be allowed the business tax, and the district in which the employees and investors are domiciled may receive the personal taxes. Moreover, business taxes can be made to yield substantial revenue. Perhaps this is fortunate because, both politically and psychologically, it may be inexpedient to load all the burdens of government on personal income and general property.

Incidence of Business Taxes. One of the more troublesome matters in business taxation is incidence. If the objective of such taxation is to impose a tax burden upon business itself, then it can be accomplished only through the imposition of a business tax that cannot be shifted forward to the consumer or backward to other producers. The consensus would probably hold that except for the net income tax (and there is considerable difference of opinion even here), almost all business taxes are usually shiftable. Thus, what is first thought to be a business tax may turn out, with further analysis, to be a tax upon the consumer. But were net income accepted as a proper measure for the imposition of a business tax, the large unprofitable concern, which absorbs as much benefit or causes as much expense to the government as the profitable one, would pay no business tax.

Personal versus Business Taxes. The traditional British policy has been to impose few taxes upon business as such. The British tax system has featured the personal income tax as its mainstay. The corporate income tax has been regarded and consistently treated as a device for collecting at the source.[1] The British tradition has much to recommend it, but there is a somewhat different problem in a country where the income tax is largely federal and where states need more revenue than they care to squeeze out of the general property tax. Perhaps it simmers down mainly to the relative merits of business, general property, and retail sales taxes, all of which are paid in considerable part by the consumer. At least it can be said for the business tax that it diversifies the tax system and attempts to measure the responsibilities of business to government, not only on the basis of capital employed (as under the general property tax) but also on some other bases which will be discussed shortly.

GENERAL PROBLEMS OF BUSINESS TAXATION

Should Unincorporated Business Be Included? If special taxes are to be imposed on business, should they cover all firms or only corporate business? If all, then a question arises as to the definition of a business.

The Model Plan of the National Tax Association approves the view that business taxes should extend to all forms of business, unincorporated as well as incorporated, but the predominant practice is to confine such taxes to corporations. There is some plausible support for special classification and treatment of corporations. As a class, corporations are identified with big business, which creates difficult problems for the government. Corporations and their stockholders are separate legal entities and are often physically as well as legally separated. This is not usually true of partnerships and individual entrepreneurs. A business tax on the corporation enables the community in which it is located to collect something for the support of public activities made necessary by its presence. The government grants certain privileges to corporations, particularly the privilege of limited liability, and sometimes this is cited as an argument for special taxation. But the argument can be answered that, in so far as this privilege is open to all, free competition should make it valueless. Immunity from personal taxation is a more important privilege, which, however, probably should be abolished rather than taxed.

If the recommendation of the National Tax Association to tax all business, incorporated and unincorporated, were accepted, where should

---

[1] Recently, under great pressure for revenue, the British have imposed a tax on corporate income and corporate dividends as such.

the line be drawn to indicate what constitutes business? Is farming a business? Is owning real estate and charging rent a business? Is practicing law a business? Is working for a salary a business? If the answer to all of these questions is "No," then the question may be put: Why tax the corner grocer on his way of making a livelihood and not any of these others? The question is not easy to answer. Perhaps everyone should be taxed once in his capacity as producer and once in his capacity as consumer. This idea, however, has never made much progress outside textbooks.

New York and Connecticut have to some extent experimented with business taxes on unincorporated business, the former with a net income and the latter with a gross income levy, but in neither has the result in terms of revenue or equity been a cause of much satisfaction.

Methods of Business Taxation. Perhaps because of the reluctance of most tax students to accept the view that there are three legs to the "tax stool"—property, income, and business—the methods employed in taxing business have proceeded on a wide but somewhat haphazard front. Whereas property and income taxes are usually based on only one measure (value in the case of the former and income in the latter), the bases of business taxes often include a great number of different measures, such as net income, property, capital stock issued, gross income, and so on. The business tax system is further complicated because some of the taxes levied on business are peculiar to business activity whereas others are laid on business along with other taxpayers; some of these taxes tend to remain on business while others are shifted; some are confined to corporations while others include unincorporated businesses as well; and some are imposed upon business in general while others are confined to specific types of business.

Although no attempt is made here to list all methods of business taxation, it is believed that those applying to business in general fall more or less into the classifications listed below. The taxes on specific types of business will be discussed later.

A	B
1. Sales taxes	1. Occupational taxes
2. Property taxes	2. Incorporation fees
3. Excess profits taxes	3. Capital stock taxes
4. Corporate net income tax	4. Corporate excess taxes
5. Gross income taxes	

The taxes listed under *A* were mentioned at the beginning of this chapter and were described as taxes more or less general in character but including business in their scope. They are discussed in more detail

in other chapters of this book. Here it may be recalled from the chapter
on income taxes that the corporate net income tax is both a device for
collection at the source and a business tax, and that the excess profits
tax, although a business tax and applicable mainly to corporations, also
has a place in the income tax picture. Gross income and sales taxes were
discussed as consumption taxes, but they deserve some additional consideration as business taxes.

The Gross Income Tax.   The gross income tax differs from the net
income tax in that the former ordinarily allows no deduction for business
expenses or cost of goods sold. In some states, such as Indiana, the
gross income tax is a general tax applying not only to what is usually
considered business but to service and investment income as well. In
other states it is more strictly a business tax (sometimes called a gross
receipts tax). This is true in Arizona and Washington.

A strong case can be made for volume of business (gross income)
as the basis of a business tax, either as a substitute for part of the property tax on business or as a supplement to it. Under such a tax the government in effect says to the taxpayer: "You have come amongst us and
have exploited our market; you have trafficked as much as your competitor; whether you have used your opportunity as well as he is not our
concern. It is the gross volume of your trade which both represents your
opportunity and causes our expense. Upon that you must pay." [2]

However, the use of gross income as the base of a business tax results in the accumulation of taxes according to the number of transactions
involved in the preparation of a commodity before it reaches the consumer. A retail sales tax based on the final exchange avoids this overlapping and in this respect is a sounder form of business taxation. The
same result could be had by applying the tax to "value added" by manufacturer and merchant rather than to gross sales. "Value added" would
differ from gross income as a base in that cost of goods sold would be
a deductible expense.

The gross income tax as a state tax on business also encounters
difficulties of interstate competition. The retailer can bear a fairly high
tax because he has little outside competition with which to contend. The
manufacturer must be dealt with tenderly since he competes with others
not paying the same taxes.

Occupation Taxes.   In some states, particularly in the south, a great
variety of special charges are imposed on business. One count tallied
over 130 separate occupation taxes in the state statutes of Alabama.
Some of those included were: special taxes on barber shops, dealers in

---

[2] T. S. Adams, "The Taxation of Business," *Proceedings of the National Tax
Association Conference,* 1917, p. 189.

coffins, dealers in dice, junk dealers, and persons engaged in the practice of medicine. Some of these levies were payable to the local units rather than the state.[3]

The outstanding characteristic of these occupation taxes is their arbitrariness. A few of them are based upon some rough measure of the volume of business, but most of them are based upon no reasonable principle whatever.[4]

Incorporation Fees. There are charges incidental to the acquisition of a corporation charter. These fees are ordinarily nonrecurrent and of small fiscal importance. They are usually based on (and sometimes graduated according to) the par value of the stock or the number of shares issued or authorized. A complementary tax may be imposed upon foreign corporations as a condition of their doing business in a state.

Capital Stock Taxes. A capital stock tax is a business tax applicable to corporations and proportioned in some way according to the capital represented by stock and employed in the business. Based, as it frequently is, upon the value of assets, it has some resemblance to a special property tax. It probably grew out of the desire to collect the general property tax on one form of intangibles (corporate stock) at the source —that is, from the company rather than the individual. But the alleged justification of the tax is the privilege of engaging in business as a limited liability concern.[5]

Capital stock taxes may be imposed upon the market value of stocks or upon the par value of either the issued or authorized issue of securities. This is the case with most state capital stock taxes. In the event of no-par stock, the tax may be based on the number of shares. Bonds as well as stocks might be included in the measure, but this is rarely done. Obviously, capital stock alone, without regard to bonds or other indebtedness, gives a distorted picture of the capital of a corporation. Par value or authorized value may have little or no relation to actual capital. Market value, although better, is open to many objections as a criterion

---

[3] See Tax Research Foundation, *Tax Systems* (New York, 1942), p. 7; Revenue Survey Committee, *Alabama Revenue System,* 1947, p. 65.

[4] Institute for Government Research, *Taxation of the State Government of Alabama* (Washington, D.C.: The Brookings Institution, 1932), vol. IV, Part III, p. 315.

[5] During and after World War I, the federal government tried out the use of a capital stock tax based on the value of the assets of corporations. But this program involved very grave administrative difficulties and was abandoned in 1926. From 1934 to 1945 the federal government levied a capital stock tax on "declared value" and supported this procedure with a so-called excess profits tax based on the same figure. The taxpayer was discouraged from declaring a low value for one tax because he might then get caught by the other. This unpopular levy was more closely related to a taxpayer's income than to his capital.

of value. For instance, it offers no means whereby the value of an inter-state corporation could be apportioned among the various states for tax purposes without going to the actual value of the assets. But the value of corporate assets is extremely difficult to determine.

Logically, a state might seem restricted to taxing only the stock represented by the proportionate assets of the corporation lying within its borders. However, it is apparently within a state's legal power to tax (at least under the "franchise tax") all the securities of a corporation which it incorporates. Corporations hold their prerogatives under sufferance; privilege to do business in this form constitutes a franchise; it is subject to excise taxation with the base measured by most any aspect of the company including *all* its gross or net income or capital stock. Thus, a tax levied on a taxable subject may be measured by a nontaxable subject. The state of Delaware, notorious for its easy incorporation laws, enjoys the benefit of this laxity by imposing a capital stock tax on all stocks authorized by the corporations it incorporates. Thus, in effect, the state imposes a tax on the assets of a corporation, even though those assets may all be located west of the Mississippi River. Delaware imposes a light tax so as not to discourage its incorporation business, but the base of the tax is large and the state receives a substantial portion of its revenue from this source. Probably it is legal for a state to tax a foreign corporation only upon some fair apportionment of capital stock employed within and without the state. This involves the difficult problem of making a fair apportionment.

About two thirds of the states employ some form of capital stock tax but with a great variety of bases, procedures, and methods of apportionment. The law of Michigan may be taken as an example. The rate in that state is 4 mills; on interstate corporations, it is based upon the portion of the value of paid-up stock and surplus represented by assets in the state. In some instances, especially on small and relatively unprofitable corporations, it represents a greater burden than would the usual net income tax.

It is probably fair to conclude that capital stock taxes in practice are only a little less arbitrary than occupational taxes. But, although they are only a rough indication of the size of the corporation, they represent one means of obtaining revenue from it. The canon of taxation to which they answer best is probably that of "getting the most feathers with the least squawking."

The Corporate Excess Tax.   The corporate excess tax is really a feature of the property tax, but it is usually associated with business taxes and may be discussed along with them. Corporate excess is the value of a corporation above that of its tangible assets and may be determined by placing a value upon the business as a whole, another value upon its tangible assets, and then deducting the latter from the former. The original method of assessment by local assessors has lost ground in favor of assessment by state officials. In some states corporate excess is taxed at special rates rather than as general property. Only a few states, of which Massachusetts is a prominent example, now retain this type of levy.

Although the corporate excess tax is a companion piece to the property tax, it serves also to tap the same values as those reached by the capital stock tax. The corporate excess tax applies only to the intangible values of a corporation, so that tangibles and intangibles shall be taxed at the same rate as real estate, whereas the capital stock tax reaches both tangible and intangible values as represented by the corporation's stock. Thus, though the base of values taxed by the capital stock levies is much broader than that reached by the tax on corporate excess, the rates are usually much lower.

The principal limitation of corporate excess taxation is in administration. If no real valuation of corporate assets is made, the tax is arbitrary like the capital stock tax, and, if such valuation is made, the task of doing a creditable job is formidable.

Toward a Better System of Business Taxation. Business taxes in the United States are characterized by much arbitrariness, complexity, and lack of coordination. Students of the subject have sought to remedy these conditions and have made a number of proposals to that end. One of these takes the form of a single coordinated business tax [6] which would include a number of alternative bases, with the tax imposed upon the base producing the highest revenue.

Among the alternative levies suggested are, first, a flat minimum tax, something like a poll tax, to cover the cost of administration or to exact a small charge for the privilege of corporate existence. The minimum charge might also be conceived as an administrative device to avoid the difficulty of applying other taxes to very small businesses. In the case of small and inactive businesses, this would probably be the only business tax paid. The second alternative tax suggested is one based on net

---

[6] Committee on State and Local Taxation, "Second Report on a Plan of a Model System of State and Local Taxation," *Proceedings of the National Tax Association Conference,* 1933, pp. 353–427.

Court dispensation of almost carte blanche discretion to tax the corporate privilege has made corporations highly vulnerable to exhorbitant taxation, multiple taxation, and extra-territorial taxation. Multiple taxation may arise from the treatment of the capital stock of companies distinct from that held by stockholders; from the taxation of both the stock of the company and its physical assets; and from the jurisdictional confusion and overlapping among states. Extra-territorial taxation arises from the right to measure an internal tax with eternal factors.

income; this tax would catch the more profitable businesses. The third proposal is a tax on gross income.

The least that can be said for a coordinated and rational system of business taxes such as the one described above is that it would be a great improvement over the present practice. However, the incidence of such a tax would be anybody's guess.

TAXES ON SPECIAL BUSINESS—PUBLIC UTILITIES

GENERAL LEVEL OF UTILITY TAXES

One of the first questions to present itself in the taxation of public utilities is that of the relative tax burden that should be imposed upon them as compared with other property and business. Some have taken the position that utilities should be entirely exempt from taxation on the ground that utility taxes are sales taxes in disguise and fall upon the consumer of utility services. On the other hand, it may be argued that utilities should pay taxes at a higher rate than that prevailing for business in general on the ground that utilities are monopolies and, therefore, special taxes should be levied upon them to recapture monopoly profits. A position midway between these extremes would call for equality of taxation with other property and business.

It is true that public utility taxes are paid in large measure by the consumers of utility services. By decision of the Supreme Court of the United States, all taxes, including income and profit taxes, may be counted as business expenses in the determination of the "reasonable return" upon the fair capital value which is used as a basis for setting rates.[7] Justice Brandeis qualified his opinion with the suggestion that the privilege to count taxes as business expenses might be weighed in the determination of what constitutes a reasonable return. However, it is doubtful whether this qualification has had any practical bearing upon rates.

The theory that utility taxes are paid in the last analysis by the consumer needs to be qualified in two respects: first, where the utility's price is set by what the traffic will bear rather than by public authority, the rule does not necessarily hold; and, second, it may take considerable time for a change in utility taxes to work itself into utility rates. There is

---

[7] *Galveston Electric Co. v. City of Galveston,* 258 U.S. 388 (1922); also *Georgia Railway and Power Co. v. Railroad Commission of Georgia,* 262 U.S. 625 (1923).

some chance that taxes will never be reflected in rates. The wheels of utility regulation grind slowly and imperfectly.[8]

To return to the problem of the general level of utility taxes, it may be said that even though the taxes are borne by the consumers of utility services, these consumers are not identical with the general public, and therefore they should pay for the special services they receive. There are many other important taxes that are probably passed on in the main to the consumer without the latter putting in a claim for exemption on that account.

The proposition that monopoly profits may be recaptured through especially heavy taxation of utilities may, of course, be countered with the fact that utility rates are now subject to state regulation and therefore there should be no monopoly profits in the business. It may be doubted that state regulation has been sufficiently effective to have eliminated all excessive or monopoly profits from the utility business, but, even conceding this, one may still urge that the public seek to strengthen its regulation rather than impose discriminatory taxes. On the whole, the middle ground that utilities should pay taxes at the same level with other businesses seems most tenable.

The history of public utility taxation has frequently been divided into three periods: one of subsidy, lasting to about the end of the nineteenth century; one of neutral treatment, lasting from then to the depression of the 1930s; and one of special burdens, from the 1930s to the present. Whether the present tax system discriminates against public utilities may be questioned, but, in general, this historical division is a useful way to describe the trend.

THE AD VALOREM SYSTEM OF TAXING RAILROADS

Local versus State Assessment. A substantial number of states attempt to apply the property tax, frequently called the ad valorem system, to public utilities including railroads. Invariably this involves difficult problems of administration. It is obvious that the usual methods of assessment, at least in the case of railroads, are quite inadequate. It is impossible to evaluate a railroad properly in the enormous numbers of segments that local assessment involves. Local assessment means valuation by hundreds of untrained and unqualified local assessors. It offers no solution for evaluating and taxing rolling stock. Nearly all railroad

---

[8] As a matter of fact, the view that public utility taxes are to be borne by consumers was somewhat modified by the rate-making authorities in carrying out the price-freezing policies of the government during World War II. Rates were not, as a general rule, adjusted upward to meet the greatly increased burden of income and profits taxation. Probably in most cases, however, income after taxes was at least sufficient to constitute a fair rate of return.

property is still locally assessed in a number of states, but the trend is decidedly toward state assessment by the tax department or a similar agency. The problems of ad valorem taxation of railroads and many other utilities are so difficult that not only state assessment is required but also a well-staffed and efficient agency to perform the task.

The procedure employed for the assessment of railroads in the ad valorem states has, to some extent, become universalized. The procedure described below is that used in Wisconsin, except as variations in other states are noted.

1. *The Unit Rule.* A railroad is assessed according to the "unit rule"—that is, as an organism or system more or less independent of the value of its parts. The reasons for this procedure have already been suggested. It is thought that each part of the railroad has value only in so far as the whole has value. Piecemeal valuation of a railroad is like piecemeal valuation of a horse. What is the value of the left hind leg of a horse? The answer depends, of course, on all the other limbs and organs of the horse. Moreover, in the case of the railroad, the whole may not be equal to the sum of all its parts. The railroad may have an additional positive or negative intangible value as a result of many factors that add to or detract from its present and future earning power. This may be taken into account by assessment under the unit rule.

2. *Evidence of Value.*[9] What evidence of value should be weighed in making an ad valorem assessment of a railroad? Usually, the general property tax statute lays down the rule that property shall be assessed at market value—what it would bring in a free exchange. But railroads are not bought and sold every day as are many other kinds of property. Thus, in place of this the following are generally accepted as evidence of value.

The Value of the Outstanding Securities. Some indication of the market value of a railroad may be ascertained by observing how its stocks and bonds are selling. Though railroads may not be bought and sold every day, fractional equities in them are constantly being exchanged. From these exchanges, security values may be ascertained and totaled. Since unit-rule assessment seeks only the value of the operating property, it is necessary to subtract from the total value of securities the value of nonoperating property of the railroad. Nonoperating property, such as idle real estate, timberland, mines, and hotels, is assessed by the local assessor like other property of a similar nature. But another complication arises in that the *XYZ* railroad may own some of the securities of the *ABC* railroad. Since the *ABC* railroad is independently assessed,

---

[9] Problems of valuing utilities for tax purposes are frequently discussed in *Proceedings of the National Tax Association Conference.*

this influence, wherever it appears, must be discounted.[10] More universal as a limitation on the usefulness of stock and bond values in ad valorem assessment is the fact that such values fluctuate more or less violently as a result of speculative trends in the security market. People may sell or buy stocks not because of their own estimate of the future earning power of the company these securities represent, but rather on the expectation of "what average opinion expects the average opinion to be." [11] The stock of one large Wisconsin corporation during the panicky market of the depression of the 1930s dropped below the worth of the company measured by its liquid assets—that is, the company had cash enough in its treasury to buy up all its capital stock at the market value. Moreover, the security markets are greatly influenced by dividend policy and do not adequately appraise undistributed earnings.

Capitalized Income. The value of a railroad company can also be determined by dividing its expected income by an appropriate rate of interest. The expected income must be gauged largely by its past record of earnings. The past record should be a representative one and, for that reason, should cover a longer period than one year. If, for example, there has been a general depression or a war inflation in the past years, these facts should be taken into account in extending the period to be considered, in the rate of capitalization, or in the interpretation of the final results.

A major difficulty in the use of capitalized earnings is the choice of a rate of capitalization. The significance of the choice is evidenced by the fact that using a 5- rather than a 6-percent rate will make a difference of one sixth in the value figure. If the rate selected is merely that at which the stock and bond market is currently capitalizing the income of this railroad, then we are back to the stock-and-bond method of valuation with its limitations and without an independent second calculation. Again, some attention must be given to the fact that the market capitalizes dividends and undistributed profits at different rates. Some attention, however, must be given to the rate of interest that business of this kind must pay in order to float new securities and draw new capital

---

[10] Moreover, special situations arise where security values are obviously a poor measure of the value of the company they represent. Such a case occurs where the company being appraised has its securities guaranteed as to interest or principal by another company. Frequently, nonoperating assets have an influence upon security values that is not easily isolated. See C. M. Chapman, "Use of Railway Statistics and Accounts in Determining Taxable Valuations," *Proceedings of the National Tax Association Conference,* 1937, pp. 242–251. See also symposia on this and other aspects of utility taxation, *ibid.,* 1949, pp. 414–433; 1952, pp. 496–538.

[11] John Maynard Keynes, *The General Theory of Employment, Interest, and Money* (New York: Harcourt, Brace & World, 1936), p. 156.

into the industry. Some attention may also be given to the average rate of return in other lines of business, making due allowance, of course, for the element of risk. Actually, rates of capitalization in practice tend to be arbitrary and to pay great respect to a traditional 6 percent.

Physical Value. In the case of property that is freely reproducible, replacement cost is usually a reliable index of value and probably has some validity even with railroads. It is a curious fact that the better a railroad is maintained, the less its capitalized past income.[12] Physical value as distinct from other measurements is independent of the quality of management. Value is always somebody's opinion, and that of original and later investors (corrected for price changes and depreciation) is entitled to respect. Physical value data has the advantage of availability— the Interstate Commerce Commission maintains such information up to date.

The weakness of physical value as an indication of a proper tax base is that it looks too much to the past. Present value depends entirely on what can be got out of a property rather than what was put into it. Imprudent investors might have "sunk" a million dollars constructing a railroad into the Desert of Sahara. But with no traffic prospects the present value of such a venture would be negligible.

3. *Determination of Value.* Given the principal evidences of value suggested in the above discussion, there still remains the question of what weight to ascribe to each in order to arrive at a single figure. A well-equipped state tax department has the services of trained statisticians and accountants for gathering information on public utilities assessed by the department. Preceding the annual assessment, the statistical division presents full information concerning all of the above measures of value, as well as many other additional facts, such as gross income, ratio of previous year's taxes to gross income, salaries of officers, dividend record, previous assessments, and other data which may be useful to the department in making an assessment. The department then "goes into a huddle" and, on the basis of the information presented, comes out with a "preliminary assessment" of the railroad. The preliminary assessment is the basis for hearings at which taxpayers or others may endeavor to show that the preliminary assessment is in error. The department then deliberates a second time and produces the final assessment.

The "huddle" system of assessing railroads may be objected to because it is not scientific. In the opinion of experts there is no specific formula that could be generally applied to different properties in reaching a value that would do equal justice to all of them. A correct formula for one year might be incorrect when applied to the same property a year hence.

---

[12] High maintenance being deductible from such income.

It has been said that judgment, not formulas, "arrived at after skilled and careful consideration of all relevant data, facts, and relationships, is the base upon which the finding as to unit value of any complex property must rest. Let us not expect the impossible by assuming that a simple or even involved formula can be written and handed to a group of calculating machine operators to grind out satisfactory final answers as to value." [13]

4. Apportionment. In the case of utilities that extend into more than one state, there is the problem of determining what value to ascribe to the various parts of the system lying in the different states. This is much the same problem as that which confronts the state corporate income tax, and it is equally difficult and important. It is well established by legal opinion that apportionment must be on some fair basis that will show approximately the true proportion of the railroad or other utility in a given state.[14] In practice, however, the states are inclined to use formulas favorable to their own interest and thus to "import" values.

Factors that have some currency of usage in railroad apportionment are track mileage, traffic units (ton-miles of freight and passenger-miles of persons transported), locomotive and car mileage, physical value, gross income, and tons of traffic originating and terminating within the state. Administrators have been trying to evolve a procedure that might be described as model. It is clear that value is a product of physical plant and activity. The first is exemplified by physical property and track mileage; the latter by such items as indicate the "line haul" and the elaborate operations of starting and ending traffic. The latest development in apportionment techniques attempts to weight three factors according to the relative expenses associated with each. The factors are line haul, terminal activity, and property. The weighting is designed to take account of the varying character of railroads. The factors themselves are measured by traffic units for the line haul; tons originating, terminating, and delivered at connections for the terminal activity; and Interstate Commerce Commission appraisals for property. There are crudities still remaining in this procedure, but it is a promising and genuine attempt to get at the realities. State apportionment of interstate busi-

---

[13] A. G. Mott, "Weight To Be Given Physical Appraisals in Determining Unit Value Assessments for Railroads," *Proceedings of National Tax Association Conference,* 1937, p. 241.

[14] The use of track mileage as the sole basis of apportionment was declared contrary to the 14th Amendment in the North Dakota case of *Wallace v. Hines,* 253 U.S. 66 (1920). This single standard takes no account of density of traffic, the location of terminal property, and as a sole criterion would result in "importation" of value by certain states. An interesting discussion of the use and misuse of apportionment factors can be found in the *Proceedings of the National Tax Association Conference,* 1937, pp. 251–301.

ness impresses many as an attempt to divide the indivisible, but it cannot be avoided if the states are to retain their tax systems.[15]

5. *Determination of Rate.*   Once an assessment has been completed, the next problem is to determine what tax rate to apply to the value obtained. In Wisconsin the rule is to apply the "average state rate." This is arrived at by dividing the total property taxes of the state (including all its subdivisions) by the *equalized* value of all the property subject to assessment. It is important to use equalized rather than assessed value in determining the rate, because it is presumed that the railroads are assessed at full value; they could legitimately protest a rate built up on assessed values for other property. These assessed values might be considerably under true value, and a tax rate calculated on the basis of assessed values would be higher than one based on equalized values. Here the importance of tax department calculation of "equalized values" is again illustrated. Railroads are the victims of much discriminatory taxation when, as frequently happens, no adequate rate equalization occurs.

In many states, the value of railroad property is allocated back to each taxing district wherein railroad property is located, to be included on the local tax rolls and taxed as other property in the district. This apportionment is usually less refined than that between states and may be based on track mileage only, thus disregarding the value of other railroad property in certain districts.

6. *Disposition of Revenues.*   When the railroad taxes are collected by the state, there is a problem as to what disposition should be made of the revenues therefrom. Certain states leave the money in the state treasury. This avoids some difficult problems of local apportionment, but it is objectionable to municipalities with valuable terminal property or repair shops within their jurisdictions. Most states attempt to apportion railroad taxes (or property) to the counties or even smaller units of government. In such cases, in addition to the problem of equity involved in the method of apportionment, there is the question of why districts that have no railroad property but contribute traffic to the railroads should be excluded from the enjoyment of railroad taxes. In a few instances the boundary lines of school districts have been manipulated or gerrymandered to include a bit of railroad so as to help pay school taxes. On the whole, there is little doubt that railroad taxes are best suited for state revenue and that apportionment is a survival of the era when railroads were locally assessed.

Variety of Procedure among the States.   In practice, the application

---

[15] See symposium on this subject in *Proceedings of the National Tax Association Conference*, 1948, pp. 429–471.

of the property tax to railroads presents considerable variety of procedures among the states. Despite the wide recognition of its undesirability, predominant local assessment of ad valorem taxes is still found in a number of states. Thus, in Texas all utility property is locally assessed except the "intangibles" and rolling stock of railroads. This time-honored custom is protected by the Texas constitution. Nebraska has a system of central assessment but permits cities and villages to make independent assessments of all railroad property within their boundaries. In Illinois one railroad, the Illinois Central, is taxed (by contract) on gross earnings; all others are under the ad valorem system, though assessment is somewhat divided between central and local agencies.

TAXING RAILROADS UNDER THE GROSS EARNINGS TAX

A considerable number of states make no attempt to tax railroads under the property tax but apply in lieu thereof a gross earning tax.[16] In Minnesota, for example, the railroad tax consists of a 5-percent levy on gross operating revenue which is assessed by the tax department. The system avoids the necessity of annual valuation and is generally conceded to be considerably simpler than the ad valorem system. It does not avoid, however, the problem of apportionment, which is much the same under both systems.

Ad Valorem versus Gross Earnings Taxation of Railroads. The relative merits of these two methods of railroad taxation have been debated at quite some length. The proponents of the gross earnings tax base much of their case on the administrative difficulties and the subjective element involved in the ad valorem system.

> If the going value of public utility enterprises is determined by a capitalization of net income, the tax commission of other assessing body is put to the laborious task of determining net income only to have the figure so obtained capitalized by a ratio determined by arbitrary rule-of-thumb methods. . . . In practice the ad valorem assessment of public service enterprises generally resolves itself into a bargaining between the assessing body and the legal representatives of the taxed enterprise, the latter defending themselves against what they consider unreasonable valuations by the threat of litigation.[17]

---

[16] The gross earnings tax is used extensively in Minnesota, Connecticut, and Maine. Many states use it to cover some utilities or to supplement other taxes.— *Tax Systems,* 1950, pp. 262–269.

[17] W. J. Shultz, *American Public Finance and Taxation* (Englewood Cliffs, N.J.: Prentice-Hall, Inc., 1931), p. 514.

On the positive side, it is argued that the gross earnings tax is simpler and involves less arbitrariness in administration than the ad valorem tax. Moreover, by using income as the base, the tax applies to some extent the ability-to-pay principle.

Proponents of the ad valorem system contend that it is not incompatible with good administration. Valuation is a feature of the general property tax and is nowhere determined by formula without the exercise of judgment. It seems probable that a tax department with a good personnel could assess railroads at least as efficiently as most other property is assessed.

And the proponents of the ad valorem system are not without ammunition for counterattack. They observe, first of all, that in states where the gross receipts tax is used, an attempt is made to adjust the rates on gross receipts so that companies as a whole will pay about the same amount as they would were they under the general property tax. This weakens the alleged advantage of the gross earnings tax as to simplicity of administration. States using the gross earnings tax must check periodically to see that rates are adequate. In doing so, they usually make an ad valorem assessment of the utility to compare the taxes under the gross earnings system with what they would be under the ad valorem system. This seems to indicate that the ad valorem system furnishes the standard of equity even in states using the other system; it also shows that these states, too, must resort to "arbitrary methods" in order to test their own system.

The end sought in the taxation of railroads is that of neutrality with other property. Neutrality is maintained with difficulty where assessment is in terms of an entirely different medium than that used generally. Moreover, gross earnings taxes are less flexible than an advalorem levy; the former can be changed only by legislative act. Gross earnings fluctuate with the business cycle more than property; this may be in accordance with ability to pay, but it again violates neutrality with other business.

It is apparent that both of these systems of taxing railways are open to important objections. Probably it is reasonable to conclude that the ad valorem system at its best is more equitable and less arbitrary than its principal alternative. But the ad valorem system requires very high-grade administration for its success, especially since assessments may have to be adjusted annually, and, in the absence of such administration, the gross earnings tax may be preferable. Taxation of railroads is by no means confined to the ad valorem and gross earnings taxes. Many states apply other forms of business taxes to these utilities, notably, the capital stock tax and the corporate excess tax.

TAXATION OF OTHER UTILITIES

Problems in the taxation of telephone and telegraph companies are not very different from those applying to railroads. Light, heat, and power companies have increased greatly in importance in recent years and, through consolidations and development of transmission lines, have assumed statewide and even interstate proportions. Local assessment survives in this field to an even greater degree than in the case of railroads. Likewise, the same objections prevail here, particularly those concerned with the inadequacy of local personnel and the impossibility of assessing adequately "one leg of the horse." As in the case of railroads, a wide variety of business taxes outside the ad valorem tax are also applied to other utilities.

OTHER PROBLEMS IN UTILITY TAXATION

Double Standard for Rate-making and Taxation. In many state legislatures at each session, and sometimes between sessions, one or more legislators demand to know why, in the name of common sense, the commission that determines the price to be charged the buying public should have one set of values for rate-making purposes while the tax department has a totally different one for taxation purposes. The legislator is convinced that a given utility is escaping its just share of taxes because it "gets away with one value for rates and another for taxes."

If it were merely a matter of two distinct bodies determining two different values, the double standard could be easily eliminated. But the explanation lies deeper than that. The rate base is not really a value at all. It is simply an estimate, made by the utility commission, on the value of the investment upon which the utility is to be allowed to make a fair return, the return being determined by the rate which would be sufficient to draw additional capital into the utility business. The price which the consumer must pay is adjusted to yield this return, on the assumption that certain demand and other market conditions will prevail. On the other hand, the tax base is truly a value. By statute it must represent, as nearly as can be determined, the selling value of the utility at the time chosen for the assessment.

If all investments in utility property were wisely made, if regulation were perfect, and if prevailing economic conditions were constant, the tax base and the rate base would approximately correspond. But none of these conditions always exists in fact. For example, if demand declines or costs rise, then the existing rate schedule cannot yield a fair return on the investment that the commission used in setting the rates. Consequently, the selling value of the utility would decline, and therefore a discrepancy would exist between the rate base and the tax base.

Thus, in the case of a defunct railroad the rate base will be much higher than the tax base. The company cannot earn a fair return upon either its investments or the cost of reproducing its plant, which are the factors that must be taken into account when a rate problem is presented to the rate commission. Were the tax department to impose an assessment upon this company equal to its rate base, it would be violating the statutory standard of assessment as well as the uniformity clause found in most state constitutions. The company must be assessed at its exchange value. And no one would buy this property without taking much account of its present and prospective earnings.

On the other hand, a strong utility presents an entirely different picture. The excess of tax base over rate base might be attributable to the unusually favorable location in which the company finds itself and its privilege of monopolizing this favorable location; it might be traceable to the failure of regulation (or at least its slowness) in reducing rates to the point where service is furnished at cost. In any case, the earning power is there and, except for the portion which is attributable to management, it can be passed on to a buyer in exchange. Therefore, it must be assessed.

A tax base is ordinarily determined in large part by a capitalization of earnings; to use this factor in setting a rate base would involve circular reasoning (earnings determine rate base and rate base determines earnings). Thus, it is clear that the rate base and the tax base are two quite different things which ordinarily cannot be reconciled. Probably this explanation will never entirely satisfy the legislator who makes the inquiry. But the double standard is usually written in both the statutory law and the constitution, and, in addition, is defensible as a matter of equity.

Taxation of Utilities under the Net Income Tax. The question of whether utilities subject to the ad valorem tax should also pay a net income tax (in states that have one) raises some interesting issues.

Utilities claim that under the unit rule and ad valorem assessment, their net income is taken into account in making their property tax assessments and that to tax them again upon their net income would be double taxation. Through a process of assessment that takes into account capitalized net income, one of the factors determining value, utilities are assessed, so they argue, upon intangible property. The intangibles, whether passing under the name of good will, franchise value, or corporate excess, are all included in the value of the franchise assessed under the unit rule. In states where intangibles are exempt from the property tax, the utilities say that they alone among property taxpayers are assessed on such intangibles and that it is no more than fair, consequently, to exempt them from the net income tax.

Those who argue that a utility should pay an income tax like any other corporation claim that the same standard of assessment holds for utilities as for other properties. In all cases, the standard of assessment is what a property will sell for at a bona fide private sale. Moreover, it is contended that under regulation a utility is expected to furnish service at cost—that is, under conditions which will yield a fair return upon its capital. Except for the lag in or failure of regulation, there would be no excess earnings upon which "intangibles" could be based. In other words, as Professor Commons has ingeniously phrased it, the "good will" of a utility is the "good will of politicians." On this reasoning it is contended that the utility has no ground for complaint if its intangibles are included under both the income and property tax.

The Disposition of Utility Tax Revenues. Under many state laws, utility property centrally assessed is apportioned among the local governments for taxation or, as in Wisconsin (except for railroads), the tax itself is in large part apportioned. Apportionment of assessment is usually on the basis of mileage or physical property; apportionment of taxes may be on a similar basis or it may include sales as a factor. Sales are less concentrated than property, but the distribution that results, even from apportionment with equal weight accorded to both factors, gives very substantial revenues to a relatively few municipalities. These few municipalities often receive more revenue than they are entitled to or can use to good advantage.

The contention will be made, of course, that any taxation district has as much right to tax the utility resources within its borders as it has to tax its soil or its factories. However, the problem must be solved by weighing the social consequences of alternative policies. There is a substantial difference between localizing the revenues from factories and farms, on the one hand, and doing the same with a public utility generating plant, on the other. The public utility plant involves very little additional public expense to the district in which it is located. Very little new education and/or public welfare programs are made necessary because a utility property is located in a district.

The likely conclusion in regard to revenues from utility taxes is that they should be earmarked for state and county use to a much greater degree than is now the rule. This conclusion would probably be accepted by most students of the subject. But important vested interests (of municipalities) have been built upon the existing practices, and these vested interests are likely to hold their own for the most part against a sounder and more equitable distribution.

Taxation of Municipally Owned Utilities. A majority of the states exempt public property from all taxes regardless of how it may be used. Of course, this includes publicly owned utility property. As far as local taxes are concerned, the exemption may result in no loss of revenue; a sum equivalent to taxes may be set aside from the earnings of the utility and transferred to the general city account. Local taxes in the case of a municipally owned utility are a bookkeeping transfer in any event. However, the bookkeeping transfer as a substitute for taxes is confusing. And, of course, it does not include the equivalent of taxes due to central units of government. The Tennessee Valley Authority pays local governments some equivalent of local taxes, but the payment is by federal legislation and is more or less gratuitous. Municipally owned public utilities pay no state or federal income taxes.

There is a strong case for the view that utility companies, whether publicly or privately owned, should be taxed on the same basis as other business enterprises. Municipal ownership is looked upon by many as a yardstick with which to measure the efficiency of private business under public regulation. This yardstick is more suitable when there are no differences in tax burdens. The consumers of publicly owned utilities owe something to the state and municipal treasures for the benefits they receive from government. There are valid grounds of support for public ownership of utilities, but avoidance of the federal income tax is not one of them. A municipally owned utility should not only make its contribution to local expenses but also to the state and county expenses.

The exemption of publicly owned utilities, especially from income taxes, is not only firmly rooted in constitutional law; it also rests upon the strategic advantage of business not conducted primarily for profit. In some respects publicly owned utilities have the same strategic tax advantages as cooperatives. Were they taxed on their earnings, they could start playing "giveaway" instead of checkers, allowing their rate payers the advantage that formerly went to their taxpayers.

Taxation of Air Transportation. The taxation of air transportation is still in its formative stages. This field was called sharply to public attention by an important decision of the United States Supreme Court [18] sustaining a personal property tax by Minnesota upon the entire fleet of the Northwestern Airlines, notwithstanding the fact that its routes traversed eight states and that the other states in which stops were made taxed some part of the fleet. Minnesota's claim to such wide jurisdiction rests upon the fact that it is the corporate domicile of the company—that is, the state from which the company received its charter. A concurring opinion expressed the view that air transportation is the special province of the federal government and that Congress might control its taxation

[18] *Northwestern Airlines v. Minnesota,* 322 U.S. 292 (1944).

(as in the case of national banks [19]) but that states had the prerogative applied in Minnesota in the absence of legislative enactment. Congress subsequently called upon the Civil Aeronautics Board for advice upon which to found legislation outlining or prescribing a tax system for airplane transportation.

The Board's recommendations, largely confined to matters of apportionment, were filed but were not enacted into law. Congress laid the matter on the table, following assurances by state administrators that they would solve the problem without legislation. The apportionment system recommended called for the use of three factors: originating and terminating traffic, originating revenues, and scheduled arrivals and departures. Minnesota has adopted an apportionment formula though with some departures from the suggested model.

Most of the states employ the property tax to tax airplane companies, some applying the unit rule, some assessing flight equipment independently. The tax is not very productive because these businesses own relatively little property. Airports are publicly provided and not taxed. Companies do pay some fees for their use but not enough to cover capital costs. The gasoline tax of the federal government extends to air transportation, but again the amount does not fully cover a very considerable outlay of expense. However, the federal government also collects a 5 percent tax on airplane tickets. Less than half the states extend motor fuel taxes to air transportation. There are other types of taxes applied sporadically along with the general federal and occasional state corporate income taxes. Thus, air transportation along with trucking is involved in the difficult problem of neutral taxation for competing forms of transportation.[20]

SUMMARY

In addition to general taxes, business in general is often subjected to special taxes. These special taxes are sometimes supported on nonfiscal grounds, mainly as a possible means of checking the size of business units. But the soundest and strongest support of them is based on fiscal grounds, contending that business enjoys special benefits for which it may

---

[19] See Chapter 17.

[20] Richard W. Lindholm, *Public Finance of Air Transportation,* Bureau of Business Research (Columbus: Ohio State University, 1948); *Multiple Taxation of Air Commerce,* House Document No. 141, 79th Cong., 1st Sess., 1945; "Final Report of the Committee on Taxation of Transportation" (George W. Mitchell, chairman), *Proceedings of the National Tax Association Conference,* 1951, pp. 347–375.

equitably be charged a tax and that such levies yield substantial revenue. The argument is somewhat confused because of the uncertain incidence of business taxes.

Among the familiar methods of general business taxation, the most common are the gross income and sales taxes, occupation taxes, capital stock taxes, and corporate excess taxes. In practice, all of these are open to important objections because of their erratic results, arbitrary classification, or weak administration. A single composite business tax based upon net income, with an alternative levy based upon gross income, would be an improvement over the existing confusion of state business taxes.

Turning to the taxation of special business, attention in this chapter was confined to the problems of taxing public utilities. The consensus is that public utilities should be subjected to the general level of taxes applied to other business. The ad valorem system of taxing railroads, quite generally applied, is conspicuously ill adapted to local assessment. State assessment may apply the unit rule and assess the railroad as an organism. This method of administration also encounters many difficult problems, chief of which is the determination of an exchange value for property that rarely exchanges. Among the evidences of value customarily employed are the value of outstanding securities, capitalized income, and physical value. Of these, most weight is usually attached to capitalized income though it encounters a major difficulty in avoiding an arbitrary rate of capitalization. Once an assessment is determined, apportionment between the taxing state and other states is necessary, and in some cases, unfortunately, values are also apportioned to local districts. Scientific apportionment involves a proper choice among many factors and proper weighting to those selected.

Railroads are also taxed by several other methods, of which the tax on gross earnings is most common. The relative merits of gross earnings and ad valorem taxation as applied to railroads has been the subject of much argument. Proponents of each system accuse the other system of being arbitrary. With excellent administration the ad valorem method is probably superior, but the gross earnings system is the choice where administration is weak.

Other utilities present much the same problems of taxation as railroads, though local assessment is more common in the case of the former. These businesses require state assessment (at least of interdistrict properties) for satisfactory results.

Special problems in the field of public utility taxation arise in the acceptance of two distinct values, one for rate making and another for taxation; in the disposition of utility taxes according to origin; and in the application of the tax system to municipally owned utilities. The taxation of airplane transportation presents interesting new problems of multiple taxation and neutrality of burdens on competing forms of transportation.

PROBLEMS

1. Assume the following facts concerning a railroad which operates in State *X:*
   a. Its net earnings in 1957 were $24 million. During the two previous years the net earnings had averaged $22 million.
   b. The road had outstanding 200,000 shares of stock and 300,000 bonds. Average quotations on New York exchanges showed the stock selling at $500 per share and the bonds at $1000 each.
   c. The Interstate Commerce Commission's valuation of the railroad was $410 million.
   d. The railroad had gross earnings in 1957 of $150 million.
   e. An average of several ratios (including mileage of road, traffic units, etc.) showed 25 percent of the railroad's total property to be located in State *X.*
   f. The assessed value of all taxable general property in the state in 1957 was $4.8 billion; the equalized value was $5.4 billion. The total general property taxes were $110 million.

   Using the above data, show quite concretely how the state would set about taxing this railroad.

2. Does determining the value of a public utility for tax purposes by capitalizing its income involve circular reasoning? Why?

3. List the factors that may result in a tax base for a public utility that differs from its rate base.

4. Why would the use of mileage as the sole factor in the apportionment of railroad property in the case of North Dakota tend to "import value"?

5. Of the corporate excess and capital stock tax, which is it that aims at all of the intangibles of a corporation?

6. On what legal theory does the Supreme Court sanction the levy of a franchise tax on domestic corporations without apportionment? How do some states take advantage of this situation?

7. Comment upon the proposition that physical value is a relevant but inconclusive datum in the valuation of a railroad.

8. What unneutralities are involved in the present tax treatment of publicly owned utilities?

9. Why is tax neutrality difficult to maintain when utilities are taxed on gross income?

10. Wherein does property tax equalization serve a useful purpose in applying the ad valorem tax to railroads?

11. Why does the stock-and-bond value of a utility often disagree with its capitalized income?

12. Explain the process (and precautions necessary) in capitalizing income to arrive at the value of a utility.

13. What has the "pay-out" policy of a railroad (proportion of earnings declared as dividends) got to do with the market value of securities and the rate at which the market capitalizes net earnings?

14. Explain the legal distinction between the subject and measure of a tax and give illustrations of this distinction.

15. Comment on the proposition: Capitalized income can be used in evaluation of utilities for taxation purposes but not for rate making.

17

SPECIAL TAXES ON BANKS, INSURANCE COMPANIES, AND CHAIN STORES

The last chapter was devoted to taxes on business in general and the special problems relating to the taxation of public utilities. Further attention is here given to the taxation of banks, insurance companies, and chain stores. The first is of substantial interest in its own right; the second brings into sharp focus the problem of neutrality in taxation; and the third affords a springboard for consideration of the relation of taxation to monopoly.

TAXATION OF BANKS

SPECIAL CHARACTERISTICS OF BANKS

From the standpoint of taxation, there are at least four important respects in which banks differ from most other businesses. The first is that banks carry a stock of intangible goods. Their assets consist mainly of various promises to pay, such as paper money, bonds, notes (some of them secured by mortgages), and the like. Banks specialize in the promises-to-pay of commercial customers who borrow when buying goods and pay when the goods are sold. A mercantile company has a stock of *tangible* goods upon which it usually pays property taxes. Perhaps the banking corporation should pay taxes upon its stock of *intangible* goods, but the fact that they are intangible and representative (of tangible goods) is an important difference.

In the second place, some banks are chartered by the federal government and are considered to be federal instrumentalities by the courts. Federal instrumentalities cannot be taxed by the states except by permission of the federal government. This goes back to an old and very important decision rendered by Chief Justice Marshall of the United States Supreme Court.[1] The decision declared unconstitutional a discriminatory state tax on a federal-owned bank. Subsequent decisions have established the fact that federal-chartered banks can be taxed by the states, with or without discrimination, only as Congress permits and prescribes.

Banks are also unique in their monetary powers. They are privileged to create credit by loaning what they do not have—that is, beyond their capital and reserves—subject to certain rules prescribed by the government.

Finally, banks are important owners of government securities, especially those of the federal government. By long-standing judicial tradition this gives them certain immunities from state taxation.

"SECTION 5219"

The separate treatment of banks in state taxation has grown mainly out of the second special characteristic. It commenced in 1863 when Congress limited the state taxation of national banks organized under the National Banking Act. The act was amended in 1868, and the legislation as amended emerged as the now familiar "Section 5219." [2] This section prescribed certain rules for bank taxation. Its two main provisions were: first, real estate owned by the bank might be taxed like other real estate; second, additional taxes might be levied on the stockholders' shares but at no higher rate than that imposed on "other moneyed capital in the hands of individual citizens." The second tax was theoretically on the shareholders rather than on the bank, and in some instances the courts held bank taxes invalid where shares were listed under the name of the bank rather than under the names of the individual share-holders.[3] Nevertheless, collection was usually from the bank itself, and the tax has been considered a bank tax.[4]

---

[1] *McCulloch v. Maryland,* 4 Wheat., 316 (1819).
[2] Ronald B. Welch, *State and Local Taxation of Banks in the United States,* New York State Tax Commission, Special Report No. 7 (Albany, 1934), p. 16.
[3] *First National Bank of Gulfport v. Adams,* 258 U.S. 362 (1922).
[4] To avoid double taxation many states provided that the value of a bank's

The rule that national bank shares could not be taxed at a higher rate than that imposed on other money capital in the hands of individual citizens was, for over fifty years, quite universally interpreted to mean that national bank shares could not be taxed at a higher rate than state bank shares. The federal statute sets no upper limit for the state taxation of state banks, but in the interest of fair competition most states have never discriminated against state banks. For the most part they have taxed all banks in the manner outlined in Section 5219. Meanwhile, however, efforts were being made in many states to modify the general property tax in order to make the tax on intangible property more effective and equitable. In some states, such as Wisconsin, modification took the form of a complete exemption of intangible property. In other states, such as Virginia, modification came about through classification of property and the application of low flat rates to intangibles. However, most states that adopted one or the other of these modifications retained the bank shares tax without any change. It was felt that this tax was well administered and that banks were generally prosperous businesses, quite able to pay taxes upon their intangible property.

The Richmond Bank Decision and Its Effect. In 1921 the United States Supreme Court, in the case of *Merchants National Bank v. City of Richmond*,[5] put an end to the special classification of bank shares. The Court held that "other money capital in the hands of individual citizens" included "not only moneys invested in private banking . . . but investments of individuals in securities that represent money at interest and other evidences, of indebtedness such as normally enter into the business of banking. . . ."[6] Broadly speaking, the Court interpreted "other money capital" to include not only state bank shares, but also a very considerable portion of the whole field of intangible property. This meant apparently, that the classified-property-tax states would have to surrender their tax on bank shares at general property tax rates or revert to the old system of including all or most intangibles in the general property tax base. The states were not prepared to accept either of these alternatives and vigorously protested the decision of the Court.[7]

In 1923, in response to numerous protests, Congress amended Section 5219 to liberalize the taxation restrictions on national banks and make them more flexible. Two other methods of taxing national banks were added to the shares tax, but only one of them might be used by any one state and then only in lieu of the shares tax. Banks might be taxed on their shares *or* their net income *or* on their dividends. If the net in-

---

real estate should be deducted from the value of its shares before they were put upon the assessment rolls.

[5] 256 U.S. 635 (1921).   [6] *Ibid.*, p. 639.

[7] Some twenty states found the validity of established practices in the taxation of banks seriously imperiled as a result of this decision.

come alternative were chosen, the rate must not be higher than that imposed on the income of other financial corporations nor higher than the highest rate imposed upon mercantile, manufacturing, and business corporations. Furthermore, the tax on dividends must not be higher than that imposed upon dividends from other moneyed capital. However, if both corporate income and dividends were generally taxed, they might both be taxed in the case of banks.[8]

Congress amended Section 5219 in 1926 to provide for a fourth alternative method of taxing national banks. By this new provision the states might impose an excise tax upon the franchise of a bank, the value of the franchise to be "measured by" or "according to" the net income of the bank. Attempts were soon made to measure the franchise by the total net income of the bank, including what would otherwise be tax-exempt interest on government bonds. The interest on these bonds is an extremely important item in the accounts of many banks. The amendment permitted the states to do indirectly what they could not do directly. After some wavering, this indirect taxation of interest received was sanctioned by the Court.[9]

EXPERIENCE OF CERTAIN STATES WITH BANK TAXATION

States have had a variety of experience with bank taxation. Some of them, Illinois for example, have continued to levy a bank shares tax, protected in this course by the fact that their other intangible property was subject, nominally at least, to the full general property tax. Other states, such as Wisconsin, have shifted from taxing the banking business (except for bank real estate) under the property tax to taxing it under their net income tax. The shift has resulted in a considerable loss of revenue and has been criticized for undue leniency to the banks. Especially conspicuous is the fact that the banks, in some cases, escape taxation even

---

[8] The amendment also added a phrase which was thought to wipe out the effect of the Richmond decision and make possible, by classification, the separation of bank stock from other intangibles for taxation purposes. It stipulated that rates on national bank shares must not be higher than those on "other moneyed capital in the hands of individual citizens . . . coming into competition with the business of national banks," and added a proviso that "bonds, notes, or other evidences of indebtedness in the hands of individual citizens not employed or engaged in the banking business and representing merely personal investments not made in competition with such business, shall not be deemed moneyed capital within the meaning of this section." Many observers were of the opinion that this proviso limited "moneyed capital" to property employed in the banking business. These people were disappointed when the Supreme Court handed down its decision in the case of *First National Bank of Hartford v. Hartford,* 273 U.S. 548 (1927). The decision held, in effect, that the proviso added nothing to the "no-discrimination" clause that had existed previously.

[9] *MacAllen v. Massachusetts,* 279 U.S. 620 (1929); *Pacific Co. v. Johnson,* 285 U.S. 480 (1932).

on their *tangible* personal property, such as bank furniture and fixtures. California and several other states have attempted to meet these criticisms by imposing a franchise tax measured by net income, a procedure which allows what would otherwise be tax-exempt interest in the tax base. Washington, with no net income tax and no tax on intangibles, has been unable to make any special levy on banks. Minnesota maintained a bank tax system for a time by "gentlemen's agreement" and now levies an income tax at a special high rate. The latter procedure is defended on the legally doubtful grounds that no discrimination can be proved so long as the total tax burden upon banks is not higher than that upon competitors. Some states try to balance burdens more precisely each year and apply a rate to the banking business based on this annual calculation. This process involves many uncertainties and questionable comparisons. Iowa and Virginia apply to bank shares the special rates applicable to other intangible property. Many state tax departments have repeatedly recommended further amendment of the federal statutes to permit a return of the old shares tax without readoption of the property tax as to other intangible property.

FURTHER PROBLEMS OF BANK TAXATION

The unique history of bank taxation suggests many problems of policy. Does the federal government need to protect not only national banks but, in effect, the whole banking business from such taxes as state legislative discretion might otherwise dictate? The franchise tax may seem to offer the states a generous alternative, but it raises many problems. Can the tax be applied to banks and not to building-and-loan associations and insurance companies? Would a compromise net income tax be acceptable under which the banks would be required to allocate expenses (pro rata) against tax-exempt income, thus reducing deductions? Can and should government securities be (specially) taxed where they are employed in the conduct of a business? Questions of bank tax policy became lost in a tangle of political and legal matters associated with the congressional legislation on the subject.

TAXATION OF INSURANCE COMPANIES

After banks, the first businesses to break away from the general property tax were insurance companies.[10] But, unlike banks, insurance companies were never protected by the federal government. In fact, they have not

---

[10] E. R. A. Seligman, *Essays in Taxation* (10th ed., New York: The Macmillan Company, 1925), p. 161.

even been accorded the federal protection that is usually extended to other interstate corporations under the commerce clause of the Constitution. This is due to the Supreme Court's decision early in the present century, which held that insurance is not commerce, either state or interstate, and might therefore be taxed without violating the Constitution. Although the Court has changed its view and has now held insurance companies subject to the operation of antitrust laws, this has as yet had no effect on taxation.[11] Thus, where there has been a relatively high degree of uniformity in the taxation of banks, there has been an impressive diversity in that of insurance companies.

SHOULD INSURANCE COMPANIES BE TAXED?

Insurance companies frequently claim they should be exempt from all except real estate taxes. They argue, first, that their property is mainly of an intangible character, consisting of such assets as bonds, notes, and mortgages. They maintain (as do the banks) that the taxation of these assets constitutes double taxation since this property is only representative of other property. Second, these companies hold that they (particularly life insurance companies) perform a valuable service for the state in preventing dependent people from becoming public charges; this service, they say, has as much claim to tax exemption as that performed by benevolent societies, which are exempt. Thirdly, they argue that much of their business is conducted by mutual companies, which are cooperatives and nonprofit-making institutions. Receipts in excess of expenses go to policyholders in payment of losses or in reduced cost of insurance. Fourth, it is claimed that the incidence of insurance taxes is on the policyholders, many of whom are poor farmers, office employees, and clerks who should be relieved of taxes rather than burdened with additional ones.

These are plausible arguments, but they have not succeeded in bringing about immunity from taxes. Probably the strongest argument for taxing the insurance companies is that even so, considering the nature of their business, they will bear no higher burdens than other lines. Strong sentiment supports neutrality in taxation; if one business is taxed, the others should be meted similar treatment. Thus we may put the question in reverse: Why shouldn't insurance companies be taxed?

Insurance, particularly in the United States, has grown to a business of enormous size. Someone has compared the insurance business to a

---

[11] *New York Life Insurance Co. v. Deer Lodge County,* 231 U.S. 508 (1913). See also *United States v. South-Eastern Underwriters' Association,* 322 U.S. 533 (1944).

Mississippi River of dollars flowing across the country; legislators, sorely pressed for new revenue sources, could hardly be expected to forego the temptation to divert a little of this stream into the public treasury.

Nature of the Insurance Business and Insurance Taxation. The insurance business is a fairly complicated mechanism but, in general, its outline may be briefly sketched as follows: Policyholders pay gross premiums to the company, and these premiums are used to meet losses and business expenses. A reserve is frequently maintained in the form of investments that provide an investment income. The company may be either building up or using up its reserves, depending upon the trend of the business and the age of the policyholders. If gross premiums and investment income exceed losses, expenses, and what is set aside for reserve, the excess may be retained as surplus or distributed as dividends to the stockholders or policyholders, or both.

In the course of this movement of wealth and property, there are many different places where the state may levy a tax. In practice, the methods of taxing insurance companies in the United States vary from state to state: levies are imposed on almost everything from gross premiums to dividends. The most common form of levy is the gross premiums tax similar in some respects to a sales tax. Gross income from investment is also used as a tax base and a few states tax stock (patterned after the old bank tax). States have indulged extensively in mercantilistic practices in their treatment of insurance companies. They have sought to aid (or protect) through retaliatory and reciprocal clauses in their tax laws the firms they have chartered. They say, in effect, "we will spare or punish your companies on the business they do in our state, depending upon how you treat our companies." This practice has created much confusion in insurance taxation. Unneutralities abound between foreign and domestic companies; different lines of insurance (as fire and life); different forms of organization (as mutual and stock); and insurance and other business.

The Net Income Tax. The federal government taxes insurance companies, along with banks, on their net income. The net income of life insurance companies is peculiarly difficult to determine because of long contracts, uncertain obligations, and (often) patronage dividends.

After much experimentation and some frustration the following method (with many qualifications) of applying the federal net income tax to life insurance companies was accepted in 1959: the base shall include (1) investment income in excess of that adequate to maintain reserves; (2) one half of other net gain (underwriting profits chiefly); and (3) the other half of other net income when distributed to shareholders. In general, mutuals and stock companies are treated alike, but the former can more readily avoid underwriting profits by declaring dividends to policy holders.[12]

Under the federal income tax, insurance received is ordinarily not taxed to the recipient unless he is the insured, and then only so far as his insurance exceeds his investment; annuities are taxed to the extent of the interest factor involved. Insurance that matures at death is ordinarily treated for tax purposes as part of the estate of the insured, though some states allow a special exemption of a specified sum. The treatment of insurance at the personal level, as previously suggested, involves many difficult problems.

TAXATION OF CHAIN STORES

JUSTIFICATION

Chapter 5 presented the alleged inequities of the property tax as applied to merchants, and particularly to chain stores as compared with independent merchants. These inequalities are said to arise because of the relatively greater inaccessibility of property tax information in the case of chain stores, their higher turnover with smaller inventory, stock manipulation, and so on. It is argued that these alleged unneutralities justify special taxation of chain stores.

In addition to and separate from the contention that chain stores enjoy tax advantages under the property tax is the contention that they enjoy certain unfair economic advantages. It is said that because of their size they are able to buy at a greater discount and that this advantage is an unfair one that should be compensated for by special taxes. Beyond this there is the argument that the chain store is a social menace and that it should be taxed either out of existence or at least to a degree that will discourage its development. The chain store tax is of principal interest as an attempt to tax business according to size.

PRACTICE

Less than a third of the states now have some kind of special tax on chain stores. The most common type of tax is one determined by the number of stores in the chain. The longer the chain, the higher the average tax per store. Usually only the stores located in the state are counted in determining the length of the chain, but Louisiana graduates

---

[12] For an elaborate discussion of the problem see Ways and Means Committee, *Tax Revision Compendium*, 1959, vol. 3, pp. 1983–2066.

its rates according to the number of stores in the chain throughout the country.[13] Until the Supreme Court held it unconstitutional,[14] another type of tax on chains was in effect in a number of states. This was a graduated tax on sales. Occasionally single-unit stores were also included in this system. Novel features in chain store legislation include the use of either floor space or the number of counters in the stores as a tax base.

LEGALITY OF CHAIN STORE TAX

Sustention of Indiana Law. An interesting series of judicial opinions have been handed down concerning the constitutional validity of special chain store taxes. In the case of *State Board of Tax Commissioners v. Jackson,*[15] the Supreme Court by a 5–4 decision sustained an Indiana law of the unit type which graduated the tax from $3 on one store to $25 for each store in excess of twenty. The issue in this case turned on whether the segregation of chain stores for special taxation was reasonable classification. Justice Sutherland, for the minority, contended that the fact that business is carried on under more than one roof is not a sufficient basis for separate classification and that there is no necessary correlation between chaining and the size of a business or the volume of its trade. A department store may do as much business as a chain of smaller stores. Justice Roberts, for the majority opinion, held that the chain feature might be considered as giving a business additional ability to pay. To support this contention, he cited the standardization of equipment and display, the more rapid turnover, the uniformity of store management, the special accounting methods, and the unified sales policy which are regular features of chain store business.

Unconstitutionality of Florida Law. Two years after the Indiana law was sustained, the Court by a 6–3 decision declared unconstitutional the Florida chain store tax.[16] The Florida law differed from the Indiana law in that it classified chains according to whether or not they extended into more than one county. The majority held this to be unreasonable classification. "There is no more reason for adopting the county line as the measure of the tax than there would be for taking ward lines in cities, or arbitrary lines drawn through the state regardless of county boundaries." [17] Justice Brandeis in his dissent stated that "size alone gives to giant corporations a social significance not attached ordinarily to smaller units of private enterprise," [18] and added that the state has as much right

---

[13] Rates in Louisiana range up to $550 per store on units in excess of 500.

[14] *Stewart Dry Goods Co. v. Lewis,* 294 U.S. 550 (1935).

[15] 283 U.S. 527 (1931).

[16] *Louis K. Liggett Co. v. Lee,* 288 U.S. 517 (1933).

[17] *Ibid.,* p. 534.　　　　　　　　[18] *Ibid.,* p. 565.

to prohibit the excessive size of a business as to prohibit the excessive size of motor trucks and the height of buildings. He contended that it is not unreasonable for a legislature to believe that certain chain stores further the concentration of wealth and power, promote absentee ownership, convert independent tradesmen into clerks, and sap "the resources, the vigor and the hope of the smaller cities and towns." [19]

Sustention of West Virginia Law. In the case of *Fox v. Standard Oil Company of New Jersey,*[20] again a 5–4 decision, the Court sustained a West Virginia statute of the unit type ranging to a top rate of $250 on stores in excess of seventy-five.[21] Justice Cardozo, in the opinion of the Court, stated that if the classification is reasonable, the Court will not examine the degree of tax. He went even further by quoting an earlier case that held that, even if the tax should destroy a business, it would not be made invalid or require compensation upon that ground alone.[22] The Indiana case was cited as precedent for holding the classification reasonable.

Unconstitutionality of Kentucky Law. In the case of *Stewart Dry Goods Company v. Lewis,*[23] the Court (with three justices dissenting) held a Kentucky statute unconstitutional. The Kentucky law differed from previous chain store taxes in two ways: first, instead of graduating the tax according to the number of units, the tax was graduated with reference to the volume of sales of a business; it varied from $\frac{1}{20}$ of 1 percent on the first $400,000 of sales to 1 percent on sales over $1 million. Secondly, no specific reference was made to chain stores; both independent and chain stores were required to pay the tax. In its operation both the large chains and the large department stores would be especially burdened. The Court held that classification by volume of sales alone was arbitrary and unreasonable. The Court said also that if some corrective for the general property tax is required it should be a net income tax or a flat sales tax.[24]

---

[19] *Ibid.,* p. 569.   [20] 294 U.S. 87 (1935).

[21] The Standard Oil Company submitted evidence that proved that this was primarily a tax on chain filling stations; that these chains, if so they might be called, paid 84.46 percent of the tax while doing only 4.6 percent of the chain store business. The Standard Oil Company alone, it was alleged, paid 42.16 percent of the tax. It was contended that filling stations were not chain stores, but the very inclusive character of the definition of the term "store" in the statute was cited to refute this contention. The law stated "the term 'store' as used in this act shall be construed to mean and include any store or stores or any mercantile establishment or establishments which are owned, operated, maintained and/or controlled by the same person, firm, corporation, copartnership, or association, either domestic or foreign, in which goods, wares, or merchandise of any kind are sold, either at retail or wholesale"—*Ibid.,* p. 95.

[22] *Alaska Fish Salting and By-Products Co. v. Smith,* 255 U.S. 44 (1921).

[23] 294 U.S. 550 (1935).

[24] Justice Cardozo for the minority contended that there might be a correlation

Importance of "Thickness" as well as Length of Chain. Whether a tax based upon sales, but graduated according to the number of outlets, would be acceptable appears not to have been decided. On the surface, it would seem that a chain store tax law might well give some attention to volume. A chain of grocery stores each doing an annual business of $50,000 would seem to have more ability to pay than a chain of filling stations each with an annual business of $10,000. And what of a chain of chewing-gum automatic vending machines? One Wisconsin law solved this problem by exempting the vending machines and by classifying other chains. A lower rate than that applied to other stores was allowed filling stations. Many state laws exempt filling stations entirely.

Sustention of Louisiana Law. In the case of the *Great Atlantic and Pacific Tea Company v. Grosjean*,[25] a 4–3 decision, the Court had before it the Louisiana chain store tax law which, as previously stated, was levied upon the stores in Louisiana but had a rate graduated according to the number of units in the chain throughout the country. Instances were cited of local chains that had considerably more Louisiana outlets than the A. and P. but yet were paying less per outlet. The majority of the Supreme Court held that

> If the competitive advantages of a chain increase with the number of its component links, it is hard to see how these advantages cease at the state boundary. . . . [All] the stores of a retail chain contribute to the central purchasing power of the chain irrespective of state lines and location of stores, and increase the per unit multiple advantage enjoyed by the operator of the system; that the greater the number of units the greater the purchasing power of the chain, the greater the rebates and allowances, the greater the advantages in advertising, the greater the capital employed, the greater the economic and social consequences, and the lower the cost of distribution and overhead.[26]

The Court was impressed by the argument that the Louisiana system was more equitable and logical than the more usual chain store tax law which graduates rates according to the "length of the chain" within the

---

between volume of business and its profitableness and that the legislature should have the discretion to choose a graduated sales tax as a supplement to the property tax. It might prefer a graduated sales tax to a net income tax on the ground that the latter is difficult to administer.

In the Wisconsin Case of *Ed. Schuster and Co. v. Henry*, 218 Wis. 506 (1935), the state supreme court held unconstitutional a Wisconsin statute similar to that of Kentucky except that it applied only to companies with more than one outlet. In this case it was argued that the law was unfair because it taxed very heavily the large department store with two outlets and exempted entirely a similar store with only one outlet.

[25] 301 U.S. 412 (1937).
[26] 301 U.S. 412 (1937), p. 420.

state. The dissenting opinion expressed the view that this amounted to one state penalizing a method of doing business in other states.

QUESTIONS OF POLICY IN CHAIN STORE TAXATION

The difficulty with chain store tax legislation is that it encourages rival merchants or groups of merchants to carry their problems of competition to the legislature, where the decisions are likely to be influenced by the more effective lobby rather than by consideration of the public interest. In every legislature there are attempts to settle competitive battles politically. A familiar case is that of restaurants seeking prohibitory legislation against the selling of sandwiches in drug stores. Suffice it to say that in the settlement of these issues the interest of the general public frequently drops out of the picture.

Some disinterested support can be found for a chain store tax which merely seeks to neutralize certain unfair advantages possessed by the chains under the property tax, and also for a chain store tax which seeks to neutralize other unfair advantages in competitive merchandising. However, only a very few disinterested students will accept a chain store tax which seeks to eliminate or discourage the chain store on the sole ground that it is socially undesirable.

TAXATION AND MONOPOLY

For many years "the monopoly problem" has commanded the attention and aroused the fears of the American people. Many are inherently distrustful of centralized power either in government or business, and they point out that the two go together. They see safety and the preservation of certain values in a plural universe. They object to the highly materialistic and mechanistic way of life that is associated with "bigness."

The chief alternatives for dealing with the monopoly problem are (1) compulsory dissolution of large combinations in restraint of competition (recently this has taken the form of an attack on dominating size as well as malpractice); (2) control of monopoly practices and prices; (3) public acquisition; and (4) taxation to recapture monopoly profits. The last of these involves as much difficulty as the others perhaps, but it could hardly solve more than part of the problem.[27]

In a country where half the business assets are owned by 200 cor-

---

[27] For a stimulating discussion of the monopoly problem in its relation to taxation and with special attention to the effect of numerous outlets, see Fred I. Raymond, *The Limitist* (New York: W. W. Norton & Co., 1947).

porations a case can be made for a tax on size as such. The principal difficulty lies in making such a tax sufficiently discriminating. Usually there is no available evidence or even a clear consensus as to the optimum size of a business in different lines. Whether the criterion in judging size should be maximum efficiency, adequacy of competition, or other factors of social welfare is also in dispute.

The author agrees with the Supreme Court's view that there is some relationship between a firm's geographical spread and monopoly power. Many states, for instance, object to branch banking yet have no fear of a big single-unit bank. But again the effect may differ in different lines of business and the nature of the establishment.

A graduated tax on corporate income is sometimes defended on the ground that it favors small business which, in turn, checks monopoly. Probably it would be much more effective to place the graduation among the giant companies instead of at the lower end of the scale. Again, however, we are confronted with the doubt that mere size, as such, is the main problem. The unneutralities in the corporate tax system favoring reinvestment over distribution of earnings are also thought by some critics to be conducive to the furtherance of megalomania among corporate officers. In taxation, as elsewhere, we are still groping for an intelligent antimonopoly program.

PROBLEMS

1. What is meant when it is said that a bank may loan money that it creates? Does this justify a special recapture business tax on banking? Are there other grounds for a special business tax?
2. Outline the different ways by which states can and do apply their tax systems to banks.
3. What special advantage, under the net income tax as applied to banks, follows from the fact that banks may deduct all of their expenses yet much of their income (derived from federal securities) is immune to tax? What are the remedies available?
4. What special features of a life insurance company make an estimation of its annual profits difficult?
5. Consider the possible unneutralities that are likely to develop in state taxation of insurance companies.
6. Make a list of the points in a tax system that are of concern to an insurance company.
7. Are the Supreme Court's decisions in the Indiana and Florida chain store cases compatible?
8. Does our present tax system discourage or encourage monopoly? Present particulars to support your answer.
9. Would our economy function better if very large companies such as

General Motors and General Electric were to operate as, let us say, a half dozen independent companies each?

10. Criticize and comment on the following propositions concerning the merits of chain stores:

   a. Chain stores are a public menace and should be eliminated;

   b. Chain stores enjoy unfair competitive advantages that warrant special taxation;

   c. Chain stores enjoy advantages under the property tax and these warrant a special tax;

   d. Chain stores are making an important contribution to merchandising, and attempts to tax them are but the unwarranted expression of frustration by less efficient distributors.

11. In the facts confronted in the Louisiana chain store case, the state was really trying to tax what lay beyond its jurisdiction. Comment.

18

NONTAX REVENUES

Many people think of taxation as the sole source of public support. There are several other government sources of revenue, however, some of which have been, at certain times and places, very important. The Cameralists, writing in the seventeenth and eighteenth centuries, "regarded taxation as the last and least of the sources of public revenue." [1] Even as recently as the late 1920s there were cities that derived more revenue from special assessments than from general property taxes. And at the present there are sizable cities that secure more revenue from the earnings of public service enterprises than from property taxes. On the whole, however, nontax revenues are of far less importance now than formerly.

DISTINGUISHING CHARACTERISTICS OF VARIOUS SOURCES OF REVENUE

Classification of Sources. In addition to taxes, the government may collect commercial revenue in its capacity as landlord or entrepreneur.

---

[1] H. L. Lutz, *Public Finance* (3d ed., New York: Appleton-Century-Crofts, 1936), p. 189.

Charges of this sort are usually referred to as *public prices*. It may also collect certain charges for special services to the individual, such as for the grant of patents, or for special costs which the government incurs on his account, such as in the issuance of hunting licenses, the funds from which help maintain the upkeep of game preserves. The former costs are usually called *fees* and the latter, *license fees*. Further, it may impose charges as a penalty, or *fines,* for violating the rules established by government. It may impose special levies for certain services rendered specific property owners. Such charges are called *special assessments.* Finally, governments sometimes gain revenue by condemning land beyond the needs of an improvement, reaping an increment on such land.[2]

Special Benefit. Considerable attention has been given to the definitions and distinguishing characteristics of these various sources of revenue. A principal distinction among them, and between them and taxes, is the degree of special as contrasted with general benefit. In the case of public prices, the special benefit is the main feature of the transaction. As in a private commercial transaction, the government and its customers engage in an exchange of equivalents, and the relation between the two is essentially contractual. In the case of fees, the special benefit or cost element predominates, but there is usually a larger factor of general interest in the transaction. Students may pay required special fees for courses of extraordinary expense even in an otherwise free state university. The students receive a special benefit, but the public, too, has considerable interest in the service. The same holds true in the case of public improvements (such as street paving) that are financed out of special assessments. Where general benefit is especially important and the special benefit less significant and less measurable, the charges made are called taxes. This is not a hard and fast rule, however. For example, the motor vehicle and social security levies are usually called taxes even though they are imposed according to more or less measurable benefits.[3] Moreover, the factor of benefit is not entirely absent nor ignored even in the distribution of other taxes, especially general property and business taxes. At best, the difference between these categories is a matter of degree, and boundaries between them are not very distinct.

Degree of Compulsion. Another possible criterion for classification of these various kinds of governmental receipts is the degree of compul-

---

[2] Occasionally the government also receives gratuitous funds that are referred to as *gifts*. Government also secure revenue from interest on public money.

[3] When motor vehicle license charges were of sufficient magnitude to pay only for cost of administration, they were fees in all certainty. When they were extended to yield a revenue far beyond these administrative expenses, they became taxes even though there remained an element of special benefit to justify their imposition.

sion involved. Public gifts are entirely gratuitous payments to the government. Public prices are contractual in character but are not compulsory except in the sense that one must make a payment if he wishes to procure a service. Certain taxes appear to be only slightly less optional; one can avoid the tobacco tax by giving up tobacco. A greater degree of constraint appears in the income and property taxes, which can be avoided only by going without these essentials. Apparently only the poll tax involves absolute compulsion, and even this could be avoided by committing suicide or "skipping the country." Any valid distinction among these revenue sources on the ground of their compulsion is certainly very much a matter of degree.

Purpose and Legal Basis. Some of these categories may be distinguished by their special purpose and the power under which they are levied. Thus fines are a form of administrative revenue levied under the penal power and are a means of enforcing laws rather than raising revenue. Licenses usually involve an element of privilege and, like fines, are imposed partly for the purpose of regulation under the police power. Special assessments are sometimes used to abate nuisances, in which case they too are levied under the police power. On the other hand, taxes and fees, as well as most special assessments, are imposed under the taxing power.[4]

Special Procedures. These categories are further distinguished in practice by certain special procedures. License payments are usually made a condition for continuing in business or some other enjoyment. Special assessments are imposed at irregular intervals and need not conform to rules of uniformity which apply to property taxes; furthermore, they are usually excluded from the application of certain statutory provisions, such as property tax exemption, and tax and debt limitations. As a rule they are confined to land and are associated with public improvements.

It will be seen that each of these categories of nontax revenue differs from the others in many respects, but usually the difference is one of degree. The boundary lines are not obvious, and the terms are used rather loosely in practice. The motor vehicle registration tax, as well as many occupational taxes, are often termed fees. Not infrequently, even gross income taxes are included under this designation. Social security taxes represent a high degree of compulsion, but they are somewhat commercial in nature and involve a measurable special benefit. It is as logical to call them public prices, premiums, or contributions as to call them

---

[4] However, it has been said by good authority that "a tax is no less a tax because its purpose is regulation or destruction." E. R. A. Seligman, *Essays in Taxation* (10th ed., New York: The Macmillan Company, 1925), p. 406.

taxes. In general, the classification of these sources of revenue into various categories is useful, even important, but the boundary lines between them must always be obscure.

THE PUBLIC DOMAIN AND PUBLIC INDUSTRIES

PUBLIC DOMAIN

Historically, the public domain has been an important source of revenue for governments. Under the feudal system the government was practically synonymous with the king, who was the principal landowner in a country. Ordinarily this land provided all the revenue the king required. During the early part of its history, the federal government of the United States also relied to some extent on the public lands for revenue. Its income might have been much greater had it not, as an objective of public land policy, placed "opening up the country" ahead of revenue, and had graft and fraud been kept out of the administration. The federal government made huge grants of land to the states for the purpose, among others, of aiding public education. However, the record of the land-grant states in managing and disposing of these public lands was no more creditable or advantageous than that of the federal government.[5]

Income from the sale of public land has not been of any importance as a source of public revenue for many years. Although in 1949 there were over 170 million acres of federal lands subject to entry under homestead and other land settlement laws, little of this land has much value for crop production.[6] In recent years, public interest has turned to the acquisition of a new public domain rather than to the disposition of the old one. The interest has been motivated in part by the desire to conserve timber resources and outdoor recreational facilities. During the depression the counties and states were in many cases forced to acquire large tracts of unredeemed tax-delinquent land.

As stated in Chapter 15, a strong defense can be made for the

---

[5] According to F. H. Swift, the domain granted specifically for schools by our federal government to its thirty public-land states amounted to 114,000 square miles, an area larger than Italy, more than twice as large as England, more than nine times as large as Maryland, and twenty-three times as large as Connecticut— Fletcher Harper Swift, *Federal Aid to Public Schools,* Bul. No. 47, U.S. Department of the Interior, Bureau of Education (Washington, D.C., 1922), p. 34. To show for all of this generosity most of the states have a meager permanent school fund. Wisconsin, for example, has a fund of about $15 million.

[6] U.S. Department of Interior, *Vacant Public Lands* (Washington, D.C., 1949).

proposition that cities should never have parted with any of their lands but should have let them instead, with long leases subject to frequent revision of rent. By this policy, large increments could have been preserved for public use. True, many city governments have shown scant qualifications for an administrative responsibility of this kind. But the large waste and cost that the practically uncontrolled private ownership of urban land has entailed could hardly have been exceeded from the public point of view had public ownership of city land prevailed. Even today there are excellent opportunities for municipalities to conserve revenue and provide service through the acquisition and management of real estate. Many European cities have made good use of this practice by purchasing large amounts of land on their outskirts to provide cheap housing as their population developed.

PUBLIC INDUSTRIES

Public Pricing and the Profits of Public Enterprises. The government may play a commercial role not only as landlord but also as entrepreneur. When successful in such a venture, it receives public revenue in the form of profits of the public enterprise. If its venture is a failure, the result may be public expenditure rather than revenue. Profits and deficits in public enterprise, however, depend not only on the success or failure of management but also upon the policy of public pricing, which in turn depends in some degree upon the purpose for which the government undertakes the particular function. If its purpose is to encourage the consumption of certain services, it may deliberately set their price below the point of maximum profit and even that of cost. For many years the federal government of the United States has provided mail service for newspapers and periodicals on this principle. At a time when postal deficits are being deplored and increases in rates are urged for other services, this point is a highly sensitive one. Public housing is undertaken largely with the view of bringing better houses within the range of low-income groups, and a deficit in the program is deliberate. Occasionally, the matter of public pricing may become a political issue of great importance. This is true in New York City where the fare on publicly owned subways has proved inadequate to pay costs of service and where political opposition to raising the fare has been a major factor. Some critics have urged a differentiation of fare according to distance and hour of travel, the latter to encourage use during times of light traffic.[7] At the other extreme are the "fiscal monopolies," such as the tobacco and lottery

---

[7] Robert M. Haig and Carl S. Shoup, *The Financial Problem of the City of New York,* Mayor's Committee on Management Survey (New York, 1952), chap. IX.

monopolies of European countries, which are operated to secure for the government the maximum revenue from certain businesses.

The typical municipally owned utility—that is, municipal water, gas, and electricity works—ordinarily seeks to charge the same prices which a privately owned utility would and attempts to earn for the local treasury at least the equivalent of the taxes the latter would pay plus a normal profit. When it succeeds beyond this point, the issue arises as to whether the taxpayers or the consumers of utility services should enjoy the benefits. In some states where municipal utilities are subject to regulation by a state public utility commission, the policy has been to order a reduction in rates as soon as a utility earns the taxpayers more than a modest profit. However, where public ownership and operation are so successful as to yield a surplus above the equivalent of taxes and a fair return upon investment, with rates no higher than those prevailing in comparable situations under private ownership and management, it seems that the city itself (or other governmental unit) might well be allowed to determine the disposition of the fruits of its success.

Other Problems in Public Pricing. The benefit and cost principles have their clearest application in the field of public prices. But even here it is extremely difficult to determine the cost of the service (cost) or the value of the service (benefit), and it is not always practical to apply the results once they are determined. The problem of differential rates in the public utility field is not confined to publicly owned utilities but applies to regulated private ones as well. In the case of railroads, the problem involves differentiation between the long and short haul, between carload and less than carload quantities, and between valuable and light commodities as against cheap and heavy ones. The problem is complicated by the fact of joint costs, as in the hauling of passengers, mail, baggage, and express all in one train. It is further complicated by the existence of overhead or constant costs which may be distributed over all or only part of the business. In the electrical utility field, differentiation among domestic, commercial, and industrial users is necessary, and the peak-load service is frequently allotted a higher cost than service at other times. In the strictly public field of postal service, a flat rate is allowed for letters below a certain weight regardless of distance to destination within the country. An exception has at times prevailed in the lower rate allowed for letters destined for delivery within the municipality in which they originate. Parcel-post charges are classified according to weight and zones of distance. Rate making is a large and intricate field, but here these few suggestions as to its nature must suffice.

Once a facility has been constructed and is not fully utilized, there is a case for charging marginal cost (less than average cost) for its services. Less than full utilization would seem to involve a social waste.

Suppose a situation where in an urban center many people need to cross (or go around) a body of water in order to get from their homes to their places of employment and return. Suppose that a bridge has been constructed to serve these people. Suppose further that the bridge is not being used to capacity and that the short-run variable costs of its operation are negligible. Say that if a charge of 10 cents is made for crossing the bridge, the latter will attract 1 million customers annually and that this will provide the revenue to liquidate the capital cost of the bridge during its expected life. However, if a 5 cent fare were charged the bridge would attract half again as many patrons some of whom at the higher fare found it more profitable to travel around the body of water. At the cheaper fare the receipts would fail to meet capital costs by $25,000 annually. But the saving to those who use the bridge might be, let us say, $50,000 under the first alternative and $150,000 under the second. Ignoring the distributive aspect, the social gain from full operation would more than offset the social loss from higher general taxes. In the long run where capital costs are marginal variable costs, a bridge of this size is not warranted perhaps (ignoring indirect benefits) unless it will pay for itself at full capacity. The problem then is one of paying for mistakes.[8]

When Should Governments Go into Commercial Ventures? This question affords a perennial subject for debate. Two answers are most frequent: (1) governments should carry on those ventures that they can do more efficiently than private enterprise; and (2) the federal government should not undertake what could be done as well by state or local governments, nor the latter what could be done as well by private enterprise. Unfortunately, these rules do not help very much; agreement will not be forthcoming on the comparative results of the two alternatives, especially if all the intangibles be included in the calculus. Experience with commercial operations by the government is spotty and affords no easy generalizations. To take a few examples, one can say with some confidence that public ownership has been successful almost universally in the field of water supply. In certain other services, such as electricity, it has been an impressive success in some of the provinces of Canada, in many municipalities in the United States, and in some European countries. The British and their dominions have gone much further in publicly owned enterprise than the United States. That these experiments have proved no panacea for all public ills is generally conceded; on the other hand, many of these ventures have been reasonably successful in rendering good service at a fair cost. In the United States an ambitious federal power, flood control, and regional development project—the Tennessee

___

[8] See Earl R. Rolph and George F. Break, *Public Finance* (New York: The Ronald Press Company, 1961), pp. 362–387.

Valley Authority—is recognized by most observers to have worked at least reasonably well. Special justification of such projects lies in their multiple purpose—a feature which is beyond the reach of private enterprise.

On the other hand, from the fiscal standpoint the North Dakota ventures into public ownership (including a state mill, elevator, bank, and insurance company) have been a source of expense rather than a source of revenue to the state; and South Dakota (except for its cement plant) seems to have had an equally dismal experience.[9] Government lending agencies such as the Reconstruction Finance Corporation have proved amenable to pressures and corruption. The dangers in public banking have long been recognized and are not absolved. There are plenty of cases where government enterprise has been characterized by lethargy and inefficiency. But there are also many cases where the same is true of private industry, and, contrary to some interpretations the public is involved and concerned in these failures also. In a sense all business, particularly corporate business, is more or less public. It is doubtful if there is anything in the annals of public business which approaches the graft and abuses found in the financing of the private American railroads.[10]

It is important to note that government production and government influence on the economy are by no means identical. Governments can exercise a powerful influence without much direct provision of goods and services; they may do this not only by exercising control but also by transfer payments. Thus, for instance, the public could support education without providing or managing schools. The propensity of some modern states for this pattern is what some critics have described as "evolving past socialism." [11]

Use of Government Corporations to Improve Administration of Public Enterprises.   Much interest has attended the use of the public corporation as an administrative device to facilitate public administration of enterprises more or less commercial in character. The public corporation allows more speed and flexibility in managerial decisions than the traditional departmental organizations. The Panama Railroad Company, a public corporate organization, has made a creditable record. The Tennessee Valley Authority is one of the more ambitious contemporary

---

[9] Gilbert W. Cooke, "The North Dakota State Mill and Elevator," *Journal of Political Economy*, XLVI (February 1938), pp. 23–51; Avon Dreyer, *South Dakota's Public Enterprise Experiments and Their Tax Effects* (unpublished doctoral dissertation), University of Wisconsin (Madison, 1952).

[10] *Hearings, Investigation of Railroad Financing*, U.S. Senate Committee on Interstate Commerce, 74th Cong., 1st Sess., 1935; this gives an interesting and revealing discussion of railroad financial manipulation.

[11] See Musgrave, *The Theory of Public Finance*, pp. 42–46.

experiments in government organization through the corporate device. Freedom from the usual checks and restraints on expenditure that corporate control allows is warranted on the expectation that competent and nonpolitical directors will be appointed to head corporate government agencies. Thus far, most of the federal appointments have fulfilled this expectation.[12]

Extent of Municipal Revenue from Public Service Enterprises. One or more utilities and enterprises are currently owned and operated by nine tenths of our urban municipalities. In some, these ventures produce little if any net revenue, while in others, such as those in San Antonio, the yield is very substantial, even exceeding that of the general property tax.[13]

A source of bitter complaint for private utilities is the tax advantages of publicly owned enterprise; no income taxes, no state and county property taxes, no personal taxes on interest paid to bondholders. From the municipality's point of view, however, these advantages may be a major point in favor of public ownership; they are at the expense of the country at large rather than the local taxpayers.

On the whole, it seems fair to conclude that a municipality with a civic-minded population and the competent administration of public affairs which goes with it can provide for itself a considerable source of public revenue through the wise choice and efficient development of public service enterprises. In times like the present, when municipalities are hard pressed for additional sources of revenue, here is a potentiality which might well be given consideration.

FEES AND FINES

Licenses and fees have never constituted an important source of revenue, but they are widely used by governments at all levels in connection with different services and to different degrees. The use of fees requires certain conditions, particularly the presence of discernible special benefits. Taxes allocate economic resources in accordance with the tastes and preferences of a majority or the consensus of the community, but they may do violence to the wishes of a substantial minority. The minority can argue plausibly: If the proponents of this outlay want it so much,

[12] John McDiarmid, *Government Corporations and Federal Funds* (Chicago: University of Chicago Press, 1938); Terence H. O'Brien, *British Experiments in Public Ownership and Control* (London: G. Allen & Unwin, Ltd., 1937); see also Frederic A. Ogg and P. Orman Ray, *Introduction to American Government* (New York: Appleton-Century-Crofts, 1951), pp. 432–433.

[13] U.S. Bureau of Census, *City Government Finances in 1960,* Washington, p. 38.

let them pay for it. Unfortunately, however, most government outlays have important indirect benefits and this is the reason why the government rather than private enterprise invests in them. The fee system is not adapted to take account of these indirect considerations. But the vast majority of public outlays provides some element of special benefit for specific persons or groups, and these may be the occasion for the imposition of fees. Such charges have been imposed for a great variety of services, ranging from the marriage ceremony by the justice of the peace to the consular and passport fees collected by the State Department of the federal government. The judicial process, particularly, is characterized by much fee taking.

One of the best known and most lucrative applications of fees is in the financing of education, particularly in the case of colleges and universities. Tuition is a major source of income for private schools of higher learning and a fairly important one in public schools at the same level, especially during recent years when the fees charged students have shown a strong upward tendency. The fee system as a support for higher education encounters the objection that it creates a financial qualification upon educational opportunities. The cost of maintenance for a student during his college period is something of a financial qualification even without fees. The objection can be met in part with a generous provision for scholarships. The fee seems most defensible in the case of professional courses, which usually add greatly to the students' earning powers, or in the case of certain special services, such as medical care or special recreational facilities, provided by the educational institution.

In recent years many cities have placed disposal of sewage upon a "public utility basis." The movement has been stimulated in large measure by property tax limitation laws. The cost of service is measured in various ways, one of the simplest of which is water consumption. The water-consumption basis ignores the use of water to maintain dooryards in dry times and areas and on this ground has been criticized as "a tax on civic pride." Some prefer the number of fixtures as a basis but this also obviously has limitations as an accurate measure of services. The benefit of sewage disposal is usually quite general, and the service is one that is appropriately supported by a general tax. The impact of a cost charge differs considerably from that of a general property levy. In the case of vacant property, the property tax applies and the service charge does not; the reverse is true in the case of tax-exempt property.

The service charge measures benefits to industry with considerably more precision than the property tax. It is much more practicable and equitable for application to sewage disposal than to some other services, such as for instance garbage disposal where a precise measure of benefits would be difficult. On the whole, the service charge for sewage disposal has considerable merit.

Highway finance provides a striking case of the usefulness and limitations of the fee system. The toll charge constitutes direct collection from specific users; motor vehicle taxes provide levies justified by benefits to highway-users as a group but less specifically pinpointed; general taxes for highways cover benefits that are thought to be primarily indirect. It is significant that the trend seems to favor the second of these means of charging over the first or the third.

Although fees are a relatively minor source of revenue, it has been thought by many critics that their use could be considerably expanded.[13a] Industries that are subject to regulation of one sort or another might well be charged directly with more of the administrative costs they create. The cost of special recreational facilities, such as tennis courts, can be paid at least in part by charging users a small fee. The charge may also help to restrict the demand to the supply in case the municipality is not in a financial position to provide sufficient free facilities. Many cities seem to have achieved considerable success, particularly in regulating traffic and rationing space, but also in securing incidental revenues by the use of parking meters.[14]

Fines are not of any importance as a source of revenue and are usually levied with no regard to filling the public treasury. The "speed traps" of some municipalities are a notorious exception. Many a motorist has had to contribute handsomely to the coffers of some small village (or worse still to the private account of some constable or justice of the peace) into whose clutches he unfortunately fell. In 1907 Judge K. M. Landis probably set an all-time record in the imposition of fines when he imposed a penalty of $29,240,000 on the Standard Oil Company for violation of the antitrust laws.[15] But his ruling was set aside, and this munificent sum was lost to the public treasury. More recently a court imposed a fine of $3 million on the United Mine Workers for the violation of an injunction. The verdict was sustained but the fine reduced to

---

[13a] See for instance, J. A. Stockfish, "Fees and Service Charges as a Source of City Revenue: A Case Study of Los Angeles," *National Tax Journal,* XIII (June 1960), pp. 97–121.

[14] Less frequently than formerly, though still quite often, a public official is allowed to keep all the fees he collects in lieu of a salary. This has worked very badly, especially in the case of county sheriffs. The office may become so lucrative that it is entirely out of line in this respect with other county offices and the object of desperate political rivalry. Moreover, the fee system may encourage a public officer to undue activity. This occurs where sheriffs are paid a fee for feeding and housing tramps. The fee system as a support for justices of the peace is particularly vicious. The justices are local officers empowered to decide petty cases of dispute. In general, each town, village, and city ward may have one, and the plaintiff in a dispute can frequently select any justice of the peace in the county. Justices who are favorable to plaintiffs get the most business and the most fees. The office is not always exploited, but the system is an open invitation to abuse. Impartial and efficient public service requires that officials be paid salaries and that fees be paid into the public treasury.

[15] *United States v. Standard Oil Co.,* 155 Fed. 305 (1907).

$700,000.[16] It has been suggested that "it is probable that in many cases a pecuniary penalty will have as satisfactory penological results as any other form of penalty" and that, "if the finance minister were also the administrator of justice . . . the revenue from fines would show a marked increase." [17] It is highly questionable whether at least the second part of this suggestion would merit any consideration for practical application.

THE PUBLIC LOTTERY

Said by some of its proponents to be the perfect and painless substitute for taxation is the device known as the public lottery. The proponent will probably not argue that gambling is not an evil. Instead he will contend that people have an innate propensity to play games of chance; given this propensity, the state may as well divert some fools' money to constructive purposes. The fact that this can be done with substantial gain for the treasury has been demonstrated in many countries; for instance, it brings large returns to some of the Australian states. People are said to enjoy particularly playing the public rather than private lottery; if they win, they enjoy their winnings, and if they lose, they are consoled by the fact that their money "went for a good cause." The use of the lottery principle in lieu of interest has long been featured in Russia to promote bond sales and in 1956 this technique was borrowed by the British.

People reared in the Puritanical tradition (as is the case with many Americans) are profoundly shocked by this line of reasoning. They start with the proposition that the state should prohibit or at least discourage gambling since it undermines "the economic virtues," persuading people to seek economic gain at the expense of others and without the usual exercise of hard work and thrift. With the lottery, they hold, the public connives at this nefarious influence and undermines its own resolution by the profits it reaps in the process. Particularly vicious is a finance system that weakens all other productive incentives and then offers this as a compensation for the acquisitive one.

Although the public lottery has little if any application in the United States, there are a substantial number of states which have legalized betting on races and share in the gains of the successful participants. This system goes under the name of "pari-mutuel tax." The racing industry is a billion-dollar business, authorized and supported by law in

---

[16] *Time,* March 17, 1947, p. 21.
[17] Jens P. Jensen, "Sources of Public Revenue Other than Taxes," M. C. Mills and C. W. Starr, eds., in *Readings in Public Finance,* p. 167.

some half the states. The governments share the commission on the business recorded by the vending machines and do very well on the concession. Parasitic or illegal gambling also attends these competitions, and it escapes the state levies.[18] The Nevada tax system exhibits impressive reliance on the gambling business.

It may be mentioned parenthetically that federal attempts to impose special taxes on gambling are quite ambitious and raise ethical and other problems. Included are fees on gambling establishments, on the volume of transactions (wagers) and on capital (coin machines). Certain activities such as bingo and card games for stakes are exempt. All this is in addition to the application of the regular net income tax to net gambling gains. There is some but not predominant support for the view that it is hypocritical to make gambling illegal (as it is in many states) and still attempt to tax it.[19]

SPECIAL ASSESSMENTS

CHARACTERISTICS

Special assessments are usually marked by the following special characteristics: (1) they allocate benefit and special charges associated with a public improvement or at least a public service to a special zone or district which may or may not be coterminous with a political unit; and (2) they allocate benefit and charges (usually) to land only and on some basis other than the value of land (such as area or frontage). However, special assessment practices differ from state to state and city to city. There are cases of ad valorem assessment and on all real estate and even all property. The absolute least common denominator appears to be some public improvement and some special allotment of its benefit.

Allocation of benefit to special districts, however, is not entirely confined to the special-assessment field. Thus in New York City, for example, certain costs of government are charged back to the boroughs presumed to benefit therefrom, and this practice is not uncommon elsewhere in public finance.

The benefit that special assessments are supposed to measure is usually conceived in terms of increment to land caused by a public improvement. However there are several differences between special assessments and land-value increment taxes, previously described. Increments may

---

[18] Rienzi Wilson Jennings, *Taxation of Thoroughbred Racing,* Bulletin of the Bureau of Business Research, University of Kentucky (Lexington, 1949).

[19] J. Henry Landman, "Government's Hypocrisy in Gambling," *Taxes,* 34: 2 (February 1956), pp. 107–108.

arise from a number of causes independent of public construction. They may be due to private improvements or to an increase in population. Land values may even decrease in spite of the fact that the land is provided with special governmental services. This does not mean that the services result in no benefit to the land. Moreover, administrators are forced to presume many benefits that do not actually materialize as increments. Attempts to check actual increments over a period of years against special assessments show that the two are frequently badly correlated.[20] Finally, special assessments may not exceed costs of the improvement while benefits (or increments) encounter no such limitation. And as a practical matter special assessments in anticipation of increments are frequently more or less arbitrary distributions of cost. The increments of the increment tax have actually been realized by a sale.

Some dispute may even occur over the question of whether a special assessment must anticipate increment. This is illustrated by the division of authority on their use for repaving. Many states do allow such use and it seems quite proper to regard the maintenance of existing values equally as important as the creation of new values.

Legal Aspects. In its *Norwood v. Baker* decision in 1898 the United States Supreme Court said: "The principle underlying special assessments to meet the cost of public improvements is that the property upon which they are imposed is peculiarly benefited, and, therefore, the owners do not in fact, pay anything in excess of what they receive by reason of such improvement." [21] The Court went on to declare unconstitutional an assessment for street construction that was assessed on a frontage basis and "excluded any inquiry as to special benefits."

This decision has never been overruled, but it has been qualified by later opinions which hold that unless administrators' allocations are palpably unjust and cannot possibly bear any relation to benefits, they will not be disturbed by the courts. In short, the courts are loath to substitute their opinions for those of designated officials.

As a rule, properties that are exempt from other taxation, such as cemeteries, churches, and lodges, are not free from special assessment and in the absence of special statutory exemption they must pay it.

---

[20] Edwin Spengler, "The Increment Tax *versus* Special Assessments," *Bulletin of National Tax Association,* XX: 9 (June 1935), pp. 258–261; XXI: 1 (October 1935), pp. 14–17; XXI: 6 and 8 (March, May 1936), pp. 163–167, 240–244. See also Herbert D. Simpson, "The Influence of Public Improvements on Land Values," *Annals of the American Academy of Political and Social Science,* CXLVIII: 237 (March 1930), p. 120. Professor Simpson shows that values may be diverted rather than created by public improvements; such improvements may result in both increments and decrements and both in unexpected places.

[21] 172 U.S. 269, 278–279 (1898).

SPECIAL-ASSESSMENT PROCEDURE AND PRACTICE

Legislation in the various states establishes a variety of purposes for which special assessments may be levied. Among the more important are the following: grading, paving, sidewalks, bridges, sanitary sewers, storm sewers, parks, extension of municipal utilities, high-pressure fire protection, ornamental street lighting, snow removal, sprinkling and oiling of streets.

Special assessments may be initiated either by petition of the property holders or the city council. The approval of a majority of the property holders may or may not be necessary, and the same is true of approval of the council. To give the council final authority independent of the wishes of the property owners represents a high degree of compulsion, but it is defended on the ground that the continuity of projects and good general city planning may require it. Procedure usually includes notice of the prospective levy and a hearing at which property owners may at least sound a protest. Many state courts require these procedures as a condition for the validity of the assessments.

The principal difficulty in the administration of special assessments is in the measurement and allocation of benefit. First, it is necessary for someone to decide what proportion of the cost of an improvement should be allotted to special assessments and what to general taxes. This is no easy task and in practice is frequently performed in quite an arbitrary manner. Once a city has been built up and everybody is served with suitable streets and sewage facilities, it is not improper to charge all of the cost of improvement of these facilities to the general taxpayer. Some may receive no special benefit from this year's improvements, but they may expect to get their "inning" next year. A through or arterial street which is of service mainly to people at or beyond the ends of the street ought not to be financed mainly by abutting property owners.

The next problem of measurement is that of determining the size of the area to be included in the special benefit charges. Following this comes allocation to specific properties. This involves choice of a criteria such as frontage, area, or value. If the former is chosen, it will confront the factor of odd-shaped and differing depths of lots. Here a leaf is sometimes taken from general property tax procedure; each square foot is assigned a value according to proximity to the improvement, and values decrease as the area recedes from the street. In the case of a park, zones may be established and the degree of benefit presumed to recede from zone to zone. Odd-shaped lots can provide puzzling exercises in geometry.

SPECIAL-ASSESSMENT FINANCE

Many problems arise in financing special assessments to which only the most general attention can be given here. Public improvements involve an arrangement for paying the contractor who does the improving. Since special assessments are usually paid in installments, some form of credit is frequently involved. The contractor may be paid in special-assessment warrants in which case he assumes the burden and the risk of collection. It is usually more economical for the city to undertake its own collection (along with the property tax) and assume its own risk of nonpayment. The city may issue special-assessment bonds to provide cash with which to pay the contractor. The special-assessment bonds may be secured by "the full faith and credit" of the city or only by special-assessment obligation. The former provides an easier market for bonds and lower rates of interest, but the latter as a rule avoids debt limitations. A third method of finance provides a revolving fund from which initial payments for improvements are made.

TREND IN THE USE OF SPECIAL ASSESSMENTS

In many cities special assessments produced from 25 to 50 percent of all municipal revenues during much of the thirty-year period before 1930. After this their use went into a substantial decline until they all but disappeared in many municipalities. Several causes account for this. One is the heavy default in assessment bonds during the 1930s; this, in turn, was due to the speculative expenditure and some abuse during the preceding decade. A second reason is that expansion is now more often confined to suburbs and does not appear in the more readily available statistics of larger cities. Special assessments are most extensively used to extend new improvements into areas about to be converted into urban use.[22]

OTHER INSTRUMENTS OF PUBLIC-IMPROVEMENT FINANCE

Excess Condemnation. Excess condemnation is the taking of more land under the power of eminent domain than is needed for an improvement. In the United States this power (where it is available) has usually been employed to wipe out uneconomic property lines resulting from the widening of a street or the construction of a diagonal thoroughfare.

---

[22] William O. Winter, *The Special Assessment Today with Emphasis on the Michigan Experience,* Bureau of Government Institute of Public Administration (Ann Arbor: University of Michigan Press, 1952), pp. 1–17.

If such land is purchased by the public, it can at least be landscaped. In Europe the power has been used considerably to resell at a profit and thus recoup the cost of the improvement.

British Town and Country Act. Postwar Britain has been characterized by great interest in planning. "As the walls came tumbling down" during the war attacks, the British found compensation in the thought that they would rebuild "according to the heart's desire." This resulted in a considerable crop of postwar legislation. Included was the Distribution of Industries Act requiring permission for the location and relocation of industry with the objective of better planning and more decentralization. Included also was the New Towns Act calling for the construction of a considerable number of completely planned "satellite" cities. Finally there was the Town and Country Act which, in addition to setting up a comprehensive framework of planning, inaugurated a new financial program to capture increments associated with improvements. Increments to land values resulting from an approved change of use would go to the government as a developmental charge; vested "floating value" would be eligible for compensation from the government to the landowner. This floating value embraced that due to anticipation of a more profitable use at the time the act was passed. Thus land on the outskirts of a city originally worth $1000, might have doubled in value before the act. Later pressed into urban use it might be worth $3000. The net developmental charge would be $1000; and if the land were excluded by the planning authority from development, compensation of $1000 would go to the owner.

The law thus extended the idea of special assessments to include a charge for increments associated with "permitted" private development. But it did not contemplate socialization of all increments; those due to a more profitable application of land without a "change of use" were immune. The program involved extremely subtle and ambiguous distinctions and the financial features proved unworkable and had to be abandoned.[23] Certainly a land-value increment tax would be much simpler.

SUMMARY

Taxes are by no means the only source of public revenue. Others include income from the public domain and public enterprise, fees, fines, and special assessments. These are distinguished from taxes and from each other by various criteria, such as the special benefit involved, but the differences are only ones of degree.

---

[23] Ralph Turvey, "Development Charges and the Compensation Betterment Problem," *Economic Journal*, LXIII (June 1953), pp. 299–317.

Income from the public domain was once very important in public finance, but in most countries this is no longer true. Public industries may be a source of revenue, depending upon their success and the pricing policy pursued by the government in selling the goods and services of the enterprise. Among the many possible pricing policies is that of marginal-cost pricing which may dictate a long-run loss to insure optimum use of existing facilities. Deliberate losses may also be accepted to allow for indirect benefits. Some municipalities derive substantial revenue from governmental undertakings. This represents a fruitful field of revenue for a municipality or state with a civic-minded population and competent administration.

Fees are widely applied in payment for public services but are only a minor source of public revenue. They involve less compulsion than taxes. They might be expanded considerably. Recent successful applications include payment for sewage disposal and the use of parking meters. The public lottery has brought considerable revenue to many countries; it is criticized on the score that it promotes gambling which in turn undermines the economic virtues.

Of considerable interest and importance, from both the theoretical and practical standpoints, is the field of special assessments. These levies receive theoretical support because they are related to special benefits (both individual and territorial) and constitute a special tax on city land values. They are frequently compared with land-value increment taxes, but they differ substantially in following benefit rather than increment and in disregarding entirely increments due to causes other than government improvements.

Legally the courts pay lip service to the rule that special assessments must correlate with benefits; however, in most cases rather arbitrary divisions of cost are sanctioned. In practice, special assessments present many grave difficulties of administration, particularly in dividing burdens between special beneficiaries and the general taxpayer, among zones of benefited territory and among the individual properties benefited. Very often the techniques employed are crude and the standards are arbitrary.

The use of special assessments is a cyclical phenomenon and, in addition, varies substantially from city to city. In the years of rapid expansion immediately preceding the depression of the 1930s, some cities collected more from special assessments than from general property. Especially in central cities, the trend, however, is one of decline. The British in their Town and Country Act experimented with the idea of extending special assessments to increments associated with a permitted change in use of land. The land-value increment tax has notable advantages over both the British innovation and special assessments.

PROBLEMS

1. Suppose a city with which you are acquainted contemplates repaving one of its main streets that passes through the entire length of the city. How should its legislators and administrators seek answers to the following:

   a. What proportion of the cost should be financed by the general property tax and what by special assessment?

   b. Should the special-assessment quota be distributed among abutting properties according to frontage? Should any attention be paid to the fact that lots in the central part of the city are more valuable? Should any attention be given to the fact that some lots are improved and others are vacant?

   c. Should any attention be given to the depth of lots? In the case of a shallow lot shall some of the cost go to lots behind that abutting on the street which is being improved?

   d. Is it proper to include the cost of intersections in the charges allotted to abutting owners?

   e. Should churches and lodges share in the cost?

   f. If the plan of repaving will damage certain abutting properties, should they nevertheless be included in the required payments?

   g. Is it reasonable to pay for repaving (as distinguished from new paving) by special assessment in the first place?

2. All taxation is said to involve compelling a reluctant minority to buy services that it does not want. Why not substitute fees and let those who want a government facility pay for it?

3. Contrast tolls and highway-user taxes as means of paying for highways.

4. Comment on the proposition: A municipality that operates a publicly owned utility at a profit is levying a sales tax in disguise. What are the several factors that may account for the profitable operation of this utility other than exploitation of consumers?

5. Is a "tax-free" town (financed by earnings of publicly owned utilities) something to boast about?

6. Many private organizations are successful in securing good attendance at meetings by offering a "door prize." Would it be a good idea for the government to harness this private propensity so as to support the treasury?

7. Who would gain and who would lose by shifting the support for sewage disposal from the general property tax to a fee for service?

8. What effects on education would result from a trend to support higher education entirely or largely by student fees?

9. Why might a deficit in the accounts of the post office department be inconclusive evidence of inefficiency in the conduct of the postal business?

10. Under socialized medicine what useful purpose might be served by charging the client a small fee?
11. Would a small charge for government publications be desirable?
12. What are some of the differences between a land-value increment tax and special assessment? What are the advantages of each? What innovation in special-benefit taxation did the British attempt with their Town and Country Act?
13. It is said that it is bad economics to charge customers of a public facility (used to less than full capacity) more than the marginal cost of providing the service even though this involves a loss in the operation:
    a. Explain the argument supporting this proposition;
    b. Should the facility have been built to begin with?
    c. Who will make good the loss and how can we compare the loss of welfare involved here with that gained by greater use of the facility?
    d. Are prices in competitive private business set at marginal cost? Is the same true of monopolistic industries?

PART 2 SPECIAL PROBLEMS OF THE REVENUE SYSTEM AS A WHOLE

19

THE POWER TO TAX

NATURE OF A FEDERAL SYSTEM

The essence of a federal system is a division of governmental power between a central over-all government and its constituent parts. This device is exceedingly well adapted to certain conditions: (1) where international unity is not fully achieved (as in the United Nations); (2) where different cultures, languages, religions, and traditions are obliged to unite for certain purposes but each insists on maintaining its own identity (as in Canada with its French and British areas); and (3) where a very large country wishes to insure a strong element of local autonomy. The last named of these conditions, except for its assured continuance, can be met as well by home rule as by federal machinery. In fact, it is not necessary to have a federal system in order to have local self-government. The alternative to a federal system is a unitary state, exemplified by Great Britain. All power in this case is lodged with the central government, though it can and does grant municipalities a large measure of home rule. But the federal system creates an intentional inflexibility; it insures local autonomy against power-hungry leadership at the central level.

It is this inflexibility that constitutes the principal weakness of a federal system. The operation of a federal system is usually thought to require a written constitution and to be facilitated by a more or less independent judiciary to interpret this document. (The unitary state, or the constituent states within a federal system, can more readily rely on unwritten tradition for direction.) The framework of the federal system, once established, may prove more resistant to changing conditions than is desired by the sovereign people or is in accordance with their interest. Australia, which has a federal system, found itself obliged to resolve questions of constitutionality on almost all of the major reform measures of a socialist government; New Zealand (which abolished its federal system some seventy-five years ago) has no such impediment. To one who is profoundly dissatisfied with the status quo, a federal system is certain to seem an unnecessary barrier. The author doubts the wisdom of its retention in homogeneous Australia. On the other hand, it is clear that without this feature of government Canada could hardly remain a united nation.

The advantages of home rule, especially in a large country, are evident. They include (1) more government *by* the people as well as for them, (2) determination of policy in close proximity to the details involved, and (3) a training school and ladder for public officials. The diversity that accompanies local autonomy is sometimes distressing and inconvenient but it can also be creative. Experimentation flourishes in this environment. Progress in nature and in civilization has thrived on diversity. On the other hand, in dealing with some problems such as unemployment, local governments lack the perspective and coordination required to solve them.

In a federal system such as our own several kinds of governmental powers are distinguished. The federal government has *enumerated powers,* a list defined in the federal Constitution and usually referred to as the powers of Congress. Certain *implied powers* are associated with the designated ones; they have been sanctioned by the courts to make the designated powers effective. The states have *reserved powers*—that is, they can exercise all the prerogatives of sovereignty not surrendered to the federal government and not denied to them by their own constitutions. By tradition, crystallized in judicial opinion, and usually by constitutional prohibition there are certain things that even sovereign governments may not do. For example, minorities are protected from majorities against violations of the right of free speech and assembly. This is the "no-man's land" in government. Finally there are powers delegated to municipalities. The municipalities are not sovereign but are merely subdivisions of the states and depend for such powers as they have upon grants from the latter. Underneath all of this structure stand the people, who are the ultimate sovereign. In general, the taxing power follows the same rules as the other powers of government. Federal powers are stated in the federal Constitution; state powers are reserved; and municipalities can tax only as the state legislature allows them.

As has been suggested, this division of authority encounters stresses and strains as new and unforeseen conditions develop. A highly interdependent economy, the giant corporation and labor union, and the urge to prevent devastating economic depressions are conditions not anticipated by the architects of the federal Constitution. Some means of adaptation to changing conditions were provided. It is possible to amend the federal Constitution though the process is long and laborious. Change by judicial interpretation is much easier, though this requires a Supreme Court congenial to a new idea; something of a revolution in constitutional law has occurred by judicial interpretation in the last two decades. In addition, it is said that "every resource of legal ingenuity is strained to bring rights and interests under the federal jurisdiction." Among the resources in the financial area are (1) federal aids (with conditions attached as to the expenditure of federal money); (2) federal credit for state taxes; and (3) taxation for nonfiscal purposes—that is, the enactment of control legislation under the guise of what is ostensibly a revenue act within the area authorized by the federal Constitution.

It should be pointed out that the federal government does not have the so-called police power—that is, the power to regulate and condition labor, business, agriculture, and other activity in the interest of the safety, morals, health, and welfare of the people. It does have three very important collateral powers: the power to spend for the public welfare, the power to tax (within a wide area), and the power to regulate interstate commerce. It is in the reinterpretation of the latter power that the revolution in constitutional law has occurred. Formerly interstate commerce was narrowly defined as transportation across state boundary lines; the manufacture of goods destined for interstate commerce was excluded. Now the definition has been broadened to include manufacture as well as transportation, and even intrastate transportation and manufacture where they affect in an important way their interstate counterparts. Thus it might be possible to control wages (minimum wage) in a plant processing milk for the local market on the ground that employment conditions in such plants had an important bearing on those of firms producing for the national market. The result has been, in effect, a handsome grant of police power to the federal government, upon which much current legislation such as minimum wage laws and industrial relations acts are based. The virtually unlimited spending power supports such federal undertakings as the Department of Agriculture, the Bureau of Education, and, of course, federal aids.

GENERAL LIMITATIONS ON THE POWER
TO TAX

TAXATION AND PUBLIC PURPOSE

As has been suggested, even sovereign legislative bodies cannot raise and spend money without some restrictions. One of these, existing usually by authority of custom and legal precedent rather than by constitutional mandate, prescribes that taxation and expenditure must be for a public purpose. What constitutes a public purpose depends upon time and place and also, perhaps, upon the disposition of the courts. A very obvious case of the expenditure of money for a nonpublic purpose occurs when a town chairman uses public funds to build a strictly private road from his own house to the hayfield on the top of his hill.

Citizen's Saving and Loan Association versus Topeka. The nonpublic purpose rule is invoked to exclude direct government aid to a specific private business. Thus, in the case of *Citizen's Saving and Loan Association v. Topeka,*[1] the Supreme Court declared invalid a Kansas statute that permitted municipalities to loan money or credit to aid private industrial concerns. The question involved arose frequently when states allowed their municipalities to grant or loan money to railroads in the era of railroad construction, but the preponderance of legal opinion permitted such practice in the absence of constitutional provisions to the contrary.

In a Wisconsin case [2] a municipality borrowed $100,000 to aid a new (private) industry, the creditors to be repaid out of taxes. The industry agreed to provide a payroll of $1 million over a ten-year period and offered a bond to secure its faithful performance. The company defaulted and the municipality sued the surety company. The state supreme court denied the right to collect on the bond. It held that the municipality's procedure was "permeated with illegality," that the contract was opposed to public policy, and that to assist the municipality to collect would encourage dishonest transactions. However, an Ohio court compelled a private corporation which had benefited by a contract with a municipality to fulfill its end of the agreement.[3]

Considerable interest attended the move of Mississippi sanctioning public borrowing and expenditure of public money to buy or build in-

---

[1] 20 Wall. 655 (1875).
[2] *Wendlandt v. Hartford Accident and Indemnity Co.,* 222 Wis. 204 (1936).
[3] *New York Central Road Co. v. City of Bucyrus,* 126 Ohio 558 (1933).

dustrial plants for leasing to private industries on terms approved by the state industrial commission.[4] The preamble stated as the major purpose of this legislation the importance to the state of providing wealth-creating work for unemployed citizens and a balance between agriculture and industry. The law was sustained by the supreme court of Mississippi in spite of the following provision in the state constitution: "The credit of the state shall not be pledged or loaned in aid of any person, association, or corporation. . . ." The court emphasized that Mississippi, in comparison with other states, has few manufacturing enterprises, "and it has long sought in vain to procure them by offering them special inducements, e.g., exemption from taxation." A positive incentive, therefore, seemed no less appropriate to the court than a negative one.[5]

Even if the decision in *Loan Association v. Topeka* were consistently applied, it would hardly support the view that state subsidies to private industry are always unconstitutional. There are many precedents for public subsidies to private business, at least where such subsidies are indirect. The protective tariff is, of course, the classic example. The defunct Reconstruction Finance Corporation loans probably carried some element of subsidy in them. And there are many other cases of this kind. These aids can be defended on the ground that they serve the public interest. What does and does not serve the public interest is usually a matter of opinion; the dividing line between the two is often scarcely visible.

Government Aid to Private Persons. There is ample precedent for ruling out special government aid to private persons on grounds similar to those used to invalidate the Kansas statute. Just two years previous to this decision, a Massachusetts court declared invalid an attempt to provide relief through public loans for the victims of a fire.[6] In 1902, however, a similar case in Wisconsin resulted in a different decision;[7] but one year later another Wisconsin case ruled out a public appropriation to provide an institution for the care and cure of drunken persons.[8] The grant of pensions to teachers already retired can be and has been challenged as a violation of the public-purpose rule. On the other hand, the soldiers' bonus acts have been generally sustained, and, of course, the

---

[4] *Laws of Mississippi,* First Extraordinary Session, 1936, chap. I.

[5] *Albritton v. City of Winona,* 181 Miss. 75, 99 (1938); a similar program in Louisiana is supported by a constitutional amendment expressly authorizing contracts between a state agency and new industries—William D. Ross, *Louisiana Industrial Tax Exemption Program,* Division of Research, College of Commerce (Baton Rouge: Louisiana State University, 1953).

[6] *Lowell v. Boston,* 111 Mass. 454 (1873).

[7] *State ex rel. New Richmond v. Davidson,* 114 Wis. 563 (1902).

[8] *State ex rel. Garret v. Froehlich,* 118 Wis. 129 (1903).

relief of personal destitution has always been regarded as a legitimate function of government.[9]

The use of public money in aid of private religious institutions—more specifically to provide transportation for children to parochial schools—has also been questioned under the public-purpose doctrine. Much will depend in a case of this kind on conditions and public opinion. In Quebec the use of the taxing power even to support the church itself (dissenters exempt) is sanctioned. In communities where all or nearly all of the population see alike on religious matters, it no doubt seems as appropriate to pay the minister with tax money as to pay the teacher with public funds.

REASONABLE CLASSIFICATION

That classification in tax legislation is not contrary to the federal Constitution, whether such classification is used by the federal government or the states, has long been established. However, it is important that the classification be *reasonable* and not arbitrary; otherwise it may be contrary to the Fourteenth or Fifth Amendments of the federal Constitution and would probably be ruled out in any event as contrary to our tradition of government. Thus a state "may, if it chooses, exempt certain classes of property from any taxation at all, such as churches, libraries,

---

[9] The rule that taxation must be used for a public purpose has also been employed to prevent public undertakings in business and industry. Several years ago the legislature of South Dakota passed an act which permitted certain state officers, if they found that gasoline prices were excessive, to buy gasoline and sell it at retail. They were permitted to use a certain portion of gasoline tax money for capital. The court, in declaring the statute void, quoted from a decision of the Kansas Supreme Court—*White Eagle Oil & Refining Co. v. Gunderson,* 48 S.D. 608 (1925) as follows:

"Our Constitution was framed, and our laws enacted, with the idea of protecting, encouraging and developing individual enterprise and if we now intend to reverse this policy, and to enter the state as a competitor against the individual in all lines of trade and commerce, we must amend our Constitution and adopt an entirely different system of government."

On the other hand, several state as well as federal court decisions have disallowed the contention that use of public money to participate in business, usually private, is taxation for a nonpublic purpose. Thus, in the leading case of *Green v. Frazier,* 253 U.S. 233 (1920), the industrial program of the state of North Dakota, which included the establishment of a state mill, bank, grain elevator, and housing corporation, all to be financed by tax-supported bond issues, was sustained. The decision rested on the grounds that inasmuch as North Dakota was predominantly an agricultural state, and this program aimed to augment its prosperity, and because the legislature, the people, and the state supreme court had all held this to be for a public purpose and for the state's welfare, the Supreme Court, in the absence of a clear violation of the Fourteenth Amendment, could not but uphold the legislation. An excellent discussion of the subject will be found in an article by B. P. McAllister, "Public Purpose in Taxation," *California Law Review,* 18 (1930), 137 and 241.

and the property of charitable institutions. It may impose different specific taxes upon different trades and professions, and may vary the rates of excise upon various products. . . . But clear and hostile discriminations against particular persons and classes . . . might be obnoxious to the constitutional prohibition." [10] In one case the Court held that taxing surface but not underground railways was a proper classification.[11] In a more recent case, a graduated tax on the gross income of merchants has been held unreasonable classification and therefore unconstitutional.[12] The Court admitted that there may be a relationship between gross income and net income (measure of ability to pay), but "denied that the graduation adopted was a 'reasonable approximation' to that increase so that the classification could be upheld." [13]

OBLIGATION OF CONTRACT

The federal constitution provides that no state shall pass any law impairing the obligation of contract, and while this does not bind the federal government (and individuals cannot sue the state in federal court) a contract made by a government is usually regarded as binding. Thus Illinois continues to tax the Illinois Central Railroad at a specified rate on its gross income (according to an old contract) notwithstanding the fact that all other railroads are assessed under another system. The railroad tax system of western Canada is dominated by the contracts made to induce extensions of railroads. However, state obligations of contract have been impaired and sustained when they came in conflict with others of its powers, such as police or eminent domain.

TAXATION BEYOND JURISDICTION

"Taxation without representation" is not banned by any tradition, but it is well settled that a legislative body cannot tax beyond its border. To support the power to tax, there must be some reciprocal relation between the government and the taxpayer.

USE OF TAXATION FOR A NONFISCAL PURPOSE

Taxation is usually primarily for revenue, but nonfiscal considerations often play a part, and may be the major objective, in tax legislation. The use of taxation to regulate rather than raise revenue may or may not be

---

[10] *Bell's Gap Railroad Co. v. Pennsylvania*, 134 U.S. 232 (1890).

[11] *Metropolitan Street Railway Co. v. New York*, 199 U.S. 1 (1905).

[12] *Stewart Dry Goods Co. v. Lewis*, 294 U.S. 550 (1935).

[13] J. B. Sholley, "Equal Protection in Tax Legislation," *Virginia Law Review*, 24 (1938), 229 and 388.

428   *Special Problems of the Revenue System*

valid, depending on the circumstances. The boundary line between what is and what is not acceptable in this field is quite obscure.

Since the federal government's powers are confined to those enumerated in the Constitution, and since economic development is in the direction of more centralized institutions, Congress has been under constant pressure to legislate on matters for which it has no specific authorization. Regulatory powers granted to the federal government are limited, and this accounts for the numerous attempts to accomplish regulatory objectives under the clearly established taxing power. Recent broadening of the concept of interstate commerce (over which the regulatory power of the federal government extends) has partially solved the problem.

The use of the taxing power by the federal government, with an apparent major or collateral purpose to regulate in fields that are beyond its regulatory power, has afforded an extremely difficult and interesting field of adjudication for the courts.

Veazie Bank versus Fenno. In an early case after the Civil War the Supreme Court was called to pass upon the legality of an attempt to tax the circulation of state bank notes out of existence. It was contended by the bank that the tax was so excessive as to indicate a purpose to destroy. In reference to this point, Justice Chase, who read the Court's decision, said: "The first answer to this is that the judicial cannot prescribe to the legislative departments of the government limitations upon the exercise of its acknowledged powers. The power to tax may be exercised oppressively upon persons, but the responsibility of the legislature is not to the courts, but to the people by whom its members are elected." [14] The Court also relied on the fact that Congress had the power to provide and regulate coinage; that it could, if it chose, prohibit state coinage altogether; that the federal tax was thus only an attempt to do indirectly what could have been done directly.

One of the most obvious instances where the federal government used the taxing power to regulate and destroy was its legislation against white phosphorus matches. The manufacture of matches with white phosphorus ingredients was extremely injurious to the employees in the industry. The federal government imposed a tax of 2 cents per 100 on such matches and by this means entirely eliminated their manufacture.[15]

McCray versus United States. The phosphorus match tax was never carried to court, but in a somewhat similar case—*McCray v. United States* [16]—an act of Congress was sustained. This involved the imposition of a heavy differential tax on the manufacture and sale of oleomargarine

---

[14] *Veazie Bank v. Fenno,* 8 Wall. 533, 548 (1869).
[15] John M. Mathews and Clarence A. Berdahl, *Documents and Readings in American Government* (New York: The Macmillan Company, 1928), p. 405.
[16] 195 U.S. 27 (1904).

colored to look like butter ($\frac{1}{4}$ of 1 cent per pound if uncolored, 10 cents per pound if colored). Legislation along these lines, frankly regulating the manufacture and sale of oleomargarine, might lie within the police power of the states, which could have justified it on the ground that they were protecting the public from fraud. However, the federal government has no such sustaining authority for this type of legislation and must resort, when necessary, to its taxing power. It was argued that Congress could not, under the guise of raising revenue, impose a tax so onerous as to make it manifest that the real objective sought was the suppression of the manufacture of the taxed article. This view, however, was rejected by the Court. Justice White, in delivering the opinion of the Court, quoted with approval an earlier case as follows: "The act before us is on its face an act of levying taxes, and although it may operate in so doing to prevent deception in the sale of oleomargarine as and for butter, its primary object must be assumed to be the raising of revenue." He added, "The decisions of this court from the beginning lend no support whatever to the assumption that the judiciary may restrain the exercise of lawful power on the assumption that a wrongful purpose or motive has caused the power to be exerted." [17]

This decision apparently gave Congress the power to levy any excise tax which appears on its face to be such, regardless of the incidental effect which the tax might have on the sale of the object taxed or on a specific business or practice related to such sale.

Similarly, the Court upheld an excise imposed upon the manufacture and sale of opium, a tax that was very clearly designed to give the federal government an effective means of regulation and control of the opium traffic.[18] A law requiring gamblers to register and purchase a $50 tax stamp was also sustained over the protest that this not only invaded the province of the states under the guise of a revenue measure but in addition compelled self-incriminating disclosures.[19]

Child Labor Tax Case. That there is a limit to what may pass as "an excise on its face" was established in the Child Labor Tax Case. In 1916 the federal government attempted to outlaw child labor under its power to regulate and control commerce, but this was declared to be an invasion of a power reserved to the states.[20] In 1919 an act was passed imposing a tax of 10 percent on net profits of firms knowingly employing children below the ages of fourteen to sixteen. To enforce the law, inspection by both the Treasury Department and the Department of Labor was provided.

---

[17] *Ibid.*, pp. 51, 56.
[18] *United States v. Doremus,* 249 U.S. 86 (1919).
[19] *United States v. Kahriger,* 345 U.S. 22 (1953).
[20] *Hammer v. Dagenhart,* 247 U.S. 251 (1918).

Chief Justice Taft, for the Court, said: "It [the law] provides a heavy exaction for a departure from a detailed and specified course of conduct in business." He went on to add that it was only where the employer knowingly departed from the prescribed course that payment was to be exacted, and concluded that, "In the light of these features of the act, a court must be blind not to see that the so-called tax is imposed to stop the employment of children within the age limits prescribed. . . . Grant the validity of this law, and all that Congress would need to do hereafter, in seeking to take over to its control any one of the great number of subjects of public interest, jurisdiction of which the States have never parted with and which are reserved to them by the Tenth Amendment, would be to enact a detailed measure of complete regulation of the subject and enforce it by a so-called tax upon departures from it. To give such magic to the word 'tax' would be to break down all constitutional limitation of the powers of Congress, and completely wipe out the sovereignty of the States." [21]

United States versus Butler.   In a case [22] now regarded as anomalous but never specifically overruled, the Court declared the Agricultural Adjustment Act of 1933 unconstitutional. This act provided for a processing tax levied on certain commodities and benefit payments under which the government gave bonuses to farmers for acreage temporarily and voluntarily taken out of cultivation.

The act applied both the taxing and spending powers, and the Court saw in the combination a clear intent to control agriculture. Subsequent to this decision new legislation, dropping the tax and stressing conservation but otherwise much like its predecessor, was enacted and sustained.[23]

In a case similar to that of *United States v. Butler,* the Court overruled a legislative act imposing a code of fair practices upon the bituminous coal industry. The act levied a tax on the sale price of coal at the mines and allowed a 90-percent credit if the code were complied with.[24]

Social Security Cases.   In May 1937 the Court, in sustaining the federal Social Security Act and the Unemployment Compensation Act of Alabama,[25] turned in the direction of a liberal interpretation of the federal taxing powers. In the Social Security Act a tax had been levied upon

---

[21] *Bailey v. Drexel Furniture Co.,* Child Labor Tax Case, 259 U.S. 20, 36–37, 38 (1922).

[22] *United States v. Butler,* 297 U.S. 1 (1936).

[23] *Wickard v. Filburn,* 317 U.S. 111 (1942); *Mulford et al. v. Smith et al.,* 307 U.S. 38 (1939).

[24] *Carter v. Carter Coal Co.,* 298 U.S. 238 (1936).

[25] *Steward Machine Co. v. Davis,* 301 U.S. 548 (1937). The Court also sustained the old-age insurance taxes and the Labor Relations Act. The latter decision considerably broadens previous interpretations of the power to regulate interstate commerce—*Helvering v. Davis,* 301 U.S. 619 (1937); *National Labor Relations Board v. Jones and Laughlin Steel Corporation,* 301 U.S. 1 (1937). Production destined for and indirectly affecting interstate commerce is now included within this power.

payrolls with a 90-percent credit for similar payments made to a state unemployment compensation system. The act prescribed in some detail the sort of state compensation system which would entitle taxpayers to the credit. It was alleged that this was coercive and an attempt to exceed federal powers. The Court held that Congress could seek to influence state action without exceeding its constitutional powers and that the conditions imposed were designed to protect the national treasury and were well within federal fiscal powers.

SPECIAL LIMITATIONS ON FEDERAL TAXING POWER

Under the Continental Congress and the Articles of Confederation, the "United States" incurred such great financial difficulties that the credit and prestige of the new union went from bad to worse. The Congress and the Confederacy had no independent powers of taxation and had to get such revenue as they could by begging or coercing the states to levy taxes on their behalf.

It is curious to observe how the situation has reversed itself in some 175 years. As a practical matter, the federal government now has far more effective powers of taxation and borrowing than do the states. Indeed, the test of World War II left many with the impression that the financial resources of the federal government are inexhaustible. Unequal financial power lies at the bottom of a developing system of federal grants-in-aid to states for meeting their responsibilities. It was mainly financial necessity which motivated the Constitutional Convention of 1787, and it was to be expected that any proposed constitution would contain much more adequate taxing powers than the federal government had theretofore possessed. Although the powers granted were very extensive compared with previous ones, and although these powers have been substantially extended (notably by the Sixteenth Amendment), they are still far from being all inclusive. The features of the federal Constitution which impose limitations on the federal taxing power will now be briefly discussed.

NO TAX ON EXPORTS

No tax or duty may be laid on articles exported from any state.[26] This limits the taxing power on articles of commerce to imports. The rule is by no means universal throughout the world. Many countries tax exports,

---

[26] *United States Constitution*, Art. 1, Sec. 9, Par. 5.

and several South American countries derive considerable revenue from
this source.[27]

DIRECT TAX APPORTIONMENT

The apportionment clause in the federal Constitution provides that
". . . direct Taxes shall be apportioned among the several States which
may be included within this Union, according to their respective Numbers . . ." and "no capitation, or other direct, Tax shall be laid unless in
Proportion to the Census or Enumeration herein before directed to be
taken." [28]

This clause raises the question as to what constitutes a direct tax, a
point that was sharply at issue in the *Pollock v. Farmers' Loan and Trust
Company* case ruling out the income tax of 1894.[29]

In 1913 the Sixteenth Amendment brought the income tax within
the power of Congress by providing that Congress might tax income
"from whatever source derived" without regard to apportionment. However, the amendment did not entirely end the controversy over apportionment of taxes aimed at net income. Subsequent decisions of the
Court have made it clear that any tax that is aimed at income, but that
is not upon net income as the Court interprets the latter, is still subject
to the apportionment clause. This interpretation of the Court makes its
definition of income a matter of first-rate importance. As has been observed, certain stock dividends were excluded from the Court's definition.[30] This makes them immune to federal taxation, but it does not
prevent a state or territory from calling a stock dividend income and taxing it as such.[31]

In 1929, in a case involving the constitutionality of the federal gift
tax, the Court held "that a tax imposed upon a particular use of property or the exercise of a single power over property incidental to owner-

---

[27] The clause has been interpreted by the Court as follows:
"The true construction of the constitutional provision is that no burden by
way of tax or duty can be cast upon the exportation of articles, and does not mean
that articles exported are relieved from the prior ordinary burdens of taxation
which rest upon all property similarly situated. The exemption attaches to the
export and not to the article before its exportation."—*Cornell v. Coyne*, 192 U.S.
418, 427 (1904). In a case involving the 1913 federal income tax, as applied to
the income of an industry engaged in exporting, the Court held that "at most,
exportation is affected only indirectly and remotely."—*Peck and Co. v. Lowe*,
247 U.S. 165, 175 (1918). On the other hand, a general excise tax on exporting
cannot be applied to sales made to a commission merchant for a foreign consignee. Such sales are regarded by the Court as a step in exportation.—*Spalding
and Brothers v. Edwards*, 262 U.S. 66 (1923).
[28] *United States Constitution*, Art. 1, Sec. 2, Par. 3, and Sec. 9, Par. 4.
[29] 157 U.S. 429; on rehaving, 158 U.S. 601 (1895). Discussed in Chapter 7.
[30] *Eisner v. Macomber*, 252 U.S. 189 (1920).
[31] *Pasados v. Warner, Barnes, & Co.*, 279 U.S. 340 (1929).

ship" is an excise and therefore need not be apportioned. A dissenting opinion contended "that a tax imposed upon an ordinary gift, to be measured by the value of the property given and without regard to any qualifying circumstances, is a tax by indirection upon the property, as much, for example, as a tax upon the mere possession by the owner of a farm, measured by the value of the land possessed, would be a tax on the land. To call either of them an excise is to sacrifice substance to a mere form of words." [32]

THE REQUIREMENT OF UNIFORMITY IN INDIRECT TAXES

The rule of apportionment previously discussed does not apply to indirect taxes; "but all Duties, Imposts and Excises shall be uniform throughout the United States." [33] Interpreting this uniformity, the Court declared that "The uniformity of taxation throughout the United States enjoined by Article I, Section 8, is geographic, not intrinsic. A graduated tax on legacies, granting exemptions . . . or on incomes . . . does not violate this clause of the Constitution . . ." [34] and even geographic uniformity means only that the tax law shall be generally applicable, not that it shall be uniform in its effect. Thus, a federal tax may be imposed on objects which exist in some states and not in others.[35]

DUE PROCESS OF LAW

The Fifth Amendment to the Constitution provides that no person shall be "deprived of life, liberty, or property, without due process of law." As applied to the tax field, this clause means that taxes must not be arbitrary or discriminatory. Classification is permitted but it must be reasonable.

The due process clause might also be invoked in the event the taxpayer is denied "a fair opportunity to assert his substantive rights before a proper judicial tribunal." [36]

TAXATION OF STATE INSTRUMENTALITIES [37]

There is no specific provision in the Constitution prohibiting the federal government from taxing state instrumentalities or the states from taxing

---

[32] *Bronley v. McCaughn,* 280 U.S. 124, 136, 141 (1929).
[33] *United States Constitution,* Art. I, Sec. 8, Par. 1.
[34] *Bromley v. McCaughn,* 280 U.S. 124, 138 (1929).
[35] *Head Money Cases,* 112 U.S. 580 (1884).
[36] Shultz, *American Public Finance and Taxation,* pp. 264–265.
[37] See Thomas Reed Powell, "The Waning of Governmental Tax Immunities," *Harvard Law Review,* 58 (May 1945), pp. 633–674; "The Remnant of Governmental Tax Immunities" (July 1945), pp. 757–805.

federal instrumentalities. The prohibitions have developed as a result of court decisions which rest upon the philosophy and theory of governmental systems existing in the United States rather than upon specific mandate. The theory upon which they are especially based is that of dual sovereignty, under which fully sovereign state governments operate within a fully sovereign government.

The following discussion of some of the more important cases pertaining to government instrumentalities includes state taxation of federal instrumentalities as well as federal taxation of state instrumentalities. It would be difficult to define exactly what a government instrumentality is; in its broadest scope it might include the following: all corporations (they get their charters from governments), all land (underlying title lies with state governments), banks, copyrights and patents, voting, college football games, sales to or by the government, government property, government bonds, and government enterprises.

McCulloch versus Maryland.   The prohibition on the taxation of federal instrumentalities by states goes back to *McCulloch v. Maryland,*[38] decided in 1819. Specifically, the issue in this case was the constitutionality of a tax imposed by Maryland "on all banks or branches thereof" not chartered by Maryland. The law required the notes of such banks to be issued upon stamped paper and in certain denominations or the payment of a lump sum in order to be absolved from this obligation. The Court declared this law unconstitutional. Chief Justice Marshall, in delivering the opinion of the Court, stated that "the power to tax involves the power to destroy," and added: "If the States may tax one instrument, employed by the government [federal] in the execution of its powers, they may tax any and every other instrument. They may tax the mail; they may tax the mint; they may tax patent rights; they may tax the papers of the customhouse; they may tax judicial process; they may tax all the means employed by the government, to an excess which would defeat all the ends of government. This was not intended by the American people. They did not design to make their government dependent on the States." [39] He made the reservation that the limitations imposed upon state powers by the Constitution as interpreted in the decision "does not extend to a tax paid by the real property of the bank, in common with the other real property within the State, nor to a tax imposed on the interest which the citizens of Maryland may hold in this institution, in common with other property of the same description throughout the State." [40]

In other words, the decision appeared to mean that the states may

---

[38] 4 Wheaton 316 (1819).
[39] *Ibid.,* p. 432.
[40] *Ibid.,* p. 436.

impose general and nondiscriminatory taxes, but not special and discriminatory taxes, on federal instrumentalities. If the decision means this, no one can quarrel with it. But subsequent opinions of the courts extended this prohibition to include all taxation by states of federal instrumentalities (subject to certain exceptions) and all taxation by the federal government of state instrumentalities (again with some exceptions).

Extension of Immunity Doctrine. In the case of *Collector v. Day*,[41] the Supreme Court ruled that the federal government could not impose and collect a general income tax upon the salary of a judicial officer of a state. This extended the limitation imposed in *McCulloch v. Maryland* to include the federal government as well as the states and a general tax as well as a specific one. A dissenting opinion aptly commented that "no man ceases to be a citizen of the United States by being an officer under the State government," [42] and wondered where the doctrine of the majority opinion would end.

In a later case [43] a federal court held the earnings of employees of the publicly owned street railway of Detroit exempt from federal income taxation.

In *Pollock v. Farmers' Loan and Trust Co.* the Court unanimously ruled out the application of the federal income tax to the interest upon municipal bonds.[44] The courts have made it clear in many cases that the Sixteenth Amendment did not alter preexisting immunities of this kind.

The exemption doctrine was carried to greater length in *Panhandle Oil Co. v. Knox*,[45] which banned a state gasoline tax on gasoline sold for use by the federal government. The Court held that the state could not exact tribute for its support on federal transactions. Justice Holmes, in his dissenting opinion, suggested that instrumentalities could be adequately protected as long as discriminatory taxation were prohibited. "The power to tax is not the power to destroy," he said, "while this Court sits." [46] Justice McReynolds added that he was "unable to think that every man who sells a gallon of gasoline to be used by the United States thereby becomes a federal instrumentality. . . ." [47]

Similarly, an attempt to apply a federal tax on manufactured goods to motorcycles sold to a Massachusetts municipality was declared in-

---

[41] 11 Wall. 113 (1870). An earlier opinion, *Dobbins v. Commissioners of Erie Co.*, 16 Peters 435 (1842), had already granted immunity to federal employees from taxation (by states) on their compensation.
[42] 11 Wall. 113, 128 (1870).
[43] *Frey v. Woodworth*, 2 Fed. (2d) 725 (1924).
[44] 157 U.S. 429; on rehearing, 185 U.S. 601 (1895).
[45] 277 U.S. 218 (1928).
[46] *Ibid.*, p. 223.
[47] *Ibid.*, p. 225.

valid.[48] The majority opinion ignored the question of incidence involved
on the theory that it was the transaction which was taxed. A dissenting
opinion argued that the matter of incidence was an important issue and
one which involved "considerations so various and complex as to pre-
clude the assumption a priori that any particular tax at any particular
time is passed on." [49] The exact status of the immunity of sales is in great
confusion, since they are made by, as well as to, governments. The conditions which determine immunity in a sale involving the government are
still not clearly defined.[50]

The taxability of sales made to cost-plus-fixed-fee contractors working on government contracts became an important issue during the early
years of World War II. In the case of *Alabama v. King and Boozer*,[51]
the Court decided that in the absence of action by Congress the state
sales tax could be applied to the purchases by the contractor. "So far as
such a nondiscrimatory state tax upon the contractors enters into the
cost of the materials to the Government, that is but the normal incident
of the organization within the same territory of the two taxing sover-
eignties." [52] The case seems to make "legal incidence" a determining
factor of constitutionality in sales tax situations. This would mean that a
vendor's sales tax would be unconstitutional as applied to sales by the
government and a vendee's sales tax would be outlawed as to sales to
the government.

In this and other cases dealing with the state taxation of federal
instrumentalities (national banks, for instance), recent decisions make
it clear that a tax by the states would not be valid unless imposed in such
a way as to come within the authority granted by Congress. It is not
recognized at all that the states have any right to tax federal instrumentalities if Congress chooses to exempt them.[53] However, the Court, as late
as 1944, decided that federally owned machinery leased to private concerns was not taxable, even in the absence of a congressional prohibition.[54]

The legal opinion in Canada concerning instrumentalities is an interesting contrast to that in the United States. The income derived from

---

[48] *Indian Motorcycle Co. v. United States,* 283 U.S. 570 (1931).
[49] *Ibid.,* p. 581.
[50] Robert Murray Haig and Carl Shoup, *The Sales Tax in the American States*
(New York: Columbia University Press, 1934), pp. 646–650.
[51] 314 U.S. 1 (1941).
[52] *Ibid.,* pp. 8 and 9.
[53] *Federal Land Bank v. Bismarck Lumber Co.,* 314 U.S. 95 (1941); see also
Northwest Airlines v. Minnesota, 322 U.S. 292 (1944) and *Carson v. Roane
Anderson,* 342 U.S. 232 (1952).
[54] *United States and the Mesta Machine Co. v. County of Allegheny,* 322
U.S. 174 (1944).

a state security or salary is taxable under the federal (Canadian) income tax.[55] The Canadian defense against attacks on sovereignty rests upon the rule that there must be no discrimination against the instrumentalities of another sovereign government with concurrent jurisdiction. This is the solution suggested in *McCulloch v. Maryland* and in many dissenting opinions in the instrumentality cases decided in the United States. Recent opinions of the Court indicate some inclination to move toward a similar rule.[56]

Limitations on the Immunity Doctrine. The rather extreme limitations placed upon the taxing power by the decisions discussed above have been subject to qualifications in others. In the case of *South Carolina v. United States,*[57] the Court ruled, with three dissents, that a state is not exempt from paying federal liquor taxes when it engages in the liquor business. Here the Court distinguished between two types of functions in which the government may engage: one is strictly governmental, the other is proprietary. Instrumentalities incidental to the performance of proprietary functions, of which the liquor business is one, are not immune to taxation. The Court may have been influenced by the possibility that, if it decided otherwise, the door would be wide open for the avoidance of much internal revenue taxation.

The criteria to be used in drawing the line between essential governmental functions and proprietary functions are the importance of the function, the time during which governments have performed it, and the exclusiveness of government performance. In a case in 1934 the Court held that, ". . . the State cannot withdraw sources of revenue from the federal taxing power by engaging in businesses which constitute a departure from usual governmental functions and to which, by reason of their nature, the federal taxing power would normally extend." [58]

The distinction between proprietary and governmental functions as a dividing line between that which is taxable and that which is not taxable is extremely unsatisfactory and has involved the Court and taxpayers in a maze of uncertainty and confusion. Functions that were not essential fifty years ago may be indispensable today. Essentiality of governmental functions is always a matter of opinion and no proper issue for the Supreme Court to decide.

In a series of further cases the Court added to the confusion; it held the compensation paid to the general counsel for the Panama Railroad

---

[55] *Abbott v. St. John,* 40 S.C.R. 597 (1908).

[56] *Helvering v. Gerhardt,* 304 U.S. 405 (1938); *Graves v. O'Keefe,* 306 U.S. 466 (1939). These decisions are discussed later.

[57] 199 U.S. 437 (1905).

[58] *Helvering v. Powers,* 293 U.S. 214 (1934).

Company [59] and to the chief engineer of a city's bureau of water supply [60] nontaxable, although with respect to salaries paid, in an earlier case to the trustee of a municipally owned railway [61] and in a later case to employees of the New York Port Authority,[62] it reached a contrary conclusion. Needless to say, the question of immunity remained more uncertain than ever.

The latest major court decision on the subject of immunities in the area of state enterprises is that of *State of New York v. United States* (Saratoga Springs Case).[63] The facts of the New York case were similar to those in the South Carolina case. A sharply divided Supreme Court sustained a federal tax on mineral water bottled and sold by the state of New York. Justice Frankfurter, for the Court, recognizing the unsatisfactory character of the rule enunciated in the South Carolina case, qualified the rule by holding that immunity should be confined to state enterprises "uniquely capable" of being conducted by the state (such as general administration and taxation). It seems very unlikely, however, that the Court will extend this doctrine to cover the general range of public utility enterprises. A strong minority would move in the other direction and grant all state enterprises full immunity.

In this and other opinions it has become clear that the powers and immunities of federal government and those of the states are not fully reciprocal. It is said that it is one thing for the part to tax the whole and quite a different matter for the whole to tax the part.

Another qualification to the immunity doctrine is that compensation received from the government by those who are employed under special contract and take no oath of office is taxable. Thus, immunity does not extend to the compensation of a consulting engineer whose work for the government is neither permanent nor continuous.[64]

A third qualification to the immunity doctrine is that no exemption will be allowed where the tax would constitute only an indirect burden upon the functioning of government. Income from patents and copyrights, once immune, is now by a reversed decision held taxable.[65] A capital gain from the sale of a government bond is taxable on the ground that ". . . neither the Federal Government nor the States have found a

---

[59] *Rogers v. Graves*, 299 U.S. 401 (1937).

[60] *Brush v. Commissioner*, 300 U.S. 352 (1937).

[61] *Helvering v. Powers*, 293 U.S. 214 (1934).

[62] *Helvering v. Gerhardt*, 304 U.S. 405 (1938). Football games conducted under the auspices of a state university have been held to be proprietary and subject to tax under the federal excise on admission.—*Allen v. Regents of University System of Georgia*, 304 U.S. 439 (1938).

[63] 326 U.S. 572 (1945); see also *Wilmette Park District v. Campbell*, 338 U.S. 411 (1949).

[64] *Metcalf and Eddy v. Mitchell*, 269 U.S. 514 (1925).

[65] *Fox Film Co. v. Doyal*, 286 U.S. 123 (1932).

tax on the profits of the sales of their securities to be a burden on their power to borrow money." [66] Interest on government securities held by banks may be taxed under a corporate franchise tax which is measured by net income.[67] At one time, the immunity allowed governmental instrumentalities was extended to include the lessee's profits on land owned by the government. Such income is now taxable.[68]

A fourth limitation to the freedom of governmental instrumentalities from taxation, one which appears to represent a fundamental change in philosophy and opens the way for a complete overthrow of the whole immunity doctrine, is that a nondiscriminatory tax creates a burden so indirect and conjectural that its application to governmental instrumentalities is permissible. This new approach has been sanctioned recently, but it is impossible to say how far the Court will apply it. In two cases involving the salaries of government employees, the Court held that the application of a nondiscriminatory tax to such income was valid. The first decision was said in the dissenting opinion to overrule by implication "a century of precedents." [69] The second specifically overruled *Collector v. Day*.[70] This leaves the exemption of municipal utilities and securities as the outstanding remaining strongholds of immunity among state instrumentalities.

Conclusion. The entire doctrine of immunity from nondiscriminatory taxation, developed in almost every case with a divided Court for well over a century, seems quite unnecessary for the preservation of sovereignty. It would have been far better, in the author's opinion, had discretion in this area been left to Congress, excepting only cases where intent to discriminate and thus interfere with the exercise of legitimate powers is manifest. The doctrine has served principally to vex the tax system. Observation of experience in other countries with federal systems reinforces this conclusion.

FEDERAL LIMITATIONS ON STATE TAXING POWERS

Limitations on the Power to Tax Commerce. Several of the federal limitations on the states' powers to tax have already been discussed or closely parallel those discussed. Like the federal government, the states

---

[66] *Wilcuts v. Bunn*, 282 U.S. 216, 232 (1931); death taxes may be applied to government bonds.—*Plummer v. Coler*, 178 U.S. 115 (1900).

[67] *Pacific Co. v. Johnson*, 285 U.S. 480 (1932).

[68] *Helvering v. Mountain Producers Corporation*, 303 U.S. 376 (1938).

[69] *Helvering v. Gerhardt*, 304 U.S. 405 (1938), p. 430.

[70] *Graves v. O'Keefe*, 306 U.S. 466 (1939).

may not levy export duties, but, unlike the former, they are also excluded from the taxation of imports. In addition, the states cannot impose tonnage taxes [71] (upon vessels, according to their size or capacity). Both limitations are qualified by the provision "without the consent of Congress." Finally, the states are excluded from taxing interstate and foreign commerce. This last prohibition is not specific, but it is inferred from the prohibition on export and import taxes and the commerce clause which gives Congress power "to regulate Commerce with foreign Nations, and among the several States, and with the Indian Tribes." [72]

The forbidden area of interstate commerce has been a prolific source of litigation. It is very apparent that the states can tax interstate commerce if they go about it in the right way. It is within the power of the states to tax property used in the transaction of interstate commerce—as, for example, the property of an interstate railroad. Such property may be included along with other wealth in a general tax, but it must not be singled out for discriminatory taxation. A state may tax the gross income of a railroad in lieu of a property tax, but it is questionable if it may impose a gross income tax in addition to a property tax.[73] The state must confine its tax on railroad property to such part as can reasonably be apportioned to its jurisdiction.[74] It is excluded from taxing goods in transit, but transportation ends when goods have been delivered or perhaps even before they are unloaded provided they have reached their destination. The rule that transit is not completed while goods remain "in the original package" is confined to foreign commerce. Even property at rest temporarily between two parts of its journey is taxable, though this does not include rebilling or reshipment en route.[75]

A state may tax the net income of corporations doing an interstate business, at least unless the income is derived exclusively from interstate commerce. In the case of *United States Glue Co. v. Town of Oak Creek,* the Court said: "The difference in effect between a tax measured by gross receipts and one measured by net income, recognized by our decisions, is manifest and substantial, and it affords a convenient and workable basis of distinction between a direct and immediate burden upon the business affected and a charge that is only indirect and incidental. A tax

---

[71] *United States Constitution,* Art. I, Sec. 10, Par. 3.

[72] *United States Constitution,* Art. I, Sec. 8, Par. 3.

[73] *Oklahoma v. Wells, Fargo & Co.,* 223 U.S. 298 (1912); *United States Express Co. v. Minnesota,* 223 U.S. 335 (1912); *Nashville, Chattanooga & St. Louis Railway v. Browning,* 310 U.S. 362 (1940).

[74] *Wallace v. Hines,* 253 U.S. 66 (1920); *Fargo v. Hart,* 193 U.S. 490 (1904); but see *Northwest Airlines v. Minnesota,* 322 U.S. 292 (1949).

[75] See Thomas M. Cooley, *The Law of Taxation* (4th ed., Chicago: Callaghan and Company, 1924), vol. 1, pp. 818–823.

upon gross receipts affects each transaction in proportion to its magnitude and irrespective of whether it is profitable or otherwise. . . ." [76] As suggested, the opposite rule holds for a gross income tax, of which the Court has said: "That portion of the tax which is measured by the receipts from foreign commerce necessarily varies in proportion to the volume of that commerce, and hence is a direct burden upon it." [77]

It has been held that where a corporation does both an interstate and an intrastate business, it may be taxed on its net income, fairly apportioned, or on its capital stock; and even if the corporation does no intrastate business, its interstate business alone can be subjected to a corporate income tax (as distinguished from a franchise tax) if there is "sufficient nexus" in the taxing state. Recent decisions [78] have made it clear that the maintenance of a sales office, whether or not owned, and the solicitation of orders is sufficient nexus.

A state may not impose a sales tax on the exports and imports over its borders even though such a tax is a part of a general sales tax that strikes equally sales made within the borders of the taxing state. On the other hand, the so-called state use taxes, levied upon the first use within the state of commodities purchased at retail outside the state and so not subject to the sales tax, have been sustained on the ground that no attempt to discriminate against interstate commerce was involved.[79] Going further, the Court has upheld the collection of a sales tax levied upon goods moving in across the border when the seller maintained a place of business in the taxing state.[80]But the state cannot collect a use tax at the source from a firm that sells over the border but maintains no place of business or makes no solicitation of business in the taxing state.

As with instrumentalities, a simple rule of nondiscrimination, plus in this case a requirement of fair apportionment, seems adequate to protect interstate commerce. However, whether sales solicitation alone constitutes an adequate basis of jurisdiction to tax is still moot. The Court has held that solicitation by independent contractors is sufficient grounds for the enforcement of a use tax against out-of-state firms.[81] There is support for the view that Congress should define the boundary lines of interstate-commerce protection. The Court, acting on a case-by-case

---

[76] 247 U.S. 321, 328–329 (1918).

[77] *Crew Levick Co. v. Pennsylvania,* 245 U.S. 292, 297–298 (1917). This decision was followed when on May 16, 1938, the Court held unconstitutional the Indiana gross income tax, in so far as it applied to business carried on in interstate commerce.—*Adams Manufacturing Co. v. Storen,* 304 U.S. 307 (1938).

[78] *Northwestern Portland Cement Co. v. Minnesota,* 358 U.S. 450 (1959).

[79] *Henneford v. Silas Mason Co.,* 300 U.S. 577 (1937).

[80] *McGoldrick v. Berwind White Coal Mining Co.,* 309 U.S. 33 (1940); *Nelson v. Sears, Roebuck & Co.,* 312 U.S. 359 (1941); but see also *McLeod v. J. E. Dilworth Co.,* 322 U.S. 327 (1944).

[81] *Scripto, Inc. v. Carson,* 362 U.S. 207 (1960).

basis and with changing personnel, has proved ill equipped to do so. Temporary legislation (pending further investigation) was enacted in 1959 attempting to define the nexus required to validate a net income tax on interstate business and collection of use tax at the source from out-of-state vendors. (Further discussed in Chapter 20.)

The Supremacy of Federal Treaties over State Tax Powers. The treaties of the United States with foreign countries are a part of the supreme law of the land, and if the federal government enters into a treaty with a foreign power providing for mutual nondiscrimination as to taxation or the property rights of the citizens of the two countries, then any state tax which conflicts with such treaty is invalid.

Discrimination against Citizens of Other States. The citizens of each state are entitled to all the privileges and immunities of the citizens of the several states.[82] This rules out any attempt to discriminate against the citizens of other states, whether resident or nonresident. Thus, assessors may not assess the property of nonresidents on a standard different from that used for the property of residents. Actually, such discrimination is a common practice, but evidence sufficient to prove intent to discriminate, or a well-settled practice of discrimination, is required to invalidate such an assessment.[83] This protection does not extend to corporations, however, since they are not counted as citizens. Thus, as a rule, the states are free to levy heavier burdens on foreign than upon domestic corporations.[84] But there are decisions which declare such discrimination invalid, particularly when applied to a corporation after it has built up a large business and valuable connections within the state.[85]

Due Process of Law. Mention has been made of the requirements that taxes must not be imposed so as to take property without due process of law. This limitation in the Fourteenth Amendment is applied to the states and is the same in substance as that in the Fifth Amendment, which restricts the federal government. The phraseology of these amendments has been applied to support decisions involving unreasonable classification and taxation beyond the jurisdiction of the taxing unit.

The state has "plenary power" over corporations of its own creation and can impose a franchise tax measured by all the capital stock of such corporations whether or not employed exclusively within the state's borders.[86] On foreign corporations, the state probably must confine such

---

[82] *United States Constitution,* Art. IV, Sec. 2.

[83] *Beeson v. Johns,* 124 U.S. 56 (1888).

[84] Nichols, *Taxation in Massachusetts,* pp. 35, 43–47. The corporation cannot be required to surrender its rights under the federal constitution, such as freedom from excise taxation on interstate business and from extraterritorial taxation.

[85] *Hanover Fire Insurance Co. v. Harding,* 272 U.S. 494 (1926); *Southern Railway Co. v. Greene,* 216 U.S. 400 (1910).

[86] *Kansas City Railway Co. v. Botkin,* 240 U.S. 227 (1916).

a tax to as much of the capital stock as is employed within its boundaries.[87]

STATE LIMITATIONS ON STATE TAXATION

There is little uniformity among state constitutions in the rules and limitations they set up for state taxation. In a few states no constitutional restrictions whatsoever are imposed on state or local taxing power. On the other hand, some states have attempted to write much of their state and local tax systems into the state constitution.

The earliest documents, written in the eighteenth century, provided only that taxes should not be levied without the consent of the people or their representatives, a provision that sprang from colonial and British experience. Constitutions of the early 1800s ignored the earlier provisions (fear of tyranny having subsided) and provided that taxes must be "equal and uniform." Later constitutions still feature "uniformity clauses" but also contain many additional details concerning such matters as exemptions, property tax limitations, occupation taxes, and so on. While the trend in the twentieth century has been away from rigid uniformity requirements, the states typically have cluttered their constitutions with all sorts of other tax restrictions: ceiling tax rates, earmarking for highway-user tax funds, restrictions on authority to levy income taxes or ceiling rates and minimum exemptions for such levies, and so on. A drastic amendment to the Arkansas constitution virtually denies the legislature the authority to increase tax rates of any kind; such increase can be authorized only by popular referendum.[88] Financial restrictions of this sort are generally disapproved of by critics who hold that they unduly curtail the freedom of legislative action and abuse the purpose of constitutions.

The most general of all state constitutional limitations is that which requires that taxes be equal, or uniform, or both. Frequently the clause applies only to property taxes, but in some states by stipulation (Texas) or court interpretation (Georgia), the uniformity provision is applied to other taxes as well. Not infrequently, state courts have held that many taxes, such as income and death taxes, are property taxes.

Uniformity provisions usually require the application of a uniform rate and assessment standard for all taxable property within the same

[87] *Cudahy Packing Co. v. Hinkle,* 278 U.S. 460 (1929).
[88] Glenn D. Morrow, "State Constitutional Limitations on the Taxing Authority of State Legislatures," *National Tax Journal,* IX: 2 (June 1956), pp. 126–133; *Arkansas Constitution,* Art. 5, Section 38.

jurisdiction. Differences of procedure based upon plausible grounds, however, are not repugnant to this provision. A few states allow almost any degree of reasonable classification even under a uniformity clause, but this is exceptional. As a rule, classification by complete exemption is permissable.

SUMMARY

A federal system calls for a division of powers between a central government and its constituent states. This provides many advantages in certain situations but is likely to prove inflexible in practice. The inflexibility may be countered by amendment, reinterpretation, and by the use of the spending power, aids, credits and taxes for nonfiscal purposes. Taxing powers, in general, are divided like other powers; those of the federal government are designated, those of the states are inherent, and those of municipalities are delegated to such units by the states.

Both the states and the federal government have broad powers of taxation, upon which, however, there are certain limitations. Among the general limitations is that taxes must be levied for a public purpose. This is sometimes used to rule out direct government aid to private corporations and individuals and might also invalidate transportation aid for children attending parochial schools. The lack of clear definition of public purpose has resulted in conflicting court decisions.

Taxation for nonfiscal purposes involves many troublesome legal questions. The difficulty here arises principally because the power of Congress to tax is much more ample than its power to regulate, and sometimes it attempts regulation in the guise of taxation. A federal tax which on its face is an excise, even though its purpose may be regulatory, is permitted, but there are limits in the degree to which this doctrine may be applied. In the Child Labor Tax Case the degree was held excessive and the tax was declared invalid. On the other hand, the social security taxes were sustained, although they are also regulatory. Here, again, the boundary lines of what is and what is not legal are hazy.

The federal Constitution includes a number of limitations upon the taxing power of the federal government, one of the most important of which is that direct taxes must be apportioned among the states according to population. This limitation was used to block the federal net income tax until the Sixteenth Amendment was adopted in 1913; moreover, it still can invalidate an unapportioned direct tax which is levied on any base other than net income.

A very important limitation on the federal taxing power, based upon court decisions rather than specific constitutional limitations, is the prohibition on federal taxation of state instrumentalities. The rule also covers state taxation of federal instrumentalities. Both applications are subject to several subtle qualifications. The immunity-of-instrumentalities doctrine has created many special privileges in the tax laws, and it is doubtful that it was ever required to protect the sovereignty of governments. The doctrine has a long history, but there are some indications that the Court is moving toward a negation of this legal development.

The federal Constitution also imposes several limitations upon the taxing power of state and local governments, including the due process clause which has been interpreted to rule out extraterritorial taxation (beyond the borders of the taxing unit) and arbitrary uses of the taxing power. By implication, states are also prohibited from taxing interstate commerce, a restriction which has been difficult to interpret and fruitful of litigation.

Finally, state constitutions frequently impose certain limitations upon state power to tax. By far the most common and important of these is that requiring uniformity in property taxation and occasionally in other taxes. Frequently this eliminates the possibility (without amendment) of state income and classified property taxes.

PROBLEMS

1. Consider briefly the legal status of the following in the context of the American federal system:
   a. A federal property tax at 10 mills on all the property in the United States.
   b. Federal tax on anthracite coal (bituminum exempt).
   c. Federal law prescribing the curriculum for elementary schools.
   d. County appropriation to cover the cost of a picnic for board members, families, and friends.
   e. Federal excise tax on sales of state-owned gasoline refinery.
   f. State corporate income tax from which companies doing only a state-wide business are exempt.
   g. A state income tax on the income from national banks including in the base the interest on federal bonds.
   h. Application of the social security system to state and municipal employees.
   i. A state income tax including in its base the interest on municipal bonds.
   j. A federal graduated personal tax, with a high exemption, on the "privilege" of owning large amounts of wealth.
   k. A local property tax on absentees' property where absentees have no right to vote.

2. In 1948 international statesmen were called upon to help devise a new constitution for Western Germany. Was it wise for them to recommend a federal system?

3. Consider the history of efforts by the federal government to control child labor. Is direct federal labor legislation now unconstitutional?

4. The federal government does not have the police power but there is not much control that lies beyond its reach through the exercise of other powers. Comment.

5. Consider the qualifications introduced by legal decisions to the rule that in our federal system it is unconstitutional for one sovereign government to tax the instrumentalities of another.

6. What are the minimum restrictions on the taxing power necessary to protect our federal system in the case of governmental instrumentalities? Interstate commerce?

7. Suppose you were called upon to recommend an ideal finance section for a new state constitution. What would you advise?

8. Define and discuss briefly the following limitations on federal power to tax:
   a. Direct taxes must be apportioned.
   b. Taxes must be for revenue and not control.
   c. State and local instrumentalities may not be taxed.

9. Consider the proposition: Federal limitation on the power of states to tax interstate commerce should be defined in a comprehensive act of Congress.

10. Comment on the proposition: The states can tax interstate commerce if they go about it in the right way.

11. Discuss the issue involved in the famous case of *McCulloch v. Maryland* and the principal qualifications that have been added to the rule there established.

20

INTERGOVERNMENTAL FISCAL RELATIONS

INTRODUCTION

The growing importance of intergovernmental relations in taxation is easy to explain. The Constitution allowed much overlapping taxation, but this developed slowly. For many years the federal government subsisted largely on customs and then on customs and excises, while the states and municipalities relied for revenue on the general property tax and business taxes. Because of the need for expanded revenues at both levels of government, a wide overlapping of fiscal sources has developed in recent years. All of the states tax alcoholic beverages and motor fuel; at least two thirds tax income and tobacco. All these sources are also used by the federal government. This has created many problems, the most obvious of which is overlapping administration by at least two layers of government, and additional cost of compliance to the taxpayer. No major source of tax revenue initiated during peacetime has been relinquished by the federal government to the states, or vice versa.

Problems of valuation, jurisdiction, apportionment, and overlapping business taxation are created by the developments of mammoth corporations. A high degree of economic interdependence has developed, taking myriad forms of which the most obvious are interstate trade, travel, communication, migration, and the nation-wide circulation of magazines and newspapers. What was once merely a local concern for government has ceased to be so under modern conditions.

The conviction that a real cause for action lies behind the coordination movement is strengthened by a listing of the complaints lodged against our present fiscal arrangements: that overlapping taxes tend to become excessive and are costly as to both administration and compliance; that the states and municipalities are left with inadequate tax resources; that the federal government is embarrassed in extending its tax system to meet emergency needs; that state taxation of a national economic system involves impossible problems of jurisdiction and multiple taxation; that state taxation under modern conditions leads to migration of wealth and industry; that economic resources are so unevenly distributed that state taxation must result in malnourishment for certain services in which there is a national interest; that mandatory expenditures imposed from above have dislocated municipal finances; that intergovernmental instrumentalities escape taxation or are taxed to the prejudice of local finances; and that the tax system as a whole has too many regressive elements and is repressive and ill adapted to such important economic ends as full employment and the maximization of national income.

"Double Taxation." Several species of double taxation in the tax system are worth distinguishing. Species A involves multiple taxation of some objects in a uniform class and not of others. This occurs in the general property tax where the state imposes a general property tax on all the operating property of a railroad and some part of the property, such as a bridge, is also locally taxed. Species B is territorial multiple taxation and occurs, for instance, where Smith pays two taxes and a larger sum than Jones by virtue of the fact that the former's wealth or income lies in more than one taxing district. Species C consists of two taxes on closely related aspects of the same object of taxation as where a taxpayer pays both a motor fuel tax and a license fee. Species D consists of the imposition of taxes on the same base by two or more layers of government. The latter species (and Species C) need involve no inequity to the taxpayer (two kinds of taxes at each of two levels of government can add up to exactly the same result as one kind of tax at each level), but the duplication can complicate the tax system and it can produce bad collateral results. However, it should be added that there are good things to be said about overlapping taxes. Two income taxes at federal and state levels do not occasion more compliance and administrative expense than a federal income tax and a state sales tax. On the contrary, the administrations can and do reenforce each other. The duplication provides the opportunity for additional economies through cooperation of administrative agencies.

FISCAL RELATIONS IN SEVERAL COUNTRIES

CANADA

An outstanding report by a Canadian Royal Commission on Dominion-Provincial Relations appearing in 1940 grew in part out of the extreme difficulties in provincial finance during the depression and draught of the 1930s. In general it recommended exclusive use of major taxes (income, business, and death taxes) by the Dominion and the distribution of equalization grants by the central government. The latter would aim to provide all provinces with means to maintain a minimum standard of government with approximately equal tax burdens. Notwithstanding the failure of a Dominion-provincial conference to implement this report, the Dominion succeeded during World War II in arranging with all provinces temporary agreements granting to the former the exclusive right to levy income and corporation taxes during the war period. The provinces accepted payments equal to 1940 income tax collections or an agreed assumption of debt-service costs.

At the close of the war another conference was held looking toward an extension of the agreements. Ontario and Quebec protested that they were being asked "to sell their birthright for a mess of pottage." They argued for a more complete separation of sources with the Dominion surrendering a considerable number of levies (including the death tax) to the provinces. Again the Dominion sought to arrange agreements with the provinces individually, and this time succeeded with all its constituents except Ontario and Quebec. The agreement in effect leased for five years all corporate income and business taxes, personal income taxes, and death taxes to the central government in return for specified financial allowances based largely on population or population and the yield of hypothetical state levies. The agreements have been extended several times and later editions included Ontario, though the latter protested against what it regarded as unfair and irrational formulas of distribution. However, the lease system was abandoned in 1962; the provinces may reenact their independent levies; subject to conformity of definitions and within prescribed limits, the federal government will collect and return the provincial taxes. Some equalization by general grant will be continued.[1]

---

[1] "A General Reappraisal of Coordination of Tax Systems in Canada and the United States" (symposium), *Proceedings of the National Tax Association Conference,* 1952, pp. 292–337. For more recent developments see current numbers of the *Canadian Tax Journal,* Canadian Tax Foundation, Toronto; R. M.

The following persuasive arguments were urged by proponents of federal-collection provincial-sharing of income and business taxes in Canada: (1) that income is really nationally created and cannot properly be localized for provincial taxation; (2) that the federal government can assure the provinces a much more stable revenue than can their own tax systems; and (3) that assurance of provincial revenues in hard times will make a contribution toward the solution of the business-cycle problem.

Watched with considerable interest on the American side of the border, these developments raised questions as to whether a similar development here would be feasible and desirable. As to feasibility, it is obviously much more difficult to secure agreement among forty-nine units of government than among eleven. More important, perhaps, is the fact that under our system of government no one has much authority to speak for any government. Our state governors, for instance, have far less authority to speak for their states than Canadian premiers have for their provinces. As to desirability, the Canadian program scored impressively in achieving simplicity in the tax system; it encountered the objections that it sacrificed local independence, left the provinces and municipalities with limited and mainly undesirable independent sources of revenue, and may have involved waste in separating decisions concerning expenditure from those to raise revenue.

AUSTRALIA

The experience of the Australian states and their federation roughly parallels that of their Canadian counterparts. Even before World War II substantial progress toward a coordinated tax system had been made. Agreements to eliminate duplicate administration had been reached; the states were to administer the federal income tax along with their own in five states; and in West Australia the federal government would manage the two levies. The arrangement worked well and was justly appraised in this country as a great achievement. Nevertheless, the system did not survive the strain of the war. The uniform tax measure of 1942 was adopted over the unanimous protest of the states. It was sustained by the Court and extended into the postwar period. However, opposition to the measure also continued and return of the right to tax income in the states was negotiated at several Premiers' Conferences during the 1950s, but without reaching agreement. In 1959 an extension of the so-called uniform tax system for six years was accepted.

Australia has several well-developed institutions of fiscal coordina-

Burns, "Recent Development in Federal-Provincial Fiscal Arrangements in Canada," *National Tax Journal,* XV: 3 (September 1962), pp. 225–238.

tion that have no counterpart in the United States. The fountainhead of policy in the area of federal-state relations is the Premiers' Conference (of Commonwealth and state ministers) which meets often and deals with a wide range of problems. Another body with federal-state representation is the Australian Loan Council which in effect rations credit and centralizes the arrangement and security for debt. Finally, there is the Commonwealth Grants Commission, a body appointed to recommend special-need grants to the weaker states (not to be confused with the distribution of "uniform tax" revenue). The standard applied is that of allowing a uniform minimum level of government (with some qualifications) at uniform state costs. On top of all this some special purpose grants are provided.[2]

NORWAY

This Scandinavian country has no federal system, but it maintains a high degree of decentralization in government. The general property tax is confined to real estate and it is much less stressed than our similar levy. The genius of the system is its major stress of an instrumentality largely undeveloped in the United States, namely, the supplement. National taxes are so selected and devised that local governments can use the same bases (with suitable modifications), and local and national taxes can be administered by a single agency and operation. The supplement, unlike the shared tax, leaves discretion to local governments to adapt the levy (within limits) to their own tastes and needs. The two taxes that constitute the core of Scandinavian revenue systems are the net income tax and net worth tax, or (personal) capital tax. The capital tax is a conservatively graduated tax on the net assets of individual taxpayers. At the national level these taxes are applied with substantial graduation; at the local level, they are appropriately less progressive (more moderate personal exemptions and little, if any, graduation).

UNITED STATES

The American approach to intergovernmental fiscal coordination may be described as pragmatic and eclectic. Institutional arrangements have been shaped and reshaped to meet changing conditions. The coordination achievement, if so it may be called, consists of a variety of devices and expedients: credits in the death and payroll tax fields; deductibility in the income tax area; separation of sources as to the property tax, automobile

---

[2] Eric D. Hanson, *Australian Commonwealth Grants Commission* (Toronto: Canadian Tax Foundation, 1960); *Commonwealth Payments To or For the States* (Canberra: Commonwealth Government Printer, 1962).

license tax, and tariffs; some supplementation of central levies in state and local sales taxes; and administrative collaboration and efforts at uniformity in many areas. The Americans have shown considerable distrust of so-called sovereign remedies, meaning a general aid or shared tax program that would break the back of the coordination problem once and for all and at one sitting. There is a strong appreciation of the value of virile local self-government. Aids have been extensively used both at the national and state levels, but they are associated with specific functions in which central and local units are thought to have a partnership of interests. Cooperation by administrative collaboration has made some progress. Conflicting jurisdiction among states has been successfully attacked by reciprocal legislation in the death tax field and by pressure to adopt standard procedures in the apportionment of the corporate income tax base; little progress has been made in eliminating this evil in the area of personal income taxes. It may be well doubted that any federal system anywhere has so plagued itself with immunities for governmental instrumentalities as has that of the United States.

Among the special agencies of coordination developed here, most outstanding is the Council of State Governments which maintains in Chicago a sort of informal capitol of the states, with subsidiaries, a magazine, and a library. Originally supported by philanthropic grants, it now receives regular support by independent state appropriations. It has taken a leading interest in the federal coordination problem.

COORDINATION DEVICES AND INSTRUMENTALITIES

Separation of Sources. The idea of separation of sources is that the federal government use certain levies, the states others, and perhaps the municipalities a third independent set of taxes. The Constitution provides for some separation in that the states may not tax foreign trade (tariffs) and the federal government cannot practically levy on general property. For many years this provided the basis for independent revenue systems, but the recent tendency has been toward more and more overlapping.

The achievement of separation of sources may be either by constitutional restriction or by forbearance. A new constitutional division would require a major operation and would also be difficult because there is major disagreement as to which taxes should be monopolized by which governments. The tax system of the United States, if so it may be called, has grown up with little if any planning. This is true of taxation within a given state but even more so of the way the tax pattern of a specific state fits into the national pattern. However, if we could begin again and lay out a system of revenue for the federal government and the states, it would not be easy to draw a satisfactory plan. Much attention would be given to the suitability of the various taxes for use by central and local governments.

Among the elements of suitability are ease of administration, jurisdictional clarity or confusion, dependability of revenue, competitive pressures, and diversity of local opinion. To cite some examples: The federal government can administer a tobacco tax much more easily than the states. It can collect the tax by selling stamps to a few manufacturers, who are required to stamp each package sold. The states may use the same technique of administration, but they have a much less centralized group to collect from and encounter difficult problems of evasion arising from the fact that they cannot tax shipments over the borders. States encounter special problems of jurisdiction in the income tax field, and they are cramped in their freedom to use this tax because of competitive pressures (threatened migration). The inheritance tax is undependable as a local source because too much depends on the uncertain death of a few rich people. Some local participation in liquor taxation is desirable because different ethnic groups react very differently to the regulation or prohibition of liquor consumption.

Using the criterion of suitability one seems to end up with far too many sources allotted to the federal government. Of course, this very fact accounts in considerable measure for the development of our grants-in-aid. Comparative advantage might still be used to determine the division, allowing the local governments those revenue sources in which they have least relative disadvantage. For example, this would probably result in motor fuel and amusement taxes being allotted to the states. The motor vehicle license tax, because of our reliance on local police to regulate traffic, is clearly most advantageously collected at the state level.

Deductibility of Taxes. A coordination device seldom recognized as such is the *deductibility of taxes* levied by other jurisdictions in calculating the net base of the tax in the taxing jurisdiction. In the United States this is most highly developed in the field of federal and state income taxes, where federal allowance for deductibility of state taxes, and in some cases the reverse materially reduces the total load of the two taxes, diminishes the differentials between income tax burdens in an income tax state and those in a nonincome tax state, and avoids threats of confiscatory burdens. It operates to check tax avoidance by migration, although this effect has generally escaped attention. Deductibility operates much like a credit, but it is less drastic as to degree.

Deductibility may be unilateral or reciprocal. States' allowance of the federal tax as a deductible item in the calculation of their own taxes, in addition to federal allowance of deduction for state taxes, presents curious results and interesting problems of policy. If both taxes are deductible from current income, taxes cannot be calculated without the aid of simultaneous equations. The result (as indicated in the accompanying footnote) is a slight decrease in taxes for the taxpayer (compared with what he would pay with unilateral federal deductibility); a considerable increase in federal revenue; and a very substantial loss for the state.[3] Moreover, it is argued that the state's allowance of bilateral deductibility makes its effective rates less progressive than otherwise, since the benefit of this procedure goes to the greatest extent to the upper brackets. On the other hand, it is claimed that disposable income should be the basis of measuring ability to pay and that the taxpayer has no real ability to support state government on the basis of what he surrenders to the federal government. The federal government can afford to be generous, perhaps, on the theory that a progressive element in state tax systems should be promoted, but were the states to go in for high and steeply graduated rates or were they to impose a levy expressly to divert federal money into state treasuries, the federal government would no doubt call a halt.

Table 4 shows the curious effect of deductibility upon a combination of state and federal taxes. Due to graduation of rates, deductibility reduces the combined federal and state tax burdens proportionately more in the middle- or higher-income brackets than in the lowest brackets. In general, exclusions from a progressive tax tend to be regressive if they constitute a larger proportion of large incomes than of small ones. However, the problem is complicated by the difficulties in comparing tax measures with different yields. This may be avoided by assuming that the federal government makes up its lost revenue by a new tax as progressive as the original. It can do this without distributional changes only if the exclusion is proportional. For reasons indicated above, to label the deduction as regressive does not warrant applying this label to the state tax itself.

Deductibility is sometimes described as a subsidy to the income tax states; however, it also applies to state excises and sales taxes though with less striking effects.

Credits. The crediting device permits taxpayers to pay federal taxes

---

[3] To calculate the two taxes, let us assume $1-million income, a federal tax rate of 80 percent, and a state rate of 15 percent; we let X equal the federal tax and Y the state tax. This leads to the two equations:

$X = \$800,000 - 80$ percent Y
$Y = \$150,000 - 15$ percent X

Solving for X and Y, we have a federal tax of $773,000 and a state tax of $35,050. Were the state tax alone deductible (against the federal) the two figures would be $680,000 and $150,000. In actual practice under cash accounting, each government allows the deduction of last year's taxes paid in the current year. This can produce erratic results where income is irregular.

with state tax receipts. It is now used to provide some coordination in the case of death taxes and payroll taxes. The credit is limited in its objectives; it is an effective antidote for interstate competition but, as used thus far, it has provided little alleviation for the evils of dual administration and compliance, diversities of laws and practices, and multiple taxation. However, the credit could be used for wider objectives. The inheritance tax credit, still attached to a 1926 schedule of federal rates, could at least be modernized and extended to cover gift as well as estate taxes. Deductibility affords only limited protection for states with high and progressive taxes, and the idea persists that the federal government

TABLE 4

Effect of Deductibility [a] on Combined Federal and State Individual Income Tax [b] for a Married Man with Two Dependents, at Selected Net Income Levels

(percent)

		Effective rate of tax			
Net income before personal exemption [c]	Federal (assuming no state tax)	State		Combined federal and state	
		New York	Minnesota (assuming no federal tax)	New York	Minnesota [d]
$20,000	25.0	4.1	6.9	27.6	27.9
$50,000	42.2	5.4	9.1	44.0	43.9
$100,000	56.0	5.9	9.8	57.5	57.1
$200,000	69.2	6.1	10.1	69.9	69.5
$1,500,000	88.0 [e]	6.3	10.5	89.3	88.9

[a] The federal government allows taxpayers to deduct State income taxes in computing net taxable income for federal purposes and, similarly, Minnesota allows deduction of federal tax in computing the state tax. New York does not allow deduction of the federal income tax in computing the state tax.

[b] Federal rates under Revenue Act of 1951, applicable to taxable year 1952; New York and Minnesota rates under income tax laws applicable to taxes paid in 1952.

[c] Prior to allowable deductions for income taxes.

[d] Taking into account reciprocal deductibility under federal and Minnesota taxes.

[e] Taking into account federal maximum effective rate limitation of 88 percent.

NOTE.—The effect of deductibility is illustrated only for net income beginning at $20,000, since most low-income taxpayers do not itemize deductions, but use the standard deduction for both federal and state income tax purposes.

SOURCE: Tax Advisory Staff of the Secretary, U.S. Treasury Department, *Federal-State-Local Tax Coordination*, 1952, p. 20.

should lend more of its income-taxing power to the states by extending to them an income tax credit. Ample justification for a credit is claimed in terms of the importance of state and local services and the growing intensity of state and local competition. But there are many difficulties. The program would cost the federal government revenue which in the present state of international relations it might be loath to lose. The program would require carefully drawn definitions; presumably it should exclude various species of gross income taxes. It is also argued that the credit would do less for the poorer states than state sharing or even than deductibility.[4]

FEDERAL COLLECTION AND STATE SHARING

One of the most commonly advocated of the coordination devices is federal collection and state sharing. It would make dual administration unnecessary and could be used effectively to achieve a completely coordinated tax system. This is a device by which the obvious advantages and the superior position of the federal government in tax administration and collection can be utilized without destroying local independence as to expenditures.

The system of central collection and local sharing is attractive for those who attach supreme importance to logical and simple mechanisms, but it encounters impressive objections. It involves a high degree of centralization as to both levies and administration. The fiscal independence of the local units under sharing is about the same as that of a minor son placed upon a revocable allowance by a generous father. Moreover, sharing on the basis of origin (enabling the smaller units to "tap their own resources") encounters not only difficulties of determining origin but also distribution beyond the point of need in the case of wealthy districts. Distribution on other bases is likely to lack an easily available objective standard and runs the danger of political abuses. Although the federal government has never developed any program of sharing revenues with the states, some of the latter have extensive arrangements of this sort with their municipalities. Liquor and sales taxes, public utility taxes and, less commonly, income and inheritance tax revenues are distributed on varying bases, such as origin or population.

Supplementation. As previously explained, supplements differ from shared taxes in that the former leave discretion (within limits) to the local governments as to whether to tax and in what degree. Supplements

---

[4] See Advisory Commission on Intergovernmental Relations, *Coordination of State and Federal Inheritance, Estate and Gift Taxes* (Washington, D.C., 1961); James A. Maxwell, *Tax Credits and Intergovernmental Relations* (Washington, D.C.: The Brookings Institution, 1962).

differ from independent overlapping taxes in that the wastes of dual administration and compliance are avoided. Single administration requires close resemblance in the terms of tax but may permit some other variations. Mississippi, for example, now uses this device in its sales tax program. The state authorizes the cities to levy a tax not to exceed a stated proportion of the state sales tax. The local taxes are collected along with the state tax. Illinois and California have more or less similar provisions.

Recently a study of New York City finances,[5] in considering a city income tax for that municipality, reviewed the various alternatives: to base the tax on the New York State levy, the federal levy, or on an independent levy of its own. At least the first of these alternatives involved the possibility of either an independent administration, or collection of the two taxes by the state. Independent administration would give the city considerably more freedom in choosing its terms of tax; state cooperation would save the expense of two administrations.

Delegation of Taxing Power. Particularly at the state level, the delegation of more taxing power (and the broadening of municipal tax systems under general home-rule powers) has been developing rapidly as an alternative to state aids, notably in New York and Pennsylvania. Thus Pennsylvania has provided that any municipality may (with minor qualifications) levy on any source which the state could use and is not now using. Some of the critics see in this development only confusion worse confounded. Others see in it the arrival at long last of some alternatives for local authorities in ordering their tax systems. If the program were to follow an alternative line and permit the duplication of state levies, we would have the basis for supplements.

GRANTS-IN-AID

Grants-in-aid, or subventions,[6] are often lumped with shared taxes, but the two are distinguishable in that the former are based on appropriations whereas the latter are based on the yield of a particular tax. The aid system permits the distribution of receipts from the federal income and death taxes (often not subject to fair localization) and relieves the financial pressure in the state and local quest for revenue. (An important further objective may be that of supporting state and local public works and welfare expenditures during depressions so that outlays may be maintained or increased without new repressive taxes.)

---

[5] Robert M. Haig and Carl S. Shoup, *The Financial Problem of the City of New York,* Mayor's Committee on Management Survey (New York, 1952), chap. VI.

[6] Further discussed in Chapter 23.

The aids are well adapted to use in a federal system, but they, too, encounter numerous difficulties. There are many ways in which aids may be distributed, and it is always difficult to agree on a formula. The circuitous routing of revenue from local communities to central units and back again is not conducive to economy or to local self-reliance and independence. Dispute also often arises concerning the control features of aids. For example, federal aid for elementary education, which seems overdue, is delayed by such controversial issues as whether such legislation ought to deny aids to the states or municipalities that persist in segregation of whites and Negroes. The selection of functions for aids at the federal level is said to be opportunistic, and this is said to have led to distortion of local expenditure patterns (vocational education favored over general education).

Joint Administration.   More collaboration between federal and state administrative officials offers promise of considerable achievement in economy and efficiency. Some achievements along this line have already been realized. It is now possible for state officials to utilize federal income tax returns for information, and such services are available on tolerably economical terms for the states. The evidence indicates that many states have employed this means of improving state administration quite extensively by photographing documents or sending state auditors to examine federal returns. Agreements between the federal government and several of the states provide for the exchange of audit information. This breaks ground because it is bilateral in character and offers potentialities for joint planning. Much remains to be accomplished; there is, for example, no exchange of mailing lists, no attempt to divide the auditing job on an orderly basis with appropriate specialization, and no division of auditing expenses on an agreed pattern. Federal and state administrations have been introduced to each other, but their association is far from intimate. Cooperation in the liquor tax field, though quite informal, has proved very effective.

Some beginning has been made, too, in developing the procedure and the habit of conference between state and federal officials. Several such conferences have been held, and they have resulted in some recommendations for legislation. Some of these recommendations have even been introduced as bills in Congress.

For many years the critics have recommended the creation of some intergovernmental agency to work continuously on coordination problems. Most recent recommendations of this order now implemented, called for a special assistant in the Executive Office of the President with a small staff and a representative advisory board devoted to this area.[7]

---

[7] The Commission on Intergovernmental Relations (Meyer Kestnbaum, chairman), *A Report to the President* (Washington, D.C., 1955), pp. 87–89.

Centralization of Governmental Functions. The present situation is one in which the central units of government have the advantage in the application of most taxes, and the local units have the major public responsibilities—highways, education, and health, for example. These local functions of government are no longer strictly local; there is now great national interest in their proper performance. It seems logical to conclude that economic centralization has proceeded faster than political centralization and that the thing to do now is to centralize the performance of certain governmental functions. Centralization lags because of tradition, vested interests, and constitutional impediments. And there are important values that are lost with the centralization of functions, among them the opportunity for a wide participation in government and the adaptation of laws to divergent local conditions. Local autonomy on local matters is a highly prized ingredient of democracy. There is danger, too, that the federal government may become too large and develop great coordination problems within itself.

PROBLEMS AND INSTITUTIONS OF INTERSTATE FISCAL RELATIONS

Multiple Taxation. A principal problem of interstate relations is that of territorial multiple taxation. Reference has been made to the many ways in which such multiple taxation can occur: the manipulation of state tax laws and administration to reach more railroad property than lies within the borders of the taxing states; the attempt to tax air transportation fleets in full in the state of the company's home office, and again in part in the states through which the company operates; double taxation of intangibles under the death tax, owing either to disagreement as to the taxpayer's domicile or to a combination of domiciliary and non-domiciliary taxation; application of the personal income tax both at the taxpayer's domicile and residence, with diverse rules for the latter as the basis of personal taxation; corporate income apportionment; capital stock apportionment and taxation of stock in full at the corporate domicile. The quantitative volume of this multiple taxation is a matter concerning which there is almost no evidence, a fact which suggests a first-rate field for future study.

Much progress has been made in the elimination of multiple taxation in the death tax field, principally by reciprocal legislation. Some progress has been made in corporate income tax apportionment, principally by the promotion of recommended uniform standard procedure. Less progress has been made in the personal income tax field where the conflict of laws centers principally on the varying use of situs and domicile as the basis of taxation and on varying standards of domicile. Since two or more states in these cases usually have legitimate grounds for imposing a tax, equity for all concerned can only be accomplished by some fair division of the revenue without prejudice to the taxpayer. Interstate compacts might be used to accomplish this purpose, but they have never made any headway in this field. Reciprocal legislation might also achieve salutary results, but it has never been applied to relieve multiple taxation by a division of revenues. Perhaps the easiest, but not necessarily the best road to achievement in this area is congressional determination of jurisdictional rules; these might be enforced by various inducements and sanctions extended by the federal government.

Following Supreme Court decisions that seemed to open the opportunity for states to tax firms that had no other nexus than sales to customers within these states, Congress has undertaken to investigate the subject and has laid down some interim rules concerning it. Under these rules nexus that is confined to sales and solicitation of sales (no office approving orders) is ruled out as inadequate.

The technical issues involved in apportionment of interstate business are formidable. What is a unitary business to which apportionment formulas should be applied? Does it include the parent of a subsidiary corporation where only the latter does business in the taxing state? When is a firm doing business in our state and does this set the limits of jurisdiction to tax? What if the firm has no office in our state but only customers (purchasers of products)? Should all of the income of a unitary business including incidental rentals and income from intangibles be apportioned? If not, where should the nonapportionable element be taxed? If the answer is that some income should be taxed at the corporate domicile, how do we define the latter? What factors should be used in an apportionment formula and how should each be defined? And so on.

Diversity of Laws and Procedure.   Another problem in the field of interstate relations arises from the wide diversity of tax laws and procedures that has developed and is still developing. Diversity may be thought to offer some advantages in that it involves widespread experimentation in new and different tax measures. But it also has many disadvantages. One is the augmented cost that private business incurs in reporting to governments and in keeping itself informed of its tax obligations.

Extraterritorial Taxation.   Occasionally it is possible for a state to tax wealth or industry beyond its borders. An outstanding illustration is the Delaware tax on all the capital stock of the companies it incorporates. A less conspicuous but oft-cited case is the taxation by New York of transfers on the New York Stock Exchange. Kentucky has achieved great success with its production tax on the liquor business though here apparently the burden is largely absorbed by the domestic producer. The Michigan "value-added" tax, as previously explained, may reach consumers of automobiles beyond the Michigan border. In a sense and to a degree, the local taxation of interstate business with incidence on the consumer inevitably involves extraterritorial taxation. But the restraints of competition tend to mitigate any territorial inequities that might result from such procedure. If one state were fortunate enough to have a monopoly on a commodity with an inelastic demand in the national market, it could hold up other states through its tax system almost indefinitely. However, the private monopoly *could* do this on its own account without any assist from the state. Such situations, however, very rarely occur.

GOVERNMENT INSTRUMENTALITIES

TAX-EXEMPT SECURITIES

The legal aspect of tax immunities for the interest on securities issued by governments was discussed in the last chapter. The immunity doctrine applies only between the federal government and the states. The relationship among the states is that of separate political entities; that between the states and their municipalities, one of legal units to their creator, so that municipalities are in a subordinate position. The immunity doctrine is responsible for the exemption of the interest on state and municipal bonds from federal income taxation and of interest on federal bonds from state and local taxation. Needless to say, this runs to a very large investment and a substantial flow of income.

Arguments against Tax-exempt Securities. It is argued against the tax-exemption feature associated with securities, first, that it involves a loss of revenue to governments. The point is not beyond dispute, however, for the exemption feature is reflected in the low interest rate at which governments are able to float securities. Interest rates have to be high enough, however, to attract the marginal buyer; when the requirements of municipalities exceed the millionaire market, the compensatory effect on the interest rate tends to disappear, leaving a large "buyers' surplus" for wealthy purchasers. More important, it is argued that the exemption of this interest is incompatible with the principle of the graduated income tax, under which all are supposed to be rated on their ability to pay. Tax exemption is worth much more to some than to others.

To the man who has too small an income to pay an income tax it would have no value at all. To the man whose income falls in the top brackets an investment in government bonds yielding 3 percent may result in as much net income after taxes as an investment in common stocks yielding 15 percent. Thus the exemption creates an attractive loophole for the avoidance of high surtaxes. Expressed conversely, a government bond that yields 3 percent to one person may be sold to another upon conditions that make it yield an equivalent to 15 percent. This is criticized on the ground that it constitutes a sort of "class price" in the sale of bonds.

Moreover, it is possible by the judicious use of borrowing to buy tax-exempts on margin and thus increase their yield after tax to incredible levels. (While interest paid for such purposes is theoretically nondeductible, it is easy to avoid disclosure of purpose.) Thus consider the following transaction. Jones, in the highest income bracket, buys a $1000 bond incurring a debt of $800 simultaneously. This could yield him 8.7 percent calculated as follows:

Yield of the bond at 2 percent	$20
Interest paid on $800 at 4 percent	32
Reduction of tax because of interest deduction	
(92 percent of $32)	29.49
Net cost of borrowing	2.51
Net yield on $200 outlay ($20–$2.51)	17.49
Rate of yield	8.7 percent

It is true that what studies have been made of the subject indicate far less of a millionaire market for tax-exempt securities than one might expect. The ownership of stock carries with it the control of strategic points in the economic system—control that wealthy families hesitate to abandon. However, there is a limit to what one can afford to pay for control, particularly since high surtaxes have aggravated the problem.

The third argument against tax-exempt securities grows out of the second. It is said that the combination of high surtaxes and abundant tax-exempt securities has produced certain undesirable nonfiscal effects. Because of the low rate of interest from government bonds, many who can ill afford to gamble are tempted to invest in more risky securities, including common stocks, whereas others who can and should do the risk bearing for society are persuaded to invest in the relatively riskless government bonds. Thus, it is contended that the tax-exemption policy will likely result in a shortage of capital for the very risky investments.[8] The conservative investor of small means who prefers government secur-

---

[8] For a more complete statement of this argument see Henry C. Simons, *Personal Income Taxation,* chap. VIII.

ities suffers a loss of income because the interest, due to tax exemption, is lower than would otherwise be the case. Income from investments may be very important for those who must live upon small savings. Those who seek security through insurance or annuities also suffer, since some of their funds are invested by the insurance companies in low-yielding government bonds.

Finally, in so far as tax-exempt bonds consist of state and municipal securities, it is contended that the exemption feature results in a federal subsidy to the states. The states are able to borrow at reduced rates of interest because of tax exemption, and the federal government pays for the advantage with reduced tax receipts. It is said that some municipalities have issued their own securities to buy federal bonds and have profited by the difference in the interest rate.

The states may render some return for this in their exemption of federal securities from state taxes. State net income taxes, however, are not universal and carry very moderate rates compared with the federal schedule. State taxes upon intangible property, which are also affected, are not well administered. The balance of gain and loss from this intergovernmental exchange of privileges is very obscure and depends upon all the vagaries in calculating the effects of tax exemption previously explained. Assuming that the balance is in favor of the states, the subsidy is thought to be particularly unfair because it is distributed to reward those states and municipalities which go in heavily for borrowing. Moreover, while municipal credit has legitimate and important functions, it is doubtful whether its use needs encouragement by federal subsidies. Direct aid for construction or for certain kinds of construction makes more sense than indirect support for borrowing particularly when the latter clutters up the tax system.

Arguments for Tax-exempt Securities. Cogent as are the arguments for the elimination of tax-exempt securities, they are stoutly resisted by proponents of the existing practice.

Increased Cost of State and Local Credit. Spokesmen for the states and cities argue that the elimination of tax exemption would result in increased cost of borrowing and that this would further aggravate an already acute property tax problem.[9] It is doubtful, however, if the credit of these government units would be seriously impaired by a sur-

---

[9] For a sympathetic presentation of this argument and a comprehensive treatment of the tax-exempt-security problem see Lyle C. Fitch, *Taxing Municipal Bond Income* (Berkeley: University of California Press, 1950). In addition to outright exemption, the literature contains many proposals for modifying the tax-exemption privilege: the use of all income to measure the tax rate even though this specific income is exempt; pegging the benefit of the tax exemption to its low-bracket value (tax credit); and taxation by a formula which would give due allowance for compensatory losses in interest resulting from market discount of the tax privilege. If the investor receives a third less on his tax-exempt investment than

render of a privilege which they have enjoyed for less than fifty years and which many other countries do not afford. Public works that are financed by taxes are hardly of less interest to the nation than those that are financed by borrowing.

Interference with State Sovereignty.   It is argued that the inclusion of interest on state and local bonds in the federal income tax base would involve a dangerous shift of power from the states to the federal government. Federal control would be enhanced by the fact that it could tax some state and local bonds and not others. This is answered with the proposition that no authority to levy a discriminatory tax is sought.

Breaking Faith with Investors.   Finally, it is argued that those who have invested in tax-exempt government securities ought not to be subject to a change in rules in "the middle of the game."

Means of Eliminating Tax-exempt Securities.   The way to eliminate tax-exempt securities in the case of governments that both issue and exempt securities is for these governments to forego further issuance with the exemption privilege. In the case of the federal government this has been the policy since 1941. Exemptions included in existing contracts are unavoidable until such contracts expire.

In the case of state and federal taxation of each other's securities, there are long and formidable legal precedents with which to cope. However, the Supreme Court might, in accord with the recent trend of its opinions, reverse these precedents. The alternative is a constitutional amendment, which would be difficult to secure because the states—particularly the nonincome tax states—appear to profit by the existing arrangement. Actually, legislation to remove this immunity, though frequently recommended by Presidents and others, encounters two very formidable vested interests: the states and municipalities, and the holders of government bonds. The former are principally interested in the exemption of future issues; the latter in the continuation of exemption on existing bonds. No breach of contract is involved in wiping the slate clean of this impediment.

TAXATION OF FEDERAL AND STATE ENTERPRISES

More difficult, perhaps, than the problem of tax-exempt securities is that of tax-exempt federal and state enterprises. Municipalities would regard any attempt by the federal government to include the earnings of mu-

---

he could have received with comparable taxable investment, he has already paid as it were a 33⅓ percent tax. As to future issues, proposals run to various schemes to compensate state and municipal governments (*ibid.*, pp. 90–91, 108–112). Although all exemptions develop their vested interests, the ones associated with investment are particularly difficult to crack and/or compensate.

nicipal undertakings in the base of the federal income tax as very men-
acing to their status. But the present exemption is open to grave criticism
in that it encourages municipalities to "take over" private enterprises
to avoid the federal income tax. On the federal side, projects such as the
Tennessee Valley Authority involve a difficult taxation problem for state
and local governments. Congress permits certain "federal payments in
lieu of taxes" to compensate state and local units in the Tennessee region
for their loss of tax base because of the federal project. The payments
take the form of a percentage of annual gross proceeds from commercial
power sales. A recent study concludes that the payments probably exceed
property tax equivalents on power property and adds that existing arrangements are working to the general satisfaction of state and local
governments in the area.[10] Exemption from income taxes (including interest on privately owned securities) complicate the problem. The debate
concerning public power would be much simpler and clearer if our federal tax system had never become entangled in intergovernmental immunities.

TAXATION OF FEDERAL PROPERTY

The federal government owned substantial amounts of real estate before
World War II, and during the war it extended its holdings considerably.
This aggravated an old issue concerning the exemption of this property
from state and local property taxes. In the case of eleven western states,
federal ownership is so widespread that these states complain of never
having been admitted to the Union. Federal holdings cover a wide variety
of purposes including housing, power, conservation, and military uses.
New acquisitions cause most dissatisfaction since they subtract from an
existing tax base. It is unthinkable, for instance, that the federal government might take over the railroads without compensating the states for
their tax interest.

A complication in federal acquisition lies in the jurisdictional status
of the acquired property. When the federal government took over the
District of Columbia, the latter ceased to be a part of the states to which
it formerly belonged and the states no longer recognized any obligation
to provide services to residents of the District. Similarly, District residents
lost their representation in legislative bodies. The same is true of some
other federal acquisitions though usually, and in the absence of specifica-
tion to the contrary, the jurisdiction after the purchase is a joint one. At
any event, it is not always clear to the states that they are obliged to

---

[10] Study Committee, *Payments in Lieu of Taxes and Shared Revenues*, Report
to the Committee on Intergovernmental Relations (Washington, D.C., 1955),
p. 62.

provide services to personnel on federal property. Some states at some times have threatened to force jurisdiction, in effect, upon the federal government. The states are not always consistent in their attitude; at one time they will solicit the location of some federal enterprise, and at another they protest that they are being cheated out of taxes.

The federal government makes some payments in lieu of taxes on some of its property, but its program in this respect has grown opportunistically and with little, if any, consistent principle. A single principle would indeed be hard to find and apply. Involved in the determination of policy in this area are such factors as the local services required by federal installations, the services or savings such federal property provides the local population, the similarity of federal property to local property now taxed, and the recency of acquisition. There is little demand for payment on such property as post offices, armories, weather stations, and prisons. There is objection to immunity of commercial and industrial property especially that of contractors and subcontractors working on government orders.[11] In the case of defense housing, the federal government proposed to pay a full property tax equivalent, reserving only the right to safeguard itself against exploitation. To accomplish the latter, the government provided its own staff of appraisers. The same type of program, however, seemed inappropriate in the case of philanthropic housing. Here the problem is complicated by the fact that the municipality usually makes its contribution to the housing project in the form of tax exemption. At the same time, tenants should be expected to make some contribution to local government. And these factors must not be allowed to raise the rent of tenants to the point where the objective of the program is defeated. Federal payments in lieu have usually taken the form of a specified percentage of shelter rents; full payments on reproduction cost would be inappropriate.

In Canada, the Dominion government once undertook to pay a portion of local property taxes in any municipality where national property exceeded 4 percent of taxable property.[12] The figure was selected by estimating the national ratio of Dominion to taxable property; any concentration in excess of the average was regarded as creating special local problems. A study committee recently considered the possibility of trying this type of program in the United States; it rejected the idea because it would make no distinctions as to kinds of federal property and would

---

[11] For an interesting discussion of some recent cases in this area see Denzel C. Cline, "Recent Developments in the Taxation of Federal Property," *Proceedings of the National Tax Association Conference*, 1958, pp. 98–106; see also symposium, Wisconsin Law Review, 1959: 2 (March 1959).

[12] J. Harvey Perry, *Taxation in Canada* (Toronto: University of Toronto Press, 1951), p. 282; the limitation was abandoned in 1957 but payments in lieu for most crown property were continued.

mean the termination of arrangements now regarded as satisfactory.[13]

A classification according to age has been suggested; for instance, properties acquired before 1939 might be excluded on the ground that they have become integrated into the economic and fiscal life of the community. Facilities classified as primarily for local service (post office) might be excluded. Facilities that serve a regional purpose might be made eligible for temporary relief only. Existing arrangements that are working without dissatisfaction (TVA) might be ignored. And so on.

SUMMARY

The present state of intergovernmental fiscal relations in the United States grew out of multiple taxation of the same revenue sources by several levels of government and the jurisdictional confusion attending the application of parochial taxes to economic institutions and activities that are national in scope. The federal constitution provides a degree of separation of sources, but in the main it establishes concurrent powers of taxation for the federal government and states. Efforts to solve the problem in the United States (as contrasted with Canada) have been piecemeal in character, and in specific areas they have utilized deductibility, credits, shared taxes, supplements, the delegation of taxing power, and joint administration, to improve intergovernmental fiscal relations. Deductibility is of particular interest because of its effects on territorial competition (for industries) and on the progressivity of the tax system. Shared taxes are highly developed in Canada and in some American states; they interfere with local freedom more than supplements which merely lend the administrative services of the state to assist localities that levy taxes similar to its own.

The states have coordination problems of their own including jurisdictional conflict, diversity of laws, extraterritorial taxation, and trade barriers. Of these, the first is the most critical and can hardly be solved (short of federal pressure) except by the little-used institution of state compacts.

An institution growing out of federal systems is the tax-exempt security which impedes the operation of progressive taxation and offers an unwanted incentive for the wealthy to invest in a riskless field of investment. These securities do aid municipalities in borrowing and thus relieve the hardpressed local-property taxpayer. The immunity of federal property from state and local taxation has also caused complaint, and various programs of federal payments in lieu of taxes have developed accord-

---

[13] Study Committee, *op. cit.,* pp. 46–48.

ingly. Some such payments attend federal housing projects, but here the benefited municipality is usually expected to make a tax concession as its contribution to the development.

It would be a pity if in our commendable efforts to make something of the United Nations, we were to neglect the fact that certain nations are a league of states and collective action among them is as undeveloped and important a field as that which challenges us in foreign relations.

PROBLEMS

1. If you were rewriting the federal Constitution, what provisions would you include that would make for satisfactory intergovernmental relations?
2. Consider the various kinds of double taxation and the degree to which, and the ground on which, each is a public concern.
3. Given federal deductibility for state taxes, what effects may be expected in making the deductibility reciprocal: (a) upon the taxpayer, (b) upon federal revenues, (c) upon state revenues, and (d) upon the progressiveness of the state tax?
4. If the federal government has the advantage in the administration of most of the major taxes in the tax system, why should it not collect the revenue for the entire country, distributing a part of each tax to the territorial divisions from which the collection was made?
5. Consider the arguments advanced in Canada for federal collection–provincial sharing of the income tax.
6. Contrast Canadian and American experience with federal grants and federal payments in lieu of taxes on federal property.
7. With a state income tax of 2 percent and a federal income tax of 20 percent of net income and with a federal credit for the state tax, how much total tax would the recipient of a $10,000 income pay? How much tax would he pay if the state tax (only) were deductible on his federal return?
8. Compare credits, sharing, aids, supplements, delegation of taxing power, and centralization of expenditure as to (a) effect on local independence; (b) elimination of costs; and (c) special difficulties.
9. If local governments are to be allowed to diversify their tax systems, should they be permitted to use only taxes also employed by the states or only taxes not used by the states? Would a system of aids or sharing provide a better solution?
10. If multiple taxation between the states were to be eliminated, what rules of jurisdiction should prevail in the case of the personal income tax, the corporate income tax, and the death tax?
11. Under what circumstances can one state collect taxes the incidence of which falls on the taxpayers of other states?

12. Explain the fact that some municipalities have been able to profit by borrowing from private parties and loaning to the federal government.

13. Explain how it is possible to add to the yield of a tax-exempt security by buying on margin.

14. Explain what determines the interest rate on tax-exempt securities and how the market compensates somewhat, but not fully, for the exemption privilege.

15. What objection would there be to the simple rule that federal housing projects should go on the local tax rolls and be taxed exactly as privately-held property is taxed?

16. Comment. As the supply of state and local bonds becomes more abundant, state and local governments profit less and high-bracket taxpayers profit more from tax-exempt securities.

PART **3** PUBLIC EXPENDITURES

21

GENERAL ASPECTS OF PUBLIC EXPENDITURE

In the preceding parts of this book consideration has been given mainly to the principles, practices, and problems involved in the raising of governmental revenues. In this and the following two chapters an attempt will be made to analyze the principles, practices, and problems involved in spending these revenues. This chapter will present a few salient observations concerning expenditures as a whole. Chapter 22 will be devoted to the component parts of the field, and Chapter 23 will consider an aspect of intergovernmental relations in public expenditure, namely, state and federal aids. These have been considered briefly as a factor, along with many others, in the general picture of intergovernmental fiscal relations. Here they will be considered in more detail.

FACTS AND TRENDS IN PUBLIC EXPENDITURES

It is a well-known fact that governmental expenditures have been increasing rapidly. The absolute figures are misleading, however, and need deflating. To be fully deflated they must be expressed in dollars of constant purchasing power per capita or as percentages of income. Public expenditures of all units of government in the United States have increased from 9.8 percent of gross national product in 1929 to 30.1 percent in 1961.[1] The deflation of absolute figures sometimes produces unexpected results. Thus New York City is shown to have spent less in terms of real purchasing power of per capita income in 1950 than in 1930.[2] And Bator calculated that the share of federal government's expense for nondefense purposes measured against real nondefense gross national product was actually less in 1957 than it had been in 1939.[3]

A moment's reflection should be sufficient to convince one of the extremely pervasive character of government in the United States at the present time. Moving from the cradle to the morgue or from the moment of rising to retirement at night, one encounters government at almost every turn. Following up the latter of these two cycles, we observe the citizen arising from his slumbers keenly aware of his alarm clock which has been set to accord with standards of time provided by the Bureau of Standards. At breakfast he glances at his daily paper and reflects with some satisfaction that the government is prepared to protect him from violence initiated abroad. The food that he eats has been amply blessed by the government: milk inspection, pure food and drug policing, and perhaps price control. He sees his daughter off to the public school where she awaits a tuberculosis test prescribed by the public health service. His trip to the office is safeguarded by traffic supervision as he traverses a public highway, perhaps on a public vehicle. The mail on his desk was delivered by a public postman. It contains a contract which he can rely on the government to enforce. It also contains a letter bearing the forms that he will use to assess his income tax. And so on.

Table 5 presents the development of expenditures by the federal government in the United States. It tells a story of rapid expansion with periodic spurts during wars and the depression of the 1930s.

Government in the United States is more decentralized than in most countries, but the changes wrought by the world wars and the depression have created a sharp trend toward centralization. Before the depression only about 35 percent of total expenditures were federal, 15 percent were state, and 50 percent local. In 1962, the percentages of the three layers of government were 64.3, 16.7, and 18.9. However, the upward trend in total outlays is shared by all layers of government. Thus, state and local expenditures more than quadrupled between 1940 and 1962 (unde-

---

[1] Tax Foundation, *Facts and Figures on Government Finance, 1962–1963* (New York, 1963), p. 27.

[2] Robert M. Haig and Carl S. Shoup, *The Financial Problem of the City of New York,* Mayor's Committee on Management Survey (New York, 1952), pp. 15–16.

[3] Francis M. Bator, *The Question of Government Spending* (New York: Harper and Row, Publishers, 1960), p. 21.

flated).[4] If military expenditures were abstracted from the picture, the three levels would be found spending not far from the same proportions of the public dollar.

TABLE 5

Federal Expenditures of the United States in Selected Years

(in millions of dollars)

Year	Expenditure	Year	Expenditure
1791	4	1935	6,802
1830	15	1939	8,966
1857	68	1941	13,387
1865	1,298	1943	79,622
1867	357	1945	98,416
1886	242	1947	39,032
1910	694	1949	39,507
1916	724	1953	74,120
1919	18,952	1954	67,537
1921	4,467	1959	80,342
1925	2,464	1962 (estimated)	89,075

SOURCE: Figures from 1791–1935 adapted from Tables in W. J. Schultz and M. R. Caine, *Financial Development of the United States;* original source, U.S. Secretary of Treasury, *Annual Reports;* 1939–1950 data from *Treasury Bulletin*, U.S. Treasury Department, August 1949, p. 1; June 1957, p. 1; June 1962, p. 1.

CAUSES OF INCREASING GOVERNMENT EXPENDITURE

The causes of the upward trend in government expenditures are numerous, and a few are worth singling out for special consideration.

Income. One study [5] suggests plausibly that the most important single factor in increasing expenses (at least among states) is income. As the economic system develops to higher levels of productivity, its resources are devoted less to primary (extractive) industry and to secondary (manufacturing and merchandising) industry and more to services. In the earlier stages of a society's economic evolution, major effort and expenditure

[4] Tax Foundation, *Facts and Figures on Government Finance*, 1962–1963, New York, p. 21.

[5] Solomon Fabricant, *The Trend of Government Activity in the United States since 1900* (New York: National Bureau of Economic Research, 1952), chap. 6.

is for food; as progress proceeds, this outlay becomes of less and less importance. It is in the service area that the government has its greatest comparative advantage. Moreover, free income (above necessities) has much the highest capacity to pay taxes. John R. Commons described the tendency of government to expand as follows: "Governments must have revenues in increasing amounts, not because they are corrupt and inefficient, which can be remedied, but because the social needs of education, ethics, morality, art, liberty, protection of the weak, highways, health, recreation grow faster in an improving civilization than do private needs of food, luxury, ostentation." [6]

Wars.   One of the major causes of mounting governmental outlay has been war in general and World Wars I and II in particular. The cost to the United States of World War II was about ten times that of the former conflict which had then set an all-time record. And war expenditures do not terminate with the end of actual conflict. They involve an aftermath of debt service and allowances for veterans. This is not all. One war is no sooner finished than it is thought necessary to begin preparing for the next. Wars accustom taxpayers to high taxation and it is rare that postwar budgets ever recede to their prewar levels. Items of federal outlay associated with war run to about two thirds of the present federal budget which in turn is about two thirds of the total outlay by all governments in the United States. Thus, the really big prizes in the search for government "economy" lie in the field of international relations. One writer has made a rough estimate that the money cost of war and war preparations to all governments during the twentieth century runs to about $2 trillion.[7] It would be a popular (but serious) sport to calculate all the good works that could have been provided in lieu of this sum had mankind learned to abstain from this folly.

Urbanization.   Undoubtedly, increased urbanization of the population is a cause of rising public expenditures. Many cities follow the rule of increasing costs. It is a well-known fact that certain city functions such as water supply, police protection, and traffic control follow this pattern, and while others offer economies of size the net effect is likely to be one of greater expense. Though it is not true that in every state cities of the first, second, third, and fourth classes will follow each other in order as to per capita outlays, the usual tendency over most of the scale is a fair correlation between size and per capita cost.

To make matters worse, central cities frequently find their tax bases depleted by suburban migration. It has long been predicted that the development of trucking and electric power would reverse the tendency

_____

[6] *Institutional Economics* (New York: The Macmillan Company, 1934), p. 831.

[7] Scott Nearing, *Economics for the Power Age* (New York: The John Day Company, Inc., 1952), p. 21.

toward concentration of population. Increasing costs themselves are a factor conducive to decentralization. And it is possible, though unlikely, that the atomic weapons may have an effect on this trend.

Development of Democracy. Quite probably the development of democracy and democratic sentiment have had a bearing on the growth of public expenditures. Democracy tends toward liberal spending. There are certain cities in Minnesota where the mine owners pay most of the taxes and the miners do most of the voting. These cities have a very high scale of public living. Somewhat the same situation prevails in the nation as a whole and has prevailed since the abolition of property qualification for voting. As far as direct taxes are concerned (the ones that make the taxpayer tax conscious), a major proportion has been paid in normal times by a minority of the voters. The poor are at a disadvantage, certainly in the economic arena, but they sometimes have an offsetting advantage in the battle of politics.

Concern for Underdeveloped Areas. Although the obligations of ethical theory for many years have embraced all mankind, it is only recently and under the pressure of awakening nationalism and the rivalry of communism that the Western world has developed a sense of the compelling need to attack poverty in other countries as well as at home. Even now it is hard to believe that most of the world's population lives in Asia and Africa and that it is desperately poor, ill fed, and discontented. Attacking this problem is no simple matter but we have begun to devote some small share of our resources to it.

Aggrandizement and Waste in Bureaucracy. It is sometimes argued that increasing public expenditures suggest increasing graft, inefficiency, and incompetence in the conduct of government affairs. This does not follow from the facts in view of the other possible explanations of the trend. Moreover, there appears to be no evidence of increasing graft and inefficiency. The consensus of informed people would probably hold that there has been considerable improvement in the methods, personnel, and standards involved in the conduct of government. "Old-timers" can still recall when railroads bought legislators as they did cattle.

Moreover, it is dangerous to generalize about the efficiency of government. Our social security system, said to be the largest insurance operation in the world, has operated for over two decades without a breath of scandal and at a level of unsurpassed efficiency. Besides, since the budget is in competition for the consumer's dollar, it is the wastes of private consumption that may be legitimately compared with those of public administration. That the American consumer spends easily, thoughtlessly, wastefully on much that is of ephemeral value is a by-word throughout the world.

Nevertheless, after a recent study of the federal government, Herbert Hoover, as head of an investigating commission, estimated that without changing the functions of government as much as $3 billion could be saved annually by improving the administration of government department ments and agencies. Undoubtedly it is possible for governments to waste a great deal of money, and the larger and more unwieldy they become the more difficult it is to eliminate inefficiencies.

Bureaucracies have very few effective checks on their quality of performance. They do not have to pass muster in the ordeal of competition as do many private undertakings. Very often they become subject to excessive red tape, to overlapping of functions, and to poor coordination of agencies. They also show a strong propensity for aggrandizement; department heads are likely to judge their success by the expansion of their responsibilities. In all of these respects, however, they do not differ from large monopolies in private business.

It may be observed in passing that no bureaucracy will bear more watching than a military one. Here the usual sins of the institution are magnified and fortified by the fact that nearly all criticism is suppressed. Moreover, military administration, whatever may be its other admirable qualities, such as fidelity, courage, and devotion, has never been distinguished by a high regard for the public purse.[8] Add to these the facts that military leadership is generally in a hurry and frequently has the task of procuring equipment for which no cost data exists, and one has the basis for the succession of exposures associated with military procurement.

Contrary perhaps to the general view, it is the author's opinion that no group should be more concerned about the evils of bureaucracy than the Socialists whose platform calls for a large degree of public ownership. The triumph of their program depends in no small degree upon an improvement in the quality of government.

Change in Predominant Attitude toward Government.   Undoubtedly some of the increase in public expenditures is due to the general change in attitude toward government. A century ago governments were feared as a source of tyranny and arbitrary power; today the more preponderant view is that a square deal for the common man and more abundant life for all cannot be achieved without relying heavily upon government.

ATTITUDES TOWARD EXPANDING GOVERNMENT

Anarchistic and Individualistic Views.   The role that government should play in the lives of men has been the topic for as much printers' ink perhaps as any other, not excepting religion. The prevailing view of

---

[8] Paul H. Douglas, *Economy in the National Government* (Chicago: University of Chicago Press, 1952), p. 146.

English and American philosophers during the nineteenth century was suggested by Jefferson's famous dictum, "That government is best which governs least," and the title of Herbert Spencer's book "Man Versus the State." Or take the following from the *London Economist* of 1847: [9]

> It may be hurtful to the pride of statesmen to discover how little they can really do to eradicate misery, to alleviate suffering, and to improve society. . . . All that can be said of the greatest statesman is that he discovered error and removed it; that he found a country harassed by restrictions and regulations, and that he freed it.

It is interesting to observe how much use was made of government in the nineteenth century notwithstanding this adverse ideological setting. Labor legislation, sanitary laws, public welfare programs, and public education all made progress on an *ad hoc* basis; that is, proponents saw problems to be solved and were convinced, despite advice to the contrary, that governments could be used to provide a solution. Nevertheless, when the Ten-Hour Bill limiting the working hours of children to ten was introduced in the British Parliament, the bishops of the Church of England, then in the House of Lords, voted overwhelmingly against the measure. Such is the power of an idea.

Most extreme of the opponents to government are the anarchists; they profess a profound faith in the individual as such and resent all attempts to apply the sanctions of coercion whether by a democratic government or an autocratic one. Even marriage should be a free union; contracts should have no enforceability beyond the conscience and good will of the parties. The philosophy envisages a spontaneous order based upon the federation of free associations. This approach has been described as the "extravagant worship of individual liberty."

Less extreme but having much in common with anarchists' views is the position of the laissez-faire individualists. Among the most celebrated was John Stuart Mill who held that "the business of life is better performed when those who have an immediate interest in it are left to take their own course, uncontrolled either by the mandate of law or the meddling of any public functionary." [10] Mill admitted that there were many exceptions but he held that the burden of proof lies upon those who favor governmental interference. He supported this general proposition on the following grounds:

---

[9] Quoted in Howard E. Bowen, *Social Responsibilities of the Businessman* (New York: Harper and Row, Publishers, 1953), p. 16n.

[10] John Stuart Mill, *Principles of Political Economy* (Ashley ed.), 1932, Book V, chap. XI, p. 952.

1. Governmental interference restricts liberty. We need constantly to be on guard against tyranny.

2. The individual is most interested in his own affairs and the best judge of his own interests.

3. Governments are inferior in the operation of industry and commerce to private enterprise.

4. People acquire education and gain self-reliance by doing things for themselves. Individual development is the great objective of society.

Modern proponents of this general view make much of the new manifestations of tyranny throughout the world and the increased difficulties in promoting a successful revolution. They are of the opinion that public interference with our economy must lead to public curtailment of civil rights; our liberties are indivisible. They add that private enterprise, even with much concentration of business, is a decentralizing factor and that a full union of all economic and political power must be regarded as a dangerous threat to democratic institutions.

Socialist and Pragmatic Views. In sharp contrast to the above views are those of Communists and Socialists who agree that governments should own and operate the essential means of production. Democratic socialism would attain these ends without the use of violence or the curtailment of civil rights. Some so-called socialists would confine government to areas where competition does not protect the public or where industry for some other reason is invested with a peculiar public interest.

An approach that might be said to lie somewhere between that of the Socialists and that of the individualists may be described as the pragmatic view. Pragmatists hold to no general theory, but they believe that in our modern world, experience and observation often support the view that government action in this case or that is the best route to the public welfare. They say that governments should assume an active and positive role both in the regulation of industry and the provision of services, but that they should leave in private hands, and mainly under private control, the chief functions of the economic system. This more positive view of government enjoyed a sharp boost during the depressed 1930s when a largely free economy brought widespread frustration and privation.

Advantages in the Use of Government. Use of government to accomplish many objectives has some very impressive advantages. One is that government provides a device for dealing with the recalcitrant who exploits his neighbors when he will not carry his share of a voluntary program from which all benefit. Familiar examples are the "scab" who poaches on the efforts of the trade union, and the farmer who chisels on the farmers' cooperative. Closely related is the fact that it is only the government that can apply effectively the financial principle of ability to pay. Thus, some despair of solving the problem of medical care by voluntary means; they say that the ultimate solution will not only require the well to pay for the ill—this can be done by private insurance—it must also require the economically strong to invest in the health of the economically weak.

Decisions on most public expenditures are not unanimous, and the same is true of the patterns of taxation used to support them. Thus, public decisions are said to involve many cases where fifty-one people out of one hundred coerce the other forty-nine; this is said to be incompatible with freedom. It is the central theme of a vast quantity of classical political philosophy.

Of course, it may be answered that even in private organizations minorities customarily bow to the will of majorities. But the government is unique in that it affords virtually no opportunity to resign.

And it may be answered, too, that minorities should not complain as long as they have civil rights; that is, they have the power to make friends and influence people for their point of view which may one day become the majority position. But this never satisfies the individualists who argue that there will still be *a minority*.

The weakness in the individualists' case seems to be that forbearance on the part of the majority to force its will on a minority is in some sense a positive decision (in which the minority coerces the majority).

Attempts have been made to apply an analysis appropriate for the market economy to the public economy as well, allotting services and applying taxes according to individual preferences. They ignore or underrate the fact that public decisions involve such important elements as spending other people's money and immeasurable indirect benefits supplied for "the good of the team." In the last analysis finances in the public sphere can hardly be divorced from value judgments in terms of national goals. This applies the rule of consensus to both the public and the private sphere, for in some sense and some degree they limit each other.

Checks on Government Spending. Democracies do seem inclined toward liberal public spending, but in the United States there are many pressures and safeguards operating on the other side. One of these is the powerful influence of modern advertising brought to bear upon the taxpayers' materialistic desires. Competitive tax rates at the local level add another impediment. Expenditure and taxes require affirmative action by a government of checks and balances. Dislike of taxes is very general and very keen, the more so because the payment is not directly associated with the benefits of public expenditure.

Some writers accordingly have concluded that the public economy in comparison with the private economy is badly lagging.[11] Examples are cited of families going to a picnic in a luxurious car through an ugly city, with food in a new gadget lunch box to be served on the banks of a polluted stream. They say that if the economists' principle of diminishing utility is valid, many families must be far down on a descending curve. The implication is that the curve is inapplicable to public services or that we are much further removed from satiety in the public sphere.

   Distinction between Government Production and Government Finance. Mention was made in Chapter 18 of the fact that governments can finance many public wants and exercise a powerful influence upon the economy without themselves being heavily involved in production. In this context government regulation is preferred over government ownership, government contracts over government plants producing defense equipment, and transfer payments over government services. We are here reminded that education, for instance, may be supported either in the form of public schools or that of assistance to students whether in public or private schools.[12]

FEDERAL, STATE, AND JOINT RESPONSIBILITY FOR GOVERNMENTAL FUNCTIONS

It is an accepted rule that the government should not perform functions that can as well be performed privately, and that the federal government should not perform functions that can be as well performed by state and local governments. However, this rule does not help very much in the practical task of allocating functions. Making for a trend toward centralization are (1) the sluggishness of state governments especially with regard to such matters as reapportionment (of legislative representation), civil service, antiquated constitutions, the long ballot, regressive taxation, and the metropolitan problem; (2) the intensity of interstate competition; (3) the increasing interdependence in the economy; and (4) the new importance of the total level of expenditures in maintaining the stability of the economy. On the other hand, points made for decentralization are the greater degree of participation in local government, the greater sense of a proprietary interest in local expenditures, and the well-recognized weaknesses of a central bureaucracy. Many functions such as health, education, and highways appear to involve strong mutual interests, and these are the areas in which grants (aids) have developed.

   Proponents of decentralized government should logically be the

---

[11] See Galbraith, *The Affluent Society.*
[12] See Musgrave, *The Theory of Public Finance,* chaps. 1–7.

most active proponents of aggressive and efficient state and local government. Actually, they are frequently found opposing state and local reforms. This leads to the accusation that their real interest is not in decentralization but rather in minimum government.

PRINCIPLE OF MAXIMUM ADVANTAGE

The main principle in public expenditure is so obvious as scarcely to require stating. It is that governments, like individuals, should determine the direction and the degree of public expenditure by balancing alternatives: one possible direction of public outlay against another, and all public outlays against the private use of the income, were it allowed to remain in the hands of the taxpayer. Thus, the government must decide which it needs most, a new city hall or higher pay for schoolteachers, and whether either should be voted in preference to more food or automobiles which the taxpayers might enjoy privately were they not taxed as contemplated. Of course, budgeting is an important aid in this balancing process. To provide public luxuries at the expense of private necessities is a violation of this principle and one that is too often exemplified in practice. Although this principle is elementary and in accord with the clear dictates of common sense, its intelligent application is neither simple nor easy.

The choices of people collectively are made quite differently from those of individuals in their private affairs. The individual may be said to vote for private services with his dollars as he does for public services at an election. But his choices in the latter instance are translated into services only through the myriad forms of politics. His vote at the polls is not circumscribed by purchasing power to the same degree as that in the market place. His decision involves a curious mixture of spending his own money on himself, spending other people's money on himself, spending other people's money on still other people, and so on.

The citizen must express himself indirectly and ambiguously in a vote for a party, a platform, and a representative. If he is interested enough, he may follow this up through correspondence with his representative and even by an appearance at hearings on particular legislation. The counterpart of advertising in the private market is political propaganda in the public one; consumers' incompetence is matched by the ignorance and indifference of the voters.

A further word should be added about providing public luxuries at the expense of private necessities. On first thought, it seems evident that there could hardly be a defense for levying taxes that compel lower income recipients to live in hovels while monumental public buildings are being constructed. Since taxes are not ordinarily earmarked, this analysis seems to force us to compare the least justifiable of our public expenditures with the most important private wants that must be sacrificed because of tax collections. Much governmental outlay would stand up under this test. For instance, reasonable expenditures for protection could be supported even though it took food from the tables of underprivileged families. But by no means could all public expenditure be so classified. The analysis gives strong support for progressive taxation, but this alternative is not practically available to some units of government such as municipalities. In these circumstances it seems unfair to compare an incremental increase in public expenditure with the sacrifice of the poorest families. The sound procedure would be to compare the total good accomplished by the public expenditure with the total damage caused by the tax, including the opportunity cost of foregoing private goods.

It is sometimes said that a good public expenditure will justify a bad tax.[13] This seems to follow from what has been said above but only, of course, if the bad tax is the sole measure that for one reason or another is available. A sales tax in Illinois for the relief of destitution in 1933 might serve as an example.

ECONOMIC EFFECTS OF PUBLIC EXPENDITURE

Effect on Consumption.   There can be little doubt that certain public expenditures do a great deal to improve the tone and raise the level of consumption in the community. Some of this influence is direct and some indirect. It raises the level directly by providing wholesome recreational and cultural facilities. Recreational outlays of governments are quantitatively far less than those made privately. But in the author's view public parks, playgrounds, libraries, and schools compare very favorably in quality with cabarets, taverns, movies, athletic exhibitions, and even pleasure driving that take the spare private dollar. On the indirect side, public schools ordinarily give the consumer about the only disinterested education he ever will get. They try to teach him some rudiments both of taste and discrimination. The outlay here can be compared with that made privately for advertising.

Effect on Production.   It is quite impossible to conceive of modern private production with the state abstracted from the picture. As ob-

---

[13] But it has also been argued that good (meaning direct) taxation is an important safeguard against unwise public expenditures.

served in Chapter 1, the roles of the private and public economies are highly complementary. Particularly through its education and health programs, the government develops and conserves the human resources that provide the working force, the leadership, and the customers of private enterprise. The government along with land, labor, capital, and the entrepreneur is a factor of production not to be despised. Too much parsimony in public expenditures would not be "good for business" in the broadest sense of that term. The interest of a particular firm, however, may be less at stake than that of all business combined. Government may also be regarded as to some extent a way by which certain social "overhead costs" (such as accident and unemployment compensation) are cared for and charged in part to business through the tax system.[14] The government, too, is engaged in production directly. The value of its services is counted in the calculation of the national income. Since there is no market to measure this value, the contribution has to be taken at cost as indicated in the government's operating statement. Certain outlays, such as interest on the public debt and social security payments, are treated as transfers of existing income rather than the creation of a new flow.

The fact that one quarter or one third of the national income passes through government is sometimes interpreted to mean that this large part of the income stream is diverted from productive into nonproductive channels. However, the fact that people invest or spend some of their money collectively does not mean that it is sterilized. To put it another way, one quarter of the national income is produced *by* as well as *for* the government. The classical economists often said or implied that the government is not productive. This attitude was due largely to a narrow definition of production or a prejudice against government or both. A publicly operated school or highway can be quite as productive as a privately operated theater or railroad.

Effect on Distribution. Government expenditures frequently alter the distribution of wealth and income in the direction of greater equality. The benefits of public expenditure may be weighted to favor the poor in comparison to the taxes they pay. In addition, adequate educational facilities permit the recruitment of a large supply of professional and skilled manual talent, and this tends to reduce the differential between the upper and lower ranks of income recipients. Some observers are worried at the present time that the output of college graduates may become so large that "suitable" positions may not be available for all of them. Logically, at least, this should lower the reward that attends these types of employment. Similarly, if there were an oversupply of physicians,

---

[14] K. William Kapp, *The Social Costs of Private Enterprise* (Cambridge, Mass.: Harvard University Press, 1950).

the cost of medical care might be brought within the range of more people's means.

One of the leading proponents of greater economic equality, R. H. Tawney, advocates public expenditures as the main instrument to attain this goal: "What is important is not that all men should receive the same pecuniary income. It is that the surplus resources of society should be so husbanded and applied that it is a matter of minor significance whether they receive it or not." [15] If education, housing, medical care, and nutrition were provided at common expense, or adequate standards in these areas were underwritten by the taxpayer as a "national minimum," the dignity of the individual and his cultural opportunities would be assured. In these circumstances inequalities would lose much of their present importance.

Since John Stuart Mill first enunciated the principle, it has been largely accepted that governments can do great damage by interfering with prices but that they can modify the distribution of economic rewards without much damage in the allocation of private resources. The modification of the distribution pattern is both through taxation and the free dispensation of benefits by means of public expenditures.

Effect on Stability of National Income. Public expenditures are recognized as one of the major tools of fiscal policy which, in turn, is one if not the major tool for coping with business cycles and inflation and deflation. Deficit spending, compensatory spending, and public investment are various names and forms of the idea that the government should act as the balance wheel of the economy, maintaining money flows at times when private business is in the doldrums. This important effect or potential effect of public expenditures will be considered in detail in a later chapter.

Operation of the Multiplier and Acceleration Principles. Under conditions of less than full employment, public expenditures may create employment and enhance income indirectly as well as directly. Those who receive income from the government's new outlay usually spend much of what they receive, and their expenditures in turn become income to others, which creates additional demand for goods and services, and so on. The new government expenditure thus sets off a chain of expenditures on the part of successive income recipients, each of whom receives somewhat less (and spends less) than the previous recipients of income. For example, if income recipients were to spend 80 percent of any increase in their incomes, and the government raised its expenditures by $100 (taxes unchanged), the following dwindling additions to national income might occur over a period of time: $100 + $80 + $64 +

---

[15] *Equality* (London: George Allen & Unwin, 1931), p. 155.

$51.20 + $40.96 + . . . etc. Hence an increase in government outlay for goods and services might raise the national income by the amount of goods and services purchased by the government *plus* the induced effects on private spending. This tendency of an increase in public expenditures (of course, the same holds for an increase in private spending) to augment business and employment has been called the "multiplier." According to the theory of the multiplier, the total effect of a new expenditure within a period of time depends on (1) the size of the initial outlay, (2) the propensity (willingness) of income recipients to spend new income, and (3) the rate of turnover involved in the process.

The last two criteria deserve further comment. It should be stressed that the repercussions of a new outlay (as illustrated above) do not occur instantaneously. How great the repercussion effect will be in a given period of time depends on the velocity of transactions. However, the *total* repercussion effect will be realized independently of time. It depends solely on people's propensity to consume an increase in income. The latter is commonly referred to as the marginal propensity to consume. In the example above, the marginal propensity to consume is assumed to be 80 percent. The student can easily verify that the greater the marginal propensity to consume, the greater will be the multiplier effect.[16]

Since in a period of unemployment spending is presumed to be the limiting factor, the saved dollar is "leakage" in the operation of the multiplier. Thus, if recipients of new income will save one fifth (20 percent) of what they receive, then the effect of a $1 million public works program is a $5 million addition to income ($1 million $\times$ 1⅕ equals $5 million). However, the impetus of the new injection is not likely to be permanent; it runs out eventually and may require a new "dose" unless business gets a psychological "lift" from the process. It is conceivable that business may react negatively rather than positively to "pump priming." More-

---

[16] This relationship can be expressed more specifically to obtain a quantitative measure of the multiplier. Let k be the multiplier, $Y =$ Income, $C =$ Consumption, $I =$ Investment (private or public), then:

$$\Delta Y = k\Delta I$$

$$k = \frac{\Delta Y}{\Delta I}$$

And since $Y = C + I$, or $I = Y - C$

Therefore $k = \dfrac{\Delta Y}{\Delta Y - \Delta C} = \dfrac{1}{1 - \dfrac{\Delta C}{\Delta Y}}$.

Since $\dfrac{\Delta C}{\Delta Y}$ is the marginal propensity to consume (m.p.c.), $1 - \dfrac{\Delta C}{\Delta Y}$ is equal to the marginal propensity to save (m.p.s.). The multiplier is the reciprocal of the marginal propensity to save. The latter term is used to describe the proportion of an addition to (or subtraction from) income that will be saved. (A somewhat more extended discussion of income determination may be found in Chapter 25.)

over, there is a chance that some of the impetus of the new investment, unless accompanied by adequate monopoly controls, will go into higher prices rather than expanded employment.

Closely related to the concept of the multiplier is that termed the acceleration principle. As demand for finished goods and services expands with an enlargement of purchasing power, new equipment may be required to accommodate it. Moreover, the fluctuations in the equipment goods industries tend to be greater than the fluctuations in consumer demand. For example, assume that 100 machines are required to produce 1000 units of a given consumer good, and each machine lasts ten years. Then at a constant volume of consumption ten machines have to be replaced every year. If now there is a sudden increase of 10 percent (from 1000 to 1100) in consumer demand, ten new machines will be needed in addition to the usual replacement requirement. Thus the 10-percent increase in consumer demand will be reflected in a 100-percent increase in capital goods production. The fluctuations of production in the equipment industries are therefore said to be largely a function of the growth in consumption rather than merely the volume of consumption. Hence, some of the saving that constitutes "leakage" under the operation of the multiplier may be offset through new investment in capital. However, if there is idle capacity to be utilized, the increase in consumption may bring about no induced investment and no magnified fluctuations in the equipment industries. The full consequences of a public works outlay thus involve very complicated considerations and are not subject to precise mathematical calculation. In times of full employment, an increase in public outlay (for example, the defense program of 1950) operates much as described above except that the increase in national income takes the form of higher prices (inflation) rather than more real output.

The economic effect of public expenditure in terms of income and employment is greatest when financed through borrowing. And borrowing from banks will be more effective than borrowing from nonbank sources. The latter might raise interest rates and discourage private investment. But its effect can be important even when it is financed through taxation.[17] Private employment need not be adversely affected by the outlay since the revenue raised by taxation is again returned to the income stream. The effect is much the same as though a new industry had been launched in the private sphere.[18]

---

[17] In this case the outlay would have a multiplier of 1.

[18] Discussed more fully in Chapter 26. For further reading on the multiplier and acceleration principle, see George N. Halm, *Monetary Theory* (Philadelphia: Blackiston Company, 1942), chap. 18; Harold M. Somers, *Public Finance and National Income* (Philadelphia: Blackiston Company, 1949), chaps. 4–6.

NATURE AND POSSIBILITIES OF ECONOMY IN GOVERNMENT

There are three types of economy in government. The first consists of the curtailment of governmental expenditures to the lowest possible figure that seems feasible at a given time and in given circumstances. This is a negative type of economy, perhaps more properly called parsimony. The second type consists of wise and intelligent selection of the purposes of public outlays and of public as compared with alternative private outlays which may become impossible if the government conscripts private funds through taxation. This is the balancing process which has been discussed in general in this chapter and will be considered more specifically in later chapters. Finally, there is the type of economy that consists of getting the most output from the least input. In subsequent chapters, particularly in Chapter 22, some possibilities for economy of this last type will be suggested.

CLASSIFICATION OF PUBLIC EXPENDITURES

SELF-LIQUIDATING, REPRODUCTIVE, PRODUCTIVE, AND NONPRODUCTIVE PUBLIC EXPENDITURES

Public expenditures may be productive in different ways and senses. The difference may be important when it comes to selecting public works in a period of unemployment. In the first place there are public outlays that are comparable in almost all respects to private investment in productive equipment. These outlays are self-liquidating from direct charges upon the beneficiaries who receive service from the outlays. The beneficiaries are willing to pay for these services in the same way that they pay for services in the private commercial world. Expenditures of this character may be called self-liquidating, reproductive public expenditures. Examples include publicly owned utilities, housing, and rural electrification. The last two named may be only partially self-liquidating.

The second class includes outlays that are reproductive in the sense that they create economic advantages for the community through which the national income and the income tax base will be enlarged in future years. They are self-liquidating in a sense, but not without the use of the net income or some other tax to help finance them. Possibly a fee might be charged to compensate for special benefits resulting from such expenditures, but it is not usually regarded as desirable. Into this class fall soil conservation, public health, and public education. Highways financed by the gasoline tax are a sort of cross between these two classes.

The third class includes outlays that are productive but not self-liquidating or reproductive. They are useful and add to the national income in the sense that they add to the current enjoyment of life. If the outlay is for a durable service, it may add to enjoyment over a period of years. However, the expenditure does not add to the income tax base, except as it, along with other expenditures, gives employment and puts purchasing power into circulation. Examples of this type of expenditure are public recreation, public parks, and most public buildings.

A fourth class of public outlays must be classed as nonproductive or wasteful. An excessive outlay for armaments (beyond the needs for defense) would go into this category. Make-work projects of little value such as "leaf raking" also belong in this class. Even this outlay, of course, adds to the income received by individuals, at least at the time of distribution and if it is financed out of credit.

Perhaps a fifth class of public expenditures should also be mentioned: the kind that involves a present governmental outlay but which may save a greater or, at all events, some governmental outlay in the future. Aids to dependent children, for example, may be defended on the ground that were they not granted, the government might have to enlarge its expenditure for dependency and delinquency when the children became adults.

Thus, government outlays may be justified on several grounds: (1) that they are investments that will add to future economic power; (2) that they add currently to human enjoyment; (3) that they save greater future outlays; and (4) that they give employment and spread purchasing power. The outlays justified on the first and third of these grounds may be thought of as investments, warranted if wisely selected and more reproductive or more conserving of future outlays than other investments, public or private, which might offer themselves as alternatives. Those based on the second are productive outlays that afford enjoyment and are warranted if they provide more enjoyment than alternative private or public outlays. Those based on the fourth are warranted, perhaps, in an emergency to stimulate private business during a depression. Needless to say, expenditures that rest only on the fourth justification are seldom warranted if alternatives that rest on one of the first three justifications exist. Also, most public expenditures are defended on more than one of the above grounds. Economy consists of an intelligent balancing of alternatives, public against private, present against future, and one object or direction against another.

Expenditures may also be classified as exhaustive or nonexhaustive (transfer payments); military and civilian; investment (capital) or non-durable.

CAPITAL AND DURABLE GOODS EXPENDITURE

In the accounting procedure used in a modern business, a sharp line is drawn between expenditures for current operating expenses and expenditures for capital outlay. An example of the former is a manager's salary; of the latter, a new truck or building. One major distinction here is that capital outlay is usually for durable goods [19] and is more properly written off through annual depreciation than as a single large negative item offset against current operating income. In addition, capital outlays of private industry are usually self-liquidating and thus more properly looked upon as an investment than as an expenditure. Their cost, less depreciation, appears on the balance sheet of the business as an asset. Outlays for such capital are more or less flexible as to time—that is, they can be hastened or delayed considerably according to the decision of the management.

Expenditures for durable goods (such as a piano or automobile) also have a distinct place in the budget of the private consumer. Such goods are not income earning like an industry's capital, but they do serve over a considerable period of time and their cost is properly budgeted in installments. Consumers' outlays for durable goods are also flexible as to time and may be greatly expanded during one period and contracted during another.

Governments also spend money for durable goods and productive equipment that may or may not be self-liquidating. Government accounts usually show capital outlays distinct from the current operating expenses of government. The purchase of a durable good such as a new schoolhouse may be a proper occasion for borrowing to spread the cost of the improvement over a considerable period. Governments, however, usually maintain nothing similar to the private corporation's balance sheet (exception: municipal utilities and other government corporations) and take no regular account of depreciation.

It is generally recognized that the capital expenditures of industry and the durable goods expenditures of consumers play a very strategic role in the cyclical movement of business and in maintaining the balance of the industrial process. Until recently, relatively little attention has been given to the equally important strategic importance of government outlays for durable and capital goods. Some present-day economists give

---

[19] Goods that are not used up or consumed within a short period, such as a year.

considerable support to the view that regulated and expanded public expenditures or investments in public works are (or might be) of major significance in coping with depressions and chronic unemployment.

LIMITS TO PUBLIC EXPENDITURE

It goes without saying that no nation can enjoy more than it produces, whether privately or collectively. Beyond that, little can be said about the capacity of governments to tax and to spend, except that it is all a matter of judgment, depending mostly on the circumstances of time and place. A great deal depends on how and where the revenue is spent. Much of the discussion of taxable capacity has concerned the question of how much a nation can afford to pay outside its borders on debts and indemnities. The limiting factor here is likely to be the inability to transfer [20] rather than inability to pay. But there is a limit to ability to pay in these circumstances. From the standpoint of those outside the country and divorcing consideration of ability to pay from that of willingness to pay, the limit is set by the fact that production may be seriously handicapped if taxation is carried beyond a certain point. The situation is quite different, of course, where revenue is expended within the country from which it is raised. Here the community gets a return for its taxes, and the problem becomes one of public versus private satisfaction of wants. Certainly something depends on how the taxes are levied and for what the expenditures are made. When the government takes taxes from *A* to pay or service *B*, it must consider the effect of the transaction on both. As Sir Josiah Stamp pointed out, the capacity to pay may be stretched a great deal if the stretching is gradual. It is interesting to observe that Bastable thought an income tax of 5 shillings on the pound (25 percent) would prove too much even for the United Kingdom.[21] Stamp calls attention to the fact that the British "were deploring the appalling weight of taxes and the absolutely suicidal policy of adding 3*d.* [1.25 percent] to the income tax" in 1910.[22] Nevertheless, during World War II, Congress concluded that taxes could not be raised without unduly damaging incentives, notwithstanding the fact that expenditures were some two or three times greater than taxes. At least one critic [23] has concluded that when a nation's taxes reach more than one quarter of its income the result will be inflationary. The taxes themselves will have a repressive

---

[20] See Chapter 28.

[21] C. F. Bastable, *Public Finance* (3d ed., New York: The Macmillan Company, 1903), p. 676.

[22] Sir Josiah Stamp, *Wealth and Taxable Capacity* (London: P. S. King & Son, Ltd., 1922), p. 131.

[23] Colin Clark, "Public Finance and Changes in the Value of Money," *Economic Journal*, LV (December 1945), p. 371.

effect on income, and private industry will seek to compensate for high taxes by borrowing. The government itself may turn to borrowing to meet its expenditures. This line of argument was seized upon by a tax-weary public during the Korean defense program to support the view that the prevailing tax level was too high.

Analysis of tax limitation may be considered in terms of psychological, political, economic, and legal inhibitions. The psychological restrictions are a matter of attitudes; they depend upon the degree of levy to which the public is accustomed and the respect of the public for the government and its program. The political barriers are similar; they include the distaste of the public for taxes and its propensity to reward representatives who reduce the levy. The economic limitations relate especially to incentive and inflation; the former relationship will depend to some extent on the type of taxes employed. Inflation will be curbed if high taxes are substituted for borrowing (at least from banks), but even taxes may be inflationary if expenditures are very high (or increasing rapidly). A country with per capita income far in excess of the cost of necessities can presumably spend and tax more than one with lower average income. To these, especially at the state level, are added the limits to taxes related to interstate competition. Legal restrictions are found in state constitutions where ceiling rates are provided in some cases for property taxes; a ceiling on federal income tax rates has also been proposed.

With so many variables in the picture it is highly doubtful if any one figure can be selected as a universal limit on taxes in a free economy. This is not to say that there are no limits.[24]

SUMMARY

Public expenditures in the United States have shown a sharp upward trend. This is true of governments at all levels but particularly of the federal government which now assumes a dominant position in the over-all picture. Many causes contribute to the trend, among them: advancing income, wars, urbanization, and a change in the predominant attitude toward government. Attitudes toward government range from those of the anarchists and extreme individualists to those of the Socialists and Communists. In between the extremes are the pragmatists who accept a governmental solution to any problem when the evidence indicates that this will promote the public welfare. A strong following supports the view that because of various checks, the so-called public sphere lags behind the private one, and that the former can be much developed with-

---

[24] Walter W. Heller, "How High Can Taxes Go?" *Proceedings of the National Tax Association Conference*, 1952, pp. 243–255.

out threatening private enterprise. Governmental action has the advantage that goes with compulsion, namely, that it can force due payment for indirect benefit and charge according to ability to pay. Centralization of governmental expenditures is now promoted by many factors, especially the sluggishness of the states, but it is tempered by fear of the federal bureaucracy.

The principle of maximum advantage in public expenditure states that governments, like individuals, should determine the direction and degree of public outlay by balancing alternatives, public and private. Public luxuries at the expense of private necessities are ruled out by this principle. This sounds simple, but it cannot be applied without many qualifications involving the nature of the tax system and the political process.

Public expenditures are classified in many ways, including the divi- of consumption, production, distribution, and the stability of national income and employment. Under conditions of less than full employment, public expenditures may create employment and enhance income indirectly as well as directly. It may do so through what has come to be called the multiplier effect and the acceleration principle, the former operating to swell consumption and the later, investment.

Public expenditures are classified in many ways, including the division into self-liquidating, reproductive, productive, and nonproductive outlay. Another useful division separates capital outlays from those contracted for recurring operating expenses. Economy in public outlay may take the form of improved rationing (better selection among alternatives) or improved engineering (more performance from each dollar expended). Attempts have been made to discover a definite limit beyond which expenditures (or taxes) threaten a private economy (or at any rate inflation), but they require consideration of the conditions of time and place.

PROBLEMS

1. It is alleged that democracy affords the poor an opportunity to encroach upon the economic gains of the rich; it is also said that governments are run by and for "big business." Which of these statements is more nearly true, and what bearing does this matter have on the trend of public expenditures?
2. Why is it necessary to deflate raw figures of increased public expenditure? How can this be done?
3. Comment on the proposition that as a nation becomes more prosperous economically, it tends to spend a larger portion of its income through government.
4. The British are currently reported to be spending through govern-

ment about 40 percent of the national income. National leaders have told the workers that if they want a higher level of public services, they will have to produce more. Does this mean that in a peacetime "mixed" economy we can accept 40 percent of income as the top limit of public expenditures?

5. A local government, let us say, is confined in its revenue sources to the general property tax. This source has already been worked substantially when a program to provide a park and playground is proposed. In favor of the program, it is pointed out that the citizenry spends substantial sums in taverns and "pool halls." In opposition, it is pointed out that the property tax hits directly some poor homeowners and indirectly some even poorer tenants. What principle of public expenditure would one apply in appraising this situation and how?

6. Comment on the proposition: A man votes every time he makes a private purchase; he votes on both commodities and brands; the result is the optimum distribution of resources for the maximum satisfaction of human needs.

7. If the government is one of the factors of production, as alleged, in what respects does it differ from the others? Why is it that businessmen, as a rule, are likely to feel that less outlay and lower taxes would be "good for business"?

8. Explain how the employment of a few building trade workers on a public works project in a depression might eventually mean more employment in the laundry trade and the machine tool industry. What would determine the addition to the national income that the outlay would create?

9. What are the advantages of government over voluntary means to achieve certain ends?

10. Contrast and compare the various attitudes with regard to the proper role of government in society.

11. It is said that the essence of government is coercion of minorities by majorities. Does this seriously curtail human freedom?

12. Make a list of some of the factors that tend to favor private as compared with public outlay in competition for the consumer's dollar.

13. Comment on the proposition that governmental activity is generally less efficient than that carried on under private auspices.

14. Are there practical economic criteria for comparing demand for public services with private demand? Are there standards of efficiency that may be applied in evaluating public activities? In what areas is the development of government most and least likely to interfere with the optimum allocation of resources in the private economy?

15. Consider the factors that should determine which level of government should undertake a given function.

16. Contrast the processes of decision making in the public and private spheres of the economy.

22

ELEMENTS OF PUBLIC EXPENDITURE

This chapter is devoted mainly to a discussion of the nature of and the financial problems associated with certain functions for which the government makes large outlays. No attempt will be made, however, to deal with all governmental functions or to treat exhaustively those covered.

An over-all picture of the outlay for the various functions of government is presented in Table 6.

EXPENDITURES FOR PROTECTION

No service of the state is more important historically or more universally provided than that of protection. The term is used to include protection from violence to persons and property by lawbreakers within the country and also by foes outside its borders. Here we shall confine ourselves to the latter aspects. It was expenditures for wars that historically ushered in many innovations in the tax system and accustomed taxpayers to levels of taxation that they might never have accepted otherwise. Military expenditures are at once the most respectable and yet probably (in more than one sense) the most wasteful of our many government outlays. Technical progress in war equipment plus more skilled international diplomacy could one day make them largely unnecessary.

TABLE 6

All Governments in the United States:
Expenditure by Functions, 1962

Function	Amount (in millions)	Percent
National defense and international relations	$ 40,387	35.59
Education	21,022	15.15
Highways	9,936	7.16
Public welfare	4,732	3.41
Hospitals and health	5,610	4.04
Police	2,184	1.58
Natural resources	11,409	8.22
Housing and urban renewal	1,320	0.95
Air and water transportation	3,073	2.21
Social insurance administration	636	0.46
General control	3,022	2.18
Interest on general debt	9,296	6.66
Other [a]	17,170	12.37
Total	$138,801	100.00

[a] Includes postal services, corrections, sewers, libraries, sanitation, fire and other unallocable services.

NOTE: The data were originally gathered by the U.S. Census and are gross rather than net, but duplication for intergovernmental transfers has been removed. Expenditures for utility and liquor stores and for insurance trust (employee retirement, unemployment compensation, OASI, and railroad retirement) are excluded. The functional classification is necessarily rough; for instance, such categories as interest on the public debt and natural resources include a considerable portion that is oriented to national defense.

SOURCE: Adapted from Tax Foundation, *Facts and Figures on Government Finance, 1962–1963* (New York, 1963), p. 19; figures are not precisely additive because of rounding.

FORMS OF MILITARY EXPENDITURES

Military expenditures fall into three categories: (1) the prewar or peacetime cost of national defense, (2) the outlays for actual warfare, and (3) the postwar expenditures for pensions to veterans and for interest and principal on war debts.

Peacetime Cost. It is quite possible that a nation that has superior resources and techniques may achieve security by outarming its potential enemy. But the effectiveness of advance military preparations is always weakened by the fact that military strength is a relative matter and that an addition to the preparation of one country is a stimulus to an equal "spurt" in the military outlays of rival powers.

Taking the Profit out of War. The people of the United States were scandalized by the extraordinary profit made in supplying the military forces during World War I. This lead to the (probably erroneous) conviction on the part of many that World War I in particular and wars in general are largely caused by "big business" in its blind quest for profits. The conviction added much support to a trend toward isolationism and pacifism. At that time proposals for the "conscription of capital" during wartime were common. Some of these proposals called for taxation that would begin at $3000 of personal income and rise by 10 percent for each additional thousand dollars of income, so that any excess of income over $10,000 would be taxed at the rate of 99 percent. Corporation taxes would be correspondingly severe.

An alternative means of preventing war profits would be direct government production of munitions. This might accomplish its objective with the highest degree of perfection, but it would involve extremely difficult problems of transition unless it were to be continued in peacetime. Moreover, war supply involves a very wide range of materials by no means all of which could be classed as munitions.

The government could reduce the risk associated with war production by providing the capital needed for war expansion. This was done to a large degree during World War II. The government also allowed accelerated depreciation under which equipment devoted to specialized war production could, for tax purposes, be written off during the anticipated period of the war. This again greatly reduced the risk factor and with it the ground for excessive profit. Where the government retained title to war plants the program created a considerable problem of disposition during the transition from war to peace.

War and Defense Contracts. Special difficulties attend the administration of war and defense contracts. Ordinary bidding is distasteful to contractors because it affords no protection from inflationary losses and because manufacturers are called upon to produce items for which they have no cost data or experience. Cost-plus contracts were widely used during World War I and the early years of World War II. They protected the supplier against all increases in the cost of labor and materials and were criticized on the ground that they "opened the floodgates to waste and inefficiency." [1] Government inspectors can be supplied to prevent this result, but they have proved largely ineffective. The fixed-price (ordinary type) contract has such important advantages that it should be employed where feasible. An incentive contract, setting a price

---

[1] Paul H. Douglas, *Economy in the National Government* (Chicago: Chicago University Press, 1952), p. 158.

target and sharing the gains of superior performance, may work well if the target set is realistic. Superimposed upon these possibilities in type of contract is renegotiation, under which the government reviews a contract after performance and recaptures profits deemed excessive. This was introduced during World War II and revived during the Korean defense program. Although recoupments by renegotiation has been considerable, the device is criticized on the ground that it divides responsibility and tends to easy acceptance of costs once they have occurred.

Excess Profits Taxation. Finally there is the excess profits tax, launched with the avowed purpose of recapturing war-caused profits. The one inaugurated during World War II contained a minor compulsory-saving feature calling for the return of part of the amount collected after the war. The tax (without the return feature) was reintroduced during the Korean conflict. In both periods personal taxes were also increased. Thus the defenses against war-caused profits are considerable, but we are still a far cry from where it can be said that no one profits from human slaughter.

Postwar Expenditures. The reabsorption of ex-soldiers into the civilian population and the postwar responsibilities of governments to veterans are old but growing problems. The obligation of government is usually conceived as ending with care and compensation for those injured in war and for their dependents. But in the United States, which has surpassed all nations in its liberality to veterans, the obligation is conceived as going much further and including care and compensation for veterans and their dependents generally, whether or not injured in war.

In foreign countries, where payments are largely limited to compensation for deaths and injuries directly caused by war, expenditures for veterans reach a high point immediately following a war and then gradually diminish. In the United States, where pensions are paid to many who were unscathed by war, the peak of payments may be long delayed and the end postponed for several generations. For example, in 1937 the United States was still paying pensions to dependents of veterans who served in the War of 1812. At this rate, the United States would not be absolved from responsibility for World War I veterans until the year 2045.

To eliminate the pension problem, an elaborate system of war-risk insurance was inaugurated in World War I. The system probably filled a useful purpose, but it failed to stop the postwar demand for bonuses and pensions. Higher pay for soldiers was added to insurance during World War II.

The demands of veterans usually extend to free medicine, special benefits to older veterans, death benefits for survivors, civil-service prefer-

ence, and adjusted compensation (bonus).[2] Allowances for readjustment
into civilian life are in a different class and are generally recognized as
justified. In the period between the world wars, veterans' organizations,
with remarkably little internal opposition, obtained such a stranglehold
on Congress that they achieved repeated successes over presidential
vetoes. The organizations thrived on this kind of program, but critics
claim that they cost the government dearly both in money and morale.
After World War II the organization of the American Veterans Committee with its platform of promoting the interest of veterans by promoting the interest of everybody seemed to proclaim the dawn of a new day.
The organization has in general had an admirable program, but it has not
succeeded in attracting a wide following among veterans.

ECONOMICS OF MILITARY OUTLAYS

If a near miracle were to happen and we were suddenly to achieve, by
diplomacy or international disarmament, complete security from foreign
attack, we would find our federal budget relieved to the extent of some
$50 billion. At first thought, this would surely be a blessing of greatest
magnitude. But on second thought, one might be troubled by the recol-
lection of the argument that under present economic institutions it is difficult to find an outlet for all idle men and resources in civilian pursuits.
One recalls in this connection that certain good news that progress might
be made in disarmament is alleged to have caused a considerable break
in the stock market in 1959. Cynics described it as a "peace scare."

One alternative (and perhaps the worst one) would be to use the
money in wholesale retirement of the public debt. This might lead to idle
or uninvested hoards with bad implications for the economy. Reducing
taxes involves the question of how taxpayers could or would dispose of
their windfalls. Businessmen now spend billions of dollars in advertising
whipping up demand for an already abundant supply of goods. There
are great alleged needs for more public services such as urban improvements and education but more expenditure on these would be regarded
by many as a case of creeping socialism. We might lend more help to
underdeveloped economies but this could aggravate our balance-of-payment difficulties.

Both after World War II and after the Korean conflict we took a
substantial drop in military spending without a depression. But special
circumstances such as pent-up demand for durable goods gave the
economy a lift in these cases. However, there are two consoling con-

---

[2] William P. Dillingham, *Federal Aid to Veterans 1917–1941* (Gainesville:
University of Florida Press, 1952).

clusions that may be ventured: (1) none of the anticipated economic trouble is inherent and inevitable; and (2) disarmament would be worth what it cost even if the price were severe economic trouble. It must surely impress more and more people that it is an absurd waste to spend billions on weapons that nobody who is sane and rational would ever dare to use.

EXPENDITURES FOR PUBLIC EDUCATION

No species in the animal kingdom requires as much time to achieve maturity as man, and this affords the older generation a prolonged opportunity to impart to youth the accumulated traditions and wisdom of mankind. Economic abundance permits leisure, and one way of taking it is by reducing the working years at the starting end. The older generation itself in a world as dynamic as our own may need some intellectual refreshment to keep abreast of the times. These simple truths support the widespread interest and faith in education. Recently, interest in education (and special opportunity for superior scholars) has been promoted by alleged shortage of technicians and the observation that Soviet Russia is doing much more to develop such talent than the United States. It is further supported by the contention that economic growth depends principally on human resources and that education is a principal means of developing and allocating talent.

PHILOSOPHY OF EDUCATION EXPENDITURES

Sponsorship. The need for education of some sort and to some degree is generally conceded, but it is not so clear what agency should sponsor the undertaking. It may be felt that this is a function that logically belongs to the church. Throughout time and space many different relationships between church and state with reference to education have prevailed and now exist. In the French-Canadian province of Quebec, tax-supported schools are at the same time both parochial and public. They are organized according to the religious practice of the taxpayer— that is, Roman Catholic or dissenting—and taxes are levied on each group independently to pay for the school. This might be called a merger of church and state sponsorship. In Russia the state has a monopoly of the schools, and in the United States the relation might be described as one of tolerance and competition. In this country most of the states prohibit the appropriation of public money for sectarian education. Sectarian schools are generally exempt from taxation, and pupils are considered as complying with compulsory attendance laws when attending such schools. Usually some measure of control is executed over sectarian schools as, for instance, in the requirement of certification of teachers. The boundary between the rival sponsors is frequently indistinct and disputed. Recent issues in this area concern the use of public money to transport children to parochial schools, the use of public school buildings for religious instruction by church-sponsored teachers, and the availability of proposed federal aid to support this or that feature of sectarian education. Legislation that would give the public schools exclusive jurisdiction in Oregon was declared unconstitutional by the United States Supreme Court; but legislation that would exempt parents of parochial school children from public school taxes has also been overruled.[3]

Private nonsectarian schools, as well as church-sponsored education, are permitted in the United States. In recent years private school enrollment has grown faster than public school enrollment. At all levels, but particularly in higher education, the private school has a prominent place in the educational picture. The private institutions of higher learning are supported by student fees, endowments, current donations, or all three.

An alternative that should not be overlooked is that of private schools with public support for scholars. This pattern is not uncommon in Europe and it was followed in the United States in distributing benefits under the GI Bill of Rights. An advantage claimed for this system is that it would provide more freedom of choice and less standardization in transmitting the traditions of society. It would, however, obviously constitute a step away from separation of church and state.[4] Public schools are further supported on the grounds that they make for "political and cultural tolerance, serve as a melting pot, and pass on a common cultural heritage.[5]

Education as an Investment.   Mention has been made in the previous chapter of the fact that expenditure for education can be very creative. The return, in money terms, however, is one of the many unverifiables in social studies. It has been shown that a high correlation exists between state income and outlay for education and also between individual income and the degree of individual education. But it is impossible to say to what degree these factors operate as cause rather than effect. The fact that some areas, richly endowed by nature, have remained backward

---

[3] David Fellman, "Separation of Church and State in the United States: A Summary View," *Wisconsin Law Review* (May 1950), pp. 427–478.

[4] Milton Friedman, "The Role of Government in Education," in Robert A. Solo, ed., *Economics and the Public Interest* (New Brunswick: Rutgers University Press, 1955), pp. 123–144.

[5] Musgrave, *The Theory of Public Finance,* p. 44.

in both educational and economic achievement is indicative but not conclusive.[6]

What proportion of its income can a state afford to spend for education? Will the proportion be larger in a rich state or a poor state? Could a poor state be justified in borrowing, if necessary, to bring its educational program to a certain minimum as has been done in some cases for highways? Data indicate that some of the poorer states are among the highest in their outlay for education in relation to state income though they rank low in outlay per pupil.

Who Should Be Educated How Long? Should some kind of minimum educational opportunity for all be underwritten by the public? Nearly everyone would give a positive answer to this question. For both civic and economic reasons, a certain minimum level of literacy and enlightenment is highly desirable to the community as a whole.

This certain minimum, however much it may include, should be available and required of all alike, regardless of race, color, sex, and aptitude. A large body of free citizens maintained in ignorance and illiteracy may properly be regarded as a first-class public menace. Compulsory education laws in the United States usually cover attendance through the sixteenth year of age, and it is established public policy to attempt to keep youth in school through their eighteenth year.

Moreover, there is a high degree of general interest in particular education. In an era of highly developed economic and social interdependence, the results of good and bad education are so widely diffused that education may properly be considered of state and nation-wide interest. The diffusion of the product can be seen in the evidence concerning migration. About 20 percent of the American people change their addresses each year, and in the case of some 5 percent this is across county lines. In South Dakota between 1940 and 1950, the rural farm population decreased from 47.7 percent of the population to 38.8 percent. The net out-migration from the State during this period was 12.3 percent of the 1940 total.[7] The out-migration involves the export of a very valuable product—namely, education. Some northern cities have acquired a large population of Negroes most of whom were educated in the south.

Beyond a minimum for all, how much opportunity for education should be offered at public expense? Should the public maintain secondary schools and colleges that all may attend? Should it adapt these institutions to the needs of very large numbers? A strong case can be made

[6] Committee on Education, United States Chamber of Commerce, *Education an Investment in People*, 1944–45.

[7] John E. Thompson, *Financing Public Education in South Dakota*, doctoral dissertation, University of Wisconsin (Madison, 1960), pp. 8, 10.

for a generous educational program beyond the minimum. It is important from the social viewpoint to maintain a recruiting ground for talent, of which much may be discovered and promoted by the equality of opportunity that public education affords. Where youth is relatively free to choose its vocation, schools may provide valuable orientation and vocational guidance. Above these and many similar considerations is the fact that education is an end in itself. Disregarding expense, the more who can be persuaded to participate, the better.

Under a private educational system the question of who should participate, and for how long, depends upon the financial ability of the prospects. This is true to some extent of a public system supported largely by the fees of participants. Under most prewar European educational systems, the question of who should continue and for how long has been partly one of finances and partly one of talent. Those who showed talent were given material encouragement to continue their education, whereas others were generally required to pay much of their own way beyond the minimum. In the United States, although both of the two criteria named above play important parts, there is a strong propensity to provide education largely at public expense for all those willing to partake of it. It is said that almost as many students are enrolled in the colleges of the United States as in all the rest of the world. The "willingness" test is a worthy and laudable one, but it is expensive. It should be qualified by the general rule of public expenditure—that is, that public outlays for any service are justified only so long as they serve a more important end than would any alternative use of the money, either public or private.

Even in the United States, the financial factor as the criterion of selection for advanced study is important and becoming more so. The evidence indicates that the trend in student fees and the private cost of maintaining oneself in college (plus the opportunity cost of forgoing a full-time job) is sharply upward. The evidence also indicates that a very large number of those who could profit by a college education do not get one. Indeed, the group that does go on to higher education is frequently not much superior in scholarship to the one that does not. This is properly regarded as a major waste of human resources. The Americans have a unique tradition of working their way through college: in some universities as many as 45 percent of the students are employed part of the time while enrolled.

The data show that for each 1000 pupils who were enrolled in the fifth grade in 1950, 885 entered high school (or the ninth grade) in the fall of 1954; 584 of the 1000 pupils graduated from high school in the spring of 1958, and 308 of the original 1000 entered college the following year. More important is the fact that less than half of the upper 25 percent of high school graduates earn college degrees. The drop-out in college is much the same story. Only 6 out of 10 of the top 5 percent of high school graduates earn a college degree.[8]

The Report of the President's Commission on Higher Education [9] suggests that eventually colleges should provide training for about one third of American youth. The report further suggests that the present economic barrier to traffic be lifted by a generous program of federal scholarships. Federal assistance to individuals at the college level has precedent in the allowances provided by the National Youth Administration (during the depression of the 1930s) and under the veterans' Bill of Rights.

SUPPORT FOR EDUCATION IN THE UNITED STATES

In 1957–1958 public elementary and high schools in the United States enrolled about 83.5 percent of the school population aged 5–17; their operating expenses were shared as follows: 54 percent from local sources, 4.0, 39.6, and 2.1 percent from federal, state, and county funds respectively. State support ranged from 86 percent in Delaware to less than 9 percent in several states such as Nebraska.[10] The general property tax supplies about half of elementary and secondary school support. For higher education, expenditures for which are about equally divided between publicly and privately controlled schools, state and local funds provide the largest share of the revenue, but fees are a strong second source with endowment and donations adding a smaller and decreasing quota.

THE SCHOOL UNIT

The typical unit of school finance in the United States is the independent school district, of which there are some 37,000 (1960) in the nation. The small rural district often finds itself unable to collect sufficient revenue to support an adequate program of education. The small-enrollment school is likely to have a high cost per pupil. The one-room school is also handicapped in the character of its instruction. Broadening the unit of support and of attendance has made some progress and offers a

---

[8] United States Department of Health, Education, and Welfare, Office of Education, *Progress of Public Education in the United States of America, 1959–1960,* 1960, p. 13; *Encyclopedia of Educational Research,* Chester W. Harris, ed. (Boston: Houghton Mifflin Company, 1960), p. 531.

[9] *A Report of the President's Commission on Higher Education* (Washington, D.C., 1947), vol. 1, pp. 41–44.

[10] United States Department of Health, Education, and Welfare, *Statistics of State School Systems 1957–1958,* pp. 18, 50.

promising opportunity for improvement in our educational machinery. The problem is not confined to elementary schools; many high schools are too small to be economical and to provide the specialized opportunities that modern education requires. However, it should be said also that many object to the size of large city schools and feel that the small rural school, though limited in some respects, provides a reasonably good opportunity and possesses inherent advantages.

Although the common school district system predominates as to number of districts, over half of the states use the township, the county, or even the state (Delaware) as the administrative and financial (though not of course the attendance) unit for schools. The centralized unit reduces the need for equalization and has other advantages of centralization though it sometimes develops coordination problems within the larger unit.

In some cases, education is organized as a department of a municipality without independent status; in others, especially where the unit of support is not coterminous with the boundary lines of other governments, school districts are independently organized, governed, and financed. Both arrangements have proponents; a strong point for the departmental organization is that it provides a single budget, facilitating a comparison of needs for educational and other functions.

STATE AIDS TO EDUCATION

The Case for State Aid. As social and economic interdependence increases in the United States, there is a growing feeling that education is of state-wide and even national interest. At the same time, the units of financial support for elementary and secondary education differ enormously in financial strength, both absolutely and in relation to the load they carry. If the local units of support are to be maintained and anything like a standard minimum program for education is to be assured, state grants-in-aid for education are necessary.

Methods of Distributing State School Aids. The two objectives most commonly sought in granting state aids to education are tax relief and equalization. The first is accomplished by providing a flat grant for each unit of educational need.[11] This method, although it does equalize school costs to a certain extent, takes no cognizance of inequalities in taxable resources between districts. It serves chiefly to lessen the burden of property taxation in all the districts and to ensure more adequate funds for education. However, where state support constitutes a major proportion of expense, equalization is inevitably substantial.

---

[11] The unit of education has been variously defined; for example, in terms of number of teachers employed or the number of pupils in average daily attendance.

Most states now attempt to distribute part of their aid on an equalization basis—that is, according to an index of need in relation to ability. About half of school aid is distributed by equalization grants. Such aids may be set up in a variety of ways but in general they are based upon the difference between the yield of a specified local tax rate and the revenue required to support a state-prescribed minimum educational program. For example, suppose a 9-mill rate is deemed proper and that this, applied to a property valuation of $250,000, will yield enough to support a standard school program for a one-teacher school. Now suppose a district has a property tax base of only $150,000. The state proceeds to pay up to 9 mills (matching the district) on the difference between $250,000 (standard) and $150,000. The maximum aid is thus $900 ($100,000 $\times$ .009 = $900). To encourage consolidation, less aid may be granted for districts with less than a specified average daily attendance, and "integrated districts" (with both elementary and high school and perhaps a minimum faculty and curriculum) may be favored. Questions are now raised as to whether aid for one function of government can be entirely separated from other demands upon the budget, especially in urban areas.

Fewer than half the states make any special provision for capital outlay. A major difficulty here is that districts may be limited in bonding power. Equalization aid may take the form of paying debt service beyond that financed by a minimum tax. Special aids are frequently provided for transportation of pupils. The problem is complicated by the fact that some districts do not operate schools, but pay tuition to other districts where their pupils attend.

As previously mentioned, educational equalization programs are badly stymied without an equalization of property assessments to serve as the index for differentials.

FEDERAL AID FOR EDUCATION

Education is a function that is traditionally and legally a responsibility of state and local government. This responsibility is included as a constitutional guarantee in Canada. Although the federal government of the United States has had one finger in the educational situation for a long time, its present financial contribution, outside of personal aid to veterans, runs to only a minor fraction of the total, and local control is jealously guarded. A movement for more general and more generous federal aid is not of recent origin, but it is becoming increasingly insistent. The movement has been restrained thus far by fear of federal control, sectional disputes over the equalization principle, disagreement over use of public money for private education, and pressure to conserve federal funds.

Proponents of federal aid have submitted a persuasive case for the view that there is a national interest in education justifying federal support. Elaborate statistics have been produced that demonstrate wide differences in per capita expenditures and educational opportunity among the states and marked variations in financial ability (almost 4–1 in terms of income per school child) and educational burdens to be borne. Citizenship interests in minimum standards for education are obvious. Local tax relief also enters the argument. Evidence concerning birth rates and the migration of population adds support. It is said further that federal money for education is an assurance that adequate resources will be allotted to the field as contrasted with highways, for instance, where federal aid is already well entrenched.

The case against an extension of federal aid has been suggested above in explaining the reasons why it has not materialized. Exception is taken to the view that the so-called ability taxes can carry indefinitely expanded loads of direct federal expenditures as well as constantly increasing grants for various state-local functions promoted by pressure groups. The general objection to aids—that they make for extravagance —is also emphasized. But most pronounced is the fear of federal control and disagreement as to the plan of distribution. A recent report went so far as to suggest that federal aid to education is a threat to individual liberty, adding that "calculated diversity is a major protection against the compulsions of a sterilizing orthodoxy." [12]

Any program of federal aid confronts major issues in the degree and manner of central controls which should be included. Aid proposals get bogged down in collateral disputes concerning segregated schools. Use of aids for this or that feature of private education sponsored by religious groups is another controversial aspect. Lack of proper equalization procedure in state aid laws is another aspect of the educational situation with which a federal aid program must be concerned, particularly if it is to involve equalization features. Obsolete state-local administrative organization, including small school units, is also involved. It would be a serious mistake merely to raise the level of school expenditure without tangible improvement in the quality and usefulness of the educational offering. A strong case can be made for federal aid to all schools including church-sponsored ones. Such practice is common in Europe. It would recognize the wisdom of maintaining diversity of opportunity in education. But it would violate the spirit if not the letter of the long-standing tradition separating church and state. The tradition grew out of profound experience in an earlier era.

---

[12] Study Committee, *Federal Responsibility in the Field of Education,* Report to the Commission on Intergovernmental Relations (Washington, D.C., 1955), p. 6.

EXPENDITURES FOR PUBLIC WORKS

NATURE OF CAPITAL AND DURABLE GOODS EXPENDITURES

Attention has already been called to the distinction between the outlays for capital and durable goods and expenditures for consumption goods and services. This distinction exists in the public as well as in the private economy. To recall some of the more obvious differences, the outlays for capital and durable goods may be more in the nature of an investment than an expenditure (this applies particularly to outlays for capital goods) and are therefore a suitable object for borrowing; they tend to be irregular; and finally, they play a very strategic part in the smooth and successful functioning of the economic system.

TREND OF PUBLIC WORKS EXPENDITURES

Public works have always been an activity of government, and in the case of the United States all units of government have been more or less involved. The promotion of canals, railways, and highways by federal, state, and municipal governments constitutes a long and interesting, if not always creditable, chapter in American history.

Although the idea of government spending to relieve unemployment was entertained and applied at least as early as the building of the Egyptian pyramids, it counted little, if at all, with the statesmen who ordered public works in the early history of the United States. The public did its building when everyone else did—that is, during the high tides of optimism when it looked as though prosperity would continue forever.

During the 1930s the public works program of the federal government became significant not only in the volume of outlay but also in the part it played in the economic strategy of the period. A large part of this program was delegated to the Public Works Administration, popularly known as the PWA. This organization claimed the following accomplishments, among others, during the first four years of its operation: it made possible four fifths of all public construction in the United States, including 70 percent of the school buildings, 62 percent of the hospitals, and 64 percent of the waterworks and sewers. In addition, it sponsored the first federal slum-clearance and low-cost housing projects.[13] How-

---

[13] *Four-year Record of PWA June 1933–June 1937*, Federal Emergency Administration of Public Works, Washington, 1937. The PWA is not to be confused

ever, it was accompanied by shrinking state and municipal outlays and a drastic drop in private construction. The federal program was hardly more than sufficient to maintain government construction at predepression levels and did very little to fill in the gap in private construction. In this connection, it may be recalled that although federal expenditures are about two thirds of the national total, federal ownership of total governmental assets amounts to only about 30 percent.

RESPONSIBILITY FOR HIGHWAYS AMONG VARIOUS UNITS OF GOVERNMENT

During the early history of the United States there was much interest in through highways (turnpikes), but by the middle of the nineteenth century this interest was displaced by that in developing a national system of railroads. The advent of the automobile brought highways once more into the limelight.[14] In 1916 the federal government inaugurated its highway aids, which have since been developed consistently. The states also extended aids and started the construction and maintenance of state highway systems.

Reason for Central Interest. The construction and maintenance of certain highways transcends local interest and, in fact, may even be of great national concern. Roads connecting important centers of population may extend through desolate country, the residents of which have neither the interest nor the resources to maintain a good road. Or, in the absence of central control, such good roads as are developed may form no connected system. Many motorists have had the disagreeable experience, after driving on a well-constructed road, of suddenly hitting a sea of mud at a town or county line. Kansas, which at one time had no state system of highways, was a good example of this.[15] Although it had many miles of highly developed highways, there were few, if any, good through routes across the state in any direction. Since then, the state has amended its constitution and has assumed sufficient authority over the highway system to ensure a fairly satisfactory system of through roads.

Grants-in-aid. Mention has been made of the fact that both the

---

with the WPA (Works Progress Administration), which also sponsored projects but usually not in the field of construction.

[14] The highway history of the United States thus covers three periods and a circle. The first period was marked by central interest to facilitate westward migration and bind the country into a closer unit. The second saw highways reduced to a role of local significance; the railways stole their place in the promotion of larger objectives. The third saw the revival of central interest in highways. Curiously, the development of the bicycle (followed by the automobile) provided the harbinger of the new era.

[15] See Jens P. Jensen, "Mud and Muddle in Kansas Roads," *Bulletin of the National Tax Association,* XII: 8 (May 1927), pp. 223–227.

federal and the state governments first expressed their revived interest in highways by means of grants-in-aid to the local governmental units. Even today, the federal government influences the highway system mainly through this means, and its control, though indirect, is very important.

In 1921 Congress authorized state highway departments, with the approval of the United States Bureau of Public Roads, to designate a system of main roads, not to exceed 7 percent of the mileage in any one state, to be known as the Federal Aid System of Highways.[16] The highways of the United States have now been classified by the federal government as follows: Some 265,000 miles of road connecting principal cities constitutes the federal primary-aid system; a secondary-federal-aid system of 590,000 miles connects the lesser communities and includes some "farm-to-market" roads; since 1944, 42,000 miles of road connecting principal metropolitan areas has been designated "the interstate system"; and finally there are local roads and streets sometimes described as "access highways." The interstate system is the major concern of the federal government (significant for defense), though federal aid is by no means confined to this area. Under its new and ambitious program of federal aid (1956), the federal government will provide 90 percent of the cost of modernizing the interstate system. The traditional formula of distribution has provided fifty-fifty matching with the federal portion divided according to the average of three ratios—area, population, and miles.

Conditions attached to federal grants have been the basis of substantial federal control of the national highway program. For example, insistence by the Bureau of Public Roads that the states assume responsibility for the maintenance of the federal aid highway system has had considerable effect in centralizing highway administration. Moreover, some federal pressure has been exerted to eliminate the so-called diversion of motor vehicle tax revenues from road building to other uses.[17]

Units of Highway Administration. Highways are administered by every important unit of government in the United States except the federal government [18] and the school districts. This includes the states, counties, towns, incorporated cities and villages, and miscellaneous local divisions of government. The relative importance of each unit and the coordination in the highway programs in the various states differ substantially. In a few states all rural roads are administered by the state

---

[16] The federal aid system is not to be confused with the marking of routes with federal numbers. The routes are marked for the convenience of interstate travel, and, although the federal numbers correspond closely with the federal aid system, there is no necessary or complete correlation between the two.

[17] See Chapter 12.

[18] The federal government, however, has direct control of certain roads in the national forests.

highway departments. On the other hand, a much larger number have state and county organizations, some have state and township systems, and others have all three of these systems: state, county, and town. In addition to these rural systems, all states have municipal organizations in charge of urban streets. The multiplicity of administrative units in the field of highway financing has proved to be very unsatisfactory in many states and, since 1930, there has been a decided trend toward centralization.

Most experts in highway finance are of the opinion that the town has no place in an efficient system of highway administration. The central units have certain advantages in the more constant utilization of machinery, the purchase of machinery and materials, and in the letting of contracts. To be sure, some towns and villages have adapted themselves quite effectively to changed conditions by arranging with other administrative units for the joint use of equipment. Central responsibility has a disadvantage in that it encourages local jealousy and dissatisfaction. But there can be little doubt that decentralized administration of rural highways is, on the whole, a wasteful system. In passing, this may be pointed out as another case where technological change has undermined local government.

ECONOMY AND EXTRAVAGANCE IN HIGHWAY BUILDING

Outlay for highways provides an excellent illustration of the two sorts of economy in government previously mentioned. First, it involves the difficulty of rationing public money well. There are certain highways that the government cannot afford not to build. Given an existing volume of traffic, the saving in time, fuel cost, and wear and tear on motor vehicles will much more than pay for the new road during its existence. On the other hand, this will certainly not be true in all cases. Moreover, the highway dollar has (or should have) to compete with dollars needed for other governmental purposes. Within the highway appropriation, through roads compete with secondary and local roads and those in one part of the state with those in another. As to the second kind of economy— engineering efficiency—there are plenty of administrative problems associated with "getting the best possible road for the least cost."

SELECTION OF PUBLIC WORKS

All public expenditures are difficult to appraise in terms of relative value and those for federal public works are no exception. If a market standard could be employed the answer would be simple: don't build a public work unless it will pay for itself in added productivity; and test the hypothesis by imposing direct charges upon the beneficiaries sufficient over the years to recoup the costs. However this leaves out of account those indirect benefits that are the major justification for public enterprise. The indirect benefits of TVA, for instance, include the very great but intangible gain for the region experienced as a result of low power costs and the expansion of industry in consequence. Some part of these benefits are local and presumably should not be financed by national taxpayers. Others are national in character; it can be argued that the federal treasury has recouped a handsome return on its outlay. Some account must be taken of the fact that many projects involve negative benefits or indirect costs in the form of injury to competitors. The development of waterways at federal expense is said to have had a very adverse effect on the profitability of American railroads. The benefit analysis is further complicated when unemployment can be relieved by public outlay and when farm surpluses raise questions about developing further land to raise fiber and food. Other refinements in benefit and cost studies include the discount (if any) to be applied to future benefits and the required rate of return.

To make matters worse, Congress has developed an unsavory reputation in its authorizations for the improvement of rivers and harbors and reclamation projects. This part of the federal budget is frequently labeled the pork barrel because of the well-known propensity of congressmen to trade votes in securing federal funds for local projects. Cost and benefit studies by various governmental agencies in this area are neither very refined or very faithfully followed but they are pioneer efforts to fortify subjective decision making with objective evidence.[19]

PUBLIC WORKS AS AN AGENCY OF ECONOMIC STABILIZATION

As previously suggested, public works as an economic stabilizer and an antidote for unemployment received much attention during the depression. Many look to an improved program of this sort to solve future unemployment problems. It is said that governments should be prepared to fill any gap in employment that the unsteady operation of private enterprise may entail.

A public works program for these larger economic objectives has been criticized on the ground that it must necessarily be too small to accomplish its purpose and that experience has proved public works to be a wasteful form of relief. In answer to the first proposition, it is said

---

[19] See Otto Eckstein, "A Survey of Theory of Public Expenditure Criteria," *Public Finances: Needs, Sources and Utilization,* National Bureau of Economic Research (Princeton: Princeton University Press, 1961), pp. 438–504.

that even though they might not solve the whole problem, well-timed public works could help substantially in counteracting depressions. At the very least, such a program would take advantage of depression prices, wages, and interest rates and thus effect economies in the construction of public works. To the second proposition, that public works are wasteful relief, the answer is made that this has been true only because the program has not been planned in advance. Moreover, public works and work relief are not to be confused. The former is designed to include only socially useful and needed projects and employs men on a going-wage basis without regard for need. The latter, exemplified by the Works Progress Administration, pays less heed to the usefulness of the work as such and employs people on a relief basis.

The degree to which public works may be utilized successfully as an economic stabilizer is in considerable dispute. Much will depend, of course, upon the volume of work which can be crowded into depression years. This in turn will depend considerably upon the cooperation of the municipalities and upon their ability to finance a public works program during depressions. In this connection, it has been suggested that municipalities should be given greater flexibility under constitutional debt limits. They should also be educated to conserve their credit for emergency periods. Of course, central units of government can expand construction directly on works which are of general interest. But experience has shown that federal expansion in construction outlays is likely to be offset by state and local reductions in building.[20] The development of a construction aid that will enable local governments to maintain or expand construction during hard times without the addition of repressive and regressive taxes should be high on the agenda of future stabilization programs. A recent proposal would make such an aid automatically available upon the indication that the level of private construction would drop below a specified point.[21] Public works (especially from borrowed funds) may give more employment and create more income indirectly than result directly from public expenditures on them. This could occur through the operation of the multiplier and the acceleration principle discussed in the previous chapter.

Other objections to public works as an economic stabilization program are that (1) such works cannot be adapted to care for diverse types of labor; (2) the work and the men may not be in the same place;

---

[20] Various complications also arise because of the international relations of the country inaugurating a works program. The program tends to raise or maintain prices, which in turn invites imports and encourages business abroad. For the fullest effectiveness of a public works program as an antidote for depressions, international cooperation would be required.

[21] James A. Maxwell, *Federal Grants and the Business Cycle* (New York: National Bureau of Economic Research, 1952).

(3) such a program may make matters worse by discouraging the deflation of costs (particularly wages) necessary to bring about recovery; (4) these outlays enlarge the ordinary budget with maintenance and operating expenditures; and (5) many works are not postponable because (*a*) they are required to facilitate private construction as the latter occurs, and (*b*) the requisite degree of transferability of capital and labor from private to public construction may not exist.

Many state and municipal public works are complementary to private developments. The most obvious case is that of highways and parking facilities required to accommodate new automobiles. Suburban development requires a large expansion of services when it occurs, and school houses have to be built when a new crop of school children overtaxes existing facilities.

If public works are to be used as an antidote for depressions, their proper timing will be an important aspect. It is thought by some that the works program should come after a certain amount of necessary deflation has occurred. At just the right moment, the program would not only give employment directly and indirectly and sustain purchasing power, but it would also check the psychological deflation that plays a large part in every depression. In spite of important difficulties that public works as a depression antidote encounter, it can be said with assurance that they are a useful instrument for dealing with economic instability.

PUBLIC WELFARE

THE BENEFICIARIES OF WELFARE

As though the responsibilities of government before the depression of the 1930s were not sufficient to engage the full capacity of the tax system, as well as the ingenuity of those in charge, there arose a new and rapacious claimant for the public dollar. This new claimant was public welfare. It was weighted with at least as many perplexing problems as any previously more important function of government. Chief among these problems was its cost, the figures for which mounted in a few brief years from a rather negligible level to sensational heights.

The dependent and delinquent population in our era is impressive in number and variety. There are the mentally ill and deficient (insane and feebleminded); the physically ill and deficient (invalids, cripples, blind, deaf); the economically handicapped (aged, dependent children, unemployed, and others); and the morally unfortunate or deficient (criminals, alcoholics, delinquents). The dependent aged, particularly, represent a large and growing group. This is attributed in part to improved medical care (increasing longevity) and in part to changes in family living and economic factors that tend to leave the older segment of the population stranded.

The trend has been toward regarding all these groups as unfortunate rather than perverse. The cost of maintaining and rehabilitating them can run alarmingly high. It is probably no more than right that the fortunate should care for the unfortunate, but the former can at least take thought as to how to accomplish this objective efficiently and how to reduce the size of the problem.

ALTERNATIVE METHODS OF CARING FOR THE POOR

The enormous volume of public welfare expenditures during the depression forced the public to turn its attention to the alternative methods of providing for the poor. Among the chief of these were the following: (1) institutionalized care; (2) outdoor or "direct" relief; (3) work relief and public works; (4) categorical aid; and (5) social insurance. Institutionalized care, which usually means the orphan asylum, the poorhouse, or the county home, was at one time the typical form of public support for the needy. However, since the welfare problem has increased in scope and the public has assumed a more humanitarian attitude toward the poor, institutionalized care has come to be regarded with disfavor and is gradually being displaced by other methods.

Outdoor or noninstitutionalized assistance may be given either by public or private agencies. Before the depression, the larger part of such care was provided by private agencies and supported not by taxes but by donations. Frequently such voluntary giving for this and other purposes has been systematized through a community union or community chest. During the depression, voluntary contributions and private agencies proved quite unequal to their task, and public agencies took over the major portion of the relief burden. It was felt by many that this was a fairer and more democratic method of raising money for relief than voluntary donations. As the depression developed, local communities found themselves overwhelmed with welfare costs and welfare demands. Consequently, first the states and then the federal government were drawn into the picture. It was plausibly and soundly contended that the destitution caused by unemployment and business failures was not local in origin and that the results of its neglect were not confined within local boundaries.

In the later 1930s the federal government withdrew from the field of direct relief and established its work relief and categorical aid programs. Work relief and public works have an advantage over direct relief in that they are better for the morale of the recipient and are intended to result in a useful return for the public outlay. However, the work programs involve greater immediate outlays. Work relief differs from public works in that it is provided on a means test, at such monthly wage and hour schedules as will finance a predetermined relief budget, and on work more or less adapted to the capacities of the applicant.

In earlier times all the needy were covered by the general term "paupers." Progress in caring for dependents has come by classifying them; instead of including all in one almshouse, each class—criminals, delinquent, insane, feebleminded, aged, ill, and so forth—has gradually been given separate treatment. One manifestation of this tendency has been the movement to substitute various "categorical aids," including the several kinds of public pensions, for the traditional general relief. The pensions differ from relief in that they are always granted in cash. They are based on a needs test, as is relief, but their dispensation is not accompanied by the same degree of supervision nor do they involve the stigma that is usually associated with direct relief. Relieved of these inhibitions, pension aids tend to be relatively generous. Categorical aids assumed great importance with the passage of the federal Social Security Act in 1935. The act provided pensions for three classes of the needy: children, the aged, and the blind; and a later act added permanent disability to the list. Federal participation took the form of generous aids to the states along with some control of state programs. Social insurance differs from pensions in that its benefit payments are distributed without regard to need.

PATTERNS OF WELFARE EXPENDITURES
AND THEIR FINANCIAL EFFECTS

From what has been said heretofore, it is apparent that there are many possible patterns of welfare expenditures, each with its own results. The pattern followed before and during the early depression years was mainly local responsibility for welfare expenditure; general assistance rather than categorical; direct assistance rather than any form of a work program. The pattern followed in 1938 was: local responsibility for relief (with help in some cases from the state); categorical aid to replace general relief to some extent; federal and state contributions toward categorical aids; a works program financed largely by the federal government. This latter pattern left the critics dissatisfied. They asked the question among others: Why should the federal government help pay for the needy aged and not for the chronic unemployables or even others on general relief?

PREVENTION OF DEPENDENCY

Constructive thought on the welfare problem must include consideration of how its magnitude can be reduced. There are several kinds of preventives that might be developed. There is the eugenics approach, which starts with the observation that probably two thirds of feeblemindedness is hereditary and that something further might be done to prevent the procreation of feebleminded children. Sterilization as a preventive is allowed in some state statutes, but it is usually limited to the inmates of institutions particularly as a condition for parole. It requires very complete and elaborate precautions to protect the individual from abusive administration. With such precautions this defense against dependency can be a humanitarian as well as a eugenic measure. Some eugenicists even look to a time when man will achieve more positive means of improving "the human stock." If we approach the problem from the environmental angle, the development that would probably help most to reduce welfare expenditures is the maintenance of a high level of opportunity, as when the economy is rapidly expanding. This is not a simple undertaking, to say the least, and may involve more radical measures than most people are willing to comtemplate. The development of a well-rounded system of social insurance can also be classed as a preventive. To avoid many welfare needs resulting from ill health, some public outlays, although inadequate, have been made. Better medical care for more people may take the form of expanded public health work or health insurance or more voluntary programs to spread costs and to make provision for illness by periodical payments.

The dispersing of very large sums for welfare is a formidable administrative job and involves important problems of fraud and other abuses. The public has been quite frequently alarmed by reports concerning the numbers of illegitimate children involved in aid for dependent children. There is general agreement that it is far better to help the poor to help themselves rather than perpetually to hand out allowances.

POSSIBILITIES OF ADMINISTRATIVE ECONOMIES

PUBLIC PERSONNEL MANAGEMENT

Government represents by all odds the largest and most important business in the United States. As in most other businesses, the successful management of personnel is a major factor in the success or failure of that enterprise.

The merit system is an attempt to apply objective standards in the recruitment, retention, and promotion of public employees. It provides for public employees minimum qualifications, competitive examinations, and permanent tenure during satisfactory performance. There are few competent critics who still believe that free appointment and removal of all administrative personnel by elected officials is conducive to maximum economy and efficiency in government. Those who have not reconciled themselves to the merit system argue that party loyalty is an important qualification in a subordinate employee and that to deprive a chief administrator of freedom in the choice of his staff is to weaken responsibility. The so-called merit system is said "to attract" large numbers of steady-going unimaginative people who rapidly sink into the bureaucratic rut.

Whatever validity there may be in these arguments, the fact remains that the excessive turnover under the spoils system is highly detrimental to efficiency. The loss of administrators' and legislators' time in attending to patronage, the employment of people who are totally unfit for the work (such as stenographers who have never operated a typewriter), and the failure to utilize heavy investments in public education must also be charged to bad personnel management. It can hardly be doubted that governments in the United States spend huge sums annually on the luxury of the spoils system. As government advances from a relatively insignificant to a major role in human welfare, the problem of proper personnel policy assumes increasingly greater importance.

Although the merit system has made rapid and consistent progress in its extension among federal employees, there still remain many whom it does not cover. It is the states and municipalities that are the worst offenders in matters of personnel. Only a minority of the states, by no means all of the large cities, and a negligible percentage of the smaller cities, counties, and other districts operate under the merit system.

Selection, retention, and promotion by merit are not synonymous with the merit system even though they are its objectives. Loopholes are available in all such systems. The sympathy of those in high office and a vigilant public opinion are important lubricants that are necessary for the successful operation of any civil service machinery. Attitudes are quite as important in good personnel management as laws. Moreover, "merit" and "spoils" in the management of personnel are always a matter of degree. The spoils system never existed in the sense that public office was universally dispensed to political followers as a reward for political assistance or as a token of friendship regardless of fitness for public office. Likewise, the merit system never existed in which merit alone guided the choice of personnel. There is no "spoils-proof" system of civil service. A good program of recruitment is only a beginning in the solution of personnel problems. There are also important problems of promotion, of in-service training, of dismissal, and of retirement.

That the governments have an unsavory reputation in the minds of many people is due very largely to their inability or unwillingness to handle personnel problems effectively. This aspect of government undoubtedly offers many opportunities for economy. Moreover, here is abundant proof of the rule that those who believe in government need to exert their constant and utmost effort to make and keep it respectable.

CENTRALIZED PURCHASING

Governments are important not only as employers but also as purchasers of materials and supplies, ranging from pickles to bridges. Although the public has never fully grasped the fact, and many public officials cannot or will not see it, herein lie many opportunities for economy. The spoils system is not confined to personnel management but can also be found in public purchasing. Proper machinery is important in this field, but no more so than a proper attitude on the part of the public and the officials.

In the past few decades, government buying has developed a technique known as centralized purchasing. Instead of allowing all departments to purchase more or less at random as their needs arise, many governments require all or most of the purchases to be made through one agency, either a separate department organized for that purpose or a division in some other department, such as the department of finance. Centralized purchasing makes possible the development of expert specialized personnel, large-quantity buying, standardization of grades, more genuine competition in bidding, and so forth. Many examples of substantial economies through the use of this technique have been cited.[22]

REORGANIZATION OF GOVERNMENTAL UNITS

The multiplicity of governmental units in the United States has, particularly in the last few years, attracted considerable attention. Recent inventories of the "governmental family" have placed the number of units at about 102,000 (1957). These governmental units run not only to large numbers but also to great diversity of pattern and function among the various states. The proponents of reorganization contend that social, political, and economic conditions have undergone momentous changes since these units were devised and that the changes have made existing machinery obsolete. Some of the claims for possible economies by reorganization have probably been extravagant; and the resistance to change in the existing pattern is certainly very strong. But it remains true

---

[22] Dickson Reck, *Government Purchasing and Competition* (Berkeley: University of California Press, 1954).

that rationalization of governmental machinery in this and other respects affords a fertile field for administrative economy.

Mention has been made in an earlier chapter of the economies that might be effected by closer collaboration between the federal government and the states in the administration of tax laws.

SUMMARY

Wars and preparation for wars loom very large in past, present, and predicted future budgets. During wars public expenditure problems center about the supply of equipment and ammunition for the fighting forces. Contracts used in military procurement cause special difficulty; many varieties have been tried and to them has been added renegotiation, but no procedure has proved entirely satisfactory. Ordinary contracts are often unacceptable because of inflation risks and lack of experience with the production of new items. The problem of minimizing war profits and of equalizing sacrifices in wartime is far from solved. After wars the problem of pensions for veterans becomes pressing. In most countries pensions are confined to persons or dependents of persons who die or become disabled as a result of war. Our own program has usually extended pension privileges to those who engage in wars generally. Finally the economics of disarmament is engaging attention: Is full employment in our "affluent society" dependent upon the most respectable form of extravagance, namely, military procurement?

Sponsorship of education is divided between state, church, and nonsectarian private initiative in various patterns throughout the world. Strong grounds are presented for the view that all should acquire a minimum of education and that many should have access to, and be encouraged to acquire, much training beyond the minimum. Education is still supported predominantly by local governments and the general property tax, though the trend is toward state support. This support usually takes the form of state aids, sometimes distributed according to school population and sometimes on bases designed to equalize school costs. The federal government frequently has been urged to extend its subvention system to cover a grant for general education. One of the impediments to this program is disagreement as to the degree of control that should accompany the aid.

Public works are capital goods expenditures and are especially significant as a tool to cope with the business cycle and underemployment. Special attention must be given to the works of state and local governments which (without federal support) tend to fluctuate with private construction. Highways are a major item of public works, in the responsibility for the provision of which all governments participate. Public works programs for depressions encounter many difficulties, among them the fact that some work is not postponable nor can labor and capital always shift with ease from private to public construction. Cost and benefit studies have been developed to facilitate the selection of public works but they are not always heeded and they are in an early stage of refinement.

Welfare outlays increased sensationally during the 1930s and are sure to occupy an extremely important place in the budgets of all levels of government in the future. There are many alternative means of alleviating poverty, including institutionalized care, outdoor relief, categorical aid, social insurance, and work relief. In addition, the unit of government and the taxes relied upon for support are vital factors in the pattern of welfare expenditures. More interest in the preventive aspects of a welfare program can be heartily recommended.

One type of governmental economy consists of getting the most in output from a given amount of input. There are many opportunities for this type of economy, including among the most conspicuous better management of personnel, better purchasing practices, and a more logical arrangement of governmental units.

PROBLEMS

1. John and Henry are brothers, the first of whom is drafted to fight in a major war. Henry escapes the draft and finds employment in a munitions factory at twice the pay he ever made before or will probably earn after the war. John gets the modest allowance paid privates in the army. Is there any inequity here? If so, should it be mitigated by allowing John a small bonus after the war or a pension at age sixty-five? Or should it be mitigated or eliminated by some other means?

2. The business cycle is said to consist mainly of fluctuations in construction and the manufacture of capital equipment. Stabilization proposals frequently advocate that the government operate a public building cycle so timed as to counteract the fluctuations in the private sphere. Consider the advantages and difficulties involved in this program.

3. Consider the proposition that our dependent and delinquent population is so indulged by government that only inadequate support can be given to the training of those who might make an important contribution to society.

4. Consider the benefit and cost problems involved in choosing public works.

5. Discuss the economic problems that would be created by disarmament.

6. Explain a technique for granting equalization aids that will take account of
    a. Different ratios of property tax assessment in different districts;
    b. Local effort to support the school;
    c. Local differences in ability to support the school;
    d. The need for consolidation of uneconomic school districts.

7. Compare the administrative problem involved in the operation of the federal government with that involved in the management of (*a*) the American Telephone Company, (*b*) General Motors Corporation, and (*c*) Midland Cooperative Wholesale.

8. Mr. White is a farmer past retirement age and unable to make a living; Mr. Brown is and has been for many years a factory employee; he is now past retirement age, and he has no independent income; Mrs. Gray is a young mother (with four small children) who has been deprived of her husband; Mr. Black is a factory worker who has lost his job but will probably get new employment in a matter of months; Mr. Green suffers a loss of income because of illness. Explain the type of welfare measure that would apply to each of these situations.

9. Why is the administration of government contracts for military procurement particularly difficult? What techniques have been developed to safeguard the public interest in this area?

10. Indicate briefly the nature of waste in public education that is associated with
    a. Undeveloped talent;
    b. Improper school units of finance.

11. Consider the proposal to extend public support for education to scholars rather than schools, thus including private institutions within the orbit of public support.

12. Would federal aid for public schools necessarily involve an undesirable degree of federal control?

13. It is said that given our present and prospective number of motor vehicles we cannot afford not to provide a very expensive system of highways; it is also said that if motor vehicles were taxed as much as they should be taxed there might be fewer of them and therefore less need for highways. Do you agree?

23

STATE AND FEDERAL AIDS

Mention has already been made of the fact that central units of government have a comparative advantage in the administration and collection of most types of taxes. At the same time local units have inherited the responsibility for many of the most important functions of government. This creates a gap to be bridged, and the bridge most often used is state and federal aids. Moreover, the collection of taxes and the distribution of funds by a central unit frees the subdivisions of inhibitions in public expenditure associated with their competition for residents. Some functions of government represent areas in which there is a partnership of interests. Aids may be the best tool for joint participation in these areas. Aids are most important in the functional fields of welfare, education, and highways. The federal government grants no aid for general education but appropriates for vocational and agricultural education. A strong trend toward more of these intergovernmental transfers is an important and persistent factor in mounting public expenditures.

Support for states and/or municipalities has usually been specific rather than general—that is, it has been associated with specific functions of government. But there is high interest in developing techniques that would aid municipalities as such independent of functions. This would recognize a partnership of interest in all locally performed functions.

GRANTS-IN-AID AND CENTRALLY COLLECTED–
LOCALLY SHARED TAXES

Differentiation. A first cousin to grants-in-aid is centrally collected-locally shared taxes. The two differ in several respects. The customary criterion of differentiation is that the grant-in-aid is distributed by appropriation, whereas the shared tax is apportioned according to fixed percentages of the yield of a certain tax. In the case of an aid, the amount distributed is largely independent of the yield of a specific tax; in the case of a shared tax, it is entirely dependent upon such yield. Appropriation from the state treasury for local education is a familiar example of aids; distribution to municipalities of a specified portion of state income tax receipts is a common form of state sharing of taxes. At times the two do not differ by a very wide margin. In general, aids are distributed on some basis of need and give more weight to the factor of control by central units than do shared taxes. The latter are more likely to be distributed where collected or on some basis designed to return the money to the community of origin. This procedure is based on the idea that the centrally collected taxes might have been levied locally and that the central government has simply loaned its superior powers of administration to the municipality.

It should be noted that whereas central distributions to junior units are frequently divided into aids and shared taxes on the criteria explained above, the more significant classification perhaps is in terms of conditional and unconditional distribution. The conditional aid is based mostly on a partnership of interests in a governmental function. The unconditional one is more likely a case of central governments' loaning their taxing power (shared taxes distributed according to origin) or of territorial egalitarianism. Unconditional grants may also aim at correcting some of the injustices that arise from splintering the community that constitutes a metropolitan area. But the measurement of territorial needs is a formidable task.

Distribution of Revenue. Distribution according to origin encounters two major difficulties. The first is that, in the case of most centrally administered taxes, origin cannot be determined with accuracy. In the case of the income tax, which is perhaps one of the easier taxes to allocate, there is the problem arising from the relative claims of the district of the recipient's domicile and of the district where the income originates. There is also the plausible claim that the whole area in which exchange is carried on creates the income of one engaged directly or indirectly in such exchange.

The second difficulty in distribution according to origin is that it frequently bestows upon some fortunate districts far more financial receipts than such districts have need of or can utilize to the best advantage. Examples abound of wealthy suburbs, tax colonies, and small districts with a big and successful factory or public utility, which get from the state in shared taxes what appears to be an inordinate proportion of state-collected taxes. Once a vested interest has been created, it vehemently resists change.

Certain shared taxes, notably the shared income tax, also suffer from grave instability. As a source of municipal revenue, they can prove highly undependable.

Some states in distributing shared taxes have taken as their standard of determining origin one which also has some bearing on need, namely, population. Thus under the new system inaugurated in New York, shared taxes are distributed on a per capita basis with some differentiation provided for municipalities according to classification (town, village, or city) and size. The program also includes a reserve to ensure stability of shared-tax distribution.

However, there is grave difficulty in setting any precise standard of need among municipalities (and states). Population with some variation by size of community may appear acceptable but it takes no account of per capita wealth and the latter takes no account of the required functions of government. The question of what constitutes equity between rural and urban regions in the distribution of state funds to municipalities seems hardly amenable to an objective answer. Wisconsin is trying an innovation by distributing part of its shared taxes inversely according to municipalities' full value tax rates. This plan may place state money where it is needed, but it is a little like saying to one's son: "If you spend modestly you are on your own, but if you are able in your budgeting to exceed the average, you will get a generous reward from your parents." Moreover it takes no account of the fact that rural wealth is not supported by income to the degree that characterizes urban wealth.

OBJECTIVES OF GRANTS-IN-AID

Partnership of Interests. It is recognized, of course, that communities are not altogether self-sufficient and that for some purposes and functions they need to cooperate with other communities through what might be called supercommunities. Thus we have regional and national governments.

This involves a division of responsibility between central and local governments, and the division is difficult enough. The experience with home-rule amendments, beginning with Missouri in 1875, indicates that what constitutes a purely local concern is vague and quarrelsome. But the principle involved is clear enough. The centralized functions, presumably, should be those where benefits are indivisible territorially—as, for instance, national defense.

It will be noted that territorial division of functions must follow a benefit rather than an ability calculus. In personal taxation, allotment according to benefit has been replaced largely by allotment according to ability to pay. Not so in territorial finance; it is a well-established rule of legal jurisdiction that one community cannot tax another for the former's benefit. Some reciprocation between government and taxpayer is required. Moreover, the long-established institution of special assessments permits additional pinpointing of benefits by geographical areas, usually within existing units of government.

However, in some functions of government there seems to be a partnership of interests. Take education, for instance. Of course, it is of direct interest to pupils and parents and of only slightly less direct interest to everybody in the local community. But, for several reasons, more remote districts also have an interest here. This is another way of saying that the interest in education is shared by central governments. Education is not the sort of good that is created and consumed in a single fiscal year; it follows its direct beneficiaries during all of their postgraduate days, and during this period many will have migrated from the city or state that provided their education. Moreover, even without migration the benefits of education have considerable extraterritoriality. If our national economic growth is as much dependent on levels of enlightenment as the proponents of education contend, then we must conclude that in some degree we are all interested in everybody's education.

The idea of a partnership of interests serves well as a rationale for state and federal conditional grants. According to this view, when central governments make these grants they are neither, as sometimes supposed, attempting to help local communities nor assuming that the latter are incompetent. They are merely bringing financial participation into line with concerns and benefits. Thus they rest on a clear and simple ideology. Not so unconditional grants which we find in some countries and a few of our states, or the so-called shared taxes which are their first cousins and which for our purposes we may lump with them. In the case of such grants, distribution must be by origin of taxes or some measure of ability and need among junior units as such.

Stimulation. Among the various objectives of aids, the first to appear historically, and the most important even today with respect to most federal aids, is that of stimulating local activity.

A central government selects a function that is thought to be of general interest and worthy of considerably more development than the local units have been able or have seen fit to allow for it. As previously stated, the subdivisions of government have inhibitions that the whole does not have; the former in some cases are also restrained by the fact that benefit of expenditure as in education is disseminated by migration. The function is promoted both by the central aid itself and by the manner of granting it. Through the device called matching, strong pressure is exerted upon the local units to spend more generously than hitherto in support of the selected function. Matching provisions specify that the central unit will contribute a certain sum for the selected function if the local unit will do likewise. The local unit is likely to feel that it cannot afford to "pass up" the funds of the central unit, in view of the fact that its taxpayers contribute along with others to the treasury of the central unit. Thus it is obliged to make the desired local outlay for the selected function in order not to lose a fair share of the central money. This device was used at one time to stimulate local expenditure for local roads. To make the pressure somewhat greater, the state in some cases provided that the county as well as the municipalities must match state outlays. Few localities could withstand the pressure to get this large proportion of "free money" for themselves.

Another statement of the local-stimulation objectives of aids is that they are a "reward for a local effort." Local units that draw upon their resources to maintain certain standards of the local services—educational standards, for instance—are allowed grants in recognition of their sacrifice for the common good.

Equalization of Costs and Opportunities. Central aids may also be given to equalize the cost of certain functions among local units and to equalize opportunities within such units. The equalization or differential grant is most plausible (1) when the function is one in which there is a strong central as well as a local interest, and at the same time (2) wide variations exist among local units in financial ability to provide the function. The equalization objective is especially prominent in state aids for education. A strong state-wide interest in educational opportunity is recognized; there is a feeling that the benefits of education are so wide and general that no particular group of taxpayers should be expected to undergo heavier, or much heavier, expense in supplying an adequate program of education than any other. Perhaps the logical course in these circumstances would be to make education a state function and pay for it directly with state-collected taxes. However, there are generally strong objections to complete centralization and, in lieu of it, a program of state aids is accepted as a fair compromise.

The equalization grant conserves funds by applying the state revenues where they do the most to raise or maintain standards. This has been aptly described as "applying the oil where the squeak is."

Relief of Local Taxation. A fourth objective of central grants is to relieve local taxation. The general property tax is the only major tax that has proved even tolerably well adapted to administration by smaller localities. The net income tax and the sales tax are far better administered by the state than by localities, and many have advocated the federal government as the proper unit to administer these taxes. Local communities in most states still have the primary responsibility for some of the important and expensive functions of government, including education and a large part of the highway system. During the depression even the states had to look for welfare aids to the federal government with its superior taxing and borrowing powers. States and municipalities are in a weak position financially because the forces of interstate competition make the levy of additional taxes, especially those based on ability to pay, a hazardous venture. Consequently, the frequent observation that aids are but the circuitous routing of the same taxes that might be levied locally is at best a half-truth. As has been previously explained, the problem thus is in getting some of the revenues that the central authorities can most efficiently collect to the local units for expenditure in the primary functions of government. There are several ways in which this gap can be bridged, one being the institution of state and federal aids now under discussion.

Central Control of Local Expenditures. A fifth objective of aids is to secure some effective central control over local expenditures through setting standards of adequacy and efficiency in the performance of a function. State educational aids are frequently granted only on condition that certain standards be observed. Such standards relate usually to length of school term, training and certification of teachers, salary schedule of teachers, and so forth. Regardless of the objectives, grants are usually featured by controls designed to ensure that central and local funds will not be wasted or spent on functions of purely local concern. In the interest of efficiency and economy, grants may also require or encourage a certain degree of consolidation of school districts, or rather small units of government, as a condition for receiving aid. Some states, for instance, provide that certain school aids shall not be distributed to districts with less than ten or twelve pupils. There are few cases where aids have been used to promote local economy (beyond the expenditure of the central funds themselves) and fewer, if any, where aids have been inaugurated for such purpose. Nevertheless, the aid institution lends itself well to a state program of promoting economy in local government.

The federal government, with its limited powers, is particularly concerned with the control aspects of federal aid. For example, it has "bought" a very high degree of control over the administration of state unemployment compensation systems by means of federal aids and credits. It is said of the British system of aids that, from 1832 on, the national government "bought" from the local authorities the privilege of audit, supervision, initiative, and control of local finances.

Compensatory Cyclical Action. A sixth objective of federal aids, now in process of development and perhaps destined for an important future, is that of compensatory action to mitigate the business cycle. The aids are a way by which the monetary power of the federal government can reach the finances of state and local governments during depressions. The use of aids during the depression of the 1930s was highly experimental and temperamental. One program went in for aids "in a big way" and the next dropped them almost entirely. The program with which the depression ended involved only the categorical social security aids that are secular in character and do not fluctuate much with the cycle. These categorical aids cover old age, dependency of children, and physical infirmities or blindness and permanent disability. Renewed interest is stirring in giving the aid program a new twist. What is needed is some kind of aid in the field of welfare and public works that will compensate effectively at the state and local level for cyclical fluctuations. If this could be established to work automatically according to a production or employment index, we might at the next downturn be spared both the delay and the uncertainty that characterized the last depression program.[1]

American federal aid programs are often criticized on the score that they follow no consistent principle or technique. Selection of functions to be aided and the degree of aid granted is supposed to be related to the intensity of central interest in the various functions. But it would be difficult to defend the federal selection of vocational education as against general education on this ground. The selection of functions, if not rationally defensible, results in further distortion of the expenditure pattern at the local level. The truth is, of course, that the aid "system" is built pragmatically, like legislative law in general. This does not result in a very rational product, but it seems nevertheless to compare reasonably well with some of the aid systems developed abroad.

METHODS OF DISTRIBUTING AIDS

Apportionment of Federal Funds. Aids may be distributed according to a rough criterion of need, such as population, or on a more refined basis of calculating "net need," with some account taken of relative local ability to support the designated function. The first method purports to measure simply the relative needs for the service; for example, in the

---

[1] James A. Maxwell, *Federal Grants and the Business Cycle* (New York: National Bureau of Economic Research, 1952), pp. 7–9.

case of educational grants, the number of children of school age in the different districts. The second method attempts to correlate this need with the relative financial abilities of the various units to provide for the need. Most federal aids have been distributed solely by the first method and have been apportioned on a basis of either total population or some specific class of the population, such as rural, farm, or urban population. During the 1930s grants for relief were occasionally left to the discretion of the administrators, who were supposed to distribute the funds according to their calculation of need. This led to quite elaborate efforts by both federal and state authorities to measure relative needs, "net need" as well as "service need."

The Social Security Act introduced the percentage grant, the volume of which was left indeterminate to depend upon the state and local requirements of service and the generosity, within limits, of state and local appropriations. This system has been criticized on several grounds but chiefly because it was alleged to result in much larger grants to the wealthy than to the poor states. Some years ago it was demonstrated that the whole federal aid system operated in general to aggravate territorial inequalities.[2] States with the highest per capita income also received the most per capita federal aid.

Since 1948 categorical welfare aids have gradually and conservatively moved in the direction of equalization. Thus the aid for old age assistance is divided into two brackets; on the first $35 of any individual grant the federal government pays about 80 percent and on the remainder, up to $50 additional, it pays about 50 percent. Total aid however is much influenced by the policy of individual states with regard to eligibility and by the generosity or niggardliness of state grants.

Recent study indicates that the federal aid system as a whole now operates to relieve territorial inequalities but that it does not do so consistently by states or by all programs. Of course the large highway aid program particularly has little or no orientation toward equalization. Even the welfare aid program shows inconsistencies in its equalization effects dependent as it is on state and local policy in granting aids.[3] It has been calculated that the progressive tax system is six times as effective in reducing the disparity in fiscal capacity between New York and Mississippi as all aids combined.[4]

---

[2] Committee on Intergovernmental Fiscal Relations, *Federal, State and Local Government Fiscal Relations,* pp. 185–225.

[3] See I. M. Labovitz and L. L. Ecker-Racz, "Practical Solutions to Financial Problems Created by the Multilevel Political Structure," *Public Finances: Needs, Sources, and Utilization,* National Bureau of Economic Research (Princeton, N.J.: Princeton University Press, 1961), pp. 135–221.

[4] Study Committee, *Federal Responsibility in the Field of Education,* Report to the Commission on Intergovernmental Relations (Washington, D.C., 1955), p. 78.

Recently, one study of federal aids for welfare recommended the elimination of open-end grants in favor of a composite grant to the states based perhaps upon population and modified by an equalization feature which would take account of per capita income. This was favored on the ground that it would reduce federal control to a minimum. It would also allow states to use federal money for general relief (outside categorical aids). It was also thought that it might reduce the erratic character of aids (quantitatively) that seems to prevail. At present, states may increase their total aid by distributing relatively small amounts to many recipients. The minority of the committee thought that no formula could be devised that would adequately recognize varying need factors.[5]

Proposals for Federal Equalization Grants.   There have been many suggestions concerning other techniques for the distribution of federal aid on a differential basis. Most of them seek to couple the aids with per capita income and to provide a higher or lower percentage of aid than some standard if state per capita income is less or more than the national average. Fortunately, reliable data on income payments (or receipts) by states are now available. It is true that local ability to support services may be more closely correlated with taxable property than with income. But the two factors are related to some extent anyway, and acceptable data on the territorial distribution of wealth do not exist. However, it would be possible to distribute aids inversely according to the yield of some standard or modal tax system. This is an old idea for which some support has continued.[6] It has the advantage that it recognizes the ability of some states to collect sales taxes from the transitory population. Per capita tax burdens in a state such as Nevada have little meaning where much of the revenue is collected from "foreigners."

For distributing federal equalization aids, the following has been proposed as a matching formula: $2x/y - 1$, where x equals a state's percent of need in terms of case load, and y its percent of ability in terms of its proportion of national income.[7] Thus, if a state had 2 percent of the work load and only 1 percent of the national income, the federal government would match its outlay 3 to 1; if need and ability were proportionate, the matching would be 1 to 1; and if relative ability were twice as great as relative need, no federal funds at all would be forthcoming.

Equalization Aids in the States.   Considerable precedent for differen-

---

[5] Study Committee, *Federal Aid to Welfare,* Report to the Commission on Intergovernmental Relations (Washington, D.C., 1955).

[6] The Advisory Commission on Intergovernmental Relations, *Measures of State and Local Fiscal Capacity and Effort* (Washington, D.C., 1962).

[7] Bryon L. Johnson, *The Principle of Equalization Applied to the Allocation of Grants-in-Aid* (unpublished doctoral dissertation), University of Wisconsin (Madison, 1947), chap. VII.

tial aids exists among the states, particularly in their distribution of aids to support education. Here the aids are distributed according to various formulas, one of the most common of which apportions in some inverse ratio to the equalized value of property within the school district, with account taken of both the educational requirements of the district and the local efforts to meet them from local resources.[8] Although distribution on a differential basis is by no means universal, it is an established feature of state aids in many states.[9]

Distribution of Aids according to a Composite Index. The so-called British "block-grant" provided for the distribution of aids according to need as measured by a composite index which was to include four factors. Nominally revenues were to be distributed according to population, but the latter was to be weighted—that is, the population of a given unit was to be increased (1) by the percentage by which the number of children under five years of age exceeds 50 per 1000 population; (2) in the proportion that the amount of per capita assessed valuation of taxable property in the unit falls below £10; (3) according to the density of population per mile of public roads; and (4) according to the number of unemployed.[10] The single formula resembles sharing in that it leaves local governments free to spend at their own discretion. After some years of application the system was abandoned or very substantially modified by the Local Government Act of 1948. The unconditional grant was retained, but it was made a more strictly equalization grant with differentials based on ratable value per head and on current expenditures. On a shortage in the standard tax base, the state pays as though it were a local taxpayer. The expenditure factor is criticized as a wide-open invitation to extravagance.[11] The equalization block grant is combined with other specific aids (as for education).[12]

The history of intergovernmental fiscal relations in Canada affords an example of a sporadic application of specific aids (for designated purposes) and a long-standing application of general grants (flat sums according to population or to replace revenues lost through the centrali-

---

[8] See preceding chapter.

[9] These aids can be operated with reasonable equity, however, only in states which have an adequate equalization of property. Here we have another illustration of the importance of better property tax administration.

[10] See Mabel Newcomer, *Central and Local Finance in Germany and England* (New York: Columbia University Press, 1937), pp. 161–290, for a more extended treatment of this act.

[11] See Reynold E. Carlson, *British Local Grants and Central-Local Finance* (Baltimore: The Johns Hopkins Press, 1947); also a review of this book by Ursula K. Hicks, *American Economic Review*, XXXIX (June 1949), pp. 794–797.

[12] See Alan T. Williams, "The Finance of Local Government in England and Wales since 1948," *National Tax Journal* (December 1958; March and June 1959).

zation of taxes). The Canadian unconditional grants have proved rather inflexible, poorly adapted to needed central controls, and a provocation of continual political bickering.[13]

The experience of Australia has been a cross between that of Canada and that of Great Britain. The distributions in lieu of income tax revenues (now nationalized) are midway between aids and shared taxes, with distribution now based largely on population. This is independent of a second aid, given by recommendation of the Commonwealth Grants Commission. This agency has for many years implemented the distribution of special grants based on fiscal need. The situation arose in part out of the alleged inequalities in loss of tariff revenues at the time of federation. The Commission, however, has with some qualification measured need in terms of the cost of standard public services at standard burden to taxpayers. The grants have decreased in importance over the years partly because of a trend toward equality in regional per capita incomes and partly because of a substantial increase in special purpose grants.[14]

ALTERNATIVE TO AIDS

Although aids have been growing, there are many who are skeptical of the merits of this device. These critics are inevitably challenged to consider alternatives. There are other ways of helping the junior units of government. One is to give them taxing power instead of money. Of course, power would not be of much help to the genuinely weak districts. But in the case of the urban centers, particularly, there are ample resources to tap if the states would but give the municipalities adequate tools for the task. Better still, the states could assist the municipalities in the administration of local taxes or permit municipalities to supplement state levies and have the state collect for both. This would still leave discretion with the local authorities. Some states, notably New York and Pennsylvania, have recently experimented with laws giving municipalities wide discretion in the diversification of their tax systems. That this introduces confusion into the tax system will be conceded. However, it provides some check on the circuitous routing of revenue to the state capitol and back again. The latter has demonstrated two limitations from the municipalities' standpoint: the money is not always intact when it gets "back home," and it has lost its proprietary connection with the taxpayer,

---

[13] J. A. Maxwell, *Federal Subsidies to the Provincial Governments of Canada* (Cambridge, Mass.: Harvard University Press, 1939).

[14] Eric J. Hanson, *Australian Commonwealth Grants Commission,* Canadian Tax Foundation (Toronto, 1960).

due to this circuitous routing. However, as we have previously suggested, the aids provide the main protection against competitive taxation, and the larger the unit that provides them, the more protection they afford.[15]

HOW FAR SHOULD AIDS EQUALIZE?

The experience with aids in Australia and the present urge to equalize our own social security grants raise sharply the question of how far aids should equalize. As previously indicated, the idea envisioned in Australia is that of a common public standard of living with common burden of taxation. In terms of our own country, this would mean that Mississippi could claim all the public amenities enjoyed by New York City at common expense to the taxpayer. The proposal raises some profound questions:

1. How far can territorial equalization of governmental services be carried as long as territorial differences in private living standards are allowed to persist? To take one illustration, what would happen if an unemployed person were paid at government expense more than he would receive from his regular employment?

2. To what degree can a community subsist on outside resources without becoming demoralized?

3. If, as alleged, distress is a symptom of maladjustment and is to be fully relieved, will needed movement of population and needed reorganization in governmental structure occur?

4. Where central units of government are financed by a graduated income tax, the tax system itself does considerable equalizing not only among taxpayers but also among territories. Is it desirable to go beyond this and carry the equalization objective into the expenditure side of the picture as well?

The equalization principle in aids is obviously related to the ability-to-pay principle in personal taxation. In both cases, probably, there is some upper limit beyond which it is dangerous to go. Moreover, self-reliance is worth cultivating, and this is as true of municipalities as of individuals. In certain of the Canadian provinces, the population has become accustomed to look to Ottawa for much public assistance. At the same time, in some places communities have employed the cooperative techniques to "do something for themselves." The two approaches, perhaps not entirely incompatible, provide an interesting contrast.

---

[15] For other alternatives to aids see Chapter 20.

PROBLEMS

1. Distinguish aids, shared taxes, block grants. Consider the proper criteria of distribution for these institutions.
2. Consider the use of aids and shared taxes to mitigate the fiscal inequalities resulting from metropolitan fragmentation.
3. Aids are said to be justified when and to the degree that central governments have an interest in local services. Is this a workable rule? Is it consistently applied in practice?
4. Would a federal equalization grant based upon per capita income and excluding the states with per capita income above the average be the most economical form of federal aid? Why? Account for infrequent use of this type of grant in the federal system.
5. The "wave of the future" in federal aids is said to be their use to stabilize and enlarge local spending power during depressions. What are some of the difficulties in implementing this idea?
6. Comment on the following:
   a. The aid system is justified to permit public expenditure for certain functions beyond that allowed by competitive local taxation.
   b. Selective federal aids, largely unplanned, may result in the distortion of local expenditure.
   c. The ideal of aids should be that every unit of government should be brought up to the average standard of local services without higher than average taxes.
   d. Aids are justified on the principle that they apply to areas the same standard of ability to pay that the income tax applies in direct personal taxation.
   e. Aids are but a way by which functions of mutual state and federal interest are mutually financed and controlled.
7. Explain and criticize federal grants for welfare.
8. Consider the proposition: It is better for a state to add to local taxing power than to grant aids. If the former alternative be accepted, should the state allow municipalities to tax what it taxes or what it does not tax?
9. Egalitarianism is the order of the day in public finance. But does territorial egalitarianism make sense? To be sure, the federal government collects more income taxes per capita in Illinois than in Arkansas, but this is solely a matter of differences among individuals. The federal government does not treat a millionaire (if any) who lives in Arkansas differently from one who lives in Illinois. Comment.

PART **4** BUDGETS,
FISCAL POLICY,
AND PUBLIC DEBT

24

BUDGETS

Budgetary procedure is sometimes regarded and treated as an aspect of public expenditure. However, any system of financial planning that makes even a pretense of being useful must involve considerations of revenue as well as expenditure. Budgetary procedure may also involve public borrowing, usually the result of unbalanced budgets. Thus it cuts across several phases of public finance and is therefore most logically given separate consideration in the study of public finance.

GENERAL PURPOSE OF BUDGETING

Governments, like individuals, cannot pass an intelligent judgment upon either a specific item of expenditure or a possible source of revenue without keeping one eye constantly focused upon the whole picture of possible expenditure and possible revenue. Most items of expenditure that offer the community a new or expanded service are desirable, but their cost must be balanced against other claims on the public revenue and against the resources of government. All taxes may appear undesirable in themselves but, balanced against the services they make possible, the decision may be in their favor. Thus, budgeting is a system of rationing and would not be necessary in an economy of such abundance that the people collectively could have everything they wanted. It is much easier to make ends meet if expenditures and revenues are planned a considerable time in advance. The planning requires some responsibility and leadership. On the federal level, budgeting requires a careful consideration of the effects of taxes, expenditures, and debt on the economy as a whole—fiscal policy. After the plan is agreed upon, discipline and technique are required to carry it out. The purpose of budgets is to facilitate this process.

HISTORY OF THE FEDERAL BUDGET

The necessity of a budget seems so obvious that one wonders at the recency of its inauguration in the United States. The budget was an essential part of the British parliamentary system two centuries ago and has been in operation in France for over a century. Among the important nations, only the United States waited until the third decade of the twentieth century to inaugurate an integrated plan of budgetary procedure. Alexander Hamilton, with all his skill in and understanding of financial matters, seems to have overlooked this important feature of fiscal administration, though it should be said for Hamilton that he presented the financial program to Congress in person and that his proposals were marked by boldness, originality, and unity. But this precedent was not followed; in subsequent administrations Congress took over financial planning, and executive initiative in budgetary matters came to an end. Much of the confusion that followed was due to the fact that Congress attempted to perform a function for which, by its very nature, it was unfitted.

During most of the history of the United States, federal finances have been characterized by a distressing lack of coordination. Appropriations proposed in Congress were not referred to any single committee but might be considered and recommended for adoption or rejection by many committees—at times, as many as twenty-nine. These appropriations were not gathered together in one bill. Revenue measures were proposed in a separate bill or bills and referred to still other committees. Very little machinery existed to keep administrative agencies within their allowances. With so little planning and discipline, it was not surprising that many retroactive appropriations had to be made in what were called deficiency bills, or that two great American institutions, the "pork barrel" and "logrolling," flourished.[1] In the states, budgetary reform has been of

---

[1] By the "pork barrel" is meant legislation of special interest to a particular local district and by "logrolling" is meant an exchange of support among legislators for such measures.

recent origin also, but in some form it has now permeated to all levels of government, although not to all units.

Creation of the Bureau of the Budget in 1921 was a major step in the direction of efficient and effective management of the financial affairs of the federal government. For the first time it was made the duty of the President to prepare the annual federal budget. The Budget Bureau was created to assist him in the preparation and execution of the budget. It was placed in the Treasury Department, with a Director of the Budget to be appointed by and directly responsible to the President. The office of Comptroller General was also created; the Comptroller was responsible to Congress and was expected to audit and authorize expenses as they occurred and to review them at the end of fiscal periods. (Most critics have thought that an error was committed here and that the preaudit as distinguished from the postaudit should be the responsibility of the administration.) Two committees in each house, one on taxes and one on expenditures, were designated to end the dispersion of financial responsibility among committees.

During the 1920s budgetary policy aimed at a balanced budget at the lowest possible level. Charles Gates Dawes was appointed the first Director of the Bureau of the Budget with the primary objective of "weeding out the deadwood" in the federal bureaucracy and achieving economy and efficiency. During the depression of 1921, when there was widespread unemployment and "want and desperation stalked abroad," the remedy prescribed was "to lift the burden of taxation from the backs of the people by a reduction in the cost of government." Even as late as 1932 the Democratic party platform stated: "We advocate an immediate and drastic reduction of governmental expenditures by abolishing useless commissions and offices, consolidating departments and bureaus, and eliminating extravagance, to accomplish a saving of not less than 25 percent in the cost of federal government." One need hardly remind the student that a revolution soon occurred in the attitude toward public expenditures, particularly as they pertain to the economics of depression.

Under the Reorganization Act of 1939, the Budget Bureau was transferred into the new Executive Office of the President. In addition to the usual financial powers, it was given the function of analyzing administrative and financial implications of proposed legislation, controlling statistics and questionnaires, acting as the administrative-management agency for the President, and, above all, planning in terms of fiscal policy.[2] Thus the Budget Bureau came into its own and became the center of administrative strategy. Financial support and staff were much expanded. Although the Bureau was reorganized in 1952, much of its

---

[2] Harold O. Smith, *The Management of Your Government* (New York: McGraw-Hill Book Company, 1945), chap. 5.

former character was preserved; the fiscal division was dropped in view of the development of other agencies in this area.

Legislation in 1946 added two innovations. One inaugurated the so-called legislative budget. It contemplated an early determination by Congress in each session of an appropriation ceiling. This was to be initiated by the four fiscal committees of Congress in joint session, and their recommendation was to be accepted or modified by the Congress as a whole. The innovation looked plausible and promising but has proved disappointing. A major difficulty seemed to be that "Congress cannot intelligently establish a budgetary total until it has examined the components in detail." [3] In the first attempt at application (1947), the two houses could not agree on a total. In the second attempt (1948), a figure was agreed upon (a cut of $2.5 billion in the President's proposal), but it was not observed in subsequent legislation and became a meaningless gesture. The 1949 Congress abandoned the attempt entirely. The legislative budget may conceivably be retrieved by altering the time schedule so that it can be developed late in a session of Congress.

Legislation in 1946 also led to what has come to be called the National Economic Budget. During the 1930s certain agencies of over-all planning had functioned within the government, among them the National Resources Planning Board and the Temporary National Economic Committee (TNEC). Mention has been made of the responsibility for planning delegated to the Budget Bureau in 1939. Now an Employment Act was added, committing the government to "promote maximum employment, production and purchasing power . . . consistent with its needs and obligations and other essential considerations of national policy." A new agency was established to implement this program, namely the Council of Economic Advisers, which was to act in coordination with the Budget Bureau. The Council is a research and advisory agency responsible for formulating an immediate and long-range program to keep the economy in high gear and on an even keel. Its reports, which are referred to Congress under the title of "The President's Economic Report," have commanded widespread interest, and the Council is evidently destined for an important future. The degree to which it must conform to the President's personal views and agree within itself (or resign?) has not become a fully established precedent. More will be said in the next chapter about the National Economic Budget and its interpretation and significance.

Since 1947 an ambitious program to improve accounting in the federal government has been underway, with the Comptroller General, the Secretary of Treasury, and the Director of Budget cooperating to-

---

[3] Jesse V. Burkhead, "Federal Budgetary Developments: 1947–48," *Public Administration Review*, VIII: 4 (1948), pp. 269–274.

ward this objective. The program involves decentralization of accounting operations to the points of operating responsibility. Accounting Office audits are based in large part on an evaluation of accounting systems and internal checks in the agencies. Recognition is being given to the need for flexibility to adapt accounting to differing management needs. Detailed reporting and other "red tape" is being reduced.[4]

Although the system inaugurated in 1921 and amended in 1939 gives the President much greater power over federal finances than he previously possessed, his power still is subject to important limitations. Congress may disregard the administration's budget entirely and pass its own program. Only through effective control of his own party (which, in the United States, requires extraordinary leadership) can the President hope to get his budget, without substantial changes, enacted into law. Of course, the President might use his veto power, but it could be overridden or circumvented by riders.[5] Complete responsibility and harmony in the federal financial program is precluded by the separation of powers [6] which, however, is a basic feature of government in the United States.

SURVEY OF BUDGETARY PROCEDURE

There are three well-recognized steps in budgetary procedure: preparation of the tentative budget, determination of a final or accepted budget, and execution of the budget as accepted.

The prevailing practice is to place the responsibility for drawing a tentative budget on the executive official of the government—the president, governor, mayor, as the case may be. The tentative budget is based upon the previous year's expenditures, requests of department heads, and the judgment of the executive. The first published draft may contain a column for each of these three sets of figures. Both in drafting the budget and in making preliminary recommendations, the executive usually has the assistance of a financial advisor—in the national government of Great Britain, a Cabinet officer, and in the United States, a "budget director." Frequently, preliminary hearings are held at which department heads explain and support their requests. It is very important for the budgetary authority to make a thorough examination and study of the departmental requests. Department heads are likely to regard their own

---

[4] T. Jack Gary, Jr., Lindsley H. Noble, and Alfred R. Golzé, "Improvements in Federal Accounting," *Public Administration Review*, X: 4 (Autumn 1950), pp. 270–280.

[5] A rider is an item (sometimes more or less extraneous) inserted into a bill in the hope of getting the former accepted along with the latter. The opponents of the rider are persuaded to accept it rather than kill the entire bill.

[6] Under separation of powers the branches of government (executive, legislative, and judicial) have a more or less independent status and check each other's acts.

function as the only one of importance and are usually expansion-minded. If the budgetary authority merely accepts the departmental requests or estimates, he is shirking one of his main functions. He should also prepare or gather estimates concerning the prospective yield of existing and proposed taxes, and expenditures should be considered in relation to taxes and vice versa. Once a tentative plan has been determined, it should be presented to the legislature (or Congress) in the form of a budgetary message. It should be printed and published as a document to serve as a basis for education and discussion.

The tentative budget is then ready for consideration by the legislature. It is introduced in appropriate legal form, and frequently in much less detail than in the budget document, by the budgetary authority himself or by a legislative committee or individual legislator. It is then referred to one or more (usually several) committees for consideration in detail and for public hearings concerning its provisions. The bill (usually several bills) is then referred to the legislature itself with the committee's or committees' recommendations for action. The legislature may have full or limited power to alter the tentative budget (as will be explained in more detail later). The legislature then acts upon the budget. In the United States, budgets, like other legislation, require executive approval to become law, except that the legislature may sometimes pass a bill over the executive's veto, usually only with a two-thirds majority vote.

Once the budget or appropriation bill has become law, it is referred to administrative officers for enforcement. Lest departments either spend more than their appropriations allow or use up their allowance in the early part of the fiscal period (thus threatening the continuity of service unless more support is obtained), budget directors are usually authorized to require quarterly reporting and approval of outlays. A designated person or section in each department is selected to deal with the budget director in these matters. In very large departments this departmental budget division should act toward the department much as the budget director acts for all departments. The departmental budgetary agent is expected to exercise a critical influence on his area. While an appropriation is a mandate not to spend more than the amount specified, it is not an order to spend all the funds available. The budget authority and department agencies should seek to conserve public funds not needed to accomplish the purpose for which they were appropriated. The authority of the budget director to require such saving has been in dispute in Washington, and the Hoover Commission Report recommends that the matter be clarified in favor of the administration.[7] The administration may wish to spend

---

[7] *The Hoover Commission Report* (New York: McGraw-Hill Book Company, 1949), p. 41.

less than authorized because (1) revenues fall below estimates; (2) change of other conditions; and (3) disagreement with the intent of the legislature. Failure to follow the intent of Congress however strikes at the traditional legislative control of the purse strings and the executive's authority in this respect is controversial. No legal precedent has been established.

It is generally agreed that the accounts of the government, like those of the private corporation, should be subject to periodic audit and that the audit should be performed by a party who has no responsibility for, or direct interest in, the government's accounts. In some states this duty is performed by independent state officers. In the case of the federal government, it is performed by the Comptroller General. There should be, in addition, a current audit of all bills and pay rolls and of other requests for funds in order to forestall irregular and illegal transactions. Preferably this audit, as distinguished from the periodic one, should be under the executive. The continual audit is for the purpose of checking on the administrators by the executive. The periodic audit is a check on the executive himself. Many states combine pre- and post-auditing in such a way that an official is responsible for checking his own work.

In some states, the state tax department or some other state agency is given the power to audit the accounts of municipalities either upon its own motion or upon requests. It is also sometimes required to make available to municipalities a uniform system of accounts. These provisions have proved highly beneficial to municipalities.

RESPONSIBILITY FOR THE BUDGET

As previously stated, the rule is to place the responsibility for preparing the budget upon the executive and his administrative staff, a procedure that is quite universally approved among the critics. Public opinion ordinarily holds the chief executive responsible for the financial success or failure of the administration, although he may have little control over either the receipts or expenditures. It is thought that the executive is in the best position to view the financial problem as a whole and to assume the responsibility for the success or failure of a financial program.

Legislative responsibility for public expenditure was an important achievement for the democratic process at the time when executive power was inherited rather than bestowed by popular vote. Complaint is made that individual legislators with little or no staff are obliged to accept most budgetary items at least as prescribed by committee. Moreover, budgets are much too large and complicated to permit much comparative evaluation even in committee. Accordingly much reliance is and must be placed on the executive and administrative bureaucracy for a satisfactory financial program and for the over-all view that makes a budget rational.

Nevertheless, executive responsibility for the preparation of the budget is by no means universal. In many states and cities, the budget is prepared by a committee of the legislature. In some jurisdictions it is formulated by a board composed of administrative or of legislative and administrative officers. Usually, in cases of board responsibility, the executive is a member of the board.

The role of the executive in the budgetary process may be a matter of degree even with an "executive budget." Among democracies, it is under the Cabinet system of government as exemplified in Great Britain that the widest responsibilities and powers are allowed the executive. The prime minister through his subordinate Cabinet officer, the chancellor of the exchequer, prepares the budget, defends it in Parliament, and resigns in case Parliament refuses to accept it in substantially the form approved by the executive and his advisors. This logical procedure centers responsibility for both the financial plan and its administration and makes impossible prolonged deadlocks between the legislature and the executive. In the United States, the executive budget is limited by "checks and balances" created in the constitutional separation of powers. Under the city manager form of municipal government, a situation somewhat similar to that of Great Britain may be found, but even in this case harmony between the legislative and executive departments may not be fully preserved. Under the American theory of government the law is supposed to be framed by the legislature, subject to some advice and checks by the executive (including, of course, the veto), and executed or carried out by the executive, subject to some advice and checks by the legislature. In these circumstances, both divided responsibility and deadlock are possible. Divided responsibility may result from the legislature's refusal to accept the executive's budget. The legislature, as a rule, may modify the recommended budget very materially and pass supplementary financial legislation of its own. The governor (or President) has the general veto to protect himself and sometimes the much more effective specific veto. But his defenses are negative rather than positive. In turn, the legislature may not secure what it wants in an appropriation bill because of the veto, and, of course, it has no power to carry out the legislation it passes.

Looking toward a greater concentration of responsibility, Maryland in 1916 provided in its constitution that the legislature could not change the governor's budget except to delete or reduce items. Separate appropriation bills might be introduced and passed by the legislature, but they must provide the revenue to finance them. A case has been made for an executive budget which the legislature has only the power to accept or reject.

On the other hand, New York City finances illustrate a situation in which responsibility is not only badly divided, but the City Council has less authority than a representative body should possess. The City's budget is first reviewed by the Board of Estimates (consisting largely of the elected city comptroller and other administrative officials). Review by the Council is limited by lack of time and staff and by the fact that the Council cannot raise the budget total. The procedure is now in process of revision.

The Item Veto. One of the most feasible and defensible means of centering responsibility for the budget upon the executive is to give him the item veto. This means that he can veto specific items of an appropriation bill. It is a safeguard against "riders," and it affords an opportunity for the exercise of selective economy. The federal Constitution gives the President a general but not an item veto power. However, the latter is common among the states. In addition to the power to strike specific items, the executive might well be given the power to reduce them.

Proposals for a so-called consolidated budget (legislative treatment of all appropriation bills in one bundle) are criticized on the score that this would invite riders. An item veto for the president would mitigate this fear. However, the item veto is resisted on the score that it might be used to victimize individual congressmen. It might be ineffective if large numbers of individual items were grouped in large categories. Moreover, as previously explained, the executive probably has some power to impound appropriations that he does not like.

PROCEDURAL ASPECTS OF TAX LEGISLATION

Many writers have commented on the contrast between tax legislation procedure under the constitutional pattern of the United States and that under the Canadian and British tradition. In the latter instance, the executive has almost plenary powers; the budget message all but has the force of law. Indeed, in the case of excises, the levy takes effect with and at the time of the announcement by the executive. In the United States by contrast, any executive or other proposal has to run the gamut of two committees, two hearings, and two independent legislative decisions. The hearings are wide open—the tradition is that anyone who wants to be heard has that privilege. However, the panel of witnesses is seldom a balanced one. Most of those appearing usually represent special interest groups and there is no cross examination except by members of the committees. The result has been so unsatisfactory in the case of the tariff that Congress has felt obliged to delegate important tariff-making powers to the president. In the case of taxation, the procedure has led to special interest legislation described as "the erosion and corrosion" of the income tax.[8]

CURRENT PROPOSALS FOR IMPROVING THE FEDERAL BUDGET

Until 1963 the current federal budget was a formidable document, consisting of more than a thousand pages and comparable in size to a large city's telephone directory. The 1963 edition was much smaller, relegating a large amount of detail to appendices. The sum of the budget's proposed commitments is no less impressive than its physique and in this respect there has been no shrinkage. These facts have brought the budgetary process into the spotlight of public attention, producing a considerable number and variety of proposals.

Consolidated Budget. It is contended that the budget should be enacted as a consolidated whole. The budget is said to be one of those things in which the parts bear on the whole and the whole bears on the parts. A middle-class family could afford a Cadillac if it were the only one of the good things of life in which the family were interested; but it may have to vote "no" on the car because there are other desires to satisfy with limited means. The idea of a consolidated budget is not new; it was embodied in the legislative-budget experiment and it was tried independently in 1950. Congressmen gulped at the prospect of having to swallow so large a morsel. Nevertheless, critics argue that piecemeal consideration by Congress along with the parceling out of the major work of revision to many subcommittees is hardly better than the fragmentary treatment of the unhappy past. States and municipalities usually employ a comprehensive budget; it is only at the federal level that nobody but the budget director and the President base decisions on an over-all view.

Control of Expenditure. It is urged that Congress must somehow disentangle its current authorizations from the proposed current expenditure. The curse of the budgetary process in Washington is "hangover appropriations." This backlog has become so large at times that the present administration could spend as much as the proposed current authorizations, were Congress to pass no budget at all. Most of this is

---

[8] See Walter W. Heller, "The Tax Legislative Process in the United States," *Canadian Tax Journal*, VII: 3 (September–October 1955), pp. 214–325; Roy Blough, *The Federal Taxing Process* (New York: Prentice-Hall, Inc., 1952), chap. 4.

due to the prevailing practice of letting contracts for military procurement that require more than a year to complete. Advance commitments, however, are not confined to the military area. Congress usually passes a highway appropriation bill, setting the amount to be spent on federal aids to highways several years in advance. It is argued that this assurance is required to facilitate agreements between the Public Roads Administration and the states. However, it is said that these many advance commitments make a "wonderland" out of what should be an intelligible budget and deprive Congress of needed control over current outlays. As to past commitments the principal control now exercised by Congress is in terms of timing.

Most extreme of the antidotes for this difficulty is the proposal to require that all appropriations lapse at the end of each fiscal year. This would be in accord with the tradition that one Congress cannot bind another. Many appropriations lapse now except for obligations incurred before the end of the year. The proposed rule would mean that Congress would have to let contracts subject to subsequent reapproval. This would create a new factor of risk which would add to the expense of procurement.

Congressional Staff.   It is said that money spent for Congressional staffing has been woefully inadequate and still might be augmented to good advantage. It was not many years ago when one committee faced the prospect of appraising a $60 billion budget with the aid of only one staff member. Understaffing is conducive either to indiscriminate cutting or none. The former has sometimes been described as pruning with a meat axe rather than a scalpel. At the state level, states with strong fiscal administration are now supplying the budget director with a corps of research analysts who review the needs and administrative performance of state agencies periodically. California goes further and also supplies a budgetary analyst for its legislative committees. How much of this sort of duplication is warranted remains moot.

Efficiency Audit.   Review of administration has several functions, one of which is to check the efficiency of administrative procedures. This is an interest distinct from that of priorities in the allotment of resources. If the Weather Bureau is not functioning properly, what it may need is new procedures rather than a cut in appropriations. Many federal agencies do have a built-in efficiency unit. Efficiency examination is also a function distinct from auditing. The audit is designed to assure that all funds have been accounted for properly and spent according to legislative intent. The General Accounting Office is headed by the Comptroller General and is a highly independent agency [9] whose major

---

[9] The Comptroller is appointed for fifteen years and can be removed only by impeachment.

function is the post audit. One alternative would be to give this office somewhat broader powers. The federal government has on occasion used an ad hoc agency like the Hoover Commission to make efficiency studies. Also recommended is an independent congressional committee for efficiency studies. This program, it is plausibly argued, would relieve Congress of a frustrating load, pave the way for a comprehensive consolidated budget, and provide the continuous criticism that Congress should give the administration. In any event, the research function like the auditing function must be divided at least between the administration (budget bureau) and Congress.[10]

Performance Budget. The Hoover Commission also recommended [11] that in the interest of intelligibility "the whole budgetary concept of the federal government be refashioned by the adoption of a budget based upon functions, activities, and projects: this we designate as a 'performance budget.' " They went on to explain that the performance budget should focus attention on the accomplishment of objectives rather than upon allocation to agencies. Current federal practice has largely incorporated this suggestion.

Performance budgeting focuses upon workloads, such as tons of garbage collected, number of schoolchildren graduated, number of income tax returns processed, and the like. It is especially serviceable in administrative management and in appraising requests.[12] In the defense department, performance budgeting takes the form of what is called programing, in which a calculation is made of what constitutes adequate defense in terms of physical units.

Traditional budgetary procedure is largely a survival from the days when the primary objective was to check legal abuses. It was not designed to facilitate comparisons in terms of priorities. More and more attention in budgeting is focused upon programs in relation to needs.

TYPES OF BUDGETS AS INSTRUMENTS OF FISCAL POLICY

Recent interest and controversy concerning the budget has focused especially on its limitations for fiscal policy. In this context three kinds or types of budgets are distinguished. First there is the so-called administrative or *conventional* budget featuring the authority for new spending

---

[10] Arthur Smithies, *The Budgetary Process in the United States* (New York: McGraw-Hill Book Company, Inc., 1955).

[11] *Hoover Commission Report*, p. 36.

[12] Jesse Burkhead, *Government Budgeting* (New York: John Wiley and Sons, Inc., 1956), chap. 6.

sought by administrative agencies. The *cash* budget gauges the sums that the federal government will take in from and feed back to the private economy. Finally there is the *national income accounts* budget developed by the Department of Commerce and designed to reflect the level of the federal government's contribution to gross national product.

The total of receipts and expenditures in these three budgets may differ substantially as may also the deficits and surpluses that they indicate. As to detail, the cash budget, for instance, ignores the accrual of interest on savings bonds; adds the net earnings or losses of some governmental enterprises; eliminates intergovernmental transactions that are completely within or between governmental agencies; and adds the receipts and expenditures of trust funds (sometimes on a net and sometimes a gross basis). These trust funds, such as the social security fund and the highway fund, cover vast areas of government operations. The income accounts budget, featuring the purchases of goods and services by the government, excludes capital transactions, such as subscriptions to the international lending agencies. Moreover its timing differs from that of the other budgets in that business taxes are gauged as they accrue and personal income taxes as they are withheld.[12a]

It is argued by some critics that the administrative budget as a guide to fiscal policy is "not simply irrelevant but positively misleading. "Moreover it is said that the conventional budget hides many billions, such as the gross receipts and expenditures of many government businesses, as that are needed to indicate the size of the government and its role in the economy."

The above criticisms of the conventional budget are not universally accepted. There are those who argue that all of this talk is but an attempt to excuse easy spending. Moreover the budgetary document has been evolving to accommodate these criticisms and present several alternative sets of data before Congress.

The Capital Budget. In addition to all of the above there is considerable support for the so-called *capital* budget which would exclude from *the* budget outlays for durable goods. This type of budget is widely used in Europe, and it is argued that the alleged greater success in balancing budgets in that area is illusory. For instance, recent exercises have purported to show that were West German budgetary accounts managed like those in the United States they would show more deficits than our own, notwithstanding the fact that they have been cited as setting an example for prudence.

[12a] Governmental accounting for budget purposes is a vastly complicated art and science. See *The Federal Budget as an Economic Document,* Dr. Roy E. Moor, Chief of Staff Joint Economic Committee (Washington, D.C., 1962), particularly pp. 110–127.

In 1933 the federal government divided its budget into two parts, one labeled ordinary, the other extraordinary. The intention was to finance the ordinary budget from current revenues and the extraordinary budget by the use of public credit. The plan was soon abandoned, however, and the budget is now presented as a unit. Divided budgets usually originate as a justification for loan finance.

A budgetary change quite in keeping with the trend of the times would be one which draws a clear line between investments, particularly in self-liquidating projects, on the one hand, and operating expenses on the other. This has been the subject for experimentation in Sweden. It leads logically to the proposition that governments should have a balance sheet (of assets and liabilities) as well as an operating statement (of expenses and income). However, considerable opinion supports the view that balance-sheet accounting or capital budgeting would provide no important advantage for the federal government outside the area of self-liquidating works.[13] In this area depreciation accounting is required for intelligent pricing. Capital expenditures are not easily identified, and it is thought that arbitrary classification might lead to an over-emphasis on public works. If an administration were to inaugurate a capital budget without due recognition of depreciation on existing assets, it would receive an unwarranted windfall. Large units of government need not encounter the factor of nonrecurrence in public works; where the pattern is affected by business cycle considerations, a deficit may be warranted and need not be associated entirely with capital goods. Local governments practice capital budgeting more or less automatically when they borrow on improvements and retire serial bonds during the lifetime of the improvement.

OTHER PROBLEMS IN BUDGETING

Techniques of financial administration associated with budgeting involve many additional problems of which a few of the more prominent can here be briefly discussed.

Comprehensiveness of Budget and Unity of Treatment. A well-accepted rule among critics of budget making is that budgets should present a complete financial plan. Very often budget presentation takes only incidental account of revenues, and it may also omit important aspects of the financial picture on the expenditure side. Among the items most frequently omitted are the assigned revenues and corresponding expenditures (as where motor vehicle tax revenue is earmarked for

---

[13] *Government Accounting and Budget Execution,* United Nations, Department of Economic Affairs (New York, 1952), pp. 16–18.

highways), the receipts and expenditures of commercial and industrial enterprises, the financial status of independent funds, expenditures and appropriations on capital account, and debt operations. Ordinarily, all of these matters have a fairly important bearing on the financial plan to be considered, and where this is true, they should be included either directly or in collateral statements.

Classification of Budgetary Data. Expenditures may be classified *functionally* (so much for health, so much for education, and so forth). This is of special value for citizen study and is usually presented in summary form. It frequently requires cutting across departmental lines where more than one department participates in performing a single function. Classification by *organizational units* reflects the departmental and agency structure of the budget. It is important for authorizations (giving legal authority to administrative units to incur obligations). For instance, expenditures for defense will transcend the Defense Department. Of special interest are the proportions of the budget that go for military and for civilian objectives. Classification may also be by *object* of expenditure (as personal services, operation, supplies, maintenance, and so forth). This affords some legislative control of allotments within departmental allowances. It raises questions as to how much detail appropriations should specify and how much freedom should be accorded administrative agencies. Finally, budgets can be broken down according to the *economic* significance of the items (transfers, purchases of goods and services, durable goods, self-liquidating outlay, and so forth). One writer divides expenditure into exhaustive and nonexhaustive outlay, defining the latter as spending "that absorbs no output but redistributes income or assets." He concludes that such outlay could conceivably run to more than the gross national product and that it is largely neutral in terms of inflationary effects.[14] All of these classifications have usefulness, at least under certain conditions and for certain purposes.[15]

Revolving Funds and Segregated Accounts. Not only should the legislature have a full picture of all accounts—in most cases it should also act annually on all accounts. Thus the widespread use of revolving and segregated or dedicated revenues in the states is a matter of considerable concern. Under this system, income from certain sources is channeled into a separate treasury or account or into a segregated part of the state general fund. There is little or no transfer of money between these separate funds. The state treasury is therefore not a single treasury but a group of more or less independent treasuries. Some state legislatures have given away their control of all but a minor part of the funds passing through their state treasuries.

---

[14] Bator, *The Question of Government Spending,* p. 9.
[15] *Ibid.,* chaps. 6–9.

Objection to segregated funds is that they deprive the legislature of the annual privilege of reviewing all expenditures and of balancing the needs in one line against those in another. It is also argued that the groups administering revolving funds tend to operate in an isolated manner and to break away from the rest of the government.

Two controversial items in the area of segregated funds are the dedication of student fees to state-supported educational institutions and the segregation of motor vehicle tax revenues for highways. The first is defended on the ground that here one finds a clear case of payment by beneficiaries for a specific service. Legislators who add to such funds from general taxes can at least obtain the facts regarding this semi-private support before they act. Highway funds have somewhat the same character, though here there is considerable dispute about the alleged impropriety of using highway taxes for other than highway support. Motor fuel taxes, viewed as general excises, are not an intolerable form of levy especially where, as is often the case, motor vehicles are granted special privileges under the general property tax.

The Public Corporation.   Unique and perplexing accounting procedures sometimes arise where they are applied to public corporations such as the Tennessee Valley Authority. The corporate form is advocated for these institutions on the ground that it enables them to break away from the "red tape" and inflexible procedures that characterize government departments. A Supreme Court decision [16] supports the view that in the absence of a statute to the contrary, public corporation's accounts are not subject to the Comptroller's preaudit. But legislation in 1945 subjected the financial operations of these agencies to the scrutiny of the General Accounting Office and the Budget Bureau. However, the Office does not control most of the ordinary expenditures of these corporations except by postaudit. Civil service rules apply, and administrative as distinguished from program outlay is subject to control. Capital expansion must be approved by Congress.

The public corporation in the United States is subject to considerably more control than its counterpart in Great Britain; on the other hand, the so-called public authorities sponsored by state and local government frequently have so much autonomy that they are not required even to submit an annual report.[17]

Balancing the Budget.   Many critics have observed that by far the most important rule in budget making is to balance the budget. Several state constitutions provide that the state must raise taxes enough to defray current expenses.

---

[16] *United States* ex. rel. *Skinner and Eddy Corporation v. McCarl,* 275 U.S. 1 (1927).

[17] Burkhead, *Government Budgeting,* chap. 16.

In the chapters on public debt, however, it will be suggested that it may not always be desirable to pay all the expenses of government from current revenues. Ordinarily, debts should be confined to irregular expenses, such as those on capital account. Where this rule is followed, debts may not be incompatible with a balanced budget, according to one definition of that term. Some have argued for balancing of budgets over a period of years corresponding with the business cycle. The principal difficulty here is the irregularity and unpredictability of business cycles. Political propensities might mean postponing or shirking responsibilities. Disciplinary weakness might lead to a strong preponderance of deficits over surpluses. Others hold that "planned deficits" are required to stimulate business during the low ebb of the business cycle. This may happen automatically if tax rates and exemptions are kept at a constant level during a business cycle. Still others believe that the government should make large investments, more or less in the nature of capital expenditures, to keep its men and resources employed. These investments might be partly or fully self-liquidating over a period of time. All of these problems go beyond the field of fiscal administration into the field of fiscal policy. More attention will be given to these problems in the next two chapters.

SUMMARY

Budgets are necessary to provide an over-all view of public finances and to facilitate the process of rationing involved in raising and spending public revenues. Until well into the twentieth century federal finances were characterized by much confusion and failure to achieve clear-cut responsibility. In 1921 responsibility for formulating the budget was centered in the executive, and a budget bureau was created to facilitate the process. Later developments added other functions to the Budget Bureau and introduced the legislative budget and the Council of Economic Advisers. Substantial progress toward more orderly financing has also been made by states and cities.

Budgetary procedure involves formulation, enactment, enforcement, and audit. Although practice in the United States (federal and state) usually lodges the function of initiating the budget with the executive, our division of governmental powers inevitably leads to confusion as to responsibility for the ultimate financial product. Budgetary personnel can be very effective in the highly important function of budget enforcement.

The size and intricacy of the federal budget have fostered many proposals for the improvement of budgetary procedure. It is suggested that the budget be considered as a consolidated whole; that changes should be made to recapture federal control of annual expenditures; that the President be given the item veto; that performance budgeting (with more attention to workloads and programs) should be more generally employed, and that Congress should more sharply distinguish traditional budget consideration from review of administrative efficiency. Not much perhaps can be done about tax procedure, but it is an open gate for vested interests.

Budgeting involves many special problems; among them are revolving funds, segregated accounts, and the treatment of public corporations. Segregated accounts are in accord with the idea that certain receipts are properly coupled with certain kinds of outlay, but the segregation is criticized on the score that it impedes the free comparison of alternatives in public spending.

Recent interest and controversy concerning the budget has focused on its limitations as an instrument for fiscal policy. Three types of budgets are distinguished: the administrative or conventional budget, which features new authority for spending; the cash-consolidated budget, which features payments to and from the government from and to the private economy; and the national income accounts budget, which is designed to reflect the level of federal government's contribution to the gross national product. The totals of receipts and expenditures in these three budgets may differ widely as may the deficit or surplus they indicate. In addition there is support for a capital budget segregating items of an investment character; it encounters the objection that it might lead to overemphasis on tangible public works.

The older view that while it is important that budgets be intelligible and comprehensive, the prime consideration in budget making is to achieve a balance of receipts and expenditure. Currently this view is often challenged, at least to the extent of contending that the balance need not be achieved in a period as short as one year.

PROBLEMS

1. Trace the principal steps in the evolution of present federal budgetary and accounting procedure.
2. Explain the role of the following in budget making: budget director; comptroller; performance budgeting; research.
3. The old tradition of English-speaking countries is that popularly elected representatives of the people control "the public purse strings." Is this compatible with the developing notion that the executive should assume responsibility for initiating the budget?

4. Indicate how a separation of the legislative functions of review and appropriation might aid the budgeting process.

5. How would performance budgeting be of aid in deciding whether a department's request for more personnel were warranted?

6. How do you account for the fact that while the President has several times asked for the item veto power, Congress has persistently refused to act favorably on the proposal?

7. Explain the function of the General Accounting Office. Would this agency be in a specially favorable position to make an annual efficiency audit?

8. Consider the significance of the rule that an appropriation act authorizes the executive to spend but does not compel him to do so.

9. Distinguish administrative, cash-consolidated, and income accounts budgets. What are the major items differently treated by these institutions? When Congress considers the wisdom of deficits and surpluses, which budget should it accept as a guide?

10. What is the importance of the classification that distinguishes exhaustive from nonexhaustive expenditures?

11. Can one consistently support revolving-fund accounting for the student fees of a public educational institution and oppose a segregated fund for motor vehicle taxes?

12. It has been said that expenditures for operation should be sharply distinguished from those for durable goods and self-liquidating projects. What are the advantages and disadvantages of this so-called capital budget?

25

FISCAL POLICY—THE PROBLEM AND ITS ELEMENTS

Financing government involves three basic fiscal functions: taxing, spending and debt management. In the broad sense fiscal theory, and the fiscal policy which derives from that theory, deals with all the problems relating to those functions. Prior to the great depression of the 1930s students of public finance were mainly concerned with three issues in this area: the welfare implications of government spending, equitable distribution of the tax burden, and the incidence of taxation. As the reader of this volume has already learned, these questions still constitute a substantial part of the public finance field.[1] During the past two decades, however, the term "fiscal policy" has come to mean a distinct area of thought and study concerning the problems relating to full and effective utilization of the nation's resources and the maintenance of price-level stability. The objective of fiscal policy in the short period is mitigation of the business cycle; over the long period, prevention of both secular stagnation and secular inflation while, at the same time, providing a favorable environment for economic growth. The financial problems in this area are partly monetary—dealing with the availability and cost of credit —and partly fiscal—dealing with taxation, the public debt, and public expenditures. It is this latter group that mainly concerns us here.

---

[1] For example, see Chapters 2, 6 and 21 of the present volume.

According to the traditional view, prudent management of government fiscal affairs called for confining expenditures to the amount essential for the performance of purely governmental functions, and the raising of sufficient tax revenue to balance the government's budget. In the event of depression it was thought that the government could make its greatest contribution to the nation's economic health by cutting its spending (and taxing) program to the irreducible minimum. Only in time of war was deficit financing tolerated, and after the end of hostilities the debt that had been incurred was to be retired as rapidly as possible.

The modern theory of fiscal policy accords government a far more active role in the nation's economic life.[2] It holds that the government's taxing and spending policies should be designed to compensate for fluctuations in the level of income and employment; that the balanced-budget orthodoxy give way to a balanced-economy objective. According to this view, falling income in the private sector of the economy should be offset by a cut in taxes and increased government spending. By the same token, inflationary pressures should be met by rising tax rates and reduced expenditures. Only during periods characterized by relatively full employment and stable prices does the balanced budget prescription apply.

This approach to fiscal policy has its theoretical basis in the modern theory of income. Before dealing, therefore, with the various schools of thought in compensatory finance, we must briefly consider the factors that determine aggregate (national) income and the ways in which statisticians have transformed these concepts into workable tools.

THE THEORY OF NATIONAL INCOME

THE INCOME FLOW

The size of the national income is determined by the total volume of production and employment. The volume of production and employment, in turn, is determined by the amount of money that individuals, business firms, and government spend for currently produced goods and services.[3]

---

[2] It should be noted that in this and succeeding chapters dealing with fiscal policy the term "government" is used in reference to national governments. Much of this discussion would not apply to state and local governments. See Eugene Meyers and Randall Stout, "The Role of States and Local Governments in National Fiscal Policy, *National Tax Journal*, X: 2 (June 1957), pp. 171–175; Harold M. Groves, "National Unity in Fiscal Policy—State and Local Aspects, *Proceedings of the National Tax Association Conference*, 1958, pp. 36–46.

[3] Net imports and exports also affect production and employment. To simplify the discussion, however, they are assumed to be in balance.

It follows, then, that the level of income is uniquely related to the level of expenditure. In fact, during any given period the two quantities are identical: money spent on the purchase of goods and services constitutes spending from the point of view of the buyer and income from the seller's standpoint. Fluctuations in the level of income and employment, therefore, are a reflection of variations in the level of expenditures. For this reason income analysis begins with an analysis of the various components that make up aggregate expenditure.

CONSUMPTION AND INVESTMENT

For the purpose of describing the fundamentals of modern income analysis it is convenient to divide total expenditures into two broad categories: consumption and investment.[4] This classification is not an arbitrary one; it is based on the fact that there is a significant difference between the factors giving rise to private expenditures on consumer and investment goods. For this reason they play quite different roles in the income generation process.

Empirical studies have established that over a reasonably short period of time (a decade for example) there is a fairly stable relationship between income and expenditures on consumer goods. As income rises consumption also rises, but at a lower rate of increase; the same relationship holds when income falls. Investment-expenditure decisions, on the other hand, while not wholly divorced from the income level, are primarily based on a variety of factors largely unrelated to the level of income: technological innovations, population growth, the development of newly discovered resources, optimistic or pessimistic expectations. Thus, while the amount consumed out of a given level of income is a fairly stable quantity, investment tends to fluctuate widely and with no predictable relationship to the level of income.

We may conclude, therefore, that consumer spending is usually the result rather than the cause of income change. As long as the level of income remains stable, there is a strong presumption that consumption spending will do likewise. Investment, on the other hand, is the unstable element in the expenditure pattern. It follows from this that changes in the level of aggregate spending, and therefore the level of income and employment, are determined primarily by variations in the size of the investment component.

---

[4] This leaves out of the picture two other expenditure categories, net foreign investment and government spending. However, this omission does no violence to the basic analysis and has the advantage of focusing attention on the private sphere of the domestic economy.

SAVINGS AND INVESTMENT [5]

The process through which fluctuations in the amount of investment spending alter the level of national income is explained by a fundamental relationship underlying modern income analysis: over any given period of time the community's savings are equal to its investments and, furthermore, this equality is continuously maintained through variations in the level of national income.

Demonstration of the equality of savings and investment is a simple exercise in elementary logic. As noted in the preceding section, expenditures are equal to consumption plus investment. Because national income and national expenditures are identical quantities, it follows that income is equal to consumption plus investment. But inasmuch as all income, be it that of an individual or a nation, must be either consumed or saved, income is also equal to consumption plus savings. Savings are therefore equal to investment (by virtue of the fact that quantities equal to the same quantity are equal to each other).[6]

While this equality of savings and investment always happens, it is never the result of conscious planning. As noted in the preceding section, saving plans are based primarily on the current level of income, whereas investment plans are governed by factors (innovations, population growth, and the like) largely unrelated to the income level. Furthermore, a substantial share of saving is done by individuals, while the bulk of investment decisions are made by business concerns. It would be the sheerest coincidence, therefore, if the two sets of plans were ever identical; that investors would want to spend for investment goods the exact amount of money savers wanted to save.

Regardless of the relationship between planned savings and planned investment, however, the former is automatically brought into equality with actual investment through changes in the level of income. Figure 19 illustrates the logic of this process of adjustment. In the diagram, con-

---

[5] Note that savings and investments are defined here in the social sense. For the community as a whole whatever income is not consumed is saved; investment is a net increase in the nation's real capital (machinery and equipment, buildings, inventories, etc.). Purchase of a share of stock previously held by someone else, a piece of land or an old building is investment from the viewpoint of the individual, but it results in no net increase in the community's real capital: the amount one man is investing, another man is at the same time disinvesting.

[6] In algebraic terms, using the standard symbols Y = income, S = saving, I = investment, and C = consumptions:

$$I = Y - C$$
$$S = Y - C$$
$$\therefore \quad I = S$$

sumption, savings, and investment are measured along the vertical, and income along the horizontal axis. The vertical distance from any point on the horizontal axis to the 45° line is equal to income at that point and reflects the fact that consumption plus savings equals income. Line *C* represents the functional relationship between consumption and income

FIGURE 19

Relation of Consumption and Investment to Income

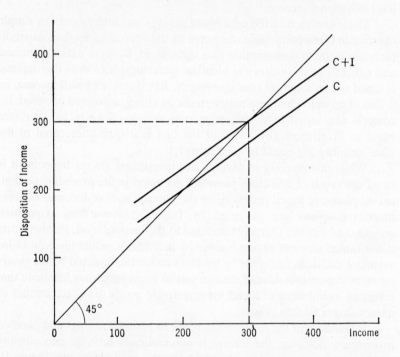

—that consumption rises as income rises, but at a lower rate of increase.[7] By adding an assumed schedule of investment to the consumption schedule the composite schedule of consumption plus investment is derived (line *C + I*).

It is clear from the diagram that given this consumption function and investment schedule, the only possible equilibrium level of income is established at the point where line *C + I* intersects the 45° line. It is only at this point that total expenditures equal total income or, stated in terms of the savings-investment relationship, that planned savings are equal to actual investment. At any income above this point business firms would

---

[7] This relationship is reversible: consumption falls as income falls, but at a lower rate of decrease.

find their costs exceeding their receipts;[8] total expenditures on consumption and investment goods would be less than total income paid out to the public (in terms of the diagram, $C + I$ would be below the 45° line). Faced with this situation, business firms would cut back output and employment until costs were reduced to the level of receipts; that is, until they no longer were producing a greater quantity of goods than the public was willing to buy at prices high enough to cover costs.

Similarly, at any income below the intersection of the $C + I$ and 45° lines, the receipts of business firms would exceed their costs; total expenditures on consumption and investment goods would be greater than total income paid out to the public (in terms of the diagram, $C + I$ would be above the 45° line). Given this very profitable situation, business firms would expand output and employment up to the point where costs had increased to the level of receipts; that is, until their rate of production had increased to the point where the quantity of goods available became sufficient to satisfy the public's demand at prevailing prices.

AUTONOMOUS CHANGES IN SPENDING

An examination of Figure 19 makes clear that a change in the level of national income will be induced by an autonomous change in either the investment or consumption component of aggregate expenditures. A shift in either the C or I schedule[9] will result in a corresponding shift in the $C + I$ schedule, causing it to intersect the 45° line at either a higher or lower level (depending on the direction of the autonomous change in spending). In the final analysis, therefore, it is the change in spending as such, rather than the source of that change, which is the causal factor in income change.[10]

---

[8] In the diagram the 45° line can be thought of as the national-income cost schedule: it is the schedule of total payments to land, labor, and capital for the production of national output. The $C + I$ line is the receipts (demand) schedule: it is the schedule of total expenditures for the purchase of national output.

[9] In the diagram the I schedule is superimposed on the C schedule. Its independent value can be derived by subtracting the C schedule from the $C + I$ schedule.

[10] It should be recalled at this point that the change in income induced by an autonomous change in spending will ultimately be substantially greater than the magnitude of the initial autonomous change. This is due to the multiplier effect which was explained in Chapter 21. If the marginal propensity to save is assumed to be one third (that is, if every $3 change in income results in a $1 change in savings and a $2 change in consumption), then the multiplier, which is the reciprocal of the marginal propensity to save, will be three. Figure 17 was constructed on the basis of this assumption. If the reader draws a new $C + I$ schedule parallel to (either above or below) the one in the diagram, he will find that the horizontal distance between the points of intersection of the old and new schedules with the 45° line (that is, the change in income) will be just three times as great as the vertical distance between the old and new $C + I$ schedules (that is, the autonomous change in spending).

Reasons have already been advanced as to why an autonomous shift is more likely to occur in the investment than in the consumption schedule. It was pointed out that while a large share of any change in consumption spending occurs in response to a change in the income level, fluctuations in investment spending are in large part independent of the income level. It is for this reason that variation in investment spending is given the most attention in modern income analysis.

It should not be assumed from this, however, that consumption can be relied upon to be a completely passive factor in the income generation process. Many economists did believe this to be true prior to World War II. As a matter of fact, the data of the prewar period tended to support the hypothesis of a highly stable, and therefore predictable, relationship between the consumption and income schedules.[11] However, postwar spending has not conformed to the precise pattern that would be indicated by projecting forward the prewar consumption-income relationship. It was just such a projection of the consumption function of the 1930s that was chiefly responsible for the numerous forecasts of a postwar depression which failed to materialize. Aggregate spending (and therefore income) turned out to be far higher than expected, mainly because a war-induced shortage of consumer durables and abundance of liquid assets combined to cause an autonomous upward shift in the consumption schedule.

Empirical studies of recent years have shown that while income remains the principal variable upon which consumption depends, the simple relationship between current income and consumption is not a sufficient explanation of consumer behavior. The consumer's spending decisions are also affected by his past earnings and future income expectations, his relative position in the community's income distribution, and the amount of wealth he has accumulated. There is support for the view that consumption is primarily influenced by the total assets of the taxpayer and for the view that expectations of future income is the major determinant. The pattern of consumption may also be influenced by institutional factors such as the age and rural-urban composition of the population, the change in attitudes toward consumer credit and the effectiveness of advertising.

National income and consumption data tend to confirm the presence of these (and no doubt other) influences on consumption spending. The consumption function appears to have shifted upward from decade to

---

[11] Lawrence R. Klein, "The Empirical Foundations of the Keynesian Economics," *Post Keynesian Economics* (New Brunswick: Rutgers University Press, 1954), p. 290. This essay provides an excellent survey of the wide range of empirical studies that have been made on the consumption function and the other variables in modern income theory.

decade,[12] and variations in the marginal propensity to consume (that is, the slope of the consumption function) have occurred from one period to the next and at various income levels.

The need to account for autonomous shifts in the *level* of the consumption function is a serious limitation on its effectiveness as a tool of economic forecasting, but is of significance from the standpoint of fiscal policy mainly with respect to the implications it may hold regarding a progressive tendency to oversave.[13] The degree of stability in the *slope* of the consumption function is of more vital concern for fiscal policy, however, because the multiplier effect (see Chapter 21) is directly determined by the marginal propensity to consume. The more stable the marginal propensity to consume, the more predictable will be the effectiveness of a given expenditure or tax program in changing the level of national income.

The fact that variables other than current income influence the slope of the consumption function reduces its stability and therefore the precision with which the quantitative effects of fiscal policy measures can be estimated.[14] Nevertheless, the fundamental relationships underlying modern income theory (which is the basis of fiscal policy) are firmly established: current income is the primary determinant of the level of consumption spending, and the ratio of consumption to income is consistently higher in the depression than in the prosperity phase of the business cycle.[15] We know, therefore, that fluctuation in investment spending is the major causal factor behind cyclical changes in the income level, and that any autonomous change in spending (coming from either

---

[12] This is the implication of the Kuznets' estimates for the period 1869–1948 and those of Goldsmith covering the years 1897 to 1949. See Simon Kuznets, "Proportion of Capital Formation to National Product," *American Economic Review, Papers and Proceedings,* XLII: 2 (May 1952), pp. 507–526, and Raymond W. Goldsmith, *A Study of Saving in the United States* (Princeton, N.J.: Princeton University Press, 1955), vol. I, pp. 12–14.

[13] It is true that the ability to make dependable economic forecasts would aid immeasurably in timing fiscal policy programs designed to nip in the bud inflationary or deflationary tendencies. However, fiscal-policy decisions usually involve the question of how much to vary government expenditures and/or taxes to compensate for an inflationary or deflationary situation which has already developed. The level of the consumption function is not a factor in this decision.

[14] It should be noted that econometricians and consumer-survey groups are making considerable progress in quantifying the relationship between consumption and a wide assortment of variables, some of which were referred to above. Their work may result in greater accuracy in the future in measuring these quantitative relationships.

[15] Raymond W. Goldsmith, "Trends and Structural Changes in Savings in the Twentieth Century," in Heller, Boddy, and Nelson, eds., *Savings in the Modern Economy* (Minneapolis: University of Minnesota Press, 1953), pp. 133–152. The conclusions in this essay are based on Goldsmith's three-volume study of savings. the first volume of which is cited in footnote 12.

the private or government sphere of the economy) will induce an income change by a multiple of the amount initially involved.[16] It follows from this that government can play an effective role during inflationary and deflationary periods by adopting tax and/or spending policies designed to increase or decrease aggregate expenditures (either directly, by varying the level of government spending, or indirectly through a tax-induced change in private spending).

INFLATIONARY AND DEFLATIONARY GAPS

In any economy there is a unique consumption-plus-investment schedule consistent with full-employment equilibrium.[17] Any attempt to spend more than that which can be produced at full employment will lead to bidding up the price level, and hence inflation. Any attempt to spend less than the full employment amount will lead to a downward pressure on prices and most commonly, unemployment. For example, in Figure 20 the full-employment schedule is represented by line $C + I$. Any lower schedule of aggregate expenditures (for example, line $C_d + I_d$) provides less than full-employment equilibrium; there is a deflationary gap equal to the amount the schedule must be raised to achieve full employment.[18] Conversely, any higher schedule of aggregate expenditures (for example, line $C_f + I_f$) results in inflation; the inflationary gap is the amount the schedule must be lowered to eliminate the inflationary pressure.[19]

---

[16] We cannot say with assurance exactly how large this multiple will be, although an estimate based on the average slope of the consumption function over the past few years will probably provide a fairly accurate working hypothesis. Goldsmith found that the marginal propensity to save varied little in the period from 1897 to 1929, averaging approximately 0.20 in each of the three nonwar decades. However, for the 1929–1941 period it amounted to 0.40. See Raymond W. Goldsmith, *loc. cit.*, pp. 144–145. The data suggest, though there is no conclusive evidence on the point, that the slope (as well as the level) of the consumption function is likely to be least predictable when major breaks in the economic structure occur (for example, the great depression of the 1930s and World War II). Between these breaks the average marginal propensity to consume (save) is probably fairly stable.

[17] The term "full employment" is used here in its most general sense to describe an economy operating at maximum capacity measured in terms of the highest attainable money income at a reasonably stable price level, and with its normal labor force employed consistent with the community's need for mobility and leisure.

[18] Note that because of the multiplier effect (assumed to be three in the diagram), closing a \$5 billion deflationary or inflationary gap results in a \$15 billion change in national income.

[19] Because the horizontal axis of Figure 20 measures income in real terms (as it must, if a change in income is assumed to represent a corresponding change in output and employment), the $C_f + I_f$ schedule cannot logically be extended to the right of the full employment line. Increased spending is actually reflected in higher prices; that is, an upward shift of the spending schedule on the full-employment

As previously noted, modern income analysis provides the rational for governments to adopt compensatory policies with the objective of closing deflationary and inflationary gaps. In regard to the former, it is argued that equilibrium (planned savings equal to actual investment) can be maintained for an indefinite period while aggregate spending is far below that required for full employment; that a nation could suffer the economic waste and the frustration of widespread unemployment for years before the necessary autonomous upward shift in investment (or consumption) would be forthcoming. By the same token, an inflationary gap is likely to generate an inflationary spiral which works severe hard-

FIGURE 20

Inflationary and Deflationary Gaps

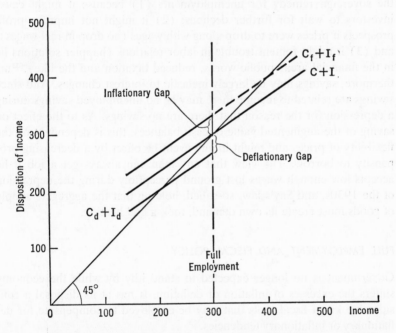

ships on fixed-income groups, saps the value of savings, and leads to other serious economic consequences. Because the nation's men and machines are already fully employed, the excess spending is drained off into higher prices rather than increased output. Moreover, the process does not stop with equilibrium at the higher price level; higher prices mean higher wages and profits, which in turn generate a further upward shift in the spending schedule. As long as the inflationary gap remains

income line. The dotted-line extension is drawn in the diagram for purely illustrative purposes.

(that is, until an autonomous downward shift in the consumption or investment schedule occurs), the inflationary spiral will continue unabated.

The view stated here that there can be equilibrium with less than full employment probably represents the consensus, but this was not always true and there are those who currently do not accept it. Prior to the publication of the late Lord Keynes' famous book, *The General Theory of Employment, Interest and Money* (1936), it was generally held that unemployment and oversaving are self-correcting phenomena; that the cure for unemployment of men is reduced wages and that for unemployment of money is reduced interest rates. Moreover, some argued that when prices fall, peoples' cash balances increase in real value and their propensity to save will therefore fall.

Keynes and his supporters took the view that cutting wages was not the sovereign remedy for unemployment: (1) because it might cause investors to wait for further declines; (2) it might not improve profit prospects if prices were to drop along with wages (no drop in real wages); and (3) it might foment trouble in labor relations (happier solutions lie in the financial area: public works, reduced taxation and the like). Furthermore, savings may be largely inelastic to interest changes. And since savings are related to income there may be no unemployed savings during a depression for the reason that there are no savings. As to the effect on saving of the augmented value of cash balances, this is dependent on the flexibility of prices and might in any event be offset by a decreasing propensity to borrow. The view that any man can always get a job if he accepts low enough wages lost ground perceptibly during the depression of the 1930s, and Say's law, so-called, holding that the aggregate supply of goods must create its own demand, took a bad beating.

FULL EMPLOYMENT AND FISCAL POLICY

Government is no longer expected to stand idly by while the economy suffers the excesses of inflation or deflation. It has at its disposal a considerable kit of fiscal tools that may be employed to compensate for deflationary or inflationary tendencies.

1. It may raise or lower the volume of public outlay (supplementing private spending to a greater or lesser extent). For instance, during a depression the government could inaugurate a public-works program.

2. It may alter the quantity (aggregate level) of taxes with the effect of either increasing or decreasing income available for private spending.

3. It may alter the quality of the tax system (increasing or decreasing its progressivity, or changing its composition) with the objective of changing the proportion of taxes coming from the savings and consump-

tion components of income.[20] These adjustments will be discussed in more detail later, but here we shall illustrate the way in which they may affect the inflationary and deflationary gap.

A change in the volume of government outlay, with taxes held constant, has the same effect on income and employment as an autonomous shift in the private spending (consumption-plus-investment) schedule.[21] If, in the deflationary situation represented by the $C_d + I_d$ schedule in Figure 20, the government increased its outlay by the amount of the deflationary gap, income would rise to the full-employment level. Similarly, in the inflationary situation represented by the $C_f + I_f$ schedule, a reduction in government outlay by the amount of the inflationary gap would restore the economy to a condition of full employment without inflation.

A change in the aggregate level of taxes, with government expenditures held constant, works indirectly on the level of national income through an induced effect on private spending and saving. A tax increase will reduce the disposable income of consumers by the amount of the tax.[22] If we assume a marginal propensity to consume of two thirds, a drop in consumption spending equal to two thirds of the cut in disposable income will result (the other third of the tax increase will be paid out of savings). In terms of Figure 19, schedule C will fall by two thirds the amount of the tax increase, as will the $C + I$ schedule (assuming that the tax increase has no effect on investment). If, as seems likely, the rise in taxes has an adverse effect on investment, the $C + I$ schedule will fall by more than two thirds the tax increase—how much more depending on how much investment falls off. The intersection of the lowered $C + I$ schedule and the 45° line will determine the new equilibrium level of income.[23] The same analysis, but in reverse, applies to a tax reduction. Two thirds of the increase in disposable income (which is equal to the tax reduction) will be spent on consumer goods, and one third will be saved. If the cut in taxes stimulates investment spending, the $C + I$ schedule will rise by something more than two thirds of the tax reduction. Income will also rise to a level determined by the intersection of the higher $C + I$ schedule and the 45° line.[24]

---

[20] Another effect of high progressivity is a relatively large fall and rise in tax collections during periods of deflation and inflation, respectively, automatically occurring through changes in the tax base. This will be discussed in more detail below.

[21] Assuming, of course, that the change in government outlay has no effect on private investment decisions.

[22] This is, of course, an oversimplification. An over-all tax increase, with no change in the quality of the tax system, will not be borne entirely by consumers.

[23] If an inflationary situation prevails, as represented by the $C_f + I_f$ schedule in Figure 20, the tax increase will reduce the inflationary gap rather than real income and employment.

[24] In either case, the amount of income change will be equal to the multiplier

Whatever effect a change in the progressivity of the tax structure (with no change in the level of taxes and government expenditures) has on income will be brought about through an induced change in private spending. Increased progressivity will shift some of the tax burden from those with low incomes to those with high incomes; conversely, reduced progressivity will shift part of the tax burden from the high to the low-income group. If those in the high-income brackets have a lower marginal propensity to consume than those with smaller incomes, increased progressivity will raise consumption spending of the latter by more than it will reduce such expenditures of the former. At the same time, however, the increased progressivity may have a repressive effect on investment spending. Making the tax structure less progressive would work in just the opposite direction. The net effect that a change in progressivity will have on total spending, therefore, depends on (1) the extent to which the marginal propensity to consume of the two groups differs and (2) the effect of a change in progressivity on investment decisions.[25]

THE NATIONAL ECONOMIC BUDGET

To create a factual basis for a national fiscal policy, the government is now expected to keep books for the people as a whole as well as for the government as such. An intelligent appraisal of fiscal activities requires some familiarity with national income accounts as well as government accounts.

The Nation's Economic Budget is a summary of such accounting and a directive for national financial planning. During the last thirty years, research organizations and government bureaus in the United States and other nations have begun to develop reliable statistics of national income. Much interest in national income as based on the recognition that it is a causal factor in the economy as well as a mere result of the economic process.

NATIONAL INCOME AND NET NATIONAL PRODUCT

Statisticians have devised a number of ways of measuring national income according to the various stages of the flow process of economic activity. Depending on the stage at which we view it, national income can be subdivided into various categories.

(assumed to be three in our example) times the *net* change in consumption plus investment spending induced by the tax change.

[25] The effectiveness of a change in progressivity as a tool of fiscal policy is discussed in the next chapter.

First, we may view national income at the stage of the distribution of money compensation for economic activity. We then speak of *the national income*. This is the summation of payments to the factors of production for current output: compensation of employees, profits of enterprise, net interest, and rental income. Measured at factor cost, national income is independent of the form in which taxes are levied, and its components are not immediately affected by any change from direct to indirect taxation or vice versa.

When we are concerned with the expenditure side of a year's operations, we express national income as the *market value* of the flow of goods to consumers and into net capital formation. National income measured at market prices includes all indirect business taxes—that is, all tax liabilities incurred by businesses, such as excise, sales, and property taxes. This is known as *the net national product*. It is useful as a measure of consumption and saving by private persons or bodies and the government.

The net national product, therefore, is simply the national income at market value. The market prices of goods sold exceed the incomes paid to the resources used in production by the amount of indirect taxes. If we measure the value of net production by the prices paid to the factors used in production, we obtain the national income at factor cost, known as the national income.

A simple example will serve to illustrate. A man buys his wife a $2000 fur coat on which there is a 20-percent luxury tax. The proceeds from the tax will pay for one month the salary of a government employee with a monthly salary of $400. Payments to the factors of production will therefore be $2400. The market price of goods and services, however, will be $2800. The former corresponds to national income, the latter to net national product (national income at market prices):

	National income	Net national product
Fur coat	$2000	$2000
Luxury tax	——	400
Salary of government employee	400	400
	$2400	$2800

Relation to Public Finance. Wherein lies the importance of the distinction between the two concepts for the student of public finance? As we noted, the national-income concept does not deduct direct taxes from or add indirect taxes to the total of incomes. Thus, for example, it includes corporate income taxes but excludes consumption taxes. Net national-product figures include consumption taxes as well as income taxes. The inclusion in the national income of taxes on corporate profits rests on the prevailing theory of the incidence of taxes levied on income. Hence, the two concepts follow the important economic distinction between taxes on income and taxes on output.

National income at factor cost is an objective and *technical concept*. It estimates the cost that has been incurred in making the goods and services that go into national income in terms of the amounts and proportions of the various factors used. National income at market prices, on the other hand, gives us a measure of the satisfactions that people actually derive at a particular set of market prices; in order to obtain a good, they have to pay the consumption taxes as well as factor costs. Net national product is therefore a subjective and *welfare concept*. It views the nation's income as a total of satisfactions, and whenever we make a statistical distribution of the national income among the different income groups, the consumption taxes which are paid as a condition of their share in the total should be imputed among the different income groups in accordance with the spending of their incomes on different lines of consumption.[26] Adjustment of the aggregate, as well as the distribution, of over $35 billion indirect taxes can be a part of public policy in maintaining a stable national income. It is contended that net national product gives us a better base for measuring the tax burden over time; deflation of factor income for price changes will give erratic results when shifts have been made from direct to indirect taxes or vice versa.

The adjustment necessary to go from national income at market value to national income at factor cost is illustrated in 1961 figures: [27]

	Billions of dollars
Net national product (or national income at market prices)	473.4
Less: Indirect taxes	48.2
Equals: National income (at factor cost)	427.8

PERSONAL INCOME

Three other totals, closely related to national income, are useful tools of public policy. To obtain a measure of payments to individuals, the Department of Commerce developed a statistical concept called Personal Income, which is not a measure of production. This figure is arrived at by

---

[26] For a more detailed discussion, see U. K. Hicks, *Public Finance* (London: Nisbet & Co., Ltd., 1947), pp. 151–158.

[27] Minor items and statistical adjustments are omitted in this and subsequent illustrations presented in this section for purposes of clarity. Therefore individual items will not necessarily add up to the total. For details, see *Survey of Current Business* (July 1957), p. 11.

subtracting from national income all undistributed corporate profits and corporate income taxes as well as contributions to social insurance funds, and by adding transfer payments of government and business to persons. Transfer payments are not included in the national income or product totals since they do not represent the equivalent of a productive service. They may be interpreted as the passing about of income rather than the creation of new income. Veterans' benefits and the interest on the government debt are so regarded. It is felt that "a comparison of the prewar and postwar volumes of production should not be distorted by the continuing interest on the national debt that arose during the war." [28] Yet government transfer payments are an important tool in fiscal policy—that is, although they are not derived from current production, they may increase disposable income and thereby purchasing power.

Personal income (as well as national income) also includes items to which no explicit cash payments correspond. Imputed income, though generally ignored by the income tax, should logically be counted in the total of goods and services. When a person saves house rent by living in his own residence or grocery bills by harvesting vegetables from his own garden, these items are part of personal income and national product. This attempt to measure nonmoney incomes is not extended to an evaluation of the services of housewives and consumer cooperatives. Capital gains are excluded on the ground that they involve a mere transfer between persons and no net addition to the personal income aggregate as such.

Always very troublesome in income calculation is the treatment of the governmental sector of the economy. It is apparent that based on the assumption of forward shifting of certain taxes, national product needs deflating to arrive at national income at factor costs. Even on the assumption that the so-called indirect taxes reduce factor incomes rather than prices, there would be a gap between the two figures, but in this case factor costs would need inflating to arrive at "true national income." The problem does not arise in the case of taxes not counted as costs.

Interest on government debt is treated as a transfer payment. This seems appropriate in the case of war debt but hardly so in the case of debt invested in government capital. In the latter case, there seems to be no reason for distinguishing between public and private investment. Under present methodology the services of public capital are not represented in national income figures.

To get from national income to personal income, the following adjustments have to be made in terms of 1961 figures:

---

[28] *Survey of Current Business, National Income Supplement* (July 1947), p. 11.

Billions of dollars

National income (at factor cost)		427.8
Less:	Undistributed corporate profits	8.2
	Corporate income taxes	22.3
	Contributions to social insurance	21.6
Plus:	Transfer payments	40.7
Equals:	Personal income	416.4

DISPOSABLE INCOME

Since some of this personal income must be paid out in the form of taxes to federal, state, and local governments, these taxes are subtracted to obtain disposable income. This also is not a measure of production since some of the items included, such as transfer payments, are not received for productive services. They do, however, represent purchasing power to the individuals who receive them. The disposable-income concept is most useful in evaluating the behavior of individuals as they distribute their income among consumption expenditures and saving.

Billions of dollars

Personal income		416.4
Less:	Personal taxes	52.8
Equals:	Disposable income	363.6
Less:	Personal consumption	338.1
Equals:	Personal savings	25.5

GROSS NATIONAL PRODUCT

As a summary measure of all economic activity, statisticians use gross national product. It is the market value of all goods and services produced before deduction of depreciation charges. It comprises the purchase of goods and services by consumers and government and by businesses for purposes of gross private domestic investment and net foreign investment. The difference between gross national product (*GNP*) and net national product (*NNP*) in 1961 figures was this:

Billions of dollars

NNP		473.4
Plus:	Capital consumption allowances (depreciation)	45.3
Equals:	GNP	518.7

Uses of Gross National Product. The *GNP* concept is particularly well adapted to short-period uses, as for instance in wartime, and for business cycle analysis. In time of war it may be desirable to ignore capi-

FIGURE 21

Five Concepts of Income

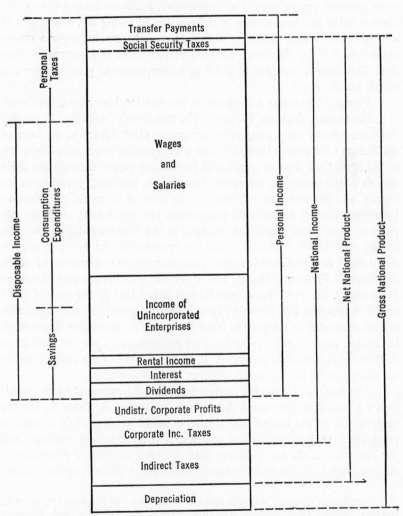

tal depreciation because maximum output irrespective of impairment of plant and capital is the goal. Since it generally moves in proportion to total business transactions, *GNP* is often considered a reasonable measure of the latter. Because national income measures only net product or contribution, gross totals are most useful as measures of economic activity and total employment. A further reason for this deliberate double counting, as compared with net national product, is that in the short period the line between capital replacements and the demand for capital additions is difficult to draw.[29] A question may be raised as to why we speak of gross national product when what we are measuring is really gross national expenditure. The explanation is closely related to our discussion in the previous section of the equality of saving and investment in any one period. Our balancing item then was changes in business inventories which is the difference between current sales and current production. This item is included in *GNP* as a component of gross private domestic investment.[30]

Figure 21 presents a diagram of the relationships above discussed.

The Nation's Economic Budget. The President's Council of Economic Advisers follows the procedure of presenting *GNP* figures in the form of the Nation's Economic Budget which is designed to summarize "in a few broad figures the flow of goods and purchasing power through the main sectors of the economy: consumer households, business, government activities, and the international area." [31] In spite of its name, the Nation's Economic Budget contains no projections into the future, since its sole purpose is to show significant changes in the economy during the preceding year. It will, however, guide the President in the policy of recommendations contained in his annual economic report to Congress of which the Nation's Economic Budget has in recent years been a part. Thus the President in his 1962 Economic Report noted that at the end of 1961 actual output was still $25–$30 billion short of potential, and urged that certain measures be adopted to close the gap. This illustrates that though the budget itself is only a record of past performance it may be used as an instrument in economic prognosis. It provides much of the subject matter for discussion in the Economic Report of the President.

The Nation's Economic Budget for 1960–61 provided by the President's Council of Economic Advisers is presented in Table 7. On the receipts side of the budget, the total consists of items relating to current production, such as wages and salaries, retained business earnings, and the like; and on the expenditures side, the total consists of purchases of current output. In the third column, additions to and absorption of sav-

---

[29] See Simon Kuznets, *National Income, A Summary of Findings* (New York: National Bureau of Economic Research, 1946), pp. 117–121; and Theodore Morgan, *Income and Employment* (Englewood Cliffs, N.J.: Prentice-Hall, Inc., 1947), pp. 13–16.

[30] M. Gilbert and G. Jaszi, "National Product and Income Statistics as an Aid in Economic Problems," *Readings in the Theory of Income Distribution* (Philadelphia: The Blakiston Company, 1946), p. 47.

[31] *The Economic Report of the President*, 1948, p. 31.

TABLE 7

The Nation's Income, Expenditure, and Saving, 1960–1961

(billions of dollars)

Economic group	1960			1961 *		
	Re-ceipts	*Ex-pend-itures*	*Excess of re-ceipts (+) or ex-pend-itures (−)*	*Re-ceipts*	*Ex-pend-itures*	*Excess of re-ceipts (+) or ex-pend-itures (−)*
Consumers:						
Disposable personal income	351.8	.....	......	364.9	.....	.....
Personal consumption ex-penditures	.....	328.9	......	.....	339.2	.....
Personal net sav-ing (+)	.....	.....	22.9	.....	.....	25.7
Business:						
Gross retained earnings ..	51.7	.....	......	54.2	.....	.....
Gross private domestic in-vestment	.....	72.4	......	.....	69.5	.....
Excess of invest-ment (−)	.....	.....	−20.7	.....	.....	−15.3
International:						
Excess of receipts (+) or of investment (−)	.....	.....	−1.5	.....	.....	−2.4
Government (federal, state, and local):						
Tax and nontax receipts or accruals	139.1	.....	......	143.6	.....	.....
Less: Transfers, interest, and subsidies (net)	37.1	.....	......	41.2	.....	.....
Net receipts	102.0	.....	......	102.4	.....	.....
Total government expendi-tures	.....	137.2	......	.....	149.8	.....
Less: Transfers, interest, and subsidies (net)	.....	37.1		.....	41.2	
Purchases of goods and services	.....	100.1	......	.....	108.6	.....
Surplus (+) or deficit (−) on income and product ac-count	.....	.....	1.9	.....	.....	−6.2
Statistical discrepancy	.....	−2.6	−2.6	.....	−1.7	−1.7
Gross national product	504.4	504.4	......	521.2	521.2	.....

* Preliminary estimates by Council of Economic Advisers.

NOTE: Detail will not necessarily add to totals because of rounding.

SOURCE: Adapted from Table B7, *Economic Report of the President*, 1962, pp. 216–217.

ings are shown. This technique of presenting statistical information is based on the truism that savings plus a government cash surplus equal investment or, as is the case when the government is borrowing funds, investment plus a government deficit equal savings. It also demonstrates that this equilibrium can be achieved on a lower or higher level of income. In order to show savings and absorption of funds in the "Excess" column, transfers of purchasing power, such as are included in personal and disposable income, have to be listed. They are not included in the *GNP* totals since they do not relate to current production. Yet, as a source of purchasing power, they do not differ from any other payments that are derived from production.

In conclusion, it should be pointed out that although the economic budget technique, as a directive of policy, derives from the Keynesian theory of income, its applicability is not confined to depression situations. The analysis has, in fact, been used to show inflationary gaps and the need for higher taxes, less government spending, and debt retirement.[32]

---

[32] Summary and problems follow Chapter 26.

26

FISCAL POLICY IN APPLICATION

Historically, our concepts of government finance have until recently differed little from those of the household budgets of the English king in colonial times. It has been the prime interest of Congress, as it was that of Parliament then, to see that in normal circumstances annual expenditures were in proper balance with annual revenues. The concept of a "proper" balance implied that expenditures should be equal to revenues. The government's budget was thus viewed much like that of a private citizen: when its receipts declined, its expenditures had to be reduced also. The analysis of the theory of national income, however, indicates that it is possible for equilibrium income to be above or below full employment income and hence cause inflation or unemployment. The theory also indicates that government can combat inflation by cutting expenditures or increasing taxes and combat unemployment by augmenting spending or cutting taxes.

This theory leads us to appreciate a very important paradox: in times of distress the citizen is obliged to cut his expenditures in order to avoid debt, while the federal government should incur debt either by cutting taxes or by augmenting expenditures. Likewise, while a citizen may feel free to spend more as the price of his services goes up, the government should spend less or increase taxes as all prices go up.

APPROACHES TO FISCAL POLICY

This modern conception of government finance developed during the 1930s as economists and politicians groped for ways of meeting the depression crisis. In the early days of the depression many thought that all that was needed was to jar the economy off dead center; that "priming the pump" with a shot of government spending would stimulate a cumulative rise in private spending and start the economy on the road to recovery. It was soon discovered, however, that the primary and secondary (consumption) effects of a nonrecurring increment in government expenditures would soon run their course. It became evident that a temporary rise in national income would not induce investors to alter their pessimistic outlook regarding profitable investment opportunities.

COUNTERCYCLICAL POLICY

Recognition of the ineffectiveness of pump priming led to the development of a countercyclical approach to fiscal policy. The government is assigned the role of varying its tax and expenditure policies with the objective of moderating fluctuations of income and employment over the business cycle. This policy calls for the government purposely to unbalance its budget during deflationary and inflationary periods: to increase its expenditures and cut taxes when private spending declines to depression levels, and to raise taxes and cut its spending during the prosperity (or inflationary) stage of the business cycle. Proponents of this approach still subscribe to a balanced-budget philosophy, but they are reconciled to the logic of a cyclically rather than annually balanced budget. Implicit in this view is the belief that with proper management of the government's budget, the depression deficit will be offset by the prosperity surplus.

Supporters of the traditional balanced-budget philosophy take vigorous exception to this line of reasoning. Maladjustments in the economy —of which inflation and deflation are merely symptoms—are regarded as self-correcting through the automatic operation of the pricing mechanism. According to this view the government's role in economic affairs should be confined largely to managing money and restraining monopoly (of labor as well as business), the growth of which destroys the flexibility of the economy and thereby inhibits the adjustment process. Countercyclical fiscal policy, they contend,[1] undermines business confidence, pre-

---

[1] For a forceful and well-rounded presentation of this point of view see B. M. Anderson, "The Road Back to Full Employment," in Paul T. Homan and Fritz

vents the restoration of a structure of relative prices (including wages and interest rates) consistent with full employment equilibrium and, because it destroys the automatic character of the free-market system, leads to the demise of private enterprise and its replacement with some form of state socialism.

COMPENSATORY POLICY

Those who argue that the exercise of an effective fiscal policy (that is, one that offsets serious inflationary and deflationary pressures) is consistent with a cyclically balanced budget, implicitly assume that surplus-producing boom years will be equal in number to deficit-incurring depression years. Many economists do not regard this as a realistic assumption. There are some in this group who think that secular stagnation is the long-run prospect—that there will be many more bad years than good ones. Others hold an opposing view that the long-run outlook is for secular inflation. If either view is correct, a countercyclical fiscal policy will not be adequate to maintain a reasonably high level of employment with stable prices. If persistent deflationary tendencies develop, long-run deficit financing will be required; on the other hand, if inflation is a continuing problem, long-run surplus financing will be necessary. In either case, adoption of a compensatory fiscal policy means that the goal of a cyclically balanced budget cannot be realized.

Secular Stagnation. The central proposition of the theory of secular stagnation is that the long-run prospects are for investment outlets to lag behind full-employment savings. If private enterprise is left to its own devices, therefore, the economy will probably experience a persistent deflationary gap. Policy suggestions to counteract this tendency include the use of devices such as social security and progressive taxation to raise the consumption schedule (and thus reduce the schedule of intended savings), and the use of compensatory fiscal policy and a long-range developmental program of public investment to offset the deficiency in private investment.

Secular stagnation does not mean a cessation of growth in the economy, but rather a failure of investment outlets to grow at a rate consistent with the economy's full-employment potential. For the United States, a relatively "mature economy," this is thought to be due to a decrease in the rate of population growth, the passing of the geographical frontier, a dearth of revolutionizing capital-consuming inventions, and the increasing ability of business to finance itself by depreciation reserves and reinvested

Machlup, eds., *Financing American Capitalism* (New York: The Twentieth Century Fund, 1945), pp. 9–70.

earnings.[2] As an affluent society with a diminishing utility of consumption goods approaches satiety, the prospect of expanding markets weakens.

Opponents of the stagnation thesis dispute its theoretical and factual basis.[3] They argue that a decline in the rate of population growth began a century ago and ask why it failed to produce stagnation long before the 1930s. Similarly, the geographical frontier in the United States was closed by 1890, forty years before stagnation is said to have developed. Moreover, they suggest that while there may be a dearth of great capital consuming innovations—although no one is sure of what lies just over the horizon—this lack can be readily offset by many smaller, but in the aggregate no less important, technological developments. Moreover, during the late 1950s we began to hear talk of stagnation combined with inflation, a situation that might arise when prices and wages are controlled by monopoly power. And with the advent of more unemployment and a slow growth rate, the stagnation thesis has enjoyed a revival.

Secular Inflation. Many who were once concerned with the threat of chronic unemployment now look upon inflation as our major long-run problem. The reason for this turnabout is not hard to find. Just as the stagnation thesis was a product of the depression-ridden 1930s, so the theory of secular inflation reflects the inflationary climate of the 1950s. In the United States, as in most countries of the Western world, an almost uninterrupted inflationary trend followed the outbreak of war in 1939 and continued for two decades.[4] All economists would agree that war and cold war have been major factors in that trend; with government spending

---

[2] This exposition of the stagnation thesis is based largely on the writings of Alvin Hansen, an American economist whose name is most closely associated with the doctrine. See his *Fiscal Policy and Business Cycles* (New York: W. W. Norton & Co., 1941), pp. 42–47, chaps. 16, 17; "Some Notes on Terborgh's 'Bogey of Economic Maturity,'" *Review of Economic Statistics*, XXVIII: 1 (February 1946), pp. 13–17; and "Growth or Stagnation in the American Economy," *Review of Economics and Statistics*, XXXVI: 4 (November 1954). It should be noted, however, that other writers who have advanced a stagnation hypothesis offer explanations quite different from those advanced here. For example, see J. A. Schumpeter, *Capitalism, Socialism and Democracy* (New York: Harper & Row, Publishers, 1947), for a theory based on changing social institutions, the growth of the labor movement and the development of the welfare state. Also see J. Steindl, *Maturity and Stagnation in American Capitalism* (Oxford: Basil Blackwell, 1952), for an analysis that points to the growth of imperfect competition and other monopoly elements as the primary causal factor. The policy recommendations of these writers quite naturally differ considerably from those suggested by Hansen.

[3] George Terborgh, *The Bogey of Economic Maturity* (Chicago: Machinery and Allied Products Institute, 1945); also "Dr. Hansen on the 'Bogey of Economic Maturity,'" *Review of Economic Statistics*, XXVIII: 3 (August 1946), pp. 170–172.

[4] As noted in the last chapter, the widely heralded postwar depression failed to materialize. The rather mild recession of 1949–1950 provided only a temporary break in the trend. After the Korean war the trend slowed considerably but did not reverse itself.

almost a quarter of the national income there was no lack of investment outlets for the nation's savings. There are those who contend, however, that a substantial cut in military spending would not eliminate the inflationary pressures inherent in present-day private enterprise economies. In essence they argue that secular inflation is inevitable because government has either tacitly or openly guaranteed full employment at all cost, and that in so doing it has abdicated its powers to resist effectively the inflationary pressures generated by the demands of organized labor, business, and agriculture.[5]

As long as deflation poses no threat to these power groups, they reason, a secular wage-price (or price-wage) spiral is inevitable. Business firms will have no fear of raising prices, secure in the knowledge that any deficiency in demand, due to a shortage of the purchasing power needed to clear the market (at the higher price level), will be offset by expansionary fiscal and monetary policies. At the same time, the workers, assured that government will not allow them to price themselves out of a job, will bargain aggressively for wage increases out of all proportion to the growth in their productivity. Resistance of employers to these demands will be weakened by the knowledge that they will have no real problem in passing on increased costs in the form of higher prices. Thus, power-group pressures in an economic environment of government-insured demand will lead inevitably to successive rounds of wage and price increases.[6]

Some economists, however, do not share this pessimistic outlook. Their appraisal of the postwar record of the United States economy does not reveal inherent inflationary tendencies.

Two basic safeguards against long-run inflation are noted: (1) the impressive capacity of the economy to expand production under pressure (as evidenced by the immediate postwar outpouring of consumer durables), and (2) the very high rate of individual and corporate saving under conditions of full employment.[7] They recognize the possibility that excessive wage demands could lead to a wage-price spiral, but note that the experience thus far indicates a higher level of industrial statesmanship than generally has been expected.

At the same time these optimistic economists point to the danger of

---

[5] The assumption by government of responsibility for maintaining employment is evidenced by the British White Paper on Employment Policy (1944) and, in the United States, by the so-called "Employment Act of 1946."

[6] For a discussion of this view and further implications for the institution of private enterprise see Martin Bronfenbrenner, "Some Neglected Implications of Secular Inflation," in *Post Keynesian Economics*, K. K. Kurihara, ed. (New Brunswick: Rutgers University Press, 1954), pp. 31–58, and the references cited in Bronfenbrenner's footnotes.

[7] Alvin Hansen, "Economic Growth and Stability," *Federal Tax Policy For Economic Growth and Stability*, Joint Committee on the Economic Report, 84th Cong., 1st Sess., 1955, pp. 14–21.

a policy of price stability at whatever the cost in terms of employment. Unemployment, they note, is likely to be even more of a drain on individual savings than moderate inflation. Moreover, depression, unlike inflation, results in the underutilization of the economy's productive capacity.

A tendency for prices to rise at a moderate rate (which is irregular and uncertain) is not disturbing to some economists.[8] They note that the periods of greatest economic growth have been associated with mild inflation, and that some inflation may be necessary in the future to promote a level of investment which will enable the economy to realize its long-term growth potential.

Finally, it is emphasized that fiscal and monetary policy is a two-way street, applicable in an inflationary as well as a deflationary period. A policy aimed at avoiding depression need not be one of full employment at all costs. Just as a budget deficit and easing of credit are useful tools to counteract deflationary pressures, a budget surplus and credit restriction may be applied in an inflationary situation.

CONCLUSION

Most economists today would agree in principle to the proposition that an attempt to balance the national government's expenditures and revenue over the business cycle is a more reasonable fiscal objective than the traditional goal of an annually balanced budget. However, the likelihood of ever accomplishing that objective is doubtful. In the first place, there is reason to suspect that incurring a deficit in the depression phase of the business cycle will have more appeal to practical politicians than producing an offsetting budgetary surplus during periods of high income and employment. Aside from this practical consideration, however, it is extremely unlikely that any one business cycle will have the degree of symmetry required for a cyclically balanced budget. Moreover, if the predictions of either the secular stagnationists or inflationists are borne out by experience, a balanced budget over any reasonable period of time would be inconsistent with the basic tax and expenditure objectives of a countercyclical fiscal policy.

It is highly probable, therefore, that a fiscal program intended to be countercyclical would in fact develop into a compensatory policy. Such a policy would be characterized by (1) a budgetary deficit during the depression phase of the cycle; (2) a balanced budget in times of full employment and stable prices; and (3) a budgetary surplus during infla-

---

[8] With a regular, and therefore predictable, rise in the price level future increases would be discounted in advance, giving rise to an explosive inflationary situation.

tionary periods. In the long run (but not necessarily over a single business cycle), the budget would be balanced only in the event that the economy was subject to neither secular stagnation nor secular inflation. If the former prevailed, the deficit years would exceed those with a balanced or surplus budget; conversely, with secular inflation the normal condition of the economy, the government would run a budgetary surplus most of the time.

MODERN FISCAL POLICY TECHNIQUES

The practical alternative policies in applying fiscal policy to the problem of economic instability are (1) changes in a balanced budget; (2) unbalancing budgets either by tax or expenditure changes; and (3) qualitative changes in the tax system.

BALANCED BUDGET

It was once thought that tax-financed government expenditures were neutral with respect to the nation's level of income and employment—that the expansionary effect of a dollar of spending would be offset by the contractive influence of the same amount of tax collections. It was recognized, of course, that there might be a redistributional effect. For example, if those who paid the taxes had a lower marginal propensity to consume than those who were recipients of the government expenditures, the net effect would be a rise in consumption spending (and, therefore, income). Aside from such redistributional considerations, however, equal changes in taxes and expenditures were thought to have no direct effect on the income level.

More recently, however, it has been shown that a balanced budget has income-generating effects even if the marginal propensity to consume is assumed to be the same among payers and receivers of government funds.[9] An increase in tax-financed expenditures will increase the *GNP* by the amount of the additional government spending; similarly, an equal cut in taxes and spending will reduce the *GNP* by the amount government

[9] A. H. Hansen and H. S. Perloff, *State and Local Finance in the National Economy* (New York: W. W. Norton & Co., 1944), pp. 245–246; H. C. Wallich, "Income-generating Effects of a Balanced Budget," *Quarterly Journal of Economics,* LIX (November 1944), pp. 78–91; T. Haavelmo, "Multiplier Effects of a Balanced Budget," *Econometrica,* XIII (October 1945), pp. 311–318; and the comments thereon by G. Harberler, R. M. Goodwin, E. E. Hagen, and T. Haavelmo, *Econometrica,* XIV (April 1946), pp. 148–158; P. A. Samuelson, "Simple Mathematics of Income Determination," in *Income, Employment and Public Policy* (New York: W. W. Norton & Company, 1949), pp. 140–143.

expenditures are reduced.[10] Because the taxpayers and recipients of government expenditures are assumed to spend equal proportions of their marginal incomes on consumption goods, a parallel change in taxes and expenditures (in either direction) can have no effect on the level of private spending—reduced consumption spending by one group will be offset by the increased consumption spending of the other. With no change in expenditures in the private sector of the economy, it follows that a net change in *GNP* equal to the change in government expenditures (and taxes) must occur. The change in *GNP* will reflect a change in output and employment when the economy is operating at less than full employment, and a change in the level of prices when an inflationary gap exists.

The process through which equal changes in taxes and expenditures result in an income change of the same amount can be demonstrated with a simple numerical example. Assume that the marginal propensity to consume is two thirds at all income levels, and that a tax-financed increase in government expenditures of $15 billion is planned. When this plan is put into effect three consequences can be expected:

1. Direct expenditures by government are increased by $15 billion.
2. Tax collections of $15 billion induce a fall in consumption equal to two thirds of this amount, or $10 billion.
3. New government expenditures of $15 billion induce a rise in consumption of two thirds of this amount, or $10 billion.

With the $10-billion tax-induced fall in consumption canceling out the $10-billion expenditure-induced rise in consumption, the net effect of the increased tax and expenditure program is an income rise of $15 billion.[11] A $15-billion cut in taxes and expenditures would have the same effect in reverse: the $10-billion increase in consumption induced by the tax cut would be canceled out by the $10-billion fall in consumption induced by the expenditure reduction; therefore, income would drop by $15 billion, the amount of the budget cut.

It can be readily shown that the change in income will be equal to the amount of the change in taxes and expenditures regardless of the

---

[10] To simplify the analysis at this point it is assumed that a change in taxes and government expenditures does not induce a change in private investment spending. As an approximation, it is assumed here that the tax and expenditure effects on private-investment outlays just offset one another. The possibility that this is not the case, of course, must be taken into account before any discussion can be complete.

[11] The same conclusion is reached through application of the multiplier concept. As explained in Chapter 21, footnote 16, the multiplier in this case is three. Increased expenditures of $15 billion are offset by a tax-induced fall in consumption of $10 billion, so that, on balance, net expenditures rise by $5 billion. Applying the multiplier to this figure gives a $15-billion rise in income.

numerical size of the marginal propensity to consume. With a marginal propensity to consume of one half, for example, a $15 billion increase in taxes and expenditures will result in a tax-induced fall in consumption of $7.5 billion and an offsetting $7.5-billion expenditure-induced rise in consumption. The net effect, as when the marginal propensity to consume was assumed to be two thirds, is a $15 billion income rise.

It should be noted, however, that this comparison takes no account of the fact that income generation is not an instantaneous process. Some time is needed for money to be collected and respent, whether the party involved is the government, a business firm, or a wage earner. It is this process of tax collection, government spending, and successive rounds of respending by the public on consumer goods that results in the ultimate rise in income by the full amount of the initial government outlay. This cumulative process proceeds at a faster rate when the marginal propensity to consume is low than when it is high. This is because the initial net increase in spending (the government's outlay less the tax-induced fall in consumption spending) is greater with a low marginal propensity to consume than with a high one: in our example, $7.5 billion and $5 billion with marginal propensities to consume of one half and two thirds, respectively. While a $15-billion rise in income will eventually occur regardless of the size of the marginal propensity to consume, it will take fewer successive rounds of spending to reach that level in the first case than in the second.[12]

Application in a Deflationary Situation. Given the conditions assumed for the foregoing analysis (for example, a stable marginal propensity to consume and no induced-investment change), use of a balanced-budget technique to offset deflationary pressures would be a relatively simple matter. As demonstrated previously, a balanced increase in expenditures and taxes would add to gross national product the amount of the new expenditures. The size of the tax-financed increase in government spending needed to raise *GNP* to the full-employment level, therefore, would be simply the difference between the present deflated level of *GNP* and the level that would produce full employment.

However, an examination of the assumptions underlying the balanced-budget hypothesis indicates that this simple and direct relationship is subject to a number of qualifications.[13] The major conditions that must be fulfilled for the balanced-budget multiplier to be unity (that is, for an

---

[12] See the section of Chapter 21 entitled "Operation of the Multiplier and Acceleration Principles" for a more detailed description of the process of income generation over time.

[13] W. J. Baumol and M. H. Peston, "More on the Multiplier Effects of a Balanced Budget," *American Economic Review,* XLV: 1 (March 1955), pp. 140–148; also, the *Comment* by Alvin H. Hansen and *Reply* by Baumol and Peston, *ibid.,* XLVI: 1 (March 1956), pp. 157–162.

increase in tax-financed expenditures to raise *GNP* by an equal amount) are briefly discussed below.

1. The increase in government expenditures must involve the purchase of currently produced domestic goods and services. Transfer payments merely redistribute income; they do not constitute an income-creating increase in effective demand for the nation's output. The latter comment also applies to the purchase of existing assets (for example, land for a road construction program) and foreign imports.

2. The taxpayers and expenditure recipients must have, on balance, the same marginal propensity to consume. Even if this is a reasonable assumption in the case of individuals, it loses validity if a substantial share of the tax burden is imposed on corporations.

3. There must be no change in the level of private investment resulting from the increase in taxes and expenditures. Tax increases, however, may induce a cut in investment because they reduce the profit expectations of businessmen; on the other hand, additional investment may result if businessmen have confidence that the government's expansionary program will increase effective demand.

It seems reasonable to conclude that the size of the balanced-budget multiplier is likely to vary over time in response to changes in these basic conditions. While it is likely to approximate unity a good share of the time, there is no assurance that a given increase in taxes and expenditures will bring forth an equal rise in the income level. A more normal expectation would be for income to rise by a somewhat lesser or greater amount.

Application in an Inflationary Situation.   From the standpoint of inflation control, the balanced-budget analysis is applicable in that a reduction in the size of the government's tax-financed expenditures reduces effective demand, and therefore inflationary pressure, by an amount equal to the budget cut.[14] Deserving of even greater emphasis, however, is the fact that once full employment has been reached an increase in tax-balanced expenditures is likely to have a multiplier effect substantially in excess of unity.

When the economy is experiencing widespread unemployment, increased spending may cause some rise in prices, but the primary effect is an expansion of output and employment. Under conditions of full employment, however, an increase in government spending (made necessary, perhaps, by a war or cold-war emergency) can only result in a bidding up of prices; with no unused productive capacity available, the only way the government can obtain the additional goods and services it requires is by diverting resources away from private employment.

Under these circumstances, the initial effect of an increase in gov-

---

[14] This is subject to the same qualifications discussed in the preceding section of this chapter.

ernment expenditures and taxes is to cause a corresponding increase in the level of prices. However, the inflationary process does not end here; with a fall in their real income (due to the price rise) consumers, in attempting to maintain their standard of living, spend a larger share of their earnings on consumption goods. In other words, the attempt to divert resources away from consumption to government is met by consumer resistance in the form of an upward shift in the consumption function. The resulting rise in aggregate demand, and therefore the level of prices, causes a further upward shift in consumption, which causes, in turn, a further price rise. Demands by labor for wage increases commensurate with the decline in its purchasing power will add additional fuel to the inflationary spiral thus generated.[15]

To offset the inflationary effects of increased government spending in times of full employment, therefore, tax increases substantially greater than an amount sufficient to balance the budget are required. The excess of taxes over expenditures must be large enough to cause a reduction in consumption equal to the rise in government spending. How large the excess must be will depend on the size of the marginal propensity to consume. Thus, if the marginal propensity to consume is one half, a $10-billion rise in government expenditures would require a $20-billion increase in taxes; $20 billion in taxes would reduce consumption by one half that amount, or $10 billion. With a marginal propensity to consume of two thirds, it would take a tax increase of only $15 billion to reduce consumption by the required $10 billion. It should be noted, however, that this will be the case only if additional taxes are imposed before an inflationary spiral develops. Otherwise a tax increase sufficient to offset the effects of an upward shift in the consumption function, as well as the increase in government spending, would be required.[16]

UNBALANCED BUDGET

Of the three basic fiscal policies available to government, the one just discussed is the only one which adheres to a balanced-budget philosophy. With the other two the budget is deliberately unbalanced. In the first case, expenditures are held constant while taxes are raised in response to inflationary pressures and lowered when deflation is the problem. The in-

---

[15] Franz Gehrels, "Inflationary Effects of a Balanced Budget under Full Employment," *American Economic Review*, 39: 6 (December 1949), pp. 1276–1278; R. N. McKean, "The Keynesian Framework and Money Income," *ibid.*, 40: 4 (September 1952), pp. 620–622; George A. Bishop, "A Note on the Overinvestment Theory of the Cycle and Its Relation to the Keynesian Theory of Income," *ibid.*, 41: 1 (March 1951), pp. 149–160.

[16] An alternative possibility of reducing consumption by tightening the money supply will be discussed in the section dealing with monetary policy.

dicated change in the level of tax collections may be brought about by varying tax rates or as a result of "built-in flexibility" in the tax structure. In the second case, the relationship between taxes and expenditures is reversed: taxes are held constant while spending is increased during deflationary periods and reduced when inflationary conditions prevail.

These two models represent, of course, pure cases which are presented in this form for purposes of clarity in depicting certain fundamental relationships. There is no reason why, in a deflationary situation, taxes could not be reduced at the same time that expenditures are expanded, or why, in the inflationary case, taxes could not be increased at the same time as expenditures are cut. Our only purpose in discussing the two cases separately is to emphasize their somewhat different policy implications.

Tax Change. As noted previously, varying the level of tax collections effects a change in the public's disposable income which, in turn, induces a parallel change (of lesser magnitude) in private-consumption expenditures. The effectiveness of a tax change of any given amount in changing the level of consumer spending depends, of course, on the size of the marginal propensity to consume. The higher the marginal propensity to consume, the lower will be the tax change needed to induce any desired change in consumer spending. By the same token, the higher the marginal propensity to consume the greater is the multiplier effect and, therefore, the lower will be the increase in consumption spending needed to generate an income change of any given amount. These relationships are illustrated in the accompanying table. In all three examples a $30 billion change in income is assumed to be the fiscal policy objective.[17] In the first case (the first line of the table), with a marginal propensity to

Tax Change Needed to Effect a Desired Change in the Level of Income

Income change desired	Marginal propensity to consume	Multiplier	Required change in consumption	Required tax change
$30 billion	one half	two	$15.0 billion	$30 billion
$30 billion	two thirds	three	$10.0 billion	$15 billion
$30 billion	three fourths	four	$ 7.5 billion	$10 billion

consume of one half and a multiplier of two, a $30-billion tax change is required to induce the $15-billion change in consumption needed to generate a $30-billion change in the income level. This is twice as great a tax change as the $15 billion required in the second example which is

---

[17] Either an increase, if deflation is the problem, or a decrease in the face of inflationary pressures. The same analysis applies to both cases.

based on the assumption of a marginal propensity to consume of two thirds and a multiplier of three. Finally, the third example demonstrates that a $30-billion income change can be achieved with a tax change of only $10 billion (which induces a $7.5-billion change in consumption), given a marginal propensity to consume of three fourths and a corresponding multiplier of four.

This tax-variation fiscal policy technique has strong support from those who fear that increased government spending during periods of depression—whether financed by taxes or debt—would too greatly enlarge government activity in the economic sphere. Politically, support for this point of view comes from the Left as well as the Right, while it is regarded very critically by the so-called New Deal school of economists. A group of economists, and particularly A. P. Lerner,[18] considers it the government's first duty to ensure an end to poverty through full utilization of all resources while at the same time interfering as little as possible with competitive markets and the price mechanism. As an anti-depression policy, therefore, they advocate tax reduction rather than public works which, they fear, may discourage competitive business. However, they leave it within the discretion of the government to lower, or raise, tax *rates* to whatever extent compensatory budget policy may require.

Considerable doubt has been expressed, however, concerning the likelihood that Congress would react quickly enough in adjusting rates to meet changing economic conditions. It is also feared that there would be great difficulty in getting Congress to increase tax rates sufficiently to offset serious inflationary pressures, or to reduce rates in periods of deflation without a parallel cut in expenditures. As a partial solution to these problems it has been proposed that Congress delegate a degree of tax-making power to administrative officials (as has been done in tariff making). However, it may be taken for granted that Congress will cling to its powers in this area with much jealousy, especially since Congress and the administration are frequently committed to widely different views regarding compensatory taxation and the proper level of different taxes.

Built-in Flexibility. The size of tax revenues may not only be altered through rate changes, but also indirectly through fluctuations of income (the tax base) itself. With high progressivity in rates, tax revenues will change proportionately more than the national income. Great reliance is placed on this relationship by the Committee for Economic Development. This school of thought takes another step toward restricting governmental action in fiscal matters: it proposes to "set tax rates to

[18] A. P. Lerner, *The Economics of Control* (New York: The Macmillan Company, 1944), chaps. 1 and 24; also his "Integrated Full Employment Policy," *International Postwar Problems*, January 1946.

balance the budget and provide a surplus for debt retirement at an agreed high level of employment and national income. Having set these rates, leave them alone unless there is some major change in national policy or condition of national life." [19] This program is generally referred to as "built-in flexibility"; that is, the greater the built-in flexibility, the greater will be the countercyclical fluctuations of revenues as income falls or rises. This automaticity produces a budget deficit as income falls, and a surplus as income rises. It has been estimated that for the present federal tax system the ratio of a percentage change in tax yield to a given percentage change in income is about 1.5.[20]

A simple example will serve to illustrate this. Assume an economy whose tax structure is progressive and whose national income is $100 billion. Tax revenues at that income are $20 billion. In the next period income rises to $120 billion (a 20-percent increase) and tax collections to $26 billion (a 30-percent increase). The income elasticity of the tax yield at that income would then be 30/20, or 1.5. Let us assume further that this nation's annual expenditures amount to $20 billion. With the assumed tax structure and a national income of $100 billion the budget would be balanced. At a national income of $80 billion, there would automatically be a $6 billion deficit; at $120 billion, a $6 billion surplus.

Income	*Taxes*	*Taxes as per-cent of income*	*Expenditures*	*Deficit or surplus*
80	14	17.5	20	−6
100	20	20.0	20	0
120	26	21.7	20	+6

The proponents of this program claim somewhat optimistically that it will "promote stability, government economy and debt reduction." Due to the automaticity of this method, no forecasting of business fluctuations will be required, and it avoids the political problems usually involved in a rate change. A further point in its favor is the avoidance of taxing persons with equal incomes in different years at changing rates. It may well

---

[19] Committee for Economic Development, *Taxes and the Budget* (New York: November 1947), p. 22; also Herbert Stein, "Stability and Flexibility in Federal Tax Policy," *National Tax Association Conference Proceedings,* 1946, pp. 260–265.

[20] R. A. Musgrave and M. H. Miller, "Built-in Flexibility," *American Economic Review, XXXVIII* (March 1948), p. 126. This study also considers the effects of transfer payments, such as social security, in arriving at an index for built-in flexibility of 1.5. The social security system accumulates funds at high levels of income when tax receipts exceed benefits, and it decumulates at low levels of income when the reverse will happen. The agricultural price-support program also automatically expands and contracts on the expenditures side as farm prices rise and fall.

be that in the Committee for Economic Development program the canon of equity is given preference over that of economy.

Spending Change. In this case, instead of varying tax rates or yields while holding expenditures constant, the process is reversed: government outlay is increased in deflationary periods and reduced in times of inflation, while the level of taxes remains unchanged. As a compensatory program this method has certain distinct advantages over the balanced-budget and tax-variation fiscal policy techniques: (1) the multiplier effect for a given magnitude of budgetary change is stronger than that for either of the other two approaches; (2) a smaller deficit in depression and surplus during periods of inflation is required with this method than when business fluctuations are countered by varying the level of tax collections; and (3) the size of the government outlay required to generate a given amount of income change is smaller in this case than when the balanced-budget method is employed.

A simple example will verify the above observations. Assume that the marginal propensity to consume is two thirds (giving a multiplier of three), and the problem is to change national income by $30 billion. The process through which the desired income change is generated by the three methods is summarized in the accompanying table which, inciden-

Comparison of the Three Methods of Compensating for Income Fluctuations

	Tax and expenditure change	*Tax change, no expenditure change*	*Expenditure change, no tax change*
Tax change	$30 billion	$15 billion	——
Expenditure change	$30 billion	——	$10 billion
Consumption change (tax-change induced)	$20 billion	$10 billion	——
Net expenditure change	$10 billion	$10 billion	$10 billion
Income change	$30 billion	$30 billion	$30 billion

tally, is designed to apply to either an inflationary or deflationary situation. Thinking in terms of the latter, in the first case a tax-financed increase in government outlay of $30 billion is required to achieve a net-expenditure increase of $10 billion (the amount needed, with a multiplier of three, to raise income $30 billion); this is because an offsetting $20-billion drop in consumer spending is induced by the tax increase. In the second case a deficit of $15 billion, resulting from a tax reduction of that amount, is required in order to induce a $10-billion rise in consumption. In the third case, a deficit of $10 billion is incurred through a direct increase of that amount in government expenditures.

For the first and third cases, it is implicitly assumed that the increased expenditures are for currently produced goods and services. If, instead, the expenditures are in the form of transfer payments, the income effects will differ from those indicated in the table by the amount of the initial outlay. This is because transfer payments do not enter the income stream directly; as in the case of a tax reduction, they enter on the second round, inducing a rise in consumption by adding to the disposable income of the transfer recipients. Thus, with a marginal propensity to consume of two thirds, the $30-billion increase in government outlay in the first case will induce a consumption rise of $20 billion. As this is just equal to the $20-billion cut in consumer spending induced by the tax increase, there will be no change in net expenditures and, therefore, no increase in the income level. In the third case, the $10-billion additional outlay will result in a $6.33-billion increase in consumption; applying the multiplier of three, the income rise will be $20 billion rather than the $30 billion indicated in the table. As long as expenditures are confined to transfer payments, no amount of increased spending will add to income in the balanced-budget case; at every level the expenditure-induced rise in consumption will be offset by the tax-induced drop in consumer spending. In the third case, however, a net increase in expenditures of $10 billion and, therefore, an income rise of $30 billion, will result if the initial amount of deficit spending is increased from $10 billion to $15 billion. In that event, it will be noted, the deficit is the same as in the second case where the tax reduction method is employed.

Both the tax-variation and spending-change fiscal-policy methods require deficit financing in deflationary periods and surplus financing when conditions are inflationary. In the deflationary case, the government has the option of borrowing from federal reserve banks, commercial banks, or the public. These alternatives (including the additional possibility of printing money) will be discussed in more detail in Chapter 27; here it will be noted that the most expansionary loan policy is borrowing from federal reserve banks. This is because the latter have, for all practical purposes, unlimited lending powers. If commercial banks are short of excess reserves, or if individuals must draw on active rather than idle balances for the purchase of government bonds, then loans raised from these sources will restrict private spending, and thus partially offset the effects of the government's spending program. However, because unused individual bank balances and excess reserves (since 1930) are typical depression phenomena, the possibility of this occurring to any significant degree appears quite unlikely.

In the inflationary case, the problem is to prevent the surplus from returning to the income stream. One possible means of accomplishing this would be to simply hold the money idle in the Treasury's federal reserve bank accounts. But this would be wasteful of interest costs and objectionable for other reasons. More likely the government will use its surplus to retire debt. If it retires bank-held debt, however, this will replenish bank reserves and make possible further lending by banks. If it retires nonbank debt, individuals and corporations will have more money to invest or spend on consumption goods without borrowing. The safest alternative would be to retire debt held by the federal reserve banks which presumably, in view of the inflationary situation and their monetary powers, will in effect sterilize the surplus.

APPRAISAL OF FISCAL POLICY TECHNIQUES

The choice of any one method, or its predominance, will depend to a great extent on the prevailing type of tax structure and expenditure pattern as well as on political preferences. The uncertain effects on investment of all three fiscal policy techniques must also be taken into account.

Balanced Budget. For those whose primary concern is the avoidance of substantial increases in the public debt during extended deflationary periods, the balanced-budget approach may seem most desirable. But in order to pull the economy out of a slump, the increases in taxes and expenditures may have to be of a startling magnitude. The large increase in tax rates would tend to have a discouraging effect on investment; the large expenditure programs necessary may actively compete with business growth. Thus, if the deficiency is substantial, a balanced increase in expenditures and tax yields may require so large a budget as to be of little practical value.

As an anti-inflationary policy, the balanced-budget approach would seem to be most appropriate in cases where inflationary pressures are relatively mild. When strong measures are called for, effective policy would require a very substantial cut in expenditures and taxes. Even in this era of high government budgets, it would not usually be feasible to cut drastically governmental functions (including national defense, which absorbs a major share of government expenditures) on solely fiscal policy grounds.

Tax Change. To those who are primarily opposed to an expansion of government, the balanced-budget route to compensatory fiscal policy must seem the least conservative and most radical. To the advocates of competitive enterprise, the tax-variation, unbalanced-budget approach will be the most desirable, since it will least interfere with the areas of private business and the decisions of private citizens. But in times of depression this route will also incur the greatest government debt. The effect on investment of a rise in the public debt will depend upon businessmen's attitudes toward deficits. However, the lowering of tax rates and the income rise generated by increased consumption may well more than offset any adverse effects due to rising debt. Depending on the degree of deflation, the tax reduction may take a variety of forms. During a deep business slump, the stimulating effect of a reduction of progressive income taxes may be very small. Instead of inducing an increase in consumption expenditures, the recipients of the tax cut may choose to merely increase their cash balances. A cut in excise taxes, which fall on consumption rather than saving, may be far more effective. The deficit required this way may be far less than that required for a reduction of income taxes. The important criterion is how much less would flow into savings by this route.

During inflationary periods an increase in taxes (along with restrictive monetary policy, which is discussed below) is likely to be a far more effective deterrent to private spending, both for consumption and investment goods, than parallel cuts in taxes and government outlays. Furthermore, because of the aforementioned difficulty in finding substantial areas of government expenditure which can be reduced in response to the requirements of fiscal policy, a tax-increase policy for combating inflation appears more promising than the reduced-spending approach. On the other hand, the practical difficulty of convincing Congress to increase tax rates for the purpose of creating a budgetary surplus should not be overlooked.

Built-in Flexibility. The CED type of tax reduction, based on "built-in" rather than rate flexibility, epitomizes the fear of an extension of government action not only with respect to expenditures but also as to variations in the composition, and rates, of the tax system. In order to be automatically compensatory, the tax system must possess a high sensitivity of yield in response to changes in income—that is, have a high income elasticity. Its success furthermore depends on a high level of taxation since the absolute amounts involved will otherwise be too small to have the desired effect.

Thus, with federal taxation at 20 percent of all income and an estimated income elasticity of tax yield of 1.5, about a third of the fluctuation of income due to a change in investment would be offset by built-in flexibility.[21] To improve the effectiveness of this method, it would obviously be necessary to raise the income elasticity of the tax yield. This would require an increase in the proportion of taxes derived from the

---

[21] Musgrave and Miller, *loc. cit.,* p. 127.

most "volatile" components of income (such as corporate profits, capital gains, and upper bracket incomes) as well as high personal exemptions. Furthermore, the use of any income-averaging devices would not be advisable from the standpoint of flexibility.[22] Likewise, a shift for reasons of greater equality from personal income to gift and estate taxes would have a similar effect.

Recent trends have pointed in the opposite direction. Postwar tax reformers have been mainly concerned with removing tax impediments to the incentive to invest. Modification of the corporate tax would reduce the income elasticity of the tax system, although the elimination of double taxation by the introduction of a dividends-paid credit, rather than an over-all corporate tax reduction, would greatly lessen this effect. This is due to the greater stability of dividend payments in comparison with total profits.[23]

To those who feel that violent fluctuations due to intermittent surges of investment activity are inherent in a modern system of private-competitive enterprise, such stabilizers as the automatic movement of tax yields and stable expenditures will "prove to be hopelessly ineffective." [24] Many critics doubt the underlying assumption of the built-in flexibility program that there is an automatic mechanism that assures that the *level* of oscillations in income will be one of high employment. It is held that even in boom years the system, if left alone, may never reach full employment. This is essentially the mature-economy thesis which argues that total income and expenditures may well be in equilibrium at less than full employment for prolonged periods of time in an economy which relies on the price system alone. It advocates reliance on a vigorous fiscal policy (changing the size of the budget) in dealing with shocklike changes in the rate of autonomous investment.

It seems improbable that automatically induced changes in spending can offset the major portion of a cumulative decline "from boom to bust." Such automaticity may be stabilizing as far as it goes, but whenever it cushions a decline, it also retards recovery by virtue of the same stabilizing mechanism. However, criticism of built-in flexibility as the sole balancing factor in the economy need not imply an objection to it as *a* balancing factor. Certainly it is better to maintain tax rates over a period of fluctuation than to raise them during deflation and lower them

---

[22] A distinction must be made in this connection between carryover and carryback. The carryover would defeat the purposes of countercycle control; the carryback, on the contrary, would amount to a tax refund in poor times of income which was withheld in times of prosperity. However, the latter may be less desirable on other grounds.

[23] Musgrave and Miller, *loc. cit.,* p. 128.

[24] Alvin H. Hansen, *Monetary Theory and Fiscal Policy* (New York: McGraw-Hill Book Company, 1949), pp. 176–180.

during inflation. Quite possibly the maintenance of rates represents the maximum of compensatory policy in *taxation that is politically feasible*. But this is not to say that a more effective compensatory program could not be achieved by using both taxation and expenditure as controls.

Spending Change. In deflationary periods, the deficit-spending route (that is, increased expenditures with no change in tax collections) attempts to achieve the best than can be attained with a given deficit by using it on planned public expenditures. This is in contrast to the induced deficit of the tax-reduction route. The impact on private investment of an increase in debt may again be doubtful. But the increase in employment and real income resulting from the public outlays may well encourage new investment. Care, however, must be taken that government outlays do not compete with, but complement, the markets for private output. A large variety of projects such as slum clearance, river-valley development, low-cost housing, education, road building, etc., may be considered in this connection. But their adaptability to cyclical variations has often been doubted. Difficulties include the problem of timing, the wastes caused by intermittent construction according to the state of the business cycle, and the fact that projects which are socially desirable should be carried out according to technical rather than cyclical considerations. It is thus often suggested [25] that projects, as for instance those on a regional level, be conducted as long-range programs to raise the general level of economic activity, for the mere existence of such projects may mitigate the violence of fluctuations and act as a stabilizer. Until recently, developments have indeed tended in that direction. During the depression the emphasis was on public works which were largely offset by the inactivity of state and local governments. After World War II attention was mainly directed at tax reduction to sustain a high level of economic activity. But the trend continued toward long-range projects such as public housing, urban redevelopment, and foreign aid programs.

The same problem confronts policy makers in regard to cutting expenditures in the face of inflationary pressures. To the extent that such a program is feasible, the creation of a budgetary surplus by reducing public expenditures would probably be a more powerful anti-inflationary weapon than either of the other two fiscal policy routes. However, the difficulties involved in adapting public-works spending programs to fluctuations in the income level lessens the likelihood that chief reliance can be placed on this means of combating inflationary pressures.

Conclusion. In conclusion it should be pointed out that while few would doubt the essential logic of the above propositions, the aggregative point of view becomes frequently guilty of serious omissions. Businesses and households do not always react along functional lines, and the eco-

---

[25] Hicks, *Public Finance*, pp. 335–336.

nomic system is not like two quart jars into which one pours economic substances until the levels are equal, and then all is well.

The view that tends to go farthest in the direction of aggregative taxation is the functional-finance approach. Its proponents hold, in essence, that "the purpose of taxation is never to raise money but to leave less in the hands of the taxpayer." [26] This, to say the least, raises many doubts as to whether the institutional aspects of taxation can be so far subordinated to the compensatory interest. For instance, what becomes of fairness and neutrality if the individual who might receive a million dollars in income during a depression escapes taxes entirely while another who "makes his pile" during prosperity is taxed to the hilt? An equitable tax system in and of itself is not to be underrated as a stimulus of economic progress in the long run.

On the expenditures side, some psychological propensities also play an important role in cyclical fluctuations. The foregoing analysis has assumed that private investment remains constant throughout the various manipulations of governmental budgets. But in a deflationary situation, effects upon private investment may be the essence of the problem. Deficit spending can add nothing to total spending if it affects business confidence so adversely that each dollar spent by the government is offset by the expenditure of a dollar less on the part of private business. Deficit expenditures on regenerative and useful public works might be "sold" to the businessman as a modified application of investment principles with which he is familiar. Business itself, of course, does not hesitate to unbalance its budget when future prospects appear to warrant expansion by borrowing. Public outlays that claim no self-liquidating character, on the other hand, might prove the occasion for more "jitters" and defeatism. One of the strong reasons for enlarging the sphere of public enterprise in the public-utility and natural-resource areas is that it would afford the public a wider field for compensatory investment.

During an inflationary period heavy reliance on taxation as a major fiscal device is limited by conflicting needs. On the one hand, the situation calls for restricted spending (consumption and investment, though the latter with some reservations) and also increased production. The trick is to discourage spending and not discourage production. But if a very high level of taxation is required to curb an excessive demand, the inflationary pressure may be strengthened rather than repressed because unusually high tax rates may curtail the incentive to produce and the expansion in productive equipment that will add to current output. This argument applies with at least equal force to monetary policy, the other major instrument of inflation control (to be discussed in the following

---

[26] See Abba P. Lerner, *The Economics of Control* (New York: The Macmillan Company, 1944), pp. 307–308.

section). A restrictive monetary policy is more likely to be effective in reducing expenditures on investment than on consumption goods.

Despite these limitations, however, the author is of the opinion that fiscal policy merits a major role in combating inflation and deflation. With the federal budget running to between a fifth and a sixth of the gross national product, its potentialities for a compensatory role are too important to be ignored. In the last twenty years, businessmen have come a long way toward full appreciation of this fact and are less likely than formerly to defeat such role by perverse reaction to it. More questions might be raised about the efficacy of fiscal policy to halt an inflation that stems from monopolistic powers (labor and business) to exert upward pressure on prices. It is not fully established that this "cost-push" cause of inflation is a serious long-run factor; anyway the sovereign remedy for coping with it has yet to be devised. Whatever this remedy may be, it will require appropriate fiscal policy as a collateral tool.

MONETARY POLICY

Prior to the 1930s stabilization of income and prices was thought to be a problem for monetary policy. With the development of modern income theory and statistics and the growth of governmental budgets, however, attention became focused on compensatory fiscal policy. The apparent ineffectiveness of monetary policy in preventing the economic collapse of 1929 or in initiating a revival in the 1930s contributed to this shift in opinion. Today most economists would agree, even though they differ as to which should play the dominant role, that an optimum approach to combating income fluctuations involves the use of both monetary and fiscal measures.

THE QUANTITY OF MONEY

Monetary policy is based on the hypothesis that there is a direct correlation between the quantity of money and aggregate spending: that changes in the money supply induce parallel changes in expenditures. The theory assumes that the public desires to hold in cash balances (currency and demand deposits) a relatively stable proportion of its income. An increase in the quantity of money increases this cash-balance ratio and, therefore, induces additional spending until income rises sufficiently to accommodate the increased money supply.[27] Conversely, a decline in the

---

[27] It should be understood that the public does not determine the quantity of money held; because the entire money supply is held by someone, the size of

money supply reduces this ratio below the desired level, resulting in a corresponding reduction in the level of expenditures.

According to the "crude"-quantity theory a change in the money supply reacts directly on spending. The more sophisticated version holds that the effect is achieved indirectly; that when the money supply is increased the public attempts to rid itself of its excess cash by using it to buy securities. This results in the bidding up of security prices with a consequent fall in the rate of interest. The interest rate reduction, in turn, induces increased investment spending which, through the multiplier effect, increases consumption and the level of income. This process continues until the desired relationship between cash balances and income is restored. By the same token, a decrease in the quantity of money results in a bidding down of security prices, a corresponding increase in the interest rate, and a reduction in the level of investment, consumption, and income.

INSTRUMENTS OF CREDIT CONTROL

The Federal Reserve System can regulate the supply of money through its power to control the reserve position of the commercial banking system.[28] It has three major credit-control instruments to accomplish this end: open market operations, changing reserve requirements, and varying the rediscount rate. In its open market operations, the System buys and sells government bonds on the open market. When it sells it restricts credit. The bond buyers write checks against their commercial banks in favor of the selling Federal Reserve banks. These checks, when they are cleared, reduce the reserves, and therefore the lending power, of the commercial banks involved. On the other hand, the open market purchase of government bonds by the Federal Reserve System makes possible an expansion of credit. In this case, checks drawn on the Reserve Bank buyers and paid to the sellers are deposited in commercial banks by the latter. When these checks are cleared, they serve to replenish the reserves of the commercial banks involved, thus increasing their lending power.[29]

Changing reserve requirements is a more direct means of controlling

---

total cash balances is at all times equal to the quantity of money. When the money supply changes, therefore, a constant ratio between cash balances and income can be maintained only if there is a proportionate change in the public's level of expenditures.

[28] Its control is considerably greater over the reserve position of member than of non-member banks. However, while about half of all commercial banks are nonmembers, a predominant share of the total volume of the nation's banking business is done by member banks.

[29] This account of the mechanics involved in open-market operations is necessarily brief. A detailed explanation can be found in any elementary principles of economics or money and banking textbook.

credit. With required reserves at 20 percent, for example, for every dollar it has in reserves, the commercial banking system can have approximately five dollars in outstanding demand deposits. Assuming that the commercial banks have a negligible amount of excess reserves (as is likely to be the case in an inflationary situation), increasing reserve requirements to 25 percent would force a 20-percent contraction in commercial-bank credit—from five dollars to four dollars in our example. A reduction of reserve requirements to, say, 10 percent, on the other hand, would double the money-creation potential of the commercial-banking system.

Some effect on the reserve position of commercial banks is also achieved by varying rediscount rates (that is, the interest rate charged commercial banks when they borrow from Federal Reserve Banks to replenish their reserves). When the rediscount rate is lowered, commercial banks find it less costly to improve their reserve position through borrowing. Raising the rate has, of course, just the opposite effect.

EFFECTS OF MONETARY POLICY

Most economists agree that monetary policy is less likely to be effective in pulling the economy out of a slump than in curbing inflationary pressures. As depression economics, the quantity theory has certain obvious deficiencies. In times of depression commercial banks follow very conservative business practices; they are far less likely to renew old loans or extend new ones than they are in more prosperous times. Consequently, while the money supply is contracted as loans are repaid, the banks usually have ample excess reserves available. Under these circumstances, Federal Reserve measures to expand the money supply will simply add to an already ample lending potential. Moreover, while such a policy may cause a reduction in the rate of interest, it offers no assurance that investors will be induced to increase their borrowing. It may well be that the profit expectations of businessmen are at such a low ebb that even a zero rate of interest would be an insufficient inducement.

This line of reasoning suggests that increasing government expenditures in times of depression will be required if rising employment and output have high priority as objectives of governmental policy. Maintaining an ample supply of money and low interest rates under these circumstances appears to be a necessary but not a sufficient condition of economic revival.

During inflationary periods, there is much to recommend a restrictive monetary policy. The continuation of inflationary pressures depends on either (or both) of two conditions: (1) an expansion in the money supply through commercial-bank loans for the financing of investment and consumption purchases; and (2) a decline in the proportion of income that the public desires to hold in the form of cash balances. While monetary authorities have no direct control over the second condition, they have ample power to reduce commercial-bank reserves, and thereby reduce the availability of investor and consumer credit. If they desire to carry these restrictive measures far enough, they can reduce the money supply by an amount sufficient to offset any conceivable rise in the velocity of circulation (that is, reduction in the desire to hold cash balances).

The degree to which such a policy would have to be carried to stop an inflationary spiral depends on the effect of a rise in the interest rate in deterring borrowing by consumers and investors and in stimulating increased saving. While little is known in this regard about consumer borrowing, most empirical studies have concluded that it would require very substantial rate increases to influence substantially investment spending. This means, in effect, that during inflationary periods profit expectations are considerably in excess of interest costs. Furthermore, while a moderate rise in interest rates would no doubt bring forth some additional saving, it is doubtful that the increase would be in significant amounts unless, again, the rise was very substantial.

One may conclude, therefore, that a restriction on the availability of credit sufficient to curb persistent inflationary pressures may be accompanied by a very substantial rise in the level of interest rates. A "tight money" policy carried to this extent would have serious secondary effects. Among these would be a rise in the cost of servicing the national debt, increased difficulty for school districts and other municipalities in providing needed public facilities, and added difficulties for the small businessman who, unlike the great corporation, is unable to finance expansion out of interest-free retained earnings. It is because of these secondary effects that many economists advocate that chief reliance be placed on fiscal policy in combating inflation, with monetary policy playing a positive, but mainly reinforcing, role.

FISCAL POLICY AND ECONOMIC GROWTH

While the matter is not beyond controversy, most economists hold it important for the economy to grow at a substantial rate and look to fiscal policy to contribute toward achieving this objective. They regard growth as important to relieve much of the still prevailing and widespread substandard living even in the United States in the 1960s; to extend greater economic assistance abroad; and to facilitate improvement in the public services, which in many areas leave much to be desired. A society that saves substantially must grow in order to avoid unemployment and over-capacity.

Growth is a complex phenomenon in which fiscal policy at most is only one element. No doubt one of its more significant factors is innovation, which in turn is related to education and research. Growth would be facilitated by the full utilization of available capital and labor involved in reducing the frequency, duration, and degree of economic recessions. This requires balance in the growth factors. There is still persistent testimony to support the view that a high rate of growth and a high rate of capital formation are practically synonymous, except that the former follows the latter as effect and cause. There can be no doubt that a fast-growing economy requires large amounts of new tangible capital and rapid replacement of obsolete equipment. But it is one thing to hold that the expansion of capital must attend economic growth, another to contend that expansion follows the growth, and still another to contend that the needed capital is not likely to be forthcoming in an economy as rich as ours.

One school of economists associates growth with the volume of savings.[30] It is prone to suggest consumption taxes and a budgetary surplus either to reduce debt or to lend funds directly to capital markets. The second school, stressing consumption, views sales taxes with disfavor and questions whether increased saving alone is enough to cause added investment without overcapacity.

Viewed in terms of the unemployment problem, one group contends that joblessness is largely associated with maladjusted areas and industries and that these will not respond readily to a program that raises over-all demand. The second school holds that adequate over-all demand would greatly facilitate other means of attacking even this specialized unemployment.

TAX BURDEN REDISTRIBUTION

In contrast to variations in the level of expenditures, much attention has also been paid to using taxation as a means of redistributing income and thereby affecting aggregate consumption. Economists who regard secular stagnation as a likely long-term prospect propose that the budget be made

---

[30] See for instance Simon Kuznets, *Capital in the American Economy*, National Bureau of Economic Research (Princeton: Princeton University Press, 1961), and a review of this book, Charles L. Schultze, *American Economic Review*, LII: 4 (September 1962), pp. 814–821.

more "progressive," by increasing the share of taxes drawn from those with high incomes whose marginal propensity to consume is presumed to be relatively low, and directing expenditures to low-income groups who are thought to consume a relatively high proportion of any additional income they receive. On the other hand, secular inflationists would encourage saving by making the budget more "regressive"; they would place heavier reliance on consumption taxes and reduce expenditures designed to foster greater equality in the distribution of income. Since public expenditures are quite often inflexible owing to the nature and needs of government activities, much of the discussion has been centered on the revenue rather than the expenditure side.

In recent years, however, much doubt has been cast on the efficacy of income redistribution as a fiscal policy device.[31] Attempts have been made to calculate changes in total consumption that would result if one were to switch between various tax structures, all of which provide the same yield. The findings generally agree that shifting between a highly regressive (consumption taxes) and a highly progressive tax structure (high surtaxes on income) produces a relatively small change in consumption. The reliability of these findings rests primarily on the available data on the consumption and saving patterns of various income groups. The data shows that whereas the average propensity to consume of a family falls considerably as income rises, its marginal propensity to consume remains fairly stable over the income range.[32] This implies that the amount consumed out of a given addition to income, or the amount of consumption forgone due to an equivalent decrease in income, will not differ greatly between groups of citizens, whether they be wealthy or poor.

It is thus generally concluded that feasible changes in the tax structure are unlikely to offset declines of consumption and investment in deflation, or an excess of consumption in inflation. It must, however, be stressed that in view of our rather insufficient knowledge of consumption

---

[31] See Harold Lubell, "Effect of Income Redistribution on Consumer Expenditures," *American Economic Review*, XXXVII (March 1947), p. 157; A. Bergson, "The Incidence of an Income Tax on Savings," *Quarterly Journal of Economics*, LVI (February 1942), p. 337; R. A. Musgrave and M. S. Painter, "The Impact of Alternative Tax Structures on Personal Consumption and Saving," *Quarterly Journal of Economics* (August 1948), pp. 475–499; and R. A. Musgrave, "Incidence of the Tax Structure and its Effects on Consumption," *Federal Tax Policy for Economic Growth and Stability*, Joint Committee on the Economic Report, 84th Cong., 1st. Sess., 1955, pp. 102–106.

[32] The student will recall that average propensity to consume is the ratio of consumption to income $\left(\dfrac{C}{Y}\right)$; the marginal propensity to consume is the ratio of the change in consumption to a given change in income $\left(\dfrac{\Delta C}{\Delta Y}\right)$.

and saving patterns once the distribution of income has been changed, the above findings are of a tentative, though interesting, nature.[33] Even if income redistribution does effect compensatory changes in consumption spending, there still remains a question as to the type of tax structure that would best serve the ends of fiscal policy. Both the theory of secular inflation and that of secular stagnation remain unproved hypotheses concerning the long-run economic outlook. Until more precise information becomes available in these areas, therefore, compensatory fiscal policy may have to rely on variations in the *level,* rather than the structure, of taxation and/or expenditures.

As has been previously indicated, a progressive tax structure has one undisputed advantage, namely, that it adds to the built-in flexibility of the revenue system. Moreover, if changes in tax patterns affect consumption and saving so little as indicated, it would seem to follow that the traditional objection to progressive taxation—that it unduly impedes saving—can have little weight. The function of saving in terms of stability and in terms of economic growth plus the relationship of the tax system to capital formation all deserve more study.[34]

INCENTIVE TAXATION

It has long been recognized that certain taxes may be used as incentives within a general framework of compensatory finance. Reference to the desirability of maintaining adequate incentives has been made in several chapters of this book. The subject may also be approached from the standpoint of elasticity of supply. Thus land is a strategic object to tax because the supply is relatively inelastic. The death tax is probably less inimical to incentives than the net income tax because the former is usually viewed by the eventual taxpayer as dated in the indefinite future. The carryover of losses in a business income tax is usually accepted as a net gain on the economic side even though it necessitates higher rates on positive income. Tax-exempt securities are suspect because they mean favor to riskless investment and entice into this area investors who should do our risk taking. And so on.

Specific Proposals. In recent times a new interest has appeared in providing a more positive program of tax incentives, a system of rewards and punishments that would regulate economic conduct in the public interest. In an earlier chapter we pointed out that taxes are first cousins to

---

[33] For example, see the discussion of statistical evidence regarding the level and slope of the consumption function in Chapter 25.

[34] See Kuznets, *op. cit.*

fines, and in these proposals there is even closer relationship, running to the point where the two cannot be distinguished. A subsidy, of course, is the opposite of a tax. The two together are thought to provide potentially the traditional whip and lump of sugar that make the donkey go.

Among the more popular of incentive proposals are the following:

1. Investment during a slump might be induced by allowing it in full or in part as a deduction from net income for income tax purposes.

2. Corporations might be required to set aside reserves during good times to become available for investment during slumps; failing such investment (following notice from the government), the funds would go to the federal Treasury by forfeiture. A program of this sort has been the subject of experimentation in Sweden.

3. Instead of rewarding investment, a tax concession might be granted for expanding employment. A scheme of this sort was tried during the depression of the 1930s in Germany, shortly before the regime of Adolf Hitler. This so-called Von Papen Plan did not lead to the desired results, however, and was abandoned after a short trial.[35]

4. Accelerated depreciation, applied during World War II in the United States and other countries, could be used as a stimulus to investment during bad years. The early write-off of capital costs would presumably encourage replacement of worn-out equipment and reduce the hazards of obsolescence.

5. Taxes might be imposed on hoarded money and idle deposits. One version of this calls for a dated currency, requiring the addition of stamps on bills as they are held over successive periods. This would be supplemented by a similar tax on holding coin and idle bank deposits.

Some of these proposals (notably the second and fourth) look promising enough to be worth some experimentation in practice. All of them suffer from the fact that they are likely to be regarded as programs of desperation, and thus they may intensify fear rather than create confidence. We should never forget that the business cycle is to a very considerable extent a psychological phenomenon.

A measure to tax hoardings could probably drive money out of hiding, but it could hardly force such money into a creative role of new enterprise. The money might simply glut the market of the safest existing investments, thus bidding up prices and pushing down yields in this area without important results in terms of employment. Moreover, the program would be very difficult to apply to banks. Undoubtedly, idle bank deposits are the hoarding of individuals rather than banks, but the failure

---

[35] Gerhard Colm, "Why the Papen Plan for Economic Recovery Failed," *Social Research* (February 1934), p. 82.

or inability of banks to loan up to the potential of their reserve is bank hoarding. However, it would probably be regarded as contrary to public policy to force banks to loan when they are restricted as to classes of loans by law and counseled to be prudent in the interest of the safety of deposits. The administrative difficulties in proposals of this sort have been judged formidable by all who have studied them intensively.

The Swedish experiment appears to have worked well and has much to commend it. By offering corporations an incentive to expand in periods of low investment, it reduces the need for compensatory federal public works.

All of the above list of incentive proposals are aimed at depression and unemployment. Another such list can be presented, the aim of which is to curb inflation. For instance, it has been suggested that during inflationary periods, employers be disallowed the privilege of deducting wage increases on income tax returns for one year after such increases have been accepted. The thought is that this would avoid the easy decision to allow wage increases beyond increasing productivity. Such wage increases are now paid with 48-cent dollars (allowing for the federal income tax) and they are passed on without much trouble to the buying public. Labor leaders are likely to press for more concessions than are economically justified partly because their leaders compete with rivals to make a showing in gains for the members. Labor might not find this proposal too unpalatable; it would support its efforts to recapture a larger share of profits.[36]

Another device of a similar character would attempt to exercise a brake on advertising during inflationary periods. This again could be done by limiting the deductibility of advertising expense. Again there is much to be said for this proposal. But would it surmount the political opposition it obviously would induce? [37]

Still other proposals have been a tax on bank loans (and perhaps those of other lending agencies) or a tax on capital goods and materials used for construction. The former would operate much like an increase in interest rates except that the government would get the benefit of higher charges and might find it easier to exempt certain borrowers (such as school districts). The tax on capital goods would extend its deterrent effects to reinvested profits. Decelerated depreciation (the opposite of accelerated) might also be used as an investment deterrent.[38]

---

[36] Sumner H. Slichter, *Creeping Inflation,* a debate with Dr. Henry Luedicke reprinted from the Journal of Commerce, 1957, p. 25.

[37] Max A. Geller, *Advertising at the Crossroads* (New York: The Ronald Press, 1952), pp. 273–275.

[38] Richard Goode, "Special Tax Measures to Restrain Investment," *Staff Papers,* International Monetary Fund, V: 3 (February 1957), pp. 434–448.

SUMMARY

This and the preceding chapter dealt with policy prescriptions designed to adapt the fiscal affairs of government to the requirements of the economy as a whole. The size of the national income is determined by the total volume of production and employment or, alternately, by the amount of money which individuals, business firms, and government spend for currently produced goods and services. Expenditure may be either for consumption goods or investment goods: that for consumption goods (with exceptions) tends to be related to and caused by income levels and changes; that for investment, to be autonomous but to cause income changes. While investment and saving gravitate to equality in the income-determining process, planned saving and planned investment are more or less independent variables and diverge to create inflationary and deflationary gaps. In any economy there is a unique consumption-plus-investment schedule consistent with full-employment equilibrium; however, equilibrium at less or more than full employment is also thought to be possible; in this case the tools of fiscal policy are recommended to relieve the perverse situation.

Statistically, the process of income flows is presented in a series of economic accounts, one of which is called the economic budget and shows the saving and spending activities of the various segments of the economy, leading to a gross national product. Other accounts present net national product and national net income, the latter differing from the former largely because the duplicating element of indirect taxes is eliminated.

In terms of budget-making, proponents of fiscal-policy control of the economy looked first to a cyclically balanced (rather than an annually balanced) budget. However, interest in this program waned as many economists became converted to the view that current factors had given the economy either an inflationary or deflationary bias (secular stagnation or secular inflation) that called for compensatory fiscal policy. The proponents of the secular-inflation thesis base their case mainly on the alleged propensity of big business and big unions to take advantage of governmental commitments to full employment.

Compensatory fiscal policy for less than full employment may utilize the technique of raising both taxes and expenditures; of keeping expenditures constant and reducing taxes; or of keeping taxes constant and increasing expenditures. Tax reduction may be automatic (built-in flexibility) or occur through a reduction of tax rates. The balanced-budget increase involves no addition to the public debt, but it requires a large expansion of government (low multiplier); reducing taxes adds most to debt but least to the scope of government; increased expenditure adds moderately to both debt and government. Compensatory fiscal policy advocated for inflation uses much the same techniques in reverse. Monetary policy (Federal Reserve programs) provide an alternative (or supplement) to fiscal policy and the relative efficacy of the two types of control is often disputed.

Other proposed fiscal-policy devices would use taxation to provide incentive for desired conduct. For instance, a tax on idle money was frequently proposed during the depression of the 1930s as a means of increasing the velocity of money. Accelerated and decelerated depreciation have been advocated to stimulate or retard investment. Taxes on bank loans or on capital expenditures are suggested to discourage excessive borrowing and investment. None of these, except perhaps the manipulation of depreciation allowances, has much benefit of experience or a wide following, but present dissatisfaction with persistent unemployment and sluggish growth rates calls for fresh thinking and ingenuity.

PROBLEMS

1. What is meant when it is said that saving and investment are independent variables? Make a list of some of the factors that determine each.

2. Comment on the proposition: Saving and investment always turn out to be equal, but that the tendency of the two to diverge is a major cause of inflationary and deflationary gaps.

3. Make a list of the so-called autonomous factors that may affect consumption. What have these to do with the reliability of predicted economic trends?

4. What is meant by equilibrium at less than full employment? What would the proponents of "Say's law" do about unemployment? What would proponents of the "New Economics" do? Is it true that any man can always get a job at the "right" pay?

5. Using a diagram that shows saving, investment, and national income in equilibrium at less than full employment, indicate what would happen if
   a. A new invention were to raise the level of investment;
   b. A successful advertising campaign were launched;
   c. Life insurance companies were to launch a successful campaign to sell more insurance;
   d. The government were to embark upon a public-works program.

6. Discuss the propensity to save as to its (a) determinants; (b) relation to propensity to invest; (c) relation to progressive taxation.

7. Two Keynesian paradoxes that seemed to fit the depression of the 1930s were: the less the propensity to save, the more will be saved; the more businessmen try to do better, the more they don't do so well. Explain the rationale of these propositions.

8. Explain why in calculating national income, the sum of the factor payments will not agree with the market value of goods and services produced.

9. Explain national income as to (a) how it differs from net national product; (b) how it differs from "productivity"; (c) its limitation as a base for measuring the burden of taxation.

10. Consider the differences in the definition of income as employed by (a) national income statisticians; (b) the income tax; (c) the private individual or business.

11. Consider the changes since the 1930s that have converted some proponents of secular stagnation to the view that we now face secular inflation.

12. Explain why a cyclical budget under secular inflation would be inadequate and inappropriate. Explain how a compensatory budget under these conditions would permit a substantial reduction in public debt.

13. What could cause inflation along with secular stagnation?

14. If we have to choose between a little inflation and a little unemployment, which would you prefer and why? If inflation is to be tolerated at all, can it be kept moderate?

15. Contrast the three so-called routes to full employment in terms of the magnitude of change required; the degree to which they can be automatic; their relative effect on public debt and the scope of government.

16. Comment on the proposition: A great war would bring inflation even though it were entirely financed with taxation. Would it bring less inflation if financed by taxes than if financed by borrowing?

17. Not everybody concedes that governments can, if they will, spend themselves out of depression. How might a failure of private confidence affect such an attempt? Why was there no such failure during World War II?

18. What creates "tight money"? Does it effectively counteract inflation? Would a tax on bank loans accomplish the same purpose with less evil effects?

19. If we are in for chronic inflation, would it make sense to shift to a tax system that places major emphasis on consumption taxes?

20. Underdeveloped countries are often characterized by underemployment (too many people on too little land); would these countries be well-advised to borrow from their central banks to provide development capital, hoping to halt inflation by the augmented output thus made possible?

21. Do so-called escalator contracts (such as those that tie wages to a

price index) provide a desirable hedge for individuals against inflation? Do they reduce or intensify the general economic problem of coping with inflation and deflation?

22. Explain how accelerated and decelerated depreciation could be utilized as a compensatory economic control.

23. Explain the difficulty in applying to banks the proposal to tax idle money.

27

PUBLIC DEBT AND ECONOMIC POLICY

The public debt constitutes a distinct section of public finance, involving public expenditures dissociated as to time from taxes, the transfer of income from taxpayers to bondholders, and significant problems of management lying at the heart of fiscal policy and monetary control. In modern times many of its issues heavily overlap those of private finance—that is, money and banking.

DEVELOPMENT OF PUBLIC BORROWING

Public borrowing is a relatively modern development. It did not appear as a regular and important feature of public finance until the latter part of the eighteenth century. Previous to this, governments borrowed occasionally, particularly during the late Middle Ages, but usually in smaller amounts and with greater difficulty than in modern times. Public borrowing in these earlier periods was more or less a personal matter between the ruler, as borrower, and the lender who was ordinarily some wealthy trader or, in the sixteenth and seventeenth centuries, a trading company (such as the British East India Company). The king had difficulty in borrowing because of his limited power to tax, the precariousness of his own existence, and the uncertainty of whether his successor would assume his obligations. Loans to him were usually for short periods at high interest rates and were frequently secured by such personal property as the crown jewels or crown lands.

Public borrowing became an important institution only with the development of certain favorable circumstances. One of these was the appearance of a money and credit economy. Before public credit could attain importance, it was essential that many people should have money to lend and that loans be sanctioned by public opinion. In medieval times lending was never fully condoned by the all-important Church, and this attitude was surrendered under new conditions slowly and reluctantly. The development of industry and trade provided both the means to support government borrowing and the sanction for credit and interest. The development of constitutionalism separated the monarch from the government as such, and it gave the creditors, who now became numerous, the security of the ballot. Security was also enhanced by the growth of wide powers of taxation. In our modern era it is hardly conceivable that, unless there be a revolution, a fully sovereign government might either repudiate, or even default on, an internally held debt. However, the creditor can be and often is undermined by the more subtle process of inflation.

The innovation of public credit was not accepted without protest. Many early writers on public finance expressed toward it the skepticism that greets most innovations. David Hume, in comparing (1752) the new practice of borrowing to pay for wars with the older one of building a "war-chest" in advance of a conflict, expressed a preference for the latter on the ground that its dispensation during the war period helped to atone for the calamities of war. His objection to public borrowing was based on the increased cost to the public arising from interest, the undue advantage alleged to attend the private ownership of securities, and the idleness that results from "living on interest." But Hume looked with favor upon the proposal to convert the national debt into individual private debt—so much per capita—a proposition which suggests the capital levy. He was of the opinion that nations, once they began to borrow, would be unable to desist until they reached the point of bankruptcy.[1] Adam Smith (1776) was hardly less hostile to public borrowing and spoke of the expedient of perpetual funding as "ruinous." [2] "The practice of funding," he observed, "has gradually enfeebled every state which has adopted it." [3]

---

[1] David Hume, *Political Discourses* (Edinburgh, 1752), chap. VIII.
[2] Adam Smith, *Wealth of Nations* (New York: The Modern Library, 1937), p. 872.
[3] *Ibid.,* p. 881.

Early writers, including Smith, Ricardo, and Mill, placed considerable emphasis upon the alleged fact that loans tend to bring about a greater depletion of capital than do taxes. Their rigorous separation of the government economy from the general economy with respect to productive pursuits led them to consider goods consumed by the government as withdrawn from the economy for unproductive use. On the other hand, the hostility to borrowing was not unanimous. Eight years before Smith's *Wealth of Nations,* Sir James Steuart propounded the view in his *Principles of Political Economy* that public debt should function as the balance wheel of the economy.[4]

In this country, Alexander Hamilton as early as 1781 considered the public debt as "a national blessing." His most urgent task was that of building up the country's credit, internally as well as externally. The key to this problem was the state, the continental, and the foreign debt. Hamilton attempted to solve the new state's plight (lack of credit and financial weakness) by satisfying the creditor class through funding—that is, redemption of the debt. It was the creditor class which had been the most ardent supporter of the new constitution. It was this same class that he chose as the cornerstone of his system and the new government. Beyond this, Hamilton found that "besides the advantage of individuals from this arrangement, the active stock of the nation would be increased by the whole amount of the domestic debt, and of course the abilities of the community to contribute to the public debt." [5] By 1892 Bastable, who was no iconoclast, was able to observe: "We may say that any State that pretends to be civilized regards the creation of a debt as one of the essential marks of having reached that position." [6]

Borrowing in the United States. With the exception of our most recent postwar experience, borrowing in the United States, as far as the federal government is concerned, has been marked by heavy additions for wars and a rapid retirement of the debt thereafter. Figure 22 presents the story graphically. Debt retirement is not a universal tradition. Many foreign countries have made slight efforts to retire war debts and have added to them by peacetime borrowing for internal improvements; in these circumstances the accumulation of debt becomes very large. Of course, economic development may also augment the ability to carry the debt. In our own experience, most wars have been financed in large part by borrowing, and the result has been a very serious disturbance in prices. Wholesale prices over a long era show a series of peaks and valleys, the former often occurring during or after war periods. Conceivably, wars

---

[4] Walter F. Stettner, "Sir James Steuart on the Public Debt," *Quarterly Journal of Economics,* LIX (May 1945), pp. 454–460.

[5] Alexander Hamilton, *Works,* John L. Hamilton, ed. (New York, 1850), II, p. 220.

[6] C. F. Bastable, *Public Finance,* 3d ed., p. 626.

could be financed entirely or at least largely by taxes, but the record here is only mildly encouraging. The financial story of the Revolutionary War is perhaps the saddest of all; the Continental Congress made some effort to levy on the states but with pathetic results; the war was financed very largely with printed money that deteriorated to the point where worthless things were, and still are, described as "not worth a Continental." As shown in Figure 22, the War of 1812 created a substantial change in the amount of government debt outstanding; it was financed with borrowing to the extent of 85 percent of its cost. This figure was lowered by 1 percent during the Civil War, but because of the costliness of that war, debt expansion was relatively greater than during World War I and World War II. A somewhat better effort was made during World War I when what then seemed a fantastically expensive war required borrowing amounting to 72 percent of the outlay. We were still more sophisticated during World War II, but the outlay was ten times higher than in the earlier world conflict, and although we bettered our previous score, we still financed about 58 percent of the war cost by bonds.[7]

The trend in the dimensions of war expense and war indebtedness is indicated by comparative per capita figures for debt at the close of the following wars: 1790–$19; 1814–$12; 1870–$78; 1920–$240; 1946–$1720. The national debt up to the Civil War never exceeded 20 percent of the estimated national income; it then rose to 50 percent, a figure that was nine percentage points above that with which we emerged from World War I; at the end of the last war this figure rose to 160 percent, but by the end of 1948 it had declined to 110 percent. More optimistic, however, are the relative figures for debt service (interest) as a percentage of national income: 0.8 percent in 1814, 2.6 percent in 1870, 2.0 percent in 1920, and 2.5 percent at the end of World War II.[8]

Periods of depression have also caused government borrowing, a fact that can be observed in Figure 22 where the debt curve shows some response to historically noteworthy bad-business periods even before the Great Depression of the 1930s. The response was due to the fact that revenues fell faster than expenditures could be cut. Since the last war, debt retirement has lost much of its political appeal. The Employment Act of 1946 made the high use of labor resources the responsibility of the federal government. The view now prevails that debt retirement during recession will aggravate unemployment. During prosperity, when surpluses have developed, tax reduction or increased defense or welfare

---

[7] For a good comparison of our major wartime borrowing experiences, see Marshall A. Robinson, "Federal Debt Management: Civil War, World War I, and World War II," *American Economic Review*, 45 (May 1955), pp. 388–401.

[8] The figures here presented are from The Committee on Public Debt Policy, *Our National Debt* (New York: Harcourt, Brace & World, 1949), pp. 1–16.

expenditures have proved more attractive politically than debt retirement. Economic growth has provided the capacity to carry a large debt with relative ease though not without some problems of debt manage-

FIGURE 22

Growth of the Gross Debt of the Federal Government, 1810–1880 and 1900–1962

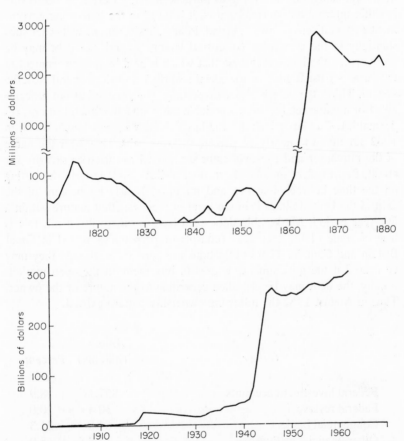

SOURCE: U.S. Treasury, *Annual Report of the Secretary of the Treasury, 1961* (Washington, D.C.: Government Printing Office, 1961), pp. 507–509. Debt for 1962 is estimated.

ment. By the end of 1960 the national debt stood at $290 billion ($1600 per capita). Because of expanding population and economic growth, both per capita debt and debt-service cost as a proportion of national income were falling.

DESCRIPTION OF THE PUBLIC DEBT

Classification of Debt Statistics.   The public debt can be classified in several categories according to purpose. First, government borrowing is either internal or external; that is, it is owed to the borrowing government's own citizens or owed abroad. Policy considerations will differ substantially in the two cases (discussed later). Second, the debt may be gross or net, the latter excluding that which is held by the government in the various trust funds (as for social security) and the Federal Reserve system. Third, the debt is either marketable (negotiable but not redeemable) or nonmarketable (nonnegotiable but, with some qualifications, redeemable). The latter includes the large class of savings bonds which in 1962 amounted to nearly 16 percent of gross debt. They bear the name of the purchaser and can neither be exchanged nor used as security for credit. Fourth, debt may be short, intermediate, or long-term depending on the time between issuance and maturity. Nearly 64 percent of the debt of the United States is in the form of securities that mature within a five-year period. Marketable debt need have no maturity at all; this is true of some of the securities (consols or perpetuals) issued in Great Britain and Canada. These obligations are permanent, though they may be retired if the government chooses to buy them on the open market. Finally, the debt may be classified according to the nature of the owner. Thus in August 1962 the following ownership pattern existed:

Owner	Amount (billions)	Percent
Federal investment accounts	$57.1	18.9
Federal reserve	30.4	10.0
Commercial banks	64.5	21.3
Other financial institutions	17.8	5.9
State and local governments	19.6	6.5
Individuals	65.9	21.8
Nonfinancial corporations	21.1	7.0
Foreign balances and international accounts	14.6	4.8
Miscellaneous	11.4	3.8
Total	302.4	100.0

SOURCE: U.S. Treasury, *Treasury Bulletin,* September 1962.

Duration and Type of Obligations. As previously suggested, public credit instruments differ in their maturities. For short-term obligations, Treasury bills and certificates of indebtedness, both ranging in maturity up to one year, are used. Bills differ from certificates in that the former are sold at auction at varying prices on a discount basis. Certificates are sold at fixed prices with specific coupon rates of interest. Up to December 1958 the Treasury issued only 91-day bills but at present there are regular issues of 91-, 182-, and 365-day bills. As of September 30, 1962 treasury bills accounted for 14 percent of the country's gross debt. Because of their liquidity bills are sold primarily to commercial banks, but they are available to all who desire to invest temporarily idle funds. Until recently certificates had been used primarily for borrowing in anticipation of tax payments. Certificates now account for only 6 percent of gross debt compared with 13 percent at the end of 1958. The advantage of relying on bills is that the Treasury is not faced with the difficult problem of setting the yield. Instead it allows the market to perform this task. The auction technique, it is felt, achieves lower interest costs.

Both tax anticipation bills and certificates are used for interim financing, that is, to smooth out the uneven flow of income tax revenues. These securities are accepted at par in payment of both personal and corporate income tax liabilities. Tax receipts are concentrated in the last half of the fiscal year (March and June primarily), while expenditures are spread more evenly over time. Thus even if the budget is in balance, there are likely to be substantial deficits in the first half of the fiscal year (July to December).

The intermediate-term security is the note having a maturity of from one to five years. Longer-term securities with over five years' duration are called bonds. Both of these types of securities carry fixed interest in coupon form which can be redeemed semiannually. Notes now account for 19 and marketable bonds for 27 percent of the public debt. These securities decline in value as general interest rates rise. For countercyclical policy, especially to check inflation, this characteristic is advantageous to the government. The losses associated with rising interest rates are greater the longer the maturity of the security. Some bondholders will prefer to wait until the obligation matures rather than accept a loss by selling the bond.

The familiar individual savings bond is on its face a long-term credit instrument, that is, it carries a maturity of something less than ten years. The length is related to the return offered and is presently seven years, nine months. The Series E Saving Bond is especially adapted to the needs of small savers and is issued in denominations as low as $18.75 (worth $25 if held until maturity). Because of their nonmarketability, these securities are insured against any loss of value from interest rate fluctuations. However, with fixed and relatively low yields, the holders of these bonds have suffered heavy losses from postwar inflation. Being redeemable at any time after sixty days, even with some cost in terms of interest, savings bonds have the same characteristics as savings deposits. Associated with them because of this liquidity is some fear of possible inflationary consequences. In some years redemptions have exceeded sales. At the end of 1954 these saving instruments totaled 28 percent of the debt and this was approximately the same percentage which existed in 1945, at the end of World War II. But by August 1962 they amounted to only 16 percent of the total debt.

Series E bonds pay no annual interest, but if allowed to mature they yield 3.75 percent. In the event of premature redemption, interest will be paid according to a graduated scale, depending on the period the bond has been held. A table indicating the redemption value appears on the face of each bond. Savings bonds are generally restricted to individuals and only $10,000 worth of them can be purchased in any one calendar year. Series H bonds are similar to Series E bonds but pay interest semiannually on a graduated scale.[9]

The above does not exhaust the list of securities issued by the federal government. Among others are the special issues designed to settle accounts between the Treasury and its various trust funds, such as social security and national service life insurance. Special issues do not bear a uniform rate of interest but are, for the most part, typewritten certificates with maturities and interest rates that vary according to the requirements of each individual trust fund. In general, government statisticians classify such securities, held by government agencies, as duplicating debt which is not included in net debt.

In state and local borrowing much reliance is placed on the serial bond, the maturities of which vary and are so arranged that only a certain proportion falls due each year. This is evidently well adapted to retirement over the life of an improvement from the steady revenue of the general property tax. Public bonds, like private ones, may be "callable" —that is, they may be so issued that the government can redeem them at any time at a stated price.

The Market for Government Securities. Marketing methods are important in the placement of government debt with desirable holders. Primary and secondary market operations are distinguished. The former refers to the sale of new issues by the Treasury and the latter to secondhand sales by security dealers. Investors interested in purchasing securities in the primary market can submit a tender at a bill auction in which

---

[9] For a brief survey of the history of the savings bond program, see Federal Reserve Bank of New York, "The Role of Savings Bonds in Government Finance," *Monthly Review*, 41 (June 1961), pp. 109–111.

they quote the price they are willing to pay and the amount they desire to buy at that price. If fixed-price securities are desired, the investor must subscribe at one of the bond, note, or certificate sales for the number of securities desired at a price and yield established by the Treasury. Speculation and market manipulation can be checked by controlling the size of the downpayment required and the allotment allowed. In the secondary market, purchases can be made on the floor of the New York Stock Exchange and through informal over-the-counter purchases from security dealers. These dealers, now numbering seventeen (five banks and twelve investment houses) handle the overwhelming volume in the secondary market.[10]

Savings bonds can be purchased at most financial institutions. The payroll savings plan, where the employee authorizes regular deductions from his paycheck, is available to employees of most large business concerns and the armed forces. Beginning in 1962, those eligible for federal income tax refunds may request them in savings bonds.

ECONOMIC EFFECTS OF DEBT AND ITS MANAGEMENT

External and Internal Borrowing. An external debt differs from an internal debt in that the former is sold in other countries in their currency. Resources are thus transferred from country A, the lender, to country B, the borrower. Expenditures by the government of country B can be temporarily increased without a corresponding increase in taxes or the money supply. When repayment of the debt is required there must be a corresponding flow of resources from B to A. This means that taxes must be increased or internal borrowing must occur. Since within the nation everybody's debt is somebody's credit, internal borrowing is government debt "within the family." The family wealth cannot be reduced because some members borrow from others. If one Jones borrows from another Jones the total Jones estate is not affected. However, if one of the Joneses borrows from a Smith, the process may involve an eventual transfer from one family to the other. This is not to say that it never makes good sense to borrow outside the family. Anyway the latter is analogous to external borrowing and illustrates the difference between it and internal borrowing. Incurring an internal debt does not reduce national resources, but it

---

[10] For more information on dealer organization, see Commission on Money and Credit, *Money and Credit* (Englewood Cliffs, N.J.: Prentice-Hall Inc., 1961), pp. 115–120; U.S. Treasury Federal Reserve, *Treasury-Federal Reserve Study of the Government Securities Market*, Parts I–III.

transfers them from the private to the public sphere. Since the United States no longer has an external debt, we shall apply the remainder of our discussion to internally held debt.

Full Employment and the Debt.   During a period of full employment, borrowing by the government transfers resources much like taxes. The difference lies in the fact that acceptance of debt is a voluntary process requiring the government to make its debt obligations more attractive (less risk, better yields, and the like) than competing private investments. The floating of the debt itself will be deflationary. But since borrowing is normally done only to pay for previously authorized expenditures, the net effect will be neutral. However, this result depends on the assumptions that the money supply and its velocity are held constant and the average maturity of claims remains constant. This will not be true if the securities are sold to the banking system.

Government borrowing during war periods is a case of issuing debt during full employment. The inflationary consequences of augmented debt during such a period is mainly due to an expanded money supply rather than to the debt as such. Financing a war by taxes is the cheapest way to get the required resources (no interest). But excessively high taxes may place too great a strain on incentives. And as we have previously observed, taxpayers may borrow their taxes so to speak, in order to maintain consumption and business at their previous levels.

To avoid high tax rates and competing for scarce capital at high interest rates, the government might inaugurate a compulsory savings plan. This device was suggested by John Maynard Keynes at the beginning of World War II.[11] It was applied conservatively in Great Britain and Canada and even more conservatively in the United States where it was confined to the excess profits tax. Keynes proposed to graft a compulsory saving feature on the personal income tax; thus part of the levy would be covered by a postwar credit. Compared with voluntary saving, it would have the advantage of a planned distribution and lower interest costs. Moreover, it need not replace voluntary saving entirely. Compared with taxes, it would have no advantage except that it might enable the government to go further in draining purchasing power into the Treasury without damaging incentives. It was also thought to have an advantage in that redemption could be timed to ease a postwar deflation, but experience in this respect has not been reassuring.[12] Compulsory saving as a possible feature of war-finance encounters the difficulty of a very unpredictable future. Curiously it has been used rather extensively by the

---

[11] J. M. Keynes, *How to Pay for the War* (New York: Harcourt, Brace & World, 1940).

[12] Walter W. Heller, "Compulsory Lending: The World War II Experience," *National Tax Journal*, IV: 2 (June 1951), pp. 116–128.

Russians. The program is faced with this dilemma: unless the date of redemption is early and certain, it is no good for incentives; if these conditions are met the government may find the debt maturing at a time that is bad for the economy.

Compensatory Financing and the Debt. During a period of less than full employment, government borrowing will normally be expansionary; the government will tap idle investment funds and put them into circulation through increased expenditures. Unlike the case of taxes, borrowing and the resulting expenditures increases the velocity of money. If banks are allowed to purchase the securities, the money supply will also be increased. Again it would appear cheaper to finance the deficits by a direct increase in the money supply thus avoiding interest. Actually printing money or the more refined technique of selling obligations to the Federal Reserve system would create more liquidity than bond sales. And there is no inherent reason why the process could not be reversed when circumstances require. The limitation of this alternative as we shall see is political rather than economic.

Means of Debt Management Policy. The decision to incur debt is the responsibility of the legislative branch of the government; debt arises from the fact that Congress fails to raise the necessary revenues to satisfy budgetary needs. But managing the debt is basically an administrative function, the responsibility of the Treasury. The managers of the public debt decide all the terms of the securities issued within any congressional restraints that may have been imposed, such as the $4\frac{1}{4}$ interest ceiling on government bonds. The terms that have by far the greatest impact on the economy are (1) the rate of interest on new obligations; (2) the type of securities that will be issued or redeemed and therefore the average maturity of the debt; and (3) to whom the debt will be sold.

Since the government is by far the largest borrower in the capital market, debt management will influence general credit conditions. If the government decides to increase the return on its securities, this will have an influence on all other financial assets, tending to increase their yields so that they may remain competitive. Thus the Treasury can have a significant influence on the level of interest rates. Further, by concentrating its borrowing in bills or bonds, the Treasury can change the liquidity structure of the economy. Reducing liquidity tends to check the velocity of money and has a deflationary effect. Increasing liquidity has an expansionary influence on the economy. By funding the debt into long-term bonds the former can be accomplished. Liquidity can be augmented by an advanced refunding which replaces bonds with securities of shorter maturities. The passage of time itself causes inflationary problems; it shortens the average maturity structure and thereby increases liquidity. For example, a ten-year bond issued in 1952 would have made the economy less liquid at the time of sale. But by the first of 1961, the bond has become as liquid as a 365-day treasury bill.

The debt manager can influence the amount of money available depending upon who is allowed to purchase the new issue. If the government sells its obligations to the commercial banks, these institutions, using excess reserves, will pay for them by creating demand deposits. This parallels the case of the bank's making loans to private corporations. The Treasury can curtail the money supply by retiring bank-held securities, but in this case unless there is further monetary control the banks might expand their private credit. At least the Treasury can curtail the money supply by retiring debt held by the Federal Reserve system.

Debt Management and Monetary Control. From the preceding section it is obvious that debt management is similar to monetary policy in that each can influence the economy indirectly through its effect on credit conditions. There has been and still is an inherent conflict between central bank and treasury policies. The primary responsibility of the Treasury is to provide the necessary funds for budgetary needs and to refund the debt as it matures. When the Treasury is borrowing it is likely to favor an "easy money" policy so that its costs will be minimized. The Federal Reserve authorities on the other hand are concerned primarily with economic stabilization. In times of deflation there is no conflict between the two agencies. During periods of inflation, proper central bank policy is to tighten credit conditions, forcing up the rate of interest. Such a policy means that the job of the Treasury will be more difficult and costly.

War Experience. During World War II of course the problem of providing the Treasury with the funds necessary to prosecute the war overshadowed all other considerations. The Federal Reserve, recognizing this, announced to the public that it would see that the Treasury was supplied with all the money needed for war finance.[13] At the same time the Treasury announced its policy: it would raise the greatest possible share of the necessary funds out of taxes. Where borrowing was necessary, policy objectives would be to (1) minimize inflation, (2) provide stability in yields on government obligations, and (3) keep the cost of borrowing to the smallest amount consistent with the other objectives. In the interest of avoiding inflation, borrowing from banks would be minimized. The government proposed to place as much of the debt as possible with low-income individuals and this would "soak up" purchasing power that would otherwise build up pressure on the prices of consumer goods.[14] The second aim—stability of yield—was the outcome of unfavorable ex-

---

[13] Board of Governors of the Federal Reserve System, *Annual Report,* 1941, p. 1.

[14] It turned out that this policy did not lighten the problem of postwar debt management.

perience with borrowing during World War I when yields gravitated to higher and higher levels during the course of the war. This resulted in discrimination against those who purchased securities early in the war and caused postponement of purchase in hope of better yields. The Treasury sought to accomplish this objective by placing much of the debt in nonmarketable securities. (The nonnegotiability of these instruments would also prevent the indirect expansion of bank credit, since individuals could not use them to support bank loans.) To the extent that marketable issues must be relied upon, open-market operations by the Federal Reserve would be used to stabilize or "peg" bond prices; the central bank would buy up existing issues at par to maintain constant yield. The third objective—minimizing the cost of borrowing and keeping the rate of interest at prewar level—conflicted with the objective of keeping the debt out of banks.

Despite the efforts of the Treasury and the Federal Reserve to place the debt with the public and nonbank institutions, the unabsorbed balance amounted to over $95 billion, or 40 percent of the total borrowed, or one fourth of the cost of the war.[15] Bank holdings of government securities rose from 40 percent of earning assets of all banks before the war to 70 percent in the early postwar period.

Postwar Experience. Following the war, and until March 1951, the pegging of the bond market virtually nullified monetary policy as a compensatory device. Bond prices continued stable and this insured successful refunding operations. The Treasury's primary fear was that if prices were allowed to drop, this might have serious deflationary effects on the economy as had been the case following World War I. There was also concern that without the central bank's support a major refunding failure might occur. This carrying over of wartime policies produced prolonged and profound controversy between the two agencies involved and within the economics profession. Most of the early postwar years turned out to be highly inflationary, and this problem became more acute with the outbreak of the Korean War. In March 1951 the Treasury and Federal Reserve reached an accord that called an end to "pegging."

Notwithstanding its new freedom, the Federal Reserve has continued to assist the Treasury in two ways. First, it has maintained a neutral position during the issuance of new government obligations. Second, the central bank continued to support the bond market to prevent disruptive price fluctuations. More recently, the Treasury and Federal Reserve have cooperated in an attempt to ease the balance-of-payments problem. The Federal Reserve entered the bond market to purchase longer-term securities and thus ease long-term interest rates. At the same time it sold

---

[15] E. A. Goldenweiser, *Monetary Management* (New York: McGraw-Hill Book Company, 1949), p. 30.

short-term securities to raise interest rates in this area. With this ambivalent policy the authorities hoped both to reduce the flow of foreign capital from the United States and to stimulate investment as an antirecession measure. But it is not fully established that short- and long-term funds are sufficiently independent to accommodate such a program.

Countercyclical Management. Critics complain that even since the accord, debt management has failed at its stabilization objective. During the first years of the Eisenhower Administration attempts were made to sell long-term securities in a period of inflation, but the bonds were poorly received and required Federal Reserve support. Because of the ever shortening maturity created by the passage of time, the need to sell some long-term debt seemed acute. The government was persuaded that long-term debt should be sold whenever practical, and this meant primarily that sales would be conducted during periods of recession and "easy money." Thus instead of increasing liquidity and reducing long-term rates to a minimum during bad economic weather, the Treasury was doing the opposite. However, a fairly large amount of these bonds were being purchased by the banking system and (on the assumption that the banks would not have made other loans with their excess reserves) this augmented the money supply.

Much more had been expected from debt management following the war with the existence of such a large and widely held public debt. A "trinity" of countercyclical tools was envisioned: fiscal, monetary, and debt management policy. The Treasury by controlling the average maturity of the debt, the price of its obligations and the general terms of new issues could support and supplement the efforts of the central bank. Actually the Treasury and central bank seem much of the time to have been pulling in opposite directions. The reason for this paradox is the cost of countercyclical debt management. The critics argue that the cost is not too much to pay for debt management's contribution to economic stabilization. Others take the view that stability can be achieved more cheaply by using only monetary policy to control credit conditions.

Debt Versus Monetary Expansion. As previously suggested, governments have the alternative of issuing notes (money) that bear no interest. In order to make such notes acceptable, it may be necessary to make them legal tender—that is, compel their acceptance at par in payment of debts.

The "greenbacks" of the Civil War period are an example of public credit extended by the issuance of legal tender notes. The treasury notes of 1890 were also credit instruments as well as money. The latter have practically all been retired, but some $318 million of United States notes (reissued greenbacks) are still outstanding. Other nations have frequently issued non–interest-bearing notes irredeemable in species. Germany, for example, built up a floating debt during the early 1920s consisting of non–interest-bearing notes of unprecedented volume. Monetary difficulties in China were due to the same cause.

No doubt the interest load of the postwar period could be reduced by "monetizing" part or all of the public debt. This could be accomplished by the purchase of bonds through the issuance of non–interest-bearing notes. It could also be accomplished by the sale of new bonds to the Federal Reserve system and the use of the proceeds to retire indebtedness held by individuals or commercial banks. The Reserve banks are limited in their dividends to 6 percent of their capital stock and, if the balance were to go to the government, monetization could be accomplished leaving no appreciable cost in interest charges.

The principal objection to fiat money is that is too easy a way to pay the government's bills. Were human beings to achieve sufficient discipline to use this tool intelligently, they could save considerable strain on the tax system to cover interest charges, amounting to $9.5 billion in fiscal 1962. The easiest way to raise money is to print it; next, to borrow it; third, to raise it by indirect tax (so that the process is invisible); and forth, to apply direct taxation. The first two have proved so tempting that it has been found necessary to surround them with inhibitions.

Greenback financing would no doubt increase the money supply far more than would debt financing, much of which is outside the banking system. To control the inflationary effects of this during a period of full employment would necessitate a revolutionary increase in reserve requirements which eventually would approach a 100 percent reserve system.[16]

CURRENT DEBT MANAGEMENT ISSUES

Management Philosophies. Several philosophies of debt management persist. The first is associated with Henry Simons [17] who suggested that the government should sell perpetual bonds during periods of inflation and refund or buy them back with cash during deflation. Converting bonds to money would stimulate the economy as government obligations moved from zero liquidity to perfect liquidity. Selling bonds during prosperous periods would be expensive. But assuming that the government is unwilling to curb inflation by augmenting taxes, the cost would be warranted. The key then is lengthening the average maturity structure during

---

[16] See Henry C. Simons, "Hansen on Fiscal Policy," in *Economic Policy for a Free Society* (Chicago: University of Chicago Press, 1948), pp. 190–191.

[17] Henry C. Simons, "On Debt Policy," *Journal of Political Economy,* 52 (December 1944), pp. 356–361.

inflationary periods and shortening it during recessions. These changes will have countercyclical effects on the money supply, velocity, liquidity structure, and interest rates.

The second philosophy [18] acknowledges the effects of changing the maturity structure, but it considers them too insignificant compared with their expense. All that can be accomplished by the cumbersome instrument of debt management can be accomplished more efficiently through monetary policy. Proper management consists in minimizing the cost of the debt: sell long-term debt during recessions when the interest cost is low, and switch to short-term obligations when interest rates are high.

Between these two extremes lies a third position.[19] This view recognizes that a cost-minimization program aggravates the cycle and works directly against monetary policy. Our compensatory tools, it is argued, have not reached the degree of sophistication where the government can afford not to use every weapon available. The least that can be asked of debt management, accordingly, is that it be economically neutral, which would be the case if the average maturity structure were to remain constant over the business cycle. The government should establish a basic maturity structure that provides for the needed liquidity at full employment. This structure should be maintained throughout the cycle. Moreover debt management should be in a position to make a more positive contribution if a strong need is demonstrated. The goal should not be to minimize interests costs but to minimize the cost of stabilization. Very likely this would require some contribution from debt management.

Maturity Structure.   As previously indicated a leading issue in debt management which continues to draw attention is the proper length for average maturity of the debt. The average length in 1946 was nine years, one month. By 1951 and the Treasury–Federal Reserve accord it had fallen to six years, seven months. The continued erosion of time and the difficulty of selling long-term securities reduced the average maturity by the end of fiscal 1960 to four years, four months. However, with the assistance of the advance refunding technique,[20] this erosion has been reversed at least temporarily. The perpetual refunding on a large scale is administratively difficult and raises the issue of excess liquidity previously

---

[18] Warren L. Smith, *Debt Management in the United States,* Study Paper 19, Joint Committee Study of Employment, Growth and Price Levels (Washington, D.C., 1960), chap. IV; Herbert Stein, "Managing the Public Debt," *Journal of Law and Economics,* 1 (October 1958), pp. 97–104.

[19] J. M. Culbertson, "A Positive Debt Management Program," *Review of Economics and Statistics,* 41 (May 1959), pp. 89–98.

[20] Advanced refunding consists of offering securities of extended maturity in exchange for existing ones. As long-term securities approach maturity, investors sell them to others who are interested in liquid debt. After bonds have matured it may be difficult to interest present holders in exchanging them for new long-term securities. With judicious advance refunding the Treasury hopes to catch these securities before they leave the portfolio of the long-term investor.

discussed. However, as an economy grows, so does its liquidity needs. Thus if the total debt is not growing, some increase in liquidity may suit the economy's needs.

The Level of Interest. It might be thought that debt management officials have no authority over the rate of interest; in order to sell securities they have to adjust the terms of their contracts to the state of the market. To some extent this is true, but the debt authorities along with the Federal Reserve Board also constitute an important factor in determining what the interest rate shall be. Witness the pegging operation of the war and early postwar period.

The function and the effects of the interest rate (if one may use this term in the singular) is the subject for a large book. Here we must confine our treatment to a few observations as follows:

1. A high interest rate is presumably a check on inflation because it tends to reduce the demand for credit and increase the supply of loanable funds. Borrowers will hesitate to seek loans at high prices and savers will be encouraged to add to their stocks of wealth. This is not so self-evident as it sounds, however; it only holds to the degree that investment and saving are interest-elastic.

2. A high interest rate obviously increases the cost of servicing the public debt. This cost has risen more than $4.5 billion since the close of World War II, and most of the increase is due to higher interest rates.

3. State and local governments suffer from the high cost of borrowing and this proves particularly embarrassing at a time when construction of school facilities is a critical need. On the other hand, endowed institutions and insurance companies complain about low interest rates. All parties here mentioned suffer from inflation.

4. Banks at the present time depend upon interest received from government securities for a considerable though decreasing part of their incomes. The war gave them a windfall in the enormous expansion of income-earning assets, most of which were created "out of the blue" and with no corresponding increase in stockholders' equity. And, of course, banks have a direct stake in the high private rate of interest that goes along with the high public one.

5. Conceding the efficacy of high interest rates in checking inflation, one may still observe that this is not the only way to check this evil. A large budgetary surplus might do the trick and there are other special alternatives mentioned in the previous chapter. A tax on loans, for instance, might afford a means whereby the government could check excess borrowing and take the profit instead of allowing the banks to have it.

Savings Bonds. As previously indicated, savings bonds as a proportion of the debt have been declining. The savings bond is ideal for small savers and encourages wide ownership of the debt, reducing distributive effects of interest payments. Moreover, savings bonds encourage general thrift. Interest costs have been below those of marketable securities and, while administrative costs are much higher, the program still appears to be less expensive than others. To reverse the net redemption pattern, the Treasury would be obliged to price these bonds more attractively, thus making them more competitive with savings deposits, saving and loan shares, and other small-saver investments. As previously explained, these securities do involve some inflationary potential.

The Purchasing Power Bond. One means of making savings obligations of the federal government more attractive is the purchasing power bond. Here the redemption value of the security would be tied to a price index and this would constitute a built-in guarantee against inflation.[21] Israel, France, Austria, and Finland have used the purchasing-power payment principle in either private or public lending, and the idea has proved popular. (In Israel, a cement company once agreed to redeem its bonds in cement.) It is said that this would give the small saver an "escalator clause" similar to those enjoyed by many wage earners and public servants. This innovation would tend to defeat inflation both by encouraging saving and by giving the government incentive to adopt other anti-inflationary measures. If it does not control inflation, these obligations could prove to be very expensive. On the other hand, the introduction of this instrument might be interpreted as a sign that the authorities have become convinced that inflation is inevitable. Moreover, the program might weaken the opposition to inflation and concentrate its effects on fewer people. Private enterprises, such as insurance companies, have expressed alarm lest they find themselves unable to compete with such an unusual species of credit. But the idea is flexible; some other features of the bonds such as early redemption privileges might be made less attractive.[22]

Agency Controlling Management. Because of the overlap in the control of the money supply and credit conditions between monetary policy and debt management, there has been support for the idea that the two should be placed under one agency. This would insure greater consistency of policy than has in fact occurred. Congress has considered consolidation under the Treasury,[23] but is loath to surrender the acknowledged advantages of an independent central bank. Others have suggested

---

[21] Richard Goode, "A Constant-Purchasing-Power Savings Bond," *National Tax Journal,* IV: 4 (December 1951), pp. 332–340.

[22] It is interesting to contemplate the economic aspects of inflation in a world in which everybody had his own private escalator privilege. For such an exercise see Amotz Morag, "For an Inflation Proof Economy," *American Economic Review,* 52 (March 1962), pp. 177–184.

[23] U.S. Congress, Joint Committee on the Economic Report, *Monetary Policy and the Management of the Public Debt,* Report of the Subcommittee on General Credit Control and Debt Management, 82d Cong., 2d sess., 1952, pp. 747–761.

that the Federal Reserve be made responsible for debt management, thus freeing the program from political pressures to minimize costs.[24] But reorganization is no guarantee of appropriate policies. And the administration and political party in power should not be so separated from such control over the economy that they cannot be held responsible for its successes and failures.

Removal of Statutory Limits. Effective debt management is constrained by two limits that were initially established under the Second Liberty Bond Act of 1917. One established a limit on the amount of debt that could be issued; it has often been amended, and only since 1954 has the ceiling been so close to the amount of debt outstanding as to restrict the flexibility of debt management.[25] The ceiling is said to stymie the Treasury's ability to take advantage of favorable market conditions and refund before near-maturing securities come due. The pressure of a ceiling requires a bond-for-bond exchange on all refunding operations. Were "tap" issues used, investors might crack the ceiling.[26]

No doubt the purpose of the ceiling is to prevent an overgrowth of claims on an uncertain future in violation of the principle of thrift. Debt is viewed by many as a means of increasing the power of government and of concealing the cost of wasteful expenditures. Critics of this view allege that the cutback in military spending in 1957, attributable to debt constrictions, contributed to the following recession. They also say that the ceiling has lead to devious budgetary methods, creating agencies which can borrow outside the Treasury and the debt limit. On balance it seems highly doubtful that the ceiling accomplishes its purpose or plays any other useful role. If Congress were to face its responsibilities directly rather than through the questionable approach of the debt ceiling, debt management would be more effective.

The second statutory restriction on debt management is an interest-rate ceiling on securities with more than five years' maturity. The impact of setting bond prices by fiat is that the Treasury, which must make its securities competitive, is forced to do its financing in shorter-term obligations. Witness the much-publicized 5 percent notes issued in 1959. Proponents of this ceiling are interested in maintaining low long-term rates of interest that may stimulate investment and in minimizing the cost of

[24] Robert L. Bunting, "A Debt Management Proposal," *Southern Economic Journal* (January 1959), pp. 338–342; G. L. Bach, "The Federal Reserve and Monetary Policy Formation," *American Economic Review*, 39 (December 1949), pp. 1189–1190; Earl R. Rolph and George Break, *Public Finance* (New York: The Ronald Press Company, 1961), pp. 539–543.

[25] See Marshall A. Robinson, *The National Debt Ceiling* (Washington, D.C.: The Brookings Institution, 1959).

[26] Abba P. Lerner, "The Burden of Debt," *Review of Economics and Statistics*, 43 (May 1961), pp. 139–141.

the debt. But again the ceiling as presently constituted fails its purpose; nothing is gained by forcing the Treasury to borrow in shorter maturities.

THE BURDEN OF THE DEBT

Whether there is a burden involved in the creation of public debt, and if so on whom it falls, is a much debated question. The generally accepted view since the end of World War II defines the burden as the sacrifice of scarce resources when the funds are spent.[27] If full employment exists, the transfer of resources is one from the private to the public sphere. If there are unemployed resources, public borrowing puts them to work and there is a gain rather than a burden. Basically what occurs at the level of the individual is a shift of resources from the lender to the taxpayer. This occurs because the creation of the debt takes the place of higher taxes.

But what of the future, if and when the debt is repaid? At that time there will be a shift of resources from the government sector, accumulated there by taxation, to the private sphere, or from the taxpayer to the bondholder. In the aggregate then, no burden can be shifted from one generation to another; the shift is between groups in the same period. In time of war it is the generation that fights the war that gives up the use of physical resources. These materials would have greatly increased real income if they had not been diverted into the war effort. The nation may have to tax future generations to pay the interest and principal of the public debt, but it is the bondholders of these later generations who receive the payments. In the aggregate we owe the debt to ourselves, and assets will always equal liabilities on the national balance sheet. Quite different is the case of municipal borrowing; here the borrowing is partly at least outside the community, and migration can materially alter the composition of the community.

This traditional explanation of debt burden is self-evident enough so far as it goes, though it has never been accepted by the man on the street, who does not differentiate between public and private borrowing or external and internal borrowing. In recent years a number of economists have also come to question the usefulness of the traditional concept. Much depends on how the term "burden" is defined.[28] The critics look to the individual's loss of real income rather than to the aggregate loss. The transfer that occurs when the government goes into debt is a voluntary

---

[27] Lerner, *loc. cit.*

[28] James M. Buchanan, *Public Principles of Public Debt* (Homewood, Ill.: Richard D. Irwin, Inc., 1958); W. G. Bowen *et al.*, "The Public Debt," *American Economic Review,* 50 (September 1960), pp. 701–705.

one. The lender sacrifices nothing; he has moved to a preferred position when he purchases government securities. The civil project or the war is not paid for in terms of individual sacrifice until taxation forces some in the economy to give up income to pay off bondholders. There is no off-setting gain to the bondholders, since payment is only a fulfillment of contractual obligations.

It is said that by looking only at the aggregative national balance sheet, the welfare effects of government borrowing are overlooked. The present generation will bear the burden only if it correctly anticipates its own and its heirs' future tax liabilities and discounts the capital value of its holdings accordingly. Such a computation appears extremely unlikely.

The analysis can pursue many further complications. The bondhold-ers who purchase the government obligations could have used this money for private investments. Since they did not, there will be higher interest charges and less private investment. Whether this reduces the capital available for production in future years then depends on the productivity of the government spending. And so on.

Incidental factors that may be overlooked are the future preemption of tax receipts for interest payments rather than welfare expenditures; the administrative cost and other problems associated with managing the debt; the effects of redistributing large sums from taxpayers to bondhold-ers. The burden argument is not very significant in establishing a prefer-ence among the three ways of raising money; taxation, borrowing, and a direct increase in the money supply.[29]

---

[29] Summary and problems at the end of the next chapter.

28

OTHER PUBLIC DEBT CONSIDERATIONS

The previous chapter concentrated on the development, description and management of the federal public debt. Here we shall attempt to round out the picture and present especially aspects of state, local, and foreign debt.

WHEN IS PUBLIC BORROWING JUSTIFIED?

When should a government go into debt? Advice to governments in this respect might not be very different from that appropriate for individuals. An individual may borrow with a good conscience to pay for an emergency. If such individual encounters catastrophic illness and has no reserves, he must borrow or suffer still more catastrophic consequences. And the federal government is also justified in paying for a war by borrowing. The federal government, however, has the taxing power and up to a point, at least, it will minimize its monetary problems by taxing rather than borrowing.

An individual may borrow for a productive purpose that shows good prospect of self-liquidating the loan. So may a government. Thus no feel-

634

ing of sin is warranted when a municipal government borrows to expand its municipal light or water plant.

An individual may borrow when he acquires a durable good that will serve him for several years. And so may a municipality borrow to pay for a new schoolhouse. In fact, if a municipality is small, it must borrow for such outlay. The existence of a huge lump in one year's budget would unduly upset the even trend of the taxing process and collect nothing from later beneficiaries of the project. Moreover, in the case of municipalities the turnover of population during the life of an improvement may be quite substantial, and the generation that enjoys a capital good should be the one to pay for it.

But in the case of a large city or state or the federal government, lumpy budgets caused by public works are no problem. An additional increment to a large stock of capital goods can be counted upon as a recurring expense.

So far in this analysis borrowing by individuals and governments are similar. We caution individuals from going into debt intemperately and too easily. The same advice is good for governments. The easiest way to raise money is to print it, the next easiest is to borrow, the third easiest is to levy an indirect (sales) tax, and the hardest is to levy a direct tax and send the taxpayer his bill before election.

But this is not the whole story. The federal government is unique in the hierarchy of individuals and governments in that it has monetary powers and responsibilities. By compensatory budgeting—deficits in bad years and surpluses in good years—it undertakes to avoid the wastes and inequities of unemployment on the one hand and inflation on the other.

In 1963 with a bullish stock market and profits at an all-time high, Congress was being asked to reduce taxes and incur a heavy deficit. This seemed to many the ultimate in irresponsible finance and the abandonment of the time-honored moral sanction that taxes are the natural restraint against excessive public expenditures. They worried about an excessive public debt that might become unmanageable. Proponents however pointed to persistent unemployment as an evil and a waste which required a remedy. Public debt that is not growing in terms of gross national product is nothing to worry about. As to moral sanctions, we must develop a new set of inhibitions to check reckless and extravagant public spending.

It will be observed that the federal government and the states and municipalities are in substantially different positions with regard to debt. The states and municipalities, to be sure, can cooperate to some degree in the federal government's compensatory finance program. They stand midway between the federal government and private corporations, but they are likely to be found much more compensated for than compensating.

DIGRESSION ON FINANCING BY INFLATION [1]

The fundamental cause of inflation in wartime is not difficult to explain. On the one hand, a flood of purchasing power is released by heavy government spending and, on the other, a shortage of civilian goods is created by the diversion of energy from peace to war production. The combination of excessive purchasing power and a shortage of goods (sometimes called the inflationary gap) produces a disequilibrium, the natural result of which is a general rise in prices. People with money to spend bid against each other for the short supply of goods and services available.

Peacetime inflation may be caused not only by an excess of purchasing power but also by the propensity of labor unions and/or monopolistic corporations to push wages beyond increased productivity and raise prices arbitrarily. Rising prices attributed to these latter causes are described as "cost-push" inflation. If the money supply were so inelastic that it could not finance the old volume of transactions at a higher level, then this price rise could not occur. But the money supply is obviously not that inelastic; it can play a role as effect rather than cause.

An extreme inflation deprives those who have long-term credits, or other long-term contracts, of some or all of the value of their assets. In this respect it is not unlike a special and extreme "capital levy." Or it can be thought of as a heavy tax on credits without benefit of graduation. In all likelihood it is responsible for more redistribution than all other institutions combined, but much of it is horizontal rather than vertical redistribution.

Both inflation and the deflation that is likely to follow it bear heavily upon the wage and salary earner; inflation because wages lag behind prices, and deflation because it involves widespread unemployment. The active entrepreneur and speculator may gain from inflation, though both are likely to suffer during deflation. The principal beneficiaries in the process of inflation are the debtors who gain what the creditors lose— that is, they are delivered from their debts. As entrepreneurs and debtors, farmers are probably likely to gain, at least temporarily. Inflation upsets the balance of an economy and is likely to have disturbing consequences in the field of labor relations. It also upsets income tax accounting, espe-

---

[1] The term *inflation* used here and elsewhere in this book is not a very precise term. It is often used to describe a time of generally rising prices. But during the late 1920s, a period commonly described as inflationary, prices showed little, if any, tendency to rise. Probably a good working definition of *inflation* is: An increase in money, or money substitutes, that threatens present or future economic stability.

cially as it deals with depreciation, inventory profits, and capital gains. It creates special difficulties in municipal finance where a spread between expenses and general property tax receipts develops.

In underdeveloped countries where the inflation danger always attends an expansionary program, rising prices are said to aggravate inequalities, favor speculation rather than productive investment, and weaken the incentive to save. On the other hand, the common existence of underemployment makes possible an increase in production that might halt the inflation.

WHEN SHOULD DEBT BE RETIRED?

Mention has been made of the fact that traditional American policy has favored paying off debt contracted for emergencies as soon as the emergency has passed. The advantages of paying off the debt are, first, that it results in a saving in governmental expenditures for interest; second, that it strengthens the credit of the government so that it can better meet emergencies; third, that in time of inflation it may serve as a tool to cope with excessive spending.

On the other hand, the consensus of the postwar period seems to hold that debt should not be retired unless conditions are favorable, meaning little unemployment, a full utilization of resources, and probably some inflationary trend. Interest in debt retirement at least for its own sake has grown decidedly feeble. By the same token there is little fear of rising debt so long as it is accompanied by rising income.

In at least two respects time tends to ease the burden of carrying debt; one is the growth of population and income that may be anticipated in a growing economy; the other (less legitimate) is the prospect of inflation. In Great Britain interest charges as a percent of income declined from 7.7 in 1818 to 6.2 in 1946, whereas during the same period British national income and debt rose twenty and thirty times their size respectively. The qualms of Smith and Hume that the propensity to borrow would lead to certain national bankruptcy seem not to have materialized.

Debt retirement accompanied by the taxes and government surplus that make it possible would seem to be definitely deflationary, but the case is not self-evident. If the government retires bank-held debt, this will replenish bank reserves and make possible further lending by banks. If it retires debt held by individuals and corporations other than banks, they will have more funds to invest or spend on consumption goods. The safest alternative would be to retire debt held by the Federal Reserve banks which are in a position to sterilize reserves. As a practical matter, however, the limiting factor in bank loans for investment and consumption spending is not likely to be the illiquidity of credit assets. Where this is true, debt retirement in any form (or the taxes that make it possible) will be deflationary.

In addition to debt retirement we have the other possibilities of debt refunding, default, and repudiation. Refunding is borrowing from X to pay off Y. Default occurs where governments are willing but unable to pay off debts. It seldom occurs in the case of a fully sovereign government because inflation is an available and more popular alternative. Repudiation indicates unwillingness to pay; it is unlikely to occur except where governments are replaced by revolution or war. New ones may be unwilling to assume old one's debts. The Soviet government has several times postponed redemption of internally held bonds. This has been regarded as equivalent to repudiation and has been explained curiously on the ground that it was forced upon the leadership by inflation. Of course, repudiation cannot be repeated often if borrowing is voluntary.

THE CAPITAL LEVY AS A MEANS OF DEBT RETIREMENT

As pointed out previously, drastic reductions in debt may be contemplated at times, particularly after a war, either because the capital of the debt may appear too large and thus be an inflationary threat, or because the annual interest cost of the debt is too high. The attempt to effect this through a once-for-all operation is known as a capital levy.[2]

NATURE AND REASONS FOR CAPITAL LEVY

A capital levy is a form of taxation designed to appropriate for the state a sum of such magnitude as to take from the taxpayer not merely a part of the income from capital but a part of the capital itself. Usually, though not necessarily, it has been coupled with the problem of the national debt and has been advocated as a means of its retirement. Postwar development of a capital levy in Germany has not been coupled with debt but has aimed at a sharing of the wealth that survived the war with those whose possessions were wiped out. Within the tax family the capital levy is most like the death tax, particularly if the latter is imposed at a high rate, since it is based upon net estate and graduated in rate. It differs from the death tax in that it is levied at a strategic time for the state rather than at the

---

[2] An excellent discussion of the theoretical and institutional aspects of capital levies may be found in Hicks and Rostas, *The Taxation of War Wealth* (Oxford: Clarendon Press, 1941), pp. 180–203; also Hicks, *Public Finance*, pp. 231–248.

death of an individual. A capital tax at the time of death would, of course, be discounted by the taxpayer at a much higher rate than a capital levy. This is because a given amount of death tax would be a far smaller sacrifice to the taxpayer in terms of loss of satisfaction than an equal amount of capital levy. Furthermore, sufficient funds for the payment of a death tax can always be provided out of the savings of other people since only a few estates become liable each year. Although death taxes are levied on capital, the sale to current savers of part of the estate facilitates their payment out of society's income stream rather than out of capital. In the case of a capital levy, the tax may lead to capital consumption unless there is a compensatory increase in real investment.

Arguments for the Capital Levy. The arguments for the capital levy as a means of relief from debts are, first, that it wipes out a supposed difficulty with one stroke of the axe and clears the budget for the service expenditures of reconstruction. It may constitute a belated attempt to apply the tax system to those who were enriched by war and inflation. It is said to be but a capitalization of ordinary taxes that might be anticipated as an alternative.

Like income taxes, capital levies can be adjusted to ability to pay, although equal amounts of capital do not always yield equal amounts of income. The social and economic advantages accruing to the owner of capital have always been considered a proper justification for differential taxation. Unlike the income taxes, which may discourage the incentive to take risks, the tax base for a capital levy is related to past action and not present effort.

Difficulties with the Capital Levy. Like the excess profits tax and the income tax, the capital levy is weakest on its administrative side. Although the tax might be equitable, it is very difficult to apply. Probably the most difficult aspect of a tax on capital is that of finding a fair value for the property involved. While it is often difficult enough to obtain reliable and equitable valuations in the case of death taxes where only a relatively small and predictable number fall due each year, the problem becomes staggering in the case of a capital levy. Property owners as well as the government are likely to experience a shortage of experienced appraisers, which may mean that assessments have to be made over a considerable period of time. But it is also probable that the levy would be made under conditions of highly unstable values which would make the determination of a fair value difficult. Considerable inequities may arise from the fact that some will pay their tax early while others may pay theirs late thus benefiting from possible declines in values as assets are being liquidated. It would be difficult to avoid forced sales and declines in relative values as great amounts of property are transferred. The government may have to support values.

In this case, the greatest danger would come from hurried and inexact valuations and subsequently a large amount of evasion. A bungled levy may have the reverse effect from the one intended, politically and economically. The outcome may well be a loss of confidence in the financial administration of the government.

The application of the tax to wealth acquired during or as a result of war would be particularly troublesome to administer. It is difficult enough to isolate war profits when they occur, and it would be much more so after several years had elapsed.

Medium of Payment. Among the practical difficulties is the medium of payment. If all payments are to be made in cash, a large amount of forced liquidation may be necessary, which may result in disturbing echoes in the security and real estate markets. If the state is to accept securities or other assets in lieu of cash, the question of which assets to accept will arise. If only certain types of assets are acceptable not all the taxpayers will be relieved, and the burden will fall quite unequally upon those who are forced to liquidate. If all assets are made acceptable, the state will have a great variety of assets to dispose of and administer. If payment on the installment plan over a considerable period is permitted, this may relieve the situation, but the original purpose of the levy is sacrificed. The levy is then likely to become merely an extraordinary income tax upon "unearned" income.

ECONOMIC EFFECTS

A capital levy, as stated, is commonly proposed to combat inflation which is the usual consequence of war finance. Indeed, the initial effects of a levy are deflationary, if only for the uncertainty that it creates in the business community. Eventually, however, the opposite may be the case. The experience of central European countries after World War I showed that without adequate exchange controls, capital flight on a grand scale is likely to take place. Second, if the levy requires additional liquidity for taxpayers to discharge their liabilities to the government, the resulting borrowing may have an inflationary effect. Third, a slow process of collection may cause great uncertainty and thereby damage enterprise as much as the high income taxes, necessary to service the debt and restrain inflation, might have done.

CONSTITUTIONALITY

In the United States the capital levy would encounter constitutional barriers. If the federal government were to contemplate using this instrument, even in an emergency, it would be confronted with the probability that it would be considered as a direct tax and available for use only if its burden were distributed among the states according to population. The states, on the other hand, have uniformity clauses in their constitutions that would generally prohibit any graduated tax on property. However, on the merits, the proposal for a capital levy recalls the idea of a periodic net worth tax, which might deserve consideration for a place in more revenue systems.

PUBLIC DEBT OF STATE AND LOCAL GOVERNMENTS

State and municipal borrowing in the United States has been mainly for the purpose of financing the construction of internal improvements, such as canals, railways, and roads. Borrowing has been sporadic, following the trend of the business cycle, and has often been intemperate. The excesses of the 1830s led to several defaults and the incorporation in many state constitutions of rigid restrictions on borrowing and on powers to construct internal improvements. Other periods of heavy borrowing were the 1870s and the 1920s.

TABLE 8

Net Public Debt of State and Local Governments
for Selected Years

(in billions)

Years	State	Local	Total	Percent of total net debt
1929	$1.6	$11.6	$13.2	6.9
1935	2.2	13.8	16.0	9.2
1940	2.1	14.4	16.5	8.7
1945	1.4	12.3	13.7	3.4
1950	4.0	16.8	20.7	4.2
1955	9.8	28.5	38.4	5.7
1960	14.5	45.6	60.0	6.8
1961	16.2	48.8	65.0	6.9

SOURCE: U.S. Department of Commerce, *Survey of Current Business,* 1950, 1954, 1960, 1961.

With the crash of 1929 and the subsequent depression, state revenues fell faster than expenditures could be cut, forcing these governments to increase their borrowing by some $2.5 billion. But by April 1933, three states and over 1000 municipalities were technically insolvent.[3] In the midst of the depression in 1933, $144 million more municipal bonds were retired than issued. Thus by the beginning of World War II the state and local net debt was below the peak that it had reached in 1933. During the war years high tax revenues and the shortage of materials for public works led to further reductions in indebtedness.

Since the end of the war there has been a rapid expansion of state and local borrowing, with debt increasing by some 300 percent in the 1950s. In recent years the largest proportion of these new loans have been for school construction, then for water, sewer, and other utilities, and thirdly for roads and bridges. Borrowing for roads was of greater importance earlier in the decade with the rapid expansion of the state toll system. With the advent of the federal highway program the importance of this reason for borrowing has declined. It is interesting to note that state and local debt though rapidly mounting is no higher now as a percentage of total debt, public and private, than it was in 1929.

SPECIAL PROBLEMS OF STATE AND LOCAL DEBT POLICY

Some governments have accumulated reserve funds for public works, but these have proved inadequate compared with postwar demands. Reserve funds have frequently played a useful role, but they have confronted legal difficulties and are vulnerable to encroachment by succeeding administrations. Some municipalities, such as Kalamazoo and Milwaukee, have attempted at times to finance public works out of current funds without benefit of borrowing. This has sometimes proved unpopular on the grounds that it resulted in postponement of badly needed projects, inequitably burdened current taxpayers with the full cost of improvements that would be beneficial to future generations, and failed to take advantage of prevailing low interest rates. As previously indicated, large units of government do have more discretion in debt policy than small ones; the former can, if they will, maintain a recurrent budgetary allowance for capital improvements.

The traditional method of borrowing to pay for local public works involves the serial bond, backed by the full faith and credit of the issuing unit of government and serviced largely from general property tax collections. The voters must generally approve a bond issue, sometimes by a two-thirds majority. Some municipal public works of the self-liquidating variety are financed by revenue bonds, payable solely from the revenue of the projects they have made possible. Authorities (such as the Port of New York Authority) and special districts are often used either to avoid debt limitations or provide desired managerial arrangements or both. Lease-purchase agreements are also used; typically, under these arrange-

---

[3] Shultz and Caine, *Financial Development of the United States*, p. 666.

ments a private company constructs a facility and leases it to the government until rental payments have covered cost with interest, after which title passes to the government. An authority may be formed to do the building, acquiring its resources from revenue bonds—revenue consisting of rentals paid by the collateral government to the authority. In some cases authorities or public corporations borrow from state trust funds the means with which to construct public buildings that are liquidated by rentals from the state, notwithstanding the fact that the state is not allowed to incur debt. This has been described as dishonest and expensive, the latter because revenue bonds usually command higher interest charges than general obligation bonds. These subterfuges pass with the courts but amendment of antiquated state constitutions would be more forthright. The federal government has also indulged in this practice to escape statutory debt limits.

The marketing of state and local bonds is normally entrusted to private financial institutions. Details of the offering may be established by a governmental unit and a bond dealer who specializes in state and local securities. In the case of large units, bond dealers may be asked to bid for the total issue at auction. But because of the small size of most municipal borrowers (school districts, townships, and the like), the unknown credit rating of the borrower to many potential purchasers, the small size of the issue (restricting secondary transactions), the expense involved in selling these obligations is likely to be extremely high. This is one reason why state and local governments stoutly resist any movement to take away their tax-exempt security privilege.[4] Centralized borrowing within a state could eliminate some of the disadvantages of small-scale borrowing. And the federal government might guarantee the principal and interest of municipal loans as it now does in the case of mortgages on veterans' and other housing.

RELATION OF STATE TO MUNICIPAL FINANCE

Self-denying Clauses in State Constitutions. The abuse of public credit during an earlier era of American history led several states to write into their constitutions provisions forbidding state borrowing except perhaps "to suppress insurrection or repel invasion." Some states are denied by their constitutions all authority to engage in works of public improvement. By constitutional amendment or otherwise, the construction and maintenance of highways is usually an exception from this restriction. Only a handful of states can borrow freely at their own discretion; some can borrow with approval by popular referendum, and some (nearly half) cannot borrow except in very unique circumstances or in very

---

[4] See pp. 461–464, above.

minor amounts (or by subterfuge). This self-imposed discipline seems to be an unwarranted and extreme reaction to the excesses and follies of the "wildcat" era. It should not be necessary to hamper a government with such restrictions and deprive it of its legitimate powers merely in order to prevent abuses. Moreover, as previously explained, tight restrictions on borrowing have led to subterfuges. Some states in effect let their counties incur debt that is really for state purposes, such as highways, and then reimburse the counties through a standing program of grants.

In the present conditions of state finances, when reliance upon the very stable property tax is rapidly diminishing and more "cycle-sensitive" taxes such as the income tax are taking its place, it is particularly important that states have some powers in the field of public credit. Unfortunately, it is impossible to say that we have reached the stage of collective intelligence and self-control where governments can be given freedom without danger of abuse. But the remedy does not seem to be the extreme one applied in these state constitutions. Whether the limitation, if any, should take the form of a larger than normal legislative majority for sanction, referendum, limitation as to purpose and duration, or amount as related to property tax base, or revenues, is a moot question. No limitation at all might be better than wide-open invitation to subterfuge. Moreover, that states should have so circumscribed their own use of credit while allowing their subdivisions substantial freedom in borrowing can hardly be explained on rational grounds. Borrowing by revenue bonds is more expensive than borrowing supported by "full faith and credit." Available subterfuges thus make present debt limitation expensive as well as futile.[5] The spectacle of setting up debt limits and then deliberately avoiding them is not calculated to enhance respect for government.

State Control of Debt Limitations.   It is generally accepted that there is an important general interest in the maintenance of municipal credit. If one municipality loses its financial head and later must default, all other municipalities suffer because their credit standing is weakened. The state, therefore, has a serious responsibility to guide and control its municipalities in their credit operations.

In this connection it may be observed that municipalities, as a rule, have very limited tax systems. They depend almost exclusively upon the general property tax and, although this has usually proved a fairly flexible and dependable source of revenue, it does have some limits, as illustrated by the fact that it broke down very conspicuously during the depression. Experimentation with tax-rate limitation laws has not added to the flexibility of the tax, especially where taxes to service debts, new or old, are included within the limitation.

---

[5] A. James Heins, *Constitutional Restrictions Against State Debt* (Madison: University of Wisconsin Press, 1963).

The most widely practiced form of state control consists of statutory and constitutional limits upon the indebtedness that any municipality may incur. This limit is usually stated in terms of a ratio to the assessed valuation of the municipality. However, debt limitations have often had many loopholes and have been otherwise ineffective. In some states the percentage has been set too high. Some states have no such ceiling, relying solely on tax limitations to prevent excessive borrowing by municipalities. Usually the limitation is applied to specific units only, whereas the taxpayer may be called upon to service debts for a variety of overlapping governments. Frequently, local assessments are subject to considerable manipulation and, of course, vary widely in relation to true taxable wealth. In several states, special assessment bonds are not included in the debt limits at all. The remedy seems to be to make the debt limit an over-all one and to set it sufficiently low to be effective. However, the over-all limit requires a central agency to apportion new debt among the overlapping units of government, a task which is by no means simple.

A major difficulty with debt limitations is that they, like tax limitations, constitute a highly inflexible control. Whether a municipality should go further into debt depends largely upon the circumstances of time and place. Certainly the purpose of the debt should be considered. Debt for improvements that have a reasonable prospect for self-sustenance should not be included within any arbitrary limits; in some cases no exception is made at present for such debts. A ratio of debt to assessed value is not a plausible basis for limitations. It ignores both revenues from other sources than the property tax and the tendency to manipulate assessments. A ratio of debt to average annual revenues would be more appropriate. For these reasons review by a state administrative agency is preferable to any form of arbitrary limit set by the legislature.

Other State Restrictions on Municipal Indebtedness. The negative controls exercised by the state cover considerably more than quantitative limitations. Municipalities are frequently required to observe certain rules of good practice in their debt policies, such as retiring the debt within a reasonable period and over the life of the improvement. In addition, they may be required to issue bonds of the serial type only and to levy taxes sufficient to liquidate the debt, thus providing for the automatic retirement of obligations. This type of control comes closer than arbitrary debt limitations to preventing abuse without undue interference with local autonomy. But unless such negative controls have a certain degree of administrative flexibility, they may not fit local situations. Moreover, they offer protection against only specific types of abuses.

State Receiverships and Assumption of Debts. Some states have set up machinery to take over the financial affairs of municipalities when the latter are unable to meet their financial obligations. It is thought that an outside authority may be more impartial than a regularly elected official in adjusting the claims of creditors, taxpayers, and those interested in municipal services. Not being dependent upon popular approval for office, the outside authority may show more courage than a local authority.

There is considerable precedent, too, for state assumption of debts of municipalities in distress. This may be better than default, but it is a last resort. It weakens local responsibility and is unfair to more conservative municipalities.

Supervision of Local Debt by a State Commission. By all odds the most constructive and promising innovation in state control is the North Carolina Local Government Commission, which has been in operation since 1931. The work of the Commission is divided into four parts: approval of applications for local bond and note issues, approval of refunding and readjusting operations, supervision of sinking funds, and supervising municipal accounting and reporting. During the depression period of widespread municipal defaults, the work of refunding and readjusting was most important.[6] An expert (though not adequate) staff is employed to keep the Commission informed and to investigate prospective new issues. The Commission rarely overrides local opinion on questions of need, but it frequently advises restraint on the ground of inability to carry an additional load. Local independence is preserved through the right to borrow (seldom exercised), notwithstanding adverse Commission decision, after a favorable referendum vote. Interest costs are said to have responded favorably to this kind of supervision and to the assistance rendered in the marketing of securities.[7] The principal merits of the North Carolina Commission are that it gives state control a positive as well as a negative aspect and makes the machinery entirely flexible. Local government departments with debt control functions are the rule among the Canadian provinces.

Positive State Assistance. There are many types of positive assistance that the state can give municipalities in the management of their debts, with or without a special department for that purpose. The state can furnish municipalities with facts concerning composite and comparative indebtedness. These facts have been scarce and difficult to procure. Expert advisory service may be made available. There is also some precedent for making state funds available for municipal borrowing. The use of state trust funds may be appropriate for this purpose. Some states assist municipalities in the marketing of securities.

---

[6] B. U. Ratchford, "The Work of the North Carolina Local Government Commission," *National Municipal Review,* XXV: 6 (June 1936), p. 319; letter from Clarence Heer, University of North Carolina, July 1953.

[7] Wylie Kilpatrick, *State Supervision of Local Finance,* Public Administration Service, Publication 79 (Chicago, 1941), p. 38.

RELATION OF FEDERAL TO STATE AND LOCAL FINANCE

Adaptation of State and Municipal Credit Program to Federal Fiscal Policy. Municipal financing has been criticized on the ground that it is usually badly correlated with federal fiscal policy. When federal policy seeks to check business and credit expansion, states and municipalities may continue to borrow heavily and may lighten local tax burdens. When federal policy seeks to encourage expansion, states and municipalities may be liquidating debts and imposing new and regressive taxes. Considering the limitation of state and municipal financial powers, not too much in the way of a countercyclical fiscal policy can be expected. To expect municipalities to act in unison for an over-all objective would be much like expecting all private industry so to behave. Nevertheless, states and municipalities can do more than they have to assure the success of federal fiscal policy. More general consciousness of the problem would itself promote such a program. Legislation to facilitate the accumulation of reserves, and debt retirement in good times, would be helpful. More flexible debt limit provisions would be conducive to sound procedure during depressions.[8]

Federal Control and Assistance. An outstanding example of federal-state cooperation in the debt field is the Australian Loan Council on which both the federal government and the states are represented. This group arose from a financial agreement between the commonwealth and the states in 1927. The Australian Loan Council in effect rations credit and centralizes the terms and collaterals for loans. Nothing approaching this is found in the United States, though some beginnings of cooperation can be cited. Loans to state and local governments from federal corporations were inaugurated during the depression of the 1930s and were very substantial. The Reconstruction Finance Corporation has been the most important lending agency, supplying funds to other governmental corporations as well as directly to private industry and to state and municipal governments. The exemption of interest on state and municipal securities from the federal personal income tax has aided, to some extent, in the marketing of these securities. A Federal Municipal Bankruptcy Act, passed during the depression, was designed to aid distressed municipalities. Federal aid has rarely taken the form of federal assumption of state debts, although even this did occur after the Revolutionary War and to a certain extent after the Civil War.

---

[8] See Harold M. Groves, "National Unity in Fiscal Policy-State and Local Aspects," *Proceedings of the National Tax Association Conference* (1958), pp. 36–46.

FOREIGN LOANS AND INVESTMENTS

The early experience of the United States was in the role of a debtor nation. The colonies borrowed during the Revolutionary War, and our national government was so weak under the Articles of Confederation that these obligations were in default and the states were threatened with intervention by foreign creditors. With the inauguration of the federal government in 1789, the foreign debt was gradually retired. Subsequently the states borrowed substantially abroad on an individual basis, or guaranteed private obligations for internal improvements, notably canals and railroads. In the difficulties occasioned by the crisis of 1837 and again after the "carpetbagger" period of reconstruction following the Civil War, there were several defaults on foreign obligations.[9]

RECENT HISTORY

The United States emerged from World War I with large debts to be collected from its allies. The latter, in turn, had reparations due them from their defeated enemies. From World War I to the depression of the 1930s, the questions of policy involved in these international obligations sorely perplexed the public. An ethical question concerned the propriety of collecting from those who had participated in a "common cause." An economic question concerned the willingness of creditors to accept goods in payment and the high tariff which blocked such means of transfer. Formerly the enemy was kept in doubt for many years as to the ultimate total of its obligations, and the large sums involved were alleged to discourage its moral and economic recuperation. It is now generally agreed that the postwar management of international obligations was one of the worst chapters in a story of badly bungled foreign relations in the period between the wars.

Fortunately, during World War II the "lend-lease" system was substituted for war debts. Under this system, goods and services were freely exchanged among the allies with an understanding that repayment would be made, if at all, in the specific goods provided (if they remained intact at the close of the war), or in such other goods as might be satisfactory to the parties involved. Settlement of lend-lease accounts proceeded smoothly, and the postwar debt problems of an earlier era have not again risen to plague us.

---

[9] Max Winkler, "Defaults and Repudiation of Foreign Loans," Foreign Policy Association, *Information Service*, IV: 11 (August 1928), p. 244.

In the early postwar period our financial relations with other countries were much involved in the Marshall Plan. It extended reconstruction aid to Western Europe, amounting to twice the size of the international debt of World War I. The program greatly accelerated postwar reconstruction and the progress of European integration programs. Only a very minor part of this transfer took the form of loans. An interesting feature was the "counterpart funds" which seemed to provide double-mileage for the aid program. Much of the aid took the form of capital goods for private parties; these parties thus encountered no exchange problem and they were expected to reimburse their own governments for part or all of the help. These governments in cooperation with the United States were then in a position to use these receipts for various works of public improvement.

The Marshall Plan has been described by one authority as a case of the rich helping the rich.[10] More recently the issues of foreign financial relations have focused on developmental grants to underdeveloped areas.

Forms of International Aid, Lending, and Investment. The species of instrumentalities and institutions in international finance run to considerable variety. Of most concern here are the transactions between governments, either loans or grants. But mention must also be made of semigovernmental loans made through the International Bank of Reconstruction and Development. The Bank grew out of the International Monetary Conference in 1944. Its capital (now authorized at $22.5 billion) was initially subscribed by forty-four member nations (now seventy-five are affiliated), and each was allotted a quota according to its ability to pay as related to economic strength. Additional capital has been raised by the sale of bonds, of which half have been purchased by public and private investors in the United States.

To complement the activities of the World Bank, which are highly selective as to economic feasibility of projects, there was established in 1960, as an affiliate of the Bank, the International Development Association. The requirements for borrowing here are less stringent; repayments may be made in local currencies, the loans are for longer periods and carry no interest, and they may be made for social projects such as educational facilities. Sixty-two nations are participating in this plan.

More exclusively American is the Export-Import Bank dating back to 1934, with capital stock of $1 billion held by the Treasury. It became a permanent and independent agency in 1945. It is authorized to make loans to foreign or domestic parties that facilitate the international trade of the United States.

Mixed loans of individuals to governments are sometimes described

---

[10] Gunnar Myrdal, *An International Economy* (New York: Harper and Row, Publishers, 1956), p. 121.

as "portfolio debt." It was voluminous during the 1920s when American bondhouses marketed among American investors many issues of foreign governments. The depression took heavy toll of these investments, however, and it is only recently that this kind of debt has made its reappearance on a considerable scale.

Private investment abroad is mostly corporate and takes the form either of branches of American firms or subsidiaries incorporated under American law. The latter type has tax advantages in that it is not taxed on reinvested earnings, but it does not share all benefits of tax treaties. American private direct investment abroad is said to be larger than government grants if those for military purposes are excluded. While American investment abroad is concentrated (especially in Canada and a comparatively small number of European countries), considerable sums are involved in many parts of the world.

Economic and Political Aspects. In general one would expect the free movement of private capital to be beneficial; it is simply a case of capital seeking an area where it can make a high marginal return and create opportunity and income where it goes. The question may be raised—as it was in connection with the international obligations growing out of World War I—whether creditor status as a nation and a continuing favorable balance of trade are compatible. On first thought, it seems evident that there is no point in foreign private investment unless it pays dividends and that these payments from abroad must take the form of imports. On second thought, two qualifications to this conclusion suggest themselves. The first is that foreign investment can be bilateral; a large amount of foreign capital is invested by foreigners in stocks purchased on the open market of the New York stock exchange. The second qualification takes note of the fact that we live in an acquisitive economy; instead of paying dividends to the home country, foreign enterprise can simply add to its wealth by reinvestment. Or as one enterprise sends money back home, others may send as much and more abroad.

Mention has been made of the view popular twenty years ago that chronic unemployment was in prospect because, among other reasons, the frontier had disappeared. Underdeveloped nations would seem to offer an adequate frontier, but it is one thing for New York to invest in Utah and another for the United States to invest in Mexico. The latter involves political risks, the greatest of which are associated with the possibility that a foreign host may choose to nationalize the resources developed by American investors. In an earlier era the answer might be to "send in the Marines." Now the risk of such casualties is assumed by the investor; no form of insurance yet developed seems adequate to handle such hazards.

Private versus Public Aid or Loans. Much debate at present centers on appropriations for international development, and one aspect of the debate concerns the question of whether the provision of capital for foreign countries should take the form of government grants, government loans, or private investment. Military and power-politics considerations are of course involved; but grants may create resentment rather than the goodwill which is their objective. Loans might avoid this reaction, but they are less potent as assistance and perhaps as a political weapon.

Vigorous proponents for private enterprise assert that the whole field of foreign assistance should be left to free private investment. They claim that public aids are an unnecessary expense to the taxpayer and that public loans had better be spent to provide loans to private investors on terms that would make a positive inducement for them to undertake risky ventures. They offer evidence that their record in technical assistance and training for local populations has been excellent.[11]

On the other side of the picture, it is said that private investment makes no contribution, directly at least, to the social overhead capital that some countries badly need: harbor facilities, education, irrigation projects, agricultural extension services, and the like. Private investment runs strongly to the extractive industries, and this has been criticized as "colonial investment" that does nothing for the host country except perhaps to provide the exchange with which industrial machinery might be bought. Moreover, the huge American companies that seek materials abroad are thought to be unequally matched in bargaining power with weak and sometimes corrupt foreign political leaders. The extractive industries as a basis for foreign economies are also said to be inherently unstable.[12]

Foreign Investment and the Tax System. A controversial point in the area of foreign investment is the application of the American tax laws to this outlay. As previously explained (Chapter 9) the American law generally applies the full corporate income tax rate to the earnings of foreign branches of American firms, but a credit is allowed for taxes paid to foreign countries. Until the Revenue Act of 1962 subsidiaries were taxed only on repatriated earnings. The new dispensation makes subsidiaries (with many qualifications) taxable on reinvested earnings.

Even the former rules had been vigorously criticized as an impediment to foreign investment. These rules denied American corporations any advantage from favorable treatment abroad (or from special con-

---

[11] American Enterprise Association, *American Private Enterprise, Foreign Economic Development, and the Aid Program,* A study for the Special Committee to Study the Foreign Aid Program, United States Senate, 85th Cong. 1st Sess. (Washington, D.C., 1957).

[12] Bernard Goodman, "The Political Economy of Private International Investment," *Economic Development and Cultural Change,* V: 3 (April 1957), pp. 263–276.

cessions often extended to attract new capital). The alleged result was that foreign countries were motivated to raise tax levels to that of the American scale. Special concessions in rates (now provided for certain western hemisphere corporations) were also sought. And foreign investors urged that the treatment formerly extended to subsidiaries with regard to reinvested earnings should also be extended to branches.

Among the factors producing a reverse trend in legislation is the balance-of-payment difficulty. While in recent years repatriated earnings have consistently exceeded the outlay of new funds invested abroad, the latter have an immediate adverse effect on the balance of payments. Moreover there is considerable concern about so-called tax havens where one foreign incorporated subsidiary may relay funds to another without incurring domestic taxation in the United States. Furthermore, intercorporate dealings afford a great many opportunities for avoidance that creates a strain on the Internal Revenue administration. Foreign investment may be desirable but does it serve the public interest so much better than domestic investment as to warrant favorable tax discrimination?

Conclusion.   As previously observed (Chapter 21), the issue of how to improve the lot of vast numbers of the world's population now emerging from colonialism is likely to trouble the conscience and perplex the judgment of the Western World for a long time to come. It would be folly to ignore the fact that there is a vast difference between the investment climate of the mid-twentieth century and that of one hundred years ago.

SUMMARY

Public borrowing assumed great importance in public finance with the development, particularly during the eighteenth century, of constitutionalism in government, the surpluses with which to make loans, public sanction of credit, and wide powers of taxation. Since then this institution has been widely, and sometimes intemperately, employed by most governments. Traditionally, federal debt has risen drastically during wars and has been retired after wars, though this tradition of retirement failed to hold after World War II.

Government debt can be classified and analyzed in several ways: internal and external; gross and net; long-term and short-term; marketable and nonmarketable; and according to the ownership of the obligations. As to maturity, federal debt instrumentalities are classified as bills, certificates, notes, and bonds. One of the most popular of these instrumentalities is the nonnegotiable savings bond. The government's chief problem with these securities is their redeemability which is said to make them hardly different from money and poor insurance against inflation.

Treasury policy of finance during World War II aimed at resistance to inflation, stability of bond yields, and low-cost borrowing. To accomplish the second of these objectives, the Federal Reserve System inaugurated the policy of buying securities at par. This led to certain difficulties in controlling bank credit and came to an end with the Treasury-Federal Reserve accord of 1951.

The managers of the public debt are mainly responsible for the terms of debt instruments: rate of interest; maturity of debt; eligible purchasers. It is conceded that to accommodate fiscal policy, the average maturity of debt should be lengthened (less liquidity) during prosperity. But this is expensive, and some critics would discard the controlling role of debt management on this account in favor of monetary policy.

Current issues of debt management also include the question of the proper controlling agency—Treasury or Federal Reserve; the statutory limits on the debt; and the use of so-called purchasing power bonds.

Many questions have been raised concerning the burden of the public debt: Is an internally held debt a burden? Can a burden through debt be shifted to a future generation? What is the nature of inflation and who bears its burden? Are there fundamental differences between federal, state, and private debt?

On a balance-sheet approach it is clearly impossible to shift the burden of the debt to future generations, but this ignores certain psychological and economic factors that lend reality to the idea of postponement. At the state and municipal level, postponement is not only real but warranted by a rapidly shifting constituency of beneficiaries. Debt retirement is now generally thought to be unwise except in times of full employment and inflation.

The capital levy, a heavy, single, personal tax upon property, involves many difficulties of administration and in finding a satisfactory medium of payment. Its use for the retirement of war debt in a single operation is counseled as a means of retroactive taxation of wealth created by emergencies and as a means of checking inflation.

Many states impose limitations and prohibitions on municipal borrowing, but a more constructive and positive form of control is provided in North Carolina by a state department with supervisory power over municipal borrowing. The self-denying clauses in state constitutions, prohibiting state borrowing, are hardly a control and not explicable on any grounds except that they are a blind reaction to excessive indulgence.

Foreign investment and the capital needs of underdeveloped areas raise such problems as the relative merits of public grants, public loans, and private investment; the alleged incompatibility of foreign loans or investment with a favorable balance of trade, and the impact of the tax system on private investment. Private investment is less burdensome on the taxpayer and less gratuitous than public grants or loans, but less conducive to a balanced development in the foreign economy. The tax system might be modified to stimulate foreign investment, but the recent trend has stressed parity of treatment and the mitigation of tax avoidance on earnings abroad.

PROBLEMS

1. Write a short history of war and postwar public debt management policy.
2. What are the advantages to the government and to the individual in the sale and purchase, respectively, of nonnegotiable debt?
3. Why does the Treasury have to raise large sums of money at frequent intervals even though the administration has a balanced budget?
4. Consider Series E bonds as to their (a) effectiveness in combating inflation; (b) avoidance of depreciation in the price of bonds; (c) soundness and convenience as an individual investment.
5. Consider the proposition: Debt management should lengthen the maturity of the national debt.
6. Comment on the proposition: Control of fiscal, monetary, and debt policy is hopelessly divided between two agencies—the Treasury and Federal Reserve—and should be concentrated in one or the other.
7. Criticize statutory limitations of the public debt.
8. Consider the claim that high interest rates benefit chiefly bankers and that they are worthless as an inflation control. What other means of controlling inflation might be offered for consideration?
9. One of the features of the national debt that makes it difficult to manage is its unequal distribution among individuals. Could this be avoided by substituting compulsion for volunteering in wartime borrowing? If compulsion is to be used anyway, why not tax rather than borrow?
10. Explain the effect of an increase in interest rates on the value of an already existing bond. Does this provide sufficient reason for attempting to stabilize interest rates?
11. Traditional business-cycle controls include, as important elements, manipulation of the rediscount rate, open-market operations, and control of reserve requirements. Explain how these were affected by war and postwar public debt management policy.
12. Would a constant-purchasing-power bond in time of inflation be a desirable innovation?

13. In a progressive economic society, what is likely to be the effect of time on the burden of public debt? What bearing, if any, does this have on public debt management policy?

14. Is there truth in the idea that to finance a war by borrowing means that those who fight a war must also pay for it?

15. Since government bonds when supported at par are practically the same as money, there is no sense in paying out billions of dollars in interest on the public debt. Comment.

16. Explain the economic differences between an internal and external public debt.

17. When the government acquires a surplus by taxation and uses the surplus to retire bank-held debt, this automatically reduces the money supply and reverses the process by which inflation got started in the first place. Comment.

18. A frontier in South America is as good an investment outlet as one in the west of the United States. Comment.

19. Every increase in the amount of national debt brings us one step closer to national bankruptcy. Comment.

20. What features of state constitutions relating to debt might well be amended if and when these constitutions are rewritten?

21. It is not inconsistent to recommend conservatism in state and local borrowing and at the same time to advocate federal deficits as a means of coping with a depression. Comment.

22. Contrast tax limitation and debt limitation from the standpoint of the legitimacy of outside interference with local home rule.

23. Compare an income tax, inflation, and a capital levy as means of financing a war or the postwar liquidation of war debt.

24. State and local governments, like private businesses, follow their individual self-interest and cannot be expected to join the federal government in countercyclical policy. Comment.

25. Compare public grants, public loans, and private investment as means of providing capital to underdeveloped countries.

26. Comment on the proposition: A country that invests heavily abroad must expect an unfavorable balance of trade and should reduce its protective tariff accordingly.

27. On what grounds is it alleged that American tax laws are prejudicial to private investment abroad?

APPENDIX

DEVELOPMENT OF PUBLIC FINANCE

HISTORY OF TAXATION IN WESTERN COUNTRIES

One needs to recall only a bit of general history to appreciate what a central place "the public purse" has had in the development of human affairs. Citation of a few of the more dramatic episodes may illustrate this. Going back to ancient history and the Bible, we find that the secession of the ten tribes of Israel, and thus the disruption of the Jewish monarchy, was in large part a tax phenomenon. The revolt is said to have been due to the refusal of Rehoboam to reduce the heavy taxes of his predecessor, King Solomon, who had embarked on an ambitious program of public works. The new king greeted a petition for tax relief with the ugly threat: "My little finger shall be thicker than my father's loins. And now whereas my father did lade you with a heavy yoke, I will add to your yoke; my father hath chastised you with whips, but I will chastise you with scorpions." As a prelude to the revolt which followed, the insurgent tribes answered the king by stoning his revenue agents to death.[1]

---

[1] I Kings, 12: 10–11.

TAXATION AND CONSTITUTIONAL DEVELOPMENT OF GREAT BRITAIN

Anyone with even superficial knowledge of English history can appreciate the role that taxation played in the political and constitutional history of that nation. A considerable portion of this history is the story of the struggle between the king and Parliament for control of the government purse strings. In describing the significance of this struggle to constitutional development, one authority writes that "no constitutional change has been more important in securing popular control over the executive government, than the voting of supplies by the House of Commons: nor has any expedient been better calculated to restrain the undue influence of the crown, than a strict settlement of its revenues by Parliament." [2]

Magna Carta, 1215.   The resentment that has been voiced against arbitrary taxation in England goes back almost to the days of the Norman conquest. It began with only a few powerful nobles and clerics who protested that they would not pay a tax to which they had not consented.[3] These were the protests of individuals. But in 1215 they joined forces and compelled King John to grant them a "charter of liberties," known in history as Magna Carta. This celebrated document, among other things, promised that "no scutage nor aid shall be imposed on our kingdom, unless by the common counsel of our kingdom, except for ransoming our person, for making our eldest son a knight, and for once marrying our eldest daughter; and for these there shall not be levied more than a reasonable aid." [4]

Notwithstanding its promises to lighten the public burden, the Great Charter is significant in taxation history not because of its actual provisions but rather because of what succeeding generations of Englishmen were pleased to read into it. The *scutage* and the aids it refers to were not taxes in the modern sense; they were feudal dues which the tenants of the king were expected to pay him as overlord. And even these restrictions were left out of the later versions of the charter. But the idea of representation, that the sovereign agreed to treat with the representatives of the nation on revenue measures, persisted from that time on. It was this principle of national consent to taxation upon which Englishmen always re-

---

  [2] Sir Thomas Erskine May, *Constitutional History of England* (London: Longmans, Green and Company, 1882), vol. I, p. 231.
  [3] *Ibid.*, p. 67.
  [4] Par. 12 (W. S. McKechnie, *Magna Carta*, 2d ed., Glasgow, 1914). Further it was promised (Par. 41) "All merchants shall have safe and secure exit from England, and entry to England, with the right to tarry there and to move about as well by land as by water, for buying and selling by the ancient and right customs, quit from all evil tolls. . . ."

lied in their long fight with their sovereigns on the question of public levies.[5]

Parliament and Charles I.   One of the major issues in the great struggle between the British Parliament and the Stuart kings was the right of the king to levy taxes without the consent of Parliament. This conflict came to a head under Charles I. He broke with Parliament and sought to raise revenue independently of its sanctions. One of the many expedients to which he resorted was the forced loan. This was a mere subterfuge, for there was no pretense that the loans would ever be repaid. Five gentlemen who refused to comply with Charles's requests were imprisoned. Shortly after this incident, Parliament submitted to the king the Petition of Rights, which he reluctantly accepted in 1628. Among other requests agreed to was that none need thereafter "make or yield any gift, loan, benevolence, tax, or such like charge" without the consent of Parliament.[6] Nevertheless, the conflict continued, and for more than a decade following, Charles attempted to govern the country without Parliament. He again resorted to various devices to secure money. One of these was the "Ship Money" which was based on an old tradition that each port must provide the monarch with a ship. Charles's version of it, however, called for payment in money rather than in kind, and payment by inland taxpayers as well as by those located in seaports.[7] But the king's financial embarrassment was not at an end, and in 1640 he resorted to the desperate expedient of buying on credit a large cargo of pepper, which had just arrived in the ships of the British East India Company, and selling it cheap for cash.[8] The culmination of this strife was a civil war in which Charles was defeated, imprisoned, and beheaded.

The Bill of Rights, 1689.   Forty years after this fateful blow to the Stuarts, James II, the last of that dynasty on the English throne, incurred the displeasure of his subjects and was deposed by Parliament. He was followed by his nephew, William of Orange, who accepted the Bill of Rights (1689). This important document included among its provisions "that levying money for or to the use of the Crown by pretense of prerogative, without grant of Parliament, for longer time or in other manner than the same is or shall be granted, is illegal." [9] Having reasserted this

---

[5] S. A. Morgan, *The History of Parliamentary Taxation in England,* Williams College, 1911, pp. 68–70; F. W. Maitland, *The Constitutional History of England* (London: Cambridge University Press, 1931), pp. 94–96, 306–311.

[6] The Petition of Rights, Par. 8.

[7] Opposition to this extortion was very strong, and at least one taxpayer, John Hampden, a courageous country squire from Buckinghamshire, refused to pay the 20 shillings which were demanded of him. He was tried by the king's judges, who, by a bare majority, sustained the tax.

[8] Samuel R. Gardiner, *History of England (1603–1642)* (London: Longmans, Green and Company, 1904), vol. IX, p. 190.

[9] The Bill of Rights, Par. 4.

principle and given it the effect of a law, the Bill closed a turbulent chapter in English constitutional history. This principle was never again seriously challenged except in connection with the colonies, and then not only the king but also his Parliament were opposed to extending its application to their outlying possessions.

TAXATION AND THE AMERICAN REVOLUTION

After the close of the Seven Years' War (known in American history as the French and Indian War), England was in great need of additional revenue to meet the resulting expenses. George III and his Parliament attempted to levy certain taxes for this purpose upon the colonists and their trade. It was argued by proponents of this policy that it was but natural to expect the colonists to make some contribution for their own protection, including the debt that had grown out of the recent war. Accordingly, Parliament passed the Stamp Act, which required the colonists to purchase stamps from the British government and apply them to leases, deeds, and other documents as a condition of their legal standing. The colonists resented these levies on the grounds that they were not represented in the British Parliament and thus had not consented to such taxation. An assembly of colonial representatives in New York in 1765 protested that the Stamp Act indicated a tendency to subvert their rights and liberties.[10]

The protest of the colonists had a familiar sound in England and won the support of a considerable following in Parliament. The Stamp Act was repealed despite the opposition of King George and the British "tories." The issue again arose, however, when the British government imposed certain tariff duties on American trade, including the importation of tea. With the exception of the latter, these duties were repealed within three years. The retention of the levy on tea was more for the purpose of soothing the feelings of the king than for raising revenue. Had it been for this duty alone, colonial dissatisfaction with taxation might have entirely subsided. But tea was destined to play a notable role in American history in yet another way. The tea trade was made a monopoly and given to the East India Company. This threatened to ruin a profitable business for both smugglers and legitimate tea merchants of the colonies. With the tariff legislation of Parliament still fresh in mind, it took but little time to arouse the ire of the colonists. Opposition to this new measure soon came to a head in the famous "Boston Tea Party," which contributed much toward bringing on the American Revolution.[11]

---

[10] Charles A. Beard and Mary R. Beard, *The Rise of American Civilization* (New York: The Macmillan Company, 1930), vol. I, p. 213.

[11] F. A. Shannon, *Economic History of the People of the United States* (New

TAXATION AND THE FRENCH REVOLUTION

The American Revolution had a profound effect upon the French, who were discontented with the conditions imposed upon them by the ruling class. The economic status of the masses during the *ancien régime,* partly because of the burdensome exactions to which they were subjected, was extremely poor. If the discontent of the colonists was justified, that of the French people was even more so, for undoubtedly theirs was one of the most oppressive tax systems of all times. The French had developed no constitutional rights of taxation by consent. In England the fight against royal arbitrariness was carried to victory not so much by the common people as by the nobles. But in France the nobles had less cause to follow suit, for both they and the clergy were exempted from many taxes, the former on the ground that their obligation consisted in fighting for the king, and the latter on the ground that the state could not encroach upon what had been dedicated to God.

The Tax System before the French Revolution. Hastily surveying some of the most important levies which the French people had to pay before the Revolution, one may observe first, that they had two "sovereigns" to support, the king and the church, both costly. The church collected the *tithe,* originally a free offering of a tenth of one's produce but becoming at a very early age of French history a compulsory contribution not only in France but throughout Europe.[12]

Far more important than the tithe were the taxes that were levied by the king. Perhaps the best known of these was the *taille,* one of the many levies originating in the feudal period. Like the English *tallage,* it was primarily a tax on the cultivators of the soil, based upon their supposed profits which were estimated by the value of their farms. But while tallage as such came to an end in the fourteenth century, the taille was made a permanent annual tax in 1439.[13] It was supposed to have been a general tax; actually, however, the nobles and the clergy, and even the wealthy bourgeois, were exempted.[14] "This tax besides," writes Adam Smith, "is supposed to dishonour whoever is subject to it, and to degrade him below, not only the rank of a gentleman, but that of a burgher, and whoever rents

---

York: The Macmillan Company, 1934), chap. VI; Harold Underwood Faulkner, *American Economic History* (New York: Harper and Row, Publishers, 1931), chap. VII.

[12] *Palgrave's Dictionary of Political Economy* (London: The Macmillan Company, 1926), vol. III, pp. 543–546.

[13] Stephen Dowell, *History of Taxation and Taxes in England* (London: Longmans, Green and Company, 1888), vol. I, pp. 39–58; E. R. A. Seligman, *Essays in Taxation* (10th ed., New York: The Macmillan Company, 1925), pp. 43–44.

[14] *Ibid.,* pp. 50–51.

the lands of another becomes subject to it. No gentleman, nor even any burgher who has stock, will submit to this degradation." [15]

The administration of this tax was its most objectionable feature. The collectors, both because they were ignorant and because of compulsion, applied arbitrary methods of assessment. Appearances were their chief basis for evaluating income. Resistance, therefore, often took the form of simulated poverty. Thus Rousseau, the eminent French philosopher, relates his visit at the house of a peasant where he had stopped to ask for dinner. At first, his host put before him only barley bread and skimmed milk and said that this was all he had. Convinced at last that his visitor was not a government spy, the peasant opened the larder and produced some ham, good wheat bread, an omelet, and a bottle of wine. The peasant concealed his stock, so he told his guest, because of the taille, for he feared that he would be ruined by taxation if the officials had any idea that he was not dying of hunger.[16]

On top of this system of direct taxes in prerevolutionary France was another and equally objectionable group of indirect taxes. During the *ancien régime,* France was cursed with an elaborate system of tariffs, effective not merely at the boundary of the country but also at the boundary lines of the provinces and even those of the cities. Their administration was not an easy task and was characterized by large-scale smuggling, with severe penalties for those who "got caught." There were also excise taxes on tobacco (through a state monopoly), wines, and ciders. The most dreaded of the indirect taxes was the *gabelle* or salt tax. The rate was higher in some districts than in others. Smuggling from low-taxed to high-taxed provinces was common. As if the physiological requirement were not sufficient, a law required every man, woman, and child over the age of seven to consume seven pounds of salt each year.[17]

Every age is most alive to its own problems. The taxpayer, whatever

---

[15] *The Wealth of Nations,* pp. 370, 805–806.

[16] Edward I. Lowell, *The Eve of the French Revolution* (Boston: Houghton Mifflin Company, 1892), p. 216. Also H. A. Taine, *The Ancient Regime* (New York: Henry Holt and Company, 1876), pp. 354–357.

This system of direct taxation was supplemented from time to time with an income tax, which in 1749 became a permanent levy until the Revolution. It was called the *vingtieme,* or twentieth, because it was supposed to claim one twentieth of the taxpayer's income. However, it was badly administered; it developed into an unreasonable levy, usually falling upon those who were least able to pay. The capitation or poll tax, graduated according to twenty-two classes of taxes, was subject to the same criticism—E. R. A. Seligman, *The Income Tax* (2d ed., New York: The Macmillan Company), pp. 50–53.

The *corvee* called for forced labor on the highways. As a service to the state, it was based on no general law but was imposed at will by the civil and military officials of the king. This imposition was confined largely to the peasants and was one of the most disliked taxes before the Revolution. It came to an end with the monarchy in 1793—Lowell, *op. cit.,* pp. 226–227.

[17] *Ibid.,* pp. 222–225.

age he lives in, is usually convinced that his generation is saddled with far heavier exactions than those of any other. If ever he was justified in this assertion, it was certainly in prerevolutionary France. There is no authentic information concerning the total tax burden that the French people had to carry. Taine, the French historian, estimated that the combined levy of all types of taxes and feudal dues took over 81 percent from the meager incomes of the peasants.[18] Some historians question this figure, although their only argument is that existence could not have been possible on one fifth of a peasant's produce.[19] It is apparent, however, that taxes took the major share of the earnings of the poor, whose patience was about exhausted. The outbreak of the Revolution in 1789 was to a great extent an indication of the desperation to which the poor were driven by the tax system of the *ancien régime*.

Abolition of the Ancient Taxes. The immediate outbreak of the French Revolution was due to the insolence of the nobles and the clergy, but important among its underlying causes were taxes and the financial troubles of the king's household. In vain did Turgot, one of Louis XVI's ablest finance ministers, labor to improve the financial situation. The expenditures of the king upon his court continued to be highly extravagant. The national finances were further strained by the indebtedness created to finance the annually recurring deficits. The time finally came when the king could borrow no more money and, because of popular resentment, could eke out no more taxes. Nothing remained for him but to consent to the summoning of the ancient Estates General, which, when it met, declared itself a National Assembly and proceeded in a series of steps to take matters into its own hands. One of its first enactments established the proposition that no tax not receiving its consent was valid. Soon the internal customs and the privileges of the tax-exempt classes were eliminated. The salt tax was abolished. For a long time, however, great confusion, incompetent administration, and inadequate funds continued to characterize national finances. In fact, it was not until the able administration of Napoleon that anything like an adequate and rational financial system was inaugurated.[20]

---

[18] *Op. cit.*, pp. 412–413. Compare, for instance, the taxation in Palestine at the time of Christ, conservatively estimated at 40 percent of a very modest income. The Romans among other levies exacted taxes on water, meat, salt, roads, and houses, and they used a so-called farming system of collection that made the term "publican" almost synonymous with "robber." Moreover, most of these taxes were not only exacted by a foreign power but went to Rome as tribute. See Sir Josiah Stamp, *Christianity and Economics* (New York: The Macmillan Company, 1938), pp. 15–16.

[19] J. M. Perkins, *France under Louis XV* (Boston: Houghton Mifflin Company, 1897), vol. I, p. 43. Also Lowell, *op. cit.*, p. 228.

[20] Leo Gershoy, *The French Revolution and Napoleon* (New York: Appleton-Century-Crofts, 1933), pp. 97–106, 153–160, 459–462.

TAXATION IN EARLY UNITED STATES HISTORY

TAXATION AND THE FEDERAL CONSTITUTION

The American colonies were ill prepared to finance the American Revolution. No national system of taxation had been developed, and the Continental Congress was forced to rely for its revenue on a combination of fiat currency, levies on the states (with no adequate machinery for enforcement), foreign subsidies, and domestic and foreign loans.[21] In fact, had it not been for the last-named assistance, particularly from France, the war could hardly have been carried to successful conclusion. When independence was finally established, the union unsuccessfully attempted to operate as a centralized government under the Articles of Confederation. One of the major weaknesses of the new government was that it had no independent powers of taxation.[22]

The necessity for a new constitution, with somewhat more generous financial powers for the government of the union, was painfully apparent. It was no small matter to induce the states to surrender sufficient power to allow the federal government its own tax system. Many saw in this the development of a tyranny more terrible than that against which they had just rebelled. Nevertheless, necessity prevailed, and a new Constitution, ratified in 1789, gave the federal government ample powers to balance its budget, reestablish its credit, and pay off its war debt, including some of the debts of the states which the new government assumed.[23]

INAUGURATION OF THE FEDERAL REVENUE SYSTEM

The new federal powers merit a more adequate treatment than can be given here. They have been discussed in Chapter 19. It may be observed, however, that the federal government was given the power to levy tariffs and excises, the former being an exclusive right. Congress speedily en-

---

[21] Shultz and Caine, *Financial Development of the United States,* pp. 47–48.

[22] Its only source of revenue, outside of borrowing, was requisitions from the states in proportion to the value of their lands and improvements. No national tariff could be levied without an amendment to the Articles, which in turn required the unanimous consent of the states. Such consent, however, was not forthcoming. The requisitions attempted were regarded by the states as voluntary contributions and were only partially paid. The Confederation government never succeeded in balancing its budgets, and interest and principal payments upon its very substantial debt were either defaulted or refunded—*Ibid.,* pp. 72–74; also D. R. Dewey, *Financial History of the United States* (New York: Longmans, Green and Company, 1928), pp. 49–50.

[23] Shultz and Caine, *op. cit.,* pp. 91–103.

acted a tariff law (1789) which at once began to bring in badly needed revenue.[24] Owners of the new industries which had lately sprung up on American soil clamored for the use of the tariff for the nonfiscal purpose of protecting their enterprises. Those new industries had taken root in the northern and central states, and the support for the protective tariff came from these sections. Planters of the south and farmers of the west, however, saw nothing to gain and much to lose in protection.[25]

SECTIONAL BATTLE OVER THE TARIFF

The first tariff law was only mildly protective, but with subsequent legislation protection gained ground. Sectional division and conflict concerning this issue grew sharper. The high protective tariff law of 1824 received only a few votes among the representatives from below the Mason and Dixon Line.[26] Four years later Congress passed the notorious "Tariff of Abominations," so called because its opponents had made it appear, with some justice, as vicious as possible in the hope of defeating it, a stratagem which proved unsuccessful. When the Tariff of 1828 became fully effective, it carried average rates of about 44 percent on dutiable goods. The Tariff of 1832 reduced rates and eliminated some of the abomination, but still it remained a highly protective tariff and very distasteful to the South.[27] It was plain that the southerners regarded the federal power to tax as a menace to their traditional liberty, for which they had fought and

---

[24] Congressional debate on Madison's bill in the House of Representatives—a very moderate measure based on a general 5-percent *ad valorem* duty and including special rates on liquors, molasses, wines, tea, pepper, sugar, cocoa, and coffee—foreshadowed the central place that the tariff would have in American public affairs.

[25] The Washington Administration had what was regarded as an ambitious program of public expenditures for that period. In addition to the assumption and retirement of the public debt, it sought to strengthen the national government by developing some military strength. To help finance the program several excises were provided, including a tax on whisky and what had some resemblance to a personal property tax on carriages. The excise met with substantial opposition. Its opponents argued that whisky was not a luxury, but a poor man's necessity. Opposition to it finally took on the proportions of an open rebellion in western Pennsylvania, and President Washington was obliged to send a small army to ensure compliance—Shultz and Caine, *op. cit.*, pp. 104–111.

[26] The South had become convinced that the tariff was a device to tax it for the benefit of the North. By that time it was becoming apparent that the South was dedicating itself to the cultivation of cotton, rice, and tobacco, which made its prosperity depend upon export trade and the opportunity of buying low-priced manufactured goods. Tariffs meant to the South higher prices for manufactured goods which the people of that region needed to purchase.

[27] Calhoun of South Carolina contended that it was unconstitutional for Congress to levy taxes for other than revenue purposes. (See Chapter 19, on the federal power to tax for nonfiscal purposes.) A bitter debate between Senators Hayne of South Carolina and Webster of Massachusetts reopened the entire question of federal versus state powers.

for which they were willing to fight again. A convention called by the legislature of South Carolina in 1832 declared the tariff acts of 1828 and 1832 null and void and any attempt to enforce the latter in that state as a cause for secession. Governor Hamilton called for 10,000 volunteers to defend this position. President Jackson wrote to the collector at Charleston that the acts must be enforced and threatened to send 40,000 troops into South Carolina. At this critical state of affairs Congress passed a compromise tariff plan sponsored by Henry Clay. The new tariff called for substantial reductions in rates over a nine-year period. It was accepted by South Carolina, and, as a result, a situation that might have led to a civil war was averted.[28]

These few historical references have been drawn to demonstrate the central place which public finance has occupied in the history of the United States and other countries.

DEVELOPMENT OF PUBLIC FINANCE INSTITUTIONS

No very clear pattern of evolution can be traced in the history of taxation and public expenditures. Most of the taxes and public expenditures known to the modern world are of ancient origin. The changes have been not so much in the tax system or in public expenditures themselves as in the nature of the institutions and the environment to and in which they have been applied. For instance it can be argued that taxes on coal and candles was a vastly different matter in the early years of the Industrial Revolution from what it is in an affluent society which provides an impressive array of services that improve the lot of the poor.

---

[28] Shannon, *op. cit.,* pp. 223–236.

Following the Civil War a period of very high protective tariffs ensued, and the issue became critical again during the Cleveland administration. With a huge surplus in the federal Treasury—$94,000,000 for the fiscal year of 1886—Cleveland denounced the tariff levies as a "ruthless extortion." He devoted his entire message of 1887 to this subject, stating that the theoretical arguments for the tariff—such as the contention that it makes for high wages in domestic industry, keeps money a home, creates a home market, and makes the country independent of foreign nations—were irrelevant since "it is a condition that confronts us and not a theory." In the election of 1888, in which he was defeated, the tariff was an all-important issue. Upon his return to office in 1892, he again sought a reduction in the tariff. He was not very successful in this endeavor, and it was not until the Underwood Act of 1913 that Congress enacted a substantial reduction in tariff rates—*Ibid.,* pp. 577–585, 785–788.

Cleveland's second administration is significant in the financial history of the United States for still another reason. In 1894 Congress enacted the first peacetime federal income tax, only to have it declared unconstitutional by the Supreme Court.

THE ANCIENT WORLD

Public Expenditures. From the earliest time of organized society the prime function of government has been the protection of the people from foreign aggression. This includes, of course, the perpetration of such aggression upon others. A second time-honored function has been the preservation of internal peace, order, and security and the administration of justice. A third function, now exercised by only a few states, has been the maintenance of a state religion. In some states, where the church has been separate from the state, the church, nevertheless, usually has had its own financial system with high powers of compulsion. A fourth function was formerly the maintenance of the king and his household, an expenditure that reached its height with Louis XIV of France, whose court probably cost the French about $100 million in addition to much forced labor. This function has its counterpart in the general national governmental expenditures of today. These four functions have been the most universal. A fifth, however, that of public works, including the building of pyramids, roads, canals, and a postal system, has also been common. Egypt incurred heavy burdens to build its pyramids. Ancient Athens had an even more extensive program of public works, which included fountains, markets, gymnasia, walls, and fortification. In addition, both the Greeks and the Romans assumed some responsibility for the welfare of their poor; the distribution of free grain in Rome is renowned. Beginnings of public recreation appear in the Greek theater and religious festivals and in the Roman amphitheater. The Roman sewers constituted a rudimentary public health program. Of all the major modern public expenditures only education appears to have been entirely neglected, and even under this heading the Greeks provided physical education in the gymnasia and wrestling schools.[29]

Feudal Forms of Taxation. A large portion of human history has passed through some form of feudal organization. Under this system, best adapted to an agricultural civilization, the king or ruler theoretically owned the country. He retained only a part of it under his personal dominion, however, and from this he received an income in produce. Since the king could not administer all the land directly, he ordinarily gave a more or less limited tenure to some of his soldiers or favorites, who in turn had their own subtenants or vassals. The tenants, like our modern sharecroppers, shared their produce with their overlords, to whom they

---

[29] A. M. Andreades, *A History of Greek Public Finance* (Cambridge, Mass.: Harvard University Press, 1933), vol. I, pp. 8–14, 114–120; Jules Toutain, *The Economic Life of the Ancient World* (New York: Alfred A. Knopf, 1930), pp. 237–238, 246–247, 256.

were also expected to render various sorts of free services. Under such organization, taxation closely resembled land rent. This system prevailed in ancient Egypt and in all Europe (with variations) during the Middle Ages.[30]

Direct Taxes. Along with these feudal contributions, many of the nations of the ancient world developed rather complex revenue systems. The gross produce tax (like our modern gross income tax) was very common, both within and without the feudal system. It depended upon the harvest and was more like our income than our property tax. More often than not these taxes were paid in produce, such as cattle, grain, wine, oil, honey, and textiles.[31] The Greeks and the Romans objected to direct taxes in any form; they regarded them as "derogatory to the dignity of a free citizen." [32] The Greeks nevertheless resorted to such taxes in times of emergency, and the Romans exacted them from the conquered provinces.

The best known of the taxes that have been handed down to us from the ancients, however, is the inheritance tax. The origin of this tax has been attributed to Rome, although there had been traces of it in Egypt many centuries earlier. In Rome it first was one twentieth of the estate (*visesima hereditatium*), but under Emperor Caracalla the rate was doubled. It applied to both inheritances and bequests, but close relatives and the very poor were exempt. An interesting feature of this tax was its nonfiscal aspects; it taxed the estates of unmarried people 100 percent and those of childless couples 50 percent.[33] Apparently, the similar features of the income and inheritance taxes of prewar Germany and Italy are no innovation in revenue legislation.[34]

------

[30] James Henry Breasted, *The Conquest of Civilization* (Harper and Row, Publishers, 1926), p. 85.

[31] *Ibid.*, pp. 66, 201, 672.

[32] Alfred Zimmern, *The Greek Commonwealth* (Oxford: The Clarendon Press, 1924), p. 289.

[33] Max West, *The Inheritance Tax* (New York: Columbia University Press, 1908), pp. 11–15; A. D. Winspear and L. K. Geweke, *Augustus and the Reconstruction of Roman Government and Society,* University of Wisconsin Studies in Social Sciences and History, No. 24 (1935), p. 161.

[34] Early governments had little need for direct taxes, since they levied tribute upon their conquered and weaker neighbors. The Greeks financed a goodly share of their public expenditures out of the generosity and patriotism of their wealthier citizens. "It was by free gifts," wrote Thucydides, the historian, "that the Athenians armed the fleets which were so long supreme on the seas, by free gifts that they formed the choirs which performed the dances and recited the songs 'taught' them by the poets"—Quoted from Zimmern, *op. cit.,* p. 290.

Another rich source of public revenue enjoyed by many of the ancient nations was the public domain. Athens and a few other of the city-states derived a considerable profit from their mines. According to one historian, Carthage obtained nearly half of her revenues from the mines in Spain, which in later years also proved to be a good source of revenue for Rome—Andreades, *op. cit.,* pp. 268–273.

Of the other direct taxes known to us, the poll or capitation tax is of very ancient origin. It was known in Egypt where it was levied upon the male population from fourteen to sixty-two years of age, but with numerous exceptions. In Rome it was levied upon all those engaged in business who were not citizens. Although it remained a poll tax in form, in time it actually developed into a kind of personal property tax.[35]

Indirect Taxes. The indirect taxes were also well developed in the ancient world. Probably the oldest of them was the customs, which first appeared in the form of gifts to the king as the price of the permission to trade. Merchants were frequently required to pay a tax upon both importing and exporting.[36] Strabo, the Greek historian and geographer, writes in his discussion of the Egyptian trade as follows: "The most valuable consignments [of India and Ethiopia come] to Egypt, and are sent on from there to the rest of the world, so that Egypt gets double duties from them, on coming in and on going out; and the duty is heavy in proportion to the value of the goods." [37]

The sales tax was also familiar to the ancients. "In Egypt . . . there was not a single stage on the way by which goods went . . . from a place of production to a place of consumption, where the exchequer did not step in and seize some proportion of the value of the goods." [38] It was also a very profitable source of revenue to the Greeks. They levied it on practically all buying and selling. To Athens especially the sales tax on slaves brought in huge sums, since that city was the chief mart for the slave trade during the fourth and fifth centuries B.C.[39]

THE MIDDLE AGES

It will be observed that most of our modern taxes were introduced before the Middle Ages. Only the net income tax, perhaps the most important of the present-day levies, appears to have been neglected. The gross produce tax had much in common with our modern property tax. It was based upon rentals or annual values, which is also true of European property taxes today. Apparently, actual yield was the base rather than an objective rating independent of management and fortune. In this respect the tax was more like the modern net income tax. Its closest re-

[35] Winspear and Geweke, *op. cit.*, p. 158.

[36] Andreades, *op. cit.*, pp. 138–143.

[37] Quotation from Toutain, *op. cit.*, p. 161.

[38] *Ibid.*

[39] Andreades, *op. cit.*, pp. 143–145, 281–285. Other revenue sources known to the ancient world included licenses and special assessments. Both of these are of ancient origin. Many of the countries of the Greco-Roman world required a license fee (occupation tax) for certain callings of shady reputation, notably, oracle mongers, jugglers, and prostitutes. Egypt levied a special payment for irrigation projects similar in many respects to our special assessments—*Ibid.*, pp. 107, 127, 284.

semblance is found in our gross income and severance taxes. Even the modern democratic tradition of no taxation without the consent of the taxed was not unknown to the ancient world. It was accepted in the Athenian democracy.[40]

During the Middle Ages public finance became closely identified with the feudal system, a system which was not unknown but less important in the ancient world. One writer has referred to this system as one of "patrimonial," as distinguished from "contributory," finance.[41] The king, dukes, counts, barons, bishops, and convents received their income partly from the land they held directly and partly from the feudal dues paid to them by their subordinates. Except during certain intervals and in certain emergencies, the king was expected to subsist mainly upon the income from the property he held directly. The exceptions included such occasions as ransoming him, knighting his eldest son, and marrying his eldest daughter. The additional revenues he sought on such occasions were designated (at least in England) as subsidies or grants. Such grants or subsidies were often made necessary by foreign wars. These revenues were "contributory" in the sense that both the expenditure and the grant itself depended upon the assent of a representative assembly. The "assent" principle, of course, was not always conceded, and it was the basis of that long constitutional struggle outlined above.[42]

Income from the Royal Demesne. In medieval England the king's demesne land was enormous, including at one time many towns and cities, among them the city of London. This domain yielded a patrimonial or rental income almost sufficient for his needs. His forests provided extensive hunting grounds for him and his friends, and a supply of venison for the royal table. In addition, they brought in revenue from fines upon

---

[40] *Cambridge Ancient History* (New York: The Macmillan Company, 1927), vol. V, p. 27.

[41] Antonio de Viti de Marco, *First Principles of Public Finance* (New York: Harcourt, Brace and World, 1936), p. 56.

[42] The medieval feudal system was an ideal instrument for arbitrary power. The king and the barons were under no obligation to render a *quid pro quo* for their revenues since they received them as a matter of right. The budget of the state was merged with the personal budget of the monarch, including the outlays for servants and entertainment. As the system developed, public expenditures increased owing to the prodigality of the rulers and to the increasing scope of collective wants. Patrimonial revenues, on the other hand, shrank owing to the gradual contraction of the public domain. For this the king himself was responsible, partly because of the generosity with which he compensated his favorites out of his lands and partly because he was forced to yield a portion of it for immediate revenue. These were auspicious circumstances for his rebellious vassals and, as we have seen, they made the most of them. The results were limitations upon the absolute power of the king both in England and on the continent—*Ibid.,* pp. 62–65; also, May, *op. cit.,* vol. I, chap. IV, and James Westfall Thompson, *Feudal Germany* (Chicago: University of Chicago Press, 1928), chap. X.

those who hunted in them without permission. Gradually, however, much of royal domain became partially or entirely alienated through the process of grant and charter.[43]

Taxes on Land and Other Property. The first known taxes in England were land taxes levied by area, or, as we would say, at so much per acre. Only the unit was not the acre, but the *hide.* The *hidage,* as the tax is sometimes known, was based upon a farm sufficient in size to support a household. It was replaced under William the Conqueror by the *carucage,* the basis of which was the carucate or plow land—an area that could be plowed by one plow and a team of eight oxen. Shortly thereafter a new imposition appeared, but fell only upon the knights to take the place of the personal services they had to render to the king under feudal tenure. This was the *scutage.* Strictly speaking this was not a tax, but it played a leading role in the history of taxation; as previously mentioned, it was one of the grievances Magna Carta was supposed to have righted.[44]

Gradually the annual value (rental value) of land became the basis of assessment. Movable or personal property was assessed either on its capital value or on a calculated annual value. During certain stages this tax, both on real and personal property, assumed a character much like our modern general property tax; at no time, however, was it as universal in its inclusions. As far as personal property was concerned, it raised much the same difficulties of administration as those confronting our modern tax. As Seligman puts it, "in actual practice virtually nothing was assessed except real estate, so that the tax soon became a land tax." [45] As a source of revenue, the land tax could not keep up with the growing expenditures of the national government in the eighteenth century. With the attempt to secure a more fertile source, it was relegated to a secondary position. In 1798 it was made permanent at prevailing rates and the landowners were allowed to pay it off in perpetuity with lump-sum payments. Many of these landowners took advantage of the opportunity,

---

[43] Dowell, *op. cit.,* vol. I, pp. 13–15, 50–55; also May, *op. cit.,* vol. I, pp. 225–229.

The revenues of the English kings were also supplemented by benevolences, gifts in token of loyalty to the king. In fact, all contributory payments to the Crown were regarded as more or less "benevolent," as is indicated by the phrases "subsidies" and "grants" frequently applied to what we would now call taxes—Dowell, *op. cit.,* vol. I, pp. 196–203.

[44] *Ibid.,* pp. 8, 34–48.

[45] *The Income Tax,* 2d ed., pp. 48–49.

To some extent, in the effort to make the tax all-embracing, a semblance to the modern income tax appeared with the inclusion of the stipends from public offices in the tax base. This feature was in effect also in the early tax systems of Massachusetts and Connecticut.

which accounts for its gradual disappearance as a source of British national revenue, although a property tax (called the rates) still remains the mainstay of local revenues in England.[46]

The Poll Tax. The poll tax was introduced in England in 1377. On its second imposition in 1379 it was graduated according to rank, for which an elaborate classification was provided. It included all males and females over the age of fifteen, except beggars. Curiously enough, it was argued that its harshness upon the poor would be mitigated because the rich were expected to aid the poor in paying it. Endless disputes arose over the age of taxpayers, and a rather insolent attempt to ascertain the age of a young girl was said to have been the immediate cause of the Kentish rebellion (in 1381) under the leadership of Wat Tyler.[47]

Indirect Taxes. Indirect taxes were also common in medieval England, particularly levies upon foreign trade. The taxes upon the latter were so well established at the time of the Great Charter that they were regarded as belonging to the king without the assent of the people and were sometimes referred to as the "ancient customs." This did not mean, however, that the king could levy customs as he saw fit. The heavy duty on wool, for instance, levied by royal prerogative during the reign of Edward I (1297), was regarded as a violation of Magna Carta and was subsequently released by the king.[48]

In the more modern era of Oliver Cromwell, inland revenues or excises were introduced into the tax system of England. In the course of English history almost every conceivable article of consumption has been taxed through either customs or excise, or both. To mention only a few, there have been taxes on salt, corn, meat, sugar, pepper, olive oil, vinegar, confectionery, tea, coffee, cocoa, glass, candles, leather, paper, newspapers, and, of course, liquor and tobacco. The tax on salt was resented in England as elsewhere, although its final repeal was not attained until 1825. The Corn Laws were a special object of criticism, but it was not until 1846 that agitation against them finally suceeded in forcing not a complete repeal but a reduction at least to a nominal rate.[49]

---

[46] On occasions the British property taxes were apportioned rather than proportioned (to use Professor Plehn's terminology)—that is, a certain sum was allotted to territorial subdivisions, and they were allowed to proceed more or less on their own in collecting the revenue. (Compare with the American system of state equalization under the general property tax discussed in Chapter 4.) This system was also used in France, including apportionment to certain orders such as the clergy. Ordinarily no special treatment was accorded to the British clergy and nobles. Once the shares of particular units were established, they remained fixed over long periods in spite of changes in wealth and population—Dowell, *op. cit.*, vol. I, pp. 95–98.

[47] *Ibid.*, pp. 91–103.

[48] *Ibid.*, pp. 76–78.

[49] *Ibid.*, vol. II, pp. 8–14, 63, 74–81, 171, 174, 269, 330.

Presumptive Taxes. A curious species of tax, not entirely extinct and savoring of both the property and income taxes, were a group of levies based on some circumstances of living, which were thought to indicate one's ability to pay as well as one's economic and social status. Such were the hearth tax, the window tax, the carriage tax, and a few other similar taxes. The hearth tax was based upon the number of stoves and chimneys, and the window tax upon the number of windows in the houses. Both encountered serious difficulties. The hearth tax had been imported from France (1662), where it had been a part of the revenue system for many years. The British resented taxes imported from France and objected to the hearth tax on the additional ground that it involved an invasion of their homes by the assessors. The window tax (1696) raised the problem of defining a window and was objected to as a tax on light and ventilation.[50]

NET INCOME AND INHERITANCE TAXES IN MODERN TIMES

The net income tax was first introduced into England in 1798 [51] and was in effect there sporadically until 1842, when it became a permanent part of the British revenue system. Like many new revenue measures, or the rediscovery of old ones, it grew out of a financial distress occasioned by war. At the outset the tax was proportional rather than progressive, but an exemption was allowed for necessary living expenses. The progressive feature was not introduced until 1907.[52] At present this tax is the mainstay of the financial system of Great Britain. The death duties were first introduced as stamp duties. Because of evasions they were not very productive and, in 1796, were replaced by a new law that levied the tax on the transfer of property itself. Owing to the strong opposition of the landowners, this tax applied only to personal property (of collateral heirs), but finally, in 1853, it was also extended to real property. It was not until 1894, however, that it assumed something like its modern form.[53]

---

[50] A curious tax, sometimes classed in the group under consideration, was the British tax on powdering of hair, a tax which contributed to a change of fashion—*Ibid.*, vol. III, pp. 163–177, 255–259.

The tax on inhabited houses (1778), exclusive of land, based on annual value appears to have been a cross between the type previously described and a special property tax. In levying this and some other taxes, Lord North, hard pressed for funds to carry on the war against the American colonies, went to the *Wealth of Nations* for inspiration. Adam Smith, the author of that famous treatise, advocated a house tax based upon annual rental value rather than upon the number of windows in a house—the type of house tax that was in effect in England in his time.

[51] Enacted into law only in 1799.

[52] E. R. A. Seligman, *The Income Tax*, 2d ed., pp. 72–80, 128–136, 202–207.

[53] *Ibid.*, pp. 452–456; Dowell, *op. cit.*, vol. III, pp. 124–140.

In this brief and rapid survey, the development of tax institutions in other countries of Europe can be largely ignored, except for the reference already made to the taxes in effect in France prior to the French Revolution. In modern times the development, on the whole, took the same course as in England, although there were many variations. The Prussian income tax with a graduated feature was introduced in Prussia in 1851. The French were slow to develop a general income tax, but after the Revolution they developed a business tax, which was a curious and complicated compound of a classified occupation or license tax, and a special income tax containing a few traces of the progressive principle.[54] The individual income tax was not introduced until 1917; it provided a two-layer structure of proportional-rate schedular taxes and a progressive rate surtax on aggregate income. It was substantially revised in 1948 to eliminate some of the differentiation in the proportional tax.

THE UNITED STATES

Early American Public Expenditures. The American colonies founded their tax institutions upon British experience, but some variations appeared in these institutions as they developed on American soil. Public expenditures in the colonial era were exceedingly modest. Many public officials served gratuitously or were compensated with fees. There were no social welfare appropriations, and public works were unimportant. It was not until the close of the eighteenth century, and especially the third decade of the next century, that large outlays were made for turnpikes, canals, and railroads. Public schooling was still in its infancy, although New England early became interested in public elementary education. The church, on the other hand, was supported by taxes in some of the colonies until after the Revolution. In Connecticut, for instance, "The inhabitants met in town meetings to appoint their minister as they did their selectmen and taxes were paid to support the minister as well as the teacher." For a time, Episcopalians and other dissenters were taxed for the benefit of the official church (Congregational). By 1729 they were relieved of this obligation, but it was not until much later that the Congregationalists themselves came to support their church through voluntary contributions instead of taxation.[55]

Colonial Direct Taxes. The direct taxes employed by the colonies (payable in tobacco in some states) were the poll tax, the so-called faculty tax,[56] and the property tax, the latter more like the English

---

[54] Plehn, *Introduction to Public Finance,* 5th ed., pp. 119, 125–127.

[55] Arthur F. Potter, "Taxation System of Connecticut in 1776," *Bulletin of the National Tax Association,* XXIII: 7 (April 1938), p. 196; Dewey, *Financial History of the United States,* pp. 8–9.

[56] The faculty tax was a substitute for the property tax and applied to the earning capacity of artisans and professional people.

"rates" than our present general property tax. These taxes were not in effect in all colonies to the same extent. The New England colonies employed all three of them, but the property tax predominated there. In the southern colonies the poll tax played the more important role, although the chief source of revenue were indirect taxes. This also held true for the middle colonies until the latter part of the eighteenth century, when greater reliance upon the property tax brought them closer to the New England system.[57]

Development of the General Property Tax. The American general property tax seems not to have developed until the nineteenth century. According to Professor Jensen there was only one case, that of the constitution of Tennessee (1796), where a semblance of uniformity and universality appeared in the property tax during the early days of the republic. This constitutional provision stated that, "All lands liable to taxation . . . shall be taxed equal and uniform, in such manner that no one hundred acres shall be taxed higher than another except town lots which shall not be taxed higher than 200 acres of land each." [58] It was uniformity by area rather than by value that this provision referred to—hardly an equitable measure of uniformity judging by our present standards. The Connecticut statute listed the items to be covered and included in the statute valuations at which they were to be listed. The assessors had little discretion and were (properly) called listers. Lacking property, artisans and professional people were also included on the list—according to their "faculties."

The new constitutions of the 1820s and 1830s (Illinois, 1818; Maine, 1819; Missouri, 1830) called for the assessment of all property (with provisions for exceptions either in the constitution or by statute), including personal property, and all in proportion to value. The Illinois constitution of 1818 contained a uniformity rule which has prevailed substantially down to the present time. This constitutional provision, however, was ignored by the legislature until 1839.[59] At this time there

---

[57] Dewey, *op. cit.*, pp. 9–14.

[58] Quotation from Jens P. Jensen, *Property Taxation in the United States* (Chicago: University of Chicago Press, 1931), p. 37.

[59] Just six years preceding this constitution, the territorial legislature set up a classification of lands—such as bottom lands, other located lands, claims to lands not yet located—and levied specific taxes against such lands at a certain sum per acre (resembling the earliest taxes of England). The best or first-class land was expected to pay $1 per acre. Although the newly adopted constitution called for a tax in proportion to the value of one's property, the tax law of the following year merely modified the classification in effect by attaching a value per acre to each of the three different classes. The present uniform tax on all property (within the same district and with specified exceptions) did not develop until after the statute of 1839.

The present provision reads: "The general assembly shall provide such revenue as may be needed by levying a tax, by valuation, so that every person and corporation shall pay a tax in proportion to the value of his, her or its property" (Constitution of 1870, Article IX).

was a strong movement toward uniformity, the principle of which was incorporated in most of the state constitutions written later. Curiously enough, in recent years there has been a reversal in this policy. The movement now is toward the classification and special treatment of different kinds of property.[60]

Colonial Indirect Taxes.   All the colonial governments employed indirect taxes, especially duties on commerce, including in many cases the commerce with the other states.[61] As we have seen, the federal Constitution of 1789 appropriated the exclusive use of the customs to the federal government, in whose hands it became the major source of federal revenue for many years.

Special excises, such as those on liquor and tobacco, have been employed by the federal government for many years, particularly since the Civil War, and more recently by the states.

Development of the General Sales Tax.   Like most other taxes, the general sales tax is no modern invention. In Roman times it was employed by Augustus, who "laid a tax of one percent upon all articles, movable goods, or fixtures, sold in the market or by auction. . . ."[62]

The modern European sales taxes, however, grew out of World War I. Most of the belligerents, with Great Britain a notable exception, adopted some form of sales tax during the period from 1918–1923. These European taxes, labeled turnover taxes, carried a broad base and were multiple-stage levies applied to each exchange of goods from the raw materials to the consumer. As explained in Chapter 11, such taxes are plagued by duplication; the French have recently pioneered with an attempt to apply the tax at the manufacturers' level to "value-added" only. The more limited single-stage tax is notable in Norway, Australia,

---

[60] Jensen, *op. cit.,* pp. 38–41, 45–47.

With the development of the general property tax came complicated problems of administration and the necessity for extensive machinery for equalization and review. This machinery began to appear as soon as the tax became universal. The difficulties with which it has been beset and the refinements which, as a consequence, have been made on it are the subjects of earlier chapters.

[61] Shultz and Caine, *op. cit.,* pp. 40–41.

[62] A. G. Buehler, *General Sales Taxation* (New York: The Business Bourse, 1932), p. 3. It was used by Spain from the beginning of the fourteenth century until the early nineteenth century. This was the famous *alcavala,* excessive application of which, with rates of 10 and 14 percent, was thought by Adam Smith to have ruined the manufacturing industries of that country. Spain also tried to introduce the system into the Netherlands but without success. However, it did successfully carry the tax to Mexico, where it has continued down to the present.—*Ibid.,* pp. 3–4. Attention has already been called to the role of sales taxes in prerevolutionary France and the contribution of these taxes to the revolution. They were also levied on various items of consumption in England and other European countries. During the Napoleonic period, special levies became so numerous in England as to constitute almost the equivalent of a general sales tax.—*Ibid.,* p. 5.

and Canada which collect respectively at the retail, wholesale, and manufacturing levels. The British Purchases Tax, originating during World War II, is characterized by steep rates but a highly selective base.[63]

The United States federal government, like the other participants in World War I, experienced an urge for a sales tax. The comprehensive excise system of the Civil War period was the nearest to a general sales tax that the federal government attained prior to this time. During the pressure of war and postwar finance, several sales tax measures were debated in Congress, particularly the "manufacturers and producers" tax of 1921 and a similar measure linked with the soldiers' bonus in 1922. Although receiving staunch and well-organized support, these measures failed to pass Congress, and another proposal in 1932, although recommended by the Ways and Means Committee, was again defeated.[64]

During World War II federal experience with the sales tax closely resembled that in World War I. Sales tax measures were debated and attracted a strong following, but they were not enacted into the revenue system. The administration countered sales tax proposals with the recommendation of an over-all expenditures tax which, however, was unacceptable to Congress. The federal government did intensify its excise tax program.

Failing to make headway in Washington, proponents of general sales taxes turned to the states where they have been so successful that the sales tax has become the leading source of state revenue. The movement began as early as 1921 when West Virginia pioneered the field with its gross income tax. Beginning with the depression, the tax spread very rapidly; thirteen states enacted sales tax measures in 1933. Although many of these levies were adopted as emergency measures, most of them have been retained. A new wave of sales tax legislation followed World War II, since which 11 states have been added to the sales tax fold. In addition to the states, a substantial number of cities, led by New York in 1934, also have enacted local sales taxes. Professors Haig and Shoup, in summarizing the spread of sales taxes over four continents during fifteen years, concluded: "In the history of public finance no other tax, save perhaps the one on gasoline, has spread so swiftly over the world." [65]

---

[63] John F. Due, "Sales Taxation in Western Europe: A General Survey," *National Tax Journal,* VIII: 2 and 3 (June and September 1955), pp. 171–185; 300–321.

[64] Buehler, *op. cit.,* pp. 116–121.

[65] Robert M. Haig and Carl Shoup, *The Sales Tax in the American States* (New York: Columbia University Press, 1934), p. 5.

CONCLUSION

This rapid survey of the development of tax institutions should convince the student that little that is entirely new in taxes or public expenditures has been invented in the modern era. The net income tax is a relatively modern innovation, and public expenditure for education is relatively new. The changes that have taken place have not been so much in the types of taxes and expenditures as in their degree and in the environment in which they operate—the economic institutions. The development of the corporation, of economic interdependence, of democracy, of monetary control, and many other aspects of economic and political life have made the profound differences in our present as compared to the past public finance problem.[66]

---

[66] Space does not permit an account of the development of public finance as a body of literature and doctrine. For this see E. R. A. Seligman, "Public Finance," *Encyclopedia of the Social Sciences,* 1930.

INDEX

Ability-to-pay principle
  in apportionment of tax burdens, 22–27
  and corporate income tax, 196–197
  and death taxes, 251–254
  and definition of income, 181–183
  and social security taxes, 329
Acceleration principle, 488
Accessions tax, 246n.
Adams, T. S., quoted, 364
Ad valorem measurement
  and mine taxation, 347–348
  and property tax, 54
  and utility tax, 369–375
Aids
  alternatives to, 534
  distribution, methods of, 530–534
  in intergovernmental fiscal relations, 457–458
  See also Federal aids; Grants-in-aid; State aids
Air transportation taxation, 380–381
Alabama
  occupation taxes of, 364–365
  single tax in Fairhope, 357
Anderson, B. M., 580n., 581n.
Arizona, gross receipts tax of, 364
Arkansas
  limitation of taxing power in, 443
Assessment (*see* General property tax; Railroad taxation; Special assessments)
Auditing
  of federal accounts, 542–543, 549–550
  and income tax, 185–186
Australia
  and aids, 534
  and income tax, 176n.
  and intergovernmental fiscal relations, 450–451
  and land taxation, 355–356
  Loan Council of, 451, 647
  and property tax, 55

Australia (*continued*)
  and sales tax, 275, 678
  voting in, 319

Bach, G. L., 631n.
Balance of payments, 233, 652
Banks, taxation of, 385–389
Barlow, Raleigh, 65n., 67n.
Bastable, C. F., quoted, 615, 492
Bator, Francis M., 474n., 553n.
Baumol, W. J., 587n.
Beck, Morris, 109n.
Benefit principle
  in apportionment of tax burdens, 18–22
  and consumption taxes, 289
  and corporate income tax, 197–198
  and highway taxation, 300–301
  and social security taxes, 328–329
  and special assessments, 411–412
  special versus general, 400
Bentham, Jeremy, quoted, 252n.
Bird, Frederic L., 66n.
Bishop, Geo. A., 589n.
Blakey, Roy G. and Gladys C., 288n., 342n., 345n.
Blough, Roy, 238n., 280n., 548n.
Blum, Walter J., 24n.
Bond interest, taxation of, 199
Boulding, Kenneth E., 137n., 151n.
Bowen, Howard E., 479n.
Bowen, W. G., 632n.
Brazer, Harvey, 90n., 96n.
Break, George F., 35n., 149n., 269n., 405n., 631n.
Bronfenbrenner, Martin, 137n., 583n.
Brownlee, O. H., 314n.
Buchanan, James M., 632n.
Budget
  capital, 551
  cash, 551
  classification of data in, 553
  economic, 554–555, 576–578

681